RJ STARR

The Psychology of Being Human

An Authoritative Guide to Mind, Emotion, and Meaning

First published by Depthmark Press | Boca Raton, Florida USA 2025

Copyright © 2025 by RJ Starr

All rights reserved. No part of this publication may be reproduced, stored or transmitted in any form or by any means, electronic, mechanical, photocopying, recording, scanning, or otherwise without written permission from the publisher. It is illegal to copy this book, post it to a website, or distribute it by any other means without permission.

Library of Congress Control Number: 2025916521

Note: Professor RJ Starr is an academic psychologist and educator, not a licensed therapist in clinical practice. This book is intended for educational purposes only and should not be used as a substitute for professional psychological advice, diagnosis, or treatment.

First edition

ISBN: 979-8-9996293-0-2

This book was professionally typeset on Reedsy. Find out more at reedsy.com

For everyone who seeks to understand themselves and others more deeply. To the curious minds willing to face discomfort in pursuit of growth. To those who embrace complexity without losing compassion. This book is for you. May it offer insight, clarity, and courage on your journey toward a more authentic and integrated life.

"The greatest journey we undertake is the one inward—where truth meets courage and understanding becomes transformation. To know the mind is to know the self, and through that knowledge, to find freedom. This path is neither simple nor linear; it demands honesty, resilience, and a willingness to embrace complexity. Yet it is here, in the depths of our own experience, that the possibility for genuine growth and lasting change unfolds."

— RJ Starr, Author

Contents

Preface   x
Acknowledgments   xiv

I   PART I: FOUNDATIONS OF THE HUMAN MIND

1 What is Psychology, Really?	3
Psychology's Many Schools of Thought	6
What Counts as Evidence in Psychology	10
Why Psychology Still Matters	14
2 Nature, Nurture, and the Stories We Live	19
Genes and Temperament: What We Inherit	21
Environment and Conditioning: What Shapes Us	24
Beyond the Binary: Interaction and Plasticity	27
The Stories We Live: Narrative as Psychological Reality	31
3 The Architecture of Mind	35
Perception and Attention: How We Take in the World	38
Memory and Mental Time Travel	41
Emotion and Cognition: Two Intertwined Systems	44
Consciousness and Self-Awareness	48
4 Self and Identity Formation	53
The Ego and the Constructed Self	56
Personality and Temperament: Stable Traits, Flexible Selves	59
Social Mirrors: How Others Shape Who We Become	62
Internal Narratives and the Story of You	66

5	Development Across the Lifespan	70
	Foundations of the Early Self: Infancy through Childhood	73
	Identity in Motion: Adolescence and Emerging Adulthood	76
	Adulthood and Integration: Purpose, Intimacy, and Responsibility	79
	Elderhood and the Search for Meaning	83

II Part II: Emotion, Regulation, and Resilience

6	What Are Emotions For?	89
	The Evolutionary Function of Emotion	92
	Affective Neuroscience and the Emotional Brain	95
	Emotions as Carriers of Symbolic Meaning	99
	Emotion and the Search for Meaning	102
7	Feeling Deeply: Emotional Granularity and Sensitivity	106
	The Language of Emotion: Why Naming Matters	109
	Sensitivity and Depth: Trait-Level Differences in Emotional Processing	112
	Cultural and Developmental Influences on Emotional Nuance	115
	The Intelligence of Feeling: Emotion as a Cognitive Tool	119
8	Dysregulation, Avoidance, and Numbing	123
	The Dynamics of Emotional Dysregulation	126
	The Psychology of Avoidance	129
	Emotional Numbing and Disconnection	133
	The Cycle of Dysregulation, Avoidance, and Numbing: Clinical and Everyday Implications	136
9	Resilience, Recovery, and Adaptive Capacity	140
	The Architecture of Resilience	143
	Recovery Is Not Reversal	146
	Adaptive Capacity and Psychological Flexibility	149
	Building the Scaffolding: Relationships, Systems, and Environments	153
10	The Myth of Healing	157

The Cultural Illusion of "Healed"	160
Scars Are Not Evidence of Failure	163
The Work of Ongoing Repair	166
Living Whole with What's Broken	169

III PART III: BEHAVIOR, HABIT, AND SELF-CONTROL

11 The Logic of Behavior	175
What Behavior Reveals	178
The Mechanics of Reinforcement	181
Loops, Triggers, and Automaticity	185
Disrupting the Pattern: Awareness and Choice	189
12 Motivation and Meaning	193
Why We Do Anything	196
The Tyranny of Achievement	199
Values, Vocation, and the Pull of Purpose	203
Reclaiming Inner Direction	206
13 Habits and Routines	210
The Architecture of Automaticity	213
The Role of Friction: Why Some Habits Stick	216
Rituals, Anchors, and the Self We Reinforce	220
Breaking, Rebuilding, and Reclaiming Agency	223
14 Self-Control and Discipline	227
The Foundations of Restraint	230
Beyond Willpower: The Systems That Support Discipline	233
Character in Practice: Integrity, Boundaries, and Moral Restraint	237
Future-Oriented Thinking and the Delay of Gratification	240
15 Change That Lasts	245
The Myth of the Turning Point	248
Identity Before Behavior	251
Structure Over Sentiment	254

Maintenance, Relapse, and the Long View   258

IV   PART IV: RELATIONSHIPS AND INTERPERSONAL DYNAMICS

16   Attachment and Early Bonds   265
    The Roots of Safety: Attachment in Infancy and Early Development   268
    Internal Working Models: The Invisible Blueprint for Relationships   271
    Insecure Attachment in Adult Life: The Echoes of Early Disconnection   275
    Rewiring the Pattern: Earning Security Through Insight and Repair   278

17   The Social Mirror: Identity in Relationship   282
    The Social Brain: How Others Shape the Self   285
    Projection and the Distorted Other   289
    Boundaries and the Shape of the Self   292
    Co-Regulation and the Shared Nervous System   296

18   Communication and Miscommunication   300
    Unspoken Rules: The Scripts Beneath Our Words   302
    What Wasn't Said: Reading the Emotional Subtext   305
    Lost in Translation: Why We Talk Past Each Other   309
    Toward Clarity: Repair, Validation, and Emotional Precision   312

19   Intimacy, Trust, and Repair   316
    The Architecture of Intimacy   317
    Trust as a Living System   320
    The Mechanics of Rupture   323
    Repair, Renewal, and the Decision to Stay   327

20   Group Psychology and Belonging   331
    Us Versus Them: The Psychology of In-Groups and Out-Groups   334
    Conformity, Loyalty, and the Cost of Dissent   338

Healing the Divide: Integration, Dialogue, and
Common Humanity   341

V PART V: BELIEF, MEANING, AND SYMBOLIC LIFE

21 The Need for Meaning   347
   Life as Question: The Existential Search for Meaning   348
   Coherence and the Construction of Reality   351
   Symbols, Systems, and the Stories We Live   354
   Meaning in Practice: Choice, Commitment, and Responsibility 358
22 Belief Systems and Worldviews   361
   The Architecture of Belief   362
   Faith, Ideology, and the Psychology of Conviction   365
   Confirmation Loops and Cognitive Blind Spots   368
   Expanding the Frame: Intellectual Humility and
   Psychological Flexibility   371
23 Memory, Narrative, and Personal Myth   375
   The Story Self: How Identity Is Narrated   376
   Memory as Meaning, Not Just Record   379
   The Personal Myth: Archetype, Role, and Repetition   382
   Rewriting the Self: Agency, Editing, and Renewal   385
24 Consciousness, Awareness, and Self-Reflection   389
   The Architecture of Consciousness   391
   The Emergence of the Observing Mind   394
   Insight, Illusion, and the Limits of Self-Knowledge   397
   Cultivating Reflective Awareness   399
25 The Search for Truth   403
   The Desire to Know   404
   The Limits of Knowing   407
   Truth, Power, and Perspective   409
   Epistemic Humility as Maturity   412

VI PART VI: PAIN, TRAUMA, AND DISCONNECTION

26 What Is Psychological Pain?	419
Pain as Signal, Not Symptom	420
The Mislabeling of Discomfort	423
Meaning, Maturation, and the Function of Suffering	426
When Pain Becomes the Identity	429
27 Trauma and Its Reverberations	432
What Trauma Is, and What It Isn't	434
Developmental Imprints: The Long Shadow of Early Pain	437
Trauma Lives in the Body: Somatic Memory and Reenactment	440
Recovery and Integration: Moving Beyond Survival	443
28 Disconnection, Numbness, and Emotional Amnesia	446
The Protective Logic of Numbness	448
Emotional Amnesia and the Loss of Inner Continuity	451
The Long-Term Cost of Emotional Disconnection	454
Reclaiming Feeling: The Practice of Emotional Reawakening	457
29 Shame, Guilt, and Inner Exile	460
The Architecture of Shame	462
Guilt as Conscience, Guilt as Burden	464
Inner Exile and the Fragmented Self	467
Integration as the Return to Wholeness	469
30 Moving Toward Wholeness	473
Acceptance Is Not Surrender	474
Making Meaning Without Erasure	477
The Discipline of Staying Human	479
Wholeness as a Lived Practice	482

VII PART VII: THE SOCIAL CONTEXT OF THE MIND

31 The Psychological Impact of Culture	487

Culture as an Emotional Blueprint	489
Belonging, Shame, and the Cost of Deviance	491
Cultural Scripts and the Construction of Meaning	494
Cultural Evolution and Psychological Adaptation	497
32 Digital Life and the Fragmented Self	500
Identity in the Age of the Interface	502
The Economics of Attention and the Collapse of Presence	504
Performative Psychology and the Illusion of Intimacy	507
Integration in a World That Splits	509
33 Emotional Culture and Collective Behavior	512
Emotional Contagion and the Amplification of Feeling	513
Polarization as an Emotional Process	516
The Performance of Public Feeling	518
Fragmented Empathy and the Struggle for Emotional Integrity	521
34 Power, Privilege, and Psychological Safety	524
The Architecture of Power: How Systems Shape Inner Worlds	526
Internalized Oppression, Internalized Superiority	529
The Fragility of Safety: Threat, Vulnerability, and Belonging	533
Toward Repair and Equity: Reconstructing Psychological Safety in Unequal Worlds	537
35 The Self in Society: Agency and Resistance	540
Adaptive Selves: How People Learn to Survive	542
The Quiet Power of Everyday Resistance	545
When Agency Costs Too Much: The Psychology of Risk and Resistance	548
Disruption and Transformation: Reclaiming the Self in a Controlling World	552

VIII PART VIII: TOWARD A PSYCHOLOGICALLY INTEGRATED LIFE

36 Integration: The Goal of Psychological Maturity	557
Beyond Fragmentation: What It Means to Become Whole	559
Emotional Intelligence as Integrative Capacity	562
Coherence Over Consistency: Making Meaning Across Time	565
Living Integrated Lives: Practices and Commitments	568
37 Becoming Ourselves	571
The Performance of Self: How We Learn Who to Be	573
Identity Under Siege: The Residue of Trauma	576
The Unwritten Self: What Emerges When We Stop Performing	579
Becoming as a Lifelong Practice	581
38 Living With Uncertainty	585
The Need for Certainty: Why Ambiguity Feels Threatening	587
Holding the Tension: Paradox as a Feature, Not a Flaw	590
The Ambiguity Within: Emotional Complexity and Internal Conflict	593
Not Knowing as Wisdom: The Psychological Strength of Open Awareness	596
39 Psychological Wisdom	599
The Slow Learning of Life	601
From Pattern to Principle	604
Letting Go of Certainty	606
Living What You Know	609
40 The Invitation of Psychology	612
Understanding the Human Condition	614
The Mirror and the Map	616
A Discipline for the Disrupted Age	619
The Ongoing Invitation	621
Afterword	624

No Finish Line, Just Forward	624
References	626
Recommended Reading List	630
On Attachment and Early Bonds	630
On Identity and Meaning	630
On Emotional Growth and Complexity	631
On Psychology and the Human Condition	631
On Living with Uncertainty	631
On Self-Discovery and Lifelong Growth	632
On the Social Nature of the Self	632
About the Author	633

Preface

I didn't write this book because I had all the answers. I wrote it because I couldn't stop asking the questions.

What makes people do what they do? Why do we love in ways that hurt? Why do we fear our own needs, hide from our own depth, or cling to beliefs that contradict our experience? How do people come apart—and how do they come back together? Why do we forget what matters until we're reminded by loss, grief, or beauty?

These questions have followed me my entire life, not as abstract curiosities but as daily realities. I have seen people unravel, reform, rebuild, repeat. I have watched as intelligence collapses in the face of loneliness, and as ordinary people find heroic strength in the middle of sorrow. I've listened to stories that defy easy explanation and felt the limits of what psychology, as a field, is often willing to hold.

And still, I believe in it.

I believe psychology matters—not because it gives us clean solutions, but because it teaches us to live with complexity. Because it reminds us that beneath every behavior is a history, behind every emotion is a logic, and inside every person is a meaning system trying to hold itself together.

This book is not a textbook in the traditional sense, but it is meant to be a serious and comprehensive guide. It is not written for academics alone, nor for casual readers looking for quick self-help tips. It is written for anyone who is serious about understanding what it means to be human through a psychological lens—for the educator trying to explain emotion to a student who can't name their own, for the clinician trying to hold space for someone whose story defies diagnosis, for the reader who wants more than pop science but less than a DSM code.

It is written in plain language, but with academic integrity. It is grounded in theory, but alive with lived experience. It honors the complexity of the mind without collapsing into jargon. It assumes the reader is intelligent, capable of wrestling with contradiction, and deserving of writing that doesn't condescend.

In writing this book, I wanted to reclaim psychology as a field of human understanding—not just measurement. Over the last several decades, psychology has become increasingly technocratic. It has leaned heavily toward metrics, diagnostics, neuroimaging, and behavior modification. These tools are useful. But they are not the field. They are not the heart of it. Psychology, at its best, is not a system of classification. It is a framework for asking better questions about what makes us who we are, and what gets in the way of our growth, connection, and clarity.

To understand human beings psychologically is not merely to name their dysfunctions. It is to notice their patterns, to track their contradictions, to hear their unspoken loyalties, to see the emotional logic of what looks irrational. It is to understand that behavior is rarely random. It is expressive, adaptive, encoded with meaning—even when that meaning is outdated, distorted, or incomplete.

Psychology helps us see those codes. It helps us ask what a person has had to believe to survive, and what they might need to believe in order to heal.

The trouble is, much of what psychology knows never reaches the people who need it most. The public is flooded with articles, soundbites, and mental health content stripped of nuance. Pop culture turns serious psychological language into memes and clickbait. Meanwhile, formal education in psychology is often buried under technical terms and outdated models, taught in ways that make it feel dry, lifeless, or reserved only for specialists. I wanted to write something that lives in the space between those two poles: rich enough for scholars, clear enough for the public, and emotionally intelligent enough to hold both.

I wanted a book that could sit on the shelf of a university library and on a nightstand. A book you could read from beginning to end, or dip into when a question arises. A book that doesn't pretend to be final, but one that offers an integrated psychological lens that can accompany you for a lifetime.

This project also reflects a deeper frustration I've had for years: that so much of what is labeled "mental health" is really about emotional pain without context. The language we use—of trauma, attachment, self-regulation, narcissism—has become part of our cultural vocabulary. But rarely do we take the time to explain what these words actually mean, where they come from, and how they function within a larger framework of mind, emotion, and identity. This book attempts to give those words their full dimensionality back.

It is not a manual for how to feel better. It is a map for how to think more clearly, feel more deeply, and relate more intelligently to the experience of being alive.

Psychology, as I use the term throughout this book, is not limited to the academic field. It includes research, yes—but also clinical observation, cultural insight, developmental logic, emotional intelligence, and symbolic meaning. It includes not only what happens in laboratories, but what happens in kitchens, hospitals, detention centers, churches, classrooms, and living rooms. It includes not only the individual, but the systems they are part of. Not only the trauma, but the defenses that were necessary. Not only the pain, but the strategies for avoiding it. Not only what is spoken, but what is felt, feared, or forgotten.

I've written this book for the full spectrum of readers: for students just beginning their journey into psychology, for seasoned professionals who want a fresh synthesis of what they've learned, and for curious readers who are tired of oversimplified content that talks down to them. This book is for the reader who doesn't want formulas, but frameworks. Who doesn't want answers, but insight.

Each chapter builds on the last, but the structure allows for movement. You can start with the architecture of the mind, or skip ahead to trauma and emotional regulation. You can begin with development or dive into identity and meaning. It's not a curriculum. It's a body of work meant to reflect the wholeness of the human condition—cognitive, emotional, social, symbolic.

I have also chosen not to write from a position of therapeutic superiority. I'm not here to diagnose anyone or to pretend that insight alone is enough. I am here to offer a framework for understanding why people struggle, how they adapt, and what possibilities exist when we understand our own internal logic with more clarity and compassion.

This book is not clinical, but it is therapeutic in the truest sense of the word: it aims to uncover, to support integration, to restore dignity to our inner lives. It is not spiritual, but it touches the sacredness of psychological depth. It is not political, but it names the ways culture and power shape emotional norms. It is not autobiographical, but it draws from decades of listening, witnessing, and studying people closely. It is not a substitute for therapy, but it may change how you approach it—or how you approach yourself.

I wrote this book because I believe there is wisdom in psychology that can help us navigate modern life. Not advice. Not prescriptions. Wisdom. The kind that doesn't eliminate uncertainty, but makes us less afraid of it. The kind that doesn't erase suffering, but helps us carry it differently. The kind that doesn't turn human beings into case studies, but treats them as whole, feeling, pattern-making creatures worthy of understanding.

So, this is not a book about what to do. It's a book about how to see.

And if we see clearly enough, we may live more fully, relate more ethically, and feel less alone in the quiet corners of our mind.

That is why I wrote *The Psychology of Being Human*.

* * *

Acknowledgments

As I reflect on the long journey that led to this book, I find myself drawn back to the earliest days of my life—not just the milestones or formal education, but the quiet, formative moments of watching. As a child, I was an observer first and foremost, keenly attuned to the rhythms of human behavior around me. I watched how adults behaved and interacted, sometimes in ways that made sense, sometimes in ways that bewildered me. I watched how my peers related to me and to one another, navigating the treacherous waters of friendship, belonging, and identity. These early observations planted the seeds of curiosity and a deep desire to understand what drives us, how we make sense of ourselves and each other, and how we carry the weight of our imperfections.

Throughout my life, I have witnessed people wrestling with their own self-inadequacies—those moments when we all feel small, unseen, or unworthy. I have grappled with these feelings myself, often trying to appear "larger than," stronger or more capable than I truly felt, not always in honest ways. This personal struggle deepened my understanding of the masks we wear and the inner battles we fight. I have watched people struggle to reconcile the truths they know with the realities they live. Some wear masks of confidence that barely conceal the tremors of doubt underneath. Others reveal their vulnerabilities in moments of raw honesty that cut through facades. I have been fascinated by the ways people behave with each other, in intimate moments and in public, how kindness and cruelty can coexist, and how empathy is often both a bridge and a battleground. I have paid attention to how others respond to these behaviors—sometimes with grace, sometimes with judgment—and how those responses shape the emotional landscapes we inhabit.

This book is deeply personal because it is the culmination of these countless moments of witnessing, reflecting, and trying to make meaning of what I saw and experienced. It is not just an academic exercise; it is a record of the human condition as I have come to understand it through lived experience and psychological inquiry. The pages here carry the echoes of conversations, the weight of silences, the tension between hope and despair that I have encountered both within myself and in the lives of others.

I am profoundly grateful to everyone who has been part of this unfolding story—the people who allowed me into their lives, shared their struggles and triumphs, challenged my assumptions, and helped me grow in understanding and compassion. Your trust and openness have been gifts beyond measure. Whether through formal collaboration, friendship, mentorship, or fleeting encounters, each connection has contributed to the texture of this work.

To those who have stood beside me in moments of uncertainty, who have encouraged me to hold complexity without retreating into oversimplification, I owe a deep debt. Your presence has been a source of strength and clarity, reminding me that the pursuit of truth is never solitary. It is woven through relationships, dialogue, and shared humanity.

I also acknowledge the invisible threads—the many faces and voices that have shaped my thinking and feeling but whose names I may never know. The barista whose smile softened a difficult day. The stranger whose kindness was a quiet reminder of human decency. The neighbor who listened without judgment. These everyday moments of connection matter profoundly. They remind us that psychology is not just about theory but about lived experience, about the subtle interactions that build or erode our sense of self and community.

This book honors the complexity of being human: the contradictions, the struggles, the moments of grace. It is written for those who seek to understand themselves more deeply, who want to live with greater honesty and compassion, who recognize that growth is often messy and nonlinear. It is for anyone who has ever felt the ache of disconnection or the hope of belonging.

Finally, I want to express my gratitude to the discipline of psychology itself. Its rich tapestry of theory, research, and clinical practice offers tools for making sense of the inner workings of mind and heart. It provides language for experiences that are often ineffable and frameworks for navigating life's challenges. This book is a humble contribution to that ongoing conversation—a conversation that is as much about healing as it is about discovery.

Thank you for joining me on this journey.

With deep appreciation,

RJ Starr

* * *

I

PART I: FOUNDATIONS OF THE HUMAN MIND

Psychology begins with how we understand the mind—our own and each other's. In this part of the book, I want to lay a foundation with you. We'll walk through how thought, emotion, memory, identity, and development actually work—not as distant concepts, but as real forces shaping your experience every day. Psychology isn't just a field of study; it's a way of making sense of how we live, relate, and grow. This is where deeper insight begins.

1

What is Psychology, Really?

Ask someone what psychology is, and you'll often hear about therapy, mental illness, or perhaps a vague reference to the brain. These associations are not wrong, but they are incomplete. Psychology includes those areas, but it also encompasses how we form habits, how we process emotion, how we remember the past, how we make meaning from experience, and how we interact with others. It includes the unseen interiority of human life as much as the observable behaviors we act out. To understand the true scope of psychology, we must first broaden our lens: psychology is not just a field of study; it is a framework for seeing, interpreting, and engaging with the full range of human experience.

Psychology is, formally speaking, the scientific study of mind and behavior. But that definition immediately invites a deeper question: what counts as "mind," and what do we mean by "behavior"? The mind is not a single organ that can be dissected and mapped like a liver. It is an emergent process—a system of perception, memory, attention, emotion, imagination, and meaning-making that arises from the brain but is shaped by countless other forces: relationships, language, belief systems, cultural norms, developmental history, even political environment. Similarly, behavior is more than physical motion; it is expressive action, chosen or conditioned, often shaped by motivations and fears that the actor cannot fully name.

In this way, psychology sits at the intersection of the internal and the external. It studies the observable, such as facial expressions, speech patterns, physiological responses, and overt choices. But it also attempts to understand what is not directly visible: beliefs, fantasies, attachments, symbolic associations, and internal conflicts. These invisible aspects cannot be captured in brain scans alone; they require narrative, introspection, clinical observation, and sometimes the willingness to sit with ambiguity.

This expansive view of psychology allows us to include many domains under its umbrella. Cognitive psychology examines how we think, learn, remember, and perceive. Developmental psychology tracks how we grow, mature, and change across the lifespan. Social psychology studies how individuals behave within groups and how group dynamics shape perception and identity. Clinical psychology deals with emotional distress, mental illness, and patterns of coping. Personality psychology explores enduring traits, internal consistency, and individual difference. Neuropsychology connects the biological structure of the brain with psychological function. Health psychology examines how mental processes influence physical wellbeing. And cultural psychology investigates how our mental and emotional lives are influenced by the societies we live in.

But even that list is not exhaustive. Psychology can also be found in places that do not declare themselves psychological: in literature, where characters enact deep unconscious drives; in art, where emotion bypasses language; in law, where intention and impulse are weighed; in economics, where human irrationality collides with predictive models. Wherever people are interpreting their world, responding to their environment, or constructing internal logic from their external conditions, psychology is operating.

This is why psychology resists reduction to a single methodology or worldview. It is not purely experimental, though it uses experiments. It is not purely interpretive, though it relies on interpretation. It does not belong solely to the therapist's couch or the laboratory. It exists in both places, and in many others. The field's strength lies in its willingness to hold complexity: to examine phenomena from multiple angles, to test ideas while also respecting subjectivity, to build models that account for patterns without erasing nuance.

This breadth of scope means that psychology is not a neutral or purely objective enterprise. It is always shaped by the questions it chooses to ask and the frameworks it employs to answer them. For example, early psychology in the West was deeply influenced by patriarchal, Eurocentric, and heteronormative assumptions. Entire populations were left out of studies or mischaracterized within them. Behavior that deviated from the dominant norm was often pathologized. Only recently has the field begun reckoning with these omissions, expanding its lens to include multiple cultural realities, forms of expression, and ways of knowing.

As the scope of psychology grows, so does its responsibility. When we study human beings, we are not studying inert matter. We are studying meaning-making systems. That requires a different kind of rigor: one that is precise but not rigid, curious but not exploitative, systematic but not dismissive of the soul. Psychology must always be willing to ask not only "What is happening?" but "What does this mean, and for whom?"

Consider a young boy who refuses to speak in school. A narrow behavioral lens might label this as oppositional. A psychodynamic lens might inquire about early relational trauma. A developmental lens might ask whether his expressive language has caught up to his receptive understanding. A cultural lens might recognize that silence is a form of respect in his community. A trauma-informed lens might ask whether school feels safe at all. All of these perspectives are psychological, and none is sufficient on its own. Together, they illustrate why psychology must remain pluralistic in its tools and humble in its conclusions.

Another case: a high-achieving adult woman who feels constant guilt for resting. A behavioral approach might note a reinforcement loop in which overperformance leads to social approval. A cognitive approach might identify maladaptive beliefs about worth being tied to productivity. A family systems approach might reveal that she was raised to meet others' needs at the expense of her own. A cultural narrative analysis might examine how her identity as a "strong woman" has been socially constructed and internalized. Each framework adds dimensionality. None cancels out the others.

This is the true scope of psychology: not a singular truth, but a multidimensional way of listening to human life. It is not merely a science of the mind. It is a practice of understanding what minds are doing as they navigate their bodies, their stories, their environments, and their internal contradictions. It is a way of asking what pain is trying to say, what adaptation is trying to protect, what emotion is trying to express, and what meaning a person has attached to what they've lived.

The psychologist—whether formal or informal, clinician or curious friend—is not someone who hands out labels. They are someone who asks better questions. Someone who can sit with ambivalence, notice patterns, hear subtext, and recognize that every person's behavior is an answer to something—even if the question is no longer visible.

Psychology is a field that asks us to hold all of that. Its scope is wide because human beings are wide. It must be, if it is to tell the truth.

Psychology's Many Schools of Thought

Psychology, as a discipline, has never settled into a single unified theory of the mind. Unlike physics or biology, which often progress through consensus around core models, psychology has evolved through disagreement, revision, and layered perspectives. Each school of thought that has emerged over the past century reflects a different attempt to make sense of the complexity of human behavior, emotion, and meaning. These theoretical traditions are not just academic postures; they shape how we ask questions, what we consider evidence, and how we interpret the lives unfolding in front of us.

Understanding these schools is not about memorizing timelines or choosing favorites. It is about recognizing that each offers a partial truth—a lens through which to view the human condition. Together, they illustrate the field's richness and its inherent tension. No one model explains everything, but each helps us see something essential that others might miss.

The earliest modern roots of psychology are often traced to Wilhelm Wundt, who established the first psychological laboratory in 1879. Wundt approached the mind as something that could be studied through introspection and controlled observation. His work laid the foundation for psychology as a scientific endeavor, distinct from philosophy, but it remained focused on consciousness and individual perception.

In sharp contrast, the behaviorists who emerged in the early 20th century rejected introspection outright. John B. Watson, B.F. Skinner, and others argued that psychology should concern itself only with observable behavior. To them, thoughts and feelings were unmeasurable, and therefore unscientific. Skinner's radical behaviorism proposed that all behavior could be explained through conditioning—stimulus, response, reinforcement, and punishment. This approach contributed enormously to fields like learning theory and behavioral therapy, but it was criticized for ignoring inner life, choice, and meaning.

Psychoanalysis, championed by Sigmund Freud, took the opposite approach. It focused almost entirely on the internal world—the unconscious mind, repressed desires, and symbolic expression. Freud introduced concepts like defense mechanisms, childhood psychosexual development, and transference. While many of his specific theories have since been critiqued or replaced, the fundamental idea that unconscious processes shape behavior remains deeply influential. His model positioned the psyche as a layered structure of competing drives, with behavior as an expression of unresolved internal conflict.

Carl Jung, once Freud's protégé, broke away to form his own school of thought—analytical psychology. He introduced the ideas of archetypes, the collective unconscious, and psychological types. Jung emphasized meaning-making, spirituality, and individuation—the lifelong process of becoming one's full self. His work is less empirically grounded than others, but it has had lasting influence, particularly in areas of narrative, mythology, and depth psychology.

As the 20th century progressed, the humanistic movement emerged in reaction to both the cold precision of behaviorism and the pathology-heavy focus of psychoanalysis. Humanistic psychologists like Carl Rogers and Abraham Maslow emphasized personal growth, subjective experience, and self-actualization. They viewed people not as collections of dysfunctions, but as beings striving for meaning, connection, and wholeness. This movement re-centered dignity, choice, and emotional richness at a time when psychology was veering toward mechanistic explanations.

Maslow's hierarchy of needs, for example, positioned basic survival needs at the base, with higher-level needs like love, esteem, and self-actualization emerging only after more foundational needs are met. While the hierarchy has been debated, the model helped frame psychological health not just as the absence of illness, but as the presence of vitality and fulfillment.

Cognitive psychology, which gained prominence in the mid-20th century, marked a return to studying the mind itself—this time with scientific rigor. Drawing from computer metaphors and information processing models, cognitive psychologists explored how people perceive, remember, think, and solve problems. The dual-process model, for instance, describes how we operate with two systems of thought: one fast, intuitive, and emotional; the other slow, deliberate, and logical. This approach helped restore mental processes to psychological study, paving the way for breakthroughs in education, therapy, and neuroscience.

At the same time, developmental psychology evolved to explore how the mind changes over time. Jean Piaget's theory of cognitive development outlined how children move through distinct stages of thinking. Lev Vygotsky emphasized the social and cultural scaffolding of thought, arguing that learning and meaning are deeply embedded in context. Erik Erikson offered a lifespan model that included identity, intimacy, and generativity as central developmental tasks. These perspectives brought a temporal dimension to psychological understanding, reminding us that people are not static—they unfold.

Later in the 20th century, systemic and relational models gained ground. Family systems theory, pioneered by Murray Bowen and later adapted by Salvador Minuchin and Virginia Satir, viewed individuals not in isolation but as nodes within interdependent systems. Behavior was interpreted not only as personal but as shaped by dynamics between people—especially within families. These models introduced concepts like triangulation, homeostasis, and generational transmission of emotional patterns.

In parallel, feminist psychology and cultural psychology challenged the field's often narrow assumptions. Feminist theorists pointed out that traditional psychological models frequently ignored gender, power, and relational dynamics. Cultural psychologists emphasized that Western norms could not be universally applied. Ideas of self, emotion, and morality differ drastically across cultures, and any psychology that claims universality must first confront its own biases.

Trauma theory also began reshaping the landscape. The work of Judith Herman, Bessel van der Kolk, and others brought attention to how traumatic experience is stored in the body, fragmented in memory, and reenacted in behavior. Trauma-informed psychology reframed many symptoms—hypervigilance, dissociation, emotional reactivity—not as pathology, but as adaptations. This shift had major implications not only for therapy, but for education, criminal justice, and public health.

Today, psychology is more integrated than ever, yet still marked by debate. Neuroscience continues to inform our understanding of emotion and cognition. Attachment theory bridges developmental psychology and clinical insight. Positive psychology, introduced by Martin Seligman, focuses on strengths, well-being, and human flourishing. Acceptance and Commitment Therapy (ACT), Dialectical Behavior Therapy (DBT), and Internal Family Systems (IFS) all synthesize older theories with new insights. These models reflect an important truth: that no one approach is sufficient. The complexity of human experience demands flexibility, humility, and an integrative stance.

Understanding these schools of thought is not just academic. Each model carries with it a particular view of the human being: as a machine, as a story, as a social animal, as a soul in search of meaning. Each one tells us what is worth paying attention to, what counts as healthy, and what change looks like. As such, theoretical orientation is not just a technical choice. It is an ethical one. It determines how we treat people, what we believe is possible for them, and how we explain their suffering.

In the chapters that follow, we will draw from all of these traditions. Not because eclecticism is fashionable, but because it is necessary. The human mind is not a puzzle with a single solution. It is a landscape, alive with contradiction and pattern, shaped by history and hope. To navigate that terrain responsibly, we must understand the tools available to us—and the theories that shaped them.

What Counts as Evidence in Psychology

Psychology is sometimes accused of being less rigorous than the "hard sciences"—too subjective, too anecdotal, too imprecise. Critics ask why its findings change, why its diagnoses evolve, or why no single theory explains it all. What they often overlook is that psychology studies the most complex and unstable object in nature: the human being. And unlike rocks, cells, or gravity, human beings live in language, culture, memory, and meaning. These layers make the question of evidence in psychology not only important, but inherently philosophical.

To understand what counts as evidence in psychology, we must first accept a basic truth: how we see the world affects what we recognize as real. This is as true for researchers as it is for the people they study. There is no neutral lens in psychology. We are always observing through some kind of framework—an assumption, a theory, a cultural script, a method that shapes what we find.

In the early days of behaviorism, for example, evidence meant direct observation. If you couldn't see it or measure it, it didn't count. B.F. Skinner famously dismissed inner life as irrelevant, arguing that science could only concern itself with stimulus and response. He believed that thoughts and feelings were epiphenomenal, a kind of noise produced by the real machinery of behavior. This approach led to elegant, repeatable studies, especially with animals, and produced powerful insights into learning and reinforcement. But it also stripped psychology of subjectivity, emotion, and meaning.

Other schools of thought, particularly psychoanalysis and humanistic psychology, leaned heavily in the opposite direction. For them, what counted as evidence included dreams, memories, symbolic associations, and emotional responses. A psychoanalyst might consider the tone of voice or the timing of a pause as meaningful data. A humanistic psychologist might treat a person's reported sense of wholeness or incongruence as evidence of psychological integration. These interpretations were not random; they were rooted in structured models. But their methods challenged traditional definitions of evidence, and that challenge still stands.

Today, psychology draws from a wide spectrum of methodologies, each with its own criteria for what is real and knowable. Quantitative research remains central. Controlled experiments, statistical modeling, and psychometric assessments allow for generalizability, prediction, and measurable outcomes. These methods are often considered the gold standard for evidence, particularly in academic and clinical psychology. Randomized controlled trials are used to evaluate the effectiveness of treatments, while large-scale surveys track behavioral trends.

But there are limits. Numbers can show correlations, not causes. They can detect patterns, but often miss the internal logic that gives those patterns meaning. A study may show that people with high anxiety avoid eye contact—but it cannot always explain why that avoidance feels like safety, or what the individual believes would happen if they looked someone in the eye. To reach that level of understanding, we must also engage with qualitative methods.

Qualitative research includes case studies, narrative analysis, ethnography, grounded theory, and open-ended interviews. These approaches prioritize depth over breadth. They aim not to predict or generalize, but to understand how a person makes sense of their own experience. A single in-depth interview can reveal the complex symbolic structures behind someone's actions. A case study can show how past trauma, cultural identity, and personality style interact in one person's life in a way that no survey could fully capture.

In clinical practice, much of what counts as evidence is relational. A therapist listens for inconsistencies, affect shifts, patterns of resistance, emotional tone, and nonverbal cues. These are not easily codified, but they are meaningful. Experienced clinicians know how to read the subtle grammar of human behavior—the way someone avoids certain words, or the way their body tightens when they speak of a certain memory. These cues, while not "objective" in the laboratory sense, are observable, repeatable, and deeply diagnostic in context.

This raises a central question: can something be evidence if it is not measurable?

The answer depends on how we define evidence. In physics, evidence must be replicable and observable under the same conditions. In psychology, the conditions are never quite the same. A person speaking to a therapist is not a constant variable; they are shaped by mood, memory, language, and relationship. Their self-report may be influenced by defense mechanisms, shame, or unconscious processes. Yet their words, reactions, and choices are data—just of a different kind.

This is why modern psychology increasingly adopts a pluralistic approach to evidence. Mixed methods research, which combines quantitative and qualitative strategies, is becoming more common. So are biopsychosocial models, which integrate biology, behavior, subjective experience, and social context. This reflects an evolving understanding that psychological truth is not flat; it is layered, contextual, and lived.

Consider how we might study grief. A quantitative approach might involve rating scales of depressive symptoms, cortisol levels, or sleep disturbance. A qualitative approach might analyze a person's narrative about the loss: their metaphors, their sense of time, their emotional expression. A cultural lens might explore how rituals, language, or expectations shape that grief. A developmental view might ask what prior losses or attachments influence the current one. Each of these provides a kind of evidence. None alone is complete.

We must also consider the role of cultural and personal bias in determining what we accept as valid. Historically, psychology privileged Western, white, male, middle-class norms as the baseline for mental health. Emotions that deviated from these norms were pathologized. Behaviors that were adaptive in one context were labeled disordered in another. This has led to generations of misdiagnosis and harm, particularly among marginalized communities. As the field reckons with this, the definition of evidence continues to expand.

For example, consider the experience of dissociation in a survivor of childhood trauma. A narrowly defined behavioral lens might see this as attention-deficit behavior. A neuropsychological test might register fragmented recall. But a trauma-informed, survivor-centered approach might recognize dissociation as an adaptive, protective function—a form of absence that once ensured survival. That interpretation is not captured by numbers alone; it is held within a narrative frame, shaped by developmental understanding and ethical awareness.

In this way, evidence in psychology must always be interpreted. It is not inert. It must be held in context, traced back to the assumptions that generated it, and considered alongside lived experience. This is not a weakness of the field; it is its realism. Human beings are not laboratory conditions. They are systems of memory, emotion, cognition, embodiment, and meaning. Studying them requires methods as complex as the phenomena themselves.

The demand for rigor remains. But rigor does not mean reduction. It means depth, coherence, and humility. It means knowing what our tools can measure and what they cannot. It means recognizing that statistical significance is not the same as psychological truth, and that lived experience, when carefully listened to, is itself a valid form of evidence.

So what counts as evidence in psychology? Behavior counts. Thought counts. Emotion counts. Narrative counts. Biology counts. Relationship counts. Context counts. What matters is not choosing one over the others, but understanding how they interact—how they shape and inform the human mind as it moves through the world, searching for safety, connection, and meaning.

Why Psychology Still Matters

Some fields survive on technical necessity, others on intellectual curiosity, but psychology survives because every one of us is living the questions it asks. A person does not need to read a single journal article to wonder why they repeat certain mistakes, why they freeze in moments that require action, or why a memory from decades ago still sends heat across the chest. These questions arise in the boardroom, the kitchen, the classroom, and the voting booth. They surface when a teenager scrolls through endless images of curated lives and wonders why theirs feels unfinished, when a new parent tries to soothe an infant and cannot locate calm within themselves, and when an elder confronts the quiet that arrives after a partner's death. Psychology is not a luxury topic; it is the study of the terrain we all must cross.

Consider Nadia, a university student who excels in every course yet feels persistent dread before turning in assignments. She tells herself, with clinical precision, that her fear is irrational. She has never received less than an A minus. Still, her stomach contracts, her shoulders rise toward her ears, and her mind rehearses catastrophic scenarios in which an overlooked typo defines her worth. A friend suggests mindfulness apps; another recommends time management tips. Nothing shifts. When Nadia eventually enters therapy, she and her clinician trace the fear back to her father's unpredictable criticism, delivered after school report cards throughout childhood. The feedback was not always harsh, but the uncertainty was. She learned to equate perfection with safety; thus, any risk of imperfection wakes up an implicit threat response. The insight does not erase anxiety overnight, but it reframes the signal. Nadia begins to understand that her dread is not evidence that she is inadequate; it is a protective strategy that once made sense. This shift—seeing symptom as adaptive—illustrates psychology's practical power. A cognitive reframe rooted in developmental and attachment theory allows new behavioral experiments; gradually, Nadia's body learns that an A minus is survivable.

Stories like Nadia's play out quietly in millions of lives. Without psychological literacy, we are left to pathologize ourselves or moralize others. We say a child is bad, a coworker is manipulative, a community is lazy, a relationship is doomed. A psychological lens interrupts that rush to judgment. It asks, What need is being met here? What threat is being anticipated? What narrative is shaping perception? When we answer these questions with care, moral condemnation often gives way to more effective strategies: limits for safety, skills for regulation, boundaries that invite mutual respect rather than domination.

Psychology matters because it decodes emotion. In everyday language, feeling is either celebrated or feared, rarely understood as information. Yet affective neuroscience demonstrates that emotion is not a distraction from rationality; it is the architecture that allows rationality to prioritize. Antonio Damasio's research with patients who lost emotional processing due to ventromedial prefrontal cortex damage showed that without feeling, choice collapses into paralysis. These patients could recite pros and cons endlessly yet could not decide where to eat lunch. Emotion supplies salience; it tells the brain what matters. When people learn to read emotion accurately—its physical sensations, its cognitive appraisals, its historical echoes—they reclaim the capacity to decide, act, and relate with integrity.

Psychology also matters at the collective level. Social identity theory explains how group membership shapes self-concept; confirmation bias shows how belief searches for evidence of itself; moral foundations theory maps the intuitive pillars that underlie political persuasion. When these processes remain unseen, societies polarize. Each side attributes malice rather than motive to the other, and dialogue devolves into caricature.

Psychological insight can interrupt this cascade. It teaches that people do not cling to beliefs solely for logical reasons. They cling because personal identity and social reward are woven into the stance. Recognizing that connection does not require agreeing, but it can reduce contempt long enough for conversation.

Trauma theory offers another example of psychology's public relevance. The recognition that chronic exposure to threat alters neural circuitry changed how courts evaluate testimony, how schools address disruptive behavior, and how emergency rooms triage survivors. Post-traumatic responses—hyperarousal, flashbacks, dissociation—once misread as attention seeking or malingering, are increasingly understood as biological memories of unsafe environments. This understanding fuels policy shifts toward trauma-informed practice. It is psychology, translated through neuroscience and social work, influencing how institutions either perpetuate harm or foster recovery.

The workplace, too, reflects psychology's reach. Organizational psychologists study how leadership style influences engagement, how perceived fairness affects turnover, and how psychological safety predicts innovation. Companies that ignore these findings often pay in hidden costs: absenteeism, burnout, and silent resignation. Conversely, leaders who grasp concepts like self-determination theory—autonomy, competence, relatedness—can structure environments that satisfy basic motivational needs. Such workplaces are not indulgent; they are strategic, harnessing human drives that have been empirically validated across cultures.

Skeptics sometimes argue that common sense suffices. People know what makes them happy; they know how to change habits. But the data show otherwise. Most smokers understand the health risks; most consumers know that credit card debt is costly; most couples realize communication is important. Insight alone rarely shifts entrenched patterns. Change requires translating understanding into practice, rooting it in the nervous system, aligning it with identity. That translation is psychological work. It involves examining reinforcement schedules, exploring attachment templates, challenging cognitive distortions, and experiencing corrective relational moments. Without these interventions, information sits on the surface of consciousness like frost on glass—visible yet impermeable.

There is a moral dimension as well. When societies adopt psychological concepts superficially, they can weaponize them. Terms such as gaslighting, narcissism, and trauma become rhetorical grenades, thrown to win arguments rather than heal wounds. Deep psychological literacy can counter this trend. It insists on precision: narcissistic personality disorder is not equivalent to selfish behavior; gaslighting is a systematic pattern of distortion, not any disagreement; trauma is a nervous system's adaptation to threat, not simply discomfort. Precision protects the integrity of suffering; it prevents serious language from eroding into labels that silence dialogue.

Finally, psychology matters because it restores scale to human suffering. Many people, facing anxiety or grief, feel defective because they cannot think their way out of feeling. Cognitive reappraisal helps, but emotion is not subordinate to thought; it is a parallel processor with roots in evolution. Recognizing that hierarchy liberates the individual from shame. It allows self-compassion to coexist with responsibility, optimism to coexist with reality. It frames healing not as the erasure of pain, but as the integration of experience into a coherent narrative that can be carried without fracture.

The chapters ahead will travel across development, emotion, behavior, relationships, belief, trauma, culture, and integration. Each domain will reveal another facet of psychology's relevance. Together they will argue that understanding mind and meaning is not optional in modern life; it is foundational. When we grasp the psychological undercurrents that move individuals and collectives, we gain leverage—not to control others, but to steer ourselves with greater honesty, resilience, and grace.

We study psychology because we live it. We write about psychology because naming patterns can set them in motion toward change. We read psychology because the mind is where every story we tell about ourselves begins and ends.

***

2

Nature, Nurture, and the Stories We Live

From the earliest moments of life, people begin trying to explain us. Family members point out familiar traits, assign inherited temperaments, and trace personality through bloodlines. At the same time, those same families shape us in real time—through caregiving, expectations, discipline, attention, and absence. As we grow, our worlds expand. School, culture, religion, friendship, geography, language—each layer adds a new contour to who we become. And somewhere in the middle of all of this, we start telling ourselves a story about why we are the way we are. That story can either clarify or confuse us.

Psychology has long wrestled with the question of what drives development. Are we shaped more by biology or by environment? Does our genetic inheritance set a fixed course, or are we fundamentally malleable? These questions have been asked for centuries, but in the last fifty years, the answers have grown more layered. We now understand that nature and nurture do not operate as opposing forces, but as interdependent systems. Biology sets parameters; environment activates or suppresses those traits; and the narratives we form about that interaction can become self-fulfilling.

This chapter examines all three: what we inherit, what we experience, and what we come to believe. Our psychological patterns emerge from this interplay. A child might be born with a nervous temperament—high reactivity, low sensory threshold—but whether that becomes anxiety or attunement depends on how the environment responds. A teenager raised in a chaotic household may develop hyper-independence—not because it is written in their DNA, but because early experiences taught them that needing others was unsafe. Later, when that same person pushes intimacy away, they may say it's "just how I am." But psychology reminds us that "how we are" is not only innate. It is adaptive.

That distinction matters. Without it, we risk mistaking conditioning for identity. We confuse survival strategies with personality. We repeat family patterns because they feel familiar, not because they are true. And we inherit not only traits, but beliefs—about worth, emotion, power, connection, and even what love should cost.

One of the more dangerous myths in Western thinking is the belief in the self-made individual, the idea that we exist outside of context and emerge from childhood as fully formed agents. But identity is always in conversation with environment. We carry traces of those who raised us, the systems that shaped us, and the roles we were asked to play. We also carry the stories those systems gave us: stories about whether we are lovable, capable, safe, or broken. These stories may not be spoken aloud, but they live in the background of every decision, reaction, and interpretation.

This is why the question isn't simply whether nature or nurture matters more. The question is how they interact, and what we make of that interaction. Some traits are inherited; some are rehearsed. Some behaviors are protective; some are expressive. Some identities reflect who we are; others reflect who we had to become in order to stay connected, avoid punishment, or protect our dignity.

By unpacking these layers, we give ourselves more room to move. We loosen the grip of inherited guilt. We stop mistaking pain for fate. And we begin to see how change is possible—not through sheer willpower, but through insight, compassion, and the slow process of rewriting what we once believed was fixed.

In the sections that follow, we'll explore the raw material we're born with, the conditions that shape how that material unfolds, the dynamic relationship between biology and experience, and the deeply embedded personal mythologies that often define us far more than genes or childhood ever could.

Genes and Temperament: What We Inherit

Every person arrives in the world with a unique biological signature. Before a word is spoken or a single parenting decision is made, we are already carrying predispositions—toward reactivity, sensitivity, sociability, attention, mood regulation, and more. These traits do not determine our destiny, but they shape the terrain. They create the emotional and behavioral contours that interact with environment to form a personality. If we want to understand how a person becomes who they are, we have to begin with what they carry from the start.

Genetics in psychology refers to the inherited blueprint passed down from biological parents. While most people associate genes with eye color or disease risk, genetic influence extends to psychological domains as well. Twin and adoption studies have shown strong heritability estimates for traits like intelligence, extraversion, neuroticism, and even certain mental health vulnerabilities. Temperament, which refers to early-emerging individual differences in emotional reactivity and self-regulation, is particularly influenced by biology. Some infants startle easily, cry more often, and struggle to adapt to changes in routine. Others are naturally easygoing, quick to soothe, and adaptable. These are not reflections of parenting style—not yet. They are reflections of innate neurobiological makeup.

One of the most widely studied frameworks for understanding temperament is the work of Alexander Thomas and Stella Chess, who identified three primary temperamental profiles in infants: easy, difficult, and slow-to-warm. Easy babies adapt quickly and have predictable routines.

Difficult babies are more irritable, intense, and less adaptable to change. Slow-to-warm babies are cautious and require time to adjust, often appearing shy or hesitant in unfamiliar settings. While these categories are broad and not universally applicable, they laid the groundwork for decades of research exploring how biological temperament interacts with environmental input.

Another significant contribution to this conversation comes from the work of Jerome Kagan, who studied behavioral inhibition in infants and its later correlation with anxiety and social withdrawal. Kagan found that some children are biologically predisposed to heightened arousal in response to novelty—essentially, their nervous systems react more intensely to new stimuli. These children are more likely to become cautious, anxious, or socially avoidant later in life, especially if their environment reinforces fear or fails to provide secure, gradual exposure to new experiences.

But temperament is not just about discomfort or difficulty. It also includes the capacity for joy, focus, persistence, and curiosity. Some children are naturally drawn to exploration. Others are more observant and reflective. These tendencies can be supported or suppressed depending on the context in which they develop. This is where the concept of "goodness of fit" becomes critical. Originally coined by Thomas and Chess, goodness of fit refers to the compatibility between a child's temperament and the expectations or demands of their environment. A highly active child in a high-structure, low-movement classroom may be seen as problematic, while the same child in a more flexible, kinesthetic learning environment might thrive. The issue is not the child, but the match—or mismatch—between their biology and their surroundings.

We also know that genetics does not act in isolation. It expresses itself through complex networks of interaction with other systems. The same genetic trait can lead to different outcomes depending on the context. A high-sensitivity trait may lead to heightened anxiety in a stressful home but may become empathy and emotional intelligence in a nurturing one. A predisposition toward impulsivity might lead to addiction in one environment, but innovation or risk-taking in another. This is sometimes called the "differential susceptibility" model—some people are simply more reactive to both negative and positive influences, depending on their genetic sensitivity.

Even in mental health, where we are quick to assume biology plays a dominant role, the picture is more nuanced. Conditions like depression, bipolar disorder, and schizophrenia do show strong heritability, but no single gene determines whether someone develops them. Rather, clusters of genes interact with life experiences, trauma exposure, social support, and personal meaning-making to influence risk and expression. This is why two people with the same genetic profile can live entirely different psychological lives.

There's also the question of how much we actually understand about our genetic influence. Popular media often overstates the certainty of genetic research. The Human Genome Project, while groundbreaking, did not reveal simple cause-and-effect relationships between genes and psychological traits. Instead, it highlighted just how complex those relationships are—polygenic, interactive, and deeply context-dependent. We know that genes matter, but we also know that what activates them often has little to do with biology and everything to do with experience.

Consider a child who is born with a genetic vulnerability to mood instability. If they are raised in an emotionally chaotic household where they are punished for expressing emotion, they may develop rigid control strategies, internalize shame, or retreat into withdrawal. If, instead, they are raised in an environment that teaches emotional labeling, offers co-regulation, and honors their feelings, they may learn how to manage that mood instability with grace. The genes are not different. The outcomes are.

And of course, this extends beyond childhood. Our biology does not stop speaking just because we've reached adulthood. We carry our temperament into our work, our relationships, our creative life, and our parenting. A person with high novelty-seeking tendencies may thrive in entrepreneurial spaces and struggle with routine. Someone with a biologically lower threshold for emotional stimulation may find themselves easily overwhelmed in crowds or under chronic sensory stress. Knowing this can help people choose environments that align with their nervous system instead of blaming themselves for not fitting into contexts that were never designed for them.

Psychological maturity often begins with accepting the shape of one's nervous system—not as an excuse, but as a reality. We cannot override every part of our biology. But we can work with it. We can understand how our inherited traits influence our reactions, our choices, and our challenges. And we can stop pretending that everything is either self-made or externally imposed.

What we inherit is not our fault. But what we do with that inheritance—that's where agency lives.

Environment and Conditioning: What Shapes Us

If our genetic temperament lays the groundwork, then our environment is the architecture that rises from it. No matter how reactive or placid a child may be by nature, the world around them—family, culture, caregiving, education, community—constructs the frame through which they learn to interpret and respond to experience. While we inherit potential, it is our environment that determines which parts of us are nourished, neglected, distorted, or overdeveloped. Environment doesn't just influence behavior; it teaches us how to exist.

From infancy forward, human development unfolds within relationship. The early caregiver-child bond is not just emotional; it is biological. Infants do not self-regulate. Their emotional states are shaped by the regulation patterns of the adults who care for them. Through thousands of daily interactions—feedings, tone of voice, facial expression, rhythm of response—the child begins to form what Bowlby called an internal working model: a template for what to expect from others and from the self. If care is attuned, predictable, and safe, the child tends to develop a secure attachment—confidence in their own worth and trust in others. If care is inconsistent, absent, or intrusive, other patterns emerge: anxious attachment, avoidant detachment, disorganized response. These patterns are not personality traits. They are strategies—unconscious systems for managing closeness, safety, and emotional exposure.

The environment teaches far more than relational style. It teaches emotional norms. A child raised in a household where anger is punished learns to suppress it. A child whose sadness is ignored may stop showing vulnerability altogether. Emotional messages are not always verbal. Children learn them through facial expression, body language, withdrawal, and approval. A parent who stiffens when their child cries is communicating something, even if they say nothing at all. Over time, these environmental cues shape how a person experiences and expresses emotion. They may learn to disconnect from feelings, to over-express to get attention, to regulate for others instead of themselves.

Beyond the family, larger cultural and societal forces take over. Schools, peer groups, religious institutions, and media all reinforce certain behaviors and beliefs. Gender norms, for example, are environmental scripts. Boys may be praised for stoicism and punished for tenderness; girls may be rewarded for helpfulness but shamed for assertiveness. These messages become embedded in behavior and often feel like natural traits. But they are environmental artifacts—internalized expectations shaped by years of reinforcement and adaptation.

Social learning theory, popularized by Albert Bandura, helps explain how we absorb patterns from the people around us. Bandura showed that people do not only learn through direct reward and punishment but through observation. A child watches their older sibling get scolded for expressing fear and learns to hide their own. A teenager sees their parent cope with stress through avoidance or aggression and internalizes that template. What we see becomes what we expect, and eventually, what we do.

This is not limited to behavior. Our sense of possibility—what life can look like, what success means, what relationships should feel like—is shaped by what we observe in our environments. A person raised in chronic scarcity may struggle to trust abundance. A child who grows up in chaos may feel unanchored in peace. The environment becomes the emotional landscape that the psyche learns to navigate. Even when we outgrow it physically, we often continue to live inside its rules psychologically.

Consider the concept of learned helplessness, originally studied by Martin Seligman in experiments with dogs exposed to uncontrollable shocks. Over time, the dogs stopped trying to escape—even when escape was possible. They had learned that their efforts were futile. In humans, this plays out in subtle and tragic ways. A child raised in an environment where effort never changes outcome may stop trying to assert themselves. They may appear passive or indifferent, but beneath that exterior is a learned belief that action is meaningless. This is not laziness. It is adaptation.

The environment also conditions beliefs about identity. Through repeated interaction, people begin to internalize not just roles, but entire narratives about who they are. A child praised only for achievements may learn that they are only lovable when they succeed. A person repeatedly treated as a burden may come to see themselves as inherently problematic. These beliefs don't come out of nowhere. They are shaped by context—by what was mirrored, rewarded, ignored, or criticized over time.

And this is where environment begins to overlap with narrative. The experiences we live through eventually become the stories we tell ourselves. Not necessarily in words, but in assumptions. "I'm too much." "People always leave." "If I show weakness, I'll lose everything." These are not abstract conclusions. They are scripts written in the body, through years of patterned experience. The environment teaches us not only how to act, but how to believe.

Importantly, environmental influence is not only about trauma or deficiency. A nurturing, responsive environment can act as a buffer against biological vulnerability. Children with anxious temperaments may thrive in homes where their fear is met with validation and gentle challenge. People raised in emotionally literate families often carry a greater capacity for regulation, empathy, and relational repair. In this sense, environment is not just what goes wrong. It is also what goes right—and what we carry forward because it gave us something solid to stand on.

But most environments are mixed. Few people grow up in purely secure or purely harmful settings. Most inherit a blend of care and confusion, safety and strain. Psychological insight involves not only naming what hurt, but also recognizing what helped, what protected, and what allowed us to adapt. Our behaviors are not flaws. They are responses to environments—some of which no longer exist, but whose rules we still follow.

To understand yourself fully, you must trace the shaping influence of your environments: the spoken rules, the unspoken fears, the roles you were assigned, and the beliefs you were asked to carry. You are not separate from these conditions. But you are not limited to them, either. By understanding the shape of the environments that formed you, you begin to recognize which parts of your behavior are inherited, which are practiced, and which no longer serve.

Beyond the Binary: Interaction and Plasticity

For most of the 20th century, the debate between nature and nurture was treated like a tug-of-war. On one side stood those who believed behavior was biologically determined, driven by genes and immutable traits. On the other stood those who emphasized environment, arguing that human beings are shaped entirely by context, upbringing, and reinforcement. But that binary framing misses the point. The most accurate, and most psychologically useful, understanding comes from examining how nature and nurture interact—how biology and environment shape each other in continuous feedback loops, across development and throughout life.

Human beings are not static products of DNA. Nor are we blank slates molded passively by our surroundings. We are dynamic systems, shaped by our biology, but also by the experiences that biology responds to, adapts within, and transforms through. The concept of interactionism—the idea that genes and environment work in tandem—has become central to modern psychology. It suggests that inherited traits and environmental inputs are not separate influences to be weighed against each other, but rather co-constructors of human development.

Take, for example, a child with a genetically sensitive nervous system. Their reactivity might lead them to cry more often, seek comfort more urgently, or become overwhelmed more easily. That same sensitivity will likely influence how adults respond to them. A responsive parent might meet their needs with patience and consistency, which helps the child develop trust and self-regulation. An impatient or punitive caregiver might respond with frustration or neglect, reinforcing the child's distress and increasing reactivity over time. In both cases, the child's biology elicits a certain environment, which in turn reinforces or reshapes the expression of their biology. This is called gene-environment correlation: the tendency for certain genetic traits to evoke specific environmental responses.

Another important concept is epigenetics—the study of how environmental factors influence gene expression without changing the genetic code itself. We now know that stress, trauma, nutrition, attachment, and even social conditions can activate or suppress certain genes. For instance, chronic early stress has been shown to alter the expression of genes related to cortisol regulation, making people more vulnerable to anxiety and depression later in life. In this way, experience gets "written into" the body—not through mutations, but through biochemical signals that influence how genes function. The genes are still there, but the way they express themselves changes in response to the environment.

Plasticity is the capacity for change—neurological, emotional, and behavioral. The brain is most plastic in early life, but it remains flexible well into adulthood. New experiences, new relationships, even new beliefs can literally reshape neural pathways. This is especially true in the context of healing and therapy. A person who has lived for decades with patterns of emotional shutdown or hypervigilance can, with consistent safety and insight, develop new ways of regulating emotion, forming relationships, and seeing themselves. This kind of change is not wishful thinking; it is supported by research in neuroplasticity, developmental repair, and trauma recovery.

Interactionism also explains why people with the same genetic predisposition or similar environmental conditions can develop in dramatically different ways. Identical twins, for example, share the same DNA, but their lives may diverge significantly if they grow up in different contexts. One may develop depression, the other may not. One may become avoidantly attached, the other securely bonded. It is not the genes alone or the environment alone that determine outcome, but the way the two combine—along with personal meaning-making, opportunity, and chance.

This helps make sense of both vulnerability and resilience. Two children may experience similar adversity, but only one develops chronic emotional dysregulation. Why? Their biology may differ, or the timing of stress exposure may differ, or the availability of protective relationships may change the trajectory. Some people are more sensitive to context—not just in a negative direction, but in both directions. A trait known as differential susceptibility suggests that certain individuals are more influenced by their environment in general. If they are raised in a chaotic setting, they may struggle deeply; if they are raised in a nurturing one, they may thrive far more than their peers. What looks like fragility in one context may be untapped sensitivity in another.

This also complicates the way we think about diagnosis and labeling. A child labeled as oppositional may be reacting to an environment that is overstimulating or emotionally unsafe. A person diagnosed with generalized anxiety may carry both a biological sensitivity and a history of unpredictability or emotional neglect. Understanding the interaction between nature and nurture helps prevent oversimplification and reduces the stigma that often comes with psychological struggle. Behavior becomes understandable, not just pathological. It becomes traceable, not random.

There are also social implications. When we recognize the plasticity of psychological traits, we stop assuming that people "just are the way they are" or that change is impossible. At the same time, we stop blaming individuals for every struggle they experience. We begin to see people within context—biological, relational, systemic. This expands both our compassion and our responsibility. Compassion, because people are responding to conditions they did not choose. Responsibility, because some of those conditions can be changed.

None of this means we are infinitely malleable. Genetics set limits. Not everyone can rewire every pattern. Some traits are enduring, and some experiences leave lasting imprints. But interactionism gives us a realistic sense of agency. It says: you are not entirely the product of your genes, nor entirely the sum of your environment. You are both, and more. You are also the meaning you make from those inputs, the choices you forge in the spaces where choice is possible, and the relationships that hold or reshape your internal world.

The binary debate between nature and nurture is no longer relevant. What matters is understanding how they relate. And more importantly, how we can use that understanding to approach ourselves—and others—with greater nuance, patience, and hope.

The Stories We Live: Narrative as Psychological Reality

By the time we reach adulthood, most of us have some idea—conscious or not—about why we are the way we are. We believe we're independent because our parents were unreliable. We say we're perfectionists because nothing we did as children felt good enough. We think we're bad at relationships because we always choose the wrong people. These stories don't come from nowhere. They arise out of experience. But over time, they become more than just explanations. They become identities.

Narrative is not decoration. It is not what we add to our lives after the fact. It is the very structure through which we experience reality. The human brain is organized to make meaning, to link events, to track cause and effect, to form a coherent sense of self through time. In psychology, this process is called narrative identity—the internalized, evolving story of the self that provides a sense of continuity and coherence. It is not always accurate. But it is always influential.

From a young age, we begin absorbing stories about ourselves from the people around us. These may be direct—what we are told about our personality, our place in the family, our strengths or flaws. Or they may be indirect—reflected in who gets attention, who is protected, who is criticized, who is ignored. Over time, these experiences settle into implicit narratives. A child who is frequently scolded for expressing anger may begin to believe they are "too much." A teenager whose efforts are never acknowledged may internalize the idea that they are invisible or fundamentally inadequate.

These stories do not simply describe our past. They shape our future. If you believe that your needs are a burden, you may avoid intimacy. If you believe that love must be earned through performance, you may seek achievement compulsively. If you believe that you are broken, you may interpret rejection as confirmation rather than coincidence. The narrative doesn't just sit in the background. It becomes the filter through which new experience is interpreted.

Narratives are also socially reinforced. The roles we play in our families, relationships, and communities often mirror the identities we've constructed internally. Someone who sees themselves as the caretaker will often find themselves surrounded by people who need care. Someone who believes they are unworthy may unconsciously seek out relationships that echo that belief. This isn't self-sabotage in the usual sense. It's the mind seeking coherence. Familiar stories, even painful ones, feel safe because they are predictable. We know how they go.

Narrative also explains why psychological insight can be so disorienting. When a person begins to question the story they've lived by, they often feel unstable. If I'm not the one who fixes everything, who am I? If my childhood wasn't fine, what does that say about how I've been coping? If I'm not unlovable, then why do I keep ending up alone? These are not just intellectual questions. They are narrative disruptions—challenges to the psychological logic that has held a person together. Change is not just behavioral. It is narrative reconstruction.

The stories we live are not always dramatic or traumatic. Some are subtle, even socially rewarded. The high achiever who always seems in control may be living a story of compensation—trying to outrun early chaos or emotional neglect. The person who prides themselves on independence may be reenacting a story of early disappointment, where relying on others led to hurt. These stories often appear as virtues. But their emotional logic tells a deeper tale.

Psychological work often involves naming and revising these narratives. This does not mean replacing a negative story with a falsely positive one. It means creating a more accurate, compassionate, and flexible understanding of how we became who we are. It means distinguishing between what was imposed and what was chosen, between what was true and what was necessary to believe at the time. Sometimes the original story helped us survive. But survival and truth are not the same.

Therapists, counselors, and reflective individuals often help others reauthor their narratives—not by denying what happened, but by reinterpreting it through a wider frame. The story of being unwanted may become a story of emotional abandonment, shaped by a caregiver's limitations rather than the child's defect. The story of being emotionally volatile may become a story of unrecognized sensitivity in a family that didn't know how to respond. These shifts matter. They change what the story allows. They make room for agency, complexity, and movement.

Culture also shapes narrative. Different cultures emphasize different emotional norms, relational expectations, and models of selfhood. In Western individualist cultures, stories of triumph and personal strength are often favored. In collectivist cultures, stories of duty, sacrifice, or family legacy may dominate. Neither is wrong, but both influence how people see their problems and their possibilities. A person raised in a context that devalues emotion may struggle to include emotional experience in their self-understanding. A person taught that obedience is moral may have difficulty separating their own desires from perceived obligation. These, too, are narrative forms.

Narratives can also fracture. In the wake of trauma, betrayal, or loss, a person may find that their existing story no longer makes sense. What they believed about the world—that it is fair, that people are safe, that they are in control—may collapse. In these moments, the person is not only grieving the event, but grieving the story that held their identity together. This narrative collapse is psychologically destabilizing. But it can also be generative. It is often the beginning of deeper inquiry, deeper honesty, and more nuanced meaning-making.

Ultimately, the stories we live are not fixed. They can be revised, expanded, challenged, or retired. But they cannot be ignored. To understand a person psychologically, we must listen for their story—not just what happened, but what they believe it means. Not just what they say, but what they protect. The narrative contains the logic of their behavior. And within that logic lies the possibility of transformation.

You are not just your genes. You are not just your environment. You are the meaning you've made from both. And in that meaning, you have more power than you think.

THE PSYCHOLOGY OF BEING HUMAN

* * *

3

The Architecture of Mind

Every day, without trying, you interpret the world. You scan for what matters, filter out what doesn't, and string your experiences into something that feels coherent. You remember what hurt you, anticipate what might happen next, respond to subtle shifts in tone, and revise your beliefs in light of new evidence—or cling to them, even when the evidence says otherwise. All of this happens within a system we rarely pause to examine: the mind.

This chapter is about that system—not as a poetic abstraction, but as a layered, working structure. Psychology's job is not to mystify the mind, but to clarify it: to name the processes that underlie awareness, memory, focus, thought, emotion, and perception. These aren't simply functions. They are the mechanisms through which reality becomes real for each of us. They determine what we see, what we miss, what we react to, and how we interpret experience. If you want to understand why people behave the way they do, you need to understand the structure behind it.

The mind is not one thing. It is a collection of systems—evolved, adaptive, interwoven—that collaborate to create what we call consciousness. Some parts are fast and automatic. Others are slow, deliberate, effortful. Some parts are shaped by biology. Others are shaped by learning, belief, emotion, and culture. The mind is not housed in one location. It is embodied, distributed, and shaped by everything it encounters. It is not a clean machine. It is a meaning-making organ.

The first layer of that system is perception. What we see, hear, feel, and attend to forms the raw material of experience. But perception is not objective. We don't take in reality as it is. We take in selected portions of it, filtered by attention and shaped by expectation. What we notice depends on what we've been trained to look for, what we fear, what we hope for, and what stands out against the background noise of everyday life. The mind is constantly deciding what matters—what to amplify, what to ignore. This filtering process determines not only what we experience, but how we interpret the world around us.

Attention is the gatekeeper. It focuses our cognitive and emotional energy on particular stimuli, while excluding others. It determines what enters conscious awareness and what remains unconscious. Attention is limited, easily hijacked, and shaped by both internal and external forces. What we attend to builds our sense of reality; what we neglect may as well not exist. In a noisy world, attention is one of the most valuable—and vulnerable—psychological capacities we have.

Memory gives experience shape over time. But memory is not a perfect recording device. It is reconstructive. We remember selectively, emotionally, and socially. The way we store and retrieve memory is influenced by mood, expectation, language, and context. Some memories fade quickly; others are etched in high detail. Some are accessible to awareness; others shape behavior without ever being consciously recalled. Our memories not only shape how we view the past, but also how we imagine the future and understand who we are in the present. They give our life narrative its arc.

Cognition and emotion are often described as separate, even opposing, forces. In truth, they are deeply intertwined. Emotions inform decisions, guide judgment, and shape belief. Cognition interprets emotion, builds schemas, and structures how we respond. You cannot think without feeling. You cannot feel without thinking. The dual-process model of cognition—system one (fast, emotional, intuitive) and system two (slow, rational, analytical)—captures this interaction well. But in everyday life, these systems are not in constant conflict. They work together, creating the texture of psychological experience.

At the center of it all is consciousness: the experience of being aware. Not just awake, but aware of the fact that you are awake. This self-referential capacity is what separates humans from many other species. Consciousness allows for reflection, choice, imagination, and insight. But it also creates problems. When we are conscious of ourselves, we are also vulnerable to self-judgment, existential anxiety, and emotional ambivalence. Consciousness lets us think about our thinking. It allows us to observe our inner world, narrate our experience, and recognize that the stories we live by are not always complete.

Self-awareness is one of the most powerful tools in psychological life. It allows for accountability, for change, for growth. But it also brings discomfort. To be self-aware is to confront contradiction, to notice the gap between values and actions, to see the parts of ourselves we would rather ignore. The mind is not always a peaceful place. But it is the only place from which meaning can be made.

In this chapter, we will walk through these foundational elements of the mind. We'll begin with perception and attention—how the world enters us. Then we'll move into memory—how the past remains with us and shapes who we become. Next, we'll explore the relationship between cognition and emotion, two systems often misunderstood as separate. And finally, we'll turn toward consciousness and self-awareness, the mechanisms that allow us to know ourselves at all.

Understanding the architecture of mind is not about memorizing terms or drawing diagrams. It is about recognizing the systems that shape how you interpret your life. It is about noticing which parts of your mind you overuse, which parts you ignore, and which parts you mistake for the truth. The mind is not just something you have. It is something you live inside every day. Learning its structure gives you more freedom to navigate it.

Perception and Attention: How We Take in the World

Every psychological experience begins with perception. Before we think, feel, remember, or decide, we are first engaged in the act of noticing—scanning our environment, interpreting signals, and selecting what to focus on. But perception is not a neutral act. It is a dynamic, interpretive process shaped by biology, experience, culture, and emotion. The world does not simply pour itself into our awareness. We take it in selectively, through the lens of what we expect, what we fear, what we value, and what we are unconsciously primed to find.

Attention acts as the mind's spotlight. At any given moment, an overwhelming amount of sensory information is bombarding the system—light, sound, temperature, posture, internal sensation, external movement. We cannot process all of it consciously, so the mind filters. It prioritizes some signals and suppresses others. This process is both adaptive and vulnerable. It allows us to function, to focus, to act. But it also means that we are always missing something. Our perception is not the whole picture. It is a curated version of reality.

The psychology of attention begins early in life. Infants are drawn to faces, particularly eyes and mouth movements, even before they understand what they're seeing. They orient toward human voices over mechanical sounds. As we grow, our attentional preferences become more shaped by learning and emotion. We develop a kind of attentional bias—toward threat, novelty, reward, or social approval—depending on our history. Someone raised in an unpredictable household may become hypervigilant, scanning constantly for signs of danger or disapproval. Another person, raised in a quiet but emotionally distant home, may develop an attentional bias toward subtle emotional cues, seeking signs of connection or withdrawal.

What we pay attention to is not just determined by personality. It is often regulated by what psychologists call salience. Salient stimuli are those that stand out—either because they are unusual, emotionally charged, or relevant to our goals. A loud noise, a crying child, a flashing light—these are all attention-grabbing. But so is a subtle shift in tone from someone we care about, or the body language of a group we feel uncertain in. Emotional salience plays a powerful role in what we notice and what we overlook. Attention is not only about stimulus intensity. It is about personal meaning.

This is why two people can experience the same event very differently. At a party, one person may be attuned to who is laughing, who is making eye contact, who seems comfortable. Another may be focused entirely on internal anxiety, bodily discomfort, or the nearest exit. Their attention is shaped by what their system perceives as most important—or most threatening. This selectivity is often unconscious, but it determines what data we take in, what we remember, and what stories we build about ourselves and others.

The process of perception is also filtered through prior knowledge and belief. If you expect someone to dislike you, you may perceive their neutral tone as dismissive. If you believe you're being excluded, you may interpret others' behavior through that filter, even if no exclusion is happening. This is called perceptual bias—a cognitive tendency to interpret ambiguous information in ways that confirm existing beliefs or fears. These biases are not signs of irrationality. They are evidence that the mind is always working to protect coherence, to avoid surprise, and to preserve emotional safety.

The cultural context also shapes perception. Different cultures train attention differently. Some cultures emphasize the individual and prioritize noticing personal achievement, status, or independence. Others focus on relational context, emotional nuance, and group dynamics. Even what we describe as "common sense" is a product of what our cultural environment trained us to see and prioritize. This has implications for everything from communication styles to conflict resolution to emotional interpretation.

Emotion and attention are inseparable. Emotional states influence what we notice, how we process it, and how we respond. Anxiety narrows attention, making it harder to see the whole picture. Joy tends to broaden it, increasing openness and creativity. Sadness can either deepen focus or fog perception, depending on its intensity. Emotional relevance gives certain stimuli priority, sometimes against our conscious will. This is why trauma is such a powerful attentional force. For someone with a trauma history, the body and mind remain alert to danger, even in seemingly safe contexts. The attentional system stays hijacked, searching for signs that it might happen again.

Modern environments often overwhelm the attentional system. With constant notifications, digital content, noise, and social surveillance, many people find their attention fractured. This state of continuous partial attention can leave the nervous system overstimulated and undernourished. It becomes difficult to engage deeply, to focus on long-form thought, or to reflect meaningfully. In psychological terms, attention becomes reactive instead of directed—drawn to whatever is loudest, most urgent, or most emotionally charged in the moment.

Attention can be trained. Practices like mindfulness, deep reading, or focused conversation help re-anchor it. So can deliberate withdrawal from overstimulating environments. But training attention is not only about productivity or calm. It is about regaining ownership of perception. When we can direct attention intentionally, we become less vulnerable to emotional reactivity and more capable of psychological flexibility. We gain the ability to see more than one frame at a time, to question first impressions, to notice what the mind would prefer to ignore.

Understanding perception and attention is foundational to all psychological insight. Before we can understand emotion, memory, belief, or behavior, we have to ask: what did the person see? What did they notice? What did they miss? These are not trivial questions. They reveal the architecture of the mind at work. They remind us that what feels real is not always the full story—but it is the story the mind is telling.

We do not perceive everything. We perceive what our minds have learned to expect and prioritize. Attention writes the first draft of reality. And understanding that process gives us the power to revise it.

Memory and Mental Time Travel

Memory is not just the faculty that allows us to recall facts. It is the system through which we construct identity, continuity, and coherence. When we say we "know who we are," what we often mean is that we remember who we've been. We remember what happened to us, what choices we made, what others said, how we felt. Memory gives our lives a through-line. It connects the past to the present and allows us to anticipate the future. Without memory, there is no sense of self, only scattered impressions and disconnected moments.

But memory is not a perfect recording device. It is not a literal archive of events stored intact in the brain. It is a reconstructive process, meaning we do not recall events exactly as they happened. Instead, we rebuild them each time we remember. Memory is shaped by emotion, language, suggestion, expectation, and later experience. What we remember depends not only on what occurred, but on how we've interpreted it, how often we've recalled it, and what meaning we've attached to it.

Psychologically, memory is both explicit and implicit. Explicit memory includes facts and events we can consciously recall: names, dates, conversations, what we ate yesterday, how a relationship ended. Implicit memory is less accessible but equally powerful. It includes skills, habits, and conditioned responses, as well as the emotional memory stored in the body. A person may not consciously remember a frightening early experience, but their body may react with tension, withdrawal, or vigilance when faced with a similar situation. This is one reason trauma is so complex: it often lives in the body and implicit systems, even when explicit recall is fragmented or absent.

There are several types of explicit memory relevant to psychological functioning. Semantic memory refers to general knowledge: facts, concepts, categories. Episodic memory, by contrast, refers to personally experienced events. Autobiographical memory blends both: it includes episodic content but also organizes it into a narrative sense of self. This narrative is not static. It evolves with time, and it is influenced by emotional state, cultural context, and even what we believe others expect of us.

The psychologist Endel Tulving introduced the idea of episodic memory as "mental time travel, "the ability to re-experience past events in the mind, with a sense of self present in those events. This capacity is central to identity. When we remember, we don't just recall facts. We reinhabit experiences. We feel the emotional texture, the visual detail, the internal responses. This re-experiencing can be nourishing or distressing, depending on what is being recalled and how it is framed.

Memory is also socially constructed. The stories we tell about ourselves—especially those told repeatedly—become more fixed in memory, regardless of their accuracy. If a person frequently tells the story of how they were always overlooked as a child, that story may become more detailed over time, even if some of those details are reconstructed or reshaped. The more we tell a story, the more familiar it becomes, and the more it feels true. This is not manipulation. It is how memory works. Recall is not passive. It is active, and it is always interpretive.

Emotion plays a powerful role in memory formation. Events charged with high emotion—especially fear, shame, grief, or joy—are more likely to be remembered vividly. This is due in part to the role of the amygdala, which helps encode emotionally salient experiences. Emotional arousal increases the likelihood that an event will be encoded and later retrieved. But high emotional arousal can also impair accuracy. Details may be distorted or lost, especially in cases of trauma. Memory may be vivid, but fragmented. Or it may be suppressed altogether, only to emerge in pieces later.

There is also a temporal dimension to memory. How we remember changes over time. An event that once felt overwhelming may later be recalled with distance or understanding. A relationship once seen as nurturing may, in hindsight, reveal a pattern of emotional manipulation. This revision is not deceitful. It reflects new information, new emotional capacity, or a broader frame. As our understanding evolves, so does the narrative scaffolding that holds memory together.

Cognitive psychology has also shown that memory is subject to numerous biases. The recency effect leads us to remember recent events more clearly than older ones. The confirmation bias leads us to remember information that supports our existing beliefs while forgetting or downplaying contradictory evidence. The peak-end rule suggests we remember experiences based on their most intense moment and how they ended, rather than their overall duration. These cognitive shortcuts are not flaws; they are adaptations. But they shape the emotional reality we carry forward.

Culturally, memory is influenced by the narratives that are permissible or encouraged within a given society or family system. Some families support open reflection and emotional storytelling. Others discourage revisiting the past, viewing it as weakness or disloyalty. These patterns influence which memories are retrieved and which are suppressed. In trauma-affected families, for example, entire chapters of history may be "forgotten" collectively, only to resurface years later when someone begins asking questions. What is remembered is not only personal; it is political, familial, and cultural.

Memory is also at the heart of psychological stuckness. People often come into therapy because they are caught in loops—of fear, regret, shame, or longing—that are rooted in memory. A client may say they feel inadequate, but beneath that feeling is a remembered experience of early criticism or rejection. That memory, often stored implicitly, becomes a template. It shapes how new experiences are interpreted. If left unexamined, it becomes a lens through which life is filtered—often in ways that confirm the original wound.

But memory is not only a source of pain. It is also the source of wisdom, intimacy, and continuity. Remembering how one has survived, how one has loved, how one has changed—these are psychologically anchoring experiences. When people are in emotional crisis, they often feel as though the past is erased. They say things like "I've always been like this," or "Nothing's ever worked." Revisiting memory can restore context. It reminds the person that who they are now is not the whole story. That they have lived through other chapters. That they are more than their current state.

Therapeutically, working with memory often involves more than just retrieval. It involves re-encoding. This means helping the person experience the memory differently—perhaps with more safety, more insight, or more support. Memory reconsolidation research has shown that when a memory is recalled and then paired with a new emotional experience, it can be updated in the brain. This is one of the mechanisms through which healing occurs—not by erasing the past, but by transforming its psychological weight.

It is important to note that memory can be distorted, influenced, and even falsely constructed. Under certain conditions, people may come to believe that they remember events that did not occur. This does not mean memory is unreliable in every case, but it does mean that memory must always be approached with humility. It is real, but not always literal. It is emotionally true, but not always factually precise.

Ultimately, memory is what gives us depth. It connects the present to the past, and the past to the imagined future. It is the foundation of identity, narrative, and meaning. When we understand how memory works, we are less likely to be haunted by it—and more likely to use it as a source of strength and clarity.

You are not just what you remember. But what you remember, and how you carry it, shapes how you live.

Emotion and Cognition: Two Intertwined Systems

For decades, emotion and cognition were studied as if they belonged to separate realms. One was seen as instinctive, irrational, and disruptive. The other, rational, deliberate, and organized. Popular culture has long echoed this division: heart versus head, feeling versus logic, impulse versus reason. But in reality, these two systems are not in conflict. They are interdependent. The mind does not think without feeling, and it does not feel without thinking. Every perception, judgment, decision, and memory is shaped by this interaction.

Emotion is often misunderstood. It is not merely a reaction, or a burst of feeling. Emotion is information. It tells us something about our needs, our values, our expectations, and our environment. It registers internal states and external cues, evaluates threat or safety, and prepares the body and mind for action. Without emotion, decision-making becomes nearly impossible. People with damage to the emotional centers of the brain often retain intellectual function but lose the ability to prioritize, evaluate risk, or make meaningful choices. They can weigh facts, but they cannot care about outcomes. This suggests that emotion is not a barrier to reason; it is its foundation.

From a neurobiological perspective, emotion and cognition are tightly linked. The limbic system, which includes structures such as the amygdala and hippocampus, processes emotional salience and links it to memory. The prefrontal cortex, responsible for executive function, judgment, and planning, works with—not against—emotional systems to regulate behavior. When we encounter a stimulus, emotional and cognitive responses occur almost simultaneously. The amygdala may fire quickly in response to perceived threat, while the cortex evaluates whether the threat is real or imagined. In this way, emotion alerts and informs, while cognition interprets and refines.

Consider how this plays out in everyday experience. You receive an email from your supervisor with an ambiguous tone. Emotion registers first—perhaps anxiety, annoyance, or defensiveness. That emotional signal primes your attention and influences what you notice. Cognition then takes over to analyze the message: Was the tone critical? Was something left unsaid? Should you respond immediately? The entire process happens rapidly, and the outcome—how you interpret the email and what you choose to do next—is shaped by both emotional and cognitive input. If your emotional state is intense, it may distort your reasoning. If your reasoning is rigid, it may override important emotional cues.

One of the most influential models of this relationship is the dual process theory, which proposes two systems of thought. System one is fast, automatic, emotional, and intuitive. It is the system we rely on when making quick judgments, reading body language, or reacting to danger. System two is slower, more deliberate, and analytical. It is the system we engage when solving problems, evaluating complex decisions, or regulating impulses. Both systems are necessary. Problems arise when one system dominates without input from the other.

People who rely heavily on system one may find themselves emotionally reactive, making decisions based on gut feeling without examining context or consequence. Those who rely too much on system two may suppress emotion to the point of disconnection, becoming overly intellectualized and disconnected from intuition. Psychological maturity involves the integration of both systems: the ability to feel fully and think clearly at the same time.

Emotion also shapes attention and memory. Events that carry emotional significance are more likely to be noticed, remembered, and rehearsed. Emotionally neutral information tends to fade more quickly. This is adaptive. From an evolutionary standpoint, remembering danger, rejection, or success helps us learn and survive. But this system also creates cognitive distortions. We may remember painful experiences more vividly than neutral or positive ones, leading to pessimistic bias. We may overestimate the likelihood of negative outcomes based on emotionally charged memories, even when those memories are not representative of reality.

Belief formation is another area where emotion and cognition merge. People often assume that beliefs are formed through logical evaluation of evidence. In practice, beliefs are often emotionally anchored first, and then rationalized later. A person may feel unsafe in certain situations, and then form beliefs that explain or justify that feeling. This is not dishonesty; it is coherence-seeking. The mind prefers consistency between what is felt and what is believed. When dissonance arises—when feelings and thoughts are out of sync—the mind will work to resolve it, often by adjusting one to match the other.

This process is especially visible in emotionally charged topics: politics, relationships, personal identity. People may ignore evidence, cling to outdated ideas, or distort facts—not because they lack intelligence, but because changing a belief would mean destabilizing a feeling. This is why cognitive behavioral therapy, or CBT, focuses not only on beliefs but on the emotional undercurrents that support them. By identifying automatic thoughts, exploring their emotional origins, and testing them against lived experience, people can shift both their feelings and their interpretations.

Emotion also plays a role in moral reasoning. Research has shown that moral judgments are often made emotionally first, then justified intellectually. When presented with moral dilemmas, people typically have an immediate emotional reaction, followed by slower cognitive reflection. This has implications for ethics, empathy, and social behavior. It suggests that moral development is not only about learning rules or principles. It is also about cultivating emotional awareness, perspective-taking, and the ability to regulate affect in the face of complexity.

Developmentally, the integration of emotion and cognition evolves over time. Young children often struggle to articulate their feelings, and their behavior reflects raw emotional states with limited cognitive regulation. As language develops and socialization deepens, children begin to label feelings, interpret intentions, and connect internal states to external outcomes. Adolescents begin experimenting with emotional logic—trying to understand not only what they feel, but why. Adults, ideally, learn to tolerate mixed emotions, revise beliefs, and think through emotional responses without invalidating them.

However, this integration is not guaranteed. Many adults remain split—either overidentified with their emotions or excessively controlled by intellectual defenses. People who have experienced emotional neglect, trauma, or rigid emotional socialization may struggle to bridge this gap. They may dismiss their feelings as irrational, or become overwhelmed by them without the tools to regulate or interpret them. In such cases, therapy often involves re-establishing the emotional-cognitive connection—helping people name, tolerate, and think about their emotional experience with both clarity and compassion.

It is worth noting that different people have different emotional-cognitive profiles. Some are naturally more emotionally attuned; others more analytical. Some process externally, needing to talk things through; others process internally, needing time and solitude. These differences are not deficits. They are variations in temperament, experience, and adaptation. The goal is not to become someone else, but to understand your own profile well enough to work with it—strengthening the weaker capacities, and making room for both clarity and feeling.

In the end, emotion and cognition are not rivals. They are partners. Emotion provides depth, urgency, and meaning. Cognition provides structure, reflection, and flexibility. Together, they allow us to navigate the world not only with insight, but with humanity.

Consciousness and Self-Awareness

Consciousness is one of the most elusive and contested subjects in all of psychology. It is the condition of being aware, the state in which we register experience, reflect on it, and hold it in mind. But defining consciousness precisely is difficult, because it encompasses so many layers of perception, thought, and awareness. At its most basic level, consciousness allows us to respond to the world. At its most complex, it allows us to observe ourselves responding, to evaluate that response, and to wonder what it means.

The study of consciousness has often fallen at the intersection of psychology, neuroscience, philosophy, and even theology. Some view it as a product of neural activity, nothing more than the result of billions of neurons firing in complex patterns. Others see it as an emergent property, something that arises not just from the brain, but from the dynamic interaction between organism and environment. Still others argue that consciousness cannot be reduced to brain function at all, but reflects a deeper or more fundamental aspect of being. Regardless of the framework used, the fact remains that consciousness is central to human experience.

In psychology, consciousness is not simply being awake. It involves the capacity to register thoughts, emotions, and perceptions while also having some reflective stance toward them. A person who is conscious knows not only what they are thinking, but that they are thinking. They can observe the contents of their mind and shift their attention voluntarily. They can imagine other perspectives. They can consider past and future, and they can ask questions about purpose, meaning, and selfhood. These are not just signs of intelligence. They are signs of consciousness functioning at a high level.

Self-awareness is a more specific facet of consciousness. It is the ability to turn attention inward and reflect on one's own thoughts, feelings, motives, and actions. While many animals display signs of consciousness—pain avoidance, problem-solving, even empathy—very few demonstrate self-awareness in the human sense. Human beings not only experience life; they experience themselves experiencing it. This recursive quality creates a unique kind of mind, capable of introspection, self-regulation, and existential questioning.

Developmentally, self-awareness emerges in stages. Infants are born with basic sensory consciousness. They can perceive sights, sounds, and touch, and they begin forming associations between sensation and response. Around 18 to 24 months, children begin to show signs of mirror self-recognition, indicating a growing awareness that the image they see is connected to their own body. As language develops, so does narrative self-awareness. Children start to describe themselves, recall past events, and imagine future scenarios. This allows for a continuous sense of identity, which is built not only on memory, but on the internal story one tells about who they are.

As adults, self-awareness expands to include emotional literacy, moral reasoning, and metacognition. Metacognition refers to the ability to think about one's own thinking. It is what allows a person to notice patterns in their own mind, question assumptions, and revise beliefs.

In therapy and self-reflection, metacognition is often the goal: helping someone step outside of automatic thought loops and see them from a wider perspective. The ability to say, "I notice that I tend to catastrophize in stressful situations," is a metacognitive insight. It opens the door for change, because it shifts the person from being inside the thought to observing it.

But self-awareness is not always comfortable. To be conscious of oneself is also to be aware of limitations, contradictions, and the inevitability of suffering. It is to live with the knowledge that life is finite, that one's choices matter, and that meaning must often be created rather than found. This burden of consciousness can lead to avoidance, denial, or distraction. It can also lead to profound insight, growth, and transformation. The difference often lies in how much safety and support a person has while navigating that awareness.

Different psychological traditions have emphasized different aspects of consciousness. Psychodynamic theory focuses on the tension between conscious and unconscious material. Freud believed that much of human behavior is driven by forces outside of awareness, and that becoming conscious of these forces is essential for psychological health. Humanistic psychology, by contrast, places consciousness at the center of personal growth. Carl Rogers and Abraham Maslow viewed self-awareness as a pathway to authenticity, agency, and self-actualization. Cognitive psychology explores the structures and processes of conscious thought, such as attention, working memory, and decision-making. Each of these perspectives adds a layer of understanding to the architecture of conscious experience.

From a neuroscience standpoint, consciousness is associated with activity in several key brain regions, including the prefrontal cortex, the parietal lobes, and the thalamus. Disruptions in these areas can result in altered states of consciousness, such as coma, dissociation, or hallucination. But there is no single "consciousness center" in the brain. It appears to arise from a networked system, rather than a localized structure. This may explain why consciousness is so difficult to study directly. It is not a thing that can be isolated. It is a process, a field, a relationship between inner and outer awareness.

Consciousness is also state-dependent. It can be altered by drugs, fatigue, trauma, meditation, or emotional overwhelm. In dissociative states, people may feel disconnected from their bodies, their thoughts, or their sense of self. In flow states, attention becomes so focused that self-consciousness fades. In mindfulness, the goal is to become aware of awareness itself. Each of these states represents a different configuration of consciousness, suggesting that it is not fixed, but fluid. People move in and out of various levels of self-awareness throughout the day and throughout life.

In clinical work, increasing conscious awareness is often the goal. Many symptoms—anxiety, depression, addiction, emotional reactivity—are maintained by automatic processes that operate below the level of awareness. Helping someone become more conscious of their thoughts, patterns, and underlying beliefs can create a pause, a moment of choice. That pause is powerful. It allows a person to respond instead of react, to reflect instead of repeat, to choose a new direction rather than being pulled by old currents.

However, too much self-focus can be counterproductive. Excessive rumination, self-criticism, or intellectualization can lead to paralysis rather than clarity. The goal is not constant introspection. The goal is flexible awareness: the ability to direct attention inward or outward as needed, to observe without judgment, and to hold one's experience with both curiosity and care. This kind of awareness strengthens emotional regulation, improves relationships, and deepens meaning.

Culturally, the cultivation of consciousness varies. Some societies encourage self-inquiry, spiritual reflection, or psychological insight. Others prioritize collective identity, social roles, or external behavior. Even within a single culture, different subgroups will hold different norms about how much self-awareness is encouraged or supported. In environments that discourage reflection, people may learn to bypass uncomfortable truths or deny emotional realities. In environments that pathologize emotion, people may learn to intellectualize their feelings rather than integrating them. The development of consciousness is not just an individual journey. It is shaped by the environment, the family, the culture, and the language available to describe inner experience.

Ultimately, consciousness allows us to be more than reactive organisms. It gives us the capacity to notice our experience, reflect on it, and change our course. It allows us to ask not only "What am I feeling?" but "Why am I feeling this?" and "What can I do with this feeling?" It gives us access to a deeper kind of freedom—not freedom from experience, but freedom within it.

To be conscious is to be able to pause, observe, and participate with intention. It is not always easy, but it is the foundation for psychological growth, ethical behavior, and meaningful connection.

* * *

4

Self and Identity Formation

From the time we first recognize ourselves in the mirror, we begin a lifelong process of answering the question: Who am I? It is a question that seems simple on its surface, yet carries infinite complexity beneath it. We do not wake up each day as a blank slate, nor do we function entirely as fixed personalities. Instead, we live inside a self that is both continuous and changing, both constructed and experienced, both authored and reflected. The self is where psychology gets personal. It is the meeting place between the inner world and the outer one. And how that self is formed—how it becomes known, shaped, tested, and reworked—is one of the most profound processes in all of psychological life.

We often talk about identity as if it were a thing we have, a possession we carry, or a label that can be printed on a driver's license. But identity is not a noun. It is a process. It is constructed over time through the interaction of temperament, emotion, memory, behavior, biology, feedback, and story. It is shaped by the families we are born into, the cultures that surround us, the roles we are assigned, the roles we choose, and the conflicts we survive. Some parts of identity feel stable across time, like core values or familiar emotional patterns. Other parts shift with age, environment, or new understanding. The experience of self is never entirely static, and that's part of what makes it difficult—and deeply human.

At the center of identity development is the ego. Not ego in the everyday sense of arrogance or pride, but in the classical psychological sense: the organizing system of the mind that creates coherence from experience. The ego holds the boundary between self and other. It mediates between instinct and morality. It protects and asserts, regulates and adapts. A healthy ego is not loud or brittle. It is flexible, clear, and capable of reflection. When the ego is underdeveloped or fragmented, the sense of self becomes unstable. When it is over-identified with roles, status, or image, the self becomes defensive or performative. Understanding the ego is key to understanding how we show up in the world, how we process reality, and how we protect our psychological coherence when that reality is challenged.

Of course, the ego does not exist in isolation. We are never just ourselves, in a vacuum. We are also the reflections others hold up to us. Identity is relational. From infancy, we come to know who we are through how others respond to us. We learn that certain traits are admired, while others are corrected or ignored. We absorb values, fears, and expectations from caregivers, culture, and community. We mirror and are mirrored. We perform and are perceived. And over time, those patterns of reflection create internal scripts that shape how we understand ourselves. Some of these scripts are empowering. Others are limiting. Many go unexamined.

This dynamic—between inner construction and outer reflection—makes identity incredibly sensitive to context. A person may feel confident and expressive in one setting, but hesitant and muted in another. They may carry different versions of themselves across different relationships, social roles, or life phases. This is not necessarily inauthenticity. It is psychological adaptability. The problem arises when a person no longer feels connected to any of those versions, or when a single version becomes so rigid that it no longer accommodates change. Identity formation is not about locking in a self. It is about learning how to relate to the self with depth, flexibility, and clarity.

Another major force in this process is narrative. Human beings are storytelling creatures. We do not just experience life. We organize it into story. We make sense of pain by explaining it. We connect moments across time by giving them emotional throughlines. We define who we are by the stories we tell about where we've been, what we've survived, what we value, and where we think we are going. This narrative capacity is both a psychological strength and a psychological vulnerability. It gives meaning to experience, but it can also trap us in patterns that no longer serve us. Some people carry identities built on shame, failure, or rejection, even when their lives no longer match those scripts. Others revise their narratives as they grow, reinterpreting old experiences with new insight. The ability to re-author one's identity story is one of the most powerful psychological tools we have.

Throughout this chapter, we will explore how identity is built from the inside and the outside. We will begin by looking at the role of the ego—what it is, how it develops, and how it functions in everyday psychological life. We will then examine personality and temperament, and how stable traits emerge alongside dynamic adaptations. From there, we will look closely at the role of social mirroring—how other people shape our self-image, and how we internalize their reactions. Finally, we will examine the personal narrative: how we tell the story of who we are, and how we can begin to revise that story in ways that foster resilience, clarity, and growth.

These are not abstract ideas. They are deeply practical. They influence how we behave in relationships, how we respond to challenge, how we define success, how we carry pain, and how we make meaning. They shape how we show up in the world, and how we feel inside ourselves. And understanding them more clearly does not just make us more psychologically literate. It helps us live with more agency, more integrity, and more self-compassion.

The Ego and the Constructed Self

We all carry some intuitive sense of self. There is a feeling of "I" that persists across our lifetime, a continuity of presence that says, "this is me." But that feeling of self is not innate in the way we often assume. It is not simply given to us at birth, nor is it a fixed object we can locate in the brain. Rather, what we experience as the self is a constructed and dynamic process—a mental architecture formed over time through psychological functions, experiences, feedback, and developmental negotiation. At the center of this constructed self is the ego.

In classical psychoanalytic theory, particularly in Freud's model, the ego is one of three psychic structures: the id, the ego, and the superego. The id represents primal drives, the superego internalized morality, and the ego the rational mediator between them. While Freud's structural model is no longer used in full by most contemporary psychologists, the concept of the ego has remained. Over time, it has evolved from Freud's internal referee to a more expansive understanding: the ego as the organizing system of consciousness that integrates thought, emotion, perception, and behavior into a coherent sense of self.

This organizing function of the ego is both protective and adaptive. It filters experience to preserve coherence. When we encounter dissonance—an experience or idea that conflicts with our self-image or beliefs—the ego steps in to protect psychological stability. It may reinterpret the event, suppress the emotion, rationalize the contradiction, or redirect attention. These defense mechanisms, while sometimes maladaptive, are often necessary for functioning. Without them, we would be overwhelmed by the sheer volume of contradiction, ambiguity, and vulnerability that life throws at us.

But the ego does more than protect. It also assembles. It gathers fragments of experience, stores memory, weighs consequences, and projects identity. The ego allows us to have preferences, goals, routines, and values. It provides the structure through which we make decisions, regulate impulses, and navigate the expectations of others. In short, it is what gives our mind a sense of center. When the ego is well-integrated, a person tends to experience themselves as real, coherent, and capable. When it is fragmented, fragile, or overinflated, the person may struggle with internal conflict, anxiety, or distorted self-perception.

One of the major tensions in ego development is the balance between authenticity and adaptation. On one hand, we want to express our true nature—to live in accordance with our values, temperament, and inner truth. On the other hand, we are constantly adjusting to our environments. Children adapt to their parents' approval patterns. Teens shape their identity in response to peers. Adults navigate the pressures of work, culture, and relationship. In each case, the ego makes necessary compromises between internal preference and external demand. Sometimes those compromises are healthy. Other times, they result in a false self.

The concept of the false self was developed by British psychoanalyst Donald Winnicott. According to Winnicott, when a child grows up in an environment that is not attuned to their emotional needs, they may develop a "false self" to maintain attachment and survive. This false self is compliant, performative, and focused on pleasing others. Over time, the child may lose touch with their authentic emotional world, resulting in an adult who functions outwardly but feels hollow inside. This pattern is not rare. Many people grow up learning that certain emotions, preferences, or traits are unacceptable, and so they suppress them. The ego adapts to preserve belonging, even at the cost of inner truth.

In therapy, one of the core goals is helping individuals differentiate between the adaptive ego and the authentic self. The ego is not inherently bad. It is necessary for navigating reality. But when the ego becomes over-identified with roles, images, or achievements, it can block deeper self-connection. People begin to believe they are their job title, their social mask, or their curated personality. When life challenges those identifiers—a job loss, a divorce, a trauma—the ego can collapse, leading to a crisis of identity. The person asks, "If I am not this, then who am I?"

This question is not a failure. It is an opening. Ego disintegration, while painful, can be the doorway to growth. Carl Jung spoke of individuation—the process by which a person moves beyond the ego's surface identity and integrates the unconscious aspects of the self. This process involves facing shadow material, examining internal contradictions, and allowing the self to become more whole. It is not about rejecting the ego, but about expanding it to include more of the truth.

Developmentally, ego strength grows through both challenge and reflection. Children build a stable ego through secure attachment, consistent feedback, and opportunities to express autonomy. Adolescents test their ego boundaries by experimenting with identity and confronting authority. Adults continue to refine the ego through experiences of success, failure, intimacy, and loss. Life's interruptions—the moments that disorient us or call us to rethink ourselves—are often the very experiences that make ego structure more flexible and integrated.

The ego is also culturally shaped. Western psychology has often emphasized an individualistic, autonomous self. But in many cultures, the self is relational, defined in terms of family, community, or collective roles. In such contexts, the ego may be more attuned to social harmony than personal preference. Neither orientation is superior. Both reveal the ways in which ego structure is not just personal, but also contextual. A well-functioning ego in one culture may look quite different from what is valued in another.

Ultimately, the ego is not an enemy. It is a tool. It helps us function, plan, protect, and engage. The goal of psychological development is not to eliminate the ego, but to work with it skillfully. When we understand how the ego is formed, what it defends, and where it limits us, we gain access to a deeper layer of freedom. We can begin to observe the ego without becoming imprisoned by it. We can hold our identity more lightly, with both seriousness and flexibility.

To live with a constructed self is not to live falsely. It is to live consciously, aware that the self we carry is a product of many forces—some chosen, some inherited, some imposed. And that we have the ongoing ability to participate in how that self evolves.

Personality and Temperament: Stable Traits, Flexible Selves

When we talk about personality, we are often referring to the consistent patterns of thought, behavior, emotional reactivity, and social engagement that make each person distinct. Someone may be described as outgoing or reserved, warm or detached, optimistic or anxious. These patterns shape how we approach relationships, handle stress, make decisions, and interpret the world. But personality is not merely a social label. It is a psychologically rooted system of traits that emerge from a combination of temperament, early experience, genetic inheritance, and learned behavior. To understand the self, we must understand how personality develops—and how flexible it really is.

At the most basic level, temperament refers to the biologically based tendencies that appear early in life. Even in infancy, children display differences in sensitivity, intensity, adaptability, and responsiveness to stimuli. Some infants are easygoing and calm; others are irritable and easily overstimulated. These early differences in behavior and arousal are not learned. They reflect variations in nervous system functioning, particularly in the reactivity of the limbic system and the regulation capacities of the prefrontal cortex. Jerome Kagan's research on inhibited versus uninhibited children, for example, demonstrated that some children show high physiological reactivity to new stimuli—fast heart rate, high cortisol levels, increased motor activity—while others do not. These differences predicted patterns of social behavior years later, suggesting that temperament lays the groundwork for personality.

However, temperament is not destiny. What a child is born with interacts with the environment in complex ways. A highly reactive child raised in a patient, emotionally attuned household may learn effective regulation and develop into a thoughtful, observant adult. That same child in a chaotic or dismissive home might instead develop chronic anxiety, mistrust, or defensive withdrawal. In other words, personality traits do not simply emerge from the inside out. They are shaped in response to how the world meets—or fails to meet—our emotional needs. Developmental psychologist Thomas Boyce has used the metaphor of "orchid and dandelion" children: some are highly sensitive and flourish only under the right conditions, while others are more resilient and adaptable regardless of environment.

As children mature into adolescents and adults, these temperamental tendencies become elaborated into personality traits. The most widely accepted model in psychology is the Five-Factor Model, or Big Five, which identifies five broad dimensions of personality: openness to experience, conscientiousness, extraversion, agreeableness, and neuroticism. Each of these traits represents a spectrum. A person may be high in extraversion (outgoing, energetic) or low (reserved, introspective). High in conscientiousness (disciplined, organized) or low (spontaneous, disorganized). What makes this model useful is not only its predictive value—personality traits are associated with a range of life outcomes, from career performance to relationship satisfaction—but also its stability. Longitudinal research shows that core traits tend to remain relatively stable over time, especially after early adulthood.

Still, stability is not the same as rigidity. While personality traits are relatively enduring, they are not fixed in stone. People change, sometimes gradually and sometimes dramatically. Experiences such as trauma, illness, major life transitions, or sustained reflection can shift how a person expresses their traits. For example, someone who has always been impulsive may develop greater conscientiousness after becoming a parent. Someone who has always been closed off emotionally may become more expressive through years of therapy or a meaningful relationship. The structure of personality is durable, but not immovable. As psychologist Dan McAdams has noted, people are not only characterized by their traits, but also by their motivations, values, and life stories—dimensions that are much more open to transformation.

This matters because personality is not just a diagnostic tool or a way of typing people. It influences how we suffer and how we thrive. People high in neuroticism, for instance, tend to experience more negative emotion, worry, and self-doubt. But they may also be more attuned to risk, detail, or interpersonal tension—qualities that can be protective in the right context. Those high in openness may be more creative and intellectually curious, but also more prone to distraction or existential distress. Traits carry costs and benefits. What matters is how they are understood and directed. When people understand their own personalities clearly—without judgment—they are better able to make choices that align with their strengths and mitigate their vulnerabilities.

Moreover, personality cannot be fully understood outside of context. Culture plays a significant role in shaping which traits are encouraged, rewarded, or discouraged. Western cultures often privilege extraversion, independence, and assertiveness. In contrast, many Eastern cultures emphasize humility, harmony, and deference to collective well-being. A personality that is considered ideal in one cultural setting may be misunderstood or pathologized in another. Similarly, family dynamics, religious traditions, gender norms, and social expectations all influence how traits are expressed or suppressed. A child who is naturally assertive may be seen as a leader in one context and as disruptive in another.

The workplace also provides a lens for how traits function. Conscientiousness, for instance, is one of the strongest predictors of job performance across industries. But high conscientiousness may also lead to perfectionism, rigidity, or workaholism if not balanced. Similarly, extraversion may be beneficial in sales or leadership roles, but can become overwhelming or performative in roles that require solitude or reflection. Personality becomes adaptive when people find environments that align with their traits—or develop the capacity to navigate environments that challenge them.

The question of whether we can intentionally change our personality has long intrigued psychologists. Traditionally, traits were viewed as largely stable, but emerging research suggests that deliberate effort, over time, can yield measurable changes. This is particularly true when change is tied to values or identity goals. For example, someone who wants to become more conscientious might begin with small habit changes, then reinforce those behaviors through feedback and self-reflection. Over time, the trait itself may shift—not just the behavior. This is not about faking a different personality. It is about reshaping the patterns that underlie one's tendencies, through repetition, motivation, and context.

From a therapeutic standpoint, understanding personality is crucial. Therapists must understand not only a client's presenting issues, but also the personality structure in which those issues live. Is the person rigid or flexible? Highly reactive or even-keeled? Open to feedback or guarded? Treatment approaches vary depending on the client's temperament. Cognitive-behavioral therapy may work well for those who are organized and reflective, while more emotionally focused work may be better suited to those with deep affective sensitivity. Personality informs how we heal—not just how we hurt.

In developmental psychology, we see that personality begins early, is shaped by both biology and experience, and remains malleable under the right conditions. In adult life, it guides relationships, values, and coping strategies. While we may not be able to change our entire structure, we can build insight, expand our flexibility, and make more intentional choices. Personality is not a prison. It is a pattern—and like any pattern, it can evolve when illuminated.

Ultimately, understanding your personality is not about boxing yourself in. It is about recognizing the themes that run through your life—where they come from, how they play out, and how they can be refined. You are not simply the sum of your traits. You are also the choices you make about how to live with them.

Social Mirrors: How Others Shape Who We Become

We do not become ourselves in isolation. Every person's identity is shaped, refined, and sometimes distorted through the eyes of others. From infancy to adulthood, we are social creatures by nature. We look outward to know who we are inward. In this sense, identity is never purely self-made. It is forged in interaction, reinforced through feedback,

SELF AND IDENTITY FORMATION

and held together by a network of mirrors—parents, peers, partners, culture—all reflecting a version of us back to ourselves. This process of social mirroring is not secondary to development; it is central. To understand how identity takes form, we have to examine the role of others in that formation.

In early development, the mirror begins with the caregiver. The concept of mirroring, introduced by psychoanalyst Heinz Kohut, refers to the way a caregiver responds to a child's expressions with attunement and emotional resonance. When a baby smiles and the parent smiles back with warmth and acknowledgment, the child begins to feel seen. This sense of being recognized—emotionally and physiologically—is foundational to a stable self. Through these repeated experiences, the child learns, "I exist, and my internal states matter." Conversely, when caregivers are inconsistent, emotionally unavailable, or misattuned, the child may struggle to form a cohesive sense of self. The message becomes, "I must perform to be accepted" or "My inner world is not valid."

This early mirroring builds what psychologists call the reflective self. The child begins to internalize the emotional responses of caregivers as part of their identity. A child who is consistently praised for being helpful may come to see themselves as "good" or "useful." A child ignored in distress may learn that their feelings are a burden. These patterns often become templates for future relationships. Without conscious reflection, we may carry those early scripts into adulthood, unconsciously seeking the same kind of mirrors we grew up with—whether healthy or not.

As children grow into adolescence, peers become the dominant mirrors. During this stage, the need for social belonging intensifies, and identity becomes more experimental. Adolescents try on roles, explore new aesthetics, adopt group norms, and observe how others react. Approval and rejection become powerful sculptors of behavior. While this stage can be turbulent, it also allows for the testing of boundaries and the refinement of self-concept. The adolescent does not simply absorb identity from others but begins to actively negotiate it. The danger arises when that negotiation is limited by rigid social expectations, bullying, or exclusion. In such cases, the mirror becomes a source of distortion rather than clarity.

Symbolic interactionism, a theory from sociology and social psychology, offers a useful framework for this process. It posits that individuals develop a sense of self through interaction with others and the meanings assigned to those interactions. According to theorist Charles Horton Cooley, we develop the "looking-glass self" by imagining how we appear to others, imagining their judgment, and then forming a self-concept based on that perceived judgment. This process happens constantly, often without our awareness. We adjust tone, posture, word choice, even interests based on the social environment, crafting a self that feels acceptable to others.

While this adaptability can foster social cohesion, it can also compromise authenticity. When the social mirror reflects only what is desirable or acceptable, parts of the self may be hidden or denied. Over time, this can lead to internal fragmentation. People feel disconnected from their own desires, unsure of their values, or trapped in performative roles. They may feel liked or admired, but not truly known. The self becomes a projection rather than a reflection. This is one of the central challenges of social mirroring: the very relationships that shape us can also obscure us.

Attachment theory adds another dimension to this dynamic. According to John Bowlby and Mary Ainsworth, the quality of our early attachments influences how we relate to others throughout life. Secure attachment fosters confidence, resilience, and openness. Insecure attachment—whether avoidant, anxious, or disorganized—can result in hypervigilance, fear of rejection, or emotional withdrawal. These attachment patterns color how we interpret social mirrors. A securely attached person may receive criticism as feedback. An anxiously attached person may receive it as rejection. In this way, our history with mirroring shapes how we read the reflections we encounter later in life.

In adult relationships, social mirroring becomes more subtle but no less influential. Romantic partners, close friends, and work colleagues all serve as mirrors. Their responses to us—spoken or unspoken—affirm or challenge our identity. A partner who sees us as capable and kind can strengthen those traits in our self-concept. A friend who consistently questions our judgment may cause us to doubt ourselves. These dynamics are not inherently manipulative. They are part of being human. We do not exist in a vacuum, and every interaction reinforces or reshapes how we see ourselves.

Cultural mirroring operates on a broader scale. Media, social institutions, and cultural narratives tell us who we are supposed to be. They reflect dominant values around gender, race, age, success, and morality. These mirrors are often distorted, favoring particular identities while marginalizing others. For individuals who do not see themselves reflected in dominant culture, the result can be a sense of invisibility or shame. This is why representation matters—not just politically, but psychologically. To see oneself reflected with dignity and depth is to feel one's humanity affirmed.

Social mirroring is also embedded in digital life. On social media, the feedback loop is constant and quantifiable: likes, shares, comments, views. People begin to curate their self-presentation for maximum affirmation. Identity becomes less about self-discovery and more about social performance. The danger is that the mirror becomes addictive. The more we rely on external validation to know who we are, the more fragile our sense of self becomes. If the algorithm changes, or the feedback slows, we are left unmoored. This is not a theoretical concern. It is a real psychological consequence of living in an image-saturated, feedback-driven world.

At its best, social mirroring can be a source of growth. Healthy relationships provide accurate and compassionate feedback, allowing us to see both our strengths and our blind spots. Good mirrors reflect without distortion. They hold us accountable without shaming, celebrate us without idolizing, and stay with us even when our reflection is messy. In therapy, this mirroring is intentional. The therapist reflects the client's thoughts, feelings, and behaviors with clarity and warmth, helping them develop a more integrated and accurate sense of self.

Ultimately, the challenge is not to eliminate social mirroring, but to become more discerning about the mirrors we use. Some reflections are warped by judgment, envy, or projection. Others are grounded in honesty and care. As we mature, we learn to recognize the difference. We begin to internalize a stable, compassionate mirror—one that allows us to navigate life with both humility and self-respect.

You are not only the product of your mirrors, but also the one who decides which reflections to keep. You do not have to believe every image the world throws at you. You can choose your mirrors wisely, and over time, become one for others as well.

Internal Narratives and the Story of You

Your life is not a list of events. It is a story. And the story you tell yourself about who you are—where you came from, what you've overcome, what matters to you, and what you expect from the future—shapes your behavior more than any isolated fact. Human beings are narrative creatures. We rely on story not just to remember the past, but to make sense of it. We use narrative to form identity, interpret experience, and construct meaning. Whether consciously or unconsciously, we are all authors of a personal myth. The way we tell that story influences everything from our emotional regulation to our moral reasoning, from our resilience to our relationships.

Narrative identity is the internalized and evolving story we develop to make sense of our lives. Psychologist Dan McAdams defines it as a personal myth that integrates past, present, and future into a coherent whole. Unlike personality traits or core values, narrative identity is not fixed. It is shaped through memory, interpretation, and reflection. A person might frame a difficult childhood as the crucible that forged their strength or as the wound that continues to define their suffering. The events may be the same, but the story changes the meaning—and that meaning determines psychological outcomes.

Narratives are built from memory, but memory is not a recording device. It is reconstructive. We remember selectively, often in ways that confirm our existing self-concept. Someone who believes they are unlucky will recall moments of failure or betrayal more easily than moments of triumph. Someone who sees themselves as resilient will remember setbacks as challenges overcome. This is not deception; it is coherence-seeking. The mind prefers stories that feel stable and emotionally congruent. But this preference can reinforce distorted or limiting beliefs if those stories are never challenged.

Our emotional lives are deeply entwined with these inner narratives. The way we explain past events to ourselves affects how we feel about them—and how we carry them forward. For instance, two people may go through divorce. One may narrate it as a failure and personal rejection, while the other frames it as a necessary transformation that created space for self-growth. The psychological difference between these interpretations is profound. The first is more likely to produce shame and rumination. The second may foster insight and forward momentum. Both are real stories. Only one supports healing.

Cognitive behavioral therapy often targets the content of these narratives, helping clients examine and reframe core beliefs that drive emotional suffering. A person might uncover a story that they are fundamentally unlovable, built on early experiences of abandonment or neglect. That narrative, while understandable, may lead to self-sabotage in relationships or chronic low self-worth. By identifying the origin of the belief and questioning its truth, the person can begin to write a new story—one that acknowledges pain without being trapped by it.

But not all change is cognitive. Sometimes it is emotional and existential. Narrative therapy, an approach developed by Michael White and David Epston, views problems as separate from the person and emphasizes the act of re-authoring one's story. This process involves identifying dominant narratives and giving voice to alternative ones that have been suppressed or overlooked. The goal is not to fabricate positivity but to recognize the richness and multiplicity of one's experience. In doing so, people begin to see themselves as agents rather than victims, capable of shaping their lives through the stories they live.

Cultural narratives also play a powerful role in shaping personal identity. The society we grow up in provides templates for what a life is supposed to look like: what counts as success, what roles are available to us, what timelines we should follow. These scripts are often internalized without question. A person may feel like a failure at thirty for not being married, not because they are unhappy, but because their inner narrative includes a cultural expectation that life should follow a certain arc. These collective myths—about gender, aging, work, happiness—become personal myths. And they can be deeply constricting.

This is why critical reflection is essential. When people begin to interrogate the narratives they've inherited, they often discover that much of their suffering comes not from their actual life, but from the story they believe it should have been. Psychological maturity involves recognizing that there is no single correct narrative. There is only the one you are creating, moment by moment, through the meaning you assign to your experiences.

In some cases, narrative identity can fracture. Traumatic events, especially those that defy explanation, can shatter a person's sense of coherence. This is sometimes called narrative disruption. After a violent assault, a car accident, or the sudden death of a loved one, a person may no longer know how to make sense of their life. The old story no longer fits, and no new story feels true. This is a psychologically vulnerable state. Healing requires not just emotional processing, but narrative repair. The person must slowly build a story that can hold the pain without collapsing under it.

Psychologists who study post-traumatic growth often find that people who are able to narrate their trauma in ways that emphasize learning, connection, or moral insight show better long-term outcomes than those who frame the event as senseless or wholly destructive. Again, this is not about minimizing suffering. It is about meaning-making. People need to locate themselves in a story where their experience has value and where their future is still possible.

Stories also shape the way we see others. We carry narratives not only about ourselves, but about the people closest to us. These stories influence how we interpret their behavior, respond to conflict, and sustain connection. In long-term relationships, people often hold implicit narratives like "She always puts work before me" or "He never listens." These stories may feel true, but they also create filters that limit new understanding. Relationship growth often involves updating the story— recognizing complexity, allowing room for change, and resisting the pull of old scripts.

Ultimately, the story of you is never finished. It is a living document, open to revision. You will add new chapters, reframe old ones, discover hidden threads that change the meaning of earlier scenes. The goal is not to have a flawless narrative, but a flexible one—one that can hold both joy and grief, strength and regret, clarity and confusion. A story that honors your humanity in its full complexity.

There is no objective, permanent self hiding behind your story. The self is the story. The way you tell it will shape who you become.

* * *

5

Development Across the Lifespan

To understand a human being, you must look not at a snapshot, but at the entire film. People are not static personalities locked in place; they are unfolding stories. And each chapter of life comes with its own psychological demands, vulnerabilities, and opportunities. In this chapter, we'll explore development not as a clinical or theoretical abstraction, but as a living, breathing process that begins in the womb and doesn't end until the final breath. From infancy to elderhood, the mind is shaped by time, relationship, memory, biology, and culture. And with each transition, our inner architecture is both reinforced and revised.

Too often, we think of development as something that only applies to children. Once someone reaches adulthood, we imagine they are fully formed, that the real growing is done. But this is not how psychological life works. Human development is continuous. We are always encountering new circumstances that demand new internal resources. We fall in love, we lose jobs, we raise children, we endure betrayals, we chase purpose, we age, and we reckon with mortality. These events don't simply happen to us—they work on us from the inside out. They deepen or fracture us. They stretch or shrink us. They become turning points in the larger arc of who we are becoming.

Each stage of life introduces new psychological tasks. In infancy, the challenge is trust: Can I depend on others to meet my needs? In adolescence, it becomes identity: Who am I, and what matters to me? In adulthood, the question often shifts to purpose and responsibility: How do I build a life that feels meaningful and stable? And in elderhood, the task is integration: Can I look back on my life with honesty, coherence, and peace?

These questions are not philosophical musings. They are the quiet pressures that shape how people feel in their own skin. They inform our emotional resilience, our self-worth, our ability to connect, and our relationship to time. When people get stuck at a developmental stage—when a need goes unmet or a trauma interrupts the process—it can echo for decades. Adults who never learned to trust may struggle with intimacy. Elderly individuals who never felt useful may withdraw prematurely from life. Understanding the psychological arc of human development gives us language for these patterns. It helps us respond with insight rather than judgment.

No stage of life is purely biological, nor purely cultural. Development happens in the intersection. A child is born with a certain temperament, but their sense of security depends on how caregivers respond. A teenager's brain is still maturing, but their choices are shaped by social norms and expectations. A midlife adult may experience hormonal shifts, but their crisis of identity is just as tied to cultural scripts about success or aging. And an elder's experience of dignity is just as psychological as it is medical.

That is why psychology must look at the whole person across the whole lifespan. We cannot understand someone's behavior without knowing what stage of life they are in, what stories they carry, what needs are pressing, and what wounds are unhealed. And we cannot offer meaningful guidance unless we respect how those elements evolve over time.

This chapter is not a dry recitation of developmental theories. It is a psychological map of human life, told through the lens of experience. In the first section, we'll begin with early childhood, where emotional patterns are first set in motion. We'll explore how attachment, cognitive development, and early relational experiences create a foundation that echoes into every later stage. In the second section, we'll examine adolescence and emerging adulthood, a period of intense identity formation and social learning. We'll look at how young people begin to define themselves in the face of both internal chaos and external expectation.

From there, we'll move into adulthood—often thought of as a period of stability, but in truth full of competing demands, private longings, and shifting roles. We'll explore how people navigate purpose, relationships, and identity in the middle decades, often under the weight of invisible pressures. And finally, we'll turn to elderhood. Not as a decline, but as a stage with its own rich psychology—one that centers on meaning, dignity, and the legacy we leave behind.

Throughout this chapter, we'll draw from the work of Erik Erikson, Jean Piaget, Daniel Levinson, and contemporary lifespan theorists. But theory will be grounded in lived experience. The goal is not just to understand how people grow, but to recognize where they get stuck, and how they might begin to move forward again. Because development doesn't end when school does. It doesn't stop with marriage or retirement. It continues for as long as we are conscious.

Understanding development across the lifespan helps us be more patient with ourselves and with others. It helps us stop expecting from a child what only a seasoned adult can offer, or demanding from an elder the drive of someone in their prime. It helps us spot when someone's behavior is not simply a flaw, but the echo of an unmet need. And perhaps most importantly, it helps us recognize that change is always possible—not because time erases pain, but because time, when paired with awareness, opens new pathways forward.

Every stage of life invites a different kind of growth. Some of it is visible. Much of it is internal. All of it matters.

Foundations of the Early Self: Infancy through Childhood

Human development does not begin with words, conscious decisions, or even memory. It begins in the quietest moments: a cry and its answer, a gaze met by another, a need met or missed. In these earliest interactions, the psychological blueprint is drawn—not in stone, but in living tissue. Before a child can speak, reason, or even recognize their own reflection, they are already learning what kind of world they live in and what kind of self they are.

Infancy is not passive. It is active absorption. A newborn does not simply observe their environment; they are shaped by it. The first task of early development is not to learn facts, but to build trust. Erik Erikson described this as the psychosocial stage of trust versus mistrust, and it is the bedrock on which all later psychological development rests. When caregivers are reliably attuned, present, and nurturing, the infant begins to feel safe in the world. This sense of safety is not intellectual. It is physiological and emotional. It becomes embedded in the nervous system, setting the tone for how the child will relate to others, to stress, and to themselves.

John Bowlby's attachment theory expanded this understanding. He emphasized that infants are biologically wired to seek closeness to a primary caregiver, especially when distressed. This attachment system is not just about comfort—it is about survival. But beyond that, it teaches the infant what to expect from relationships. Mary Ainsworth's observational studies later identified distinct attachment styles: secure, avoidant, ambivalent, and disorganized. These styles are not labels—they are adaptive patterns formed in response to early caregiving environments. A securely attached child has learned that their emotional needs will be met with consistency and care. An avoidantly attached child has learned that expressing need leads to rejection or discomfort in the caregiver, and so suppresses emotion. An ambivalently attached child has experienced inconsistency—sometimes comfort, sometimes not—and so becomes hypervigilant and emotionally intense in seeking connection. A disorganized attachment reflects fear and chaos, often associated with abuse or neglect.

These early patterns matter because they set the stage for emotional regulation. A child who feels safe can begin to explore, take risks, and develop autonomy. A child who feels unsafe may cling, withdraw, or struggle to self-soothe. Emotional regulation is not taught by instruction. It is learned through co-regulation—how a caregiver helps the child process emotion in real time. Over time, these interactions become internalized, forming the basis of what psychologists call the "internal working model" of self and others. If the caregiver's face consistently says "You're okay, I've got you," the child internalizes a sense of worth and security. If the caregiver's face says "You're too much" or "You're on your own," the child learns a different lesson—one that can last well into adulthood.

But development does not pause at attachment. As the child grows, so too does their cognitive world. Jean Piaget's theory of cognitive development outlines four major stages: sensorimotor, preoperational, concrete operational, and formal operational. In the first two stages, which span infancy through early childhood, the child is learning that objects exist even when they are out of sight (object permanence), that actions have consequences (causality), and that symbols can stand for real things (language and play). Piaget's model has been refined over the years, but its central insight remains: children are not miniature adults. They think differently. They reason through experience, and their understanding of the world expands in stages.

Emotion and cognition are not separate tracks during development—they are intertwined. A child's ability to think is influenced by how safe they feel. Stress impairs learning. Trauma can delay language, distort perception, or lead to hypervigilance. Conversely, a secure and stimulating environment can promote not just faster learning, but more adaptive ways of thinking. When a child is consistently validated and encouraged, they begin to internalize a sense of efficacy: I can do things.

I can solve problems. My ideas matter.

Social learning also begins in childhood, long before we give it that name. Albert Bandura's work on observational learning showed how children absorb behavior by watching others. They don't just imitate, they infer. They begin to understand social rules, power dynamics, gender norms, and emotional expression based on what they see and hear. If anger leads to control, they learn that anger is powerful. If sadness is punished or ignored, they learn to hide it. These lessons become templates for how they will behave in future relationships.

Language acquisition is another milestone of early development with deep psychological implications. Language is not just a communication tool—it is a cognitive organizer. It allows children to name feelings, ask questions, and construct narratives. As soon as children can talk, they begin to tell stories about themselves and their world. These stories—though simple at first—are the beginnings of identity. A toddler who says, "I'm brave," or "I don't like loud noises," is practicing self-definition. They are building a psychological boundary between self and other, past and present.

It is also during early childhood that the moral self begins to form. Lawrence Kohlberg's stages of moral development begin with simple obedience: doing what avoids punishment. But even at these early stages, children are absorbing the emotional tone of morality—what brings praise, what elicits shame, what earns love. If morality is taught through fear or humiliation, the child may comply outwardly while internalizing a sense of unworthiness. If it is taught through dialogue, empathy, and consistency, the child can begin to develop an inner compass rather than an external performance script.

Development in childhood is not a straight line. There are spurts and regressions, breakthroughs and delays. What matters most is not perfection, but presence. A caregiver who can rupture and repair, who can admit mistakes and still offer safety, teaches the child resilience. It is not about avoiding failure, but about modeling recovery.

By the end of early childhood, much of the child's psychological architecture is already in place: a basic sense of self, a working model of relationships, a style of emotional regulation, and a framework for understanding the world. These are not fixed in stone, but they are influential. Later stages of development will revise and expand them, but the blueprint often remains. This is why early experiences matter; not because they doom us, but because they shape the terrain on which we continue to walk.

Identity in Motion: Adolescence and Emerging Adulthood

Adolescence is not just a time of hormonal chaos or mood swings, though those are common. It is a psychological crucible—a period where everything internal is being reshaped in response to everything external. This is when a person begins to ask, often without words, the most destabilizing and important questions of human life: Who am I? What matters to me? Where do I belong? What kind of adult am I becoming?

Developmentally, adolescence marks the second great wave of psychological transformation, following early childhood. But unlike infancy, where the primary task is attachment, the adolescent is tasked with differentiation. That is, they must begin to separate from their caregivers not just physically, but emotionally and ideologically. This is the psychological work of individuation: the gradual formation of a distinct, coherent identity that is separate from parental scripts and early childhood roles. And it is not a peaceful process. In fact, it is often messy, emotionally volatile, and marked by tension between autonomy and dependence.

One of the central psychological tasks of adolescence, as Erik Erikson famously noted, is identity versus role confusion. This is the developmental crisis that defines the stage: the need to define oneself while navigating conflicting roles, values, and social feedback. Teenagers are trying on different selves in rapid succession—not because they are fickle, but because they are experimenting. They are comparing their internal sense of who they might be with the external cues they receive from peers, authority figures, and cultural narratives. And while this search can look superficial from the outside, it is profoundly serious on the inside.

Neurologically, adolescence is a period of rapid brain development. The prefrontal cortex—the seat of executive functioning, planning, and impulse control—is still under construction. Meanwhile, the limbic system, which governs emotion and reward, is highly active. This creates a psychological state where feelings are strong, but regulation is weak. A teenager may fully believe in a value system one week and abandon it the next. They may appear defiant, but feel lost. They may perform confidence in public and quietly panic in private. What they need is not correction, but guidance. They need adults who can tolerate the chaos without collapsing into control or criticism.

The importance of peer relationships cannot be overstated during this stage. While parents remain emotionally significant, peers become the primary mirror. Adolescents begin to define themselves through friendship, social comparison, and romantic connection. These relationships are not shallow. They are emotionally intense and deeply formative. A betrayal from a friend can cut deeper than a disciplinary consequence. A sense of exclusion or alienation from peers can feel existential. This is not simply about popularity—it is about belonging. Human beings are wired to attach, and in adolescence, that wiring shifts from the family to the wider social world.

Emerging adulthood, a term popularized by Jeffrey Arnett, extends this period of identity development beyond the teenage years. Especially in industrialized societies, many individuals now experience their twenties as a distinct stage—not yet fully embedded in adult roles, but no longer adolescents. This stage is marked by exploration in love, work, worldview, and lifestyle. It is also a time of great instability. People may change jobs, cities, partners, and goals multiple times in the span of a few years. But behind the surface movement is a deeper process: the gradual consolidation of identity.

During these years, people begin to make sense of their earlier experiences, reframe their childhood narratives, and make more intentional decisions about who they want to be. They start asking whether their values are inherited or chosen. They begin to understand what kind of relationship patterns they carry and whether those patterns are serving them. This is where early attachment wounds often reemerge—not in the same form, but through repeated relational dynamics that force reflection. Someone who felt unseen as a child may now unconsciously seek partners who are emotionally distant. Someone who was overly parentified may now feel overwhelmed by responsibility or secretly long for care.

Vocational identity is another major theme of this period. For many, the twenties are marked by anxiety over purpose, direction, and adequacy. The pressure to "figure it out" can be crushing, especially in cultures that equate productivity with worth. But identity does not form through a single choice. It forms through repetition, reflection, and correction. People begin to notice patterns: what excites them, what drains them, where they feel most themselves. Over time, these patterns become part of a more stable self-concept.

Culturally, this stage is also shaped by the narratives available to young adults. If the culture tells them that success means marriage, wealth, and status by thirty, they may feel chronically behind. If the culture offers no viable models for diverse forms of adulthood, they may feel unseen or illegitimate. The psychological burden of comparison is acute in this stage, especially in the age of social media. Images of curated perfection can distort the internal compass. This is why narrative coherence becomes so important. A young adult who can craft a meaningful personal narrative—one that honors their pace, values, and history—is far more psychologically grounded than one who blindly chases external validation.

Another underappreciated aspect of this stage is grief. Emerging adulthood is full of small losses that often go unacknowledged: the loss of childhood simplicity, the fading of old friendships, the disillusionment with authority figures, the collapse of inherited beliefs. These are developmental deaths, and they deserve mourning. People are not only growing during this time—they are also shedding. They are letting go of roles, dreams, and illusions that no longer fit. And that process, while necessary, is often lonely.

The psychological resilience built during adolescence and emerging adulthood is not about never falling apart. It is about learning to hold contradiction. A young adult who can say, "I don't know who I am yet, but I'm learning," is already more integrated than one who adopts a rigid persona to avoid uncertainty. The goal is not to arrive at a fixed identity, but to develop the capacity for ongoing revision. Because identity is not a destination. It is a lifelong process of becoming.

The work of this stage is not easy. It requires courage, reflection, risk, and repair. But it is also full of beauty. This is the stage where people discover their deepest values, form their most enduring bonds, and begin to see the outline of a life that feels authentically theirs.

Adulthood and Integration: Purpose, Intimacy, and Responsibility

There is a quiet shift that happens as people enter adulthood. It is not a single moment or event. It is a psychological turning inward, a reorientation from possibility to responsibility, from identity formation to identity enactment. Adulthood is the stage where the internal work of earlier life begins to show up in the external shape of one's relationships, work, values, and choices. It is where coherence either takes root or begins to unravel.

Psychologically, adulthood is often understood through the lens of integration. Integration means bringing together disparate parts of the self—dreams and duties, needs and roles, contradictions and commitments—into a whole that can function with relative consistency across time and context. But integration is not the same as perfection. It is not about achieving balance in every area of life. It is about developing the capacity to hold multiple truths, navigate competing demands, and sustain one's identity even as circumstances evolve.

One of the most central themes of adulthood is purpose. Whether defined through career, contribution, parenting, creative work, or service, adults seek to matter in ways that extend beyond the self. This need for purpose is not simply a cultural expectation. It is a psychological drive. Viktor Frankl, whose work emerged from the devastation of the Holocaust, wrote that meaning is the primary motivational force in human life. Without a sense of purpose, even the most materially successful life can feel hollow. Adults want to know that their days are not just filled, but meaningful.

For many, career becomes the primary container for purpose in adulthood. It offers structure, identity, financial stability, and often, social validation. But the psychological significance of work goes deeper. Work allows people to actualize values, express competencies, and feel part of something larger. When work is aligned with one's sense of self, it can be deeply fulfilling. When it is misaligned, it can become a source of quiet despair. People who feel trapped in meaningless work often report symptoms of depression, not because of laziness or entitlement, but because of a disconnect between effort and meaning.

Alongside purpose, intimacy emerges as a defining task of adulthood. Erikson described this stage as intimacy versus isolation, highlighting the developmental need to form close, enduring relationships that require vulnerability and reciprocity. Intimacy is not limited to romantic partnership. It includes deep friendship, chosen family, and emotionally honest companionship of any kind. These relationships serve as mirrors, support systems, and containers for growth. But they also require psychological maturity. Intimacy demands the ability to tolerate difference, manage conflict, express need without shame, and offer care without control.

For many, the pursuit of intimacy in adulthood is complicated by unresolved patterns from earlier stages. People bring their attachment styles, communication habits, and unhealed wounds into their adult relationships. Someone who grew up needing to suppress their emotions to maintain connection may now struggle to assert boundaries. Someone who learned that love is earned through perfection may now feel unworthy in moments of vulnerability. These dynamics often surface not as conscious beliefs, but as emotional reflexes—pulling away, becoming defensive, over-functioning, or collapsing into silence. Recognizing these patterns is the first step toward intimacy that is not just consistent, but emotionally nourishing.

Parenting, for those who take it on, introduces another layer of psychological complexity. Raising children is not just a logistical or biological task. It is an emotional and existential experience. Parenting evokes one's own childhood, reveals hidden traits, and exposes the limits of patience and control. It can be a profound source of meaning, but also of stress, guilt, and identity diffusion. Adults who become parents often wrestle with competing needs: to protect and to empower, to guide and to let go, to nurture and to maintain their own personhood. The healthiest parenting often comes not from perfection, but from conscious reflection and emotional presence.

Another major theme in adulthood is the negotiation of competing roles. Adults often wear many hats simultaneously—professional, partner, parent, caregiver, citizen, friend. These roles come with expectations, both internal and external. The stress of adulthood often arises not from any single role, but from their collision. Someone may feel torn between caring for aging parents and meeting work deadlines, or between being emotionally available at home and staying alert in a demanding job. These tensions are not signs of failure. They are the psychological reality of modern adulthood. What matters is how individuals navigate these conflicts—whether they do so with self-compassion and adaptability or with rigidity and self-blame.

Midlife introduces a specific form of psychological reckoning. It is not simply a crisis, as popular culture suggests. It is a period of deep questioning: Is this the life I intended to live? Are my relationships real? Do my achievements reflect my values? This stage often brings unresolved losses to the surface, invites re-evaluation of identity, and opens space for new priorities. It can be unsettling, but also liberating. Many people use midlife as a chance to recalibrate—to leave jobs, repair relationships, pursue long-abandoned interests, or confront long-avoided truths. The work of integration often intensifies here, not as a tidy project, but as a lived process of sorting what to keep, what to grieve, and what to grow into.

The adult years also demand resilience. Life does not slow down or simplify. It introduces illness, financial strain, family conflict, and unexpected turns. Resilience in adulthood is not just about bouncing back. It is about making meaning in the face of change. It involves emotional regulation, social support, cognitive flexibility, and the capacity to maintain hope without denial. Adults who cultivate resilience are better equipped to adapt to losses, hold steady during uncertainty, and continue to develop rather than simply endure.

Responsibility, too, is a defining feature of adulthood. This is not only the external responsibility of tasks and dependents. It is the internal responsibility of self-awareness. Adults are responsible for managing their triggers, examining their impact on others, making ethical decisions, and contributing to relational health. This does not mean being flawless. It means being accountable. The mature adult is not the one who never causes harm, but the one who recognizes it, repairs it, and evolves from it.

Psychologically, adulthood is not a plateau. It is an active, ongoing phase of development that invites deeper integration of self and sustained engagement with life's complexity. Those who view adulthood as a stage of stasis often feel disillusioned or emotionally dulled. Those who embrace it as a site of continued growth tend to experience greater fulfillment and relational depth. Adulthood is where the themes of earlier development come into sharper relief—not as problems to solve, but as patterns to understand and work with.

This stage may lack the drama of adolescence or the tenderness of childhood, but it holds a quiet profundity. It is where people live out their values, form families of origin or choice, build legacy, and deepen their understanding of love, failure, and meaning. It is not always visible from the outside. But internally, adulthood is where some of the most important psychological work happens.

Elderhood and the Search for Meaning

There is a kind of clarity that comes with elderhood that no other life stage quite offers. Not because the questions are resolved, but because the noise starts to quiet. By the time a person reaches their sixties, seventies, or beyond, something irreversible has taken place: the majority of life is now behind them. This shift in temporal orientation transforms the psychological landscape. The concerns of youth and midlife—achievement, comparison, reputation—begin to lose their grip. What remains are the deeper questions. Did my life matter? Did I love well? Do I feel at peace with who I've become?

The psychological task of elderhood is integration with finality in view. Erik Erikson described this stage as integrity versus despair. Integrity is not about perfection or accomplishment; it is about coherence. It is the ability to look back on one's life and find a sense of narrative consistency, emotional resolution, and internal peace. Despair, on the other hand, arises when there is too much regret, too many unhealed relationships, or an overwhelming sense that life was misused. But despair is not inevitable. With honest reflection, relational repair, and the chance to tell one's story, many people move toward integrity in their later years—even if the road was turbulent.

Elderhood often invites a process of life review. This is not merely an act of remembering, but a psychological sorting. What mattered? What themes repeated? What wounds remain? Life review allows people to revisit experiences with the insight of distance. Events that once seemed confusing or painful can be reinterpreted through a broader lens. A betrayal in youth may now be seen as part of a pattern in one's life choices. A long-forgotten kindness may emerge as a defining moment. This is the psychological work of harvesting meaning.

There is also a relational aspect to this stage. Elders are the keepers of emotional memory—family history, cultural legacy, moral perspective. When given the space to share, their reflections can serve as guideposts for younger generations. But modern culture is not always structured to honor the elder voice. Many societies prioritize productivity, novelty, and youth. As a result, older adults may feel invisible or dismissed, particularly when their pace slows or their needs increase. This creates a profound psychological wound: to have lived so much, and yet feel erased by the very systems one contributed to.

One way to restore dignity in elderhood is to restore relevance. Older adults still have emotional wisdom, moral insight, and relational presence to offer. But they must be invited, not just accommodated. Psychological research confirms that a sense of generativity—feeling useful, needed, and connected to something larger—has a direct impact on wellbeing in later life. Those who volunteer, mentor, teach, or remain socially active tend to report greater life satisfaction and lower rates of depression. The ability to continue contributing, even in modest ways, helps preserve identity and vitality.

Aging also introduces a new relationship with the body. Physical limitations, illness, and the inevitability of decline are not abstract fears; they become daily realities. This can provoke grief, fear, and frustration, especially when independence is compromised. But it can also soften the ego. The body's slowing creates an opportunity to reprioritize, to focus on presence over performance. Many elders describe a shift from doing to being. They are no longer trying to prove themselves. They are simply trying to live honestly, comfortably, and with a sense of emotional clarity.

There is a kind of intimacy that becomes available in elderhood that is hard to reach earlier. With the urgency of productivity gone, many older adults find themselves drawn toward reflection, forgiveness, and reconnection. Estranged relationships may find their way back to tenderness. Unspoken hurts may be addressed with honesty that once felt too risky. Regret does not have to define elderhood; it can also refine it. When people are willing to face their past without defensiveness, a gentler kind of truth can emerge—one that accepts imperfection without collapsing into shame.

Of course, not all elders have the same psychological experience. Some carry trauma that was never named or treated. Some experience cognitive decline that limits memory, language, or self-awareness. Others are isolated by death, distance, or disability. These realities make the need for emotional and psychological support in elderhood all the more pressing. A society that does not invest in the wellbeing of its elders is a society that forgets its own future. How we treat our oldest members reveals what we believe about dignity, worth, and the arc of a life well lived.

Death, too, becomes more present. Not necessarily in a morbid way, but as a fact to be faced. The psychological orientation toward death in elderhood can shape how someone lives their final years. Those who have avoided the topic often carry unresolved anxiety. Those who have made peace with mortality often radiate a quiet calm. This does not mean they welcome death. It means they are not run by the fear of it. They have turned toward the truth that their life, like every life, will end—and that meaning must be made within that boundary.

End-of-life psychology offers powerful insights here. Studies show that people near death do not fear the loss of breath as much as the loss of coherence. They want to know that their lives had value, that their pain was not wasted, that someone remembers who they were. Even small gestures—a listening ear, a family ritual, a spoken word of love—can offer profound peace. Dignity-conserving care, pioneered by clinicians like Harvey Chochinov, emphasizes the need to preserve identity and personhood even in decline. A dying person is still a full person, and their emotional world remains rich with meaning.

Elderhood is often viewed as a period of decline, but psychologically, it can also be a culmination. The years that stretch behind offer not just memory, but depth. The task of this stage is to live in alignment with one's accumulated truths, to forgive where possible, to release what no longer matters, and to savor what does. It is to tell the story of one's life—not as a perfect tale, but as a deeply human one.

And perhaps more than anything, elderhood is the final invitation to become oneself without pretense. With nothing left to prove, the question becomes simple: Can I live this final chapter with presence, honesty, and peace?

* * *

II

Part II: Emotion, Regulation, and Resilience

Emotion shapes how we experience the world—how we understand ourselves, connect with others, and respond to stress. In Part II, we'll explore the architecture of emotion, the development of regulation, and what makes resilience possible. This isn't about mood management. It's about reclaiming emotional clarity as the foundation for maturity, relationship, and meaning.

6

What Are Emotions For?

Most people think of emotions as something personal, something private that happens inside us in response to the world. But from an evolutionary perspective, emotions were never meant to be internal experiences alone. They evolved as tools—for survival, for communication, and for motivation. We are emotional creatures not by accident, but by design. And yet, in modern life, many people are disconnected from that design. They see emotion as irrational, dramatic, or inconvenient. They treat feelings as weaknesses to be hidden, rather than signals to be read. But when you understand what emotions are for, they begin to make a different kind of sense.

Emotions are not random. They are patterned responses shaped by millions of years of evolution to help organisms detect opportunities and threats, connect with others, and prioritize behaviors that increase survival and reproduction. Fear helps us avoid danger. Anger mobilizes us to address injustice or violation. Sadness slows us down so we can grieve and integrate loss. Joy reinforces behaviors that lead to safety, intimacy, or reward. Even shame, as painful as it is, evolved to keep us from violating group norms that could lead to social exclusion. Emotions, in other words, are information systems.

That's why we can't simply dismiss emotions as irrational. They may not always feel logical, but they are functional. They arise for a reason.

And when we ignore or suppress them, we cut off access to vital data about our needs, our values, and our environment. A person who cannot feel fear may take reckless risks. A person who cannot feel anger may allow themselves to be mistreated. A person who cannot feel joy may lose the ability to recognize what makes life meaningful. Emotional awareness is not indulgent; it is adaptive.

Still, we have to distinguish between emotion and emotional literacy. Everyone has feelings. But not everyone knows how to name them, understand them, or respond to them wisely. Emotional literacy involves being able to notice what we feel, make sense of why we feel it, and choose how to act on that feeling in a way that honors both the self and the situation. This is where development and environment matter. A child who grows up being punished for showing anger may learn to repress it entirely. An adult who was never taught how to comfort themselves may interpret sadness as failure. And across cultures, some emotions are elevated while others are taboo, leading to emotional habits that may or may not serve mental health.

Affective neuroscience has helped illuminate what happens in the brain during emotional experiences. Emotions are not just "in the heart"; they involve complex interactions between neural circuits, hormones, and cognitive interpretation. The amygdala evaluates threat and relevance. The insula processes visceral and bodily sensations. The prefrontal cortex assesses context and applies judgment. When these systems work well together, emotion guides action in a balanced way. But when they are misaligned—because of trauma, developmental disruption, or chronic stress—emotion can either become overwhelming or absent altogether. The brain may overreact to mild threats, or fail to respond to serious ones.

It's also important to recognize that emotions are layered. On the surface, we may feel anger. But beneath that, there may be fear, shame, or grief. A person who lashes out in traffic may not be reacting to another driver, but to a broader sense of powerlessness in their life. A partner who becomes emotionally distant during conflict may not be cold, but overwhelmed and uncertain how to respond. Emotions point to deeper stories. They are never just about the moment. They are about patterns, expectations, and past experience, all converging in the body's response.

That's why therapy, introspection, and even art can be so powerful—they allow us to uncover the emotional meanings we carry, many of which operate below conscious awareness. What we feel is shaped not just by biology, but by memory and meaning. The same event can trigger joy in one person and fear in another, depending on their history. This is where the symbolic layer of emotion becomes essential to understand. Emotions carry messages, not just impulses. They reveal what matters to us, what wounds we still carry, and what we long for.

But sometimes emotions misfire. They arise too strongly, not strongly enough, or in inappropriate contexts. A person may feel panic in safe situations or numbness in the face of real danger. These distortions are not signs of weakness—they are clues. They suggest that something in the emotional system has been disrupted. Trauma, in particular, can hijack the brain's threat-detection systems, leading to chronic hyperarousal or emotional shutdown. In these cases, emotional regulation becomes a survival strategy rather than a path to insight. And until safety is restored, emotional clarity remains out of reach.

In this chapter, we'll explore these dimensions of emotion in full. We'll begin with the evolutionary roots—why emotions exist in the first place, and how they function in animals and humans alike. From there, we'll dive into the brain, looking at how affective neuroscience helps us understand the physical basis of feeling. We'll then turn to the symbolic function of emotion: how our feelings encode meaning, identity, and memory. And finally, we'll look at what happens when these systems break down—and what it takes to rebuild emotional coherence.

Emotion is not just a feeling. It is a form of intelligence, a compass, and a connector. When we learn to listen to it—not obey it blindly, but listen—we become more attuned, more resilient, and more human. Most of what people call emotional problems are not caused by feeling too much. They are caused by not knowing what to do with what they feel.

And the work of maturity, in many ways, is learning to feel wisely.

The Evolutionary Function of Emotion

To understand the role of emotion in human life, we have to begin at the level of survival. Long before language, before moral codes, before symbolic thinking, organisms needed a way to respond quickly and appropriately to their environments. Emotion was the answer. It provided a rapid signaling system that helped creatures detect threats, pursue rewards, and maintain vital social bonds. While the modern human brain has evolved far beyond its early ancestors, the emotional systems we carry remain deeply rooted in those early survival tasks.

Consider fear. In evolutionary terms, fear evolved to help organisms recognize and respond to danger. The moment an animal detects a predator, its body mobilizes: heart rate increases, pupils dilate, blood rushes to the muscles. This isn't a conscious decision; it's an automatic response honed by natural selection. The animals most attuned to danger were the ones most likely to survive long enough to reproduce. Their emotional reactivity became a trait passed on through generations. And though the threats in modern life have changed—traffic, job loss, social exclusion—the systems remain.

Anger, too, has adaptive roots. It energizes the body to overcome obstacles, assert boundaries, or correct perceived wrongs. In group-living species, anger helped maintain fairness and deter exploitation. A primate that didn't react to stolen food or physical aggression would be at risk of losing status or safety. Anger, in this sense, is a protective force. It signals that something in the environment is violating a need or expectation and primes the individual to act.

Sadness evolved in part to conserve energy during loss or failure. When an organism is injured, defeated, or grieving, slowing down can prevent further harm and allow time for recalibration. Sadness also serves a social function. In many species, expressions of distress elicit comfort or aid from others. A whimper, a cry, or a downturned posture draws attention and activates caregiving responses. Emotion, in this way, facilitates interdependence.

Even joy and pleasure play essential evolutionary roles. They reinforce behaviors that promote survival and connection—like eating, mating, nurturing offspring, or forming alliances. Dopaminergic and opioid systems in the brain create rewarding sensations that strengthen memory and learning. When something feels good, we are more likely to repeat it. This basic principle helped guide creatures toward behaviors that enhanced their fitness and social cohesion.

The most striking thing about these emotional systems is how consistent they are across species. Researchers have found evidence of emotional analogues in mammals, birds, and even some reptiles. While the complexity varies, the functional architecture—detection of relevant stimuli, physiological arousal, behavioral response—is widely shared. Human emotion builds on this scaffolding. We feel with nuance and self-reflection, but the roots of those feelings are deeply biological.

This is where the work of evolutionary psychology and ethology becomes essential. By comparing human emotion with animal behavior, we can better understand which emotional capacities are ancient and which are shaped by culture. Take the facial expressions of emotion. Charles Darwin was one of the first to suggest that certain expressions—like wide eyes in fear or a furrowed brow in anger—are universal across cultures because they reflect evolved responses. More than a century later, Paul Ekman's research confirmed this with empirical evidence: people from vastly different cultures could reliably identify basic emotions based on facial expressions alone.

These basic emotions—joy, anger, fear, sadness, surprise, and disgust—are often referred to as primary emotions. They are thought to be hardwired, rapid, and difficult to suppress. Secondary emotions, such as guilt, pride, embarrassment, or shame, are more culturally influenced. They require a sense of self and social awareness, making them more complex and context-dependent. But even these build on the evolutionary foundation of primary emotional systems.

Emotion also plays a central role in decision-making. Antonio Damasio's research on patients with damage to the ventromedial prefrontal cortex—a region critical for integrating emotion and judgment—showed that without emotional input, people struggle to make even simple choices. They can analyze facts but feel no guidance toward action. Emotion, it turns out, gives weight to options. It helps us prioritize, evaluate, and commit. A life of pure reason is a myth. Even the most calculated choices are infused with affect.

Social behavior is another key arena where emotions show their adaptive power. Group living requires cooperation, empathy, and shared norms. Emotions regulate these dynamics. They alert us to violations, signal intentions, and foster trust. A smile invites connection. A glare warns against intrusion. A tear invites comfort. These signals create social order and allow humans to live in complex, cooperative societies. Without emotion, the glue of human relationships would dissolve.

Importantly, emotion is not simply reactive—it can be anticipatory. Anxiety, for example, prepares the body for potential threats before they occur. Anticipatory emotions allow organisms to simulate outcomes and adjust behavior in advance. This gives humans a critical edge: we don't have to wait for danger to respond; we can plan, imagine, and prepare. This capacity to forecast emotional consequences underlies moral behavior, long-term planning, and conscience.

Still, the evolutionary advantages of emotion come with trade-offs. A system designed to detect threat quickly can become hypersensitive. The same fear response that kept our ancestors alive in the savanna may now be activated by social rejection or financial stress. A brain shaped for cooperation and belonging can become vulnerable to shame and exclusion. Evolution doesn't aim for happiness. It aims for fitness. Sometimes that means we feel more than we can bear.

This helps explain why people can become emotionally overwhelmed in modern environments. Our systems were built for immediate, embodied threats, not chronic, abstract stressors. The brain still activates the same circuits, but the threats are harder to escape—emails, deadlines, news cycles, and social comparison. Our emotional systems are being pushed in ways evolution never prepared for.

Understanding the evolutionary function of emotion helps reframe these experiences. Emotions are not flaws to overcome. They are the legacy of what helped us survive. And when we feel too much or too often, it is not because we are broken—it is because our environment has changed faster than our wiring. This perspective can reduce shame and open the door to more compassionate self-understanding.

The task, then, is not to rid ourselves of emotion, but to learn how to relate to it wisely. To recognize its evolutionary origins, its strengths, and its limits. Emotion is here to help. But it must be integrated with awareness, reflection, and context. Only then can it serve its intended purpose—not to rule us, but to guide us toward a life that makes sense.

Affective Neuroscience and the Emotional Brain

If evolution explains why emotions exist, affective neuroscience explains how they work. Emotional experience is not something that happens in a vacuum. It is a dynamic interplay between the brain, body, and environment, shaped by specific neural systems that evaluate, process, and respond to internal and external stimuli. These systems don't operate in isolation; they're deeply interconnected, influencing not only how we feel, but how we interpret those feelings, regulate them, and assign meaning.

Affective neuroscience is the study of the neural mechanisms of emotion. It examines how different brain regions contribute to emotional perception, arousal, expression, and regulation. Though the science continues to evolve, there is a foundational understanding of the key players in emotional processing. The amygdala, for instance, is central to emotional salience. It acts like an alarm system, rapidly assessing the relevance of stimuli—especially those that signal threat or novelty. When you jump at a sudden noise or feel uneasy in a dimly lit hallway, the amygdala is involved.

The amygdala is also crucial in the formation of emotional memories. It helps tag certain experiences as significant, particularly those involving fear or reward. That's why some memories feel emotionally charged even years later. They were encoded in concert with strong amygdalar activation, which prioritized them in storage. These emotionally tagged memories can shape future responses, often outside of conscious awareness. A child who grew up in a chaotic household may flinch at raised voices, even as an adult in a safe environment. The brain remembers.

Adjacent to the amygdala, the hippocampus plays a role in contextualizing emotional events. While the amygdala signals importance, the hippocampus helps determine when and where it occurred. This partnership matters. It allows us to distinguish between past and present, memory and current reality. In trauma, this contextual separation often breaks down. The emotional brain reacts to reminders as if the original event is happening again, because the hippocampal input has been bypassed or silenced.

The insular cortex, or insula, is another crucial region. It processes interoception—the awareness of internal bodily states. Emotions begin in the body: a quickened heartbeat, shallow breath, tightened chest, or flushed skin. The insula translates these physiological changes into conscious feeling. When you say you have a "gut feeling" or feel sick to your stomach from stress, you are describing interoceptive awareness. The stronger your connection to bodily sensation, the more tuned in you are to your emotional states.

The prefrontal cortex, particularly the ventromedial and dorsolateral regions, serves as a regulator. It evaluates emotional input, suppresses inappropriate impulses, and integrates social and moral considerations. This is the area most involved in emotional regulation and conscious decision-making. It helps you choose not to yell in a meeting, even if you feel angry, or to keep walking when afraid rather than freezing in place. The prefrontal cortex is also involved in reappraisal—changing the meaning of a situation in order to change your emotional response to it.

Importantly, these brain areas are not arranged hierarchically. The older, limbic regions like the amygdala are not simply primitive relics, nor is the prefrontal cortex a purely rational override. They work together. Emotion and reason are not separate domains; they are part of the same system. Effective regulation involves coordination between emotional salience and contextual judgment. Problems arise when that coordination is disrupted.

In depression, for instance, there is often reduced activity in the prefrontal cortex and increased activity in regions associated with rumination and emotional pain. In anxiety disorders, the amygdala is hyper-responsive, leading to exaggerated fear responses even in relatively safe environments. In both cases, there is a mismatch between the perceived emotional significance of a stimulus and its actual context. Treatment often involves helping the brain recalibrate, either through cognitive restructuring, medication, or exposure-based therapies that retrain the system.

Neurochemistry plays a central role as well. Neurotransmitters like serotonin, dopamine, norepinephrine, and GABA help modulate emotional tone. Dopamine is associated with reward and motivation. Serotonin influences mood stability and impulse control. Norepinephrine ramps up alertness in response to stress, while GABA has calming, inhibitory effects. Imbalances in these systems can shape emotional experience dramatically, which is why pharmacological interventions target these pathways.

But emotional processing isn't confined to isolated areas or molecules. It's an emergent property of distributed networks. One such network is the default mode network (DMN), which is active during rest, self-reflection, and mind-wandering. It is implicated in the construction of internal narratives and the processing of social and emotional information. Overactivity in the DMN has been linked to depressive rumination, while underactivity can correlate with certain types of dissociation or emotional numbing.

Another important network is the salience network, which includes the amygdala and insula. It helps determine what deserves attention and emotional investment. When functioning properly, it helps us prioritize what matters most in a given moment. But in chronic stress or trauma, the salience network can become dysregulated, making everything feel urgent or threatening, or alternately, causing a sense of deadened apathy.

Developmentally, these systems mature over time. Children are not born with fully developed emotion regulation capacity. Their limbic systems develop earlier than their prefrontal regions, which helps explain why young children can be emotionally volatile. Emotional development is scaffolded by caregiving: a caregiver who helps a child name, soothe, and understand feelings is helping to build the child's brain. This is more than metaphor. Repeated co-regulation helps wire the connections between emotion and reason. Inconsistent, neglectful, or frightening caregiving can lead to dysregulated emotional systems that persist into adulthood.

Experience shapes the emotional brain. Neural plasticity allows emotional patterns to be strengthened or weakened over time. This is the premise behind both psychotherapy and learning: the brain can change. Repeated emotional experiences—whether of safety, empathy, conflict, or threat—reinforce specific pathways. Healing often involves repeated corrective experiences that help rewire those patterns. A person who never felt safe enough to cry may learn, over time, that vulnerability can lead to connection. That is not just psychological insight; it is neurobiological change.

Cultural factors also influence emotional processing. While the neural hardware is largely shared, the interpretation and expression of emotion vary across cultures. Some cultures value emotional restraint; others emphasize expressive openness. These values shape how emotions are encoded in the brain, what is emphasized or suppressed, and how individuals come to relate to their own affective lives. The brain is not a static machine; it is an interpretive organ, constantly shaped by context and meaning.

Ultimately, affective neuroscience reveals that emotion is a whole-body, whole-brain process. Feeling is not a single location or a fleeting response—it is an integrated experience involving perception, memory, sensation, meaning, and regulation. Understanding the emotional brain gives us insight into why we react the way we do, how patterns become entrenched, and where change is possible. Emotion is not a flaw in our wiring. It is the expression of that wiring, in real time, shaped by biology and refined by experience.

Emotions as Carriers of Symbolic Meaning

Emotions are not only biological signals or evolutionary adaptations; they are also deeply symbolic. They carry meaning that reaches beyond survival responses and physiological arousal. In the human experience, emotion becomes a language—one that encodes values, identity, memory, and significance. Affective neuroscience can tell us where emotions are processed, but it cannot fully explain what they mean to us. For that, we turn to psychology's interpretive branches: depth psychology, narrative theory, symbolic interactionism, and cultural analysis.

To say an emotion is symbolic is to say it points beyond itself. Anger can be more than a reaction to a boundary violation—it can be a symbol of betrayal, a cry for dignity, or a protest against invisibility. Sadness might reflect the pain of loss, but it can also represent the longing for a past self, an unspoken dream, or a sense of unworthiness carried from childhood. Joy can be a fleeting pleasure, or a profound affirmation that life is worth living. The same emotion can mean something entirely different depending on the person, context, and story it is embedded in.

Carl Jung's work is essential here. For Jung, emotions were not just feelings to be managed, but expressions of the unconscious. He viewed emotion as the bridge between the conscious ego and the deeper layers of the psyche. In his view, emotional disturbances often arise when the individual is out of alignment with their deeper symbolic life—when the archetypes of meaning, purpose, or identity are misrecognized or suppressed. An inexplicable sadness might not be just about recent events, but about a soul-level disconnection from the life one is meant to live.

The symbolic dimension of emotion is especially visible in dreams, where feelings often appear in exaggerated or displaced form. Fear in a dream might manifest as a tsunami. Joy might appear as flight. These emotional images are not just dramatic flourishes—they are the psyche's way of encoding and communicating truths that words alone cannot carry. When people say they feel something "in their bones" or that a situation "just feels wrong," they are touching on this symbolic register. The emotion carries meaning beyond logic.

Narrative psychology deepens this idea. Our emotional responses are shaped by the stories we tell ourselves about who we are, what has happened to us, and what matters. Emotion is not simply reactive; it is interpretive. It arises in response to what something means within our personal narrative. A breakup feels different depending on whether one sees it as abandonment, liberation, failure, or justice. The same event evokes different emotions based on the story it fits into.

This is why therapy so often centers on reframing. Changing the story changes the emotional response. When someone begins to see their anger not as evidence of being "out of control," but as a signal of unmet needs or a history of being silenced, the emotion shifts. It may not disappear, but it becomes intelligible. Meaning transforms feeling. And in many cases, it is the absence of meaning that makes emotions unbearable. People often say they can endure pain if they know why they're experiencing it. When there is no meaning, emotion can feel like chaos.

Culture also shapes the symbolic vocabulary of emotion. Different cultures assign different meanings to the same emotional expression. In some traditions, tears are signs of weakness; in others, they are sacred. Anger may be interpreted as aggression or passion, depending on the cultural lens. These differences affect how people interpret their own feelings. A person raised in a culture that stigmatizes emotional expression may feel shame not only about what they feel, but about the fact that they feel at all.

Symbolic meaning is also influenced by language. The words we have for emotions influence how we experience them. Some languages have emotional terms that do not exist in others. The Portuguese word *saudade* refers to a deep, melancholic longing for something absent—a complex emotional state that English might only approximate with "nostalgia" or "yearning." Having a word for a feeling gives it shape. It allows it to be named, shared, and reflected upon. Without language, the emotion remains inchoate. With language, it becomes part of consciousness.

Personal history plays a role too. If a child was punished for crying, that child may grow into an adult who experiences sadness with shame. The emotion is not just about the current situation; it is tangled in symbolic meaning built over time. That adult may feel sadness as dangerous, weak, or unworthy—regardless of the facts. Similarly, someone who received affection only when performing well may associate pride with love, and failure with emotional abandonment. These learned emotional associations shape the symbolic landscape of a person's life.

In ritual and religion, emotions are given collective symbolic meaning. Grief rituals, celebrations, confession, or communal chanting all invite emotional states to be expressed and shared within structured, symbolic frames. These practices validate feeling while also transforming it. The mourning process, for example, is not just about the release of sadness, but about recognizing the significance of loss. Symbol and emotion are intertwined. Without ritual, grief can feel meaningless. With it, grief becomes a form of honoring.

Art, too, carries symbolic emotion. A song, painting, or film can evoke powerful feelings—not because it tells us something factual, but because it touches a symbolic chord. People cry at fictional stories not because they forget they are fiction, but because the story symbolizes something real and important to them. A painting might move someone to tears not because of its technical skill, but because it represents something they cannot put into words. The emotional reaction is symbolic resonance. The feeling tells a truth the intellect cannot articulate.

This symbolic function of emotion also explains why feelings are often hard to explain. When someone asks, "Why are you upset?" there may not be a clear answer. The feeling might be responding to something unspoken, a history, a memory, or an internal conflict that has yet to be named. Insisting that emotions always be rationalized or justified misunderstands their nature. Emotions are not always about the surface. They are messengers from deeper realms, encoded in symbols that take time to interpret.

Understanding this symbolic layer of emotion opens the door to self-inquiry. Rather than asking only, "What am I feeling?" one can ask, "What might this feeling represent? What is it pointing to? What story am I living out right now that makes this feeling arise?" These questions are not about analysis for its own sake, but about reclaiming the intelligence of feeling. Emotions are not roadblocks to logic. They are carriers of meaning. And when interpreted with care, they can guide us toward deeper alignment, healing, and purpose.

Emotion and the Search for Meaning

Emotion is one of the deepest conduits through which meaning flows into our lives. It is not only a response to what happens to us, but also a signal of what matters most. When we are moved, we are not merely reacting; we are registering significance. Whether we are awed by beauty, gutted by loss, or pierced by longing, emotion reveals the presence of value. Meaning is not constructed only in the intellect—it is felt. And it is often in our emotional lives that we encounter the raw materials from which meaning is made.

Consider grief. It is not just sorrow over someone's absence; it is the measure of their importance. The more we grieve, the more the relationship meant. Grief is the emotional echo of love, even when the mind cannot fully process the reality of loss. In that sense, grief is a form of meaning itself. It insists that what we lost mattered and still does. In the silence that follows a death, it is not the facts that sustain us—it is the capacity of emotion to hold the sacredness of what was shared.

The same is true of awe. Whether standing beneath the vastness of the night sky or hearing a symphony that stirs something ancient in the soul, awe reminds us that we are small, but not insignificant. It repositions us in relation to something greater—nature, time, mystery, creation—and opens the door to questions of purpose and belonging. These experiences often resist explanation. They live in the body, in the tremble of the chest or the lump in the throat. Emotion makes meaning felt before it is understood.

Psychologist Viktor Frankl, who survived the concentration camps of Nazi Germany, wrote powerfully about the centrality of meaning in emotional life. In *Man's Search for Meaning*, he argued that suffering without meaning is unbearable, but suffering with meaning can be endured. He observed that those who found emotional reasons to live—love for a family member, a sense of unfinished purpose, a deep commitment to belief—were more likely to survive. Meaning did not eliminate their suffering, but it gave it shape, orientation, and dignity.

Emotion also shapes the stories we tell about our lives. In narrative identity theory, people are understood to build their sense of self by crafting a story that integrates past, present, and future. Emotions are not just details in that story—they are what give it emotional truth. A story about childhood doesn't matter simply because it happened. It matters because it carries emotional weight. The meaning of a memory is determined less by the facts than by the feelings that surround it. A parent's absence, a sibling's jealousy, a teacher's kindness—each becomes part of the self not because of what occurred, but because of what it meant emotionally.

This emotional scaffolding is what allows meaning to change. A painful event can be reinterpreted over time, especially if new emotional experiences offer fresh perspectives. An early betrayal might once have symbolized personal failure, but with healing, it might come to symbolize survival or strength. Emotion is the portal through which reinterpretation becomes possible. Without it, meaning remains cold and abstract. It is the feeling that lets us live into a new story.

Emotion also guides our ethical lives. Moral development is not merely a set of cognitive rules—it is grounded in empathy, guilt, compassion, indignation, and outrage. These feelings help us distinguish between right and wrong. When people say they have a "gut sense" that something is unjust, they are describing an emotional response that carries moral meaning. And when people become desensitized to suffering or injustice, it is often an emotional numbness that has taken hold, not just a lapse in reasoning.

This connection between emotion and morality is present from early development. Young children show signs of empathic distress when they see others cry. They attempt to comfort, to share, or to seek help. These are not learned scripts. They are spontaneous expressions of emotional attunement. As children grow, these feelings become more nuanced and socially shaped, but they remain central to our ethical compass. A society that suppresses emotional intelligence is a society at risk of losing its moral bearings.

Relational meaning is also shaped by emotion. Our sense of connection, trust, loyalty, and betrayal are all emotionally encoded. We remember how people made us feel more vividly than what they said. The emotional fabric of relationships often defines their meaning. A marriage may be sustained not just by shared goals, but by the enduring experience of being emotionally seen. A friendship may dissolve not because of one argument, but because of the accumulation of small emotional injuries that altered its meaning.

In moments of crisis, it is often emotion that guides us back to meaning. When everything else falls away—status, certainty, routine—it is emotional clarity that reveals what matters. People often report, after traumatic experiences or major life changes, that their priorities shift. They may become less interested in achievement and more focused on connection. They may find purpose in helping others, telling their story, or creating beauty from pain. These are not rational calculations. They are emotional reckonings that reorganize the self around a new center of meaning.

Even in spiritual life, emotion plays a central role. The numinous, the sacred, the transcendent—these are often felt before they are believed. People describe feeling "called," "moved," "convicted," or "healed." These are emotional states with deep symbolic meaning. They orient the individual toward something greater, whether conceived as God, the universe, or a moral imperative. For some, these experiences become foundational. They reshape identity, values, and behavior. Without the emotional dimension, these transformations would remain superficial.

Ultimately, emotion is not the opposite of reason. It is the soil from which meaning grows. When we feel deeply, we are not losing control—we are gaining access to the deeper truths of our own lives. Emotions connect us to our values, illuminate our needs, and guide us toward what is real. They are not always comfortable. But they are always meaningful. And when we listen to them with care—not as enemies to be silenced, but as messengers to be understood—we begin to build a life that is emotionally honest, ethically grounded, and rich in meaning.

* * *

7

Feeling Deeply: Emotional Granularity and Sensitivity

We live in a world that rewards performance but rarely teaches precision when it comes to feeling. Most people can tell when they're upset, but fewer can distinguish between frustration, disappointment, resentment, or despair. This lack of precision isn't a flaw of character—it's a skill gap, and an important one. The difference between saying "I'm sad" and "I feel disillusioned" is more than vocabulary. It's the difference between general discomfort and deep psychological insight.

This chapter is about that difference. Emotional granularity—the capacity to recognize, label, and differentiate between specific emotional states—is a form of psychological sophistication that often goes unnoticed. It's the invisible thread that separates emotional reactivity from emotional intelligence, confusion from clarity, and impulsive behavior from thoughtful response. The more finely attuned we are to what we feel, the more agency we gain over our inner world.

This isn't about being overly sensitive or endlessly introspective. It's about building a map. In the same way that learning geography helps us navigate the physical world, learning emotional vocabulary helps us move more skillfully through the psychological landscape. When you know the difference between envy and admiration, or between shame and guilt, you can respond in ways that reflect your values and protect your integrity. Without that granularity, everything gets flattened—and when everything feels the same, nothing can be truly understood.

The human brain is wired to notice and respond to emotion. Evolutionarily, this was essential for survival: fear signaled danger, anger prepared us for defense, and joy reinforced connection. But those were broad strokes. Modern life demands more nuance. In close relationships, in parenting, in leadership, and especially in healing from trauma, the ability to name and interpret emotion with clarity becomes central. Emotional granularity allows us to understand our needs before they explode. It allows us to comfort others in ways that are accurate, not just well-intentioned.

There is growing empirical support for this. Research from the fields of affective neuroscience and emotion theory has consistently shown that individuals with high emotional granularity tend to have better psychological outcomes. They manage stress more effectively, show greater resilience, and have a lower risk of mood disorders. Importantly, they're not necessarily "less emotional"—they're just clearer on what they're experiencing. And that clarity allows for more adaptive regulation.

Still, granularity isn't just a cognitive skill. It has emotional and existential depth. Being able to name your feelings doesn't just help you manage them—it helps you live them more fully. You can't metabolize what you haven't digested. And you can't digest what you haven't named. In this way, emotional granularity becomes a tool for depth, not detachment. It supports authenticity by anchoring emotional experience in language that reflects reality.

But not everyone has the same baseline sensitivity. Some people simply feel more. They experience emotional life with more vividness, more permeability, and more impact. This isn't pathology—it's temperament. And when paired with high granularity, it can become a remarkable strength. These individuals often make excellent therapists, artists, educators, and leaders—not in spite of their emotional depth, but because of it. Yet, when granularity is low, emotional sensitivity can become overwhelming, disorienting, or even paralyzing. The key isn't to dull feeling—it's to refine it.

This chapter also addresses emotional intelligence more broadly. While often reduced to a vague notion of empathy or likability, true emotional intelligence includes the disciplined ability to identify, understand, and regulate emotional states in oneself and others. That requires granularity. Without it, even well-meaning people struggle to connect meaningfully. Emotional intelligence is not about being "nice" or "agreeable"—it's about being accurate, honest, and attuned.

Culture plays a role here too. Many people grow up in emotional environments where only a narrow range of feelings is allowed. Boys may be taught to suppress sadness; girls may be discouraged from expressing anger. In some families, any emotional expression may be seen as weakness. In others, volatility may be normalized. These early emotional climates shape how we interpret and respond to our own emotions for years to come. Emotional granularity, then, is not just learned through language, but shaped by environment, values, and emotional permission.

We'll also look at how granularity intersects with trauma. In the aftermath of emotional injury, many people find themselves flooded by undifferentiated affect. Everything feels overwhelming, or nothing feels accessible. The internal compass gets scrambled. Part of healing is learning to make emotional distinctions again—to learn, slowly and gently, that fear is not always danger, that sadness is not always a collapse, and that anger can be constructive. Emotional granularity becomes a pathway back to self-trust.

The ability to feel deeply is not something to be managed away. It is a form of intelligence that, when cultivated, helps us become more honest, more connected, and more grounded. In this chapter, we will explore what emotional granularity looks like in practice, what psychological research tells us about its benefits, and how individual sensitivity and emotional nuance can be understood not as liabilities, but as core components of mature psychological life.

This is not a call to overanalyze your every mood. It's an invitation to understand what you're actually feeling—so you can live with more truth, relate with more clarity, and build the kind of inner life that can withstand the pressures of the outer world.

The Language of Emotion: Why Naming Matters

There's a difference between being emotional and being emotionally literate. Emotional literacy begins not with behavior but with language—the capacity to describe what we feel with accuracy, nuance, and clarity. Without that capacity, even the most emotionally charged life can remain psychologically shallow. We might react, we might feel overwhelmed, but we won't really know ourselves. And without knowing what we're feeling, it becomes nearly impossible to regulate those feelings or communicate them meaningfully to others.

Emotional granularity is the term psychologists use to describe the ability to make fine distinctions between emotional states. Someone high in emotional granularity doesn't just feel "bad"—they feel disappointed, irritated, ashamed, envious, or despondent, and they can tell the difference. Someone low in granularity, by contrast, may experience all distress as a single, undifferentiated emotional blur. The research is clear: people with greater emotional granularity are better at coping with stress, more resilient after setbacks, and more skilled at forming close, honest relationships.

This isn't surprising when you consider how language shapes cognition. The act of naming an emotion is not just expressive—it's regulatory. Neuroscientific research has shown that labeling an emotion recruits activity in the prefrontal cortex, helping modulate limbic reactivity. In simple terms, putting feelings into words gives the brain something to work with. It creates space between stimulus and response. That space is where self-awareness lives.

But it's not just about using any word. Precision matters. The difference between saying "I'm anxious" versus "I'm dreading a conversation that feels overdue" reflects not only greater clarity but also greater control. Broad labels like sad, mad, or fine often mask much richer emotional terrain. We say "mad" when we really mean hurt, "tired" when we mean discouraged, "anxious" when we mean unprepared. And when we mislabel emotion, we treat the wrong wound. Granularity is what allows us to identify the real problem.

This is particularly true in conflict. Consider how differently a conversation might unfold if someone said, "I feel overlooked," instead of, "You never listen." The first invites understanding. The second invites defensiveness. The specificity of emotion changes the dynamic. When people speak from a clear emotional vocabulary, they reduce confusion, increase connection, and create the conditions for resolution. Miscommunication thrives on vagueness. Clarity disarms it.

Granularity also supports internal coherence. When we don't know what we're feeling, or we can't put it into words, we become fragmented. Our behavior may shift unpredictably. We may misread our own needs or react to the wrong cues. But when we can name what we're feeling with specificity, we begin to align our inner world. We make sense to ourselves. That internal congruence is a major foundation of psychological well-being.

Children begin developing emotional granularity as early as toddlerhood, depending on how adults around them respond to their emotional expressions. A child who is taught to distinguish between frustration and embarrassment is learning more than vocabulary—they are learning how to organize their emotional world. And when those distinctions are consistently supported over time, they lay the groundwork for emotional maturity. Adults who can say "I feel conflicted" rather than "I don't know what's wrong with me" are often those who had, or later developed, access to environments where feelings were both allowed and understood.

This makes emotional granularity a fundamentally relational skill. You can't grow what isn't modeled. Many adults come into therapy or adulthood never having been taught the difference between fear and shame, or between guilt and regret. Their emotional vocabulary is either too narrow or distorted by early experiences. For instance, if someone was punished for expressing anger as a child, they may grow up interpreting all assertiveness as aggression. If someone was only rewarded when they smiled, they may struggle to identify sadness, even in their own body.

Emotionally intelligent people are not simply more empathetic—they are more precise. They notice subtle shifts in feeling, both in themselves and in others. They don't just sense tension in the room; they intuit whether it's anxiety, resentment, boredom, or uncertainty. This precision allows them to respond appropriately, rather than generically. And this response fosters trust. People feel seen not when someone guesses their emotion, but when someone accurately names it without judgment.

But accuracy doesn't mean rigidity. Part of emotional granularity is the ability to sit with ambiguity until the right name emerges. Sometimes it takes hours, days, or even weeks to understand what a feeling actually is. The goal is not to label quickly, but to label well. We live in a culture that prizes immediacy, but emotional clarity is often slow work. It requires self-reflection, pattern recognition, and the willingness to tolerate discomfort.

There's also a cultural layer here. Emotional vocabulary varies across languages and societies. Some cultures have dozens of words for what others might call sadness. Others have unique terms for social feelings like embarrassment, pride, or longing. Learning to feel with nuance sometimes means expanding the emotional vocabulary beyond your first language or beyond what was taught in your family system. The emotional lexicon of a person is shaped by both language and life experience.

Emotionally precise people don't just speak differently—they process differently. They're more likely to pause before reacting. They're less prone to emotional flooding. They can communicate needs with clarity and set boundaries that make sense. Most importantly, they can tend to their own emotional lives with compassion, rather than confusion or shame.

There's power in being able to say: I'm not just angry—I feel disregarded. I'm not just sad—I feel obsolete. I'm not just nervous—I feel exposed. Each of those sentences opens a door. It brings us closer to truth. And truth, emotionally spoken, is the foundation of all relational and psychological healing.

Emotional granularity is not elitism. It is not therapy-speak or indulgent introspection. It is self-respect. It is the ability to name your own life as it unfolds, with words that dignify what you feel, and what it costs you to feel it.

Sensitivity and Depth: Trait-Level Differences in Emotional Processing

Some people are more affected by life than others. They cry at commercials, feel drained by tension in a room, or replay conversations for hours wondering what someone meant. Others move through the same world with less friction. They seem to brush off insult, deflect pressure, and compartmentalize emotional chaos with little visible struggle. This chapter looks directly at that difference—not as pathology or personal flaw, but as a real trait-level variation in how emotion is processed, stored, and integrated. Emotional sensitivity is not about being weak. It's about how finely the nervous system responds to internal and external cues.

We begin by examining temperament. From birth, infants show distinct patterns of reactivity. Some cry easily, startle frequently, and require more soothing. Others are placid, unfazed by noise or disruption. These early signs of what researchers call "affective sensitivity" don't vanish with age—they become the emotional scaffolding upon which personality is built. Temperament doesn't dictate destiny, but it sets a tone. Children with heightened sensitivity often develop a rich internal world, keen observational skills, and high attunement to others. But they may also be more vulnerable to anxiety, overstimulation, and emotional overwhelm in unpredictable environments.

This is supported by empirical models like Jerome Kagan's work on behavioral inhibition and Thomas and Chess's temperament research. These models suggest that individual differences in emotional responsiveness are both stable and biologically grounded. High reactivity doesn't make someone emotionally unstable. It simply means their threshold for activation is lower, and their system processes stimuli with more depth and intensity.

But this sensitivity is not always understood—or welcomed—by others. Emotionally sensitive individuals are often mislabeled as dramatic, overreactive, or too much. In families or cultures that prize stoicism, this mismatch between inner reality and outer expectation can result in shame. Many people learn to hide their reactions, not because they lack control, but because they've been taught their reactions are unacceptable. The result is a chronic dissonance between what is felt and what is expressed.

This emotional masking can lead to self-doubt. Sensitive individuals often struggle with questions like: Why does this bother me so much? Why can't I just let things go like everyone else? Why do I always feel like I'm on high alert? The answer lies in how their systems are wired. Their emotional radar is more attuned. They pick up subtleties that others miss. They don't just notice the obvious—they feel the undercurrent. That doesn't make them fragile. It makes them accurate. But without tools for regulation and clarity, that accuracy can become a burden.

A useful framework here is the concept of High Affective Sensitivity, a proposed trait model that integrates depth of processing, emotional resonance, and internal reactivity. People high in this trait are not only more affected by emotional events—they also spend more time thinking about them, integrating them, and attaching meaning to them. They may be prone to rumination, but they're also capable of remarkable insight. Their emotions are not superficial fluctuations. They are enduring, meaningful, and often central to how identity is formed.

Research on Highly Sensitive Persons (HSPs), particularly the work of Elaine Aron, further elaborates on this. While her model has limitations and overlaps with other personality constructs, it does highlight something important: a portion of the population exhibits consistently deeper cognitive and emotional processing. These individuals are more impacted by both positive and negative experiences. They don't just react—they metabolize. And in doing so, they often grow in ways others do not.

Emotionally sensitive individuals also tend to be empathic. They intuit the emotional states of others, sometimes even before those states are named. This interpersonal sensitivity can be an extraordinary gift, especially in roles that require emotional labor—teachers, therapists, artists, caregivers. But it comes at a cost. The emotional permeability that allows deep connection can also lead to burnout, compassion fatigue, or emotional merging. Without boundaries and support, sensitivity becomes exhaustion.

Importantly, this isn't a call to toughen up or shut down. It's a call to understand how emotion is processed differently across individuals. The same comment that barely registers with one person might linger for days in another. The same film might be moving for one viewer and life-altering for another. This doesn't mean one person is overreacting. It means their nervous system, shaped by temperament, experience, and biology, responds with more amplitude.

That amplitude can be harnessed. Emotionally sensitive individuals are often deeply creative. Their capacity to feel, imagine, and reflect enables them to create work that resonates across time and culture. Their intensity, when channeled, becomes wisdom. But when left unacknowledged or misunderstood, it can turn inward, breeding self-doubt, isolation, or chronic dysregulation.

Therapeutically, the goal is not to diminish sensitivity, but to scaffold it with understanding and strategy. Sensitive individuals benefit from practices that help ground them in the present, regulate their physiological arousal, and organize emotional input. Techniques from dialectical behavior therapy (DBT), mindfulness-based cognitive therapy (MBCT), and compassion-focused therapy (CFT) are particularly effective for individuals with high affective sensitivity, offering tools for naming, holding, and working through emotion rather than avoiding it.

It's also worth noting that emotional sensitivity exists on a continuum. People may be more sensitive in one domain than another. Someone might have strong emotional responses to music but not to interpersonal conflict. Another might be unshaken by tragedy yet devastated by perceived rejection. Emotional depth is not a fixed global trait. It is dynamic, context-dependent, and shaped by both internal wiring and life history.

Finally, there is a developmental arc to consider. Over time, sensitive individuals often become wiser about their emotional processes. They learn to distinguish between intuitive truth and emotional projection. They learn to discern when their reactions are useful signals versus old patterns. They become less afraid of their feelings, and more curious. Sensitivity, when matured, becomes discernment. And discernment is one of the clearest markers of emotional intelligence.

To feel deeply is not to be defective. It is to be alive in a particular way. It is to walk through life without armor, but with awareness. For those with this trait, the challenge is not to feel less—it is to understand more.

Cultural and Developmental Influences on Emotional Nuance

We don't come into the world knowing how to feel. We learn it. The range of emotions we can recognize, name, and appropriately express is shaped not just by biology, but by culture, upbringing, and social norms. Emotional nuance is not simply a matter of having a larger vocabulary or deeper sensitivity. It is a developmental achievement—scaffolded over time by the way our emotions are mirrored, responded to, and given meaning by others. This means emotional intelligence, granularity, and maturity are inseparable from the contexts in which we are raised.

In early childhood, a child's emotional world is co-regulated by the adults around them. A toddler doesn't yet have the capacity to manage fear or name sadness, but when a caregiver names those emotions for them—"You're frustrated because your tower fell," or "It looks like you're feeling shy"—they begin to associate internal sensations with language. That process of mirroring is foundational. It tells the child not only what emotion they're feeling, but also that it's safe to feel it. When this kind of attuned response is consistent, the child builds a secure internal map of emotion. When it is absent or misattuned, that map becomes distorted or underdeveloped.

Cultural values determine which emotions are emphasized and which are suppressed. In many Western contexts, especially in the United States, emotional expression is often encouraged, even celebrated—particularly for emotions like pride, joy, and excitement. In East Asian cultures, by contrast, emotional restraint and social harmony are prioritized, making overt displays of emotion less common and less socially acceptable. Neither approach is inherently superior, but each shapes the emotional palette people use to interpret and express their internal states.

This becomes particularly clear when looking at linguistic differences. In English, we might use the word "sad" as a catch-all for dozens of subtly distinct states. But in Russian, there are specific terms for different kinds of sadness, such as "toska," which captures a deep spiritual ache without clear cause. In German, the word "schadenfreude" captures the experience of taking pleasure in another's misfortune—a feeling that exists across cultures but may not be linguistically represented in all of them. The vocabulary we are given informs the distinctions we're able to make. It literally limits or expands the categories we have for emotional experience.

Family dynamics also play a major role. Some families operate on a principle of emotional openness, encouraging discussion of feelings, processing of conflict, and reflection. Others function more rigidly, with rules—spoken or unspoken—about what can and cannot be felt. In some homes, anger is off-limits. In others, vulnerability is punished. A child growing up in an emotionally repressive household will not only have

FEELING DEEPLY: EMOTIONAL GRANULARITY AND SENSITIVITY

fewer words for their emotions, but also fewer internal permissions to experience them at all.

This creates emotional blind spots that often persist into adulthood. Someone raised in an environment where emotional displays were mocked may feel shame every time they cry. Another person, never taught to name emotional discomfort, may only recognize their distress once it manifests physically, as fatigue, stomach pain, or restlessness. Emotional nuance requires both linguistic tools and psychological safety. Without one or the other, people learn to default to general states like "fine," "stressed," or "pissed off"—all of which fail to capture the specific experiences underneath.

Educational systems also shape emotional nuance, albeit unevenly. Some schools now integrate social-emotional learning (SEL) into their curricula, teaching students to identify, name, and work through emotions in structured ways. But these programs are far from universal. And even when present, they are often deprioritized compared to cognitive development and academic performance. Yet research consistently shows that emotional competency is linked to academic success, mental health, and long-term well-being. When students can name what they're feeling, they are less likely to act out, shut down, or withdraw.

Peer culture adds another layer. In adolescence especially, the emotional norms of a peer group can override those learned at home. A teenager who cries easily in a family where feelings are accepted may learn to suppress tears if friends ridicule vulnerability. Or conversely, someone who grew up in an emotionally restrained home may learn to open up through peer relationships where sharing is normalized. Emotional fluency is dynamic; it grows and contracts depending on the social incentives surrounding it.

Media, too, plays an outsized role in shaping emotional expectations. Film, television, and social platforms portray stylized emotional experiences that often distort reality. Grand romantic gestures, explosive arguments, and perfect closure create emotional scripts that real life rarely follows. Viewers internalize these portrayals, often without realizing it. The result can be a mismatch between what people feel and what they think they're supposed to feel. Someone grieving, for example, may feel guilty that they're not crying more—because they've absorbed the idea that grief should look dramatic.

For those growing up in marginalized communities, emotional nuance can be further complicated by systemic pressures. Racial, gendered, and socioeconomic norms often dictate which emotions are permitted and which are penalized. Black boys in the United States, for example, may be socially punished for expressing anger or defiance, while girls may be silenced when they assert themselves. These constraints narrow the emotional vocabulary available to entire groups of people—not because the feelings aren't there, but because their expression is unsafe or invalidated.

The developmental arc of emotional nuance is not linear. Many people don't begin expanding their emotional range until adulthood, especially if earlier environments were emotionally impoverished. Therapy, close relationships, artistic practices, and reflective writing can all serve as vehicles for growth. Each time someone names an emotion they've never named before—disenchantment, longing, pride, ambivalence—they open new territory within themselves. And in doing so, they gain not only self-awareness, but also relational clarity.

The more differentiated our emotional awareness becomes, the more flexible our responses. A parent who can tell the difference between a child's fear and fatigue can respond more appropriately. A partner who knows the difference between being annoyed and feeling disrespected can communicate more constructively. A leader who understands when a team is anxious versus when they are demoralized can make better decisions. Emotional nuance translates directly into relational effectiveness.

Emotional development is lifelong. Just as language becomes richer with reading and writing, emotion becomes more refined with introspection and engagement. No one is born with complete access to their emotional life. It must be cultivated—through words, through safety, through reflection, and through relationship.

The Intelligence of Feeling: Emotion as a Cognitive Tool

The relationship between emotion and cognition has often been framed as a dichotomy: emotion is seen as impulsive, irrational, and disruptive, while cognition is viewed as rational, deliberate, and orderly. This framing, however, misrepresents the true nature of human psychological functioning. Emotion is not a barrier to clear thinking; it is an essential component of cognition itself. The ability to integrate emotional experience with reflective thought is what gives rise to emotional intelligence. This capacity to feel deeply and think clearly simultaneously is fundamental to adaptive decision-making, moral reasoning, creativity, and relational health.

Pioneering research by neurologist Antonio Damasio challenged longstanding assumptions about the separateness of emotion and reason. In studies of patients with damage to the ventromedial prefrontal cortex, a brain region critical for integrating emotion and cognition, Damasio observed a profound impairment in decision-making despite preserved intellectual ability. These patients could articulate facts and logical arguments but failed to make sound personal choices. They lacked the emotional signals that assign value to options and guide prioritization. This demonstrated that emotion serves as a critical evaluative function in cognition, providing what might be called an internal compass. Emotions highlight what matters to us in the moment and help organize thought around those priorities.

Emotions act as rapid, heuristic signals that influence attention, memory, and behavior. A feeling of unease may subtly direct attention away from potentially harmful choices. Excitement may energize pursuit of opportunity. These affective cues often operate beneath conscious awareness but exert powerful influence on cognitive processing. When emotion and cognition are in harmony, decisions tend to be both efficient and aligned with personal values. When these systems are out of sync, decisions may become erratic, shortsighted, or disconnected from core needs.

A key factor that enhances this integrative process is emotional granularity—the ability to identify and label emotions with precision. Rather than simply feeling "bad" or "good," individuals with high emotional granularity can distinguish between nuanced states such as frustration, disappointment, resentment, or wistfulness. This fine differentiation supports metacognition, the capacity to reflect on one's own mental and emotional states. Metacognitive awareness creates a space between stimulus and response, allowing for thoughtful modulation rather than reactive impulsivity. The more clearly one understands what one is feeling, the more effectively one can regulate those feelings and choose appropriate actions.

Beyond facilitating personal decision-making, emotion is deeply implicated in moral reasoning. Our ethical judgments arise not only from abstract principles but from embodied feelings such as empathy, guilt, outrage, and compassion. These emotional experiences provide motivational force and moral salience. The perception of injustice evokes anger or sadness, which compels action. Feelings of remorse or shame motivate repair and reconciliation. Emotional intelligence involves recognizing and navigating these feelings within oneself and in others. It is essential for prosocial behavior, relational harmony, and social cohesion.

Emotion also enhances creativity and complex problem-solving. Emotional intuition—an instinctive sense of what "feels right"—often precedes moments of insight. Emotions broaden cognitive flexibility, facilitating novel associations and divergent thinking. Conversely, emotional rigidity, such as chronic anxiety or anger, can narrow attention and limit perspective, impeding adaptive problem-solving. Emotional intelligence supports resilience by balancing stability with openness and by fostering constructive engagement with challenges.

Interpersonal effectiveness depends heavily on the integration of emotion and cognition. The ability to accurately perceive and interpret the emotions of others is the foundation of empathy. Emotional intelligence enables us to respond compassionately without losing boundaries or becoming overwhelmed. It supports conflict resolution by revealing underlying feelings rather than focusing solely on surface behavior. It allows relationships to be grounded in authenticity, understanding, and trust. Social intelligence is rooted in emotional literacy and regulation.

The development of emotional intelligence is a lifelong process. While children begin with rudimentary emotional recognition and regulation, the sophisticated interplay between feeling and thinking matures over adolescence and adulthood. Educational systems, therapy, and reflective practices can enhance emotional intelligence by cultivating awareness, vocabulary, and regulatory skills. Importantly, emotional intelligence is not about suppressing or controlling feelings, but engaging them with clarity and skill. It involves discerning when emotions provide useful information and when they distort perception.

Modern life presents unprecedented emotional demands. The complexity of social environments, the speed of information flow, and the intensity of interpersonal interactions require high levels of emotional skill. Emotional intelligence is a critical survival skill, supporting mental health, adaptive functioning, and ethical engagement. It enables us to navigate ambiguity, manage stress, and maintain connection in a fast-changing world.

Understanding emotion as a cognitive tool transforms our relationship with ourselves and others. It invites us to respect the wisdom embedded in feeling while cultivating the discipline to interpret and apply that wisdom thoughtfully. This integration marks the threshold of psychological maturity, where self-awareness, empathy, and reason coalesce into a coherent, grounded way of being.

The intelligence of feeling is the foundation of a life lived with presence, depth, and meaning. It allows us to embrace complexity without fragmentation and to respond to our inner world with both honesty and compassion. It is the cornerstone upon which resilience, growth, and relational richness are built.

* * *

8

Dysregulation, Avoidance, and Numbing

Emotions are supposed to help us. They signal when we're in danger, when we're safe, when we belong, and when something is off. At their best, emotions serve as a kind of internal navigation system, helping us adapt, respond, and make sense of what matters. But for many people—especially in adulthood—emotions no longer feel like helpful signals. They feel like problems to be managed, suppressed, or outrun. For some, they arrive like tidal waves—overwhelming, destabilizing, and unpredictable. For others, they seem to have disappeared altogether, leaving behind a kind of quiet detachment or pervasive dullness. This chapter explores what happens when our emotional systems go off course: when we can't feel what we need to feel, or can't stop feeling what we wish we didn't.

The psychology of being human cannot be understood without reckoning with emotional pain. Most people do not shut down because they're weak. They shut down because their internal systems have been overwhelmed. Emotional dysregulation is not a character flaw. It's the result of an internal signaling system that has been compromised by trauma, chronic stress, underdeveloped emotional skills, or relational chaos. Whether someone explodes in anger, withdraws into silence, or self-soothes through substances, what we see on the outside is rarely the whole story. Beneath it lies a disorganized, often frightened, internal landscape. Understanding that landscape—and how it leads to avoidance and numbing—is central to understanding how emotional dysfunction takes root.

At the center of this dysfunction is dysregulation: the inability to stay within a tolerable emotional range. A regulated emotional system allows us to feel anger without breaking things, sadness without collapsing, anxiety without shutting down. Dysregulation means the system overshoots or shuts off. People become reactive or unreachable, volatile or vacant. These are not arbitrary reactions. They're survival strategies. When people have not been taught how to process emotion—when no one modeled how to make room for hard feelings, to name them, or to trust that they won't destroy you—it makes sense to fear your own internal experience. Dysregulation is not about bad behavior; it's about an untrained or overwhelmed system doing the best it can with what it has.

But because feeling too much is unbearable, the most common psychological solution is avoidance. Avoidance isn't always obvious. It can look like perfectionism, intellectualizing, humor, caretaking, or staying busy. It can also look like procrastination, shutting down, self-harm, or addiction. What ties these behaviors together is that they offer an escape hatch—some way out of the emotional heat. Avoidance protects us in the short term. It numbs the pain. It helps us keep moving. But over time, it also keeps us from building the very emotional capacity we need to grow. Avoidance makes feelings the enemy. It teaches us that discomfort is dangerous, and that anything that stirs us too much should be silenced, managed, or ignored. In this way, avoidance becomes its own trap: the more we avoid what we feel, the harder it becomes to feel anything at all.

Eventually, for many people, that effort to avoid emotional pain becomes total. They don't just avoid certain feelings—they stop feeling much at all. This is emotional numbing: a muted internal life, where joy, sorrow, and connection all seem to lose their color. Numbing is often misinterpreted as apathy or indifference, but it is neither. It is self-protection. Numbing is what happens when a system becomes so saturated with pain or confusion that it shuts itself down. In trauma studies, this is often referred to as hypoarousal—a state in which the nervous system lowers its energy in response to perceived helplessness. But numbing doesn't only follow trauma. It can come from chronic invalidation, emotional neglect, or long-term emotional overexertion. And the most painful irony of numbing is this: while it protects people from unbearable pain, it also cuts them off from vitality, pleasure, and intimacy.

These three experiences—dysregulation, avoidance, and numbing—often feed each other in a cycle. A person becomes dysregulated, finds the experience intolerable, and begins avoiding emotional triggers. But the more they avoid, the less resilient they become. Eventually, the system begins to shut down, and numbing sets in. But even numbness doesn't eliminate the underlying emotional material. It simply buries it. And when those buried emotions resurface—often suddenly, under stress or through triggering relationships—they do so with intensity and confusion, reactivating the cycle of dysregulation. Over time, this loop can become a kind of emotional identity. People begin to see themselves as "too sensitive," "emotionally broken," or "shut down." They lose confidence in their ability to feel things cleanly, express them constructively, or live with emotional aliveness.

The goal of this chapter is not to offer a roadmap to perfect regulation—no such map exists. Instead, it aims to demystify what these emotional patterns actually are: how they develop, how they function, and why they persist. Emotional dysregulation is not the result of personal weakness. Avoidance is not just laziness or denial. Numbing is not apathy. These are complex, layered responses to a world—and often a childhood—that did not provide the emotional scaffolding people needed. They are also, in many cases, reversible. While not everyone will return to the full emotional range they once had, understanding the mechanics of these patterns is often the first step toward reintegrating what was shut down.

We cannot talk about the psychology of being human without talking about pain. But it is not pain itself that distorts us. It is the inability to process, express, and integrate that pain. In this way, emotional distress is not a sign that something is wrong with a person—it's a sign that something within them is still trying to work itself out. This chapter looks at that effort, that struggle, and the deeply human strategies people use to make it through. And in doing so, it invites a deeper question: What would it take—not to feel better—but to feel again?

The Dynamics of Emotional Dysregulation

At its core, emotional dysregulation refers to the inability to manage and respond to emotional experiences in a way that is appropriate to the situation. This may sound simple, but it touches some of the most complex systems in human psychology. Emotions, by nature, are fast-moving and often ambiguous. They arise from sensory input, memory, prediction, belief, and social context all at once. When a person is regulated, they are able to tolerate discomfort without collapsing into it or running from it. When they are dysregulated, they become either overwhelmed or shut down—and sometimes both in the same day.

To understand how emotional dysregulation develops, we have to start with the nervous system. The human brain is not simply a thinking organ; it is also a regulatory organ. The limbic system, particularly the amygdala, acts as an emotional alarm center, constantly scanning the environment for threat and interpreting stimuli in terms of danger, safety, or reward. In a well-regulated system, the prefrontal cortex helps moderate these limbic reactions, interpreting them in light of memory, context, and social norms. But when regulation is impaired—whether by trauma, early neglect, neurodevelopmental patterns, or chronic stress—the balance between emotional reactivity and higher-order control breaks down. People begin to feel hijacked by their own internal experience.

This hijacking can take many forms. For some, it shows up as explosive anger, panic attacks, or emotional meltdowns. For others, it looks like inconsolable sadness or disproportionate guilt. Dysregulation doesn't always mean more emotion—it can also mean difficulty accessing emotion, becoming emotionally frozen or paralyzed under stress. Either way, the key feature is that the emotional response does not match the situation. The intensity, duration, or volatility of the feeling is out of proportion to the actual trigger. The person might recognize this mismatch intellectually, but they cannot stop it. This is because dysregulation is not a choice; it is a systems problem.

Psychologically, emotional regulation is a skill, and like all skills, it is developed over time through modeling, repetition, and safe practice. In early childhood, primary caregivers play the central role in what developmental psychologists call "co-regulation." A baby does not soothe itself; it is soothed by another. Over time, those external patterns of regulation are internalized. A child who is comforted when distressed, validated when scared, and guided rather than punished for emotional outbursts begins to build a map for managing their inner world. But when caregivers are emotionally unavailable, inconsistent, or themselves dysregulated, the child receives a fragmented or chaotic emotional blueprint. They may learn that feelings are dangerous, shameful, or unwanted. Or they may learn that their emotions are only met with indifference or volatility. In either case, regulation does not develop; survival strategies do.

Many adults live out the legacy of these early blueprints without realizing it. They might describe themselves as "emotionally intense," "high-strung," or "too sensitive," never realizing that these are not fixed traits but patterns that emerged in response to unstable emotional conditions. Others might see themselves as "emotionally detached" or "numb," unaware that those traits, too, often originate in environments where emotional expression was punished, ignored, or never modeled. In both cases, the core issue is not the presence or absence of emotion but the inability to stay within a window of tolerance—that middle zone where feelings are manageable and communication is possible.

The concept of the "window of tolerance," coined by Dr. Dan Siegel, is especially useful here. When a person is within their window, they can engage, reflect, and respond without becoming overwhelmed or shut down. Outside that window, the nervous system shifts into either hyperarousal (fight or flight) or hypoarousal (freeze or collapse). Dysregulation occurs when a person cannot remain in that window or return to it once they've left. Some people live their entire lives outside it, lurching between emotional chaos and emotional flatness, not because they're dramatic or damaged but because no one helped them find the tools to stay anchored.

Complicating this further is the cultural landscape. Modern emotional culture tends to reinforce both overexpression and repression, depending on context. In some environments, emotional outbursts are rewarded as authenticity or passion; in others, they are punished as weakness or instability. This inconsistency only deepens the confusion. People learn to mask certain feelings, amplify others, and distrust their own internal compass. The more fragmented their emotional literacy becomes, the more likely they are to misread their own reactions or to believe that something is fundamentally wrong with them.

From a clinical perspective, dysregulation is a common feature across a range of psychological conditions—borderline personality disorder, bipolar disorder, PTSD, generalized anxiety, and even ADHD. But it also shows up in people with no formal diagnosis, just trying to hold their lives together while feeling out of control inside. Importantly, dysregulation is not limited to negative emotions. Some people struggle to regulate joy, excitement, sexual arousal, or even success. Anything that produces a surge of emotion—positive or negative—can become difficult to manage when the internal system lacks adequate scaffolding.

A common misunderstanding is that the goal of emotional health is to feel good. But the real goal is to feel fully and respond skillfully. Dysregulation interferes with both. It clouds perception, distorts communication, and makes meaningful self-reflection nearly impossible. When people are dysregulated, they are not thinking clearly. They are reacting, defending, protecting, or escaping. Relationships suffer. Work becomes a battlefield. Everyday challenges feel like crises. And eventually, this chronic internal volatility becomes exhausting.

But the good news is that emotional regulation can be learned, even in adulthood. Neuroplasticity ensures that new emotional patterns can be formed through repeated, consistent, and supported experiences of co-regulation, mindfulness, and emotional exposure. It is not easy. It requires trust, practice, and often therapeutic support. But it is possible.

Before any of that learning can begin, though, a person must understand what dysregulation is and what it isn't. It is not just being emotional. It is not moral failure. It is not immaturity. It is a signal that the internal system is misfiring—and often has been for a long time. Recognizing this with compassion, clarity, and psychological precision is the first step in building an emotional system that can handle life's intensity without collapsing under it.

The Psychology of Avoidance

Emotional avoidance is one of the most widespread psychological coping strategies in the modern world—and also one of the least acknowledged. It often begins as a reasonable, even adaptive, response to distress. When an emotion feels too strong, too overwhelming, or too likely to disrupt daily functioning, it can feel logical to push it aside. The problem is not that people avoid discomfort; the problem is that they come to rely on avoidance as their primary means of emotional survival. Over time, this habit reshapes how they experience life, relationships, and even themselves. Avoidance becomes not just something they do, but a lens through which they perceive what is safe, what is possible, and what is true.

Psychologically, avoidance is rooted in fear—specifically, fear of emotional pain. That pain may come in the form of grief, shame, rejection, helplessness, or the destabilizing anxiety that follows uncertainty. These are all universal human experiences, but not all of us are taught what to do with them. Some people learn early that expressing emotion leads to punishment, embarrassment, or neglect. Others learn that strong feelings make them a burden to those around them. In both cases, the emotional system concludes: it is safer not to feel. And from that point forward, the avoidance begins.

Avoidance takes many forms. It can be overt or covert, active or passive. Some people avoid emotion by staying busy: overworking, overcommitting, or constantly tending to others. Others do it through distraction: scrolling endlessly, binging media, or numbing with food, alcohol, or substances. Still others intellectualize, analyzing their pain instead of feeling it. Even excessive humor, charm, or competence can become forms of emotional evasion—tools that allow someone to navigate social life without ever truly revealing what they feel. In this way, avoidance is not a singular act but a system: a system designed to keep a person functioning without having to touch what hurts.

This strategy works, to an extent. Avoidance can allow people to maintain jobs, relationships, and routines even while holding deep unprocessed pain beneath the surface. But the cost is subtle and cumulative. Avoidance robs people of emotional fluency. Over time, the capacity to name, interpret, and express emotions begins to atrophy. They may not even realize what they're feeling, only that they're tense, irritable, or flat. This internal fog makes it harder to set boundaries, form close relationships, or feel confident in one's decisions. Because emotions are a core part of intuitive reasoning, moral judgment, and social connection, the long-term effects of avoidance go far beyond discomfort—they undermine agency.

The paradox of avoidance is that it eventually creates the very problems it was meant to prevent. People avoid feeling shame, only to act in ways that generate more of it. They avoid grief, only to feel a vague, persistent emptiness. They avoid vulnerability, only to end up disconnected. Avoidance doesn't eliminate emotion; it delays and distorts it. And when that emotion finally breaks through—because it always does—it often comes with increased force and confusion. A minor conflict may spark an outsized reaction, not because of the issue itself, but because it punctures months or years of buried frustration and fear.

From a psychological standpoint, avoidance is a protective mechanism that has been overgeneralized. Originally, avoidance evolved to help organisms survive: to withdraw from threats, danger, or harm. But in humans, this same mechanism can misfire when internal states like sadness, anger, or fear are treated as threats. The brain begins to code discomfort as danger, and the person responds not with curiosity or reflection, but with retreat. This leads to chronic emotional underprocessing, a state in which life becomes a series of tasks to manage rather than experiences to engage.

Developmentally, avoidance is reinforced through both direct and indirect social cues. Children may be told not to cry, not to talk back, not to "make a scene." Or they may watch caregivers model emotional denial—smiling through pain, avoiding hard conversations, or numbing with alcohol or detachment. These early patterns send a clear message: feeling is dangerous. And the child, eager to maintain attachment and stay safe, learns to bypass or bury emotional responses. By adulthood, these habits are so well-rehearsed that avoidance becomes second nature. People don't say, "I'm avoiding sadness"; they say, "I'm just too busy to think about it."

Importantly, avoidance is not always conscious. In fact, many people who are avoidant believe they are being strong, rational, or productive. And sometimes, they are. There are situations in which setting aside emotion temporarily is adaptive—when parenting a child through an emergency, for example, or managing crisis at work. The problem arises when temporary emotional suppression becomes a lifestyle. When people never return to what they felt. When they build entire lives around emotional avoidance, mistaking it for control.

In clinical practice, avoidance is central to many forms of psychopathology. It plays a core role in anxiety disorders, particularly panic disorder and agoraphobia, where people come to fear the sensations of anxiety itself. It contributes to depression, where emotional suppression can lead to flatness and loss of meaning. It's a core feature in trauma-related disorders, where individuals avoid reminders, feelings, and even parts of themselves that are associated with overwhelming experiences. Even substance use disorders are often rooted in a desire to avoid emotional pain, not just to chase pleasure.

One of the more damaging outcomes of long-term avoidance is the erosion of self-trust. When a person avoids their internal states, they begin to lose confidence in their own perceptions. They may become overly reliant on others for validation or excessively wary of emotional intimacy. They may second-guess their boundaries, their desires, even their sense of identity. This is because emotions are not optional. They are part of the infrastructure of being human. When we cut ourselves off from them, we don't become stronger—we become disoriented.

Breaking the pattern of avoidance requires more than willpower. It requires a shift in how emotion is understood and valued. People must learn to reclassify discomfort not as a threat, but as a signal—one that carries information worth listening to. This often involves a deliberate reengagement with feeling: practicing emotional exposure in small, manageable doses; developing language for inner experience; and learning to stay present with sensations rather than fleeing from them. In therapy, this might involve techniques like exposure, emotion-focused processing, or mindfulness-based interventions that help build emotional tolerance. In daily life, it means slowing down long enough to feel something before moving on.

Avoidance is seductive because it offers immediate relief. But it never provides resolution. It keeps people alive, but not fully living. And perhaps most importantly, it sends a quiet message to the self: that your feelings are too much, too dangerous, or too embarrassing to face. Undoing that message takes time. But it is possible. And it begins with this understanding: avoidance is not weakness—it is a learned strategy for protection. And like all strategies, it can be revised.

Emotional Numbing and Disconnection

While dysregulation often looks loud and avoidance looks busy, emotional numbing is quieter. It doesn't draw attention to itself in the same way. There are no explosions, no obvious retreat. Instead, there is a stillness that many people mistake for composure. But behind that stillness is often a profound loss: the inability to feel fully. People who are emotionally numb may not look like they're in pain, but that's precisely the trap. Numbing does not erase emotional distress; it just dulls it. It creates a kind of internal distance where not only is pain kept at bay, but so is joy, excitement, longing, and even love.

Emotional numbing is often confused with emotional regulation, especially in cultures that prize stoicism, self-control, and emotional restraint. But the two are fundamentally different. Regulation means the ability to move through emotions without becoming overwhelmed or overtaken by them. Numbing means not moving through them at all. It is not an active skill but a shutting down of the emotional system itself. People who are emotionally numb often describe feeling like they're on autopilot, going through the motions of their lives without a real sense of presence. They may laugh, perform, or even comfort others—but privately, they report a kind of inner flatness or emptiness that feels difficult to name.

In clinical terms, emotional numbing is most often associated with trauma, particularly in post-traumatic stress disorder (PTSD). In such cases, numbing is a protective adaptation. The brain, faced with experiences it cannot process, begins to dampen the emotional response in order to preserve psychological functioning. This is often referred to as hypoarousal: a physiological state in which the nervous system suppresses activation to minimize distress. But the phenomenon is not limited to trauma survivors. Chronic stress, emotional neglect, burnout, and long-term avoidance can also lead to a similar shutdown. Over time, the system learns that feeling is unsafe, and so it stops trying.

From a developmental perspective, emotional numbing can emerge early in life, particularly in environments where emotional expression is discouraged or ignored. A child who grows up being told to "toughen up," or who is repeatedly met with indifference when expressing hurt, learns not to expect emotional resonance. That child may eventually stop reaching for it altogether. In this context, numbing isn't just a reaction to stress; it's a strategy for relational survival. The child protects themselves from further rejection by dampening the emotional system itself. The price of that protection, however, is the loss of felt experience.

In adulthood, emotional numbing can manifest in many ways. Some people lose interest in things they once enjoyed. Others feel detached from relationships, unable to connect even when they want to. Many report feeling like observers in their own lives—technically present, but not really alive in the moment. This is especially common in high-functioning individuals who appear competent, productive, and socially integrated, but privately feel hollow or emotionally distant. They may have careers, families, even achievements, but experience no internal resonance. The milestones don't land. The victories don't feel real.

This detachment can be deeply confusing. People wonder what's wrong with them. They may ask why they can't feel joy, why they're not more excited, why nothing seems to move them anymore. They may begin to self-diagnose as depressed or broken, when in fact what they're experiencing is a protective withdrawal of their emotional system. The tragedy of numbing is that it is often invisible—not only to others, but to the person experiencing it. Because the absence of feeling doesn't scream for attention the way panic or sadness might, it often goes unaddressed. It becomes the water people swim in, the background condition of their lives.

In relational contexts, emotional numbing creates distance. It becomes harder to connect, harder to empathize, harder to feel present with others. Intimacy requires access to emotional reality, both one's own and another's. But when emotional signals are muted or absent, relationships begin to feel shallow or performative. Partners may complain that they "can't reach" the person. Friends may sense that something is off, even if they can't name it. And the person who is numb may feel a growing sense of guilt or confusion, knowing that something essential is missing but not knowing how to retrieve it.

From a psychological standpoint, emotional numbing often operates alongside cognitive distortions. People may begin to believe that emotions are useless or dangerous, that vulnerability is a weakness, or that their inability to feel makes them fundamentally flawed. These beliefs reinforce the disconnection. And because numbness dulls the internal warning system, people may also fail to recognize when they are in unhealthy environments or toxic relationships. Without emotional data to guide them, they may rely solely on rationalization or habit, remaining in circumstances that no longer serve them.

There is also a cultural layer to emotional numbing. In many societies, especially those that prioritize productivity and external achievement, the absence of feeling is not always viewed as a problem. In fact, it is sometimes rewarded. The ability to "push through," "not let things get to you," or "stay focused no matter what" is often praised. But beneath that praise is a dangerous normalization of emotional suppression. People are taught to override their internal states for the sake of efficiency, stability, or image. Over time, this devalues the emotional system itself. And when the culture supports that devaluation, numbing becomes not just a personal strategy but a shared norm.

Reconnecting with emotion after numbing is not a simple reversal. It requires not only permission but safety. The emotional system will not fully reawaken unless it trusts that it can do so without being overwhelmed or punished. This is why therapeutic spaces, trauma-informed relationships, and mindful re-engagement with feeling are so essential. The goal is not to force emotion back online, but to gently invite it. To make space for its return. And to trust that what went dormant can, under the right conditions, begin to stir again.

Ultimately, emotional numbing is not a sign of failure. It is a sign that something inside has been trying to survive. It is a form of emotional self-anesthesia, one that keeps the system intact at the cost of vitality.

The work, then, is not to shame the numbness but to understand it. And to begin the long, often fragile process of coming back into contact with life as it actually feels—not just as it appears.

The Cycle of Dysregulation, Avoidance, and Numbing: Clinical and Everyday Implications

Dysregulation, avoidance, and numbing do not appear in isolation. While each can be analyzed individually, they rarely exist without the others. Instead, they operate in a looping system, a kind of emotional feedback cycle that keeps people trapped in reactive or disconnected states. The emotional system swings from chaos to shutdown, from overactivity to absence, with avoidance acting as the pivot. What begins as a response to pain becomes a system of coping that eventually becomes a way of being. Understanding how these states reinforce each other—and how they affect daily life—is essential for making sense of both clinical pathology and the quieter emotional dysfunction that many people live with undiagnosed.

This cycle often begins with dysregulation. A person experiences intense emotional activation—fear, anger, shame, grief—that feels too overwhelming to manage. Because they have not developed the capacity to process that emotion in real time, they instinctively seek relief. That relief often takes the form of avoidance. The avoidance may be behavioral (retreating, distracting, self-medicating) or cognitive (minimizing, rationalizing, denying). In either case, the emotion is pushed aside rather than processed. Over time, repeated avoidance dampens the emotional system itself, leading to numbing. But numbness is not a resolution—it is a suppression. The underlying emotional content remains unprocessed, stored in the body, memory, and nervous system. And when it finally surfaces—often through triggers, stress, or relational rupture—it reactivates the dysregulation. And the cycle continues.

In everyday life, this cycle doesn't always look dramatic. It can manifest in subtle patterns: irritability that erupts unexpectedly, exhaustion that feels unshakable, relationships that remain shallow despite desire for closeness. People may appear to be functioning, but inside they feel misaligned. They describe feeling "off," "hollow," or "out of sync." They may pursue external changes—new jobs, relationships, routines—hoping to correct the internal misfire, only to find that the numbness or volatility follows them. This is because the cycle is internal. Until the person addresses the underlying emotional mechanisms, external adjustments rarely bring lasting relief.

In clinical settings, this cycle underlies a wide range of conditions. In mood disorders, it often shows up as emotional lability—mood swings that feel disproportionate to events, followed by periods of shutdown or disengagement. In anxiety disorders, the pattern of dysregulation and avoidance becomes particularly pronounced: people experience anxiety, avoid the situations that trigger it, and then become more sensitized to those triggers over time. In trauma disorders, the entire cycle is heightened. The nervous system is on constant alert, swinging between hyperarousal (panic, anger, reactivity) and hypoarousal (numbness, detachment, dissociation), with avoidance as the only stable ground.

But even outside of clinical contexts, the cycle of dysregulation, avoidance, and numbing affects how people live, relate, and make decisions. It shapes communication styles—people lash out or shut down, then avoid hard conversations altogether. It influences parenting—adults project unresolved emotional patterns onto their children, responding to their needs with either overcontrol or emotional absence. It affects work—people become paralyzed by perfectionism, drained by burnout, or detached from their sense of purpose. And most quietly, it affects identity—people lose access to their authentic selves because their emotional lives have become so distorted or inaccessible.

This cycle also has systemic and cultural implications. In environments where emotional expression is stigmatized or where productivity is prioritized over wellness, dysregulation is misunderstood as laziness or volatility, avoidance is rewarded as discipline, and numbness is praised as composure. These misinterpretations reinforce the cycle. People are less likely to seek help when dysregulation is shamed, or when numbing is seen as strength. They are less likely to build emotional resilience when avoidance is equated with maturity. And so the loop continues—quietly reinforced by cultural norms that prize stability over emotional honesty.

Breaking this cycle requires multiple interventions, and not all of them are clinical. Therapeutically, approaches like dialectical behavior therapy (DBT), emotion-focused therapy (EFT), and somatic experiencing help people build the capacity to stay with emotion, rather than flee or suppress it. These methods emphasize emotional tolerance, regulation skills, and bodily awareness, all of which help widen the window of tolerance. But outside of therapy, change often begins with awareness. People must first recognize the pattern: not just that they feel "off," but how and why their emotional system keeps looping. From there, they can begin to experiment with small acts of emotional engagement—naming a feeling, staying present in a difficult moment, choosing not to distract right away.

This kind of emotional re-entry is slow and uneven. People may swing back into dysregulation, fall into avoidance again, or retreat into numbness when overwhelmed. But with time, they can learn to pause the cycle, even if they can't stop it completely. The goal is not to feel everything all at once, nor to avoid all discomfort. It is to regain access to feeling and to trust that it won't destroy them. That they can tolerate hard emotions, stay present with them, and come out intact.

Support systems play a critical role in this process. Emotionally attuned relationships—whether with friends, partners, or professionals—offer a kind of external regulation that helps rebuild internal capacity. Safe others model what it looks like to feel, to stay, and to recover. This is why emotional recovery is rarely a solitary process. While the work of facing one's emotions must ultimately be done internally, it is often made possible by the presence of someone else who says, in word or action, "You're not alone in this."

The cycle of dysregulation, avoidance, and numbing is not a flaw in the human design—it is part of it. It reflects the incredible flexibility of the emotional system, which adapts to survive whatever conditions it is given. But surviving is not the same as living. When emotional coping becomes rigid, habitual, and invisible, it stops protecting us and starts limiting us. And if we are to understand the psychology of being human, we must confront the fact that most people are not fighting their emotions—they're fighting the consequences of not being able to feel them.

Breaking that cycle is not about forcing ourselves into a different emotional state. It is about cultivating the conditions—internal and external—that allow for the return of emotional aliveness. This may not look dramatic. It may begin quietly: with a pause, a feeling named aloud, a moment stayed with instead of escaped. But in those small moments, the system begins to reorganize. Not through force, but through permission.

And when that happens, people do not just regulate better. They return to themselves.

* * *

9

Resilience, Recovery, and Adaptive Capacity

Not everyone breaks the same way. Some people collapse under strain, while others bend and return. Some emerge from hardship hollowed out and brittle, while others somehow grow deeper, wiser, more alive. This difference is not about superiority. It's about systems—internal and external—that allow one person to recover while another remains stuck. Resilience is one of the most misused words in psychology and public discourse. It is often flattened into a slogan, held up as proof of grit or individual toughness. But real resilience has little to do with slogans and everything to do with structure: how the mind, body, and relationships work together to absorb disruption without losing coherence. Resilience is not just surviving. It is adapting without becoming someone you're not.

This chapter explores the psychology of resilience not as a fixed trait, but as a dynamic process—one that involves recovery, flexibility, and the ability to reorganize meaning in the aftermath of adversity. It is about what happens after the rupture. How people respond when what they counted on is taken from them. How they rebuild after a loss, a betrayal, a collapse in health, a failure of imagination, or the quiet shattering of what they thought they believed. In this sense, resilience is not about optimism or toughness; it's about how people stay intact without staying the same.

To understand resilience, we have to begin with the reality of human vulnerability. No one escapes injury—not physically, emotionally, or existentially. Whether through trauma, illness, relational loss, systemic harm, or the slow erosion of hope, every life is touched by pain. But pain alone does not determine the outcome. What matters more is what surrounds the pain: the internal capacity to regulate emotion, the relational context that makes suffering bearable, the cognitive frameworks that interpret meaning, and the systems of support that allow repair. Resilience is the term we give to this entire ecosystem—the process by which people navigate hardship without losing their sense of self.

Importantly, resilience is not the same as endurance. A person can endure immense suffering by shutting down, numbing out, or pushing forward at any cost. That is not resilience; that is survival. And while survival is necessary, it is not sustainable. What separates resilient adaptation from rigid coping is the presence of elasticity—psychological give. Resilient people may feel fear, grief, rage, or hopelessness, but they don't stay frozen in it. They metabolize what happens to them. They move with the pain rather than around it. They adjust their expectations, rewrite their stories, and stay connected to the parts of themselves that are still intact.

Much of this capacity is built long before adversity arrives. Resilience is seeded in childhood through secure attachment, emotional validation, and the gradual development of self-trust. It is reinforced through experiences of co-regulation and emotional repair. People who have been allowed to break without being abandoned learn that recovery is possible. They don't learn this through lectures. They learn it through being held while crying, being heard without being fixed, being seen without being dismissed. Over time, this becomes an internal template: I can fall apart and come back together. I can bend without breaking.

But resilience is also built in adulthood. Life continues to offer opportunities for integration—moments when we discover that we can face what once felt unfaceable, stay present with what we used to run from, or reimagine what once felt like a dead end. In these moments, something shifts internally. Resilience is not just about enduring bad things; it is about responding to them in ways that expand, rather than shrink, our humanity. That expansion is often uncomfortable. It may involve grieving what will never return, accepting an irreversible change, or learning to carry something that has no resolution. But through that discomfort, new patterns of strength emerge—not the kind that protects us from pain, but the kind that holds us inside it without falling apart.

There are also profound cultural misconceptions about resilience that need to be confronted. In many social narratives, resilience is portrayed as individual heroism: the lone survivor, the comeback story, the one who beats the odds. But this framing ignores the role of environment. Resilience is never entirely self-made. It is relational, systemic, and contextual. People are more likely to recover when they are not punished for breaking, when they are surrounded by people who hold them in their struggle, when their pain is not pathologized or politicized. In this way, resilience is not only a psychological phenomenon—it is also a social justice issue. Who gets to be resilient? Who is expected to be? Who is supported in the process, and who is left to do it alone?

This chapter takes a layered approach to resilience. It begins by exploring what resilience really is: a form of psychological architecture that enables recovery without collapse. It then differentiates recovery from reversal, making the case that growth after adversity does not mean returning to how things were, but integrating what has changed. It explores the mechanisms that allow for that integration—flexibility, meaning-making, cognitive reappraisal, and emotional endurance—and how these can be developed and strengthened over time. Finally, it turns outward to examine the external scaffolding that supports resilience: relationships, institutions, cultures, and collective systems of care.

To be human is to face rupture. But the story does not end there. Resilience is the capacity to let life shape us without letting it deform us. It is the process of becoming more whole, not in spite of pain, but through a deeper relationship to it. In this sense, resilience is not just a psychological function. It is an ethical commitment: to remain available to life, to ourselves, and to one another—even after everything has changed.

The Architecture of Resilience

Resilience is often misunderstood because it wears many masks. It can look like strength, grit, determination, or composure. But psychologically, resilience is something more nuanced. It is not simply about enduring hardship—it is about withstanding disruption without losing coherence. It is the capacity of a person's inner system to absorb stress, integrate pain, and reorganize in a way that allows for continued functioning without fragmentation. To call someone resilient is not to say they are unaffected by difficulty; it is to say that they remain intact in the face of it. And that intactness is not luck. It is built, layer by layer, through biological, developmental, relational, and environmental systems.

The first layer is neurological. Human beings are born with nervous systems that are inherently responsive to their surroundings. From the moment of birth, the infant's autonomic nervous system is shaped by patterns of interaction—how consistently they are held, soothed, mirrored, and responded to. These early experiences don't just create emotional expectations; they physically shape the architecture of stress response. When caregivers are responsive and predictable, the infant learns that distress is temporary and manageable. Over time, this expectation becomes internalized. The child develops a nervous system capable of self-soothing, anticipating repair, and regulating arousal. In short, they begin to build the biological foundation of resilience.

But resilience is not simply a matter of biology. The next layer is psychological, and it centers around what attachment theorists call "secure base" experiences. Children who have at least one reliable caregiver develop not only better emotional regulation, but also the confidence to explore, make mistakes, and return for comfort. This dance of separation and return—of moving out into the world and coming back to safety—forms the core of psychological resilience. It teaches the child that the world is not only survivable, but also recoverable. That they can encounter stress without being abandoned. That they can fall without shattering.

These early relational experiences become internalized as working models—mental representations of how relationships function and how the self is treated in times of need. Secure working models support resilience because they allow people to believe that connection is possible, that help will be available, and that their distress is worthy of attention. Insecure models, by contrast, undermine resilience. They teach the child that needs are dangerous, that emotions lead to rejection, or that survival requires self-erasure. People with these models may appear tough or independent, but beneath that exterior is often a fragile structure—one that has not been supported, only armored.

Social learning also plays a critical role in resilience. Children observe how adults respond to setbacks, failure, and distress. Do they recover with grace or fall apart? Do they name their emotions or bury them? Do they ask for help or isolate? These patterns become scripts for how to deal with adversity. In resilient environments, people see that mistakes are survivable, that conflict can be repaired, that suffering can be witnessed without shame. These social cues shape how people interpret their own distress and whether they believe recovery is possible.

In adolescence and adulthood, resilience begins to expand beyond the family system. Peer relationships, mentorships, school environments, community structures—all contribute to the scaffolding that supports or erodes resilience. During this period, identity becomes a key mediator. People who develop a coherent sense of self—who have language for their experiences, values that guide them, and a basic narrative of who they are—are more likely to integrate difficulty than be undone by it. This is because identity provides continuity. When life is disrupted, resilient individuals can still locate themselves. They know who they are in pain.

They can narrate what is happening without collapsing into it.

Crucially, resilience is not a personality trait. While temperament may influence how easily someone recovers, resilience itself is not static. It can be built, eroded, rebuilt, and expanded over time. It is sensitive to context, relational dynamics, and repeated exposure. Even someone who was not resilient as a child can develop profound adaptive capacity later in life, especially when given access to supportive relationships and opportunities for safe self-expression. This challenges the myth that people are either "resilient" or "not." In truth, resilience is more like a muscle: it can atrophy or strengthen depending on how it is used, how it is supported, and what kind of strain it is asked to endure.

One of the most powerful contributors to adult resilience is the presence of meaning. Viktor Frankl, in his work with Holocaust survivors, argued that the ability to find or create meaning in suffering was central to psychological survival. This insight has since been echoed in trauma research, grief studies, and existential psychology. Meaning provides structure to chaos. It gives pain a place in the narrative. Without meaning, hardship feels random, senseless, and defeating. With meaning, even devastating loss can be integrated into a coherent life story. This does not eliminate the pain, but it allows the person to remain oriented within it.

Flexibility is another hallmark of resilient systems. Rigid belief systems, perfectionism, and black-and-white thinking are all enemies of resilience because they leave no room for adaptation. When things do not go according to plan, the rigid mind breaks. The flexible mind bends. Psychological flexibility allows a person to update their expectations, change strategies, and reframe challenges without losing their core values or sense of purpose. This kind of flexibility is often learned in adulthood—through experience, reflection, or therapeutic work—and it is one of the most important predictors of emotional recovery after trauma.

Finally, it is worth emphasizing that resilience is relational, not just individual. People are more resilient when they are not alone. This is true biologically—co-regulation helps calm the nervous system. It is true psychologically—being seen and heard helps integrate experience. And it is true socially—access to support networks, care systems, and community resources all increase the likelihood of recovery. When people are surrounded by others who reflect their worth, hold space for their struggle, and believe in their capacity to grow, they recover faster and more fully. In this way, resilience is not merely an internal capacity but a reflection of the emotional and relational ecology in which a person lives.

The architecture of resilience is not one thing. It is an intricate, layered construction made up of biology, attachment, belief, identity, and social connection. It is neither fragile nor invincible—but it is repairable. And that may be the most important insight of all: resilience is not what keeps us from breaking. It is what helps us come back together when we do.

Recovery Is Not Reversal

When people talk about recovery—after trauma, illness, loss, or personal collapse—they often imagine a return. Back to normal, back to who they were, back to how things used to feel. This longing is understandable. Pain creates rupture, and the desire to undo rupture is one of the most deeply human impulses we have. But recovery does not mean reversal. It does not mean going back to a previous emotional state or resurrecting a prior identity. It means integrating what happened and reorganizing around what is now true. In this way, recovery is not a path to the past; it is a process of constructing a future that makes space for what changed.

The fantasy of reversal is seductive. After heartbreak, people want to unlove the person who left. After grief, they want to feel joy the way they used to. After trauma, they want their nervous systems to forget. This fantasy is often reinforced by cultural scripts that equate healing with erasure. Phrases like "move on," "get over it," or "return to yourself" imply that healing is a form of deletion—removing the impact of pain so that life can resume uninterrupted. But this is not how the human system works. The psyche does not forget. The body does not un-experience. True recovery doesn't involve deletion; it involves transformation.

Psychologically, recovery is a reorganization of the self. It requires a person to absorb what happened and make room for it without letting it consume or define them. This is an active, often uncomfortable process. After trauma, for example, people may need to re-learn basic trust—trust in the world, in others, in their own perceptions. After loss, they may need to revise their narrative of identity: not just "I was someone's partner" or "I was healthy," but "I am someone who lost and kept living." After collapse—of a belief, a career, a worldview—they may need to build a new framework from the ground up, one that can accommodate the disillusionment without losing integrity. These are not returns. They are remakings.

This process is rarely linear. Recovery often involves setbacks, disorientation, and moments of deep internal conflict. People can feel better for weeks, only to be triggered by a smell, a song, a date on the calendar. These moments do not indicate failure; they are reminders that integration takes time. The nervous system does not follow a calendar. The emotional body does not conform to the logic of closure. Instead, it moves in spirals, revisiting the same places with slightly different awareness each time. In this way, healing is not a clean arc. It is a recursive unfolding.

Clinically, this recursive process is well-documented in trauma research and grief theory. The dual process model of bereavement, for instance, proposes that grieving individuals oscillate between confronting the pain of the loss and engaging with the demands of daily life. This oscillation is not avoidance—it is regulation. It allows people to metabolize intense emotional material without being swallowed by it. Similarly, in trauma recovery, the phase-oriented model suggests that healing begins with stabilization, followed by the processing of traumatic memory, and eventually a reintegration of identity. These frameworks highlight that recovery is not a single act, but a series of internal negotiations.

Perhaps the most important of these negotiations is the shift from why to how. In the aftermath of a disruptive event, people often become stuck in questions of meaning: Why did this happen? Why me? Why now? While meaning-making is essential, it can also become a trap when pursued obsessively. At some point, resilient recovery shifts the focus from explanation to movement. How do I live with this? How do I carry what I cannot change? How do I build a life around what remains? These are not easy questions, but they are livable ones. And they mark the beginning of a different kind of healing—one based on presence, not perfection.

Identity plays a central role in this process. People cannot recover without reevaluating who they are. This doesn't mean reinventing oneself completely. It means integrating the pain into a self-concept that still feels coherent. A person who once saw themselves as optimistic may now see themselves as clear-eyed but hopeful. Someone who once prided themselves on invulnerability may now value softness, boundaries, or discernment. These identity shifts are not betrayals of the former self—they are evolutions of it. And the more people are supported in making sense of these shifts, the less alienated they feel from their own recovery.

Language is also a powerful tool in this reorganization. The words people use to describe what happened to them shape how they experience it. Saying "I was destroyed" creates a different internal reality than saying "I was broken open." Saying "I can never trust again" is different from saying "I'm learning what trust means now." These shifts are not about sugarcoating pain. They are about claiming authorship of the narrative. When people feel that their story is being written for them—by circumstance, by diagnosis, by others' interpretations—they feel disempowered. Recovery begins when they begin to reauthor that story in a voice they recognize.

This is why social context matters so much in the recovery process. People do not heal in a vacuum. They heal in relationship: to others, to language, to culture, to systems of meaning. A supportive environment can help make sense of suffering. An invalidating one can deepen it.

Recovery is harder when people are told they're taking too long, when their pain is minimized, or when their experiences are pathologized instead of honored. The quality of the relational environment—both personal and institutional—shapes the trajectory of recovery more than most people realize.

None of this means that recovery always results in growth. Sometimes, people do not become stronger or wiser. Sometimes they are simply changed. They carry a scar, a limp, a quieter voice. They go on, but not triumphantly. And that, too, is recovery. It does not need to be spectacular to be real. It does not need to inspire others to be valid. Recovery is not a performance. It is a private reckoning. A decision, sometimes daily, to stay in relationship with what happened rather than dissociate from it. To live, even when it hurts. To keep constructing meaning in a world that does not guarantee it.

In this sense, recovery is not about erasing damage. It is about continuing to live in its aftermath with honesty and integration. It is not a return. It is a re-entry—into life, into relationship, into the fragile, ongoing project of being human.

Adaptive Capacity and Psychological Flexibility

When a person bends without breaking, it is not because they have eliminated vulnerability. It is because they have developed *adaptive capacity*: the ability to adjust to changing demands, reorient after disruption, and continue functioning even under strain. Adaptive capacity is not a shield against discomfort. It is a form of psychological agility—an internal readiness to respond, pivot, or reframe when life does not unfold as expected. It is not always visible from the outside. Often, it looks like calm, composure, or quick problem-solving. But at its core, adaptive capacity is built on something far more subtle: the willingness to remain engaged with reality, even when that reality is painful, inconvenient, or unfamiliar.

Psychological flexibility is the engine of adaptive capacity. Defined by researchers in the field of contextual behavioral science, psychological flexibility refers to the ability to hold one's thoughts and emotions lightly, to stay present, and to take values-based action—even when faced with discomfort. This concept is a cornerstone of Acceptance and Commitment Therapy (ACT), a therapeutic model designed to help individuals move away from avoidance and toward meaningful engagement with life. Unlike models that prioritize symptom reduction, ACT focuses on increasing a person's capacity to live well with what cannot be controlled. In this way, it reflects a fundamental truth of emotional resilience: it is not suffering that derails people, but rigidity.

Rigid minds break more easily. When people insist that life must follow a particular path, that emotions must behave in certain ways, or that they must never fail, they set themselves up for collapse. This rigidity can take many forms: perfectionism, black-and-white thinking, catastrophizing, moral absolutism, or an obsessive need for certainty. These patterns are understandable—they provide the illusion of control in an unpredictable world. But they also narrow the range of possible responses. When life inevitably deviates from expectation, rigid thinkers panic, shut down, or double down on failing strategies. In contrast, those with psychological flexibility are able to update their thinking, shift expectations, and experiment with new behaviors without losing their core sense of self.

Adaptive capacity is also deeply tied to emotional tolerance. People who cannot tolerate discomfort tend to avoid it at all costs. This avoidance limits their behavioral repertoire, reduces their exposure to new experiences, and reinforces a belief that they are incapable of surviving hard emotions. Over time, their world shrinks. But those who learn to stay present with emotional discomfort—even briefly—expand their range. They begin to trust that sadness won't annihilate them, that anger doesn't mean danger, that anxiety can be moved through rather than escaped. This trust is not abstract. It is learned, often through repeated exposure to emotional risk followed by repair. And the more this trust develops, the more capacity a person has to adapt under stress.

Cognitive flexibility is another critical component. This refers to the ability to take on multiple perspectives, adjust mental frameworks, and shift problem-solving strategies in response to new information. Developmentally, cognitive flexibility begins in childhood as children learn to manage competing rules, switch tasks, and navigate contradictions. But it continues to develop throughout life, especially in environments that reward open-mindedness, curiosity, and critical thinking. Flexible thinkers are more likely to reinterpret adversity in constructive ways. They are able to entertain alternative explanations, reconsider assumptions, and remain open to the possibility of change. In contrast, inflexible thinkers are more likely to ruminate, blame, or collapse into helplessness.

Meaning-making plays a vital role in this process. Adaptive individuals are not just cognitively agile; they are also existentially engaged. They can revise the meaning of their experiences without invalidating their pain. For example, someone who loses a job may reframe the event not as personal failure, but as a forced redirection toward work that better aligns with their values. Someone who experiences a betrayal may eventually come to understand it not as proof of their unworthiness, but as a painful clarifier of who and what they can trust. These reappraisals do not deny the hurt. They contextualize it in a way that restores agency.

Importantly, adaptive capacity does not eliminate emotional intensity. Some of the most resilient individuals feel deeply, react strongly, and struggle openly. What distinguishes them is not a lack of suffering, but a willingness to remain in process. They do not demand immediate resolution or perfect clarity. Instead, they stay in relationship with the problem, returning to it over time with new angles, new questions, and new strategies. This kind of adaptive persistence is what psychologist Carol Dweck calls a "growth mindset"—the belief that abilities, traits, and understandings can evolve with effort and feedback. It is a psychological posture that privileges learning over certainty.

Social and cultural factors also shape adaptive capacity. Environments that reward experimentation, normalize failure, and support emotional expression tend to foster greater flexibility. Conversely, environments that punish mistakes, enforce rigid norms, or stigmatize vulnerability tend to produce defensive rigidity. In this way, adaptive capacity is not simply a matter of will. It is a response to the ecosystem in which a person is embedded. This has important implications for education, healthcare, leadership, and mental health care: systems that want to support resilience must create conditions in which flexibility is possible.

There is also a moral dimension to psychological flexibility. Rigid thinking is often the root of moral polarization, ideological extremism, and relational breakdowns. The inability to hold multiple truths, entertain ambiguity, or tolerate difference leads to black-and-white narratives that simplify reality but destroy complexity. Adaptive individuals, by contrast, are able to remain grounded in their own values while making space for the perspectives and experiences of others. They do not collapse into relativism, but they do resist the seduction of certainty. This moral flexibility allows for connection, dialogue, and growth in ways that rigid systems cannot tolerate.

Finally, adaptive capacity is not a guarantee against collapse. Even the most flexible individuals can be overwhelmed by grief, destabilized by trauma, or undone by sudden change. But when this happens, they are more likely to rebuild. They have more tools, more mental pathways, more practiced habits of reorientation. They know how to shift posture without abandoning their principles. They know how to grieve without turning to despair. They know how to try again, not because they are immune to pain, but because they are practiced in the art of adjusting.

In this way, adaptive capacity is not about invulnerability. It is about responsiveness. A resilient person does not stay the same—they stay intact by staying in motion. They move toward what matters, even when the ground keeps shifting. They remain available to life, even when it does not cooperate. And that availability—rooted in flexibility, emotional endurance, and meaning—is what allows them to bend without breaking.

Building the Scaffolding: Relationships, Systems, and Environments

Resilience is not only an internal trait. It is also a function of context. While psychological flexibility, emotional regulation, and meaning-making matter, they do not emerge in isolation. People develop resilience within relational systems—families, friendships, communities, workplaces—and within the larger social, political, and economic structures that either buffer or compound distress. To understand resilience in real terms, we must move beyond the individual and examine the scaffolding around them. That scaffolding is not peripheral; it is foundational. It determines not only how someone survives adversity, but whether they are allowed to recover at all.

At the center of this scaffolding are relationships. From infancy through adulthood, co-regulation with others is the first and most enduring source of psychological strength. A regulated nervous system is often a borrowed one. When a child falls apart and is met with calm, steady attention, they begin to internalize the expectation that pain can be witnessed, not just endured. That lesson carries forward. In adulthood, relationships that offer presence, not pressure; support, not solutions—help buffer the effects of trauma and stress. People recover faster when they are not alone in their suffering. They recover more deeply when they are seen and believed. And they are more likely to remain intact when they are loved not in spite of their brokenness, but through it.

Relational scaffolding does not require perfection. It requires consistency. A friend who checks in regularly. A partner who knows when to listen without fixing. A therapist who helps name patterns without judgment. A teacher who believes in a student's potential even when they falter. These relationships build the sense of safety, trust, and coherence that make resilience possible. Without them, people may survive—but they survive through emotional contraction. They armor themselves. They isolate. They develop rigid coping structures to make up for the absence of dependable human connection. What looks like independence is often relational malnourishment in disguise.

Beyond one-on-one relationships, social environments play a critical role. Communities that promote emotional expression, normalize struggle, and provide collective rituals for loss and reorientation tend to foster greater resilience. This is why cultural traditions matter—not as quaint customs, but as frameworks for integrating disruption. Ceremonies for grief, storytelling circles, rites of passage, communal caregiving—all of these provide emotional containment. They signal to individuals that their pain belongs somewhere. That it is part of a shared human story. In Western contexts, where individualism and emotional privacy are prized, this communal scaffolding is often underdeveloped. People are expected to manage their pain privately, efficiently, and without too much disruption. The result is not resilience. It is emotional isolation.

Systems of care are another essential layer. Access to mental health services, safe housing, healthcare, food security, and financial stability all impact how resilient someone can be in the face of adversity. A person who loses their job and still has access to unemployment benefits, community support, and healthcare is far more likely to recover than someone who faces the same loss with no safety net. This may seem obvious, but it directly contradicts the myth that resilience is purely about willpower or mindset. When basic needs are unmet, the psychological system shifts into survival mode. In this state, flexibility shrinks. Emotion becomes reactive. Executive functioning declines. The brain does not prioritize growth when the body is under siege.

These structural realities mean that resilience is inherently unequal. It is easier to be resilient when you are resourced. It is easier to adapt when the world around you allows for rest, repair, and re-entry. This does not diminish the courage of those who persevere under oppressive conditions—it makes their resilience even more remarkable. But it does require a reframing of how we talk about strength. Too often, the most vulnerable populations are asked to be the most resilient: communities impacted by poverty, racism, violence, or displacement are praised for their strength while denied the support that would reduce the need for it. In this way, resilience discourse can become a smokescreen for systemic neglect.

To counter this, resilience must be understood not as a demand placed on the individual, but as a collective responsibility. Families, schools, workplaces, healthcare systems, and governments all shape the conditions under which resilience can flourish or falter. This begins with emotional education. Teaching children emotional literacy, conflict resolution, and help-seeking behavior is a form of early scaffolding. In workplaces, fostering psychological safety—where employees can admit mistakes, express concerns, and receive feedback without fear—strengthens both individual and organizational resilience. In healthcare, integrating trauma-informed care practices reduces retraumatization and supports recovery. These are not luxury interventions. They are the architecture of a psychologically functional society.

Environments also signal what kinds of emotions are permissible. In some cultures, resilience is linked to silence—bearing pain without complaint, enduring hardship stoically. In others, it is linked to faith or spiritual surrender. In still others, it is associated with action, protest, or artistic expression. These cultural narratives shape how individuals understand their own pain. They can empower or constrain. A person raised to believe that asking for help is weakness may delay or avoid support even when it is urgently needed. A person taught that anger is destructive may suppress it, only to erupt later in ways that damage trust and self-respect. Resilience is not just what a person can do. It is what they are permitted to do—by their culture, their environment, and their relationships.

Technology also influences this scaffolding. In digital spaces, people can find community, resources, and representation that may not exist in their immediate environments. Online forums, support groups, educational platforms, and social media movements all contribute to emotional scaffolding in new ways. But these same platforms can also undermine resilience by accelerating comparison, misinformation, and emotional overstimulation. A constant stream of crisis without regulation or communal processing can erode rather than support the nervous system. The challenge is not to reject technology, but to curate it—intentionally seeking out digital environments that promote understanding, connection, and emotional coherence.

Finally, we must acknowledge the role of time. Scaffolding is not only about who and what surrounds you—it's also about when. People need time to process, recover, and rebuild. Cultures that demand quick recovery—whether after childbirth, loss, trauma, or illness—truncate the healing process. Resilience cannot be rushed. It unfolds according to rhythms that are often unpredictable. A system that prioritizes speed over sustainability will produce outwardly functional but internally exhausted individuals. Real scaffolding includes temporal space: time to feel, time to reflect, time to rest. Without this, even the most emotionally intelligent individuals will begin to fray.

When we talk about resilience, we must talk about infrastructure. Not just emotional tools, but the environments that allow those tools to be used. Not just individual traits, but collective practices. Resilience is not an inner fortress. It is a network of supports that holds a person upright while they reorganize themselves. It is the friend who shows up, the community that affirms, the therapist who listens, the policy that protects, the school that accommodates, the workplace that understands. These are not nice additions to resilience—they are resilience.

And if we are serious about fostering psychological health at scale, we must build for it. Not just in individuals, but in the worlds they inhabit. The more we recognize resilience as a relational and systemic achievement, the more humane, adaptable, and enduring our cultures will become.

* * *

10

The Myth of Healing

There is a story many people tell themselves, or are told by others, about what it means to heal. In this story, healing is a clean break from pain. The wound closes, the past loses its charge, the patterns dissolve, and the person moves forward with clarity and peace. This version of healing is compelling—it is orderly, satisfying, and complete. It offers hope that the pain will one day be irrelevant. That we will be able to look back at what hurt us and feel nothing. That we will no longer be affected by what we've lived through.

But this is a myth. Not because healing isn't real, but because it rarely fits this narrative. For most people, healing is not a moment of triumph. It is not the absence of pain. It is not a state one reaches where the past has no fingerprints on the present. Instead, healing is uneven, recursive, and often quiet. It is the process of learning to live with what remains. It is not the deletion of trauma, grief, or shame—but the integration of it into a life that still has meaning, love, and movement. Healing is not a finish line. It is a form of relationship—with oneself, with memory, and with the parts of us that do not fully return.

This chapter examines the false promises and quiet truths surrounding healing. It begins with the cultural narrative—the story we are sold about what it means to be emotionally whole. Popular psychology, social media, and even parts of the wellness industry often promote a version of healing that looks like transcendence. You let go. You release. You ascend. But for many people, this vision does more harm than good. It sets them up to feel like failures when pain resurfaces, when old patterns return, when grief lingers longer than expected. It creates the impression that true healing is evidenced by the total absence of symptoms. That anything short of that is inadequacy.

In reality, psychological healing is more like adaptation than elimination. A person learns to carry what once felt too heavy. They learn to name what once was unspeakable. They recognize triggers more quickly. They pause before reacting. They feel things more cleanly. They soften in places where they once hardened. But they may still carry sadness. They may still struggle with trust. They may still have days when the past feels unbearably close. These experiences are not failures of healing. They are signs of a nervous system that remembers, a psyche that is still integrating, and a life that continues to be shaped by what it has survived.

Some scars never fade. And they shouldn't have to. Scars are not shameful; they are evidence of healing in progress. They are the body and mind's way of saying, "Something happened here—and I lived." But because our culture often associates recovery with erasure, people feel pressured to hide these marks. They pretend to be over things they're still struggling with. They apologize for needing more time. They rush through grief rituals. They fear that their lingering pain makes them emotionally unwell or spiritually underdeveloped. In this way, the myth of healing becomes a source of new pain layered on top of the old.

What's often missing from mainstream narratives is the concept of ongoing repair. Healing is not a binary state. It is a layered, living process that requires continual attention. A person may make peace with their past, then find new pain in how it shapes their relationships. They may set boundaries, then feel guilt for doing so. They may understand where their trauma came from, but still struggle to trust others. These moments do not mean healing has failed. They mean healing is alive. The work continues—not because the person is broken, but because they are still growing, still encountering the world, still discovering the shape of their needs and limits.

This chapter also explores the relational dimension of healing. Some wounds are interpersonal, and so is their repair. A person cannot resolve betrayal, abandonment, or emotional neglect solely through individual reflection. They must re-enter relationship—first with themselves, then with others. They must test out new dynamics, risk new levels of honesty, learn how to receive care in ways that once felt unsafe. This work is delicate and difficult. It does not guarantee neat resolution. But it is the heart of what makes healing relational rather than conceptual. Without this layer, healing remains an intellectual exercise. With it, healing becomes embodied, contextual, and alive.

Finally, this chapter offers a reframing: that psychological maturity is not about becoming someone unmarked by pain, but someone capable of living with what they carry. Some pain will always ache. Some losses will never be filled. Some questions will never be answered. But this does not mean healing is impossible. It means healing must be understood differently—not as a return to purity, but as a movement toward integrity. Not as a solution, but as a commitment to wholeness that includes the broken places.

In a culture obsessed with optimization, closure, and personal transformation, there is something radical about accepting that some wounds stay open in subtle ways. That some healing processes never fully conclude. That we are not meant to be scrubbed clean of our histories, but to be shaped by them with care. Growth does not require erasure. And being whole does not mean being unchanged.

Healing, then, is not about becoming someone new. It is about becoming more fully yourself—even in the aftermath of pain. It is about turning toward your life, not away from it. And it is about recognizing that the goal is not to be unscathed, but to be unhidden. To live in such a way that even your scars have a place, and even your unfinished parts can belong.

The Cultural Illusion of "Healed"

In the popular imagination, healing is often portrayed as a clean, upward arc. A person suffers, reflects, transforms, and then emerges lighter, wiser, and free of the burden that once defined them. It is the redemptive arc, the narrative closure, the satisfying ending. Movies show it in montages. Memoirs are built around it. Self-help books sell it in five steps or less. This vision of healing is emotionally seductive because it promises something definitive: a future in which pain is no longer part of the story. But this image is not just oversimplified—it is damaging. It creates a false binary between those who are "healed" and those who are not, and it teaches people that the ongoing presence of emotional pain is a sign of personal failure.

The cultural illusion of healing rests on several intertwined beliefs: that pain can and should be eliminated, that healing has a clear end point, and that emotionally healthy people no longer feel haunted by their past. These ideas are woven into public language and therapeutic culture alike. Terms like "closure," "letting go," and "moving on" are often used with moral urgency, implying that to linger in pain is to be stuck, to revisit old wounds is to regress, and to still be affected is to be unwell. In this framing, healing becomes a social performance as much as a psychological process. People may rush to declare themselves "over it," suppress ongoing struggles, or force forgiveness before it is authentic—all to meet an external expectation of emotional finality.

This pressure is especially acute in cultures that prize independence, emotional self-sufficiency, and forward momentum. In such environments, grief is expected to be discreet, trauma is pathologized if it persists, and anger must be metabolized quickly or redirected toward personal growth. While some of these pressures are subtle, others are institutionalized. Bereavement leave, for example, is often capped at a few days, regardless of the depth of the loss. Mental health support is frequently oriented around symptom reduction rather than long-term integration. Even in supportive settings, the underlying message is clear:

healing is measured by how little evidence remains of the pain.

But healing rarely looks like disappearance. In psychological terms, it is more accurately described as reorganization. The nervous system doesn't forget trauma; it learns to regulate around it. The psyche doesn't erase grief; it builds new narratives to hold it. The body doesn't reset to a baseline untouched by pain; it adjusts, often in visible and invisible ways. This means that healing is not about removal—it is about adaptation. And adaptation is not linear, predictable, or complete. It unfolds in fits and starts, often revisiting the same emotional ground with different levels of awareness each time. It can feel like progress, then regression, then uncertainty. This is not failure. It is fidelity to the complexity of being human.

The myth of healing as erasure also sets people up to mistrust their own emotional experiences. A person may begin to feel okay, then be undone by a song, a memory, an anniversary. Under the influence of the cultural script, they may interpret this as relapse—proof that they are "not as healed as they thought." But this interpretation misses the point. Emotional waves are not evidence of dysfunction; they are reminders of attachment, meaning, and lived history. They are not interruptions in healing—they *are* healing, continuing its work at a depth that cannot always be predicted or controlled.

This false ideal of healing also pathologizes slowness. People who grieve for years, who continue to flinch at certain triggers, or who carry unresolved anger are often viewed as emotionally undeveloped or unwilling to let go. In reality, these experiences may reflect not weakness, but depth. The more central a loss or injury was to a person's sense of self, the more time, space, and repeated integration it will require. Just as physical injuries heal differently depending on depth, location, and context, so do psychological wounds. There is no universal timeline. Yet people internalize shame when they do not "bounce back" quickly enough, often compounding their suffering with the belief that something is wrong with them for still hurting.

Even clinical frameworks can unintentionally reinforce this myth.

Diagnostic criteria, treatment protocols, and evidence-based interventions are sometimes oriented toward achieving symptom relief in short windows. While this focus is understandable—especially in healthcare systems with limited time and funding—it risks framing ongoing pain as noncompliance or resistance. Patients who still struggle after treatment may be labeled "treatment-resistant," when in fact their suffering is reflective of a system that expects too much too quickly. Healing cannot always be accelerated, and pressure to do so often leads to defensive suppression rather than true integration.

Part of dismantling the cultural illusion of healing involves reclaiming the right to be in process. This means creating emotional environments—both internal and external—where people do not have to pretend they are finished. It means honoring recurrence, recognizing that old wounds may resurface not because they are unhealed, but because new layers of life have invited new layers of reckoning. It means naming the parts of ourselves that still ache—not for the sake of wallowing, but for the sake of honesty. Because the moment we stop requiring ourselves to be "over it," we create space to actually be *with* it—and that is where healing begins to take on texture, nuance, and truth.

This shift also opens the door to a different kind of strength—one rooted not in resolution, but in capacity. The capacity to feel without collapsing. To speak without apologizing. To ask for help without shame. To stay in relationship with what has hurt us, not as victims of the past, but as narrators of it. This is the strength that cultural myths about healing tend to overlook. It is quieter, less cinematic, and more sustainable. It does not promise that nothing will hurt again. It promises that we will still be here, even if it does.

When we dismantle the illusion of "healed" as a final state, we are not lowering the bar for human growth. We are raising the standard for what it means to be whole. Wholeness is not untouched. It is not unscarred. It is full contact with the self, in all its contradiction and continuity. And that is a far more honest—and more humane—foundation on which to build a life.

Scars Are Not Evidence of Failure

Scars have long served as metaphors—etched proof that something happened, and that the body survived it. They are not the injury itself, but its trace. They are what remains after rupture begins to mend. Yet when it comes to emotional and psychological wounds, many people expect themselves to emerge unmarked. They want the pain to vanish without residue, the patterns to dissolve without reminder, the grief to pass without altering their view of the world. In this pursuit, they confuse scars with failure. They see the lingering effects of pain—sensitivity, hesitation, emotional depth, a guarded heart—as signs they haven't done enough, haven't healed well enough, or are somehow stuck in the past.

But scars do not mean you failed. They mean you lived. They mean your system did what it had to do to keep going. In the human psyche, scars show up as adaptive patterns: defense mechanisms that once protected you, stories you tell yourself to make sense of pain, triggers that form around unresolved rupture. They may be inconvenient. They may resurface at inopportune times. But they are not evidence that healing failed. They are part of the healing. They are what's left after the damage has been survived, and the system has done its best to reorganize.

One of the reasons scars are so often misread is because we are taught to associate health with invisibility. If you're truly over it, the logic goes, there will be no trace of the problem. You won't flinch when someone raises their voice. You won't panic when a relationship deepens. You won't replay conversations or spiral into shame. You'll just be okay. But this standard is not only unrealistic—it's cruel. It sets people up to doubt their own growth every time an old pain surfaces. It encourages them to minimize their histories or present a polished version of recovery to gain social acceptance.

In truth, the human system is designed to remember. Memory is not limited to the mind—it is stored in the body, in the nervous system, in relational habits and affective patterns. Painful experiences leave impressions. And even when healing occurs, those impressions do not disappear. They become part of the emotional landscape. A person who has been betrayed may become more discerning. A person who has experienced neglect may develop a heightened awareness of emotional absence. These are not flaws. They are adaptations. They reflect what the system has learned to look out for. And while these patterns may need refinement, they are not proof of failure—they are signs of survival intelligence.

Scars also signal continuity. They link the present self with the past self. They say: I remember. And for many people, this continuity is part of how they make meaning. The pain they lived through may inform their values, their boundaries, their purpose, or their way of relating to others. They are who they are in part because of what they've endured. Trying to erase all traces of pain would be to erase the threads that shaped their character, their discernment, their depth. Wholeness, in this view, is not about removing all evidence of the wound—it's about including the wound in the narrative of who you are.

Developmentally, we see this dynamic in how children process emotional injuries. A child who is consistently invalidated when expressing sadness or fear will often develop ways of masking or redirecting those feelings. These strategies may persist into adulthood—through perfectionism, emotional detachment, or chronic people-pleasing. When these patterns are later uncovered in therapy or reflection, the goal is not to pathologize them, but to understand their origin. These patterns are emotional scar tissue—evidence of how the child survived a relational environment that did not meet their needs. Healing does not always mean undoing these patterns entirely. Often, it means softening them, learning to choose them rather than be ruled by them, or creating new options that weren't available in the past.

This reframe matters because it changes the goal of healing. Instead of striving to become someone untouched by pain, the person begins to see themselves as someone shaped—sometimes beautifully—by what they've endured. The question becomes not "How do I get rid of all traces of this?" but "How do I live well with what remains?" This shift reduces shame and allows for greater self-compassion. It honors the reality that pain alters people, but that altered people are not broken. They are simply different. And often, they are deeper, more relationally attuned, more empathetic, and more capable of holding space for others.

Still, not all scars feel noble. Some feel like they compromise function—making intimacy harder, trust slower, or joy more fleeting. These are real effects. They deserve acknowledgment. But even these scars do not mean healing failed. They mean the system is still adapting. In some cases, the residue of pain will always be part of the person's internal experience. A trauma survivor may always be startled by sudden noise. A grieving parent may always ache on birthdays. A person who lived through abandonment may always feel tension around closeness. These reactions do not mean the person is emotionally stuck. They mean the original injury mattered—and still does. Healing allows us to move forward. It does not always eliminate the pull of what once wounded us.

Socially, we need more accurate language for this reality. Phrases like "unhealed trauma" or "emotional baggage" are often used dismissively—as if people who carry visible scars are somehow less whole or emotionally responsible. But visible pain is not a liability. It is a kind of emotional transparency. It signals that someone is still engaged with their experience—that they haven't buried it, denied it, or turned it into a weapon. Scars are a sign that something is being metabolized, not avoided. That should not be punished. It should be respected.

The same is true in relational contexts. Partners, friends, and family members often struggle to understand why someone they love still reacts strongly to certain stimuli or continues to process old events. The temptation is to urge them to "move on" or "let it go." But this rush to resolution rarely helps. It reinforces the idea that ongoing emotional residue is a burden rather than a reflection of complexity. In contrast, relationships that make space for scars—without trying to minimize or fix them—help normalize the deeper truth: that being impacted is not the same as being impaired. That healing can coexist with reactivity. That being emotionally affected is not a moral flaw.

Ultimately, to carry scars is to carry testimony. They are not proof that the injury should have happened, but that it did—and that something in the person chose life in response. Scars tell the truth: that people break and mend, fall and stand again, lose and still reach for connection. They are not signs of failure. They are the signatures of persistence.

The Work of Ongoing Repair

Healing, when honestly lived, is less like a destination and more like a rhythm. It is not something you arrive at and check off a list. It is a form of ongoing repair—a relationship you continue to cultivate with yourself, your history, your relationships, and the narratives that have shaped you. This repair does not always happen in therapy rooms or grand life decisions. More often, it happens in the daily choices to respond differently, to speak more truthfully, to stay present for what once made you retreat. It is not glamorous. It is not always visible. But it is where real transformation takes place—not all at once, but over time, in the repeated effort to meet yourself and others with greater integrity and care.

One of the most misunderstood aspects of emotional healing is its recursive nature. People often expect that once a trauma has been named, a wound acknowledged, or a pattern identified, the work is done. But psychological injuries—especially those formed over time or in relational contexts—require sustained attention. The same pain may resurface across years, but each return brings a slightly different opportunity: to feel it more fully, to respond with more skill, or to understand it from a new perspective. In this way, healing is less about fixing something broken and more about developing the capacity to stay in relationship with what's unresolved.

This is where the concept of ongoing repair becomes essential. In developmental psychology, rupture and repair are central concepts in the formation of secure attachment. No relationship is without rupture—what matters is whether the rupture is acknowledged and whether repair follows. The same holds true within the self. There will be days when old habits reemerge, when the inner critic speaks loudly, when grief returns unexpectedly. The work is not to prevent these moments from happening, but to meet them with less self-abandonment. To acknowledge the rupture, and then engage in conscious repair.

This repair can take many forms. Sometimes it is behavioral: choosing to respond to a trigger with breath instead of blame. Sometimes it is narrative: rewriting the internal story from one of failure to one of resilience. Sometimes it is relational: apologizing for a pattern you've enacted or offering forgiveness where possible. And sometimes, it is simply presence: sitting with an emotion that once felt unlivable, and letting it move through without shame. What makes these acts powerful is not that they resolve everything instantly, but that they reinforce a new pattern. The system learns, over time, that it is safe enough to try again.

Internal repair is often the most difficult, because it requires facing the parts of ourselves we were taught to disown. The angry part, the needy part, the ashamed part. These aspects of the self are not accidents—they were formed to protect us, to adapt, to survive. But they are often pushed into exile by a culture that rewards composure over expression and control over vulnerability. The process of re-integrating these parts—sometimes referred to in therapeutic models like Internal Family Systems (IFS)—is not about indulging them, but about recognizing their purpose and helping them evolve. You don't heal the wounded child by scolding her for still being hurt. You heal her by listening, validating, and letting her know she is no longer alone.

Reparenting is one form of this internal work. It involves consciously offering yourself the emotional responsiveness you did not receive when you needed it most. This might mean setting boundaries where there used to be none. It might mean offering comfort rather than criticism when you make a mistake. It might mean creating rituals of care—cooking a nourishing meal, taking time to rest, writing down what you feel—to show the self that its needs matter. Reparenting is not a one-time intervention. It is a practice. One that may feel awkward at first, especially for those who were taught to suppress their needs or prioritize others. But over time, it builds self-trust—the foundation for any real emotional repair.

Narrative repair is another crucial aspect. Human beings make meaning through story. The way we tell the story of our pain shapes how we experience it. This does not mean sugarcoating reality or bypassing grief with platitudes. It means examining the language we use and asking whether it reflects our truth—or someone else's interpretation of it. For example, "I'm damaged because of what happened" is a story. So is "I've been reshaped by what happened, and I'm still learning how to carry it." Both may contain truth, but one offers more room to breathe. Narrative repair means reclaiming authorship over the way you understand your own life. It means choosing metaphors that honor your pain without collapsing your identity into it.

Ongoing repair also extends into the realm of interpersonal relationships. Many emotional injuries are relational in origin—formed in families, friendships, romantic partnerships, or systems of power. For that reason, they often require relational engagement to fully heal. This does not always mean reconciling with the person who hurt you. But it does mean examining how your patterns show up in current relationships. Do you retreat when intimacy deepens? Do you try to earn love through self-erasure? Do you become hyper-vigilant to signs of rejection? These patterns are not evidence of failure—they are invitations for repair. And that repair happens not just by insight, but by practice: staying present in discomfort, communicating needs clearly, and tolerating the vulnerability of being seen.

In some cases, healing within relationship means taking accountability. Offering a genuine apology for harm done—not to erase guilt, but to restore trust. In other cases, it means setting boundaries—not as punishment, but as a form of self-protection and integrity. In still others, it means forgiving—not to forget or condone, but to release yourself from the ongoing burden of resentment. These acts of repair are not always mutual. Sometimes they happen alone, in internal dialogues or private rituals. But even when they are not shared, they can shift something fundamental in the psyche. They reaffirm your agency. They remind you that you are not bound forever to the roles and injuries of your past.

It's important to note that ongoing repair is not a sign that something went wrong. It's a sign that something continues to matter. You revisit the pain because you're still in relationship with what it means. You work through it again and again because your system is still integrating. This is not weakness. It is fidelity. To your own depth. To the truth of your experience. To the belief that you are worth the effort of reweaving your emotional life, one thread at a time.

Ongoing repair is not a failure of healing. It is the shape that real healing takes. It is the slow, repeated decision to treat your pain with respect, your patterns with curiosity, and your growth with care. It will not always feel like progress. But it is. Because every time you choose not to abandon yourself in the face of your own history, you're doing something radical. You're refusing to disappear. You're standing inside your life—not as someone who is finally fixed, but as someone who is still here, still trying, still whole.

Living Whole with What's Broken

What does it mean to live a whole life, knowing you carry parts that will never fully mend? This is one of the central questions of psychological maturity—and one that healing culture often tries to answer too cleanly. The dominant narrative suggests that wholeness is achieved through resolution: that the broken parts must be fixed, the past rewritten, the pain finally transcended. But real life rarely follows that arc. Some pain doesn't end. Some relationships never reconcile. Some emotional patterns soften but never vanish. And yet, despite all of that, people go on to live meaningful, connected, even beautiful lives. Not because they have resolved everything, but because they have stopped waiting to.

Living whole with what's broken requires a shift in worldview. It asks us to abandon the fantasy of emotional completion—the idea that we will eventually become fully healed, perfectly integrated, unshakably grounded. Instead, it asks us to accept contradiction as a feature of our inner landscape, not a flaw. This is the essence of integration: not eliminating pain, but incorporating it into a broader sense of self. Integration allows for contradiction. It says: you can still carry grief and love again. You can still be triggered and trust yourself. You can feel afraid and move forward. These are not signs of hypocrisy. They are signs of capacity.

This capacity is not given—it is built. Through experience, through relationship, and through the deliberate choice to remain present to your own life. One of the greatest misunderstandings in contemporary emotional culture is the belief that healing makes us *more* perfect. In reality, it often makes us more human: less polished, more honest, less concerned with performance, and more connected to what matters. When people begin to accept that their broken parts are not enemies but evidence of a life deeply lived, something shifts. They stop posturing. They stop pretending. They begin to tell the truth—not just about what happened, but about how it shaped them.

That truth-telling is a form of self-respect. It is not self-pity, nor is it self-indulgence. It is the act of refusing to edit your life to fit someone else's narrative of progress. Living whole with what's broken means recognizing that some chapters don't conclude neatly, some relationships remain ambiguous, and some inner dynamics don't follow a therapeutic timeline. This is not a sign that you've failed to grow. It's a sign that growth does not always tidy up the past. Sometimes it simply helps you live alongside it with more grace.

Existential psychology offers a useful lens here. In contrast to models that aim to resolve or cure, existential thought centers around the inherent tensions of human life: freedom and responsibility, love and loss, meaning and absurdity, hope and despair. These tensions cannot be eliminated. They must be navigated. To live well, then, is not to remove discomfort but to relate to it differently. To stop fearing the presence of emotional messiness as a threat to wholeness—and instead see it as part of the texture of being alive. As the philosopher Paul Tillich wrote, "The awareness of the tragic dimension of life is the condition for understanding the depth of life." In other words, we don't mature by escaping pain. We mature by integrating it.

This integration takes different forms for different people. For some, it means maintaining a relationship with the dead—not in a supernatural sense, but by allowing grief to coexist with daily life. For others, it means accepting that certain emotional triggers may always exist, but learning how to move through them without shame. For many, it means no longer hiding their story. They begin to speak plainly about their history, not seeking pity or shock, but claiming their full humanity. This shift in tone—from secrecy to ownership—is one of the clearest signs that integration is underway.

There is a kind of dignity that comes from no longer needing to pretend that you're finished. This is what allows people to step into their lives more fully, even when the scaffolding is imperfect. They build families, write books, fall in love, raise children, take risks—not because they are unscarred, but because they have stopped waiting for the scars to disappear. They accept that fear may always be a companion, that certain anniversaries may always sting, that some nights may still bring nightmares. And they choose to live anyway—not in denial of those realities, but in relationship with them.

Living whole with what's broken also creates new relational possibilities. When we stop demanding perfection in ourselves, we stop demanding it in others. We become more tolerant of imperfection, more able to forgive, more capable of intimacy that is rooted in reality rather than projection. We recognize that everyone is carrying something. And we no longer confuse being "put together" with being emotionally trustworthy. This shift moves us out of comparison and into connection. We no longer feel behind for struggling. We feel less alone for admitting it.

Narrative identity theory helps illuminate this point. According to this framework, people build their sense of self through stories—how they interpret and sequence the events of their lives. Those who are able to create *redemptive narratives*—in which suffering leads to growth or purpose—often report higher levels of psychological wellbeing. But redemptive doesn't mean erasure. The most psychologically healthy narratives are not those that gloss over pain, but those that incorporate it with nuance and compassion. They allow for unresolved grief, lingering anger, and unanswered questions. They affirm that even when a story contains tragedy, it is still worth telling. And that the teller is still whole.

In spiritual traditions, too, we often find models for living with what's broken. In the Japanese art of kintsugi, broken pottery is repaired with gold, highlighting the fracture rather than concealing it. The object is seen not as ruined, but as more beautiful for having been broken. This metaphor is overused in popular culture, but its essence remains profound. It challenges the aesthetic of flawlessness. It values the visible history of an object. And it echoes what mature healing often looks like in people: not hidden, but revealed. Not flawless, but embodied. Not finished, but fully alive.

To live whole with what's broken is to reject the premise that healing requires erasure. It is to stop measuring your worth by your level of painlessness. It is to accept that your tenderness, your vigilance, your uneven edges are not deviations from wholeness—they are part of it. You are not whole *despite* what you carry. You are whole *with* it. And that truth, once integrated, creates a kind of freedom that no amount of perfect functioning ever could.

Because in the end, healing is not the return to who you once were. It is becoming who you are now—fully, honestly, and without apology. Even if you still ache. Even if you still don't know what to do with some of the pieces. Even if you are still learning how to hold them.

Especially then.

* * *

III

PART III: BEHAVIOR, HABIT, AND SELF-CONTROL

Behavior shapes our lives in ways we often don't notice. In this part, I want to explore with you how habits form, how self-control works, and why some patterns feel so hard to change. These aren't just abstract ideas—they are the invisible forces guiding your daily choices, your struggles, and your successes. Understanding how behavior works gives you the tools to live more intentionally and align your actions with what truly matters.

11

The Logic of Behavior

People often explain their actions by referencing personality, morality, or emotion. They say they snapped because they were tired, helped because they're generous, or stayed silent because they were raised that way. These explanations may be partially true, but they're rarely complete. Much of human behavior is not driven by conscious decision-making or stable traits. It is shaped, reinforced, and repeated through a more fundamental process: conditioning. The things people do, avoid, or crave are often not expressions of identity, but the residue of learned patterns—loops that were trained, rewarded, or unconsciously repeated until they felt automatic.

This chapter explores the psychology of behavior, not as a moral judgment or a reflection of character, but as a system governed by principles of reinforcement, environmental feedback, and psychological need. It draws from behaviorist traditions that emphasize observable action, but also integrates cognitive and emotional layers that explain why certain behaviors stick even when we consciously want to change them. In doing so, it aims to help us see behavior not as mysterious or fixed, but as logical—understandable when viewed through the right lens.

To understand human behavior, we must begin with a simple truth: people do what works. Not in the moral sense of what is right, but in the functional sense of what reduces discomfort, increases reward, or maintains emotional equilibrium in the moment. If raising your voice gets people to listen, you may keep doing it, even if you feel guilty afterward. If withdrawing from conflict avoids shame or overstimulation, you may repeat it every time closeness threatens to overwhelm you. These patterns are not random. They are learned. And once learned, they become reinforced—not just by outcomes, but by internal relief, anticipation, and social feedback.

This learning process begins early. Even infants learn quickly which cries bring attention, which gestures elicit soothing, and which behaviors are met with silence. Over time, these associations expand. Children learn which behaviors get them praise, which get them reprimanded, and which get them ignored. They internalize patterns about how to gain approval, avoid rejection, or escape discomfort. Some of these behaviors persist long into adulthood—not because they still serve the person, but because they were never interrupted. In this way, behavioral patterns can become outdated solutions to long-past problems. They continue to operate not because they make sense in the present, but because the nervous system remembers them as effective.

Modern life is filled with reinforcement loops that shape our behavior without our full awareness. The buzz of a notification, the comfort of food after stress, the dopamine hit from a like or share—these are all examples of conditioned responses. But conditioning isn't limited to habits around devices or consumption. Emotional responses, interpersonal dynamics, and even self-sabotage can be reinforced over time. A person who shuts down when criticized may have learned that silence prevented escalation. A person who people-pleases may have learned that approval kept them safe. These behaviors may frustrate us when they persist, but they are not illogical. They are adaptations—trained by history and maintained by internal or external reward.

This chapter will examine those mechanisms in detail: how classical and operant conditioning shape behavior, how reinforcement schedules determine habit strength, and how behavioral loops become self-perpetuating. It will explore the tension between intention and automation—why people can want to change but keep repeating the same actions, why insight alone is often insufficient for behavioral transformation, and how the brain's preference for predictability reinforces familiar patterns even when they are painful or dysfunctional.

But this chapter will also offer a way forward. Behavior may be conditioned, but it is not irreversible. Patterns can be interrupted. New associations can be formed. Habits can be retrained. What makes this possible is awareness: the ability to observe our behavior with curiosity rather than judgment, to map its triggers and consequences, and to build in moments of pause where choice can emerge. Through strategies rooted in behavioral psychology, cognitive reframing, and mindfulness practice, people can begin to reshape their responses—not through willpower alone, but through repetition, reinforcement, and environmental redesign.

This approach removes moral weight from behavior. It helps us see that people are not lazy because they procrastinate, weak because they overreact, or broken because they repeat destructive patterns. They are responding to conditioning. And when we understand the logic behind behavior, we gain not only compassion—but leverage. We can change what we reinforce. We can rewire what we repeat. We can work with the system, rather than against it.

At its core, this chapter argues for a humble view of human behavior—one that acknowledges how much we operate on learned loops, how sensitive we are to reinforcement, and how complex change really is. But it also affirms that those loops are not destiny. With enough awareness, structure, and support, people can interrupt cycles that once felt inevitable. They can replace reflexes with intention. They can build habits that reflect who they are becoming, not just who they've been.

Behavior is not always a reflection of belief. It is often a reflection of what has been rewarded, avoided, or reinforced over time. When we understand that, we stop asking, "What's wrong with me?" and start asking, "What is this behavior trying to accomplish—and what could I offer myself instead?"

That shift—from blame to curiosity, from judgment to pattern recognition—is the beginning of real behavioral freedom.

What Behavior Reveals

Behavior is often misunderstood as either surface-level action or moral expression. In one view, it's mechanical—what someone *does* rather than who they are. In the other, it's personal—an indication of character, values, or intent. But neither interpretation tells the whole story. Human behavior is a layered signal. It expresses psychological need, learned history, relational memory, and situational context all at once. A single behavior—shutting down during conflict, overexplaining an error, checking a phone repeatedly—may look simple, but underneath is a map of past reinforcements, emotional associations, social cues, and internal strategies for survival. To understand a person's behavior is not to decode their personality—it is to understand their conditioning.

The behaviorist tradition in psychology emphasized observable action for this very reason. Early thinkers like John Watson and B.F. Skinner argued that internal mental states could not be measured with scientific rigor and that psychology should instead focus on stimulus and response. Though limited in scope, this perspective offered an important corrective to models that overemphasized introspection. It reminded us that behavior follows patterns—and that those patterns are shaped by environment, consequence, and repetition. What you do repeatedly becomes what your nervous system expects. What is reinforced becomes automatic. In this view, behavior is not random; it is trained.

But this chapter goes beyond classical behaviorism. While early models excluded internal states like belief, motivation, and memory, modern psychology integrates them. Cognitive-behavioral models, developmental frameworks, and social learning theories now help us understand that behavior is both *shaped by* and *shaping of* internal experience. What you do affects what you believe; what you believe affects what you do. And all of this occurs in a context—cultural, relational, and situational—that constantly provides feedback. Behavior is not merely reaction. It is interpretation, regulation, protection, communication, and learned association, all acting simultaneously.

When someone behaves in a way that puzzles or frustrates others—or themselves—it's tempting to assign a personality label. "I'm just lazy." "She's manipulative." "He's insecure." These labels may provide shorthand, but they rarely offer clarity. They focus on description rather than function. A more useful question is: *What does this behavior accomplish?* What need is it attempting to meet? What discomfort is it avoiding? What outcome is it predicting based on past experience? Asking these questions moves us from judgment to understanding. It allows us to approach behavior as adaptation—an attempt, often unconscious, to preserve safety, dignity, belonging, or control.

Take, for example, someone who habitually avoids difficult conversations. A surface analysis might label them as conflict-avoidant or emotionally immature. But deeper investigation might reveal a history of being punished or ignored when expressing difficult feelings. Over time, they learned that speaking up leads to rupture or rejection. Avoidance, then, is not passivity—it's strategy. It is what once protected them. And until something more effective is learned and reinforced, it will likely remain their default. This doesn't excuse all behavior, but it does contextualize it. Understanding behavior as adaptive helps us intervene not with shame, but with skill.

This principle applies to almost all human conduct—from self-sabotage to perfectionism, from addiction to withdrawal, from micromanaging to people-pleasing. These behaviors may look irrational from the outside, but they make perfect sense when viewed through the logic of reinforcement. If overworking once helped you avoid emotional pain, you'll keep doing it. If lashing out made people back off, you'll associate anger with safety. If self-silencing helped preserve attachment, it will feel dangerous to speak up. These associations are rarely conscious, but they are powerful—and they shape not only how we act, but how we interpret others' actions as well.

Importantly, behavior is always contextual. The same behavior can have entirely different meanings depending on the environment. A child who talks constantly in one classroom may be seen as disruptive, while in another they are encouraged as expressive. An employee who hesitates before speaking may be read as disengaged in one workplace and as thoughtful in another. Behavior is never just behavior—it is always embedded in a system of cues, expectations, and histories. That's why interpreting it accurately requires zooming out. Asking not just *what* is happening, but *where, with whom,* and *under what conditions.*

Another layer to behavior is emotional regulation. People often behave in ways that help manage emotional intensity—whether through expression, avoidance, or distraction. Yelling, withdrawing, overeating, overexplaining, checking out—all of these can serve to regulate emotional states. When we treat behavior as irrational, we miss its regulatory function. A person who procrastinates, for instance, may not be lazy. They may be overwhelmed. The delay provides temporary relief from anxiety, even if it causes long-term problems. A person who criticizes others may not be cruel—they may be displacing their own internalized fear of failure. In both cases, the behavior is functioning to contain something that feels unmanageable.

Social modeling also plays a role. People mimic behaviors they've seen rewarded in others. Children learn to manage emotion not just by being taught, but by observing how adults behave under stress. If a child grows up watching caregivers shut down, lash out, or pretend everything is fine, those behaviors become templates. The child doesn't need to understand them cognitively to absorb them emotionally. This is how behavioral patterns become generational—passed down not through genetics, but through modeling and reinforcement. These patterns can persist across decades, shaping how people show up in their relationships, workplaces, and sense of self.

That said, behavior is not destiny. Even deeply ingrained patterns can be interrupted. But change begins with observation. Before a pattern can be altered, it must be seen. This requires curiosity without condemnation. When people can watch their behavior with a neutral, even compassionate lens—when they can ask, "What am I trying to accomplish right now?"—they begin to regain authorship. They stop acting on reflex and begin experimenting with choice.

This is especially important in relationships. Often, conflict escalates not because of intent, but because of behavioral loops. One person withdraws, the other pursues. One becomes critical, the other defensive. These patterns feel personal, but they are often just well-rehearsed responses to fear, shame, or disconnection. When both people can step back and ask, "What are we doing, and what are we reinforcing?" the loop can begin to break. New options become visible. Old reactions soften.

Understanding behavior in this way doesn't make it easy to change—but it makes it possible. It replaces the question "What's wrong with me?" with "What is this doing for me?" And that question leads to other, better ones: Is there a different way to meet this need? Can I tolerate what this behavior is protecting me from? What would it look like to choose a new pattern?

Behavior, in the end, is not a moral statement. It's a pattern of learning, reinforcement, and regulation. It's a map. And when you can read it, you're not just reacting to life—you're beginning to navigate it.

The Mechanics of Reinforcement

If behavior is the surface, reinforcement is what lies underneath—the quiet force shaping what sticks, what fades, and what comes to define us. Most people think of reinforcement as reward, but in behavioral psychology, reinforcement refers more broadly to anything that increases the likelihood of a behavior recurring. That increase can happen because something pleasant follows an action, because something unpleasant goes away, or because the action itself creates a reliable emotional shift. Reinforcement is not always obvious or conscious. Often, we don't realize we're being trained. But the consequences of reinforcement shape nearly every behavioral pattern we have—from how we communicate to how we soothe ourselves, assert control, or avoid shame.

The distinction between classical and operant conditioning is foundational here. In classical conditioning, originally studied by Ivan Pavlov, an organism learns to associate two stimuli. For example, if a dog hears a bell before receiving food, it will eventually salivate to the sound of the bell alone. This model helps explain how emotional associations form: why certain smells trigger nostalgia, why certain tones of voice make us defensive, why the sound of a text alert produces a surge of anticipation. But most complex human behavior is better explained by operant conditioning—the process by which behavior is shaped through consequences.

Operant conditioning, developed by B.F. Skinner, focuses on how behavior is modified by what follows it. If a behavior is followed by something desirable, it becomes more likely to occur again. This is positive reinforcement. If a behavior removes something unpleasant—like silencing an alarm or avoiding a confrontation—that behavior is also reinforced. This is negative reinforcement. Importantly, "positive" and "negative" here refer to the *addition* or *removal* of a stimulus, not to its moral value. Both types strengthen behavior. And in both cases, the reinforcement doesn't need to be big. Subtle emotional payoffs—relief, comfort, validation, escape—can be just as powerful as material rewards.

Punishment, by contrast, is anything that decreases the likelihood of a behavior. It can be positive (adding an unpleasant consequence, like criticism) or negative (removing something valued, like attention). While punishment can suppress behavior temporarily, it is often less effective over time than reinforcement, especially if no alternative behavior is offered. Moreover, punishment can backfire by reinforcing avoidance, secrecy, or defiance. A child who is yelled at for expressing anger may learn not to show anger—but the feeling doesn't disappear. It goes underground, potentially resurfacing in anxiety, physical symptoms, or displaced aggression.

THE LOGIC OF BEHAVIOR

What makes reinforcement so powerful is its ability to shape behavior long after the original consequence is gone. This is especially true when reinforcement is *intermittent*—that is, when the reward doesn't come every time, but comes just often enough to keep the behavior alive. This is the principle behind gambling: the unpredictability of the payout makes the behavior resistant to extinction. The same pattern can be seen in emotionally volatile relationships, where occasional moments of warmth or validation keep a person engaged despite repeated harm. In such cases, the intermittent reinforcement doesn't just maintain behavior—it creates a powerful attachment to the pattern itself.

Reinforcement schedules—the timing and frequency of rewards—also matter. Behaviors that are reinforced every time (continuous reinforcement) are learned quickly but extinguish quickly when the reward stops. Behaviors that are reinforced unpredictably (variable ratio schedules) are learned more slowly but become more deeply ingrained. This helps explain why some habits are so hard to break even when they no longer serve us. They're not tied to a predictable payoff—they're tied to the *possibility* of one. This variable reinforcement keeps us checking our phones, hoping for a text. It keeps us staying late at work, hoping to be noticed. It keeps us returning to people who hurt us, hoping this time will be different.

Anticipation plays a powerful role here. In many cases, the reward is not the actual consequence but the internal state we anticipate. A person who drinks to relieve stress may find that even thinking about drinking brings relief. This is known as a *conditioned response*—the behavior is reinforced not only by its outcome, but by the emotional shift it promises. Anticipation itself becomes reinforcing. And this can create powerful loops. Over time, we begin to seek the feeling *of* the reward, not just the reward itself. We check our email, not because we expect something important, but because we want to feel that something might be waiting. We reach for snacks not out of hunger, but out of the hope that comfort is coming.

These loops don't require conscious belief. The reinforcement doesn't have to be logical or even still active. Many people continue behaving in ways that no longer provide reward—because at one point they did. A person may continue overworking because it once led to praise, even if that praise no longer comes. A person may continue apologizing excessively because it once prevented punishment. This is one of the most frustrating aspects of reinforcement: it's sticky. It creates behavioral grooves that persist long after the original context is gone. This is why understanding the *history* of reinforcement is essential to changing behavior. You have to know not just what the behavior does now, but what it *used* to do.

Reinforcement is also socially mediated. Much of what we do is reinforced by others—through approval, attention, agreement, or disapproval withheld. These social reinforcers are often more powerful than we realize. A person who jokes to deflect tension may be reinforced by others' laughter, even if internally they feel dismissed. A person who keeps the peace may be reinforced by others' gratitude, even as their own needs go unmet. These reinforcements shape identity. Over time, we internalize not only the behaviors that are rewarded, but the roles associated with them: the peacemaker, the performer, the achiever, the caretaker. These roles are not fixed, but they feel stable because they've been practiced—and reinforced—over time.

Even internal dialogue can become a source of reinforcement. Self-talk that soothes, validates, or rationalizes behavior can strengthen patterns just as surely as external feedback. If telling yourself "I deserve this" justifies impulsive spending, or "They probably didn't mean it" keeps you in a harmful relationship, then the behavior is being reinforced internally. This is why changing behavior often requires more than willpower. It requires altering the internal script that maintains the reinforcement loop.

Importantly, reinforcement is not inherently good or bad. It is neutral. It simply reflects what works—for the nervous system, for the emotional self, for the perceived outcome. But because reinforcement operates beneath the surface, it can be hard to spot. Many people don't realize what they're reinforcing in themselves or in others. A parent who gives in to a tantrum is reinforcing escalation. A manager who avoids giving feedback reinforces underperformance. A partner who disengages during conflict may inadvertently reinforce emotional distancing.

This isn't about blame—it's about clarity. When we understand how reinforcement works, we stop moralizing behavior and start mapping it. We ask, "What's being rewarded here? What's being avoided? What pattern is being strengthened by this reaction?" And once we can name the reinforcement loop, we gain leverage. We can shift what we reinforce. We can design consequences more intentionally. We can create space for new behaviors to take root—not by punishing the old, but by cultivating and rewarding the new.

Behavior may seem like a mystery from the outside. But beneath every pattern is a logic of reinforcement—an emotional or situational payoff that once made sense, and often still does. When we uncover that logic, we can begin to intervene—not with shame, but with strategy.

Loops, Triggers, and Automaticity

Most of what people do in a given day is not the result of deliberate decision-making. It is habitual, cued, and often unconscious. From the moment a person wakes up and reaches for their phone, to the way they respond to an email, shift their tone depending on who enters the room, or reach for food in response to stress, their behaviors are largely governed by loops—predictable sequences of trigger, routine, and reward. These loops are not inherently bad. They allow the brain to conserve energy by automating repeated actions. But when these loops become misaligned with a person's values, needs, or long-term goals, they begin to feel like prisons. The person knows what they are doing, yet feels unable to stop.

Understanding behavioral loops requires understanding how the brain economizes. The human nervous system is wired for efficiency. Novel tasks require full attention, but repeated tasks are quickly offloaded into automatic systems. Walking, brushing your teeth, typing your password, and reacting with sarcasm when embarrassed—these can all become automatic once practiced. Automaticity means the behavior is executed with minimal cognitive effort and often outside of conscious awareness. This is adaptive, but it also means that many self-defeating patterns are not being chosen, they are being activated.

The behavioral loop, often described in habit psychology, consists of three parts: the cue, the routine, and the reward. The cue is the trigger—a time of day, a feeling, a location, an interaction. The routine is the behavior itself. The reward is the outcome that reinforces the loop. For example, the feeling of anxiety (cue) might lead to scrolling through social media (routine), which provides distraction or dopamine release (reward). Over time, the loop strengthens. The behavior becomes the brain's default response to the cue, even if the reward is only partial or fleeting.

Not all loops are harmful. Many are neutral or beneficial. Brushing your teeth when you wake up, exercising at a certain hour, or journaling to regulate emotions—these are all functional loops. The challenge is that the brain does not distinguish between helpful and unhelpful patterns. It simply follows reinforcement. If an action reduces discomfort or delivers pleasure, even briefly, it gets encoded. This is why so many emotional behaviors—snapping in anger, withdrawing during conflict, self-medicating with food or alcohol—persist despite a person's insight or regret. The loop continues because it works on some level, even if the larger impact is negative.

Triggers are a key component in this system. A trigger is not just an event, but a signal that the brain associates with a needed behavioral response. Triggers can be internal or external. A raised voice, a deadline, or a certain smell can cue a reaction. So can an internal sensation: a racing heart, a wave of shame, or a memory fragment. These triggers do not need to be dramatic to activate a loop. Often, they are subtle and embedded in everyday life. A person may feel defensive every time they sit down at a dinner table—not because of the food, but because of long-standing associations between meals and conflict. The current moment becomes fused with past experiences, and the behavior unfolds automatically.

Automaticity becomes most problematic when a person is no longer making contact with the present moment. Instead, they are reacting to a felt prediction. The body and mind are responding to an anticipated outcome based on past reinforcement. This creates what some therapists call "emotional time travel." A person who learned to go silent when criticized may fall into that pattern with a partner who is not criticizing them, simply because the internal cues feel familiar. The loop is not responding to reality. It is responding to memory—physiological, emotional, and behavioral.

These loops can be social as well. In relationships, behavioral loops often form without discussion. One person withdraws when overwhelmed. The other becomes more insistent. The first retreats further. The second escalates. Over time, this pattern becomes automatic. Neither person may remember how it started. They simply know that it keeps happening. These interpersonal loops are not reflections of personality flaws. They are co-created systems of response, often shaped by earlier conditioning and sustained by mutual reinforcement.

Breaking a behavioral loop requires more than insight. Knowing what you are doing is not the same as being able to stop. The first step is recognizing the cue—what sets the behavior in motion. This requires paying attention not only to events, but to internal states. What were you feeling just before the behavior began? What were you anticipating? What associations might be hidden beneath the surface? This kind of attention slows the loop down. It makes it visible. And once it is visible, it can be disrupted.

The second step is understanding the reward. What is this behavior giving you, even temporarily? Relief? Escape? A sense of control? Validation? These rewards are often layered. A person who lashes out in anger may feel powerful for a moment, but the deeper reward may be the prevention of vulnerability. A person who avoids responsibility may feel relief, but the deeper payoff may be the avoidance of shame. When you can name the reward, you can begin to ask whether there are other, less costly ways to meet the same need.

This leads to the third step: inserting a pause between cue and routine. This pause does not have to be long. Even a breath, a gesture of physical interruption, or a moment of acknowledgment can create enough space for a different choice. This is the foundation of behavioral flexibility. You cannot always control the cue. You may not be able to eliminate the trigger. But you can learn to pause before the automatic response—and that pause can change everything.

The final step is to reinforce the alternative. New behaviors do not take root simply because they are rational or desirable. They must be reinforced. This means associating them with reward, consistency, and emotional safety. If taking a breath before reacting is followed by calm and understanding, that behavior becomes easier to repeat. If setting a boundary leads to clarity rather than chaos, the loop begins to shift. Over time, the new behavior becomes more efficient, more reliable, more automatic. And that is when the old loop begins to dissolve—not through willpower, but through repetition and reinforcement.

Behavioral loops are not signs of brokenness. They are signs of learning. And like all learned systems, they can be restructured. What once protected can be updated. What once relieved pain can be replaced with something more sustainable. But this requires a shift in focus—from controlling the behavior to understanding its function. When people begin to see their habits not as failures, but as patterns with logic and purpose, they gain the power to interrupt them. Not perfectly, not instantly, but consistently.

And in that consistency, new possibilities emerge—behaviors that reflect not only survival, but choice.

Disrupting the Pattern: Awareness and Choice

Behavioral change is often framed as a matter of willpower: the idea that if a person wants something badly enough, they will simply stop doing what harms them and start doing what helps them. But human behavior rarely changes through force. Patterns that have been reinforced over time do not disappear because someone decides they should. They change when the system that supports them is interrupted—gently, repeatedly, and with awareness. Disrupting behavior is not about brute strength. It is about precision: learning to recognize cues, observe responses without collapse, and choose alternatives that the nervous system can actually tolerate.

Awareness is the starting point for any real change. Not awareness in the abstract, but grounded, pattern-based observation. This means tracking what happens before, during, and after a behavior. When does the loop start? What precedes it? What does the behavior protect you from or soothe you through? What follows it—both externally and internally? Many people try to change behavior without mapping it first, and as a result, their efforts remain conceptual. They try to stop drinking without noticing the conditions that drive them to drink. They try to stop people-pleasing without noticing how early discomfort cues the behavior. This lack of clarity keeps them stuck. Behavioral loops cannot be disrupted until they are understood.

Mindfulness, in this context, is not a spiritual add-on. It is a skill for pausing pattern execution. When people can notice an impulse without immediately acting on it, they create space for alternative responses. This pause does not guarantee a different outcome, but it does create an opening. Even a one-second window of awareness can shift the brain from reflexive activation to a more conscious state. In that space, the person can ask questions: What am I feeling? What am I trying to solve right now? Is this behavior aligned with what I actually want, or is it just familiar? These questions do not require immediate answers—they require willingness to stay with discomfort rather than flee from it.

Cognitive-behavioral therapy (CBT) offers specific tools for disrupting behavioral patterns. One of the most effective is the ABC model: Antecedent, Behavior, Consequence. This model encourages individuals to observe the trigger (A), the action taken (B), and the outcome that follows (C). By mapping these sequences repeatedly, people begin to see patterns that were previously invisible. They notice that stress always precedes overeating, or that rejection cues withdrawal, or that shame leads to overexplaining. This awareness builds a vocabulary of behavioral logic. Once that logic is known, intervention becomes possible—not by force, but by informed experimentation.

Another powerful method involves *replacement*. Simply removing a behavior without replacing it leaves a psychological vacuum. The nervous system still wants regulation; the psyche still wants relief. If nothing new is offered, the old behavior will return, even if it no longer feels good. This is why behavior change is more about *substitution* than suppression. For every habit you aim to break, there must be something else to reach for—something that meets the same need with less long-term cost. A person who stops numbing with alcohol may need new rituals for soothing. A person who stops checking their phone compulsively may need new practices for managing anxiety. Without this layer, change cannot hold.

The challenge is that alternative behaviors often feel uncomfortable at first. This is because they are not yet reinforced. The reward they offer may be delayed, unfamiliar, or subtle. And the person's nervous system may not yet trust the new path. For example, speaking up instead of staying silent may lead to short-term anxiety, even if it ultimately results in clearer communication. Choosing rest over workaholism may produce guilt before it produces relief. These emotional reactions are not signs that the new behavior is wrong; they are signs that it is new. The body resists what it has not yet learned to predict. This is why consistency matters. Reinforcement takes time.

Emotionally, disrupting behavior also requires tolerance for disappointment. Change rarely happens in a clean line. There will be regressions, slip-ups, and moments of reactivity. Many people interpret these as failure and give up prematurely. But from a behavioral standpoint, these moments are part of the learning process. They provide feedback. They reveal where the system is still vulnerable. And they offer another opportunity to practice the pause, observe the cue, and choose something different. Perfection is not the goal. Pattern interruption is.

Environment matters as well. Behavioral loops are often sustained by surroundings—people, objects, routines—that cue certain responses. Someone trying to stop late-night binge eating may struggle if their home is stocked with high-reward snacks. Someone trying to assert themselves more clearly may struggle if their workplace punishes dissent. Disrupting behavior sometimes means altering the environment to reduce triggering cues and support new habits. This may involve setting boundaries, creating buffers, changing routines, or even altering physical spaces. These changes are not avoidance; they are structural supports for behavioral change. They give new patterns a place to grow.

Relationships play a role in this, too. People do not behave in isolation. Their loops are often mirrored or reinforced by others. If someone is always met with panic when they set a boundary, they may retreat to avoid the emotional cost. If they are met with appreciation and stability, they are more likely to repeat the action. Behavior change is accelerated in environments that validate the new response and reward the attempt—even if imperfect. This is why support systems matter. Not because they fix the behavior, but because they shape the field in which behavior is practiced.

Reinforcement must be reimagined in this context. It is not just about rewards in the behavioral sense; it is about what makes a behavior sustainable. This includes emotional congruence (the behavior feels aligned), psychological permission (the behavior feels allowed), and relational safety (the behavior is supported). When these conditions are present, the behavior is more likely to take root. When they are absent, the system defaults to what is familiar—even if harmful.

Ultimately, disrupting behavior is about reclaiming agency. Not through pressure, but through process. It is the practice of making the automatic visible, of slowing down the reactive mind, and of offering yourself new paths in place of old loops. It is the steady work of becoming someone who can feel discomfort without escaping it, who can respond without reenacting, and who can live according to values rather than conditioned reflex.

This does not mean controlling every impulse. It means choosing which ones to follow. It means understanding what your behavior is trying to do for you—and then deciding whether that path still serves you. Change happens not through resistance, but through awareness paired with permission. When people feel safe enough to notice, curious enough to map, and supported enough to try again, they begin to act from choice rather than pattern.

That is the logic of behavior. And that is the beginning of freedom.

* * *

12

Motivation and Meaning

Why do we get out of bed in the morning?
It seems like a simple question, but at its core lies one of the most complex and defining aspects of human life: motivation. Every action we take, from the most mundane to the most life-altering, is driven by something. Hunger may push us toward food; loneliness may pull us toward others; ambition may propel us toward achievement. Even inaction has its motive—comfort, avoidance, fear, resignation. Whether we are aware of it or not, our lives are built on a series of motivations, layered and often competing, that direct how we use our time, what we pursue, and what we avoid.

Motivation is not just the fuel of behavior—it is the architecture of meaning. What we strive toward reveals what we value, whether consciously chosen or unconsciously absorbed. Some motives are biological and universal: survival, safety, social belonging. Others are learned, shaped by culture, family dynamics, or early reinforcement. We are taught what to want, how to want, and what it means to succeed. Over time, these messages fuse with our internal experience, forming the blueprint for how we evaluate progress, define fulfillment, and determine our worth.

But not all motivation is equal. Some motives leave us feeling alive, energized, and deeply engaged. Others exhaust us, disconnect us from ourselves, or lead us into cycles of chronic striving and emotional depletion. At the heart of this difference is a psychological distinction that cuts across decades of research: the difference between *intrinsic* and *extrinsic* motivation.

Intrinsic motivation refers to doing something for its own sake—because it is interesting, enjoyable, or aligned with one's values. It is the drive to learn, create, connect, or challenge oneself without needing an external payoff. Children exhibit this kind of motivation naturally: they explore, ask questions, and play for the joy of discovery. Adults, too, can access this inner drive—when they become absorbed in a task, lose track of time, or feel pulled toward a goal that resonates with who they are.

Extrinsic motivation, on the other hand, refers to doing something for a separable outcome: praise, approval, money, avoidance of guilt, or fear of consequences. It is the logic of the external world: performance reviews, report cards, social likes, promotions, gold stars. While extrinsic motivation can be useful—especially in structured environments or short-term goals—it often becomes problematic when it overshadows intrinsic values. When people start doing things primarily for reward or to avoid disapproval, the quality of engagement declines, and so does the emotional payoff.

Modern life is saturated with extrinsic motivators. From early schooling to professional careers, people are taught to measure their success in external terms: grades, income, status, visibility. This can lead to a chronic disconnection from internal motives, replacing personal curiosity with performance anxiety, or replacing emotional satisfaction with a compulsive drive to achieve. People may wake up one day with a resume full of accomplishments and a profound emptiness inside—not because they did nothing, but because they never paused to ask *why* they were doing it.

Psychologists have long studied what happens when intrinsic motivation is undermined. One consistent finding is known as the *overjustification effect*: when a person is rewarded for something they already enjoy, their intrinsic motivation tends to decrease. The act begins to feel like a job, a means to an end. Over time, the internal joy of the activity fades, replaced by a sense of pressure or obligation. This is why turning passions into professions can be so emotionally complicated—and why some of the most talented, driven people find themselves burned out, disillusioned, or lost.

But motivation is not fixed. It can be remembered, reclaimed, and restructured. Even when someone has spent years operating on external fuel, it is possible to return to intrinsic roots. This requires more than setting goals—it requires identifying values. What actually matters to you? What gives your life a felt sense of direction, even when it's difficult? What do you find yourself drawn to, even without being told? These are the questions that reawaken inner motivation and point toward authentic meaning.

Meaning is a central, though often neglected, dimension of motivation. People are not motivated only by pleasure or success—they are motivated by coherence. They want their actions to make sense in the context of their identity. They want to feel that their choices reflect something deeper than habit or expectation. This is why some people walk away from lucrative careers, why others devote themselves to causes that offer little material return, and why so many crises of motivation are actually crises of meaning. The problem is not laziness. The problem is misalignment.

This chapter will explore the architecture of human motivation, beginning with foundational theories and expanding into the lived realities of drive, depletion, and desire. We will examine the psychological cost of living by extrinsic rules, the emotional power of rediscovering intrinsic engagement, and the critical importance of value-based motivation for long-term wellbeing. We will also address the quiet collapse of motivation—when nothing feels worth doing—and reframe that collapse not as pathology, but as a psychological signal: an invitation to reassess, realign, and reconnect with what matters.

You will not find a formula here. But you will find a framework. A way to understand the difference between what pushes you and what pulls you, between what keeps you running and what keeps you grounded. Because at the end of the day, motivation is not about how much energy you have. It is about what direction you are facing.

Why We Do Anything

Human behavior is rarely random. Even when it appears irrational or inconsistent, it reflects a deeper motivational structure—an emotional or cognitive logic that organizes action, attention, and effort. At its core, motivation is the mechanism by which we translate internal states and external stimuli into movement. Hunger leads to food-seeking. Fear triggers withdrawal. Curiosity draws us into the unknown. From the biological to the existential, every action we take has a psychological driver beneath it. To understand motivation is to understand the scaffolding of human life: how we survive, adapt, strive, avoid, and make sense of ourselves.

Theories of motivation have long tried to organize this complex terrain. One of the earliest and most influential was Abraham Maslow's hierarchy of needs. Maslow proposed that human motivation is structured in layers, beginning with physiological needs like food, water, and shelter. Once those are met, individuals seek safety, then belonging, then esteem, and finally, self-actualization—the desire to live in alignment with one's potential. Though Maslow's model has been critiqued for its rigid structure and cultural assumptions, it remains a useful starting point. It reminds us that motivation is not static. It shifts as our circumstances, developmental stage, and internal life evolve.

Beyond basic survival, what drives people most consistently is the pursuit of needs that are emotional, relational, and symbolic. These include autonomy (the sense that one's actions are self-directed), competence (the belief that one can affect outcomes), and relatedness (the feeling of being connected and valued by others). These three elements form the foundation of self-determination theory, one of the most robust contemporary frameworks for understanding human motivation. According to this theory, people are most engaged and psychologically healthy when their environment supports these three needs. When any of them is thwarted, motivation tends to collapse—or contort into reactive forms like compulsive achievement, withdrawal, or external validation-seeking.

Children demonstrate the raw expression of these needs. They reach, explore, mimic, and challenge without needing to be pushed. Their questions are constant, their curiosity endless. This is intrinsic motivation in its purest form: doing something because the activity itself is satisfying. But over time, this natural motivation can become displaced by external pressures. A child praised only for high performance may begin to equate their worth with achievement. A teenager punished for independent thinking may learn to suppress authentic engagement. These early experiences shape how motivation is encoded—not just what a person wants, but how they believe wanting is supposed to work.

As individuals grow older, the sources of motivation become more diffuse and more culturally coded. External motivators like money, status, recognition, and praise are introduced early and often. Academic settings reward performance over process. Social systems reward visibility over depth. Over time, people learn to chase certain goals without examining whether those goals actually matter to them. This is one of the central dilemmas of modern life: individuals are surrounded by motivational cues, yet many find themselves deeply disconnected from any sense of internal direction. They continue moving forward, but the effort feels hollow.

It is important to clarify that extrinsic motivation is not inherently negative. Many worthwhile tasks—paying bills, exercising, following laws—are motivated by external outcomes. Extrinsic motivation can initiate habits, provide structure, and reinforce important social functions. The concern arises when these motivators override internal signals. When people stop doing things because they care, and start doing them only to be seen, rewarded, or deemed acceptable, motivation begins to lose its grounding. The activity becomes a performance, and over time, the internal compass grows quieter.

One of the most powerful dynamics within motivation is the shift from autonomy to compliance. Autonomy is the felt sense that one's actions are chosen, even within constraint. It is not about freedom from limits, but freedom within them. Compliance, by contrast, is the internalization of pressure. It involves doing what is expected to avoid punishment or disapproval, often while suppressing one's real desires or emotions. While both may result in outwardly similar behavior—studying hard, meeting deadlines, showing up on time—the emotional experience is entirely different. Autonomy brings vitality. Compliance breeds resentment, exhaustion, or numbness.

This is why intrinsic motivation tends to be more sustainable. When people act in ways that align with their interests, values, or passions, they engage more fully. They persist longer, learn more deeply, and report higher satisfaction. Their energy comes not from fear or pressure, but from the internal coherence between their actions and their identity. Conversely, when people act solely to meet external standards, they often experience emotional depletion. The work may get done, but it leaves a residue of fatigue or self-alienation.

Of course, few situations allow for purely intrinsic engagement. Most people live within systems—families, workplaces, institutions—that impose certain demands. The challenge, then, is not to eliminate extrinsic motivators, but to anchor them in something personally meaningful. A teacher may need to prepare students for standardized tests, but their deeper motivation might be helping students think critically. A physician may be bound by billing systems and bureaucratic constraints, but still find purpose in easing suffering. When external tasks are linked to internal values, motivation stabilizes and deepens.

Another key concept in the study of motivation is goal orientation. People tend to pursue goals either to achieve something positive (approach orientation) or to avoid something negative (avoidance orientation). Both forms of motivation can drive behavior, but they carry different emotional tones. Approach-oriented goals are associated with curiosity, ambition, and creative risk-taking. Avoidance-oriented goals tend to generate anxiety, rigidity, and short-term thinking. Over time, a dominant avoidance orientation can lead to a chronic sense of threat and a narrow motivational field—one where people are always trying to stay out of trouble, but rarely feel pulled toward growth.

Motivation also changes with context. What feels motivating in one phase of life may not in another. A person might be driven by ambition in their twenties, stability in their thirties, and meaning or contribution in their later years. These shifts are not failures of consistency. They are signs of psychological development. As individuals change, so do the motives that feel legitimate and life-giving. Part of emotional maturity is learning to recognize these shifts and respond accordingly, rather than clinging to outdated definitions of success or identity.

Crucially, the absence of motivation does not always indicate apathy or laziness. Often, it reflects disconnection. When a person cannot feel what matters to them—because of trauma, burnout, depression, or chronic adaptation—they may lose access to motivational energy. Their goals may feel abstract, their routines hollow. In these moments, the work is not to "get motivated," but to gently reconnect with meaning, safety, and self-trust. The flame of motivation is not extinguished—it is obscured. And with the right conditions, it can return.

Understanding why we do anything begins with recognizing that motivation is not simply a matter of effort. It is a reflection of relationship: to self, to others, to the world. It is shaped by context, history, emotion, and need. And it is sustained when people feel that their efforts matter— not just in outcomes, but in alignment with who they are becoming.

The Tyranny of Achievement

In cultures built around competition, performance, and visible success, achievement is rarely optional. From childhood, people are taught that their value is linked to what they can produce, how well they can perform, and how others evaluate the results. Metrics are everywhere—grades, test scores, likes, promotions, rankings—and the pressure to rise through them is relentless. Achievement becomes not just a goal but an identity, something that must be constantly maintained to preserve social worth. For many, this begins as ambition. Over time, it mutates into compulsion.

This pressure operates quietly at first. A child learns that praise follows high performance. A student internalizes that disappointment follows anything less than excellence. Slowly, the act of learning is replaced by the pressure to prove. The process of growth becomes less about curiosity and more about measurement. Teachers, parents, peers—all become agents of surveillance. What begins as encouragement turns into expectation. And when expectations are chronic and high, motivation becomes less about joy and more about avoidance: avoiding failure, avoiding shame, avoiding the perception of inadequacy.

At the center of this shift is a subtle psychological trade: people learn to seek *worth* through achievement, rather than experiencing achievement as a byproduct of intrinsic worth. This reorientation is not immediately noticeable. In fact, many high achievers appear confident and focused. But under the surface, their motivation is increasingly tethered to external validation. They begin to perform rather than participate, striving to maintain appearances rather than engage with depth. The consequence is not just stress—it is disconnection from the internal compass that once gave their efforts meaning.

Social media accelerates this disconnection. Visibility becomes currency. Accomplishments are no longer private milestones but public performances. A graduation, a job promotion, a creative success—all are filtered, posted, and measured by engagement metrics. The need to be seen eclipses the satisfaction of the experience itself. This externalization of meaning distorts motivation. People begin to curate their lives not around what fulfills them, but around what performs well. The goal is no longer to do meaningful work—it is to appear impressive.

In psychology, this shift is well documented. Research on extrinsic motivation shows that when individuals are primarily driven by external rewards—praise, money, status, approval—their engagement tends to suffer. They may continue the behavior, but with less creativity, less persistence, and less satisfaction. This is known as the *undermining effect*: external incentives can reduce intrinsic interest, especially when those incentives are perceived as controlling. In short, the more a person feels *pushed*, the less they feel *drawn*. And when this dynamic persists, even high-functioning individuals may experience a quiet motivational collapse.

Achievement, then, becomes a double-edged sword. On one hand, it provides structure, opportunity, and a sense of progress. On the other, it creates a fragile self-concept—one that depends on constant performance. When people are praised for being exceptional, they often begin to fear being anything else. This fear produces rigidity. Risk feels dangerous. Rest feels irresponsible. Vulnerability feels incompatible with identity. Over time, the individual becomes trapped in their own reputation.

The tyranny of achievement is not always loud. In many lives, it hides behind busyness: overworking, overcommitting, constantly striving. These patterns are often rewarded socially. High achievers are praised for their dedication, their output, their success. But underneath the praise is often depletion. Burnout is not caused only by doing too much—it is caused by doing too much of what feels misaligned, unsupported, or unsustainable. When the drive to achieve disconnects from a sense of purpose, the result is a life full of motion but empty of vitality.

Perfectionism is one of the psychological byproducts of this system. Not the healthy pursuit of excellence, but the compulsive need to avoid mistakes, to be above criticism, to never disappoint. Perfectionism masquerades as ambition, but it is rooted in fear: fear of failure, of judgment, of being exposed as inadequate. And because perfection is unattainable, the person lives in a constant state of tension. Even success feels temporary, because the next challenge is always waiting. The motivational engine never shuts off—it just runs hotter.

This chronic striving also alters how people interpret their value. Many come to believe they are only as good as their last performance. Rest becomes difficult. Saying no feels risky. Pleasure without productivity feels undeserved. Even leisure is filtered through the lens of usefulness: vacations are curated for social media, hobbies are monetized, self-care is scheduled like a job. In this environment, it is not just motivation that suffers—it is identity.

What gets lost in the process is the capacity to experience meaning outside of measurement. When every action is judged by its outcome, people forget how to be present with the process. A student stops reading for interest and reads only to pass. An artist stops creating for expression and creates only for acclaim. A parent stops connecting with their child and focuses instead on whether they're raising a "successful" one. These shifts are not intentional. They are systemic. And they are emotionally corrosive.

It is worth asking: what is the cost of achievement when it eclipses all other motives? For some, the answer comes in midlife, when the external rewards begin to feel hollow. For others, it comes in burnout, anxiety, or a creeping sense of futility. They may have done everything "right," but something essential is missing. That something is not just passion—it is permission. The permission to want what matters, to value what isn't measured, to define success in terms that nourish rather than deplete.

Reclaiming motivation from the tyranny of achievement requires a psychological reorientation. It means asking different questions: not "What will they think?" but "What feels aligned?" Not "Am I winning?" but "Am I becoming who I want to be?" This shift is not easy. It often involves grief: letting go of goals that were never really yours, dismantling identities built on compliance, and confronting the fear that without achievement, you might not be enough.

But on the other side of that grief is freedom. The freedom to pursue goals that reflect your actual values. The freedom to create without performance. The freedom to rest without guilt. These are not indulgences. They are necessary conditions for sustainable motivation. They restore the internal structure that achievement culture has eroded.

Achievement will always have a place in human life. But it must be held in context. It must be guided by values, supported by emotional grounding, and balanced with self-awareness. When achievement becomes the only acceptable form of value, motivation collapses into performance. But when achievement is one expression of a larger internal framework, motivation becomes a source of energy, engagement, and meaning.

In the end, the question is not how much you can do. The question is whether what you do reflects what matters.

Values, Vocation, and the Pull of Purpose

Most people, at some point in their lives, wonder what they are meant to do. It may begin as a quiet curiosity or arrive suddenly during a crisis. It may take the form of discontent in a job that no longer fits, a longing for deeper impact, or a persistent sense that something essential is missing. This pull is not always loud, but it is persistent. It signals that motivation is not just about doing things, but about doing the right things—right not in the moral sense, but in the personal, authentic sense. The things that fit. The ones that echo inward.

Intrinsic motivation is grounded in this sense of internal pull. It is what drives a person to engage with something not because they have to, but because they feel drawn to it. This is the energy behind meaningful work, artistic expression, enduring curiosity, and service that nourishes both giver and receiver. It does not require applause or permission. Its reward is the process itself—the feeling of being inside something that matters.

But this kind of motivation doesn't flourish in every environment. It needs psychological safety, space for exploration, and freedom from constant judgment. It also requires a degree of internal clarity: a person must be able to distinguish between what they've been taught to value and what they actually value. Without that distinction, intrinsic motivation is easily overridden by habit, performance norms, or inherited expectations. People may spend years pursuing goals that belong to someone else's version of success, wondering why their energy feels hollow.

Purpose, like motivation, is not a fixed object. It is less a destination and more a direction. People discover it not by waiting for revelation, but by paying attention to where their attention naturally goes. What do they care about? What stirs them? What problems do they feel compelled to solve, even when no one is asking them to? These questions are not easily answered, but they reveal something essential about identity. Not the curated one, but the internal structure that gives shape to desire and meaning.

Psychology offers several frameworks for understanding how purpose influences motivation. One is the concept of *vocation*—the idea that certain activities or paths resonate so deeply with a person's values, temperament, and worldview that they feel called to them. This does not mean everyone has a singular "calling," nor does it suggest that purpose is always tied to profession. Rather, vocation is the alignment between inner values and outer action. It is the experience of moving through the world in a way that feels coherent, not just efficient.

When people act in accordance with their values, several things happen. They tend to experience less inner conflict. Their motivation becomes more consistent. They are more likely to enter states of deep engagement—what Mihaly Csikszentmihalyi called "flow"—where time dilates, self-consciousness fades, and the activity becomes its own reward. These states are not just enjoyable. They are nourishing. They replenish energy rather than depleting it. Over time, they contribute to a felt sense of meaning, fulfillment, and personal coherence.

Values themselves are not static. They are shaped by lived experience, developmental stages, and cultural context. What matters at age twenty may not matter at forty. Life events—loss, illness, parenting, trauma—can reorder priorities overnight. When these shifts occur, motivation often shifts with them. A person who once thrived on ambition may become more drawn to caregiving. Someone who built a career on competition may suddenly long for collaboration or mentorship. These changes are not regressions. They are recalibrations of the motivational system in

MOTIVATION AND MEANING

response to changing inner landscapes.

Yet, aligning with purpose is rarely straightforward. It often requires difficult trade-offs. Some people discover what they care about most only to realize that their current life is incompatible with it. Others know their values but lack the resources, support, or courage to act on them. The dissonance between internal motivation and external circumstance can be emotionally painful. It breeds restlessness, resentment, and sometimes despair. But that tension is also a signal—it points to the gap between who someone is and how they are living. And it invites change.

One of the barriers to acting from intrinsic values is the fear of insignificance. People worry that what truly matters to them won't be impressive, profitable, or socially validated. They hesitate to follow their curiosity or commit to work that feels meaningful if it doesn't come with a recognizable badge of success. This anxiety is understandable in a world that measures worth in metrics. But it is also one of the great distortions of modern life. The most meaningful contributions are often quiet, local, and uncelebrated. They don't need to be large to be significant.

Consider the teacher who helps students feel seen. The community organizer who protects a neighborhood. The hospice nurse who eases someone's final days. These roles may not carry prestige, but they are saturated with purpose. Their motivation is not rooted in outcomes alone—it is embedded in values: dignity, service, compassion, justice. And because of that alignment, the work sustains rather than drains.

Purpose is not the same as passion. Passion is emotional, sometimes fleeting. Purpose is grounded. It holds through difficulty. People who are guided by purpose are not always enthusiastic, but they are anchored. They can persist through tedium, frustration, or setbacks because they are motivated by something deeper than reward. They are not immune to fatigue, but their fatigue has context—it is in service of something chosen, not just something endured.

There is a kind of quiet authority that comes with living in alignment. It does not need to shout or prove itself. It is recognizable not in words, but in steadiness. In motivation that endures not because of pressure, but because of clarity. This clarity is often hard won. It requires turning inward, listening carefully, and making decisions that might look strange from the outside. But over time, it builds a life that fits—not perfectly, not without friction, but with integrity.

Ultimately, the pull of purpose is the pull toward coherence. It is the psychological alignment between values, behavior, and identity. When people live from this place, their motivation becomes less volatile. They may still struggle, but they do not feel directionless. They know what matters. They know where they are going. And even when the path is unclear, the compass is intact.

Reclaiming Inner Direction

When a person's motivational system becomes hijacked by external demands, internal clarity often fades. The question is no longer, "What do I care about?" but "What am I supposed to be doing?" The shift is subtle but powerful. Without realizing it, people begin orienting their decisions, energy, and time around expectations rather than alignment. They accumulate tasks, goals, and identities that do not originate from within. Over time, they may find themselves outwardly successful but inwardly unmoored, moving forward without feeling moved.

Reclaiming inner direction is not about abandoning responsibilities or withdrawing from the world. It is about reestablishing the internal authority to discern what matters and why. It requires slowing down enough to hear what has been drowned out: intuition, desire, discomfort, longing. These inner signals do not shout, and they do not compete well with urgency. But they are the foundation of self-directed motivation. They point not to what is expected, but to what is essential.

The first step in this process is usually recognition. A person must notice that their current pattern of motivation no longer works. This might come in the form of burnout, disengagement, irritability, or a persistent lack of meaning. These signals are not failures; they are indicators. They suggest that the system is out of sync—that the person is acting from obligation rather than conviction. In many cases, this realization brings relief. It makes sense of the fatigue. It names the fog.

From recognition comes the difficult work of disentanglement. This means identifying which motivations are inherited, which are internalized, and which are still alive. People often discover that they have been chasing goals that once made sense but no longer do—or worse, that never belonged to them in the first place. The pressure to be impressive, to meet certain milestones, to perform competence can become deeply embedded. Reclaiming direction means challenging these scripts and allowing space for new values to emerge.

One of the most effective tools in this process is values clarification. This involves naming the principles that feel most true and important— independent of outcomes or approval. Values are not goals. They are directions, ways of being. A person might value creativity, integrity, service, adventure, or kindness. These values provide a map. They make it possible to assess choices not in terms of productivity, but in terms of alignment. They help answer the question, "Does this fit the life I am trying to build?"

Rebuilding intrinsic motivation also involves restoring the conditions that support it: autonomy, competence, and relatedness. Autonomy is the freedom to make meaningful choices. Competence is the belief that one's actions can be effective. Relatedness is the sense of connection and belonging. When these needs are met, people tend to feel more energized, more engaged, and more resilient. When they are absent, even meaningful goals can begin to feel burdensome.

In practical terms, this means restructuring daily life to support these conditions. For autonomy, it may involve reducing unnecessary obligations, saying no more often, or adjusting how and when tasks are done. For competence, it might mean setting smaller, more achievable goals, or focusing on areas where growth feels possible. For relatedness, it often requires fostering relationships that support rather than pressure— spaces where motivation is encouraged, not coerced.

Many people fear that if they loosen their grip on external motivators, they will become lazy or aimless. But intrinsic motivation is not the absence of structure—it is structure that arises from within. It is entirely possible to be both self-directed and disciplined, both free and focused. The difference is in the origin of the energy. Discipline that comes from alignment is sustainable. It builds strength rather than resentment.

Reclaiming inner direction also requires a shift in how success is defined. Traditional markers—status, money, productivity—are not inherently wrong, but they are often too narrow. They fail to capture qualities like integrity, presence, curiosity, or compassion. When success is expanded to include these dimensions, motivation becomes more inclusive, more human. It becomes less about achievement and more about engagement.

Another key element in restoring intrinsic motivation is the ability to tolerate discomfort. Choosing alignment over approval, or clarity over certainty, often feels unsettling. It may mean disappointing others, changing course, or sitting with ambiguity. But these are not signs of failure. They are signs that the person is reclaiming authorship of their life. Discomfort is not always a problem to solve. Sometimes, it is a sign of growth.

There is also a deeper emotional layer to this process: the grief that comes with recognizing how much of one's life has been lived under the guidance of misaligned motivations. This grief is not only about time lost—it is about the parts of self that were silenced, the joys that were postponed, the directions never taken. Allowing space for that grief is essential. It honors the cost of disconnection and opens the door to more honest engagement.

In clinical and developmental psychology, this process often parallels what Erik Erikson described in his theory of psychosocial development as the task of *identity vs. role confusion*. Although traditionally associated with adolescence, this stage recurs across the lifespan. People continually confront the question: "Who am I in this phase of life?" Reclaiming motivation is part of answering that question with greater fidelity and depth.

It is also important to remember that intrinsic motivation is fragile in certain contexts. Environments that are punitive, excessively evaluative, or chronically demanding tend to suppress it. In these settings, people often survive through compliance rather than engagement. When possible, changing the environment can be transformative. But when change isn't feasible, it becomes even more important to carve out spaces—however small—where internal motivation can breathe. A daily walk, a creative practice, a conversation that doesn't revolve around output. These small acts accumulate. They reawaken a sense of choice.

As people begin to live from this reclaimed direction, their relationship with effort also changes. Effort is no longer something extracted, but something offered. It comes with more presence, more care, and more satisfaction. Even in difficulty, there is a sense of being aligned. This does not eliminate struggle, but it reframes it. Struggle becomes part of the process of staying close to what matters.

In the end, reclaiming motivation is an act of psychological sovereignty. It is the decision to make one's life internally coherent, even in a world that rewards performance over authenticity. It is the commitment to value what is felt, not just what is measured. And it is the return to a kind of freedom that is not the absence of responsibility, but the presence of meaning.

The motivational system is not just a mechanism. It is a reflection of how well a person can hear themselves—and how willing they are to follow what they hear.

* * *

13

Habits and Routines

There is no aspect of daily life untouched by habit. From the moment we wake to the way we brush our teeth, brew our coffee, check our phones, speak to others, respond to stress, or end our day, much of what we do is automatic. The structure of habit is so deeply embedded in human behavior that most people move through their lives unaware of the degree to which they are governed by it. And yet, it is often habits—more than decisions—that determine whether our lives align with what we value or drift from it entirely.

Habits are not just convenient; they are neurologically efficient. They allow the brain to conserve energy by shifting repetitive actions into procedural memory. This automation is adaptive. It reduces cognitive load, allowing attention to be directed elsewhere. But there is a tradeoff. The more a behavior becomes habitual, the less conscious it becomes—and the more difficult it is to examine, interrupt, or change. What begins as a choice gradually transforms into a pattern, and what was once deliberate becomes reflexive.

This transition from conscious action to automatic behavior is central to human psychological functioning. But it also introduces a powerful tension. If habits make life more efficient, they can also make it more rigid. A person's routines can become so entrenched that even when they are misaligned with health, values, or goals, change feels psychologically expensive. This is why knowledge is often insufficient for behavioral change. People may know what they want to do differently—eat better, exercise more, engage more mindfully—but find themselves unable to translate intention into action. The culprit is rarely willpower alone. It is habit architecture.

Understanding the mechanics of habit provides insight into this struggle. Habits are constructed through loops: cue, routine, reward. A cue triggers the behavior, a routine is the behavior itself, and the reward reinforces it. These loops are reinforced over time, often without conscious awareness. The reward doesn't have to be dramatic. It might be the relief of distraction, the comfort of familiarity, or the momentary pleasure of a dopamine hit. But over time, these loops create grooves in the brain. And the deeper the groove, the harder it is to steer elsewhere.

Yet, habits do not exist in a vacuum. They are shaped by environment, stress, social modeling, cultural norms, and emotional needs. A person may eat automatically not just because of hunger, but because of loneliness or boredom. Another may check their phone compulsively not out of interest, but out of a need to escape discomfort. These behaviors are not irrational. They are adaptations—ways the brain has learned to soothe, distract, or stabilize itself. But when these adaptations go unexamined, they become barriers to agency.

One of the most misunderstood aspects of habit formation is the role of friction. Friction refers to anything that increases the effort required to engage in a behavior. High-friction habits are harder to start and easier to abandon. Low-friction habits, in contrast, slide easily into place— and often remain there, even when they conflict with long-term goals. Much of the modern environment is designed to reduce friction for consumption and convenience, while increasing friction for reflective or effortful actions. This has profound implications for how we live, what we value, and how much control we truly have over our routines.

Just as habits influence behavior, they also reinforce identity. People come to see themselves as the kind of person who meditates, or who doesn't. The kind of person who writes, or who procrastinates. These identities are not abstract—they are built through repetition. The actions a person takes each day become the scaffolding of their self-concept. And once that identity takes shape, it further shapes behavior in return. This feedback loop is powerful. It helps explain why change is not just hard, but disorienting. It requires not just doing something new, but becoming someone new.

Yet within that difficulty is also possibility. Habits can be broken. New ones can be built. And even deeply ingrained routines can be restructured with the right understanding and strategy. The key is not to rely on force or willpower alone, but to understand how motivation, context, and timing intersect with the human nervous system. Behavioral change becomes possible when it is designed with both psychological and environmental leverage in mind.

This chapter examines the science and psychology of habit through four lenses. First, we will explore the architecture of automaticity: how habits are built in the brain, why they persist, and what cognitive mechanisms support their formation. Next, we will look at the role of friction—why some habits take hold easily while others fall apart, and how small environmental changes can shift the odds of success. From there, we will explore how habits shape identity, not just behavior, and how everyday routines reinforce or distort our sense of self. Finally, we will turn toward change: what it takes to dismantle destructive habits, construct sustainable ones, and reclaim agency over the routines that govern our lives.

Habits are the invisible infrastructure of experience. They make up the majority of our day-to-day behaviors, shape our identity over time, and influence how we feel, think, and relate to others. But they are not fixed. They are plastic, adaptable, and open to revision. When people learn to work with the grain of human psychology rather than against it, they discover that motivation is not a mystery—it is a system. And within that system lies the potential to build a life that reflects not just routine, but intention.

The Architecture of Automaticity

Every human brain is built for repetition. It learns by doing, remembers by association, and economizes by automating. The sheer volume of decisions, movements, and perceptions that people navigate daily would overwhelm the nervous system if every action required conscious deliberation. Fortunately, it doesn't. Through a process known as automaticity, the brain stores frequently repeated behaviors in a kind of neurological shorthand, allowing them to be executed quickly and with minimal effort. These behaviors are called habits, and they are not merely conveniences. They are structural elements in the architecture of identity, behavior, and experience.

The formation of a habit begins with a behavior repeated under consistent conditions. If the action reliably leads to a reward—something pleasurable, useful, or emotionally stabilizing—the brain begins to associate the context with the outcome. Neural circuits in the basal ganglia, a region involved in motor control and procedural learning, begin to encode the cue-behavior-reward loop. As the loop repeats, the behavior becomes faster and less effortful, gradually migrating from deliberate action to automatic response. Over time, the brain comes to rely on this automation. It becomes the default setting.

This efficiency comes at a psychological cost. The more a behavior becomes automatic, the less it is subject to reflection. Habits reduce cognitive load, but they also reduce conscious oversight. This is not inherently negative—brushing one's teeth or driving a familiar route are examples of useful automation—but it becomes problematic when maladaptive behaviors follow the same path. A person may find themselves compulsively checking their phone, snacking at night, or reacting with irritation, not because they have chosen these behaviors, but because the loop has been cemented. The decision has already been made, neurologically speaking.

Psychological research has helped to formalize this understanding. In the 1990s and early 2000s, studies on habit formation began to emphasize the importance of context, reward, and frequency. Wendy Wood and colleagues found that nearly 45 percent of daily behaviors were performed in the same location, at the same time, in the same way—not because of intention, but because of habit. The implication is sobering: much of what people believe to be volitional is actually habitual. That is, they are not choosing in the moment, but repeating what was once chosen long ago.

This insight shifts the focus of behavior change. If habits are a product of automaticity, then change is not merely a matter of willpower or resolution. It is a matter of disrupting the loop, modifying the environment, and reengineering the reinforcement structure. To do this, it is necessary to understand the anatomy of the habit loop.

Each loop begins with a cue—an internal or external trigger that signals the brain to initiate the behavior. This could be time of day, a particular emotion, a social context, or a sensory stimulus. The cue sets off a routine, the actual behavior performed in response. Finally, there is a reward—something that satisfies a need, eases discomfort, or provides a dopamine surge. Over time, the brain begins to anticipate the reward as soon as it encounters the cue. This anticipation itself becomes reinforcing, creating a self-perpetuating cycle.

Take, for example, the common habit of evening snacking. The cue might be the end of the workday. The routine is heading to the kitchen and grabbing chips. The reward is a brief sense of relief, pleasure, or distraction. Repeated often enough, the brain no longer evaluates whether this action is helpful. It simply recognizes the cue and initiates the loop. Disrupting this habit is not as simple as saying no to chips. It requires identifying the cue, understanding the underlying need being addressed, and substituting a different routine that offers a comparable reward.

Automaticity is not limited to physical actions. Emotional habits—ways of reacting to stress, conflict, or ambiguity—follow similar loops. A person may habitually withdraw during arguments, escalate conflict when criticized, or numb out when overwhelmed. These reactions, too, were once responses that served a purpose. Over time, they became default behaviors, reinforced by emotional relief or avoidance of pain. Changing these patterns means addressing the underlying emotional cue, not just the visible behavior.

One of the challenges in modifying habits is the delayed cost. Habits form because they produce an immediate reward, even if the long-term outcome is negative. Procrastination, for instance, offers immediate relief from pressure, even if it ultimately leads to stress. Scrolling through social media provides stimulation and escape, even if it results in disconnection or regret. The brain, biased toward short-term rewards, privileges the immediate. This creates a motivational mismatch: people want the long-term benefits of change but are hooked by the short-term rewards of habit.

To counter this bias, habit change strategies often involve amplifying immediate feedback for new behaviors. This might include visual progress tracking, small personal rewards, or social reinforcement. These interventions help bridge the motivational gap by making the benefits of change more tangible. Over time, as the new behavior becomes associated with positive outcomes, it begins to take on its own momentum.

The concept of keystone habits adds another layer to this picture. Some habits have a disproportionate influence on the rest of life. Regular exercise, for example, often improves sleep, mood, and time management. Daily journaling can enhance emotional regulation, self-awareness, and goal clarity. These keystone habits serve as anchors—behaviors that stabilize and support the development of other routines. Identifying and focusing on these pivotal habits can accelerate the process of change, making transformation feel more organic and less effortful.

Automaticity also intersects with identity. As habits repeat, they begin to send messages to the self: "This is what I do," which becomes, "This is who I am." The person who writes every day starts to see themselves as a writer. The person who consistently avoids conflict may come to see themselves as passive, even if that's not how they want to be. These identity cues are powerful motivators. They reinforce behavior through self-concept. To change a habit, then, often requires revising the story a person tells about who they are.

The architecture of habit is not a prison, but it is a structure. It supports, limits, guides, and shapes. Recognizing that structure allows people to work with it, rather than against it. It moves the conversation away from blame—Why can't I just stop?—and toward design: How can I build a system that supports what I care about?

Behavioral freedom is not found in rejecting structure altogether. It is found in choosing it consciously. In using the brain's preference for automaticity to support rather than sabotage. And in understanding that every repeated action is not just a behavior, but a vote for the person one is becoming.

The Role of Friction: Why Some Habits Stick

Most attempts to change behavior fail not because people lack discipline, but because they miscalculate effort. They overestimate motivation and underestimate friction. Friction, in the context of habit formation, refers to anything that slows or complicates the execution of a behavior. It is the invisible force that resists momentum, the quiet drag that turns simple actions into persistent challenges. A behavior that feels effortless in one setting becomes laborious in another, not because the behavior itself has changed, but because the friction around it has.

Understanding friction allows us to answer a fundamental question: Why do some habits stick while others fall apart? The answer often has less to do with willpower and more to do with architecture. When a habit is easy to perform, contextually supported, and emotionally neutral or positive, it becomes likely to persist. When a habit is logistically difficult, emotionally taxing, or cognitively overloaded, it struggles to take hold. And because friction tends to operate below conscious awareness, it is often misattributed to character. People don't say, "The friction was too high,"—they say, "I failed again."

There are two main types of friction: physical and psychological.

Physical friction includes anything that adds literal steps, distance, or complication to a behavior. For example, if the gym is a 30-minute drive away, the chances of maintaining a consistent workout routine decrease sharply. If healthy food requires lengthy preparation, but junk food is within arm's reach, the latter will likely win. Reducing friction for desired behaviors—and increasing it for unwanted ones—is one of the most practical strategies for sustainable habit change.

Psychological friction is subtler. It includes emotional resistance, decision fatigue, ambiguity, or negative association. For instance, if a person associates exercise with shame, judgment, or prior failure, they may avoid it even if they value their health. If writing feels tied to perfectionism or criticism, sitting down to write may trigger avoidance, no matter how strong the intention. Psychological friction often appears as procrastination, distraction, or self-sabotage, but underneath these behaviors is a system trying to protect itself from discomfort.

One of the most effective ways to reduce friction is through environmental design. This means adjusting the physical space to make desirable behaviors easier and undesirable behaviors harder. If a person wants to read more, placing a book on the nightstand and keeping the phone in another room creates a lower-friction pathway to reading. If the goal is to cut back on alcohol, removing it from the house raises the effort required to consume it. These changes are not about restriction; they are about removing the obstacles that trip the brain into defaulting to easier, less aligned choices.

Behavioral economist B.J. Fogg introduced the concept of "tiny habits" to emphasize the importance of low-friction starting points. His research suggests that new habits are most successful when they are extremely easy to begin. Doing two push-ups instead of committing to a full workout. Writing one sentence instead of finishing a chapter. The principle is simple: reduce the activation energy. Once a behavior begins, momentum often carries it forward. But the barrier to entry—the initial friction—must be low enough to cross without resistance.

James Clear, in his work on atomic habits, expands this insight by suggesting that habit formation is not about intensity but consistency. He emphasizes the importance of stacking new habits onto existing routines—tying a desired behavior to a well-established one. This strategy, called habit stacking, reduces cognitive friction by embedding the new behavior into an existing pattern. It minimizes the number of decisions required and increases the likelihood of automatic follow-through.

Friction can also be emotional, particularly when a new habit threatens an existing identity. A person who sees themselves as "not a morning person" may find it harder to build a morning routine, not because mornings are inherently difficult, but because the new behavior conflicts with their self-concept. In these cases, the psychological resistance is rooted in dissonance. The habit feels like a lie. The way through is to make the behavior feel congruent—not by forcing identity change upfront, but by reinforcing it through repetition. Every completed action becomes evidence: maybe I am the kind of person who can do this.

There is also social friction, which includes the reactions, expectations, or pressures from others that either support or hinder behavior change. If a person's peer group mocks their attempt to eat differently, go sober, or engage in mindfulness, the likelihood of success plummets. Habits are socially contagious and socially constrained. Changing them often means either enlisting support or creating boundaries around influence. Some of the most successful habit changes occur not through internal discipline alone, but through changes in environment, affiliation, and accountability.

Another important factor is what researchers call implementation intention. This is the practice of deciding in advance when and where a behavior will occur. Instead of vaguely committing to "meditate more," a person commits to "meditate for 10 minutes at 7 a.m. in the living room." This clarity removes ambiguity, which is a major source of friction. It also helps the behavior get anchored in context, which increases the likelihood of automaticity over time.

It is worth noting that friction works both ways. Just as reducing friction helps build habits, increasing friction helps break them. If someone wants to reduce social media usage, making the login process longer, deleting the app, or turning the phone to grayscale can increase just enough effort to create a pause. That pause reintroduces decision-making—turning an automatic behavior into a conscious one. Even a few seconds of friction can be enough to shift the trajectory.

Despite these tools, some forms of friction are internal and complex. Trauma, depression, ADHD, or anxiety can dramatically alter the relationship with behavior. What seems like laziness or lack of discipline may be a symptom of nervous system overload. In these cases, the most compassionate—and effective—approach is to shrink the task to match the available capacity. Reducing friction might mean accepting a different pace, redefining success, or seeking support that lowers the emotional toll of the behavior.

Ultimately, friction is not the enemy. It is information. It reveals where the path is blocked, where energy is leaking, and where the system needs support. By identifying and modifying sources of friction—physical, emotional, social, or cognitive—people can create conditions in which habits are not just possible, but inevitable. Behavior becomes less about force and more about flow. And motivation becomes less about trying harder and more about designing better.

When we stop blaming ourselves for lack of discipline and start examining the architecture of effort, we begin to see behavior in a new light. It becomes a conversation between the person and the environment, between intention and access. And in that conversation, friction is not failure. It is a signal: this needs adjustment. Not because you're broken, but because the conditions aren't yet aligned with who you're trying to become.

Rituals, Anchors, and the Self We Reinforce

Most people think of habits as things they do. But at a deeper level, habits are things they become. Each repeated behavior does more than fill a moment—it shapes the internal narrative of identity. The person who exercises before dawn isn't just building strength; they are reinforcing a self-image: someone who shows up for themselves. The person who takes a nightly walk after dinner isn't simply moving their body; they are embodying a rhythm, a closing ritual to the day, a psychological anchor. Over time, these patterns become more than behaviors. They become the threads that stitch together the story of who someone is.

Habits don't just arise from identity—they contribute to it. This idea is central to the work of narrative psychology, which explores how humans make sense of life through internal storytelling. People are meaning-makers by nature. They interpret experience through the lens of "What kind of person does this make me?" And the answer is often influenced more by repeated action than singular moments. While dramatic events shape memory, it is the quiet repetition of daily behaviors that constructs identity scaffolding. Who we believe we are is built not only through what we think, but through what we consistently do.

Rituals are habits with emotional weight. They carry intention, symbolism, or meaning beyond the task itself. A person might light a candle before journaling, not because it's necessary, but because it creates a threshold—a signal to the body and mind that something inward is about to begin. Rituals can be spiritual, personal, or entirely secular. What matters is that they stabilize time and identity. They punctuate experience. They help people feel a sense of continuity between the self they were yesterday and the one they are today.

The power of ritual lies in its anchoring function. In a world of distraction, overstimulation, and role switching, rituals become anchors to a stable self. They tether people to patterns of meaning and emotional coherence. The ritual of brewing tea, walking a dog, meditating, or even checking in with oneself before sleep creates a rhythm that settles the nervous system. These anchors are especially important during periods of change, loss, or ambiguity. When identity is in flux, rituals offer reassurance: some part of me is still intact.

But not all rituals are healthy, and not all anchors stabilize in helpful ways. People can also become anchored to patterns that reinforce negative self-concepts. The person who numbs with nightly drinking, isolates when stressed, or spirals into self-reproach after failure is also engaging in ritualized behavior. These too become identity-reinforcing. They send messages to the self about who one is, what one deserves, and how one copes. And with repetition, these messages take root.

The difficulty is that habits operate below conscious thought. They reinforce identity quietly, incrementally, and often without examination. This is why reflective practices are so crucial. The simple act of asking "What is this behavior telling me about who I am?" interrupts the loop. It makes the implicit explicit. And once conscious, habits can be evaluated: Are they aligned with who I want to be? Do they serve my values? Or are they relics of an old survival strategy I've outgrown?

A helpful lens for examining these questions is the distinction between identity-congruent and identity-incongruent behavior. Identity-congruent habits feel internally coherent. They align with values, aspirations, and self-concept. Identity-incongruent habits create friction. They feel like betrayals of self or reminders of failure. When someone engages in identity-congruent behavior—even if it's small—they tend to feel energized. When they repeat identity-incongruent behavior, even if it provides short-term relief, it often leaves behind shame, self-doubt, or regret.

Over time, people gravitate toward identity-congruent behavior because it feels like coming home to oneself. This is the psychological mechanism behind what researchers call "self-reinforcing loops." A person behaves in a way that feels authentic. That behavior affirms identity. The affirmed identity increases motivation to repeat the behavior. The cycle strengthens. This is how daily meditation turns into "I'm someone who takes care of my mind." How practicing gratitude becomes "I see myself as someone who reflects." It is not just the act but the story the act tells about the actor.

There is also an important cultural dimension to this. The environments people inhabit shape which habits are available, celebrated, or discouraged. A person surrounded by hustle culture may develop habits of constant productivity that reinforce an identity of worth through output. Another raised in a community that values emotional reserve may struggle to build habits of open expression. These dynamics are not neutral. They exert pressure, signal norms, and influence the palette of behaviors a person believes they are allowed to access.

Because of this, building new habits is often a process of unlearning. Not just unlearning old behaviors, but unlearning the identities they were attached to. The person recovering from perfectionism must unlearn the identity of the overachiever. The person healing from avoidance must unlearn the identity of being "bad at follow-through." This is not merely behavioral. It is existential. Letting go of an identity—however limiting—means stepping into uncertainty. The brain resists it. But with repetition, new anchors can take hold.

Anchoring rituals can be deliberately chosen and cultivated. A morning stretch, a three-minute breath after meetings, writing a sentence a day—these are not dramatic acts. But they accumulate. They create touchpoints with the self. Over time, they become part of one's lived narrative: "This is how I start my day," or "This is how I come back to myself." And these small rituals, once automatic, begin to radiate outward. They influence mood, behavior, even interpersonal patterns. In this way, habits become culture—not only of the self but of the spaces one moves through.

There is deep psychological power in asking: What are the rituals I already live by? Which ones do I want to preserve, and which ones do I want to rewrite? The answers are often surprising. People may find that their strongest habits are not the ones they consciously chose, but the ones they fell into—reactions to stress, modeled behaviors from childhood, shortcuts through emotional discomfort. Naming these rituals does not invalidate them. It simply restores choice.

Habits are rarely just about efficiency. They are about identity, meaning, and self-anchoring. In a fragmented world, rituals remind people who they are. They create coherence not through grand statements, but through daily repetition. They are the slow etching of selfhood into time. And in that slow carving, a person becomes someone they recognize.

Breaking, Rebuilding, and Reclaiming Agency

Every habit begins with a choice. But not every habit remains a choice. Over time, repeated actions become default patterns—hardwired responses that operate beneath conscious control. This is both the gift and the burden of habit: it allows for efficiency, but often at the expense of agency. The purpose of breaking and rebuilding habits is not just to change behavior. It is to reclaim authorship. To move from being shaped by one's routines to becoming the architect of them.

Breaking an entrenched habit requires more than resistance. Habits are not just actions—they are associations, reinforcements, and often emotional coping strategies. A person who wants to stop doom-scrolling at night may find that it is not the content they are addicted to, but the feeling of escape, of delay, of numbing the stress of the day. To disrupt the behavior, they must understand what it is accomplishing beneath the surface. What is the need being met? What is the discomfort being avoided? Until those questions are answered, behavior change will feel like deprivation rather than redesign.

The first step in reclaiming agency is awareness. This includes both pattern recognition and emotional context. What time of day does the habit occur? What precedes it? What emotions are typically present? Simply tracking behavior for a few days can illuminate loops that felt invisible. The act of noticing is not passive. It is an intervention in itself. By naming the loop, the person begins to loosen its grip. And by observing without judgment, they make space for curiosity, which is essential to lasting change.

Once a habit loop is identified, the next step is to create intentional friction. This involves placing barriers between the cue and the routine. If late-night snacking is the issue, moving snacks out of immediate reach, brushing teeth earlier, or creating a "kitchen closed" ritual can add just enough resistance to create a pause. That pause is critical. It reintroduces the possibility of decision. It gives the person a moment to ask, "Do I want this? Or am I simply following a script?"

But friction alone is not enough. Habits are not broken in a vacuum. They must be replaced. This is where the concept of substitution becomes central. The goal is to meet the same emotional or psychological need through a different, more aligned behavior. If the old habit soothed anxiety, the new one must also offer calm. If the old habit provided stimulation, the new one must also engage. Substitution honors the function of the original behavior, even as it transforms its form.

For example, someone trying to reduce alcohol use may not succeed by removing alcohol alone. They must build rituals that replicate the emotional rhythm: a special glass with a non-alcoholic beverage, a moment of decompression, a sensory cue. The nervous system responds not only to substance but to ritual. By preserving the ritual while changing the content, the person signals safety to the body. It says: You are still held, just in a new way.

This is also why timing matters. Behavior change is more effective during periods of transition—times when routines are already in flux. Moving to a new city, starting a new job, or even returning from vacation can offer windows where the brain is more flexible. These liminal moments are prime for redesign. Because the usual cues are disrupted, the loops are more malleable. The person can seize that instability to install new patterns before the old ones reassert themselves.

But even in stable environments, change is possible with the right scaffolding. One powerful tool is the use of keystone habits—habits that initiate cascading effects across multiple areas of life. Exercise is a common keystone habit. People who begin to move regularly often report better sleep, improved mood, more disciplined eating, and even greater patience. The key is that the habit creates a shift in identity: "I am someone who takes care of myself." That shift increases motivation, coherence, and behavioral follow-through.

Rebuilding habits also requires emotional regulation. Change brings friction—not just practical, but psychological. There is loss involved: loss of comfort, familiarity, and sometimes even social connection. A person who stops engaging in gossip may find themselves excluded from social circles. A person who wakes early to write may miss out on late-night socializing. These losses are real, and they must be acknowledged. Pretending that change is only gain ignores the emotional complexity of transformation.

Ambivalence is normal. Most people want to change and not change at the same time. They want to be healthier without giving up comfort foods. They want to be more present without reducing stimulation. This tension is not a flaw in character—it is a reflection of competing values. Motivational interviewing, a therapeutic approach to resolving ambivalence, teaches that people move toward change when they feel heard, not coerced. Applying this to oneself means holding space for both sides: the part that resists and the part that desires. Both have reasons. And both deserve a seat at the table.

Another useful framework is the use of "if-then" planning. This involves identifying potential obstacles and pre-planning a response. For example: "If I feel the urge to scroll TikTok before bed, then I will open my sleep app instead." This strategy increases psychological preparedness. It transforms moments of vulnerability into opportunities for redirection. Over time, the brain begins to automate the new response. What began as a deliberate intervention becomes part of the default.

Support also matters. While habit formation is personal, it is rarely solitary. Sharing goals, enlisting accountability partners, or even joining communities aligned with desired habits can dramatically increase adherence. Social connection creates reinforcement. It makes new behaviors feel less isolated and more meaningful. It also provides mirrors: others who reflect back the kind of person one is becoming.

The final phase of habit change is integration. This is when the new behavior is no longer something the person is trying to do—it is something they are. It feels natural, inevitable, almost obvious. This is not to say it is effortless. Habits still require maintenance, especially under stress. But the person now has tools, awareness, and a narrative. They see themselves not as someone who breaks habits, but as someone who rebuilds them with care and agency.

Agency, in this context, is not control. It is ownership. It is the ability to respond with intention rather than react with inertia. It is the quiet dignity of choosing again, even after lapses. It is the refusal to let old loops dictate the future. And it is the deep knowing that every new pattern is not just a change in behavior, but a vote for the kind of life one is willing to live.

When habits become conscious, they become flexible. When behavior aligns with values, it becomes meaningful. And when action reflects identity, it becomes sustainable. This is the psychology of habit not as productivity, but as authorship. It is how people reclaim the pen from their patterns and begin, again, to write themselves forward.

* * *

14

Self-Control and Discipline

The ability to say no—to pause, hold back, or wait—is one of the clearest indicators of psychological maturity. It appears in childhood when a toddler learns to resist a tantrum, and again in adulthood when someone walks away from an argument, a temptation, or a self-defeating pattern. The capacity for self-control is rarely celebrated with fanfare. It unfolds quietly, in the spaces between impulse and action, between desire and decision. And yet, in those spaces, the foundation for long-term stability, achievement, and moral coherence is laid.

Self-control has often been mischaracterized as a simple matter of willpower, as if grit alone could hold the human psyche together in the face of conflicting urges and internal chaos. But restraint is not born from force. It is born from integration. True discipline is not the suppression of desire but the capacity to prioritize one value over another without losing touch with either. It is not the denial of emotion but the ability to act with intention even when emotion surges. At its highest form, it becomes the expression of character: a reflection of internal alignment rather than external compliance.

To understand discipline, we have to begin with biology. The human brain evolved to prioritize immediate rewards because, for much of evolutionary history, survival depended on it. Scarcity, danger, and unpredictability made it advantageous to seize what was available, to act before thinking, to gratify rather than delay. The prefrontal cortex—the region responsible for foresight, planning, and impulse regulation—is a relatively recent addition in evolutionary terms. It is also one of the last areas of the brain to mature in individual development. This means that restraint is not a default—it is a capacity that must be developed and supported.

But biology only sets the stage. Whether a person develops self-control depends just as much on their environment. A child raised in chaos, unpredictability, or neglect is less likely to learn that waiting pays off. If rewards are inconsistent, or if promises are routinely broken, the brain internalizes a lesson: act now or lose your chance. What appears to others as impulsivity may be, in fact, a form of adaptation—a learned distrust in the future. Conversely, in environments where stability, consistency, and responsiveness are present, self-regulation becomes more likely. Discipline grows best in conditions of psychological safety.

Still, no matter how favorable the early context, discipline requires continual reinforcement. Adult life presents endless opportunities for avoidance, indulgence, and reactivity. To remain oriented toward long-term goals, people must actively cultivate habits, environments, and belief systems that make restraint sustainable. This is why systems matter. The most successful forms of discipline are not heroic acts of denial. They are well-structured lives—designed to minimize unnecessary decisions, reduce exposure to temptation, and anchor people in values that are stronger than their moods.

Self-control is not a monolith. It shows up differently across contexts. For some, it means resisting the urge to procrastinate. For others, it means walking away from toxic relationships, refusing to retaliate, or holding a boundary that costs something emotionally. In each case, discipline is not merely behavioral—it is symbolic. It tells the self something about who they are, what they believe, and how much power they have over their own trajectory. People who possess strong self-regulation tend to feel more agentic, more capable of navigating life without being pulled off course by every inner wave.

That said, the conversation around discipline has often been distorted. Cultural narratives frequently turn restraint into a performance—proof of toughness, superiority, or moral purity. In this view, the disciplined person is someone who suffers visibly, who pushes through pain and emerges with pride. But this glorification of suffering often masks emotional rigidity, self-denial, and disconnection from pleasure. True discipline does not require martyrdom. It requires discernment. It is not the ability to endure anything, but the wisdom to know what is worth enduring—and what is not.

This is especially important in a culture saturated with immediate gratification. Digital media, fast consumption, and algorithmic feedback loops create an environment where pleasure is always one click away. In such a context, discipline becomes more than a private virtue; it becomes a psychological defense against overstimulation and erosion of attention. The modern world does not merely tempt people with indulgence. It conditions them to expect it. And in doing so, it chips away at the mental muscles needed to tolerate discomfort, sustain focus, and choose long-term meaning over short-term relief.

But discipline cannot be separated from meaning. Without a larger story—one that gives context to the sacrifices being made—restraint becomes brittle. People can grind themselves into disciplined shapes and still feel hollow if the effort is not connected to purpose. This is why some of the most disciplined individuals are also the most emotionally grounded. Their restraint is not a rejection of pleasure. It is a commitment to something greater. It is rooted in clarity, not compulsion. And it reflects an inner structure that can withstand stress without collapsing into chaos or avoidance.

The psychology of self-control, then, is not simply about saying no. It is about building a life in which one can say yes with integrity. It is about constructing routines that protect mental bandwidth, boundaries that preserve dignity, and practices that strengthen the bridge between intention and action. It is not discipline for its own sake, but discipline in service of a life that feels coherent, principled, and self-authored.

This chapter will explore how that life is built—from the early foundations of regulation and trust, to the behavioral systems that support disciplined living, to the deeper character traits that emerge through consistent alignment with one's values. It will also examine the role of future thinking, delayed gratification, and the emotional scaffolding that allows restraint to feel like freedom rather than restriction.

The Foundations of Restraint

Self-control is often presented as a moral trait, something a person either possesses or lacks. But psychological research suggests that restraint is not a fixed characteristic. It is a developmental process, one that depends on both biology and environment, on neurological maturation and relational trust. Before it becomes a character strength or a behavioral strategy, self-control must be learned. And for most people, the earliest lessons begin not with punishment or praise, but with pattern recognition and emotional containment.

In childhood, the first glimpses of self-regulation emerge in infancy. A baby cries, then quiets when picked up. Over time, that same baby begins to anticipate comfort, understanding that discomfort will not last forever. This shift, subtle but foundational, forms the bedrock of trust: the belief that needs will be met, and that waiting is not the same as abandonment. Without that foundational trust, restraint often calcifies into fear or control rather than true patience. With it, the child begins to internalize the possibility of delay without panic.

One of the most well-known studies on restraint is the "Marshmallow Test," conducted by Walter Mischel in the 1960s and 70s. In it, children were given a choice: eat one marshmallow now, or wait and receive two later. The experiment seemed simple, but what it revealed was not merely about preference. It was about future orientation, emotional regulation, and symbolic thought. Children who were able to wait often employed creative strategies: turning away, singing to themselves, imagining the marshmallow as something else. These strategies reflected more than willpower. They reflected executive function, imaginative flexibility, and cognitive self-soothing.

The original findings suggested that those who could delay gratification were more likely to have positive life outcomes—better academic performance, healthier relationships, and more stable careers. But later studies added important nuance. The capacity to wait was not just a matter of internal strength. It was deeply influenced by the environment. Children from unstable or unpredictable homes were less likely to wait—not because they were impulsive, but because their experience had taught them not to trust that rewards would come. In other words, their behavior was not deficient. It was adaptive.

This understanding complicates simplistic narratives about discipline. A person who struggles with self-restraint may not be lacking character. They may be operating from a worldview shaped by inconsistency, scarcity, or betrayal. If you have learned that people do not keep their promises, that food may not be there tomorrow, or that emotional needs will be dismissed, waiting becomes irrational. This insight reframes discipline as something that must be supported, not demanded. It also highlights the importance of attachment: people develop self-control in the context of reliable relationships.

As children grow, the ability to regulate impulses becomes more nuanced. It expands from physical restraint—such as waiting to open a gift or refraining from hitting—to cognitive control, such as holding a thought in working memory, resisting distraction, or shifting attention voluntarily. These skills are governed by the prefrontal cortex, which continues to mature into early adulthood. This is why adolescents often show dramatic swings in self-control: their emotional systems are fully online, but the cognitive systems that regulate them are still catching up. What looks like recklessness is often neurological imbalance, not a moral failure.

This developmental timeline has real consequences. It means that restraint must be taught, modeled, and reinforced consistently through childhood and adolescence. Punishment alone does not produce discipline. In fact, harsh or inconsistent punishment often backfires, creating anxiety or defiance rather than internal regulation. Children learn restraint not just by being told to control themselves, but by observing adults who manage their own emotions, delay their own gratification, and create structured environments that support intentional behavior.

One of the most effective ways to build self-control in children is through routines. Predictable schedules, clear expectations, and consistent consequences reduce the cognitive load of decision-making. They create an external structure that the child can internalize over time. Rather than relying on moment-to-moment willpower, the child learns to operate within rhythms. These rhythms become behavioral templates, guiding action even in the absence of immediate supervision.

Language also plays a key role. Teaching children to name their emotions, to use words like "frustrated" or "tempted" or "overwhelmed," expands their capacity for regulation. When a child can say, "I'm mad and I want to hit," they are already creating space between impulse and action. They are moving from reactive behavior to reflective processing. Over time, this verbalization builds a bridge between emotion and executive function—a bridge that becomes sturdier with each use.

But restraint is not only a childhood task. In adulthood, the stakes of self-control become more complex. The impulses may be subtler—reaching for a phone during a conversation, interrupting someone mid-sentence, spending impulsively after a hard day. But the core dynamic remains: there is a moment when desire pulls one way, and something deeper must intervene. That something is rarely brute force. It is often a form of inner reasoning: a remembered value, a goal, a mental image of the future.

To support this kind of reasoning, adults must also cultivate environments that reinforce restraint. This might include limiting exposure to triggering stimuli, creating systems for accountability, or surrounding themselves with people who model the kind of control they wish to embody. As in childhood, discipline grows in context. Even high-functioning adults are more successful in regulating behavior when their surroundings support that regulation. It is not weakness to design a life that minimizes temptation. It is wisdom.

Emotion plays a complex role in self-control. While some emotions—like fear or guilt—can temporarily increase restraint, sustainable self-discipline is more closely linked to emotional clarity and regulation. A person who can tolerate anxiety without reacting, who can sit with frustration without escape, who can acknowledge desire without acting on it—this person possesses the emotional maturity that makes restraint feel like a choice rather than a punishment. Emotional regulation, then, is not separate from self-control. It is its foundation.

At its core, restraint is the capacity to remain anchored in a chosen value while navigating the pull of competing impulses. It is the ability to act with coherence over time, even when the immediate moment offers an easier out. This is not a trait one either has or lacks. It is a skill, a structure, a process. And it can be built—again and again—through the practices, relationships, and decisions that shape a life.

Beyond Willpower: The Systems That Support Discipline

The idea that discipline comes down to willpower is deeply rooted in popular culture. Movies, motivational speeches, and self-help literature often frame personal transformation as a dramatic battle between weakness and resolve, between indulgence and grit. In these stories, the person who succeeds is the one who tries harder, who fights through temptation with sheer force of will. But the psychological evidence tells a different story. The most disciplined people are not fighting harder—they're designing better.

Willpower is a limited resource. Like attention or working memory, it can be depleted. In fact, research on decision fatigue shows that the more decisions people have to make throughout the day, the more their capacity to regulate themselves weakens. By the evening, a person who has made hundreds of micro-decisions may be significantly less able to resist temptation. This is why people often eat junk food at night, or scroll for hours instead of sleeping. Their cognitive resources are exhausted.

The implication is clear: if you rely on willpower to maintain discipline, you will lose. Not every time, but often enough that your self-concept begins to erode. You start to think you're weak, lazy, or undisciplined, when in fact you're simply human. To build real discipline, the solution is not to fight temptation at full strength, but to reduce the number of times you need to fight at all.

Systems thinking offers a path forward. Systems are structures, routines, and environments designed to make desired behavior easier and undesired behavior harder. A person who keeps a clutter-free home doesn't spend their day resisting the urge to leave messes—they've developed systems that make tidiness automatic. A writer who produces consistently doesn't spend hours conquering resistance—they've created habits, tools, and rituals that support flow. Discipline becomes sustainable when the systems do most of the heavy lifting.

One powerful system is habit automation. When a behavior becomes habitual, it no longer requires conscious effort. Brushing your teeth, locking your door, tying your shoes—these actions happen without negotiation. The same principle can be applied to goals that require discipline. A person who wakes up at the same time every day to exercise will, over time, find that the behavior becomes expected. The friction decreases. The cognitive load disappears. The discipline has moved from conscious choice to unconscious rhythm.

But habit alone is not enough. The surrounding environment must also be optimized. Environments can either cue unwanted behavior or support restraint. Consider the person who wants to eat more healthfully. If their home is filled with processed snacks, every moment becomes a test of willpower. If, instead, their kitchen is stocked with nourishing options and the snacks are not visible—or better, not present—their environment reduces the need for constant regulation.

The same logic applies to digital environments. A person trying to reduce screen time will struggle if their phone is always within reach, notifications are constantly pinging, and apps are optimized for endless scrolling. By removing triggering apps, turning off notifications, or placing the phone out of reach during focused work time, they make discipline easier. What looks like strength from the outside is often good design on the inside.

Time management is another key system. People are more likely to act with discipline when their days have structure. This doesn't mean rigid schedules, but rather intentional planning. When tasks are assigned to specific blocks of time, there is less space for procrastination. When breaks and rest are built in, there is less need for escapism. A disorganized day invites impulsivity. A structured day supports intentionality.

Accountability systems are equally powerful. While self-discipline is an internal process, it is often strengthened by external scaffolding. This can take the form of goal tracking, public commitments, or even social contracts. A person trying to maintain sobriety may find strength in a recovery group. A person writing a book may stay consistent by checking in with a writing partner. When behavior is witnessed, it gains weight. When it is mirrored by others, it gains meaning.

One of the most underestimated aspects of discipline is environment design. James Clear, in his book *Atomic Habits*, emphasizes the idea that behavior is often the product of one's surroundings. If you want to drink more water, keep a water bottle visible. If you want to read more books, keep one near your bed. If you want to stop staying up late, install lights that dim in the evening. People often assume they need to change their mindset, but sometimes what they need is to change the room.

Of course, not all environments are within one's control. A person working three jobs or living in a chaotic household cannot simply design their way into discipline. This is why compassion matters. Discipline is easier for those whose environments support it. The rest must work harder—and often feel worse for failing. Understanding this doesn't mean abandoning responsibility; it means acknowledging context. It means helping people build what they can, where they are, with what they have.

Another layer to systems thinking is energy management. People assume discipline is about time, but it is more accurately about energy. If your body is under-slept, underfed, or overstimulated, your ability to regulate impulses drops sharply. This is why one of the best "discipline hacks" is simply to protect your physiological baseline. Sleep, nutrition, movement, and rest are not luxuries. They are prerequisites for restraint. When the body is depleted, the mind has less to work with.

Internal systems matter too. These include scripts, affirmations, and decision frameworks. For example, a person may develop a rule that they never argue online after 9pm. Or that they don't open email before finishing their most important task. These rules reduce ambiguity, which in turn reduces emotional strain. When you already know what to do in a given situation, you save yourself the exhaustion of deciding.

But perhaps the most essential internal system is self-trust. People are more likely to act with discipline when they believe their actions matter. If you think your efforts are futile, if you think the goal is unreachable, or if you think you'll sabotage yourself eventually anyway, discipline becomes brittle. Every setback feels like confirmation of failure. By contrast, when people feel that their behavior is aligned with a meaningful goal—and that their future self is worth investing in—they are far more likely to act with integrity over time.

This is why discipline cannot be reduced to behavior alone. It is not just about the act of restraint. It is about what that act represents. A vote for a future self. A signal to the psyche that one's choices have weight. When that meaning is supported by good systems—external and internal—discipline becomes less a matter of constant struggle and more a matter of quiet structure.

In the end, the most disciplined people are not always the strongest. They are often the most prepared. They've built systems that support their values, reduce unnecessary decisions, and protect their energy. They've learned to stop relying on willpower alone—and in doing so, they've built lives that work for them, not against them.

Character in Practice: Integrity, Boundaries, and Moral Restraint

Discipline is often framed as a skill, a tool to achieve goals or maintain focus, but it is also a reflection of character. Beyond impulse control and delayed gratification, discipline intersects with morality, identity, and self-respect. The person who chooses not to retaliate when provoked, who honors a commitment in private with no recognition, who tells the truth when lying would be easier, is practicing discipline of a different kind. This is not merely behavioral regulation. It is the expression of internal values through consistent action, especially when no one is watching.

To understand how restraint becomes character, we must first distinguish between compliance and integrity. Compliance is the act of following rules, often in response to authority or fear of consequence. Integrity is the act of aligning behavior with values, even when disobedience would be safer or easier. Children may comply with rules to avoid punishment. Adults with character act out of coherence with who they believe themselves to be. In this way, character-based discipline emerges not from fear, but from a clear internal compass.

That compass is shaped by many forces: early moral instruction, cultural values, relational models, and personal experiences. But at its core, it depends on the ability to hold competing values without collapse. The person who values honesty must sometimes hold that value against the desire to protect someone's feelings. The person who values kindness must weigh it against justice. Discipline, when grounded in character, is the ability to navigate these tensions without betraying one's deeper commitments.

This does not mean rigid perfectionism. In fact, the healthiest forms of moral restraint come from a flexible yet principled core. People who are overly rule-bound often struggle with moral nuance. They may obey laws or codes without understanding the spirit behind them. True character involves discernment. It asks not only "What should I do?" but "Why?"

and "What will this choice say about who I am becoming?" In this way, discipline becomes a developmental process—not of obedience, but of identity formation.

Psychologist Lawrence Kohlberg proposed a model of moral development with six stages, ranging from obedience to avoid punishment (Stage 1) to principled conscience driven by universal ethical principles (Stage 6). Most people, he argued, plateau in the middle stages, where they act morally to gain approval or maintain social order. Higher stages, marked by internalized ethics, are rare—but they are also where discipline becomes most authentic. At that level, people restrain themselves not to be seen as good, but to remain in alignment with a self they respect.

Boundaries are another form of moral discipline. To set a boundary is to restrain one's own behavior and to assert limits on what one will tolerate from others. This is a particularly complex form of self-regulation, because it often involves both discomfort and confrontation. It is far easier to give in, keep quiet, or adjust oneself to avoid tension. But people who maintain clear boundaries demonstrate a discipline of self-worth. They act not from control, but from clarity. They know what they are responsible for—and what they are not.

In relational contexts, boundary discipline shows up in many ways. A person may resist the urge to check their partner's phone, even when they feel insecure, because they value trust more than temporary relief. A parent may allow their child to experience the natural consequences of a decision, even though rescuing would be emotionally easier, because they value responsibility over comfort. These moments reveal how discipline extends beyond personal goals and into the moral fabric of relationships.

This kind of restraint can be emotionally taxing. It asks people to sit with discomfort, to delay gratification not for future rewards, but for moral congruence. This is especially true when the benefits of disciplined action are invisible or misunderstood. Someone who walks away from a toxic dynamic may be seen as cold. Someone who holds a boundary may be called difficult. Someone who refuses to betray a confidence may suffer loss. In these cases, the reward for discipline is internal: a sense of integrity that may be hard-won and privately held.

But this kind of moral restraint also builds something essential: self-trust. When people act in alignment with their values, even in hard moments, they reinforce the belief that they can count on themselves. They become less dependent on external validation. Their worth becomes less fragile, their decisions more grounded. Over time, this deepens both their sense of agency and their relational capacity. Others begin to feel that they are trustworthy not because they are agreeable, but because they are consistent.

There is a quiet strength in someone who knows their limits and upholds them without drama. Who says no when yes would be easier. Who stays when it matters and leaves when it's time. Who acts from principle rather than pressure. This is the kind of discipline that does not announce itself. It does not seek applause. But its effects ripple outward—into relationships, into communities, into the culture. It changes what people expect from one another. It raises the standard for what is possible when restraint is rooted in care.

Of course, character-based discipline is not always rewarded. In some environments, it may be punished. Whistleblowers are often ostracized. People who resist corrupt systems may be cast out. Children who challenge unjust authority may be labeled defiant. In such cases, discipline takes courage. It becomes an act of moral resistance, not compliance. And it often requires a support system—a community, a mentor, a belief system—that reinforces the value of doing what is right, even when it costs something.

For this reason, moral restraint often flourishes in community. Not because people are trying to impress each other, but because they share values that reinforce and reflect their aspirations. When restraint is mirrored by others, it becomes easier to sustain. When it is normalized, it becomes less lonely. This is why cultures, families, and institutions have such a powerful influence on discipline. They either support it—or sabotage it. And when they do the latter, even the most principled individuals can falter under the weight of contradiction.

Yet there is something enduring about character. It persists even when circumstances do not reward it. It reasserts itself after failure. It invites people back to their values even after missteps. The person who betrays themselves is not ruined—they are called. Back to integrity. Back to boundaries. Back to the quiet, steady practice of being who they say they are.

Discipline, when practiced in this way, is not about restriction. It is about coherence. A life of character is not one of constant struggle against impulse, but of frequent alignment between value and behavior. It does not require perfection. It requires honesty. The person who can admit failure without excuse, who can recommit without self-punishment, is not weak. They are strong enough to face themselves—and to begin again.

In the end, discipline grounded in character is not something others can measure. It is an inner posture, a way of moving through the world with clarity and care. It is revealed in how a person handles temptation, power, provocation, and loss. It is tested in silence. Affirmed in solitude. And cultivated in the small, private decisions that shape the architecture of a life.

Future-Oriented Thinking and the Delay of Gratification

Delaying gratification is not a matter of simply saying no. It is a capacity rooted in time. To delay gratification, a person must believe in a future that is worth waiting for. They must be able to imagine themselves in that future, feel connected to the consequences of their actions, and trust that what they resist now will bring something better later. Without that psychological infrastructure, restraint collapses under the weight of immediacy. When the future feels unreal, discipline feels irrelevant.

This is where future-oriented thinking becomes essential. It is the cognitive ability to simulate outcomes, to project oneself forward in time, and to make current choices based on distant rewards. This ability is not equally developed in all people. It grows with age, social learning, and a stable emotional environment. It also depends on neurological development, particularly in the prefrontal cortex, which governs planning, foresight, and regulation. People who have stronger future-orientation tend to be better at budgeting, health maintenance, long-term planning, and resisting impulsive behavior. But this isn't just about cognition—it's also emotional.

To delay gratification, a person must be able to tolerate the emotional discomfort that comes with postponement. That discomfort may take many forms: boredom, frustration, restlessness, anxiety, longing. Discipline requires not just the mental ability to see the long-term benefit, but the emotional endurance to stay grounded while that benefit is still out of reach. For many people, this is the true difficulty. The reward is too abstract. The discomfort is too immediate. In that gap, the present wins.

This is why emotionally driven behaviors—such as compulsive spending, overeating, substance use, or doom-scrolling—are so difficult to interrupt. They offer immediate relief. They create a sense of control in the now. And when the future feels uncertain, those short-term comforts often seem like the only guaranteed pleasure. Discipline in these contexts requires more than willpower. It requires a reason to believe that the discomfort of waiting will be worth it.

Meaning plays a crucial role here. The ability to delay gratification is strengthened when the future is tied to something meaningful. A student may study for hours because they envision a life of purpose on the other side of a degree. A parent may resist an impulse to lash out because they want to be the kind of role model their child can count on. A recovering alcoholic may pass a drink not because they are repressing desire, but because they are protecting a future self they are learning to value. These are not acts of repression. They are acts of commitment.

In this light, future-oriented discipline becomes an identity act. The person is not just resisting an urge. They are affirming who they are—or who they hope to become. This shift is powerful because it reframes restraint from deprivation to alignment. Instead of seeing discipline as saying no to pleasure, the person sees it as saying yes to integrity, to growth, to a future self they respect.

There are tools that can strengthen this future connection. Visualization exercises, journaling, and long-term goal tracking can help make the distant feel closer. Concrete reminders—photos, calendar events, visible goals—can make abstract futures more tangible. Even simple questions like "Will this matter in a week?" or "What would future-me want right now?" can disrupt the pull of impulse and insert a moment of perspective.

But it's not always enough. For many people, the future is not simply distant—it is unstable. Those who have experienced trauma, economic instability, or systemic discrimination often develop a compressed time horizon. This is not a failure of imagination; it is a survival adaptation. When tomorrow has historically brought chaos or disappointment, investing in the long-term feels foolish. The logical choice becomes seeking safety and comfort now, before the opportunity disappears.

This is why shaming people for their "lack of discipline" often misses the mark. It fails to account for the psychological cost of hope. To delay gratification, a person must believe that their efforts will be honored by time. If they have no reason to believe that, their choice to act on impulse is not a weakness—it is a way of managing existential uncertainty. Discipline cannot be demanded from people who have never been shown that restraint leads somewhere safe.

Support systems are essential here. People who have mentors, communities, or role models that embody long-term investment are more likely to mirror that capacity. This is especially true for young people. Adolescents who see adults setting goals, maintaining boundaries, and honoring commitments develop a template for what disciplined living looks like. They begin to internalize the idea that the future is real, and that their actions matter.

Narrative also matters. People need a story about who they are becoming. A future-oriented self is not just an image—it is a plotline. And discipline is what moves that story forward. Without narrative continuity, people become unmoored. Their choices lose context. Their sacrifices feel pointless. To delay gratification, a person must be able to say, "This is part of something bigger." That bigger thing might be family, career, service, faith, or simply personal growth—but it must exist. Without it, restraint becomes empty.

This connection between narrative and discipline is especially apparent in recovery communities. People who stay sober long-term often describe their journey not in terms of resisting temptation, but in terms of reclaiming a life story. They see themselves as participants in a redemptive arc. They are becoming someone they were always meant to be. Their discipline is not about deprivation; it is about choosing coherence over collapse.

The most effective forms of discipline, then, are those rooted in meaning, connection, and future vision. They do not rely solely on suppression. They depend on clarity. The person who sees where they're going, who feels the future as something alive and real, is far more capable of regulating the present. This doesn't mean the struggle disappears—but it becomes bearable. The tension between now and later becomes a space of purpose, not punishment.

Finally, it's important to recognize that delayed gratification is not always virtuous. Sometimes the right choice is immediate. Sometimes joy should not be postponed. Sometimes restraint is misused to avoid vulnerability or spontaneity. Discipline becomes dysfunctional when it is used to suppress emotion, avoid intimacy, or maintain control at the cost of vitality. The goal is not to delay everything. It is to delay the right things, for the right reasons, at the right time.

This is where maturity comes in. A mature person can distinguish between the impulse that needs to be paused and the joy that deserves to be seized. They can tell when the future is calling, and when the present is already enough. Their discipline is not rigid—it is responsive. It adapts to context. It honors complexity. And it serves a life that is not only productive, but meaningful.

Discipline, in its most evolved form, is not about denying life. It is about choosing the shape of a life over time. It is the quiet, consistent act of becoming. Not in defiance of desire, but in service of a future self who is worth every patient step.

* * *

15

Change That Lasts

Change is seductive. It promises relief, redemption, renewal. From New Year's resolutions to spiritual awakenings, from therapy breakthroughs to viral self-help mantras, people are drawn to the idea that transformation is possible—that something profound and irreversible might happen, allowing them to become who they were always meant to be. But change, real change, rarely looks or feels like that. It is not always inspiring. It is not often glamorous. And it almost never happens the way stories tell it.

If psychology has made one thing clear, it is this: transformation is not an event. It is a process. The idea that people can change overnight, through insight or crisis or motivation alone, has a certain emotional appeal. It flatters the imagination. But it also sets people up for disillusionment. When the moment passes and nothing is different, when the inspiration fades and the old habits return, people blame themselves. They assume the change failed because they weren't strong enough or serious enough. In truth, the model they were given was flawed from the start.

Lasting change is slow because it moves through multiple layers of the self: thought, emotion, habit, environment, and identity. It does not move cleanly from intention to outcome. It meanders. It pauses. It regresses. It often becomes invisible just when it is working most deeply. This frustrates the modern mind, conditioned by productivity culture and instant feedback. But it reflects the nature of psychological development. People do not merely adopt new behaviors—they unlearn old ones, integrate new frameworks, and reorganize their sense of who they are.

This is why transformation cannot be forced through willpower alone. The individual might be ready, but the conditions must also allow for movement. A person cannot become someone new while embedded in an environment that only recognizes the old version of them. A child cannot thrive in a classroom that labels them broken. A spouse cannot heal in a marriage that punishes vulnerability. Change must be reinforced, mirrored, and given space. It is an ecological phenomenon, not a private one.

It is also cyclical. Behavioral psychologists have long noted that change tends to follow stages: precontemplation, contemplation, preparation, action, and maintenance. Most people cycle through these stages many times before lasting change takes root. They may prepare to change, act on it, relapse, reflect, and start again. This is not a sign of failure. It is the rhythm of adaptation. The key is not avoiding regression, but expecting it and using it.

Insight plays a role, but not always the role people assume. A powerful realization can initiate change, but it cannot complete it. Knowing why a behavior exists does not eliminate the pattern. Emotional breakthroughs may create new awareness, but that awareness must be embedded into daily decisions. A person who understands that their anger is rooted in childhood fear must still learn how to respond differently the next time they feel threatened. Insight opens the door, but repetition walks through it.

Equally important is emotional regulation. Change requires discomfort: disrupting routines, facing uncertainty, tolerating awkwardness. People who expect change to feel good are often surprised by how destabilizing it is. The nervous system does not distinguish between good and bad unfamiliar—it simply reacts to difference. As a result, people may sabotage growth not because they don't want it, but because their bodies have not yet learned to feel safe within it. This is why trauma-informed approaches to change emphasize safety, pacing, and embodiment—not just mindset.

The role of identity cannot be overstated. People struggle to maintain new behaviors when those behaviors conflict with their self-concept. A person who sees themselves as unreliable will unconsciously disrupt routines that prove otherwise. A person who believes they are inherently broken may reject experiences of progress because they contradict the core narrative. Until the identity is updated, the behavior will remain fragile. Change becomes stable when the person says, "This is who I am now"—and believes it.

There is also a paradox at the heart of transformation: it requires both acceptance and effort. People must accept where they are, without denial or shame, and still work toward something different. If they skip acceptance, they build on self-rejection. If they skip effort, they mistake self-love for passivity. True change honors both truths. It says, "I am enough as I am"—and also, "I am capable of more." This tension—between compassion and responsibility—is where most sustainable growth begins.

Cultural narratives often obscure this complexity. They celebrate radical reinvention, glorify the before-and-after, and spotlight the individual hero. But real transformation is quieter. It happens in the repetition of hard conversations, the steady decline of self-destructive coping, the invisible work of waking up one morning and doing the right thing again. It is not the single moment of resolve, but the accumulation of moments that follow. Most of them unremarkable. Most of them unnoticed.

This chapter aims to dismantle the fantasy of sudden change and replace it with a grounded, psychologically rich understanding of how transformation really unfolds. We will explore the myths that keep people stuck in loops of disappointment. We will examine why identity, environment, and structure matter more than emotional motivation. And we will affirm that lasting change is not a matter of personality strength or willpower. It is a matter of alignment: between belief, behavior, and the systems that hold them in place.

There is no magic formula, but there is a map. Not everyone will follow it in the same order or at the same pace, but the terrain is familiar: insight, resistance, practice, setback, recalibration, endurance. Through this process, the old self is not destroyed, it is restructured. The scars remain. The flaws are not erased. But something new takes form: a self that is more integrated, more congruent, and more trustworthy to live within.

If transformation sounds slower, messier, and more ordinary than you hoped, that's because it is. But it's also more durable. And ultimately, more human.

The Myth of the Turning Point

Stories of transformation are often told through the lens of a single moment: the rock bottom, the wake-up call, the flash of clarity that changes everything. These moments are emotionally powerful because they satisfy a deep cultural longing—the desire for immediate, redemptive change. They suggest that if we just suffer enough, or realize enough, or try hard enough, everything can be different by morning. But the truth is more complicated. Transformation does not hinge on moments. It hinges on systems. Lasting change is not born in a turning point; it is forged in repetition, structure, and gradual reconfiguration of self and behavior.

Psychology, particularly in its clinical and developmental branches, consistently finds that the mechanisms of change are cumulative. The human brain is wired for plasticity, but it rewires slowly, through experience and consistency. A single decision can feel pivotal—and often is the catalyst—but it is rarely sufficient. For example, a person may decide to leave a toxic relationship, and that decision may feel monumental. But what follows is a series of smaller, more difficult decisions: how to resist returning, how to rebuild self-worth, how to navigate loneliness without numbing, how to create new boundaries. The change is not the leaving—it is the living that follows.

What we often call a turning point is better understood as a threshold: the moment when a person becomes psychologically available for change. This might be triggered by crisis, loss, shame, love, exhaustion, or even sudden insight. But the threshold is just the opening. Whether someone steps through—and stays on the other side—depends on the scaffolding available. That scaffolding includes behavioral routines, social supports, emotional skills, environmental reinforcements, and above all, a reason to continue that is stronger than the impulse to return.

People return to what is familiar, even when it hurts, because familiarity provides predictability—and predictability feels like safety to the nervous system. Neuroscientific studies on habit formation and addiction have demonstrated that behavioral loops are reinforced not just by dopamine or pleasure but by relief from uncertainty. To break a loop, the alternative behavior must offer more than just theoretical value; it must offer real, embodied relief. This is one reason why insight alone fails so often. Knowing something is harmful is not enough. It must also feel safer to stop than to continue—and that safety takes time to build.

The allure of the turning point also stems from how we remember and narrate our lives. Memory compresses complexity. People tend to anchor their personal stories in moments that felt emotionally intense or symbolically important. Someone might say, "Everything changed when I had that conversation," or "The day I got that diagnosis was the day I decided to live differently." But that's the retrospective story. In the moment, things were usually murkier. There was doubt. There were hesitations. There were partial commitments. What looks like a clean break in hindsight was, more often than not, a slow unraveling followed by gradual reconstruction.

Cultural narratives reinforce this distortion. Films, memoirs, and self-help genres often hinge on scenes of dramatic change. The protagonist has a revelation, takes a risk, or suffers a loss—and from that point forward, the trajectory is clear. This is compelling storytelling, but poor psychology. In real life, change often looks like contradiction. A person may make a healthy choice on Monday, relapse on Tuesday, recommit on Wednesday, question everything on Thursday, and start again on Friday. These fluctuations are not evidence of failure. They are evidence of process.

Even in therapy, the idea of a breakthrough can be misleading. Clients often describe a session that felt transformative, a moment when something clicked, or tears flowed freely, or a truth was spoken aloud for the first time. These moments matter. They are sacred in their own way. But what matters more is what happens afterward. Does the insight translate into new behavior? Does the emotional release lead to deeper responsibility? Can the person tolerate the changes that new awareness demands? True transformation is measured not by what is felt, but by what is integrated.

This distinction matters because the myth of the turning point can do real harm. It sets up unrealistic expectations. When people do not feel transformed after a powerful moment, they assume they did it wrong. They begin to chase the next insight, the next retreat, the next moment of clarity—believing that maybe the next time will stick. This leads to a cycle of inspiration and disappointment. Meanwhile, the actual work of change—mundane, effortful, unglamorous—is neglected or avoided.

The myth also creates shame. If someone hits a "rock bottom" and still doesn't change, they may feel broken. But there is nothing broken about resisting change, especially when change feels unsafe. Many behaviors, even harmful ones, serve psychological functions: they regulate emotion, maintain identity, or preserve relational roles. Until those functions are addressed and replaced, change will be resisted; not because of weakness, but because of structure. The problem is not that the person lacks willpower. The problem is that they lack an alternative that works under pressure.

Change becomes more accessible when we stop waiting for a turning point and start building a turning process. This means creating the conditions under which new behavior can survive. It means recognizing that transformation is not a burst of effort, but a sustained shift in how one relates to time, choice, emotion, and self. It means valuing small, consistent action over dramatic declarations. It means giving up the fantasy that one moment will do what only a system can sustain.

James Clear, in his work on habits, reminds us that we rise to the level of our systems, not our goals. This holds true not only in behavior change but in identity transformation. The person who wants to be healthier cannot rely on one powerful decision—they must change their environment, their routines, their self-concept. The person who wants to stop people-pleasing must do more than say no once—they must learn to tolerate disapproval, build boundaries, and redefine their relational worth. These are not singular moments. They are living systems.

It is more honest—and more compassionate—to tell the truth about change. It is slow. It is non-linear. It is full of setbacks and second-guessing. But it is also real. And it is available. Not to those who wait for the lightning bolt, but to those who learn to move in the dark. Who take one small step, then another. Who allow the discomfort of uncertainty. Who trust that something is shifting, even when nothing is obvious.

In the end, transformation does not usually arrive with fanfare. It sneaks in through repetition. Through ordinary choices made in unremarkable moments. Through a thousand small refusals to become who you no longer want to be.

Identity Before Behavior

When people try to change their lives, they usually start with behavior. They download a fitness app, cut out sugar, start journaling, or commit to waking up early. These actions often work for a short time. But if the underlying identity remains the same, the behaviors eventually fall apart. The psychology behind this is not mysterious. People act in ways that are consistent with who they believe they are. If the behavior and the identity are misaligned, identity will win.

This is one of the central insights in psychological models of self-regulation. Theories from cognitive psychology, including self-perception theory and identity theory, make it clear that behavior is not just the result of decisions. It is shaped by internalized narratives. People behave in accordance with the roles they believe they are playing. A person who sees themselves as "the responsible one" may take on more than they can manage. A person who sees themselves as "unlovable" may sabotage intimacy. A person who sees themselves as "bad with money" may unconsciously reinforce that belief through careless spending. The behavior is not arbitrary. It is anchored in self-concept.

The problem is that most attempts at change try to modify actions without confronting identity. People push themselves to do new things while silently holding onto old labels. They say things like, "I'm trying to be more disciplined," or "I'm working on being less reactive," but they still believe, deep down, that they are undisciplined or emotionally unstable. These contradictions create psychological friction. The behavior feels inauthentic, because it does not yet match the internal map. When the old identity reasserts itself, the person feels like a fraud. And so they revert.

This is why change is more sustainable when it flows from identity rather than opposing it. If someone begins to believe, "I am someone who follows through," then completing a task becomes an expression of that identity. It feels natural. If someone begins to see themselves as emotionally regulated, then calming down during an argument feels like self-affirmation, not self-denial. This principle is often used in cognitive-behavioral therapy, where clients are encouraged to test new identities by behaving "as if" they already are the person they want to become. The goal is not to fake it, but to allow behavior to shape self-image gradually, in parallel with deliberate cognitive restructuring.

But identity is stubborn. It is often rooted in early experiences, internalized feedback, and unresolved emotional pain. Children who are called lazy, dramatic, or selfish by caregivers tend to absorb those labels. Over time, they organize their expectations around them. They stop trying to prove otherwise, and instead behave in ways that confirm what they already believe. This is not a failure of will. It is the result of conditioning. People internalize the roles they are given, especially when those roles are reinforced by family, culture, or environment.

To change behavior meaningfully, then, people must engage in identity revision. This does not mean inventing a new self out of thin air. It means questioning the inherited assumptions. It means identifying which stories no longer serve. It means updating the map to reflect new experiences. This process can be emotional. It often brings grief. Letting go of an identity, even a painful one, can feel like a kind of death. It can also create social disruption. When someone stops playing the role that others expect—whether that role is caretaker, rebel, clown, or victim—they may meet resistance. Others may feel threatened, confused, or betrayed. This is why identity change requires courage. It is not just a personal act. It is relational.

Psychologically, identity revision involves both top-down and bottom-up processes. From the top down, people use reflection, language, and insight to name who they want to be. They reframe old beliefs. They examine what they have been told about themselves and decide what to keep. From the bottom up, they gather new evidence through behavior. They make small choices that align with the new identity. Over time, these choices accumulate into proof. The brain begins to update its sense of self not because someone said it should, but because it sees that the pattern has changed.

Narrative work can accelerate this process. When people begin to see their life as a story, they gain the ability to edit it. They can place a period where they used to put a comma. They can turn a chapter of shame into one of learning. They can begin to imagine what kind of character they want to become and what kind of story would honor that choice. This is not self-deception. It is conscious authorship. It is the use of meaning-making to reinforce psychological coherence.

Social mirroring is also essential. Identity does not form in isolation. It is co-constructed. People need others to reflect back a version of them that aligns with who they are trying to become. This is why change is more likely to stick when people surround themselves with those who support the new identity. If someone wants to be sober, they are more likely to succeed in communities that normalize sobriety. If someone wants to become confident, they will grow faster around people who treat them with respect. The new self needs witnesses.

There is a practical lesson here: if a person wants to change, they should start by asking not "What should I do differently?" but "Who am I becoming?" Behavior is important, but it is downstream from identity. When the self-concept begins to shift, the behaviors that match it become easier to maintain. They stop feeling like obligations and start feeling like expressions of who the person is.

This is why shame is such a poor tool for change. Shame reinforces the old identity. It says, "You are still that person. You haven't changed." Even when people are trying their hardest, shame pulls them back into the past. It erodes the fragile hope that something else is possible. In contrast, affirmation nurtures new identity. It says, "You are growing. You are learning. You are showing up differently." These messages create space for the self to evolve.

There is nothing passive about identity change. It is one of the most demanding forms of growth a person can undergo. It requires honesty, repetition, support, and time. It requires stepping out of the familiar narrative and living without the script for a while. But when the new identity takes hold, the change becomes less effortful. It becomes self-reinforcing. The person no longer has to ask themselves what to do. They already know, because they know who they are.

Structure Over Sentiment

People often assume that change happens when they feel ready. They wait for motivation to strike, for clarity to arrive, for emotional certainty to carry them forward. But the most consistent psychological research on habit formation and behavioral change tells a different story. It is not emotion that makes change stick—it is structure. Systems, routines, environmental design, and accountability matter more than inspiration. Feeling ready may help someone take the first step, but only structure will carry them through the thousand steps that follow.

Emotions are fleeting. They are responsive to mood, energy levels, context, and memory. A person can feel determined in the morning and defeated by afternoon. They may leave a therapy session or a seminar feeling inspired, but that inspiration rarely survives the return to ordinary life. This is not a failure of character. It is the reality of emotional regulation. Feelings do not provide a stable foundation for behavior. They are too reactive, too context-dependent. What sustains change is what surrounds it—not what sparks it.

Behavioral psychology has demonstrated this principle clearly. In B.F. Skinner's work on operant conditioning, behavior is shaped by consequences, schedules of reinforcement, and environmental cues. The more predictable and repeatable the structure, the more likely a behavior is to persist. Later theorists expanded on this by examining how habits form through cue-routine-reward loops. If the context cues a behavior, and the behavior is followed by a meaningful outcome, the brain will automate that loop. The behavior becomes easier, not because the person wants it more, but because it now fits the groove of their daily life.

This is why changing behavior often begins with changing the environment. People who want to eat healthier are more successful when they remove processed snacks from their home and stock easy, nutritious options. People who want to focus at work do better when they silence notifications, clear their desks, and schedule blocks of uninterrupted time. These structural interventions reduce friction. They make the desired behavior more accessible and the undesired behavior more inconvenient. The result is a shift in default action.

James Clear, Charles Duhigg, and other modern voices in habit psychology have emphasized the same idea: people do not rise to the level of their goals. They fall to the level of their systems. The most effective way to make a change last is to design the conditions that support it even when motivation fades. For example, a person who wants to exercise regularly will benefit more from laying out their workout clothes, scheduling the session in their calendar, and keeping the gym bag in their car than from watching another motivational video. The action becomes part of the infrastructure of the day. It no longer requires a fresh surge of willpower each time.

Accountability systems are another form of structure. When people know that someone else is tracking their progress, offering support, or simply bearing witness, they are more likely to follow through. This is not about external pressure or shame; it is about external reinforcement. Humans are social creatures. We behave differently when we are seen. In group therapy, peer coaching, or structured programs like Alcoholics Anonymous, accountability is built into the process. The person is not expected to maintain change in isolation. They are held in a system that makes consistency more likely.

Routine itself functions as a stabilizer. When a behavior is tied to a specific time or place, it becomes easier to access. Morning and evening rituals, structured work hours, and designated spaces for focused activity reduce the cognitive load required to make decisions. This is known in psychology as decision fatigue—the idea that the more choices we have to make, the more our mental resources are depleted. Structure removes the need for choice. The behavior is not negotiated each time. It is simply done.

Even creativity and spontaneity benefit from structure. Artists, writers, and performers often speak of the discipline required to produce work consistently. They do not wait for the muse to appear. They create the conditions in which the muse is most likely to visit. The same applies to psychological growth. Insight is more likely to arise in a mind that has been made ready through regular reflection, consistent journaling, or time spent in stillness. Change does not require drama. It requires design.

One of the most overlooked aspects of structure is emotional scaffolding. People do not need their feelings to be perfectly aligned before taking action, but they do need a way to soothe and stabilize themselves when feelings get in the way. This includes skills like emotional labeling, distress tolerance, and self-compassion—all of which can be practiced deliberately. A structured emotional routine might involve checking in with oneself at the end of each day, rating emotional states, or identifying recurring triggers. These small rituals teach the nervous system what to expect. Over time, they create internal conditions that support behavioral consistency.

Resistance to structure often comes from a mistaken belief that structure is rigid or punitive. People associate it with control, rules, and the loss of freedom. But in reality, well-designed structure creates freedom. It reduces chaos. It allows energy to be focused where it matters most. For someone trying to heal from trauma, structure can provide safety and predictability. For someone managing ADHD, it can reduce overwhelm. For someone pursuing a major life change, it can act as a scaffolding during moments of doubt. Structure is not the enemy of authenticity—it is its container.

This understanding has implications for everything from therapy to education to leadership. Helping someone change does not require convincing them to feel differently. It requires helping them build a structure that will carry them forward when their feelings falter. Therapists who work with behavior change focus not only on insight but on systems. Teachers who want students to thrive structure their classrooms with clear routines. Leaders who want cultural change in organizations build new norms and reinforcements. In each case, the shift happens not through inspiration, but through design.

To live differently, a person must often build a new life around the self they are becoming. This includes not only what they do, but what they allow into their environment, whom they spend time with, how they organize their day, and what signals they send to themselves about who they are. Every cue matters. Every system sends a message. When those messages are aligned with the goal, the path forward becomes less about willpower and more about rhythm.

Lasting change is not about being in the right mood. It is about building the right mechanisms. When the emotional weather changes—as it inevitably will—the structure remains. It keeps the person moving, not because they are always inspired, but because they no longer need to be.

Maintenance, Relapse, and the Long View

When most people think about change, they picture a clean, upward trajectory. Once the decision is made, the line should move forward, maybe even accelerate. Success is imagined as a straight path: from unhealthy to healthy, from reactive to regulated, from avoidance to engagement. But the psychology of real change tells a more complicated story. Progress is rarely linear. Growth is often jagged. And relapse is not the exception—it is part of the process.

The idea that relapse means failure is one of the most damaging assumptions in personal development. It turns any setback into a source of shame, which often leads to giving up altogether. But from a psychological and behavioral standpoint, relapse is expected. In addiction studies, behavioral loops, and habit research, the return to previous behaviors is seen not as a collapse, but as an opportunity to examine what the new system could not yet support. Something about the context, the stressors, or the emotional terrain overwhelmed the fragile new pattern. That information is valuable. It shows where the structure needs reinforcement.

This is why recovery models emphasize the importance of planning for setbacks. In dialectical behavior therapy, clients are taught that urges and regressions are part of the cycle, not proof that progress has been erased. In cognitive-behavioral therapy, relapse prevention is built into the treatment plan. And in trauma-informed care, reactivity is understood as the body protecting itself in the absence of safety, not as evidence that healing has failed. These approaches recognize that long-term change requires stamina, not perfection.

People who stay committed to change over time do not succeed because they never slip. They succeed because they build systems that make it easier to return after slipping. This includes routines, social supports, emotional regulation strategies, and a mindset that honors process. The mindset piece is especially critical. If someone believes that one bad day invalidates all the good ones, they will stop trying. But if they believe that change is measured in patterns, not moments, they can recover quickly. They can see relapse as a deviation, not a reversal.

It helps to replace the word relapse with return. Return is a neutral term. It acknowledges that behavior has shifted back to a familiar place without the moral baggage. From there, the person can ask useful questions: What led to the return? Was I overwhelmed, isolated, triggered, exhausted? What structure failed? What emotional need went unmet? How can I respond differently next time? These questions turn the moment into a learning opportunity. Shame shuts that learning down. Curiosity reopens it.

Another useful reframing is to focus on maintenance, not just achievement. Too often, people set goals with no plan for what comes after. They work toward a number, a title, a relationship, or a milestone—and then feel lost when they arrive. The achievement gave them a direction, but not a structure. Maintenance requires an entirely different set of skills. It is less about striving and more about sustaining. It involves paying attention to the small actions that hold things in place, even when no one is watching.

Maintenance also demands a realistic view of motivation. No one feels motivated all the time. Even deeply committed people experience doubt, boredom, and resistance. What keeps them going is rhythm. Just as the body relies on circadian rhythms to regulate sleep, the psyche benefits from predictable behavioral rhythms. Morning routines, weekly reflections, structured mealtimes, consistent exercise, and regular check-ins all create a sense of psychological gravity. The person is not floating—they are tethered.

There is also a cognitive shift that occurs when a behavior becomes part of identity. The person no longer thinks, "I'm trying to stay sober." They think, "I don't drink." They no longer say, "I hope I can keep going to the gym." They say, "I'm someone who trains." The behavior is not just something they do—it is something they are. This shift makes relapse feel less like a personal failure and more like a break in alignment. The question becomes, "How do I return to myself?" rather than, "Why did I mess up again?"

Maintenance is about continuity. It is about building a life where the behavior makes sense, where it belongs. This means considering context. If someone changes but their environment stays the same—if they are surrounded by triggers, undermined by relationships, or drained by work—they will struggle. Change must be embedded in reality. It must be compatible with the life the person is actually living. Otherwise, the effort becomes unsustainable.

Psychological resilience plays a role here. Resilience is not just about bouncing back from major trauma. It also refers to the small recoveries that happen every day. A person wakes up in a bad mood and chooses to move anyway. They feel rejected and decide to journal instead of shutting down. They forget their goals and remember them an hour later. These moments of self-righting are invisible from the outside, but they are foundational. They are what make long-term change possible.

A final element in the psychology of lasting change is time perspective. When people view change through a short lens, they panic at every fluctuation. When they zoom out, they see the broader arc. One week of emotional chaos does not erase six months of effort. One month of disconnection does not define a relationship. Time allows for gentleness. It reveals the truth of what has been built. And it reminds people that they are not starting from scratch, even when it feels like they are.

Long-term change is not about avoiding relapse. It is about building a relationship with yourself that can withstand it. A relationship that is honest, structured, forgiving, and grounded in rhythm. A relationship where progress is measured not in perfection, but in persistence. Where the question is not "Did I slip?" but "Did I come back?"

And when the answer is yes, that is the proof of change. Not that the person never left, but that they knew how to return. They knew how to face themselves without collapse, how to re-enter their commitments without humiliation, and how to keep moving forward even when the path blurred beneath them. This is what distinguishes temporary effort from sustainable transformation: not intensity, but consistency over time.

The deeper truth is that most enduring change looks boring from the outside. It is not fireworks and reinvention. It is quiet repetition. It is the decision to keep showing up—when the mood is flat, when the future is unclear, when nobody is watching. It is in those uneventful moments that identity is reinforced and trust in the self is rebuilt. Emotional life is dynamic, and so is behavior. What matters is the gravity of return. The inner compass that keeps pointing the person back to what they chose when they were clear.

That compass becomes stronger through use. Every time someone returns to their values after a detour, they carve a path. Each return lowers the resistance for the next. This creates a feedback loop of integrity: small acts of alignment that build inner credibility. Eventually, the person begins to trust themselves. They believe that they will come back, not because they always do everything right, but because they have a track record of repair. And that belief becomes self-sustaining.

This long view of change requires patience. It is easy to romanticize rapid transformation, to imagine a life remade overnight. But the psychology of being human tells a slower story. People grow through seasons. They become stronger not by skipping struggle, but by integrating it. They become wise not by avoiding mistakes, but by learning to face them directly and recover with grace.

Change that lasts is not driven by fear, nor held in place by shame. It is built on structure, nurtured by identity, supported through relationship, and affirmed over time by return. It bends, it falters, it drifts. But it holds. That is what makes it real.

* * *

IV

PART IV: RELATIONSHIPS AND INTERPERSONAL DYNAMICS

Relationships are at the heart of what it means to be human. In this part, I want to walk with you through how we connect, communicate, and sometimes clash with others. These dynamics aren't just theories—they are the living, breathing realities that shape your sense of belonging, your identity, and your wellbeing every day. By understanding the psychology behind relationships, you'll gain insight into building deeper connection and navigating the challenges that come with being close to others.

16

Attachment and Early Bonds

No relationship begins in adulthood. Long before people choose friends, partners, or colleagues, they learn how connection feels. They learn whether comfort is accessible, whether closeness is safe, whether needs will be heard or ignored. These lessons come not from language or logic, but from the earliest experiences of being held, fed, soothed, or left alone. In the silent spaces between cries and response, the human nervous system begins to map the emotional landscape of the world. That map becomes the blueprint for how connection is sought, feared, or avoided later in life.

Attachment theory, one of the most influential frameworks in developmental psychology, offers a clear premise: the way a child bonds with their primary caregiver sets the stage for nearly every emotional, relational, and cognitive pattern that follows. First developed by John Bowlby and expanded by Mary Ainsworth, the theory proposes that human beings are biologically wired to seek closeness and protection, especially in times of distress. This drive is not a weakness; it is an evolutionary safeguard. A child who can reliably access a caregiver's support is more likely to explore the world, regulate emotions, and form trusting bonds in adulthood.

But not all children receive this support consistently. Some experience caregivers who are emotionally distant, erratic, or frightening. Others learn to suppress their needs to preserve fragile attachment. These adaptations are not conscious—they are survival strategies. They become internal working models: deeply ingrained beliefs about the self (Am I lovable? Am I too much?) and about others (Can I depend on you? Will you stay?). These models are not based on isolated incidents. They are built from repeated interactions. They become so automatic that most people never realize they are operating from them.

In adulthood, attachment patterns do not disappear. They re-emerge in intimacy, often disguised as personality. A person who clings tightly to partners may believe they are just "intense." Someone who avoids closeness may see themselves as "independent." These behaviors are not random—they are echoes of early lessons. And unless examined, they tend to repeat. A person may keep choosing unavailable partners, overfunction in friendships, or misinterpret healthy distance as abandonment. They are not trying to suffer. They are trying to stay safe, according to a script written before they could read.

Secure attachment is not about perfection. It is about trust. It forms when a child experiences a caregiver as consistently available, emotionally attuned, and responsive to distress. This does not mean the caregiver never fails—it means they repair. The child learns that misattunement is tolerable and that emotional needs can be met without fear. This forms the basis of what Bowlby called a "secure base": a reliable emotional home from which the child can explore, return, and explore again. In adulthood, this becomes the capacity to love without losing the self, to seek comfort without shame, and to tolerate emotional distance without panic.

The tragedy of insecure attachment is not only that it hurts—but that it becomes familiar. People often prefer the pain they know to the vulnerability they don't. They may reject secure relationships because they feel too foreign. Safety itself can feel dangerous when the nervous system has been conditioned to expect threat. This is why healing attachment wounds is not merely an intellectual task—it is a somatic, relational, and often disorienting process. It requires new experiences of connection that are consistent enough to rewrite the body's expectations.

Therapy can play a powerful role here, not because the therapist gives advice, but because the relationship itself becomes a new attachment experience. When the therapist shows up reliably, responds with warmth, and repairs ruptures without punishment, the client begins to internalize a different model of connection. Over time, this new model can extend to other relationships. In some cases, romantic partners, friends, or mentors serve as corrective emotional figures. This process is known as earning security. It does not erase the past. But it expands the future.

Attachment theory also helps explain why some people struggle with self-regulation. Emotional regulation is learned through co-regulation: the caregiver's ability to soothe the child becomes the template for the child's ability to soothe themselves. If a child's distress is met with indifference or punishment, they may learn to suppress emotions, or be consumed by them. In adulthood, this can manifest as emotional shutdown, chronic anxiety, or explosive reactivity. Healing requires not just insight, but practice: learning to stay with emotion without being overwhelmed, to ask for comfort without shame, and to regulate through presence rather than performance.

Importantly, attachment styles are not fixed. They are tendencies, not destinies. People can shift toward greater security through reflection, relationship, and repair. The first step is awareness: naming the pattern, understanding where it came from, and recognizing how it plays out. From there, the person can begin to intervene in the cycle. They can notice the urge to pull away or cling. They can pause before interpreting silence as rejection. They can ask, "Is this about now—or is this about then?" And in that pause, they gain the chance to respond differently.

This chapter will explore the foundations of attachment and the lifelong impact of early emotional bonds. It will examine how internal working models shape self-concept and behavior, how insecure styles manifest in adult life, and how people can move toward earned security. Attachment is not just about childhood. It is about the patterns that live on in our nervous systems, our relationships, and our sense of what love can be.

The Roots of Safety: Attachment in Infancy and Early Development

Before a child can form words, they form expectations. These expectations are not intellectual; they are physiological, emotional, and sensory. They live in the body as impressions of safety or danger, of connection or abandonment. In the earliest months and years of life, these expectations are shaped primarily through one channel: the caregiving relationship. Whether a caregiver responds consistently, unpredictably, or not at all determines the child's basic orientation to the world. Will I be seen? Will I be comforted? Can I reach out and expect to be met?

John Bowlby, the originator of attachment theory, described this early bond as a biologically embedded system. Like hunger or thirst, the need for proximity to a caregiver is innate. Human infants are uniquely vulnerable; they cannot survive without sustained adult care. Evolution thus shaped them to seek closeness and connection as a survival mechanism. When they are frightened, overwhelmed, or in distress, they instinctively reach out. And when those gestures are reliably met, the child learns that the world is safe enough to explore. This secure base, as Bowlby called it, becomes the foundation for all future development—cognitive, emotional, and social.

Mary Ainsworth expanded on Bowlby's work through observational research, most notably the Strange Situation Procedure. In this structured study, toddlers were observed during brief separations and reunions with their primary caregivers. Their behavior revealed distinct patterns of attachment, which Ainsworth categorized as secure, avoidant, and ambivalent (also referred to as resistant). Later researchers added a fourth category: disorganized attachment, which emerged in children who displayed contradictory or fearful behavior toward their caregivers, often in the context of abuse, trauma, or severe emotional inconsistency.

Children with secure attachment show distress when separated but are quickly comforted upon reunion. They use their caregiver as a secure base, venturing out to explore but returning when unsure. They trust that help is available and that their emotions will not be met with rejection or neglect. This is not because the caregiver is perfect. Rather, the caregiver is consistently good enough—present, responsive, and emotionally attuned. Over time, this consistency allows the child's nervous system to develop with a baseline of trust and emotional resilience.

In contrast, children with avoidant attachment minimize their distress. They appear independent or emotionally flat, even in stressful situations. This is not a sign of confidence—it is an adaptation to emotional unavailability. These children have learned that expressing need leads to rejection or indifference. Suppressing those needs becomes a strategy for preserving connection, albeit at the cost of emotional intimacy. The cost grows over time, often shaping adults who struggle with vulnerability or see dependency as weakness.

Ambivalent or resistant attachment arises from inconsistency. The caregiver's responses are unpredictable—attuned at times, neglectful at others. As a result, the child becomes hypervigilant and emotionally reactive. They cling tightly, protest separations, and have difficulty being soothed. They are not sure whether comfort will come, so they amplify their signals in a desperate attempt to ensure a response. In adulthood, this often manifests as anxious attachment: preoccupation with relationships, fear of abandonment, and difficulty trusting that love will last.

Disorganized attachment is the most complex and distressing pattern. It emerges when the caregiver is both the source of comfort and the source of fear. This paradox scrambles the child's nervous system. They may approach and then flee, reach out and then freeze. The system designed to seek safety cannot find it. Over time, this can lead to dissociation, emotional dysregulation, and fractured identity development. In adulthood, disorganized attachment may present as a chaotic pattern of intense connection followed by withdrawal, or an inability to form coherent relational strategies.

These attachment patterns do not exist in isolation. They are shaped by the caregiver's own attachment history, the child's temperament, the broader social context, and cultural norms around emotional expression. A caregiver dealing with unresolved trauma may struggle to attune to their child, not out of neglect, but because they are overwhelmed themselves. In this way, attachment patterns often span generations. What is not repaired tends to be repeated.

The neurological implications of early attachment are profound. During the first three years of life, the brain undergoes rapid growth, particularly in areas related to emotional regulation, stress response, and social processing. Secure attachment supports the development of the prefrontal cortex and calms the reactivity of the amygdala. This allows the child to experience distress without being overwhelmed. They learn that feelings are tolerable and can be soothed. Insecure attachment, by contrast, often leaves the nervous system on high alert, creating a baseline of anxiety, hypervigilance, or numbness that follows the child into adulthood.

Attachment also shapes the internal voice. The way a caregiver responds to a child becomes the template for the way the child will later speak to themselves. A child who is soothed learns to self-soothe. A child who is shamed learns to self-blame. These patterns become internalized, often beneath conscious awareness. They influence how a person experiences failure, interprets conflict, or navigates emotional needs. The early relationship becomes the mirror through which the self is seen.

None of this is deterministic. Children are remarkably adaptive, and the human brain retains plasticity well into adulthood. But understanding these early bonds is crucial for understanding later behavior. Many adults find themselves reenacting patterns that no longer serve them, not because they are broken or irrational, but because they are following a script written before they could write their own. Recognizing where that script began allows them to revise it.

The roots of safety are planted in relationship. When those roots are deep and stable, the person grows with confidence, resilience, and emotional clarity. When they are shallow or fractured, the person may grow in unpredictable directions—twisting, bending, bracing against imagined winds. But even then, the possibility of new growth remains. Later experiences, especially consistent and emotionally safe ones, can offer new soil.

Attachment is the first story the body learns to tell itself: Am I safe? Am I held? Am I worthy of comfort? And the answer to that story shapes not only how people connect with others, but how they come to know themselves. When those answers are secure, life feels navigable. When they are not, the search for safety continues, often disguised as independence, intensity, or control.

Internal Working Models: The Invisible Blueprint for Relationships

By the time a child reaches adulthood, most of what they believe about themselves and others is no longer being taught. It has already been learned. These beliefs don't sit at the surface of awareness. They live deeper, behind habits of attention, interpretations of conflict, and instinctive emotional reactions. Psychologists call these internal working models: cognitive-affective templates formed through early attachment experiences that organize the way people relate to others, to themselves, and to the world.

John Bowlby coined the term to explain how past relational experiences become predictive frameworks. These models are not just memories of what happened. They are expectations about what will happen. A securely attached child, for example, who consistently experienced a caregiver as emotionally available and attuned, will tend to expect that others will be responsive. Their internal working model includes the assumptions: I am worthy of care. Others can be trusted. Emotions can be expressed and met with support. Conversely, a child who learned that closeness brought punishment, chaos, or neglect will internalize very different beliefs: I am too much. Others will reject me. Vulnerability leads to harm.

These models become so embedded that they often feel like truth. The person is not thinking about attachment styles; they are reacting. They may withdraw in the face of intimacy, assume malice where there is none, or cling too tightly out of fear of abandonment. Each of these behaviors makes sense within the logic of their original attachment pattern. They are not strategies selected at random; they are responses encoded through repetition, held in memory, emotion, and the nervous system.

Internal working models affect every dimension of adult life. They shape how people interpret tone and silence, how quickly they trust, and how they navigate closeness or conflict. A securely attached individual may approach relationships with curiosity and flexibility. They assume goodwill until shown otherwise. But someone with an anxious model may hear neutral feedback as a rejection, interpret distance as a sign of collapse, and live with a constant hum of relational threat. This is not immaturity; it is memory, activated through present conditions.

The most difficult aspect of internal working models is their invisibility. Because they develop before the child has language, they operate beneath conscious awareness. People do not wake up and decide to sabotage their relationships. They are simply living out the map that was drawn for them before they could draw their own. And because the same model tends to produce similar relational outcomes, it often appears to be confirmed. The person who expects abandonment becomes hypervigilant, which may overwhelm or push others away—reinforcing the sense that people always leave.

Psychological flexibility comes from learning to recognize and revise these models. This is difficult work. It requires not only intellectual insight but emotional exposure. A person must be willing to question the assumptions that have kept them safe. They must tolerate the dissonance between old expectations and new experiences. For example, if someone has always expected closeness to end in betrayal, they may instinctively push away a partner who shows steady care. Letting the connection deepen would mean letting go of a model that, however painful, has been predictable.

Therapeutic relationships are especially powerful sites for this kind of revision. In psychodynamic therapy, the therapist-client relationship is understood as a living space where old models can be activated, examined, and reshaped. The client may unconsciously test the therapist, expecting disappointment, rejection, or disinterest. If the therapist responds with consistency and attunement, a new pattern begins to emerge. Over time, the client internalizes a different set of expectations—not because the therapist says the right things, but because the experience of emotional safety is repeated and embodied.

Other therapeutic models also target internal working models, though with different mechanisms. In cognitive-behavioral therapy, distorted core beliefs are challenged and restructured. In internal family systems therapy, parts of the self that carry attachment wounds are brought into conscious dialogue and reparented internally. In emotionally focused therapy, couples learn to recognize their attachment cycles and reach for each other in more regulated ways. All of these approaches acknowledge that the past does not vanish—but it can lose its grip.

Importantly, not all internal working models are wholly secure or insecure. Many people carry mixed models. They may trust in some contexts and collapse in others. They may feel secure in friendships but fearful in romantic settings. Attachment is not a fixed trait; it is a dynamic system that responds to context, stress, and relationship history. A person who is secure with one partner may become anxious with another, especially if that partner behaves in ways that trigger unresolved patterns. Understanding this variability can help reduce shame. Struggling in one relationship does not mean someone is incapable of connection. It may mean the relationship is activating an old wound.

Beyond close relationships, internal working models shape self-concept. People who were consistently validated as children tend to internalize a sense of worth. They believe their emotions make sense and that their needs matter. Those who were dismissed or punished for their feelings may learn to distrust themselves. They might invalidate their own experiences, assume they are "too sensitive," or chronically second-guess their instincts. Over time, this internalized self-rejection can lead to depression, anxiety, or persistent self-doubt.

Even one corrective emotional relationship can shift the model. A friend who consistently listens, a teacher who sees potential, a partner who stays present—these relationships offer lived experiences that contradict the old story. But for the contradiction to take root, the person must be open to letting the new experience matter. This is one of the paradoxes of attachment healing: it requires both new relational data and the willingness to integrate it. Without that openness, even healthy connections can be misinterpreted or dismissed.

Self-reflection is essential. Individuals can begin to trace their own models by asking: What do I expect from people when I'm vulnerable? What do I believe about myself when I'm in conflict? Do I assume that people want to understand me—or that I have to protect myself? Do I trust that I can repair after rupture—or do I panic at the first sign of tension? These questions help illuminate the lens through which relational life is being filtered.

Once seen, these models become editable. Not instantly, not perfectly, but meaningfully. A person can learn to pause before interpreting silence as abandonment. They can remind themselves that safety is not always a trap. They can choose to stay present when they want to flee, or to speak up when they've always shut down. Each new behavior becomes a small revision in the script. With time, those revisions accumulate. The story begins to change.

Internal working models are not destiny. They are blueprints—and blueprints can be redrawn. What matters is not whether someone had a perfect childhood, but whether they are willing to understand how their past has shaped their present, and whether they are open to building something new. The invisible patterns can become visible. And once they are visible, they can be changed.

Insecure Attachment in Adult Life: The Echoes of Early Disconnection

The patterns set in early attachment don't disappear when people grow up. They mature into personalities, preferences, defensive strategies, and emotional reflexes. A child who learned to suppress emotional needs may grow into an adult who prides themselves on self-reliance. A child who learned that love is unpredictable may become an adult who clings tightly, trying to prevent loss before it happens. The original need—for safety, connection, and understanding—remains unchanged. But the adult expression of that need often becomes more complex, more camouflaged, and harder to trace.

Insecure attachment in adulthood does not always look insecure. In fact, it often masquerades as independence, ambition, intensity, or high standards. What distinguishes it is not appearance but function. Is the behavior protecting the person from a perceived threat to connection? Is it serving as a buffer against vulnerability? Is it a strategy designed to keep others at just the right emotional distance—close enough to avoid abandonment, but far enough to avoid disappointment?

Avoidant attachment in adulthood often appears as emotional self-containment. These individuals may seem calm, logical, and undemanding. They typically value autonomy and are uncomfortable with overt displays of emotion—both their own and others'. But beneath the surface is often a deep-seated mistrust of intimacy. Their early experiences may have taught them that emotional needs are met with indifference or punishment, so they adapt by needing less. Or at least appearing to. Relationships are tolerated, sometimes even enjoyed, but only on terms that protect emotional independence. This can lead to patterns of emotional withdrawal, stonewalling during conflict, or difficulty offering comfort when a partner is in distress.

Anxiously attached adults, on the other hand, tend to hyperactivate the attachment system. They often seek excessive reassurance, fear abandonment, and are sensitive to shifts in emotional availability. Small relational changes—a delayed text, a shift in tone—can feel catastrophic. These individuals may become preoccupied with the relationship, constantly monitoring for signs of rejection. Their early experiences likely included inconsistent caregiving: sometimes attuned, sometimes unavailable. As a result, they learned to amplify distress as a way to maintain connection. In adult life, this can manifest as clinginess, emotional reactivity, or difficulty trusting that love will stay.

Disorganized attachment in adulthood often presents as chaotic or contradictory relational behavior. The person may crave intimacy but fear it. They may idealize partners and then devalue them. They may alternate between anxious pursuit and avoidant retreat. This pattern is often rooted in early experiences where the caregiver was both the source of safety and the source of fear. As adults, these individuals may struggle to form coherent relational strategies. Emotional intimacy may trigger unresolved trauma, leading to dissociation, panic, or rage. They may find themselves drawn to relationships that replicate the unpredictability of childhood—not because they want pain, but because it feels familiar.

These patterns are not chosen. They are inherited through experience. And they often go unrecognized because they become normalized. The person does not feel anxious or avoidant—they feel like themselves. Only through reflection or repeated relational struggles does the pattern begin to reveal itself. Unfortunately, many people blame themselves or others without understanding the underlying dynamic. An anxious person may see themselves as "needy." An avoidant partner may be labeled "cold." The relationship may fail, not due to lack of love, but due to incompatible attachment systems playing out without awareness.

Attachment styles do not only influence romantic relationships. They affect friendships, workplace dynamics, family systems, and parenting behavior. An anxiously attached person may overfunction in friendships, taking responsibility for others' feelings. An avoidantly attached leader may struggle to offer emotional attunement to employees. A disorganized parent may swing between overinvolvement and emotional withdrawal, confusing the child's sense of safety. Recognizing these dynamics is crucial—not to assign blame, but to create space for self-understanding and growth.

One of the challenges in adult attachment is the reenactment of early dynamics. People often choose partners who reflect their internal working models. An anxiously attached person may be drawn to an avoidant partner, and vice versa. This creates a common dynamic called the anxious-avoidant trap: one partner pushes for closeness, the other pulls away, both feeling misunderstood and unsafe. These patterns can be deeply painful, but they are also opportunities for growth if both partners are willing to examine their roles and learn new ways of relating.

Therapy can help individuals begin to identify their attachment patterns and understand how those patterns play out in current relationships. For those with anxious attachment, therapy might focus on building internal sources of validation, learning to tolerate uncertainty, and reducing the urge to overfunction. For those with avoidant attachment, therapy may involve increasing emotional awareness, building comfort with intimacy, and exploring the fears that drive emotional distancing. For those with disorganized attachment, therapy often involves trauma work, nervous system regulation, and the gradual development of safe, coherent relationships.

Importantly, insecure attachment is not a diagnosis. It is not a defect. It is a set of adaptations to early environments. And it can change. Relationships are not just sources of wounds—they are also sites of repair. With awareness, intention, and consistency, people can learn to offer themselves and others the emotional availability they may have missed in childhood. This does not require erasing the past. It requires learning to relate differently in the present.

Real change often begins with naming the pattern. A person might start to notice that they shut down in conflict, or that they panic when someone needs space. They might trace that response back to childhood experiences of emotional invalidation or unpredictability. From there, they can begin to pause, reflect, and choose a new response. Instead of withdrawing, they might stay present. Instead of clinging, they might ground themselves. Each moment of awareness becomes a moment of choice—and each choice becomes a step toward security.

Insecure attachment is painful, but it is also a doorway. It reveals the unmet needs still asking for attention. It points to the parts of the self still longing for connection, safety, and trust. And it reminds us that, while the past cannot be changed, the way we relate to it—and to others—can. When those patterns are made visible, they can be softened, rewritten, and eventually replaced.

Rewiring the Pattern: Earning Security Through Insight and Repair

While attachment begins in infancy, it does not end there. The patterns laid down in early life are deeply influential, but they are not permanent. Just as the human brain is shaped by experience, it can also be reshaped by new experiences—especially those that are emotionally safe, sustained over time, and coherent with the person's unmet relational needs. This is the foundation of what psychologists refer to as "earned secure attachment": the process by which an individual moves from an insecure attachment style to one that more closely resembles the emotional flexibility, resilience, and openness of secure attachment.

The notion of earned security challenges the myth that people are trapped by their childhoods. While early experiences do shape the nervous system, internal working models, and relational reflexes, they are not set in stone. They are, in essence, stories—stories told to the self about what relationships mean, what emotions cost, and what kind of love is possible. When those stories are recognized, challenged, and interrupted by new kinds of connection, the internal narrative begins to shift. The result is not a clean slate, but a deeper and more integrated sense of self.

Rewiring attachment begins with awareness. This awareness is not merely intellectual; it must include emotional recognition. A person must learn to observe their own patterns without shame or defensiveness. For example, someone who consistently pulls away when a relationship deepens might begin to ask: What am I afraid of? What am I protecting? Where did I learn that closeness equals danger? The goal is not to shame the protective behavior, but to understand it. Behavior that makes sense in one context often becomes maladaptive in another. Recognizing that shift is the first step toward choosing differently.

Therapy can provide a critical space for this work. A strong therapeutic relationship offers something rare: a consistent, attuned presence that allows old models to be questioned in real time. For the anxiously attached client, the therapist's reliability helps regulate the fear that abandonment is inevitable. For the avoidantly attached, the therapist's non-intrusiveness allows exploration of emotional intimacy without threat. For those with disorganized attachment, the therapist may serve as the first relationship in which closeness and safety coexist. Over time, this repeated experience becomes a new template—not because it's perfect, but because it's emotionally coherent.

But therapy is not the only path. Any relationship—romantic, platonic, familial—can become a site of attachment repair if it is marked by consistency, empathy, and emotional safety. What matters is not the title of the relationship, but the quality of presence within it. A friend who shows up without judgment, a partner who listens without defensiveness, a mentor who sees potential where others saw threat—these experiences begin to challenge the core assumptions of insecure attachment. Each moment of attunement says: Maybe you are not too much. Maybe connection can survive your full emotional range.

Rewiring is also a physiological process. The nervous system plays a central role in attachment. People with insecure attachment often live in a state of hyperarousal (anxious attachment) or hypoarousal (avoidant or disorganized attachment). Regulating the nervous system is essential for creating the internal conditions that allow for new patterns. Practices like deep breathing, grounding exercises, somatic therapies, and body-based mindfulness can help stabilize physiological responses to relational stress. Without this regulation, insight alone is rarely enough; the body must feel safe before the mind can fully engage.

Internal parts work can also support attachment repair. Many people carry internalized voices or sub-personalities that echo the messages they received in early life. For example, a person might have an inner critic that shames them for needing help, or an inner protector that blocks intimacy out of fear. Engaging with these parts through frameworks like Internal Family Systems or ego-state therapy allows the person to recognize and re-negotiate with these internal voices. Over time, the harsh protector can soften, the frightened child can be comforted, and the self can become a more secure internal leader.

Language also matters. Learning to name emotions, express needs clearly, and communicate boundaries without fear is part of building secure functioning. People with insecure attachment often struggle with this. An anxiously attached person might fear that expressing a need will drive others away. An avoidant person might feel that admitting need is equivalent to failure. Rewiring involves reclaiming the right to ask, to say no, to state clearly what is felt and wanted. These are not just communication skills—they are acts of reorganization, replacing confusion with clarity and fear with self-respect.

It's also important to understand that healing is non-linear. Old patterns do not vanish overnight. Even in the presence of secure relationships, moments of regression are common. The key is not to avoid these regressions, but to respond to them with curiosity rather than judgment. Why did that trigger me? What need was activated? How can I repair now, rather than retreat? These questions support a growth mindset around attachment. They treat the work as developmental, not as a binary of healed versus broken.

Another crucial piece of the puzzle is grief. Rewiring attachment often involves grieving what was not received. For many, this is the most difficult part. It means confronting the fact that some early needs went unmet and cannot be retroactively fulfilled. This grief is not self-pity. It is a form of honesty, an acknowledgment of the emotional reality that shaped the person's world. Naming that loss creates room for integration. It also allows the person to stop unconsciously chasing what was missed and begin building something new from a grounded place.

As secure behaviors accumulate, the internal model becomes more coherent. The person starts to interpret distance not as danger, but as difference. They experience conflict without assuming catastrophe. They learn to trust that connection can survive rupture. They become less reactive, more responsive. Their relationships feel less like tests and more like conversations. And perhaps most importantly, they begin to trust themselves. This is the essence of secure attachment: not the absence of need or conflict, but the presence of emotional flexibility, internal safety, and the belief that connection is possible—even when it's hard.

Rewiring attachment is not about perfection. It is about repair. It is about creating relationships, both external and internal, where emotional honesty can be met with care. Where needs can be spoken without fear. Where the past is not denied, but held in perspective. Over time, this becomes the new pattern: not a fantasy of constant comfort, but a reality of earned security. A sense that no matter what has happened, connection is still within reach. And that the person you are becoming is worthy of it.

* * *

17

The Social Mirror: Identity in Relationship

Human beings do not form in isolation. From the moment of birth—and arguably even before—our nervous systems, sense of self, and emotional responses are shaped through relationship. This chapter explores that relational dimension not as a secondary layer on top of a fully formed identity, but as one of its primary architects. To understand who we are, we must understand how we exist with others. And to understand how we exist with others, we must recognize that identity is not a fixed property we possess; it is a process that emerges in context, interaction, and reflection.

The title of this chapter, *The Social Mirror*, speaks to a phenomenon that is both psychological and physiological. Our emotional states are mirrored, moderated, and in many cases made meaningful through other people. Infants cry and are soothed. Children perform and are praised, scolded, or ignored. Adults learn to regulate based on facial expressions, vocal tones, and the subtle or explicit feedback loops of their social environment. At each stage, our internal states are shaped by our perception of how others see us. That feedback loop—sometimes affirming, sometimes distorting—can solidify into identity. I am someone who is cared for. I am someone who is too much. I am someone who is lovable when quiet. These are not conclusions drawn from logic; they are adaptations to what relationships have taught us is safe, expected, or tolerated.

Psychologically, this is framed through concepts like co-regulation, projection, and boundary formation. Co-regulation refers to the emotional calibration that happens between people, especially in early life. A calm caregiver helps a distressed infant return to baseline. Over time, this repeated experience wires the nervous system to expect that emotional arousal can be tolerated and soothed. Conversely, in the absence of such regulation, the child learns that distress is either ignored or punished, and internal chaos often becomes normalized. Adults who struggle with emotional regulation frequently carry nervous systems that never fully learned to settle in the presence of another. They may appear self-reliant or emotionally volatile, but at root, they are lacking the foundational experience of being emotionally met by another human being.

Projection, a more defensive mechanism, is another way relationships shape identity—by providing a surface onto which unconscious material can be cast. When people cannot tolerate certain aspects of themselves, they often attribute those traits to others. A person who fears their own anger might see others as consistently hostile. Someone ashamed of their neediness may perceive their partner as overly dependent. These projections often go unnoticed, because they confirm internal beliefs. But over time, they distort both relational dynamics and self-perception. We become confused not only about who others are, but about who we are when we are with them.

Boundaries, then, become critical. Without a clear sense of where one person ends and another begins, identity becomes diffuse, reactive, and unstable. In enmeshed families, children may take on emotional roles they are unequipped for, such as serving as a parent's confidante or emotional regulator. In adulthood, these blurred boundaries can show up as people-pleasing, emotional fusion, or chronic guilt for asserting needs. On the other end of the spectrum, overly rigid boundaries can signal a defensive withdrawal—walls instead of limits. Both extremes inhibit the development of a mature identity: one that is both connected and distinct, emotionally available and self-defined.

Part of growing into psychological adulthood involves learning how to be in relationship without losing oneself. This is harder than it sounds. Many people enter adulthood still searching for external validation, approval, or safety they never received in childhood. They may unconsciously attempt to recreate early dynamics, hoping this time the story ends differently. Others avoid intimacy altogether, fearing that to connect is to be controlled or erased. In both cases, the early relational mirror has left a distortion—one that must be actively re-examined and revised in adulthood.

Relational healing does not come from avoiding others; it comes from engaging with new relational experiences that disconfirm the old narrative. A person who has always felt ignored may begin to trust their voice in the presence of a partner who listens without judgment. Someone who learned to equate love with sacrifice may learn, slowly, that their needs can coexist with closeness. These new experiences provide alternative reflections—clearer mirrors through which the self can be seen more accurately, and perhaps more compassionately.

One of the most powerful psychological shifts occurs when a person moves from being defined by others to engaging with others as a full, differentiated self. This shift does not mean becoming emotionally detached or fiercely independent. It means learning to stay emotionally grounded in the presence of another's difference. It means holding on to one's values in the face of disagreement, expressing needs without fear of abandonment, and navigating the inevitable tensions of relationship without collapsing into old scripts of self-betrayal or blame.

This chapter traces that developmental arc. It begins with how identity is shaped by early relational experiences and the fundamental role of co-regulation in emotional development. It then turns to projection, not simply as a defense mechanism but as a lens through which people often misread themselves and others. From there, we explore the concept of boundaries—how they form, how they fail, and how they can be repaired. Finally, we consider what mature relational identity looks like: the capacity to engage in dialogue without losing oneself, to connect without fusing, and to stand firm without isolating.

In a culture that often emphasizes individualism, it can be easy to forget how deeply social we are. But psychology reminds us that autonomy and connection are not opposites—they are mutually reinforcing. When people are secure in themselves, they are more available to others. When they are genuinely connected to others, they are more able to know themselves. The social mirror, when clarified, becomes not a trap but a tool: a way to refine the self through relationship, to test assumptions through dialogue, and to grow not despite others, but with them.

The Social Brain: How Others Shape the Self

Human beings are wired for connection. Long before we form abstract ideas about who we are, we come to feel ourselves into existence through the presence and response of others. The self is not born in a vacuum; it is sculpted through interaction, carved through the thousand small cues we absorb about our worth, our effect on others, and our place in the relational world. From infancy through adulthood, our nervous systems remain responsive to these social signals, constantly interpreting and adapting based on emotional cues, facial expressions, tone of voice, proximity, and presence.

This deep interpersonal sensitivity is not a weakness of the human system. It is the foundation of our survival and our social intelligence. The same neural structures that allow us to process physical pain are activated when we feel socially excluded. The amygdala, so often thought of in terms of fear, also lights up in response to ambiguous or threatening social feedback. The prefrontal cortex, essential for decision-making and moral reasoning, plays a central role in interpreting relational context. We are biologically predisposed to notice others. And in noticing them, we come to organize ourselves.

Developmental psychology has long recognized the essential role of early caregivers in the construction of self. The infant does not yet have a self-concept, but it has a nervous system that registers safety and danger. When a caregiver responds consistently to distress—picking the child up, soothing them with tone and rhythm—the infant's system begins to associate presence with regulation. These repeated moments of co-regulation gradually teach the child that emotions can be tolerated, and that connection is a source of safety, not threat. In contrast, when a caregiver is neglectful, intrusive, or inconsistent, the infant learns that emotional cues may be ignored or punished, and that closeness may lead to pain.

This process—of being emotionally seen, felt, and regulated by another—is the core of what attachment theorists call "mirroring." It is not merely mimicry; it is the act of attuning to and reflecting back the child's internal state in a way that helps the child make sense of that state. When a baby cries and the caregiver says, "Oh, you're upset, aren't you? You're hungry," the child begins to link inner sensations with meaning. Over time, this scaffolding gives rise to emotional literacy. Without it, feelings can remain unformulated, chaotic, or overwhelming. Adults who grew up without adequate mirroring often struggle to name their own emotional experiences. They may know something is wrong, but not what or why.

This early pattern becomes the blueprint for social self-construction. If a child consistently receives the message that they are lovable, interesting, and emotionally safe, they carry those assumptions into later life. If they receive the message that they are a burden, confusing, or too much, they internalize those identities as well. These impressions form what internal family systems therapy and attachment theory both describe as internal working models: unconscious maps of what to expect from relationships, how much space to take up, and what must be done to maintain connection.

Yet identity does not form in childhood and stop. It is always in motion, shaped by the relational ecology we inhabit. A child's early experiences may be formative, but adult relationships—romantic, platonic, professional—continue to update or reinforce the sense of self. A workplace where someone is consistently ignored may reignite old feelings of invisibility. A partner who consistently listens without judgment may begin to undo the shame that once seemed fused to emotional expression. In this way, each relationship becomes an interpretive lens: not just a space to perform identity, but a space in which identity is either confirmed, challenged, or revised.

Neuroscience backs this up. Social baseline theory suggests that the brain assumes the presence of others as part of its standard operating conditions. Emotional regulation, threat response, and problem-solving are all more efficient when we feel socially supported. Functional MRI studies show that the presence of a trusted other during a stressor reduces activation in brain regions associated with threat. The implication is profound: the human brain is not built to regulate alone. Isolation increases the load on the brain's stress systems. Support decreases it. Co-regulation is not a luxury. It is a structural feature of the human nervous system.

This helps explain why interpersonal neglect or betrayal can feel like an existential injury. It is not just emotionally painful; it disrupts the very system designed to make sense of emotional pain. When a child cries and is punished for it, or a partner reaches out in vulnerability and is met with mockery or silence, the injury runs deeper than the moment. It confuses the nervous system about what is safe, what is real, and whether connection is a viable path to regulation or just another source of dysregulation.

For this reason, identity is not best understood as a fixed trait, but as a dynamic set of patterns—patterns that emerge, stabilize, and adapt in response to the social environment. This is what makes change possible. When people enter into relationships that offer new forms of mirroring, the sense of self can begin to shift. A person who was once terrified of abandonment might, through consistent relational presence, begin to internalize a new message: that they can be valued even when they are not performing. That they can be loved even when they are struggling. That they do not have to manage someone else's emotions in order to be safe.

Social mirroring also operates at cultural and systemic levels. Identities are not only shaped in personal relationships; they are shaped by the broader social gaze. Race, gender, class, body size, ability, and other social markers become mirrors through which identity is reflected. When society offers narrow, distorted, or dehumanizing images of certain identities, those images become part of the internal social mirror. A child growing up in a culture that denigrates their ethnicity or body type is receiving a form of misattunement—not from a single caregiver, but from the collective. Healing at this level requires not only personal work, but collective redefinition: expanding the cultural mirrors so that more people can see themselves with dignity, clarity, and truth.

Still, even in oppressive systems, interpersonal relationships can become sanctuaries. A mentor who affirms a student's intelligence, a friend who consistently shows up, a partner who makes space for vulnerability—these moments counterbalance the toxic reflections of the wider world. They become anchors, slowly reshaping the self not through ideology but through lived experience. Over time, a new message becomes possible: I am real. I am not too much. I belong.

This is the power of the social brain. It takes in the emotional signals of others, integrates them into the sense of self, and uses that composite to navigate the world. When the signals are safe and consistent, identity stabilizes. When they are threatening or absent, identity splinters. But because the brain is plastic—changeable through experience—new social environments can give rise to new internal structures. Not immediately, not easily, but consistently and with care.

The self is not a solo project. It is an emergent property of the emotional fields we inhabit. And when those fields are marked by safety, respect, and clarity, the self doesn't just survive—it organizes, clarifies, and grows.

Projection and the Distorted Other

One of the most powerful, and often invisible, forces in relational life is projection. At its core, projection is the act of unconsciously attributing one's own thoughts, feelings, or traits to someone else. It is not an intentional lie, nor a deliberate manipulation; rather, it is a protective psychological maneuver that allows a person to disown something internally uncomfortable by experiencing it as coming from the outside. Projection is common, automatic, and deeply human. But when left unchecked, it distorts perception, damages relationships, and freezes growth by preventing individuals from engaging with their own emotional reality.

Projection begins as a defense. The psyche uses it to preserve stability, especially when the truth feels too threatening to hold. A person who carries guilt may experience others as judgmental. Someone afraid of their own aggression may see the world as hostile and antagonistic. A person overwhelmed by shame may be hypersensitive to criticism, even when none is present. These reactions are not invented out of thin air. They often feel intuitively true because they align with what the person already believes, deep down, about the world and themselves.

In clinical psychoanalytic tradition, projection is often discussed alongside its counterpart, introjection. Where projection casts unwanted parts of the self outward, introjection absorbs external attitudes, expectations, or criticisms as if they were self-generated. Together, these processes shape the inner world and affect how a person relates to others. When projection dominates, the world becomes a screen upon which internal drama is played out. The other person ceases to be fully real—they become a character in the projector's psychological script.

Projection is especially common in emotionally charged relationships, where the stakes feel high and the vulnerability is acute. Romantic partnerships, parent-child dynamics, and close friendships often carry unresolved emotional material from early life. When someone unconsciously associates a partner with a critical parent or an abandoning caregiver, they may begin to react not to the person in front of them, but to the projection they have cast. This can lead to repeated misunderstandings, chronic conflict, and a sense that the relationship is always teetering on the edge of collapse.

One of the more painful aspects of projection is that it tends to reinforce itself. When someone believes others are untrustworthy, they may behave in guarded, skeptical ways—inviting reciprocal distrust. When someone believes they are unlovable, they may unconsciously sabotage closeness to confirm that belief. The projection, then, becomes a self-fulfilling prophecy. The behavior elicited from others seems to prove the original assumption, even though it was the assumption that shaped the behavior in the first place.

Projection does not always come from overt trauma or obvious emotional wounds. It can also stem from internal conflict: parts of the self that feel unacceptable, weak, contradictory, or embarrassing. A person who wants to be seen as competent may disown their insecurity by accusing others of incompetence. Someone who is terrified of needing others may label others as overly dependent. These projections act like psychological shields. They protect the ego from rupture, but in doing so, they limit relational intimacy and distort perception.

In group dynamics and social identity, projection can become systemic. Prejudices, stereotypes, and scapegoating often operate through large-scale projection. An in-group disowns its fear, aggression, or shame by attributing it to a targeted out-group. Historical examples abound, from racial scapegoating to moral panics. The social mirror becomes fractured, no longer reflecting shared humanity but broadcasting projections of fear, inferiority, or threat. This is one reason why projection must be understood not just psychologically, but ethically. When people fail to recognize their own internal material, they often place the burden of it on others—sometimes with devastating consequences.

In everyday life, projection is often subtle. It can take the form of reading hostility into a neutral comment, assuming disinterest where there is simply distraction, or interpreting silence as rejection. These distortions may seem minor, but over time, they accumulate. They interfere with honest dialogue and create unnecessary distance. What could have been clarified in a simple conversation becomes a source of simmering resentment or unnecessary rupture.

The antidote to projection is not to eliminate it altogether—that would be impossible. Instead, it is to become more curious about one's reactions. When a strong emotional response arises, particularly one that feels out of proportion to the situation, it can be an invitation to look inward. What part of me is being activated here? What story am I telling myself about this other person? Is there a chance I'm reacting to something old rather than something current?

This is the work of psychological ownership. It involves reclaiming what has been disowned and examining the parts of the self that are difficult to hold. This may mean confronting one's own envy, fear, vulnerability, or entitlement. It often involves grief—the grief of recognizing how past experiences shaped current expectations, and how much of one's relational suffering has been rooted in misunderstanding rather than malevolence.

Projection is particularly seductive because it offers temporary relief. It allows someone to preserve a certain self-image, to feel more in control, or to avoid difficult emotions. But it also imposes a cost: relationships become warped by misperception, and growth is arrested by the refusal to face what is inwardly true. Over time, this can lead to loneliness, chronic dissatisfaction, and the painful sense that no one ever really sees or understands the self—when, in reality, the self has been hiding behind projections all along.

In healing-oriented relationships, projection can be gently interrupted. A partner might say, "That's not what I meant, but I wonder what that brought up for you." A therapist might reflect, "It sounds like you're feeling judged—have you felt that way in other relationships too?" These interventions do not accuse or invalidate; they invite reflection. They create space for the person to retrieve what has been cast outward and explore it safely, without shame.

Mature relational identity depends on the gradual reduction of projection. It requires the courage to see others as they are—not as stand-ins for our fears, disappointments, or unmet needs. And it requires the humility to admit that sometimes, what feels true is really just familiar. As people learn to recognize and take responsibility for their projections, their vision becomes clearer. The social mirror becomes less distorted. Relationships become more authentic, more mutual, and more capable of growth.

The goal is not perfection. Everyone projects. But with awareness and practice, people can learn to pause before reacting, to reflect before assuming, and to look inward before blaming outward. This capacity—for psychological containment, relational honesty, and self-inquiry—is one of the foundations of emotional maturity. And it is what allows the self to emerge, not in isolation, but in dialogue—with the truth, with others, and with the full complexity of what it means to be human.

Boundaries and the Shape of the Self

Boundaries are among the most misunderstood aspects of psychological health. Often equated with walls or emotional distance, boundaries are in fact the architecture of selfhood. They define where one person ends and another begins. They govern what we allow in, what we express out, and how we manage the emotional transactions of daily life. Without boundaries, there is no coherent identity. With distorted boundaries, identity becomes reactive, unstable, or rigid. With healthy boundaries, the self has both permeability and protection—the ability to engage without absorption, to give without depletion, and to connect without collapse.

Boundaries are not merely abstract concepts. They are experienced somatically, relationally, and behaviorally. They show up in how people say no, how they tolerate conflict, how they handle guilt, and how they negotiate closeness. A person with collapsed boundaries may feel responsible for others' emotions, struggle to assert their needs, or shape-shift to avoid rejection. A person with overly rigid boundaries may isolate themselves, shut down emotionally, or avoid vulnerability at all costs. Both extremes reflect an internal uncertainty about whether it is safe to be separate, whether needs can coexist with connection, and whether the self is allowed to take up space.

The formation of boundaries begins in childhood. Infants and young children are, by nature, boundary-less. Their sense of self is still forming, and they rely on caregivers to reflect, regulate, and protect. When caregivers respect the child's signals—pausing when the child pulls away, honoring their hunger or satiety, responding to distress with presence rather than intrusion—the child begins to internalize a sense of bodily and emotional autonomy. They learn that their cues matter, that they are not extensions of another's will, and that closeness can happen without engulfment.

When boundaries are violated in early life—through neglect, enmeshment, overcontrol, or abuse—the child adapts, often by over-accommodating or over-defending. A child who grows up being emotionally parentified may learn to suppress their needs and attune entirely to others. A child who is constantly criticized may become emotionally armored, fearing exposure. These adaptations serve a purpose: they allow the child to survive in an environment where the self is not fully respected. But over time, they calcify into relational templates that make mutuality difficult.

Boundaries are not synonymous with disconnection. In fact, the presence of clear, healthy boundaries makes deep connection possible. When people know where they end and others begin, they can engage authentically. They are not reacting from fusion or withdrawal; they are choosing to relate from a place of agency. This is why mature boundaries are not static. They are responsive. They shift based on context, relationship, and emotional bandwidth. A person may disclose more in one context and less in another. They may be available to support a friend one day and need to protect their energy the next. The boundary is not a rule; it is a living expression of self-awareness.

One of the key misunderstandings about boundaries is that they are something we set once, declare, and then enforce. In reality, boundaries are ongoing negotiations. They are not just statements ("I won't tolerate that"), but patterns of behavior, self-regulation, and relational feedback. They require internal clarity: What am I feeling? What am I responsible for? What am I not responsible for? And they require the courage to act in alignment with those insights, even when others are displeased.

The social mirror plays a significant role here. People often learn what boundaries are "allowed" based on the reactions they receive. A child who is scolded for saying no may learn that asserting limits leads to punishment or shame. A person whose family mocks emotional expression may learn to wall off vulnerability. These early social cues shape not only how people treat others, but how they treat themselves. They may override their own limits, gaslight their own discomfort, or minimize their own pain—internalizing the distorted reflection they received.

Boundary repair involves more than confrontation. It begins with recognition: noticing when one has been chronically overextended, chronically withholding, or chronically uncertain. It involves grief: acknowledging the years spent living without adequate self-protection or relational clarity. And it requires practice: small acts of saying no, honest disclosures, decisions not to explain oneself, or moments of sitting with discomfort rather than reflexively people-pleasing. These practices build internal coherence. They signal to the self that it is safe to exist—not as a reflection of others, but as a distinct center of experience.

The work of developing boundaries is not just personal; it is also relational. Others will often resist new boundaries, especially if they have benefited from their absence. A person who suddenly stops overfunctioning in a friendship or family system may be accused of being selfish or cold. A partner who begins to ask for emotional reciprocity may be labeled as needy. These reactions are not signs that the boundary is wrong; they are signs that the dynamic is changing. And when a dynamic changes, everyone involved is forced to confront their own emotional habits.

For boundaries to hold, they must be maintained even in the face of discomfort. This does not mean rigidity. It means returning to the self, over and over, to ask: Is this true for me? Is this sustainable for me? Is this aligned with my values? These questions orient the self in relationship. They prevent collapse into other-focus and prevent isolation through over-defensiveness. They anchor the person in a position of emotional integrity—one where they can love others without losing themselves.

Healthy boundaries also allow for differentiation, a concept in family systems theory that refers to the ability to stay connected to others while maintaining one's own thoughts, feelings, and identity. A highly differentiated person can remain close to someone with different beliefs or emotional reactions without needing to change them or merge with them. This capacity is essential for mature relationships. It allows for tension without rupture, disagreement without contempt, and intimacy without fusion.

The presence of boundaries is often most noticeable in their absence. When someone consistently feels drained, resentful, over-responsible, or emotionally confused, there is usually a boundary issue at play. These feelings are not moral failings; they are signals. They indicate that the self is not being honored, that the emotional ecology is out of balance. Listening to these signals—without judgment—opens the door to change. It allows the person to begin constructing boundaries not out of fear, but out of self-respect.

Ultimately, boundaries are not about controlling others. They are about defining the conditions under which the self can remain whole in relationship. They protect time, energy, emotional safety, and psychological coherence. They allow for choice, for mutuality, and for genuine connection. And they provide the structure within which the self can be both stable and flexible, resilient and responsive, individual and relational.

Co-Regulation and the Shared Nervous System

The idea that we regulate emotion entirely within ourselves is a comforting fiction. In reality, our nervous systems are not independent operators; they are open, permeable, and deeply attuned to the emotional states of those around us. This process, known as co-regulation, is the mutual exchange of emotional cues that helps people manage stress, settle arousal, and maintain a sense of internal balance. Though often unnoticed, co-regulation is happening all the time—between lovers, friends, parents and children, coworkers, and even strangers in public spaces.

It is present when a baby quiets in a parent's arms, not because anything changed in the environment, but because the parent's calm presence offered a stabilizing force. It is present when a partner walks into the room and can tell instantly that something is off, simply by reading the subtle shifts in posture, tone, or expression. It is present when a friend holds eye contact during a story that is hard to tell, offering a kind of emotional holding that keeps the teller from spiraling into overwhelm. In all of these cases, regulation is not generated in isolation—it is scaffolded, supported, and sustained through relationship.

From a neurobiological perspective, co-regulation is grounded in the principles of polyvagal theory, developed by Stephen Porges. This theory describes the vagus nerve as a key player in emotional regulation and social connection. When people feel safe, their parasympathetic nervous system facilitates a calm and engaged state, supporting connection and communication. But when the nervous system perceives threat—whether real or symbolic—it shifts into defensive modes: fight, flight, or freeze. Co-regulation occurs when another person's presence, voice, or touch signals safety to the nervous system, allowing it to return to a regulated state.

Importantly, co-regulation is not something we grow out of. It is not a developmental phase that ends in adulthood with the rise of independence. While it is true that emotional maturity involves developing internal regulatory skills, these skills do not replace relational support—they work alongside it. Adults still need connection to stay regulated. A soldier in a combat zone may stabilize emotionally just by hearing a familiar voice on the phone. A stressed executive may feel their entire body relax during a walk with a trusted friend. Regulation happens between bodies as much as within them.

Co-regulation is also reciprocal. While one person may take on a more stabilizing role in a given moment, the process flows in both directions over time. Parents co-regulate their children, but children also affect their parents. Partners soothe each other in cycles. Even in professional settings, calm leadership can regulate a tense team, while collective anxiety can spiral when left unaddressed. This reciprocity means that people are constantly shaping each other's internal states. Emotional contagion is real—one person's anxiety, joy, frustration, or calm does not stay contained; it reverberates through the system.

Because of this, relationships are not emotionally neutral. They are regulatory systems. Some relationships consistently increase stress and dysregulation. Others offer steadiness and grounding. This is why it matters who we spend time with, how conflict is handled, and whether vulnerability is met with attunement or dismissal. A person in a chronically invalidating relationship may find themselves in a near-constant state of emotional exhaustion—not because they are emotionally fragile, but because their nervous system is being pulled out of balance again and again without relief.

The quality of co-regulation is deeply shaped by attachment history. Those who grew up with emotionally attuned caregivers tend to have a more finely tuned capacity to both receive and offer co-regulation. They are able to notice subtle emotional cues, respond without overcorrecting, and stay present even in the face of strong emotions. Those who lacked this kind of attunement may struggle. They may shut down in the face of distress, escalate quickly, or misinterpret cues. These challenges are not signs of moral failure or emotional immaturity—they are adaptations to relational environments where co-regulation was unreliable, unsafe, or absent.

Healing in these areas often begins not with internal strategies, but with external experiences of consistent, attuned presence. In therapy, a client may slowly learn that their feelings are not too much. In friendship, a person may feel emotionally met for the first time. These relational experiences create new neural pathways. They signal to the nervous system that connection does not have to be threatening, that emotions can be held, and that the self can be known without being engulfed or rejected.

Of course, co-regulation is not always positive. Just as someone can offer emotional grounding, they can also become a source of dysregulation. This can happen through volatility, neglect, emotional manipulation, or simply misattunement. Over time, these patterns corrode trust in others and reinforce the belief that regulation must happen in isolation. The result is often a false independence: a stance of emotional self-sufficiency that functions more like defensive withdrawal than genuine autonomy.

To move from dysregulation to regulation, people often need help identifying what co-regulation feels like. Many have no template for it. They may confuse control with care, or mistake avoidance for calm. They may feel unnerved by genuine attunement, interpreting it as a setup for later abandonment. For these individuals, learning to co-regulate involves more than receiving support; it involves tolerating it. It means noticing the impulse to pull away when someone offers warmth and resisting the urge to downplay distress in order to avoid burdening others.

Developing the capacity to co-regulate also involves being able to offer it to others. This does not mean becoming someone's emotional regulator full-time; that is unsustainable and ultimately disempowering. But it does mean cultivating emotional presence: listening without fixing, naming without judging, and staying grounded in the face of someone else's dysregulation. This presence is often more powerful than advice or solution-giving. It says: I am here with you. I can tolerate your emotion without being overwhelmed by it. You are not alone.

In mature relationships, co-regulation becomes a shared skill. Each person learns when to reach for the other and when to hold their own emotional center. They develop rhythms of support and repair, moments of checking in, and patterns of mutual presence. These habits are not dramatic; they are quiet, subtle, and often unspoken. A hand on the shoulder. A pause in conversation. A phrase that grounds both people in shared reality. Through these moments, emotional safety is built—and with it, the freedom to be vulnerable, real, and whole.

In the end, co-regulation is not weakness. It is a foundational expression of what it means to be human. To need others. To be affected by others. And to find, in the presence of another, the strength to feel, to settle, and to keep going.

* * *

18

Communication and Miscommunication

Human beings talk constantly. We talk to connect, to persuade, to regulate, to defend, to soothe, and to escape. We use words to perform roles, express identity, and claim space in the social world. Yet for all the communication that takes place in a day, so little of it leads to true understanding. Miscommunication is not the exception; it is the default. People talk past each other while thinking they're on the same page. They hear what they fear instead of what was meant. They speak in code without realizing the other person is using a different key. Language fails, not because people are careless, but because communication is layered, emotional, and shaped by histories that few conversations make explicit.

This chapter examines why human communication so often breaks down, and what that breakdown reveals about how people perceive, interpret, and relate. The surface of a conversation rarely tells the whole story. Beneath every exchange are scripts: internalized patterns that guide tone, phrasing, and timing. These scripts come from culture, family, past relationships, and unspoken emotional logic. They shape not only what is said, but what is expected in return. A simple question like "Are you okay?" may register as a loving check-in to one person and as invasive scrutiny to another. The words are the same. The meanings diverge.

Much of the work of being human, emotionally and relationally, involves learning to navigate this divergence. Communication is not the transfer of data. It is an emotional transaction. Every sentence carries subtext: the felt sense behind the words, the mood carried in the voice, the hidden need behind the message. Most people don't say what they mean directly. They imply, hint, gesture. They want to be understood without the risk of vulnerability. They fear rejection or conflict, so they speak in softened terms, hoping the other will intuit their real meaning. When that intuition fails, miscommunication follows.

And it fails often. People are conditioned by different emotional dialects. One person may come from a family that values directness; another may have learned that politeness and subtlety are signs of respect. One partner may try to solve problems through practical suggestions, while the other is seeking emotional validation. Neither is necessarily wrong. But when each assumes the other shares the same frame, the conversation becomes a maze of missed cues. Both walk away feeling unseen, even though both were trying to connect.

Miscommunication is not merely annoying. It shapes the contours of trust, intimacy, and safety in every relationship. When people consistently feel misunderstood, they begin to retreat. When their efforts to connect result in criticism or confusion, they may stop expressing themselves altogether. Over time, these micro-misattunements accumulate. They harden into emotional distance. And ironically, the more emotionally important a relationship is, the more likely it is that these misunderstandings will matter. With strangers, miscommunication is shrugged off. With loved ones, it hurts.

Understanding communication at its psychological core means seeing it not as a skillset to be mastered, but as a mirror of internal life. The way someone speaks, listens, interprets, and responds is deeply connected to their emotional development. A person who was shamed for expressing anger may struggle to name frustration in adulthood. A person who grew up managing a parent's emotions may listen for threat rather than content. These patterns are not random. They are adaptations—often unconscious, sometimes protective—that shape how people use language to navigate closeness and distance.

The process of translation is always in play. Each person interprets what they hear not just through the words spoken, but through a filter of memory, belief, and emotional expectation. This filter can distort or enrich. It can open space for empathy, or it can harden into defensiveness. Meaning is not delivered; it is co-created. Every exchange between two people involves two separate internal worlds trying to reach one another through the fragile bridge of language.

Repair becomes essential. Miscommunication is inevitable, but it does not have to be permanent. What matters is whether people can recognize when something has gone awry, pause long enough to clarify, and offer emotional precision in the aftermath. This means asking, not assuming. Listening beyond rebuttal. Speaking not only to be heard, but to be known. And learning, sometimes, to say: That's not what I meant. Let me try again.

In this chapter, we will explore the psychological architecture behind communication: the scripts that drive it, the subtext that colors it, the distortions that block it, and the practices that can restore it. At the heart of this exploration is a deeper question: not just how people talk, but what they are really trying to say beneath the words—and whether anyone is truly listening.

Unspoken Rules: The Scripts Beneath Our Words

Communication is rarely neutral. Beneath every exchange lies a network of assumptions, roles, and preconditioned responses that shape how we speak, what we hear, and how we interpret others. These are the scripts of human interaction—internalized rules of engagement that operate just beneath awareness. They tell us when to speak and when to stay silent, how much emotion is appropriate to show, which topics are safe and which are not. These scripts are not chosen consciously; they are absorbed from early life, enforced by culture, and refined by social experience. And once internalized, they can become invisible, even as they dictate the rhythm and content of conversation.

Every family system has its own linguistic code. In one household, vulnerability might be spoken openly, even encouraged. In another, emotional openness may be met with discomfort, sarcasm, or avoidance. Some families communicate primarily through teasing or criticism, others through silence and gesture. Over time, children learn what kind of speech earns attention, what kind of tone signals danger, and what kinds of topics are best avoided altogether. These lessons sink deep. They become not only social habits but identity markers. A child who learns that emotions are disruptive may grow into an adult who speaks in controlled, matter-of-fact tones even when discussing deeply painful subjects. A child who learns that conflict is dangerous may become an adult who smiles through discomfort, deflects confrontation, or struggles to assert their needs.

Scripts also emerge from cultural context. Language is not merely a set of words but a set of values. In some cultures, directness is prized—saying exactly what you mean is a sign of respect. In others, indirectness is a form of care, a way of preserving harmony and saving face. These norms influence not only what is said but what is expected in return. A direct speaker may interpret a softer communicator as evasive or passive-aggressive, while the softer communicator may interpret the direct speaker as rude or aggressive. Neither is wrong; both are operating from internalized rules about what communication should feel like.

Complications arise when people with different scripts interact. In romantic relationships, for instance, a person raised in a home where problems were named and processed may be paired with someone who learned to keep emotional distress private. When conflict arises, the former may want to talk through everything immediately, while the latter may shut down or withdraw. What looks like avoidance to one feels like self-protection to the other. Without awareness of these background scripts, each person may interpret the other's behavior through their own lens—leading to frustration, accusation, and misattunement.

These scripts are not always dysfunctional. Many are adaptive and necessary. They allow for shared meaning, efficient interaction, and social cohesion. But problems occur when scripts remain unexamined, especially when they conflict with the emotional needs of the present moment. A person may find themselves repeating patterns—minimizing their feelings, overexplaining, placating anger—not because those choices make sense now, but because they once ensured survival or approval. The script remains, even as the context has changed.

Scripts also dictate emotional pacing. Some people move quickly in conversation—responding fast, interrupting, filling silence with words. Others need more time. They pause, reflect, and choose their language carefully. These differences are often rooted in personality, trauma history, or cultural upbringing. But when left unspoken, they can become points of tension. One person may feel steamrolled; the other may feel ignored. What is needed is not just awareness of one's own pace, but curiosity about the other's.

In high-stakes communication—conflict, confession, repair—the influence of internal scripts becomes even more pronounced. People fall back on learned patterns. They speak in ways that once protected them, often unaware that these strategies may now be misfiring. For example, someone may use humor to defuse emotional tension, unaware that their partner experiences it as dismissive. Another may become overly formal during difficult conversations, not because they don't care, but because vulnerability was once punished or mocked.

Awareness of scripts is the first step toward flexibility. When people can name the patterns they learned, they begin to see them as one way of being, rather than the only way. This opens the door to choice. It allows someone to ask, "Is this way of speaking still serving me? Is it allowing me to be understood? Is it helping or hurting the connection I want to build?" These questions are not about blame; they are about expanding capacity. They invite people to step out of reflex and into intention.

Therapeutic work often involves surfacing these hidden rules. Clients may come in believing that their communication problems are about vocabulary or assertiveness, when the real issue lies deeper—in the assumptions about safety, belonging, and worth that underlie how they speak. A therapist might ask: "What would it mean if you said that out loud?" or "Where did you learn that certain emotions weren't allowed in conversation?" These inquiries reveal the architecture of the script, making space for revision.

In relationships, a shared language around scripts can be transformative. Partners who learn to identify their own patterns—and communicate about them without shame—can begin to co-create new ones. They might say, "I tend to shut down when I feel overwhelmed; it's not that I don't care," or "I grew up in a house where silence meant trouble, so when you go quiet, I get anxious." These disclosures make room for understanding. They replace accusation with context. They offer both people a chance to see the conversation not just as a moment, but as a reflection of a deeper map.

Ultimately, scripts are part of what it means to be human. No one communicates in a vacuum. Everyone brings a past, a culture, a set of emotional habits. The work is not to erase those influences, but to become fluent in them—to understand the language one speaks, and the language others may be using. When this fluency grows, communication becomes less about getting it right and more about staying engaged. Less about fixing misunderstandings and more about understanding where they come from.

What Wasn't Said: Reading the Emotional Subtext

In every conversation, something is left unsaid. Sometimes it is intentional—a held breath, a redirected sentence, a glance that says more than words could. Other times, it is unconscious: a feeling too vague to name, a need not yet known, a discomfort dismissed before it finds language. Beneath the spoken message lies the emotional subtext—the tone, posture, timing, and silence that frame meaning and give it emotional weight. Subtext is not an accessory to communication. It is central to how people interpret each other. And when it is misread or ignored, communication collapses into confusion, resentment, or emotional disconnect.

Human beings are wired for subtext. Before children have access to language, they learn to attune to facial expressions, voice inflection, and physical touch. These early experiences form the basis of emotional literacy: the ability to read cues, intuit mood, and navigate relational space. A caregiver's raised eyebrow, a change in vocal tempo, a soothing rhythm of touch—all of these communicate long before words are formed. As language develops, these nonverbal cues do not disappear. They integrate with verbal communication, creating a multilayered form of interaction in which what is said and how it is said are equally meaningful.

But this integration is fragile. Subtext depends on mutual awareness, cultural familiarity, and emotional safety. When these conditions are disrupted, subtext becomes noisy, distorted, or unintelligible. In emotionally charged conversations, for instance, subtext may overwhelm content. A partner may say, "I'm fine," while their tone signals anything but. A friend may insist, "I don't mind," yet their clipped phrasing and withdrawn body language reveal otherwise. The message is split between language and emotion. If the listener takes the words at face value and misses the tone, they may walk away falsely reassured—only to discover later that trust has eroded or that pain was quietly dismissed.

This tension is especially visible in cultures or families where direct expression of emotion is discouraged. In these environments, people often develop sophisticated subtextual communication as a workaround. Sarcasm, humor, passive phrasing, or exaggerated politeness become vehicles for expressing dissatisfaction or setting boundaries. But these indirect forms require interpretation. When others do not pick up on the subtext, or interpret it differently, frustration builds. The speaker feels they have communicated clearly—after all, they dropped hints, changed tone, withdrew affection. But to the listener, no message was ever explicitly delivered. Misattunement becomes inevitable.

Emotional subtext also becomes scrambled when the speaker and listener are in different emotional states. A person in distress may overinterpret a neutral comment as critical. Someone in a calm state may miss the rising agitation in another's voice. Even the same sentence can carry radically different meanings depending on context. "You're late," said with amusement, invites play. Said with tension, it signals frustration. Said with resignation, it carries sadness. Words are carriers of emotion, and emotion modifies meaning.

Part of the difficulty lies in the fact that many people are unaware of the subtext they emit. Emotional signals are often automatic. People may raise their voice, fold their arms, or speak faster without realizing it. These cues may contradict their verbal message, causing internal incoherence. A parent might say, "You can tell me anything," while their expression signals judgment. A supervisor may insist, "I'm here to support you," while their posture communicates disinterest. The dissonance between words and subtext erodes trust. Listeners pick up on the emotional tone, even if they can't articulate why something feels off.

Conversely, some people become hypersensitive to subtext—especially those who grew up in environments where safety depended on accurately reading others' moods. These individuals may overread tone, looking for hidden meanings even when none exist. A slightly delayed text response might trigger anxiety. A flat expression might be interpreted as anger. Their nervous system has been trained to scan for threat in the emotional atmosphere. For them, emotional subtext is not subtle background; it is primary data.

This hyperattunement can create its own communication challenges. When one person is reading between the lines and the other is communicating only at the surface, frustration grows. The highly attuned individual may expect the other to be equally sensitive to tone and pacing, and feel wounded when that sensitivity is not reciprocated. The less attuned person may feel accused or confused by reactions they didn't anticipate. Each is speaking a different emotional language—one of subtle signals, the other of direct speech.

To navigate this complexity, people must cultivate dual awareness: attending to both content and emotional tone, listening not just to what is said, but how it lands. This requires slowing down. Many communication failures happen not because of malice or apathy, but because of speed. In fast-paced interactions, tone is overlooked, cues are missed, and emotional feedback loops are never completed. The body speaks more slowly than the mind. To read subtext accurately, one must first be emotionally present.

Developing this presence involves internal regulation. A dysregulated listener cannot attune to others' cues. When flooded by their own anxiety or anger, their capacity to pick up subtle emotional signals shuts down. Likewise, a dysregulated speaker sends confusing signals—shifting tone, erratic pacing, or emotional leakage that contradicts intent. Subtext clarity emerges from emotional clarity. When a person is internally grounded, their subtext becomes more coherent, and their capacity to interpret others improves.

Repairing misattuned subtext also means learning to name it. This is where metacommunication becomes valuable: the ability to talk about how one is talking. "I'm noticing that your tone changed—can we pause?" or "I might be misreading you, but I'm sensing some tension" are invitations to clarify subtext. These moments can feel awkward at first, but they are essential for building relational accuracy. They move communication from assumption to inquiry, from performance to authenticity.

Emotional subtext, at its best, is a powerful force of connection. A wordless glance can communicate deep understanding. A shared silence can feel more validating than paragraphs. Subtext is how people say, "I see you," without speaking it aloud. But when misaligned, it becomes a source of confusion, alienation, or emotional injury. Learning to read and regulate emotional subtext is not a communication skill, it is a relational capacity. It is the ability to feel, to notice, to care about how one's presence affects others.

And perhaps most importantly, it is the ability to stay with the complexity of what is not said, knowing that sometimes the deepest truths arrive quietly, carried not in language, but in tone, timing, and shared presence.

Lost in Translation: Why We Talk Past Each Other

Two people sit across from each other, exchanging words that are technically correct, even polite. On the surface, it seems like a conversation is taking place. But emotionally, something is missing. They leave the interaction confused, irritated, or oddly alone. This is the experience of talking past each other—of using the same language but speaking from entirely different emotional or psychological coordinates. It happens in marriages, workplaces, friendships, and therapy offices. And it is one of the most common and overlooked forms of relational breakdown.

The problem often starts with assumptions. Most people enter conversations with the implicit belief that meaning is shared. They assume that their words mean the same thing to the listener as they do to themselves. They believe that tone is neutral, that intent is obvious, that their context is understood. These assumptions create a false sense of clarity. Communication becomes performance rather than inquiry: a delivery of thoughts, not an exploration of meaning.

What's often missing is recognition of the listener's interpretive frame. Every person filters conversation through a complex internal system: memory, mood, relational history, cultural background, emotional sensitivity, and cognitive bias. These filters color what is heard, how it's interpreted, and what response is deemed appropriate. A sentence that sounds like kindness to one person might feel like pity to another. A question meant to show care may come across as interrogation. Words are not universal tokens; they are context-dependent signals. When context is mismatched, interpretation fails.

This failure becomes even more pronounced in emotionally loaded situations. When people are upset, anxious, or defending themselves from perceived threat, their ability to hear accurately decreases. Cognitive narrowing occurs. The brain prioritizes safety over nuance. A mildly critical comment might trigger shame in someone with a history of rejection. A factual correction might feel like domination to someone who grew up being talked down to. In these moments, people don't just hear what is said—they hear what their nervous system has been trained to expect.

This is especially evident in conflict. Arguments often escalate not because of what was said, but because of how it was interpreted. One partner says, "I need more space," intending to set a healthy boundary. The other hears, "You don't love me anymore." The first defends their intent; the second defends their pain. Neither is wrong. But both are locked into defending a version of the conversation that feels true to them. They are no longer discussing the same moment; they are reacting to different realities.

Much of this dynamic can be explained by what psychologists call *confirmation bias*: the tendency to notice, interpret, and remember information that confirms existing beliefs. In relationships, this means that once someone expects to be misunderstood, dismissed, or rejected, they begin to see evidence of that everywhere. A neutral tone is perceived as cold. A delayed response is taken as proof of disinterest. These interpretations may be partially accurate—but they are also shaped by expectation. The listener is not only hearing the speaker; they are hearing their own fears, projections, and memories layered onto the message.

Trauma exacerbates this dynamic. People who have experienced emotional neglect, abandonment, or abuse often develop protective listening habits. They scan for cues of danger, control, or dismissal, even when none are present. They may mishear intention, interrupt tone, or prepare counterarguments before the other has finished speaking. Their goal is self-protection. But the result is often relational friction. They may seem defensive, difficult, or closed off—not because they don't want connection, but because connection feels risky.

Another barrier to mutual understanding is semantic drift: the way language changes meaning over time or between groups. In some families, "I'm fine" really does mean fine. In others, it means "don't ask." In one workplace, "urgent" might imply a same-day turnaround. In another, it means "within the week." These differences seem trivial until they produce breakdowns in trust or performance. Shared vocabulary does not guarantee shared meaning. Clarity requires explicit calibration.

And then there is emotional literacy—the ability to name and describe internal states accurately. Many people struggle with this. They might say, "I'm tired," when they are actually discouraged. Or "I'm angry," when the deeper emotion is shame. This imprecision creates further confusion. The listener may respond to the stated emotion rather than the real one, leading to mismatched support. Without a shared understanding of what's truly being felt, people offer the wrong kind of empathy—or none at all.

Technology adds another layer. Text-based communication strips away tone, body language, and facial expression—all crucial cues for interpreting intent. Misunderstandings multiply. A period at the end of a sentence may feel cold. A delayed reply may feel like rejection. Emojis, punctuation, and timing carry disproportionate emotional weight. In digital spaces, where subtext is harder to read, people project even more of their own internal state onto what they receive.

Repairing these misfires starts with humility. People must learn to approach conversation not as performance but as co-construction. This means letting go of the need to be right, and embracing the work of being clear. It means checking interpretations—"Did you mean that the way I heard it?"—and listening beyond rebuttal. It means being willing to pause when communication goes sideways, to name the moment rather than escalate it.

It also means slowing down. Most miscommunications happen not because people lack the right words, but because they're moving too quickly to notice misalignment. The nervous system speeds up under stress. Speech becomes clipped. Listening becomes reactive. Slowing the pace of interaction creates space for checking assumptions, asking questions, and adjusting tone. Clarity is rarely found in urgency.

Finally, it means honoring difference. Not every misunderstanding is a problem to fix. Sometimes it reveals a deeper divergence in worldview, emotional need, or relational style. The goal is not to eliminate all misunderstanding, but to create enough mutual understanding that connection remains possible. This requires patience, emotional maturity, and a shared commitment to navigating the messiness of meaning.

Talking past each other is not just a communication error. It is a psychological event—a clash of interpretations shaped by experience, emotion, and memory. To bridge that gap requires more than better language. It requires better listening, more honest self-reflection, and a shared willingness to slow down and try again.

Toward Clarity: Repair, Validation, and Emotional Precision

Every relationship worth keeping eventually runs into miscommunication. Words miss the mark, tone falls flat, meanings get twisted by stress, history, or emotion. The goal of meaningful connection is not to eliminate these breakdowns, but to become skillful in recovering from them. This is the work of emotional precision: the ability to identify what went wrong, to validate the other person's experience without defensiveness, and to communicate in a way that honors both clarity and care.

Repair is not an apology alone, though an apology may be part of it. Repair is a set of relational practices that restore trust after a rupture. In the context of communication, this means acknowledging misalignment, asking for clarification, and demonstrating genuine curiosity about the other person's experience. "That's not what I meant" is a common impulse, but it often lands as invalidation. A better starting point is, "I can see how that landed differently than I intended—can we talk more about what you heard?" This signals willingness. It affirms that the goal is understanding, not control of the narrative.

Emotional validation is one of the most powerful tools in this process. To validate is not to agree, nor to accept blame for someone else's projections. It is to recognize that their emotional reaction makes sense given their internal context. A partner might say, "When you walked away, I felt abandoned." Even if the other did not intend to abandon, that feeling is real. Responding with, "That wasn't my intent" short-circuits the emotional process. Responding with, "I didn't realize that felt like abandonment to you—thank you for telling me," opens space for mutual repair.

Many people resist validation because they fear it implies guilt. But validation is not confession. It is respect. It is the capacity to acknowledge that two people can experience the same moment differently, and that both experiences matter. It is also an antidote to defensiveness. When people feel heard, they soften. When they feel dismissed, they dig in. Defensive communication is often a response to feeling erased, not just misunderstood.

Emotional precision supports this work. Precision does not mean robotic detachment. It means developing the vocabulary and self-awareness to name what is actually happening inside. Many communication breakdowns occur because people use vague or inaccurate emotional labels. "I'm upset" could mean angry, disappointed, betrayed, embarrassed, or lonely. Each of these requires a different kind of response. Without precision, the speaker may feel increasingly isolated and the listener increasingly helpless.

Therapeutic traditions like nonviolent communication (NVC) emphasize the importance of distinguishing between observation, feeling, need, and request. Rather than saying, "You made me feel ignored," a person might say, "When I shared and didn't hear a response, I felt alone. I think I need more acknowledgment when I open up. Would you be willing to let me know what you're thinking in those moments?" This approach clarifies the emotional landscape without blame. It invites dialogue, not defensiveness.

But emotional precision is not only about phrasing. It depends on internal regulation. A person who is flooded with emotion cannot access the language centers of the brain effectively. Their speech becomes reactive, imprecise, or impulsive. Part of developing communication skill is learning to pause long enough to down-regulate before speaking. This may mean taking a breath, stepping away, or simply acknowledging, "I'm not in a good state to talk right now. Can we come back to this?" That, too, is a form of precision—knowing when not to speak.

Clarity also involves recognizing habitual distortions. People often have filters shaped by childhood, trauma, or chronic insecurity. These filters warp perception: a neutral comment sounds critical, a disagreement feels like abandonment. Without self-awareness, these distortions are projected onto others. But with reflection, they can be managed. A person might say, "I'm realizing that I heard judgment in your tone, but I think that may be coming from my own fear of being wrong." This level of ownership transforms the conversation. It makes it safe for the other person to be honest without becoming the target of displaced emotion.

In relationships, communication is never just information exchange. It is always about emotional positioning: Who is safe? Who is in control? Who matters in this moment? Repair depends on noticing these positions and adjusting accordingly. A listener might need to step back from problem-solving and simply witness. A speaker might need to acknowledge their own part in the dynamic. Both might need to reaffirm their shared purpose: to understand each other better, even when it's hard.

Moments of repair, when handled well, are not signs of weakness in a relationship. They are its strength. Couples, teams, and families that communicate well are not those who avoid rupture, but those who repair consistently and without shame. They treat miscommunication not as failure but as feedback. They notice the tone shift, the tightened jaw, the dropped gaze—and they circle back. "I think we lost each other for a second. Can we try again?" These small moments build trust, coherence, and relational safety over time.

Communication is both an art and a discipline. It requires emotional fluency, cognitive awareness, and above all, humility. No one gets it right all the time. But the goal is not perfection—it is presence. When people stay present through misunderstanding, stay kind through frustration, and stay curious through conflict, they build relationships where clarity is possible and where being human—messy, imprecise, vulnerable—is not a liability, but the very thing that deepens connection.

* * *

19

Intimacy, Trust, and Repair

Intimacy is one of the most sought-after human experiences and one of the most poorly understood. It is mistaken for warmth, conflated with sex, confused with comfort, and idealized beyond recognition. Most people long for it; few can define it clearly. At its core, intimacy is not a feeling, not a mood, not a spark—it is a pattern of relating in which both people feel seen, safe, and significant. It is not automatic, nor is it passive. It must be constructed and maintained, often in the face of fear.

Trust, in a similar way, is misunderstood. It is imagined as something you either have or do not, like a light switch or a bank balance. But trust is relational. It is a pattern, not a promise. It is built through repeated interactions where someone proves that they are accountable to both reality and to you—that their behavior lines up with their words, that they regulate their emotional impact, and that they can take responsibility when they fall short. People do not earn trust with grand declarations. They earn it in the small, quiet moments when they could deflect blame but do not. Or when they could lie, and choose not to.

The reason this chapter matters is because most of what breaks love is not cruelty, but disconnection. Misattunement. Avoidance. Defensiveness. A slow retreat from vulnerability. The people who love each other may still love each other, but without repair, without the tools to process rupture or renegotiate emotional needs, even deep love can become distant, brittle, or unrecognizable.

There are predictable reasons relationships erode. And just as predictably, there are things that can stabilize and restore them. This chapter will walk through both sides of the equation: what makes love work, and what makes it fall apart. It will explore intimacy as a psychological and relational structure—one that can be intentionally strengthened or unintentionally dismantled. It will look at trust not as a fixed commodity, but as a living process. And it will focus deeply on rupture: how it happens, why it matters, and what is required for repair.

There is no single formula for keeping love alive. But there are clear psychological patterns that determine whether a relationship thrives, stagnates, or collapses under pressure. This chapter is not about romance or conflict resolution in the traditional sense. It is about emotional architecture: how people build something between them, brick by brick—and what happens when that structure is neglected, undermined, or destroyed. More importantly, it is about the repair process, and how to recognize when repair is truly possible.

The Architecture of Intimacy

Intimacy begins not with passion, but with presence. It is not something people fall into by accident or sustain through chemistry alone. It is a relational structure built slowly over time, through mutual risk-taking, emotional attunement, and shared psychological space. The mistake many people make is assuming intimacy means simply feeling close to someone or enjoying their company. But real intimacy is not about proximity—it is about emotional exposure. It means allowing another person access to your inner world, and being careful, skilled, and attentive enough to do the same for them.

This kind of vulnerability requires more than affection. It requires psychological maturity. People must be able to tolerate discomfort, name their needs, regulate their reactions, and stay present in moments of tension or uncertainty. They must be able to differentiate between their own thoughts and feelings and those of their partner, without collapsing into emotional fusion or withdrawal. Intimacy is not built on constant agreement or identical worldviews; it is built on the ability to stay connected across difference.

At its core, intimacy involves the feeling of being understood and accepted. This is not a one-way street. Emotional intimacy is co-created—it requires that both people attune to each other's emotional states without losing touch with their own. This is where the concept of co-regulation becomes central. In an intimate relationship, partners do not merely express emotions; they help each other manage them. They become safe harbors in moments of emotional turbulence. This kind of emotional responsiveness strengthens the bond and fosters security.

Psychologically, intimacy depends on a foundation of attachment. Bowlby's attachment theory helps explain how early relationships shape our capacity to form and sustain closeness. A securely attached individual will generally feel comfortable both giving and receiving affection, setting boundaries, and recovering from conflict. Anxiously attached individuals may pursue closeness in desperate, consuming ways, while avoidantly attached individuals may retreat or deflect when intimacy begins to deepen. These patterns do not just appear in childhood; they echo into adulthood, shaping how people experience love, trust, and emotional closeness.

Internal working models—our unconscious expectations about how relationships work—also play a decisive role. These models are formed early, often shaped by how caregivers responded to our emotions, how safe we felt in conflict, and whether we were taught that our needs were valid. As adults, these models filter how we interpret our partner's behavior. If you were raised in an environment where love was inconsistent or conditional, you may read neutrality as rejection, or conflict as abandonment. You may subconsciously push people away just to see if they come back. These patterns are not destiny, but they are powerful. Unless brought into awareness, they can quietly distort how intimacy is experienced and expressed.

Cultural expectations complicate matters further. In many Western societies, people are taught to equate intimacy with romantic or sexual connection. But psychological intimacy can exist in many forms: between friends, siblings, long-term companions, even within therapist-client relationships. What all forms of intimacy share is a kind of emotional closeness rooted in authenticity, not performance. It is not about being impressive, but being honest. Not about being perfect, but being open.

Intimacy also requires boundaries—not as walls, but as clarity. Emotional closeness does not mean total merger. In fact, true intimacy cannot exist without separateness. Two people must have distinct identities, needs, and inner lives, or else the relationship becomes enmeshment, not intimacy. Boundaries allow people to show up fully without fear of emotional engulfment. They protect the conditions that make vulnerability possible: safety, agency, and trust.

When intimacy is strong, it creates what psychologists call a secure base—a sense that you can be fully yourself and still be loved. This is the paradox of intimacy: it is built on repeated evidence that someone can witness the parts of you that feel unlovable, and love you anyway. But this process is never automatic. Even the most loving relationships can falter if the conditions for emotional openness are not continually maintained. Trust must be reaffirmed, safety must be reestablished, and communication must be recalibrated as both people grow and change.

In that sense, intimacy is a practice. It is not a static state, but a living dynamic. And like any practice, it requires attention, adjustment, and care. When it is absent, relationships may still function—but they begin to feel hollow. When it is present, people feel not only connected, but expanded. They are able to see more clearly, feel more deeply, and grow more fully within the context of relationship.

Trust as a Living System

Trust is not a promise. It is not a personality trait, a static agreement, or a blind belief in someone's goodness. Trust is a living psychological system that adapts, degrades, and regenerates in response to behavior. It is built not through intention, but through impact—through a consistent pattern of reliability, truth-telling, self-regulation, and emotional accountability. And while it can be strong and resilient, it is never invincible. Even deeply rooted trust can be damaged through avoidance, inconsistency, or self-protection disguised as kindness.

Psychologically speaking, trust forms through exposure. You do not trust someone because they reassure you, but because you observe how they behave under pressure. You learn whether they respond to your vulnerability with care or defensiveness. You track whether they follow through on commitments, tell you the truth even when it is uncomfortable, and acknowledge their impact when harm is done. These are the micro-behaviors that build or corrode trust—not declarations of love, not gifts, not promises of forever.

Trust grows in environments of emotional congruence. When someone says one thing and does another, when they act kind but seethe with resentment, or when they deny the obvious to preserve their image, trust erodes. The human nervous system is exquisitely attuned to misalignment. Children raised in emotionally incongruent environments often develop hypervigilance, scanning for subtle cues that the emotional reality does not match the verbal one. As adults, they may struggle to trust others even when no threat is present—not because they are paranoid, but because they have learned that words are not always reliable indicators of safety.

At the same time, trust is relational; it exists not in isolation, but in interaction. You may trust one person deeply while remaining guarded with another. This is not about paranoia or favoritism—it reflects how trust adapts to the psychological dynamics of each relationship. If one partner consistently meets repair with defensiveness, or disappears in times of need, trust cannot be sustained. If another partner is honest, emotionally available, and willing to make themselves known, trust can flourish—even in the face of conflict.

In attachment theory, trust functions as the operational glue of secure bonds. It allows for exploration, conflict, individuation, and reunion without fear of abandonment or retaliation. When trust is present, couples can disagree without feeling like the entire relationship is at risk. They can name needs without fearing rejection, set boundaries without guilt, and admit fault without collapse. But when trust is fragile, even minor disagreements can feel threatening. Emotional safety disappears, and partners often shift into protective modes—criticism, stonewalling, avoidance, or control.

There is a difference between earned trust and assumed trust. Many people, especially in the early stages of relationships, give trust as a default. They assume good intent, project their values onto others, and hope that mutual affection is enough. But psychological trust must be earned—not through dramatic gestures, but through mundane consistency. You trust someone when they have shown, again and again, that they can handle the truth, show up when it matters, and take responsibility when they fail.

Responsibility is a crucial component. When people harm others—whether through dishonesty, neglect, or emotional injury—and then minimize, justify, or shift blame, trust collapses. Not necessarily because of the original rupture, but because of the response to it. People often tolerate mistakes far more easily than they tolerate betrayal of accountability. Trust can survive imperfection. It cannot survive gaslighting.

This is where the concept of rupture and repair becomes essential. In close relationships, rupture is inevitable. People will say the wrong thing, miss a cue, act out of fear, or retreat when they should have leaned in. The strength of the relationship does not lie in the absence of rupture, but in the capacity for repair. Repair requires both vulnerability and skill. It involves acknowledging the rupture clearly, taking ownership of the emotional impact, and making real behavioral change—not just offering an apology.

Many people, however, are unpracticed in this. They mistake appeasement for repair, or conflict avoidance for trust maintenance. But trust is not maintained by sweeping things under the rug. It is maintained by facing the rupture directly, even if it is uncomfortable. This is especially true in long-term partnerships, where unresolved tensions can calcify into distrust that poisons even the affectionate moments. When someone avoids addressing a pattern that hurts the other person, they are essentially asking them to swallow that pain in the name of harmony. Over time, this silencing breeds resentment, and with it, a quiet erosion of trust.

Another common misunderstanding is the idea that love and trust are interchangeable. People say "I love you" as if it guarantees trustworthiness. But love without trust is not intimacy; it is longing. You can love someone deeply and still not trust them with your emotions, your pain, or your truth. And if you do not trust that they can hold your vulnerability with care, your nervous system will remain on guard, even in their presence. This is why relationships that lack trust often feel emotionally exhausting. You are constantly managing what can be said, what must be hidden, and how much of yourself is safe to bring forward.

Trust is also shaped by each person's psychological history. If someone has been betrayed, abandoned, or dismissed in past relationships, their baseline level of trust may be lower. This is not a character flaw; it is a survival adaptation. Their mind and body have learned to protect them from future harm. In healthy relationships, trust can be slowly rebuilt—not through persuasion, but through attuned presence. If you are in relationship with someone who has been hurt, the task is not to convince them to trust you. It is to behave in a way that makes trust possible again.

Ultimately, trust is not about never hurting each other. It is about what happens afterward. It is about knowing that when hurt occurs, both people will move toward repair rather than away from responsibility. That each person is willing to face the discomfort of truth, not retreat into justification. Trust is made of many small choices over time: to listen, to pause, to stay curious rather than reactive, to speak honestly when it is easier not to. These choices, made consistently, become the nervous system of the relationship. They carry the signals of safety or danger, connection or threat.

And when trust breaks, it is rarely because of a single act. It is because of a cumulative sense that the other person is no longer emotionally accountable to you—or perhaps never was. Rebuilding trust is possible, but it requires time, truth, and effort that matches the depth of the rupture. No shortcuts. No quick fixes.

In a psychological sense, trust is the environment that makes all other relational processes possible. Without it, intimacy becomes dangerous, conflict becomes war, and communication becomes strategy. With it, love becomes something expansive—something that can hold the complexity of human emotion without fear.

The Mechanics of Rupture

Love rarely breaks all at once. More often, it erodes in increments—through missed signals, repeated misunderstandings, unattended injuries, and the slow decline of emotional responsiveness. The mechanics of rupture are deceptively simple: when one partner feels unsafe, unseen, or emotionally alone—and that feeling persists over time—trust begins to decay, and with it, the conditions for intimacy start to collapse.

Rupture is not always dramatic. Most of it unfolds quietly, below the threshold of conscious awareness. A dismissive remark that goes unacknowledged. A moment of vulnerability met with silence. A pattern of avoidance that leaves one partner carrying the emotional weight of the relationship. These moments might seem small in isolation, but cumulatively, they chip away at the felt sense of connection. What begins as subtle discomfort becomes resentment, emotional shutdown, or volatility. Left unaddressed, the system tilts out of balance.

Psychologically, ruptures often arise from the collision between unmet needs and emotional defense. Every person in a relationship brings with them a blueprint—formed by childhood experience, cultural messaging, and past relational trauma—of what love is supposed to look like. When reality doesn't match that blueprint, when needs are not recognized or honored, disappointment takes root. And if those needs are not even acknowledged—if the other person seems unwilling or unable to engage—emotional defenses come online. Withdrawal, criticism, sarcasm, caretaking, control. Each one serves a purpose: protect the self from pain, rejection, or shame. But in doing so, each one creates more distance.

Ruptures are accelerated when partners operate from different emotional languages. One might value direct conversation; the other avoids conflict. One might need closeness to feel secure; the other needs space to self-regulate. These differences are not inherently incompatible, but without communication and mutual interpretation, they become sources of tension. One person's need for autonomy feels like abandonment. One person's need for reassurance feels like smothering. The more misunderstood each partner feels, the more likely they are to default to their own coping strategies, even when those strategies hurt the relationship.

John Gottman's research on the "Four Horsemen"—criticism, contempt, defensiveness, and stonewalling—offers a clinically grounded understanding of how rupture unfolds. Criticism attacks the partner's character rather than addressing behavior. Contempt introduces mockery, disgust, or moral superiority, which is especially toxic to trust. Defensiveness blocks accountability, signaling that the partner's perspective is invalid or unreasonable. Stonewalling shuts down the conversation entirely, often through silence, disengagement, or physical withdrawal. These behaviors are not just unpleasant; they are corrosive. When they become habitual, they create a climate of emotional unsafety in which repair feels impossible.

Rupture is also intensified by avoidance. Many people, especially those socialized to keep the peace or suppress emotion, will tolerate harm without speaking up. They fear conflict, want to be seen as easygoing, or do not believe their needs are valid. But emotions do not disappear; they accumulate. When the need for safety or recognition is ignored repeatedly, the body keeps score. Over time, tolerance becomes bitterness. Quiet endurance turns into rage. And when rupture finally surfaces, it often does so with disproportionate force—not because of that moment's content, but because of the emotional backlog behind it.

One of the most damaging forms of rupture occurs when one partner minimizes or denies the other's emotional reality. This might take the form of gaslighting, but it can also show up in more subtle ways: dismissive tone, repeated interruptions, rolling eyes, or strategic redirection. These behaviors signal that one person's perception is invalid, excessive, or irrelevant. Over time, this undermines emotional safety and destabilizes the partner's sense of internal coherence. What was once a secure connection becomes a minefield of self-doubt.

Power dynamics complicate rupture as well. In relationships where one partner holds more social, financial, or emotional leverage, rupture can be perpetuated by imbalance. The more powerful partner may dictate the terms of communication, demand forgiveness on their timeline, or weaponize vulnerability. The less powerful partner may comply out of fear, dependence, or confusion. This creates a relational ecosystem where rupture becomes embedded in the structure of interaction—not a deviation from the norm, but the norm itself.

Rupture is not always relational. Sometimes it is internal. A person may feel torn between staying and leaving, between being who they are and who they think they need to be to maintain love. Internal contradictions—such as wanting closeness but fearing exposure, or needing support but fearing dependence—can lead to chronic ambivalence. This ambivalence often goes unspoken, but it seeps into the relationship through irritability, lack of affection, or inconsistent engagement. Partners may feel the shift but not understand it, leading to confusion and further disconnection.

A rupture becomes dangerous not when it happens, but when it is left unacknowledged. Relationships can survive extraordinary difficulty when both people are willing to face what is true. But when rupture is denied, when its impact is downplayed, when one partner moves on while the other is still bleeding—something fractures. The emotional ledger becomes unbalanced. The injured partner begins to carry not just the pain of the original hurt, but the loneliness of being the only one still feeling it.

Another sign of rupture is emotional asymmetry. When one partner consistently initiates repair, raises concerns, or carries the burden of relational upkeep, the relationship begins to feel more like management than mutuality. Even if the love is real, the weight becomes unsustainable. Emotional labor without reciprocity breeds exhaustion. It is not the presence of conflict that drains people; it is the feeling that they are alone in caring about it.

Children who grow up in environments where rupture is ignored or punished often become adults who either fear conflict entirely or unconsciously recreate rupture as a familiar dynamic. They may provoke, withdraw, or cling—not because they want to destroy the relationship, but because it is the only way they know how to feel seen. This is why rupture must be understood in developmental terms. Many of the patterns that break love in adulthood were first learned in childhood as strategies to survive disconnection.

But rupture is not simply about pain. It is also about unmet expectations. Many people enter relationships with implicit contracts: If I love you, you will love me back. If I am loyal, you will never hurt me. If I make myself small, you will never leave. These contracts are often invisible until they are broken. And when they are broken—by infidelity, indifference, emotional distance, or betrayal—the resulting rupture can feel existential. It is not just the relationship that is in crisis, but the person's entire framework for safety and meaning.

Understanding the mechanics of rupture allows us to see relational pain not as random or hopeless, but as patterned and repairable. Relationships break for specific reasons. Not because people stop loving each other, but because the behaviors that sustain love are no longer being practiced.

When partners become adversaries rather than allies, when emotional truths are avoided rather than integrated, rupture becomes the logical outcome.

The good news is that rupture does not have to be the end. But it does have to be faced. With clarity. With courage. With enough psychological humility to name what has happened without sugarcoating it. Only then can repair become possible—not as an act of forgiveness, but as an act of emotional integrity.

Repair, Renewal, and the Decision to Stay

Repair is not the same thing as resolution. It is not a tidy ending to a period of difficulty, nor is it the erasure of pain. Repair is the ongoing process of restoring emotional safety after rupture, of rebuilding trust where it has been fractured, and of deciding—deliberately, actively—to stay in relationship with one another, knowing the full complexity of what that requires. It is not reactive; it is architectural. Repair is how relationships become resilient, not because they avoid injury, but because they learn how to metabolize it.

Psychologically, repair is most effective when it is both specific and embodied. Generic apologies—"I'm sorry you feel that way," "Let's just move on," or "I didn't mean it like that"—often fail to land. They signal discomfort rather than responsibility. Effective repair requires emotional precision: naming the injury, acknowledging the emotional impact, and taking ownership of what contributed to the rupture. It also requires behavioral follow-through. Without change, repair becomes performance. And performance erodes trust.

Many people struggle with repair because they have never seen it modeled. In families where conflict was denied, exploded, or punished, the idea of facing rupture with openness may feel foreign or unsafe. As adults, they may default to defensiveness, minimization, or appeasement—none of which restore connection. This is where psychological maturity becomes crucial. Repair depends not just on love, but on the ability to self-regulate, to tolerate discomfort, and to see the relationship as a shared system rather than a battlefield.

Gottman's research has shown that what separates stable couples from those who dissolve is not the absence of conflict but the presence of repair attempts—and, more importantly, whether those attempts are received. A bid for repair might be subtle: a hand on the arm, a softened tone, a pause in the argument. But for it to work, the receiving partner must recognize it, allow it in, and respond to it. This mutual willingness to de-escalate—to prioritize connection over victory—is the core skill that makes renewal possible.

Still, not all relationships can or should be repaired. Some patterns are so deeply entrenched, or so fundamentally out of alignment, that staying becomes a form of self-abandonment. When repair efforts are consistently dismissed, when vulnerability is met with contempt, or when one partner is doing the emotional labor of both, the relationship may no longer be a viable container for mutual growth. In these cases, the decision to leave is not a failure. It is an act of psychological clarity.

For those who do choose to stay, however, repair must be more than episodic. It must become embedded in the relationship's culture. That means building habits of emotional check-in, creating shared language for naming needs, and setting clear agreements about how to handle conflict. It also means recognizing that the repair process is cumulative. Every time rupture is acknowledged and metabolized, the relationship becomes more capable of holding future complexity. This is what resilience looks like—not immunity to pain, but integration of it.

Forgiveness may or may not be part of the repair process. Contrary to popular belief, forgiveness is not a requirement for healing. It is a personal, internal process that cannot be forced or expected. What matters more in repair is accountability: a partner's willingness to acknowledge their role, validate the other's pain, and make meaningful changes in behavior. Forgiveness, if it comes, should be the byproduct of trust restored—not its substitute.

Another key element in relational repair is the reestablishment of

INTIMACY, TRUST, AND REPAIR

emotional safety. After betrayal, neglect, or rupture, even small moments can feel threatening. A glance, a sigh, a delayed response—all can trigger old pain if the nervous system has not yet recalibrated. Repair, therefore, must be paced with care. It requires transparency, predictability, and co-regulation. One partner cannot demand that the other "get over it"; instead, they must help create the conditions in which healing becomes possible.

For some couples, especially after major ruptures like infidelity, abuse, or abandonment, repair may involve creating an entirely new relational contract. The old structure—based on assumptions, unspoken agreements, or fantasy—has collapsed. What is needed is not a return to the past, but a reimagining of the future. This might involve therapy, boundaries, renegotiated roles, or new forms of emotional practice. It is not a rewind, but a rebuild. And for many, this process becomes a surprising source of growth—not in spite of the rupture, but because of how it was handled.

There is also a need to grieve. Even in relationships that survive and thrive after rupture, something has been lost: innocence, a version of the story, a sense of invincibility. Grieving this loss is part of emotional repair. When it is skipped, partners may feel pressured to "move on" without fully integrating the experience. But integration is not forgetting—it is remembering differently. It is carrying the story in a way that makes you wiser, not harder.

Deciding to stay in a relationship after rupture is not a one-time event. It is a daily recommitment. Every meaningful relationship asks this question over and over again: Are we still choosing this? Are we still building this together? The answer may shift over time. Some relationships make it through storm after storm, weathered but alive. Others dissolve, not because the people stopped loving each other, but because they no longer had the same vision, values, or psychological capacities. Both outcomes are valid. What matters most is that the decision is made consciously, not by default.

For those in long-term partnerships, renewal often comes in seasons.

After a rupture, couples may need to slow down, reestablish rituals of connection, or invest in shared meaning-making. This might look like creating new routines, rediscovering what they appreciate about each other, or reconnecting through play, affection, or shared purpose. Intimacy is not revived through guilt or obligation. It is revived through presence. And presence takes practice.

Ultimately, repair is not about erasing what happened. It is about affirming who we are to each other now, in light of what has happened. It is about asking: Can we still be safe with each other? Can we still be honest, curious, kind? Can we still choose to make this relationship a place where both people can become more whole, not less?

When the answer is yes—not perfectly, not painlessly, but earnestly—then love does not just survive. It deepens. And with that deepening comes something rare: a bond that has known rupture, navigated truth, and emerged not unscarred, but unbroken.

* * *

20

Group Psychology and Belonging

Human beings are not designed for isolation. Our nervous systems are wired for connection, our sense of self is shaped in relation to others, and our survival—both physical and psychological—has long depended on belonging to a group. From early childhood through late adulthood, people organize their identity through the lens of social membership: Who am I to others? Who is us, and who is them? These questions are not just cultural; they are psychological scaffolding for how we understand ourselves in the world.

Group belonging is not a preference. It is a psychological need. Maslow placed it at the center of his hierarchy, just above physiological safety. Social identity theory reinforces this, showing that much of our self-esteem and worldview is anchored in the groups we identify with—whether those are defined by culture, religion, race, gender, profession, politics, or something as simple as a favorite sports team. These affiliations shape not only how we see ourselves, but how we treat others. They guide empathy, influence perception, and determine whose pain matters.

The darker side of group psychology emerges when belonging becomes conditional, when identity becomes oppositional, or when fear is used to reinforce loyalty. Groups are powerful precisely because they create structure and meaning—but that same power can lead to division, distortion, and violence. In-group favoritism and out-group derogation are not fringe behaviors; they are common responses to psychological threat, amplified by culture and reinforced by reward systems. Tribalism is not limited to warzones or political echo chambers. It shows up in everyday choices, judgments, and loyalties.

This chapter explores the mechanics of group behavior—how people form social identity, how groups create cohesion, and how the human need to belong can lead both to profound connection and profound division. It examines the dynamics that govern conformity, loyalty, and moral disengagement. It looks at the conditions under which group membership becomes more important than truth, and why dissent within a group can feel like betrayal, even when it is principled.

But the chapter also moves toward integration. It investigates the psychology of bridge-building: what helps people see beyond tribal narratives, what fosters empathy across lines of difference, and how shared identity can expand rather than constrict our sense of humanity. Belonging does not have to mean uniformity. It can mean interdependence. And when approached with psychological flexibility and courage, it can become a site of healing rather than harm.

Group psychology is not just about them. It is about us. It is about the choices we make, consciously or unconsciously, when we decide who belongs, who matters, and who we are when we stand among others. This chapter asks us to look closely at those decisions—not to judge them, but to understand them. Because until we understand the pull of belonging, we cannot fully grasp the risks or rewards of what it means to be human together.

reward and regulation.

But the fear of exclusion is equally powerful. Being cast out of a group, or even anticipating rejection, can activate the same brain regions as physical pain. Social exclusion is not just uncomfortable—it is psychologically threatening. This threat can lead to a variety of defensive behaviors: conformity, overcompensation, suppression of dissent, or the adoption of group norms that may conflict with personal values. The fear of being alone can drive people to do things they would otherwise resist, not out of malice, but out of a desperate need to remain inside the circle.

The power of belonging can be seen in how easily groups form. In Tajfel's minimal group paradigm, participants were divided into groups based on arbitrary criteria, such as a preference for one painting over another. Despite the meaningless distinction, participants consistently showed favoritism toward their in-group and discrimination against the out-group. This suggests that the desire to belong and to differentiate between "us" and "them" is deeply rooted—not in logic or shared experience, but in the basic architecture of social cognition.

Belonging is not always healthy. A group can offer identity and protection while also demanding compliance, loyalty, or the suppression of individuality. When belonging becomes conditional—based on adherence to rules, ideologies, or performances—the psychological cost rises. People may begin to shape-shift to stay included, hiding parts of themselves that feel inconvenient or controversial. Over time, this can lead to alienation from the self, even while remaining accepted by the group. The person is included, but not known.

This tension is especially pronounced in adolescence, when peer groups become primary arenas for identity experimentation. The adolescent mind is intensely focused on status, acceptance, and social rules—not because teenagers are shallow, but because they are in a developmental stage where belonging defines their place in the world. For some, group membership becomes a crucible for growth. For others, it becomes a site of harm. Bullying, exclusion, and identity policing are not deviations from group behavior; they are often its enforcement mechanisms.

Adult group dynamics are more subtle, but no less powerful. Workplace cultures, family systems, religious communities, and online forums all serve as social ecosystems that shape thought, behavior, and emotion. The need to belong remains constant, but the rules for belonging shift depending on context. Some groups require emotional loyalty, others demand intellectual alignment. Some encourage individuality within connection, while others punish deviation. The psychological consequences depend not just on whether one belongs, but on what kind of belonging is being offered.

At its best, group belonging fosters mutual recognition, shared purpose, and emotional support. It becomes a mirror in which the self is reflected back with clarity and care. At its worst, it becomes a cage—a place where people lose access to complexity, curiosity, and contradiction. The quality of the group matters. So does the individual's ability to remain differentiated while staying connected. Healthy belonging does not ask people to disappear; it asks them to show up, fully, and be met with respect.

The need to belong is not a flaw. It is a feature of what it means to be human. But to belong well—to belong without disappearing, contorting, or excluding others—requires psychological flexibility. It requires the capacity to see groups not as absolutes, but as evolving contexts. And it requires the courage to ask hard questions about who we are among others, and who we are when we stand alone.

Us Versus Them: The Psychology of In-Groups and Out-Groups

The human mind categorizes quickly. It is how we survive complexity—by creating order out of chaos, clarity out of ambiguity. One of the most persistent and powerful forms of categorization is social: Who is with me, and who is not? Who is safe, and who might be a threat? Who belongs to my group, and who stands outside of it? This is the core of in-group/out-group psychology—a built-in function of social cognition that begins early in life and shapes how we perceive, evaluate, and relate to others.

In-group favoritism and out-group bias are not learned behaviors in the traditional sense. They are instinctual tendencies, later reinforced by culture, experience, and social conditioning. Even infants as young as six months demonstrate a preference for faces and voices that resemble those of their caregivers. By preschool, children show marked favoritism toward others who share their language, accent, or stated preferences. These early inclinations form the basis for later group dynamics, especially when identity becomes fused with morality, value, or perceived safety.

Henri Tajfel's minimal group experiments famously demonstrated how little it takes to create group boundaries. When participants were divided into arbitrary groups—based on random choices or meaningless traits—they still displayed preferential treatment toward their own group and negative assumptions about the out-group. This occurred even when there was no shared history, no emotional bond, and no material benefit. Simply knowing that someone was "not one of us" was enough to trigger bias. This finding has been replicated countless times, underscoring how quickly the mind moves to categorize, and how readily it assigns meaning to those categories.

This "us versus them" orientation has evolutionary roots. In early human societies, distinguishing friend from foe had life-or-death consequences. Those who could rapidly identify allies and threats were more likely to survive. Over time, this pattern became neurologically embedded. The amygdala—an area of the brain involved in emotional processing and threat detection—responds more strongly to images of out-group members, especially when they are unfamiliar or portrayed in ambiguous ways. This does not mean people are naturally hostile. It means they are naturally cautious. And that caution, in the absence of reflection or empathy, can easily become prejudice.

Group membership shapes perception in profound ways. Studies in social psychology show that people are more likely to remember positive traits, excuse negative behavior, and extend trust to members of their in-group. Conversely, they are more likely to view out-group members as less trustworthy, less intelligent, or more dangerous. This phenomenon is not limited to extreme settings. It appears in schools, offices, neighborhoods, religious communities, and digital spaces. It operates beneath the surface of everyday interaction, shaping tone, attention, and assumption without conscious intent.

Moral judgment is deeply influenced by group boundaries. People are more likely to rationalize harm done to out-group members or to view their suffering as less significant. This moral distancing can pave the way for exclusion, cruelty, or even violence—justified not by overt hatred, but by implicit bias and narrative framing. The language of "they"—as in, they always do this, they're not like us, they deserve what they get—becomes a psychological shield against empathy.

Out-group bias intensifies under conditions of threat. When individuals or groups feel insecure—economically, culturally, or emotionally—they often cling more tightly to group identity. The need for certainty and safety leads to sharper boundaries, more rigid norms, and greater hostility toward perceived outsiders. Politicians, media outlets, and ideological movements often exploit this dynamic, presenting the out-group as a threat to survival, purity, or tradition. The result is not just fear, but moral panic—an emotional frenzy that justifies extreme behavior in the name of protection.

Dehumanization is the most dangerous consequence of out-group bias. It occurs when people come to see others not just as different or wrong, but as fundamentally less human. Dehumanization has many faces. It can look like slurs, stereotypes, or jokes. It can look like laws that strip people of rights or dignity. It can look like silence in the face of harm. Once someone is placed outside the circle of moral concern, their suffering becomes easier to ignore—or even to justify.

But in-group psychology is not always sinister. It also fosters solidarity, mutual aid, and identity formation. It allows people to feel anchored, to experience pride, to build cultures and traditions. The problem is not group identity itself. The problem is what happens when group identity becomes exclusionary, inflexible, or fused with superiority. When "us" cannot exist without a diminished "them," psychological rigidity sets in.

One of the key mechanisms that reinforces in-group cohesion is narrative. Groups tell stories about themselves: who they are, what they value, what makes them good or chosen or victimized. These narratives are often selective, emphasizing positive traits and downplaying flaws. They create emotional coherence, a sense of shared meaning. But they can also become tools of distortion. When group narratives become sacred, they are protected from critique. Dissent becomes betrayal. Complexity becomes threat.

Confirmation bias plays a major role here. Once someone identifies strongly with a group, they are more likely to accept information that supports the group's worldview and dismiss information that contradicts it. This self-reinforcing loop makes it difficult to challenge internal assumptions, even when evidence points in a different direction. Identity becomes tied to belief. And belief becomes immune to reality.

Social media platforms have amplified these dynamics. Online spaces often sort users into ideological silos where in-group validation is constant and out-group demonization is rewarded. Algorithms prioritize outrage and tribal loyalty, not nuance or bridge-building. As a result, people are more likely to experience the world as a series of "us vs. them" battles—over values, truth, morality, and even basic facts.

Still, the human capacity for empathy remains. In controlled settings, when individuals from different groups are placed in close contact under conditions of mutual respect and shared goals, prejudice can decrease. This is the foundation of contact theory, which suggests that structured intergroup interaction can lead to more accurate perception and deeper understanding. But it requires effort, trust, and the willingness to see the other not as a category, b ut as a person.

In-group/out-group dynamics are not inherently bad. They are psychological tools. They help us organize the world. But like all tools, they must be used with awareness. When left unchecked, they foster division, rigidity, and harm. When understood and reflected upon, they can be softened, restructured, and expanded. The goal is not to eliminate groups, but to enlarge the circle—to see that "us" can be bigger than we thought.

Conformity, Loyalty, and the Cost of Dissent

Group belonging has a price. Sometimes the cost is minor: wearing the team colors, laughing at the inside jokes, using the right language. Other times, the cost is much higher: suppressing doubts, denying personal values, staying silent in the face of harm. This is the paradox of social identity—while groups provide safety and connection, they also exert pressure. That pressure can keep people aligned. It can also keep them complicit.

Psychologically, groups maintain cohesion by enforcing norms. These norms can be explicit, like formal rules or expectations, or they can be unwritten, absorbed through tone, behavior, and silence. Norms tell people what is acceptable, what will be rewarded, and what will provoke backlash. Once internalized, these expectations often go unchallenged, even when they conflict with individual judgment. The desire to remain in good standing with the group outweighs the desire to question its assumptions.

Solomon Asch's classic conformity experiments offer a clear illustration of this process. Participants were placed in a group with actors who gave clearly incorrect answers to simple visual tasks. Despite seeing the obvious right answer, many participants conformed with the group's false consensus. They knew it was wrong—but the fear of standing out, being judged, or making others uncomfortable led them to override their own perception. These findings are not about visual perception. They are about psychological safety. When faced with group consensus, people often choose belonging over truth.

Conformity is not weakness. It is survival. In evolutionary terms, being cast out of the group was often a death sentence. Even today, the fear of social exclusion activates the same brain regions associated with physical pain. To belong is to be safe; to dissent is to be at risk. The brain understands this, even when the stakes are low. As a result, people often self-censor—not because they are insincere, but because they are socially attuned.

Loyalty reinforces this dynamic. In most groups, loyalty is treated as a virtue. It signals commitment, solidarity, and dependability. But psychologically, loyalty can become a trap when it is weaponized to demand silence or obedience. When people are told that questioning the group is disloyal—or worse, that loyalty means defending the group even when it causes harm—the result is emotional and moral distortion. The individual becomes bound not just by affection, but by fear of abandonment or exile.

This is particularly evident in tight-knit groups: families, religious communities, political organizations, friend circles. When someone challenges the dominant narrative or refuses to conform, they often experience rejection, guilt-tripping, or character attacks. Their concerns are reframed as disloyalty, bitterness, or attention-seeking. This emotional pressure discourages future dissent and reinforces the illusion that the group is unified, righteous, and secure.

Stanley Milgram's obedience studies deepen our understanding of this phenomenon. In his famous experiment, participants were instructed to administer what they believed were painful electric shocks to another person, simply because an authority figure told them to. The majority complied, even as the recipient screamed in protest. These findings are not just about authoritarianism; they are about the psychological power of perceived duty and group hierarchy. When people feel responsible to an authority or a collective cause, they are more likely to suspend their own moral compass.

The cost of dissent is often isolation. Whistleblowers, truth-tellers, and those who leave rigid systems frequently report feelings of loss, alienation, and grief. They are not only separated from the group; they are separated from the version of themselves that existed within it. That version may have felt loved, respected, or certain. Without it, the dissenter must rebuild identity from scratch, which can be disorienting and painful. This is why many people remain in groups that no longer serve them—because leaving feels like losing not just community, but self.

Group dynamics also shape how dissent is perceived. When dissent comes from within—when it is framed as love, concern, or loyalty to higher principles—it has the potential to spark reflection. But when it is framed as opposition, or when the group is in a defensive posture, dissent is more likely to be rejected. Timing, tone, and relational capital matter. In psychologically healthy groups, dissent is expected and valued. In rigid or insecure groups, it is punished.

Cognitive dissonance plays a key role in silencing dissent. When people are confronted with evidence that contradicts their group's behavior or values, they experience psychological discomfort. To reduce that discomfort, they may rationalize, deflect, or attack the source of the contradiction. This is not always conscious. It is a protective reflex. Admitting that the group is wrong—or worse, that you were wrong to support it—requires a level of vulnerability that many find intolerable.

The emotional cost of dissent is also influenced by personality and background. Those with high agreeableness may find conflict especially distressing. Those with histories of abandonment or relational trauma may experience dissent as dangerous to their survival. Cultural background matters too. In collectivist cultures, maintaining group harmony is often prioritized over individual expression. In such settings, dissent is not just risky—it is taboo.

Yet dissent is necessary for psychological and social health. It is what keeps groups honest, flexible, and responsive. Without dissent, groups become echo chambers, immune to correction. They drift toward rigidity, exclusion, and self-deception. The dissenting voice, though often unwelcome, serves as a vital check against groupthink and moral stagnation.

There is also a difference between healthy conformity and coercive conformity. Healthy conformity reflects alignment with values—when someone joins a cause, community, or tradition because it resonates with their sense of meaning. Coercive conformity, by contrast, emerges from fear, pressure, or the desire to avoid rejection. The outward behaviors may look the same, but the psychological experience is profoundly different. One is chosen; the other is endured.

In intimate relationships, conformity can show up in subtle ways: agreeing to avoid conflict, suppressing needs to seem easygoing, mirroring preferences to feel connected. These behaviors often go unnoticed until resentment builds. What looks like harmony may be compliance. And over time, that compliance erodes authenticity and connection.

The solution is not to abandon loyalty or group identity. It is to make space for truth within them. This requires emotional maturity on both sides: the courage to speak, and the courage to hear. It means cultivating environments where disagreement is not just tolerated, but welcomed. Where loyalty is not measured by silence, but by a shared commitment to growth and integrity.

Ultimately, the cost of dissent must be weighed against the cost of silence. When groups cannot tolerate internal challenge, they become brittle. When individuals cannot name what feels wrong, they become numb. Conformity may keep people safe in the short term—but in the long run, only honesty keeps them whole.

Healing the Divide: Integration, Dialogue, and Common Humanity

The antidote to division is not sameness. It is integration. Psychological integration is the process of holding complexity without collapse—of recognizing that people can be different and still belong to each other. In a world increasingly organized around identity and allegiance, integration offers a path out of tribal rigidity. It does not ask people to abandon their group affiliations, values, or loyalties. It asks them to widen the circle of moral concern, to develop the psychological flexibility to see humanity on both sides of the divide.

Healing social fractures begins with recognition: that in-group and out-group distinctions are not absolute. They are narratives, mental shortcuts, and emotional defenses. They can be softened, rewired, and reimagined. Social psychology has shown repeatedly that people's attitudes toward others are malleable, shaped by contact, empathy, and shared experience. This is not naive optimism. It is a finding supported by decades of research in intergroup relations, particularly Gordon Allport's contact hypothesis, which holds that under the right conditions, sustained interaction between groups reduces prejudice and increases understanding.

But those conditions matter. Contact alone is not enough. For dialogue to transform perception, it must occur in environments where participants have equal status, shared goals, and institutional support. Power asymmetries must be acknowledged, not ignored. Safety must be established. And the conversation must move beyond polite exchange into vulnerable territory—where people can share lived experience, name pain, and make room for emotional truth. Otherwise, the dialogue becomes performance, reinforcing the very hierarchies it seeks to dissolve.

Psychologically, integration also requires the dismantling of internal binaries. Many people have been trained to think in moral absolutes: good versus evil, right versus wrong, us versus them. These binaries are seductive because they reduce uncertainty. But they also distort reality. People are not consistent. They are contradictory, layered, and context-dependent. Integration begins when someone can hold two seemingly opposing truths at once: that they have been harmed and have also caused harm, that their group has real grievances and is not beyond critique, that loyalty to a community does not require the denial of its shadow.

One tool for this kind of inner work is narrative complexity. Instead of framing people as entirely heroic or villainous, individuals can be encouraged to tell richer, more nuanced stories—about themselves, their histories, their choices. Research shows that when people reflect on their lives through the lens of complexity rather than coherence, they display higher levels of empathy and openness. The same applies to group identity. When a group can hold its own contradictions without collapsing into defensiveness or shame, it becomes more capable of ethical growth.

Another avenue for healing is the cultivation of identity complexity—the psychological flexibility to see oneself as belonging to multiple, sometimes conflicting, social categories. When people recognize that they are not just one thing—not just a race, religion, nationality, or political position—they become less likely to demonize others. They see common ground where previously there were only fault lines. Identity complexity disrupts the machinery of dehumanization by reminding people that every "them" contains multitudes.

Restoring common humanity also involves what psychologists call perspective-taking: the cognitive and emotional act of imagining the world from another's viewpoint. This is not the same as agreement. Perspective-taking does not require endorsing another person's choices or beliefs. It requires recognizing that those choices and beliefs emerge from real psychological landscapes—landscapes shaped by memory, culture, trauma, and longing. When people engage in perspective-taking, even briefly, their attitudes soften. Their sense of moral superiority loosens. They become more capable of listening, less reactive, and more willing to learn.

But perspective-taking is emotionally expensive. It requires energy, humility, and the willingness to be uncomfortable. In moments of social stress—when people are overwhelmed, threatened, or uncertain—perspective-taking is often the first capacity to disappear. That is why healing cannot be left to individuals alone. It must be supported by systems: educational institutions that teach critical thinking and emotional literacy, media that prioritize nuance over outrage, communities that value dialogue over purity.

Restorative practices also offer a model for bridging group divides. Originally developed for use in criminal justice and education, restorative approaches emphasize dialogue, accountability, and repair. Instead of punishing or exiling those who cause harm, restorative circles invite all parties into a shared conversation about impact, needs, and commitments going forward. These practices are difficult, but they foster a different kind of justice—one that centers relationship and mutual responsibility rather than retribution.

In some cases, healing requires ritual. Humans are symbolic creatures. We need ways to mark transition, to grieve what was lost, and to affirm what we hope to build. Group conflicts that have festered for generations cannot be resolved by reason alone. They require symbolic gestures—apologies, memorials, shared ceremonies—that communicate emotional truth. These rituals do not erase history, but they create a context in which new relationships can emerge.

Crucially, integration does not mean erasure. It does not mean abandoning identity, silencing pain, or pretending everyone agrees. It means staying in relationship across difference. It means developing the emotional and cognitive stamina to live inside tension without resorting to violence—internal or external. In practice, this means inviting dissent into group spaces, encouraging complexity in public discourse, and making empathy a cultural norm rather than a private virtue.

The work of healing is long. It does not always yield dramatic results. It is not about "fixing" people, but about making space for them to show up more fully—more honestly, more vulnerably, more responsibly. And when enough people begin to do this work—not perfectly, but persistently—the culture begins to shift. People learn to ask better questions. They become less reactive. They stop needing every conversation to end in agreement. And they begin to recognize that common humanity is not a sentimental idea—it is a psychological fact.

We are wired to belong. But we are also wired to divide. The challenge of maturity is learning how to do the former without being captured by the latter. That is the work of integration: to reclaim complexity, to restore perspective, and to remember—again and again—that behind every category is a person. A person who breathes, and breaks, and tries. Just like you.

* * *

V

PART V: BELIEF, MEANING, AND SYMBOLIC LIFE

Belief and meaning are the stories we live by—sometimes quietly, sometimes loudly shaping how we see ourselves and the world. In this part, I want to explore with you how we construct meaning, how symbols guide our experience, and why our beliefs matter so deeply. These aren't abstract concepts; they are the emotional and cognitive threads weaving the fabric of your life. Understanding this symbolic world helps us find clarity, purpose, and coherence amid complexity.

21

The Need for Meaning

To be human is to need meaning. Not simply as a philosophical luxury, but as a psychological imperative. Meaning organizes our experience, stabilizes our identity, and anchors us in the face of chaos. It is the invisible structure behind motivation, memory, emotion, and belief. People do not live in reality as it is. They live in a version of reality that makes sense to them—a version filtered through the story they tell about who they are, why things happen, and what it all means.

Existential psychology begins here. Rather than treating meaning as a cognitive abstraction or cultural artifact, it treats it as a fundamental psychological need. Viktor Frankl, a Holocaust survivor and psychiatrist, argued that the search for meaning is the primary motivational force in human life. Even in the most extreme suffering, he observed, those who could find meaning in their experience—however painful—were more resilient, more grounded, and more likely to survive with their dignity intact. His work, along with that of Rollo May, Irvin Yalom, and others, formed the foundation of a psychological approach that takes seriously the interior terrain of human existence: death, freedom, isolation, and the absence of inherent purpose.

These existential givens are not abstract concerns. They shape emotional life in profound ways. The knowledge that life is finite, that no single belief system can offer certainty, that we are responsible for our choices and ultimately alone in our experience—these truths create both anxiety and opportunity. Meaning is the way we respond. It is the framework we build to withstand uncertainty, to create coherence, to make suffering bearable and joy comprehensible.

But meaning is not handed to us. In modern life especially, traditional sources of meaning—religion, family structure, national identity—have lost some of their organizing power. What remains is a more personal, more fragile project of meaning-making. People build meaning through work, love, creativity, service, and belief. They construct systems of values, interpretive frameworks, and internal narratives that help them navigate life's ambiguity. When these systems are strong, they offer clarity. When they collapse, the result is often despair.

This chapter explores the psychology of meaning—not just what people believe, but why they need to believe something at all. It looks at how the mind seeks coherence, how identity is stabilized through symbolic frameworks, and how meaning can be both a source of liberation and a mechanism of control. It also investigates what happens when meaning is threatened—by trauma, loss, disillusionment—and how people begin to rebuild.

Meaning is not a destination. It is a process. It is shaped by time, context, relationship, and emotion. And while it can be borrowed from others, it must ultimately be claimed. This chapter is about that claiming. About the deeply human impulse to orient oneself within the mystery of existence—and to find, even in the face of uncertainty, a reason to go on.

Life as Question: The Existential Search for Meaning

Human life does not come with instructions. We are born into a world already in motion, surrounded by people with their own hopes, fears, and unfinished stories. We arrive without a map, yet with a deep, unspoken sense that we are supposed to figure something out. From childhood onward, that sense develops into questions—some conscious, others implicit: What is the point of all this? What is my role here? What does it mean to live well, and what makes it all worthwhile? These are not distractions from psychological life. They are its foundation.

Existential psychology begins with the premise that these questions are not only valid but essential. Unlike traditional models that pathologize distress or seek to eliminate discomfort, existential approaches view anxiety, uncertainty, and doubt as natural responses to the human condition. Life is ambiguous. Time is limited. We are ultimately responsible for our choices, and no belief system can fully shield us from pain, loss, or death. Underneath every personal struggle—whether it presents as depression, indecision, relationship conflict, or addiction—is often a crisis of meaning: a felt disorientation, a rupture in coherence, a loss of the "why" behind the doing.

Viktor Frankl famously argued that meaning is not a luxury for the privileged, but a necessity for survival. In *Man's Search for Meaning*, he describes his experiences in Nazi concentration camps, noting that prisoners who maintained a sense of purpose—even a fragile one—were more psychologically resilient than those who succumbed to meaninglessness. Frankl believed that humans are motivated not merely by pleasure (as Freud suggested) or power (as Adler proposed), but by a will to meaning. This will is not a passive desire—it is a drive, a need, a compass pointing toward a life that matters.

Irvin Yalom, another central figure in existential therapy, identified four core "existential givens": death, freedom, isolation, and meaninglessness. Each poses a psychological challenge. Death reminds us that time is finite. Freedom demands that we take responsibility for our lives. Isolation highlights the unbridgeable distance between one consciousness and another. And meaninglessness confronts us with the fact that life has no built-in purpose. These givens are not problems to be solved; they are conditions to be engaged. The way we relate to them determines much of our emotional landscape.

Meaning, in this framework, is not the same as happiness. It is deeper and more durable. Happiness is emotional, often fleeting. Meaning is existential—it structures one's sense of self, value, and purpose over time. A person can be grieving and still feel their life is meaningful. They can be anxious and still feel that what they are doing matters. Meaning holds even when mood does not.

At different stages of life, the search for meaning takes different forms. In adolescence, it might involve questions of identity and belonging—Who am I, and where do I fit? In early adulthood, it often centers on direction and purpose—What should I do with my life, and how do I choose well? In midlife, it may turn toward reflection and recalibration—Is this the life I meant to build, and if not, what now? And in later life, the search often becomes more contemplative—What has it all meant, and what legacy am I leaving behind?

Some people find meaning through service to others. Some through creativity, spirituality, activism, or relationships. Others locate meaning in discipline, learning, or survival itself. The path is never identical, but the need remains constant. Even those who claim to reject meaning often construct a kind of anti-meaning in its place—an attachment to nihilism, rebellion, or the performance of indifference. This, too, is a meaning system. It tells the person who they are and how they relate to the world.

The absence of meaning, by contrast, is not simply blankness. It is often experienced as despair. Existential despair is not always loud. It can appear as apathy, listlessness, avoidance, or chronic distraction. The person may feel disoriented, unmotivated, emotionally flat. Their life no longer feels tethered to anything that justifies effort or care. This is not depression in the clinical sense, though the two can overlap. It is a crisis of orientation—a psychological vertigo that arises when the frameworks that once made sense of life begin to unravel.

Trauma often catalyzes this unraveling. When something catastrophic happens—loss, violence, betrayal—it can fracture the person's assumptions about the world, about safety, fairness, or order. What once felt coherent becomes incoherent. The brain scrambles to rebuild a story that can hold the experience, but often fails. The person is left with unanswered questions: Why did this happen? What does it mean now?

Who am I in the aftermath? Healing, in these cases, is not just about emotional regulation or cognitive restructuring. It is about reweaving the fabric of meaning.

Religious and spiritual traditions have long served as meaning-making systems. They offer stories, symbols, rituals, and moral codes that help people locate themselves in a larger context. But even in secular societies, people gravitate toward frameworks that offer orientation: nationalism, political ideology, career identity, family roles. These systems serve psychological functions. They tell the person how to be, what to value, and how to interpret experience. When they work well, they provide structure. When they become too rigid, they can also become cages.

Importantly, meaning is not found. It is created. Life does not hand out coherent narratives. People construct them—imperfectly, creatively, and often under pressure. This construction process is both cognitive and emotional. It involves memory, imagination, and judgment. It requires vulnerability and honesty. And it is rarely finished. Meaning evolves. What felt meaningful at twenty may feel hollow at forty. What gave purpose in one season may no longer apply in the next. The task is to keep rebuilding.

The search for meaning is not a sign of immaturity or weakness. It is a sign of engagement. It means the person is awake to the depth of life, to its risks and its wonder. It means they are willing to ask the hard questions—not because they expect easy answers, but because the asking itself is part of what makes life meaningful.

Coherence and the Construction of Reality

The human brain is not a passive recorder of events. It is an active meaning-making organ, constantly interpreting, shaping, and organizing experience into patterns that feel coherent. This process begins automatically and continues throughout life. It is how people remember, how they plan, how they sustain identity over time. Psychological coherence—the sense that things make sense, that experiences fit together—is not a bonus feature of mental life. It is a central operating system. When coherence is intact, life feels navigable. When it breaks down, the result is confusion, anxiety, or collapse.

At the center of coherence is narrative. People understand their lives as stories: this happened, and then this, and it meant that. These stories are not simply factual timelines. They are interpretive frameworks that link events to values, emotions, and goals. They give shape to experience and allow the self to remain stable across time. You are the protagonist of your story, and the story has to make sense—for your decisions to feel justified, for your emotions to feel valid, for your future to feel imaginable.

Jerome Bruner, a leading figure in cognitive psychology, argued that humans organize experience in two primary modes: the paradigmatic and the narrative. The paradigmatic mode is analytical, logical, and rule-based. It seeks objective truths. The narrative mode is interpretive, subjective, and story-based. It seeks coherence. While both modes are necessary, most people rely heavily on narrative to structure personal meaning. This is why even seemingly irrational beliefs can feel stabilizing—they keep the story intact.

Trauma often disrupts this narrative mode. When something happens that cannot be integrated into the existing framework—something too shocking, too senseless, too overwhelming—the narrative fractures. The person may struggle to make sense of what occurred, to understand why it happened, or to locate themselves in its aftermath. They may question their identity, doubt their perceptions, or lose trust in the coherence of life itself. This is not simply an emotional response. It is a cognitive dislocation—a failure of integration that leaves the person adrift.

Narrative therapy, a model developed by Michael White and David Epston, is grounded in this insight. It treats people not as bundles of pathology, but as authors of meaning. The goal is not to deny the reality of suffering, but to help people re-author their stories in ways that restore agency, coherence, and dignity. By externalizing problems ("the problem is the problem, not the person") and by reconnecting people to forgotten strengths or neglected values, narrative therapy helps rebuild a framework where meaning is possible again.

Psychological coherence also depends on temporal continuity—the sense that past, present, and future are connected. When people feel stuck in the past, detached from the present, or hopeless about the future, coherence falters. This is often seen in depression, where the future feels collapsed, or in PTSD, where the past feels intrusively alive. Therapy in these cases often focuses on restoring a coherent timeline: locating the person's current self within the larger arc of their life story, and helping them see that their experience, however painful, is part of a trajectory—not the endpoint.

But coherence is not just personal. It is also social. People rely on cultural scripts to interpret their lives: what a "normal" childhood looks like, what success means, how grief should be expressed. These scripts provide structure, but they also constrain. When someone's experience deviates from the cultural script—say, they grieve too long, leave a marriage for reasons others don't understand, or struggle with a role society says should bring them joy—they may begin to doubt themselves. The disconnect between inner truth and outer narrative creates a kind of double disorientation: the self feels incoherent internally and misunderstood externally.

This is why representation matters. Seeing one's experience reflected in literature, film, religion, or public discourse helps validate personal meaning. It signals that your story is not an anomaly. That others have walked this path and found language for it. Without such reflections, people may internalize the belief that their experience is wrong or illegible. This belief does not just hurt; it undermines the entire structure of self-understanding.

Memory plays a central role in constructing coherence. But memory is not a fixed archive. It is a dynamic, reconstructive process. Every time a memory is recalled, it is subtly reshaped by current mood, context, and belief. People remember selectively. They emphasize some details, omit others, and impose narrative arcs that were not originally present. This is not deception; it is function. Memory serves identity, not accuracy. It helps maintain a coherent sense of self in the face of constant change.

Still, coherence is not the same as truth. A story can feel coherent and still be incomplete, distorted, or protective. This is especially true when coherence is built on denial—on suppressing contradiction, avoiding conflict, or maintaining illusion. People may cling to narratives that cast them as victims or heroes, that flatten others into villains, that omit complexity in favor of simplicity. These narratives can be comforting, but they often come at a cost: emotional rigidity, relational stagnation, or an inability to grow.

Psychological maturity involves the ability to tolerate a less tidy kind of coherence—one that includes contradiction, ambiguity, and emotional range. It is the difference between a story that explains everything and a story that holds everything. This form of coherence does not require perfection or resolution. It requires integration: the weaving together of disparate experiences into a self that can make sense of them without needing to distort them.

In this way, coherence is less about certainty and more about livability. Can the person wake up and feel like their life, however complex, makes enough sense to keep moving forward? Can they locate themselves in a story that feels honest, meaningful, and flexible enough to grow with them? If so, coherence has been restored—not as a rigid structure, but as a dynamic frame for meaning.

Symbols, Systems, and the Stories We Live

People do not live by logic alone. They live by symbols, rituals, metaphors, and myths. They live by the stories handed down from generations before them, by the banners of belief under which they gather, and by the frameworks that make sense of life's unexplainable moments. From birth to death, humans reach for systems that help them interpret the world—not because these systems are empirically verifiable, but because they are emotionally stabilizing. In the absence of absolute knowledge, symbols become bridges between chaos and coherence.

Symbolic frameworks serve many functions. They offer meaning, identity, continuity, and moral orientation. Religion is perhaps the most enduring of these frameworks. Across cultures and centuries, religious systems have provided answers to the most fundamental existential questions: Why are we here? What happens when we die? How should we live? They offer not just doctrine but narrative—a cosmic story in which the individual plays a meaningful role. Rituals, sacred texts, and moral codes provide structure and predictability. Even for those who no longer identify with organized religion, the psychological blueprint remains: a need for belonging, purpose, and symbolic anchoring.

But symbols are not limited to religion. Ideology functions symbolically as well. Political movements, social causes, national identities, and even consumer brands serve as meaning-making structures. They tell people who they are, what matters, and who to stand with. They offer not only values, but enemies—those who threaten the system's coherence. This is part of what makes symbolic systems powerful: they not only unite, they divide. They clarify identity by creating boundaries around it.

Carl Jung understood symbols as psychological tools that speak to the unconscious. He believed that archetypes—universal symbolic patterns—emerge spontaneously in dreams, myths, and art because they represent core human concerns. The mother, the hero, the shadow, the trickster—these are not just literary devices; they are containers for psychological truths too complex to be expressed in literal terms. A symbol, in this view, does not explain; it reveals. It points to something deeper, more ambiguous, more emotionally resonant than analysis alone can reach.

Metaphor functions similarly. When people say they are "carrying a heavy burden," "walking through fire," or "finding light at the end of the tunnel," they are not describing physical events. They are translating emotion into imagery. This translation helps the experience feel real and sharable. It gives form to the formless, allowing pain, hope, or confusion to be communicated and understood. In therapy, metaphors often emerge naturally—and they are rarely arbitrary. They reflect how the person sees their struggle, and sometimes, how they see their potential for healing.

Ritual is another form of symbolic meaning-making. Whether religious or secular, rituals create order in transitional spaces: birth, coming of age, marriage, death, loss, recovery. They mark time, honor change, and offer a sense of continuity. Even simple rituals—lighting a candle, saying a mantra, visiting a grave—help structure emotional life. They provide a container for feelings that are otherwise overwhelming or ambiguous. In times of crisis, people often return to ritual not because they believe in magic, but because ritual restores rhythm to psychological life.

However, symbolic systems are double-edged. When held flexibly, they support growth and reflection. When held rigidly, they can become authoritarian, exclusionary, or oppressive. Literalism is one of the main psychological risks of symbolic thinking—when people lose the capacity to see symbols as metaphor and begin to treat them as concrete fact. This is where religion turns fundamentalist, ideology turns dogmatic, and culture turns intolerant. The symbol becomes a command rather than an invitation. The story becomes a script rather than a canvas.

This rigidity is often driven by fear. In uncertain times, people cling to symbols as anchors. They want clear answers, firm boundaries, and absolute truths. Symbolic systems provide these—at a cost. When systems demand obedience, suppress dissent, or vilify outsiders, they no longer serve psychological integration. They serve control. People may still feel oriented, but at the price of critical thinking and emotional complexity.

Yet the answer is not to abandon symbolic thinking. It is to mature within it. Symbols are not childish; they are essential. They allow people to speak the unspeakable, hold mystery, and stay connected to meaning in ways that logic cannot fully contain. The mature relationship to symbolism is not literal belief, but reflective engagement. It means asking: What does this mean to me? What part of myself is being expressed here? What does this ritual, image, or narrative allow me to feel, understand, or become?

This kind of engagement also opens the door to cross-cultural empathy. When people view symbols as lenses rather than walls, they can appreciate the depth of other traditions without needing to adopt them. They can recognize that another's myth is not a threat to their truth, but a reflection of a different emotional landscape. In this way, symbolic frameworks can become sites of dialogue rather than division.

In secular contexts, people often create their own symbolic systems—personal rituals, family traditions, internal philosophies. These may not look like religion, but they serve similar functions: stabilizing identity, marking transition, orienting action. A person might find meaning through creative work, athletic discipline, or caregiving. They may tell themselves a guiding story: that they are a survivor, a protector, a seeker, a builder. These roles carry symbolic weight. They help organize life, even when the external world offers no clear answers.

The stories we live—about who we are, what matters, what life is for—are rarely fixed. They evolve as we evolve. Symbolic systems, when held with flexibility, allow us to grow without losing orientation. They become living frameworks, not static blueprints. And when we reflect on the symbols that shape us, we reclaim agency over how meaning is made—not by dismantling every structure, but by understanding the architecture well enough to renovate it when needed.

Meaning in Practice: Choice, Commitment, and Responsibility

Meaning is not just a concept to ponder; it is a force that shapes how people live, decide, and act. Existential psychology emphasizes that meaning becomes real not in abstract thought but through choice and commitment. Humans are confronted with freedom—the freedom to choose how to respond to their circumstances, to define their values, and to take responsibility for their lives. This freedom is both a burden and a gift. It is the source of existential anxiety, but also the wellspring of authenticity and growth.

Choice is the moment when meaning moves from theory into practice. Every decision—large or small—is an expression of what a person values and how they interpret their existence. Choosing a career, ending a relationship, speaking a truth, or simply getting out of bed all carry symbolic weight. They are acts of self-definition. But freedom also entails risk. Every choice closes off alternatives, and every commitment creates limits. This is the paradox of existential agency: to be free is to be bound.

Commitment anchors freedom in reality. Without commitment, choice can become paralyzing, leading to avoidance or despair. Commitment provides direction, purpose, and a framework within which meaning can flourish. Yet commitment is not blind adherence. It is a conscious embrace of values, goals, and relationships that matter enough to warrant investment—even in the face of uncertainty and difficulty. Commitment transforms meaning from an idea into a lived reality.

Responsibility accompanies choice and commitment. It means owning the consequences of one's actions, accepting the impact on oneself and others, and navigating the complexities of moral and practical accountability. Responsibility is not external obligation; it is an internal stance. It is the recognition that while the world may be indifferent, one's response is not. This stance is foundational to existential maturity.

Existential therapists often describe this triad—choice, commitment, responsibility—as the core of psychological health. People who embrace these dimensions tend to report greater well-being, resilience, and coherence. They are more able to tolerate uncertainty, ambiguity, and suffering because they perceive themselves as active agents rather than passive victims. Meaning is not given; it is claimed through the exercise of freedom within constraints.

This does not mean that meaning is always easy or stable. People continually renegotiate their commitments as circumstances change, values evolve, and knowledge deepens. Existential freedom demands ongoing reflection and adjustment. It requires courage to confront ambiguity and to revise previously held beliefs without losing a sense of self. This dynamic process keeps meaning alive and relevant.

Psychologically, living with meaning involves integrating existential realities with day-to-day experience. It means balancing the tension between autonomy and connection, hope and despair, permanence and change. Meaningful living includes embracing vulnerability, seeking growth, and accepting mortality. It entails making peace with paradox and complexity rather than seeking simplistic answers.

The practice of meaning also unfolds in relationships. People find and sustain meaning through connection with others—through love, service, shared goals, and mutual recognition. Meaning is rarely a solitary pursuit. It is embedded in social and cultural contexts that provide language, symbols, and support. Yet it remains deeply personal, unique to each individual's experience and choices.

Philosophers such as Søren Kierkegaard and Jean-Paul Sartre emphasized that meaning is a project, not a possession. It must be continuously created through authentic engagement with life's challenges and opportunities. This engagement often involves confronting existential anxiety, the "dizziness of freedom," and the responsibility that comes with radical choice. Meaning is found not in certainty, but in the courage to live without it.

In practical terms, cultivating meaning requires mindfulness of one's values and intentional action aligned with them. It involves reflective practices—journaling, dialogue, meditation—that help clarify what matters. It demands willingness to face discomfort and ambiguity rather than retreating into distraction or denial. Meaningful living is a journey of becoming, not arriving.

In summary, meaning emerges through the interplay of choice, commitment, and responsibility. It is a lived process that shapes identity, behavior, and emotional resilience. Existential psychology invites people to embrace this process fully, recognizing that the search for meaning is not a problem to be solved but a condition to be inhabited. Through this embrace, life gains depth, coherence, and purpose—even amid uncertainty and impermanence.

* * *

22

Belief Systems and Worldviews

Every person lives inside a worldview. Whether consciously adopted or unconsciously inherited, that worldview shapes how reality is interpreted, what is considered true, and what counts as evidence. It influences perception, memory, emotion, and behavior. It is not simply what a person believes; it is the frame through which all believing occurs. And for most people, that frame is so familiar, so self-reinforcing, that it feels less like a perspective and more like the world itself.

Belief systems serve essential psychological functions. They provide structure in the face of uncertainty, meaning in the face of suffering, and orientation in the face of complexity. Religious faith, political ideology, cultural norms, and personal philosophies all offer narratives that explain how things are and how they should be. They tell the person who they are, what is valuable, and whom to trust. In doing so, they simplify a chaotic world and make action possible. But they also filter out information that doesn't fit. Every belief system comes with blind spots.

This chapter explores the architecture of belief—how worldviews are formed, sustained, and sometimes defended at all costs. It draws from cognitive psychology, neuroscience, and social theory to examine how people make sense of their world, and why changing that sense is so difficult. It looks at how beliefs are emotionally charged, socially reinforced, and cognitively protected through confirmation bias and motivated reasoning. It also explores how systems of faith and ideology offer belonging and coherence, but can become rigid, tribal, or intolerant when challenged.

At the heart of this inquiry is a paradox: belief systems are both necessary and dangerous. Necessary because no human can function without some interpretive framework. Dangerous because those frameworks can become closed systems, impervious to evidence, hostile to difference, and resistant to growth. What begins as a tool for meaning can become a fortress of certainty.

The chapter does not argue against belief. It argues for awareness of belief. For understanding the difference between faith and fact, identity and ideology, confidence and certainty. It asks what it means to believe responsibly—to hold convictions without weaponizing them, to stay grounded without becoming rigid, to recognize one's own blind spots without collapsing into relativism. In an age of polarization, misinformation, and tribal morality, this is not just a philosophical task. It is a psychological one.

The Architecture of Belief

Beliefs are not simply ideas held in the mind. They are structures—emotional, cognitive, and often social—that shape perception and behavior at every level. From childhood onward, people begin to construct belief systems not through abstract reasoning, but through lived experience. A child learns what is safe, what is dangerous, who to trust, and what the world is like based on patterns they observe and internalize. These early impressions harden into assumptions. And assumptions, over time, become beliefs—often so deeply woven into the fabric of thought that they operate invisibly.

Psychologically, beliefs provide order. The brain is constantly filtering and organizing sensory information into patterns. Without a coherent framework to interpret that data, people become overwhelmed. Belief systems function as templates for reality; they tell the person what to notice, how to evaluate it, and what it means. In this way, belief is not a reaction to evidence—it is often the frame that determines what counts as evidence in the first place.

This filtering process is necessary. The world is too complex to process in its raw form. But it also introduces bias. Once a belief is in place, new information is not evaluated neutrally—it is interpreted through the lens of the existing framework. This is not a moral failing; it is a cognitive shortcut. The brain, designed to conserve energy and reduce ambiguity, defaults to confirmation. It prefers coherence over contradiction.

Social reinforcement strengthens this architecture. Beliefs are rarely private. They are shaped and sustained within families, cultures, communities, and institutions. People tend to adopt the beliefs of those around them, not just because of influence, but because belonging requires it. Agreement signals loyalty. Dissent can threaten the social fabric. As a result, beliefs often become entangled with identity. To question a belief may feel like questioning the self—or betraying the group.

This identity-bonded nature of belief explains why rational arguments rarely change minds. Beliefs are not just conclusions drawn from evidence; they are emotional investments, tied to safety, status, and self-understanding. A political ideology, for example, is rarely just a policy preference—it is often a worldview that reflects core values, social affiliations, and moral convictions. Challenging that ideology is not just a debate. It is a disruption of the person's psychological scaffolding.

Neurologically, belief involves multiple brain regions. The prefrontal cortex is responsible for evaluating information, making judgments, and regulating doubt. But beliefs also activate the limbic system—the emotional center of the brain. This means that beliefs are felt before they are analyzed. In fact, studies in cognitive neuroscience show that people process threatening information about their beliefs in the same way they process physical threat. The defensive response is fast, automatic, and emotionally charged.

This is why belief systems tend to self-reinforce. Once a framework is established, it selects for evidence that confirms it and dismisses or reinterprets evidence that contradicts it. This selective processing creates what psychologists call a "closed belief system"—a worldview that cannot be falsified because it has mechanisms to explain away any challenge. For example, a conspiracy theory may account for all disconfirming evidence by claiming it was planted or manipulated. A rigid ideology may label opposing views as immoral, ignorant, or dangerous, making dialogue impossible.

Yet not all beliefs are rigid. Some are open, provisional, and subject to revision. These belief systems are characterized by psychological flexibility. The person holds their beliefs with curiosity rather than certainty, and is willing to update them when presented with new evidence or deeper understanding. This capacity is not innate—it is cultivated through experience, education, and introspection. It requires the development of metacognition: the ability to think about one's own thinking.

Importantly, belief systems are not limited to grand ideologies or religious creeds. People hold beliefs about themselves, others, relationships, success, failure, love, power, and worth. These personal beliefs often operate in the background, shaping behavior and emotion without conscious awareness. A person who believes they are fundamentally unlovable may interpret neutral interactions as rejection. A person who believes the world is dangerous may perceive threat where none exists. These core beliefs often originate in early attachment patterns, trauma, or cultural conditioning—and they can be as powerful as any political doctrine.

Therapeutically, identifying and reframing these beliefs is a central task. Cognitive-behavioral therapy, for example, focuses on uncovering maladaptive beliefs—such as "I must never make mistakes" or "If I'm vulnerable, I'll be hurt"—and replacing them with more accurate, compassionate alternatives. But this process is not purely logical. Changing a belief involves emotional risk. It requires the person to tolerate uncertainty, to give up the illusion of control, and to face the possibility that the story they've lived by may need to change.

Belief systems also serve existential functions. They help people answer questions that are not empirically solvable: What is the meaning of life? What happens after death? What is my purpose? Whether grounded in religion, philosophy, or secular humanism, these frameworks provide symbolic scaffolding for human consciousness. They help the individual locate themselves in a vast, indifferent universe—and offer a sense of coherence where none is guaranteed.

The architecture of belief is powerful, intricate, and deeply human. It allows people to function, to relate, to make decisions, and to find meaning. But it is also susceptible to rigidity, distortion, and error. Understanding how beliefs are built—emotionally, cognitively, and socially—allows for a more compassionate and more critical engagement with the worldviews that shape human behavior. The goal is not to eradicate belief, but to bring awareness to its construction—to live inside our frameworks with both conviction and humility.

Faith, Ideology, and the Psychology of Conviction

Faith and ideology are often treated as opposites: one emotional, the other intellectual; one sacred, the other secular. But psychologically, they function in remarkably similar ways. Both offer coherent worldviews that answer existential questions. Both provide systems of meaning that organize values, guide behavior, and establish group identity. And both rely on conviction—a deep emotional investment that grants the belief system authority over thought and action.

Faith, in its broadest sense, is not synonymous with religion. It is the act of placing trust in something that cannot be fully proven. For some, this takes the form of belief in a divine order, a spiritual path, or a transcendent purpose. For others, it may show up as a deep trust in justice, in love, in human progress, or even in the scientific method. What distinguishes faith from mere preference is that it asks for commitment beyond evidence. It is not a hypothesis to be tested; it is a lens through which the world is interpreted.

This interpretive function is central. Faith shapes perception at every level—from what a person notices in the world to how they experience suffering. A religious worldview, for example, may reframe hardship as divine testing, or joy as spiritual reward. These interpretations do not arise from objective data. They arise from narrative, symbol, and the emotional logic of a system that makes life coherent. And coherence, more than accuracy, is often what the psyche craves.

Ideology functions similarly. Though grounded in political or philosophical claims, ideologies operate as closed systems of belief, complete with their own heroes and villains, sacred values, and explanatory models. They provide purpose, belonging, and moral clarity—especially in times of uncertainty. Like faith, ideology offers a way to feel right. It organizes not only what to think, but how to feel: who to trust, what to fear, where to place one's hope and anger.

The psychology of conviction reveals how both faith and ideology can become emotionally fused with identity. When a belief system becomes part of who someone is, disagreement feels like threat. This is known as identity fusion: the merging of personal and group identity so thoroughly that any perceived attack on the belief is experienced as an attack on the self. This fusion strengthens loyalty, but also limits flexibility. It makes dialogue difficult and dissent dangerous.

Conviction has a physiological dimension as well. Studies using neuroimaging have shown that strongly held beliefs—especially moral or ideological ones—activate emotional centers in the brain rather than areas associated with logical reasoning. This suggests that when people defend their beliefs, they are often defending a felt sense of security or moral order, not simply a set of propositions. This helps explain why evidence alone rarely shifts deeply held beliefs. What's at stake is not logic, but meaning.

Faith and ideology also serve relational functions. They bind people together. Shared belief fosters intimacy, trust, and collective identity.

Religious rituals, political movements, and even internet subcultures use this shared conviction to create emotional bonds. These bonds are not incidental—they are often the glue that keeps the belief system intact. To question the belief, then, is to risk social exclusion. Many people stay aligned with worldviews they no longer fully accept because the social cost of honesty feels too high.

This dynamic can be both supportive and oppressive. On one hand, shared belief provides a sense of belonging and emotional resonance. On the other, it can create environments where conformity is enforced, dissent is punished, and complexity is erased. When faith becomes dogma, or ideology becomes orthodoxy, the belief system loses its reflective capacity. It stops asking questions and starts demanding allegiance.

Authoritarian systems exploit this dynamic. They use ideology not just to guide behavior, but to control thought. Dissent is reframed as betrayal. Alternative views are delegitimized. Language is weaponized to enforce belief conformity. In such systems, belief is no longer a personal journey—it becomes a test of loyalty. The psychological effect is profound: people begin to censor not just what they say, but what they allow themselves to think.

But rigidity is not inevitable. Faith and ideology can also support growth, justice, and compassion—when held with humility. The key difference lies in how conviction is approached. Mature belief systems encourage self-examination, acknowledge mystery, and tolerate doubt. They recognize that belief, like identity, is dynamic. It evolves in response to experience, reflection, and dialogue. Immature systems, by contrast, seek purity and permanence. They collapse ambiguity into certainty and punish those who challenge the narrative.

In therapy and in life, people often wrestle with inherited belief systems that no longer fit. This process—sometimes called deconstruction—is psychologically demanding. It can involve grief, confusion, and relational rupture. But it also opens the door to more authentic conviction. To believe again, not because one must, but because one has looked deeply and chosen freely.

Ultimately, conviction is not the enemy of psychological health. It is the quality of the conviction that matters. Beliefs that allow room for complexity, that recognize their own limits, and that remain in dialogue with reality can support resilience and integrity. Beliefs that demand certainty, suppress curiosity, or substitute loyalty for truth tend to produce fear, division, and emotional stagnation.

Faith and ideology are powerful psychological tools. They help people orient to a world that is often chaotic, painful, and uncertain. But their power comes with responsibility: the responsibility to examine not only what we believe, but why—and to ask whether our convictions make us more alive, more connected, and more open to the fullness of human experience.

Confirmation Loops and Cognitive Blind Spots

Once a belief system is in place—whether religious, ideological, or personal—the mind begins to protect it. This is not always conscious or deliberate. It is a byproduct of how human cognition evolved: to preserve coherence, minimize uncertainty, and reduce psychological discomfort. These protective mechanisms create what psychologists call confirmation loops—self-reinforcing patterns that filter information, reinterpret challenges, and maintain the integrity of the belief system, even in the face of contradictory evidence.

Confirmation bias is the best-known mechanism in this loop. It refers to the tendency to seek out, favor, and recall information that supports one's existing beliefs while dismissing, ignoring, or distorting evidence that challenges them. This bias operates at every level—from selective attention and memory to how people interpret events, conversations, and even scientific data. Once the mind has committed to a particular worldview, it begins to curate reality in its favor.

The process is efficient and automatic. People rarely notice it happening. They are not lying to themselves or intentionally avoiding the truth. Rather, they are experiencing reality through a cognitive filter designed to protect internal consistency. Dissonance—the discomfort of holding two conflicting ideas—requires effort to resolve. The brain prefers shortcuts. It chooses the path of least resistance: double down on the original belief, reinterpret the evidence, and move on.

This cognitive rigidity is reinforced by social dynamics. People tend to surround themselves with others who share their views—a phenomenon known as homophily. In these echo chambers, dissenting information is rare, and when it does appear, it is quickly reframed as biased, threatening, or uninformed. Online algorithms further intensify this effect by feeding users content that aligns with their interests and beliefs, creating informational bubbles that feel expansive but are in fact narrow.

The result is epistemic closure: a condition in which a person or group no longer has access to outside perspectives. Any contradictory evidence is seen not as a challenge to engage with, but as a threat to be neutralized. In political or religious contexts, this can lead to ideological insulation, moral absolutism, and an inability to tolerate ambiguity. In personal life, it can show up as emotional inflexibility, stubbornness, or chronic misinterpretation of relational feedback.

Motivated reasoning adds another layer to the loop. This refers to the tendency to reason in a way that supports a desired conclusion rather than an objective truth. For example, a person who believes they are unlovable may interpret a friend's delayed response as evidence of rejection—even if the delay had nothing to do with them. Similarly, someone committed to a political ideology may dismiss a well-supported critique as propaganda. The belief comes first; the reasoning follows.

Cognitive dissonance theory, originally proposed by Leon Festinger, explains how people resolve internal conflict when confronted with information that contradicts their beliefs. Rather than update the belief, most people adjust their interpretation of the new information—or shift the emotional weight they assign to it. This is not deception; it is a defense. It helps preserve identity and stability in a world where complexity is constant.

These mental habits are not limited to the uneducated or the ideologically extreme. Highly intelligent people are often better at rationalizing their beliefs, not revising them. Intelligence enhances the ability to construct convincing arguments, but it does not necessarily increase self-awareness or openness. In fact, strong analytical skills can make a person more skilled at defending flawed ideas, particularly when those ideas serve emotional or social needs.

Blind spots are inevitable. The human mind cannot process all information objectively. But when those blind spots become entrenched—when people cannot see what they do not want to see—they begin to lose touch with reality. Relationships suffer. Learning stalls. Growth becomes impossible. What begins as a mechanism for emotional safety becomes a barrier to psychological development.

Therapeutic work often involves identifying and gently challenging these blind spots. A therapist might notice a repeated pattern in how a client interprets rejection or avoids responsibility. Rather than confront it head-on, they might ask curious, non-threatening questions: "What else could that have meant?" or "What do you think someone else might see in this situation?" These questions introduce a crack in the closed system—an opening for new interpretation.

But it is not only therapy that allows for this. Life itself can interrupt the loop. Crises, losses, transitions, and unexpected encounters often shake the foundations of belief, making space for something new. When a tightly held worldview no longer explains experience—when the story begins to collapse under the weight of contradiction—the mind is forced to adapt. This moment is disorienting but also full of potential. It is the beginning of reflection.

Still, openness must be cultivated. People must develop the psychological capacity to tolerate discomfort, to admit error, and to remain curious in the face of difference. These are not natural tendencies; they are learned practices. They require humility, emotional regulation, and a willingness to be changed by what one encounters.

In an era of information overload, belief protection has become more urgent and more automatic. People are bombarded with stimuli, opinions, and conflicting narratives. The instinct to simplify, to anchor, to insulate is strong. But the cost is high: intellectual rigidity, moral polarization, and emotional fragility. The mind that cannot tolerate contradiction becomes brittle. And a brittle mind, no matter how brilliant, cannot grow.

To live consciously is to know that you have blind spots, and to seek them out—not to shame yourself, but to expand your field of vision. It is to ask: What am I not seeing? Whose voices am I excluding? What assumptions am I making, and are they still serving me?

Awareness of confirmation loops does not eliminate them. But it creates room to step outside them. And in that space, something essential becomes possible: the freedom to change.

Expanding the Frame: Intellectual Humility and Psychological Flexibility

Beliefs provide structure, but it is flexibility that keeps them alive. Psychological growth does not require abandoning convictions; it requires the capacity to hold them lightly, revise them when necessary, and recognize their limits. This is the work of intellectual humility—not weakness or indecision, but the disciplined willingness to question one's own certainty. In a world of complex problems and conflicting truths, the ability to expand the frame of one's thinking may be the most important cognitive skill of all.

Intellectual humility begins with the recognition that no perspective is complete. Every belief, however carefully formed, is partial—shaped by culture, experience, personality, and access to information. No one sees everything. No one knows everything. To acknowledge this is not to undermine conviction, but to ground it in reality. Arrogance distorts perception. Humility clarifies it.

This humility does not mean detachment or relativism. It does not require people to treat all views as equally valid or to withhold judgment where action is required. Rather, it invites a posture of ongoing inquiry. It means remaining open to the possibility that you might be wrong, or that there might be more to the story than you have considered. It means listening with the intent to understand, not just to respond.

Psychological flexibility supports this posture. Defined by acceptance and commitment therapy (ACT) as the ability to stay in contact with the present moment while adapting behavior in service of one's values, flexibility is what allows people to respond to new information without falling apart. It is what enables someone to let go of a cherished but outdated belief without losing their sense of identity. And it is what allows complex conversations to continue, even when they are uncomfortable.

Flexibility and humility are not merely intellectual traits; they are emotional achievements. To remain open in the face of disagreement requires emotional regulation. To tolerate ambiguity without retreating into rigidity requires self-trust. Many people defend their beliefs aggressively not because they are confident, but because they are afraid. Fear hardens. Shame shuts down curiosity. In this sense, belief rigidity is often a symptom—not of deep knowledge, but of unmet emotional needs.

Cultivating a more flexible mind often begins with metacognition—the capacity to think about one's own thinking. This involves noticing the moment when certainty arises and asking: Where did this belief come from? What function does it serve? What assumptions underlie it? These questions are not always easy to answer. They require stillness, reflection, and the willingness to be changed by the answers.

Some of this flexibility is developed through exposure to difference. When people engage regularly with ideas, cultures, and people outside their immediate worldview, their cognitive boundaries expand. This does not mean adopting every new perspective, but rather encountering enough complexity to soften the idea that one's current view is the only possible one. Travel, literature, meaningful dialogue, and even conflict—

when approached with openness—can all serve this function.

Educational systems also play a role. When students are taught not just what to think but how to think—how to evaluate evidence, recognize bias, and articulate uncertainty—they are better equipped to navigate a pluralistic world. The goal of education should not be ideological compliance but cognitive maturity: the ability to hold competing ideas, wrestle with complexity, and still act with integrity.

Importantly, flexibility does not eliminate the need for boundaries. Being open does not mean being porous. A psychologically flexible person can say, "I understand where you're coming from, and I still disagree." They can distinguish between empathy and agreement, between tolerance and capitulation. This is the strength of flexibility—it allows for clear boundaries without closing the door to dialogue.

There is also a generative aspect to this mindset. When people hold their beliefs reflectively, they remain capable of growth. They can adapt to changing circumstances, repair ruptured relationships, and make better decisions over time. Their sense of identity is not tied to any single idea or affiliation. It is rooted instead in values, intentions, and a commitment to learning. This creates psychological resilience.

In therapy, developing this capacity is often a turning point. A client who once saw the world in binaries—right or wrong, success or failure, love or rejection—begins to see nuance. They become less reactive, more curious. They stop needing their beliefs to protect them from discomfort and begin allowing those beliefs to evolve in response to it. This shift is quiet but profound. It marks the transition from defensiveness to depth.

Culturally, the need for flexibility has never been greater. We are living in an age of information saturation, ideological polarization, and rapid social change. The temptation to cling to certainty—to fortify belief systems against the complexity of modern life—is understandable. But it is ultimately self-defeating. Rigid minds cannot solve complex problems. Closed systems cannot adapt. A society that cannot reflect cannot heal.

Expanding the frame of belief does not mean having no convictions. It means understanding the frame itself. Seeing how it was built. Noticing where it narrows the field of vision. Asking who gets excluded, what gets left out, and what might be waiting on the other side of certainty. It means knowing the difference between a belief that serves life and one that merely serves fear.

In the end, belief systems are tools. They can build, they can destroy, and they can evolve. The question is not whether we have them. The question is how we hold them—and whether we are willing, when needed, to set them down, look again, and rebuild something wiser.

* * *

23

Memory, Narrative, and Personal Myth

You are the story you tell yourself. Not in a poetic sense, but in a literal psychological one. Identity is not a static trait or a fixed essence; it is a narrative—crafted over time, revised with experience, and shaped by memory, emotion, and meaning. Who you are is, in large part, who you believe yourself to be. That belief is constructed, moment by moment, in the stories you tell about where you've been, what it meant, and what kind of person it made you.

Psychologists call this *narrative identity*—the internalized and evolving story that gives your life continuity. It links past to present, present to future, self to society. It allows you to interpret experience, navigate change, and decide what matters. But narrative identity is not a record of facts. It is a framework of meaning. It is memory filtered through values, emotion, and perspective. And like all stories, it is shaped by what is emphasized, what is omitted, and how events are connected.

Memory plays a central role in this process. But memory is not a neutral archive—it is dynamic, reconstructive, and emotionally driven. People remember selectively, interpretively, and sometimes inaccurately. They edit the past not out of deceit, but out of a psychological need for coherence. The mind wants the story to make sense. It wants the person to appear consistent, understandable, and justifiable. When memory threatens that coherence, it is often reinterpreted—or buried.

Beneath the conscious story, deeper patterns are at work. Many people live within a personal myth—a symbolic narrative that defines their place in the world. This myth may cast them as the rescuer, the exile, the underdog, the martyr, the survivor. These roles are often unconsciously inherited, shaped by family dynamics, cultural narratives, and early emotional experience. They are not inherently pathological. In fact, they can be adaptive and meaningful. But when the myth becomes rigid—when it prevents growth, limits self-perception, or traps the person in repetition—it needs to be rewritten.

This chapter explores the psychology of self-narration: how people form identity through story, how memory functions as a meaning-making tool, how symbolic roles become scripts, and how individuals can revise their internal narrative to reflect greater truth, agency, and integration. It draws from narrative psychology, trauma theory, and depth psychology to illuminate the dynamic relationship between memory, identity, and transformation.

To know yourself is not just to catalog facts. It is to understand the story you've been telling—and to decide whether it still serves you. Stories can wound. Stories can heal. And sometimes, the most important psychological act is not to find a better answer, but to find a better frame.

The Story Self: How Identity Is Narrated

Who are you? Ask most people, and they will answer with a story. Not a list of facts or traits, but a narrative: where they came from, what shaped them, what they've survived, what they value, and what they hope to become. This storytelling is not incidental. It is foundational. People do not simply have experiences—they interpret them. And those interpretations, layered over time, become the framework through which identity is understood.

Psychologists call this *narrative identity*: the internalized and evolving story of the self that gives life meaning and continuity. It is not about what happened, but what it meant. This narrative links past to present and anticipates the future, providing coherence across shifting roles, changing circumstances, and inner contradictions. It is how people make sense of themselves—how they explain their actions, regulate their emotions, and find purpose in what they endure.

The building blocks of narrative identity are autobiographical memories—memories of personally significant events that are emotionally charged and interpreted through a sense of self. But memory is not a file drawer. It is a living process. When someone recalls a moment from childhood, they are not retrieving a fixed recording. They are reconstructing it, often influenced by who they are now, what they need to believe, and what their current emotional landscape demands. This reconstruction is not deception; it is function. The goal is coherence, not historical accuracy.

Over time, people develop narrative patterns—recurring themes, roles, and plotlines that shape how they tell their story. Some stories are redemptive: the person frames hardship as a path to growth, a crucible for wisdom or resilience. Others are contaminating: the person views their life as a downward spiral, where good things are spoiled by inevitable failure or betrayal. These narrative structures, studied extensively in the work of psychologist Dan McAdams, are predictive of psychological well-being. The redemptive storyteller tends to be more hopeful, more resilient, and more able to adapt. The contaminating storyteller often struggles with depression, rumination, or learned helplessness.

But narrative identity is not just emotional; it is moral. People use their stories to define right and wrong, to justify their choices, and to frame their suffering within a moral universe. "I did what I had to do." "They never gave me a chance." "I've always looked out for others." These statements are not just explanations—they are identity markers. They signal how the person wants to be seen, and how they see themselves.

Culture plays a major role in shaping these narratives. Every society offers dominant story templates—about success, gender, family, justice, trauma, and redemption. These cultural scripts inform what kinds of stories feel believable, admirable, or possible. A person's self-narrative does not emerge in a vacuum. It is shaped by what their culture values, what their community reinforces, and what roles are available to them based on race, class, gender, and history.

Family systems provide another powerful template. Children often internalize the implicit stories told around them: who the hero is, who the scapegoat is, what traits are rewarded, and what truths are allowed. These stories form early blueprints for identity. A child who is always told they are "the strong one" or "the difficult one" may unconsciously adopt that identity into adulthood, reinforcing it through choices and interpretations that align with the role—even when it no longer fits.

Yet even the most entrenched stories can change. Life disrupts narrative coherence. A diagnosis, a betrayal, a new relationship, a moment of grace—these experiences can open space for reinterpretation. A person may come to see their past with new eyes, to question the meaning they once assigned to events, or to explore versions of themselves they had long disowned. These narrative shifts can be quiet or dramatic. What matters is not the speed of change, but the honesty of it.

Therapy often supports this process. Narrative therapy, in particular, helps people externalize their problems ("The problem is not who you are, it's the story you've been living") and identify alternative storylines. Through dialogue, reflection, and curiosity, clients are invited to question inherited scripts, highlight overlooked strengths, and author new meanings for old pain. This is not about denial. It is about reclaiming agency over interpretation.

Agency is central. Narrative identity is not only descriptive; it is directive. The story we tell influences the future we imagine—and therefore, the choices we make. A person who sees themselves as perpetually broken may avoid risks, relationships, or opportunities for healing. A person who frames themselves as a learner, a survivor, or a work in progress may feel more permission to grow. These shifts are not magical. They are narrative.

The "story self" is not a final answer to the question of identity, but it is a powerful starting point. It reminds us that we are not only shaped by what has happened to us, but by the meaning we assign to those events. It reminds us that coherence is a need, but not at the cost of truth. And it reminds us that while the past cannot be rewritten, the story can—and often must be.

Memory as Meaning, Not Just Record

Memory is often misunderstood as a record of the past, a mental archive of what has happened. But psychologically, memory functions less like a filing cabinet and more like a living document—revised, edited, and shaped by the present. What people remember, how they remember it, and what it means to them is far more about identity than about chronology. Memory does not preserve the past. It constructs the past in service of the self.

This reconstructive nature of memory has been demonstrated repeatedly in psychological research. Elizabeth Loftus's studies on eyewitness testimony revealed how susceptible memory is to suggestion, expectation, and narrative framing. A single word—*smashed* versus *bumped*—can change how people recall a car accident. Participants who were asked misleading questions often incorporated those distortions into their recollections, sincerely believing the false version to be true. These findings were not just about legal accuracy. They pointed to a deeper truth: memory is shaped by what we believe, not the other way around.

Emotion plays a central role in this shaping. Highly emotional experiences are encoded differently in the brain than neutral ones. They are often more vivid, more persistent, and more likely to be remembered in detail. But emotion also colors the memory itself. A person recalling a breakup during a season of grief will likely experience that memory differently than when recalling it during a season of gratitude. The events may remain the same, but the emotional tone changes the meaning. And meaning is what memory retains.

Psychologically, people do not store memories to catalog the past; they store memories to interpret the present and anticipate the future. The mind keeps what is useful—what supports the self-concept, explains relationships, or protects against threat. Traumatic memories, for example, are often fragmented or dissociated—not because the brain failed, but because coherence in those moments would have been too psychologically overwhelming. The memory system protects survival, not continuity.

This has significant implications for how people understand themselves. When someone says, "I've always been this way," they are not just reporting a timeline—they are organizing memory around a dominant narrative. They may selectively recall examples that support the story of being anxious, unlucky, overlooked, or resilient. Other memories, those that contradict the dominant self-image, may be minimized or forgotten entirely. This is not a flaw in the system. It is the system. The mind preserves the version of the past that keeps the story coherent.

However, coherence is not the same as truth. And sometimes, the demand for narrative consistency comes at a cost. A person might cling to a story of betrayal so tightly that they overlook moments of connection. Or they might preserve a self-image of being "the strong one" and in doing so, erase all memories of vulnerability, support, or softness. These omissions create a distorted picture—not because the person is lying, but because the story they needed to survive eclipsed other parts of the past.

Therapeutic work often involves retrieving those eclipsed memories—fragments that were disallowed by the dominant narrative. A client may suddenly recall a small act of kindness from a parent they had long viewed as entirely neglectful, or they may begin to see how their story of failure left out the context of impossibly high expectations. These recovered elements do not negate the original memory; they complicate it. And in doing so, they offer a more integrated sense of self.

Trauma complicates memory further. Traumatic memories are often stored in a raw, sensory form—flashes of sound, image, or body sensation unmoored from time. These "implicit memories" do not feel like the past; they feel like the present. They intrude, disrupt, and confuse. Trauma survivors may struggle to trust their own recall, torn between emotional certainty and cognitive doubt. This is not because they are broken. It is because trauma disrupts the brain's ability to organize experience into narrative. The story fractures, but the pain persists.

Healing from trauma often requires transforming memory into story—linking fragmented sensations and emotions into a coherent narrative that can be held, shared, and eventually integrated. This is not the same as forgetting. It is the process of relocating the memory from raw survival into reflective awareness. It means saying: This happened, and this is what it means to me now. That shift—from re-experiencing to remembering—is the essence of post-traumatic growth.

But memory is not only disrupted by trauma. It is also edited by need. A person in a new romantic relationship may reinterpret past relationships in light of what they now understand about love. A parent may remember their childhood differently after having children of their own. A person facing terminal illness may recall their life through the lens of legacy rather than struggle. These are not manipulations of truth. They are the mind's way of making peace with what was, in service of what now is.

This editing process is not inherently bad. In fact, it reflects a kind of psychological wisdom. People do not need perfect recall to be well—they need stories that are meaningful, coherent, and flexible enough to grow with them. The danger comes when memory becomes too rigid or too sanitized. When people cling to a version of the past that is overly idealized, chronically negative, or frozen in grievance, their present becomes limited. They cannot revise the self if the past is fixed.

One way to approach memory more flexibly is through re-authoring practices. These involve looking at the same events through different emotional lenses or from different vantage points. What did this experience cost me—and what did it teach me? How did it hurt me—and how did it shape me? What part of this story have I never told? These questions open space for complexity. They allow the person to be both harmed and wise, both unfinished and growing.

Culturally, memory is also shaped by collective narratives. People often remember their past through shared lenses—national history, family lore, social trauma. These collective memories can unify or divide, depending on how they are framed. A community that remembers itself as victimized may pass down intergenerational mistrust. A family that remembers itself as resilient may foster pride and hope, even through hardship. These social memory systems affect individual identity in ways that are often unconscious but deeply influential.

The challenge, then, is not to seek a pure or objective memory—that does not exist. The challenge is to recognize memory as a tool of meaning-making. To notice how stories about the past support or constrain the present. And to ask: If I could hold this memory differently, what else might be possible in how I live now?

Memory, like narrative, is not a final truth. It is a lens. And when that lens becomes more flexible—more willing to include forgotten details, untold emotions, and revised interpretations—the self becomes more whole. It is not about rewriting history. It is about reclaiming the ability to live beyond it.

The Personal Myth: Archetype, Role, and Repetition

Every person carries a story beneath the story—a deeper, often unspoken myth about who they are, what life is, and how the world works. This personal myth is not always conscious, but it is powerful. It shapes behavior, relationships, expectations, and even memory. It is the symbolic framework through which life is interpreted and enacted. And while it often begins as a survival strategy, it can become a script people perform without knowing they are performing.

Carl Jung referred to this as the archetypal layer of the psyche. In Jungian psychology, archetypes are universal symbolic patterns—primordial images or roles that arise from the collective unconscious and express themselves through dreams, fantasies, and cultural stories. The orphan, the hero, the wise old man, the shadow, the trickster—these are not just literary devices. They are emotional structures, psychological templates that organize human experience across cultures and generations.

The personal myth draws from these archetypes, but it does so in individualized ways. A person may unconsciously live out the role of the martyr—constantly sacrificing their needs to earn love or moral superiority. Another may embody the hero—driven to prove worth through achievement or conquest. Others play the caregiver, the exile, the rebel, the rescuer, the invisible one. These roles are not inherently pathological. They often reflect adaptive responses to early environments. The problem arises when the role becomes rigid—when the myth no longer fits, but the person cannot stop playing it.

Children absorb these roles through both explicit and implicit messages. A child raised in chaos may become "the fixer," learning to calm tensions or mediate conflict. A child who feels unseen may become "the performer," earning love through excellence or charm. A child who is overcontrolled may become "the rebel," defining selfhood through opposition. These roles become not just responses, but identities. They offer coherence in environments where safety or recognition is scarce.

Over time, these roles organize perception and behavior. The fixer scans for problems to solve, even when none exist. The performer seeks applause, even when exhausted. The rebel resists guidance, even when it is kind. Each role carries an emotional logic. It creates predictability. But it also creates repetition. The person reenacts the same dynamics across relationships, workplaces, and life stages—often confused about why the same patterns keep emerging.

The repetition is not random. It is the unconscious mind seeking resolution. Freud called this the repetition compulsion—the tendency to recreate early relational dynamics in an attempt to master or undo them. Jung saw it more symbolically: the psyche repeats what has not been integrated. The story keeps resurfacing until the person becomes aware of it and claims authorship. Until then, the myth runs the show.

These personal myths are not always tragic. Some are empowering. A person may carry a myth of being a survivor, a truth-teller, a healer, a seeker. But even positive roles can become limiting if they are too narrow. The healer who cannot ask for help. The survivor who cannot feel safe. The truth-teller who alienates others. The seeker who never arrives. When a role becomes the entire identity, it can imprison the very person it once protected.

Narrative therapy and depth-oriented approaches often focus on making these myths conscious. Rather than simply analyzing behavior, they explore the story beneath the behavior. What role are you playing? Where did that role come from? What did it cost you to keep it? What are you afraid might happen if you let it go? These questions do not shame or pathologize. They invite reflection. They ask whether the story that once saved you is still serving you.

Symbolic thinking is central here. When people see their lives as symbolic—as layered with meaning, metaphor, and pattern—they gain psychological distance. They can look at their story rather than only from within it. They begin to notice motifs: "Why do I always end up in relationships where I have to prove my worth?" "Why do I always feel like I'm on the outside looking in?" These are not just personal complaints. They are echoes of a larger myth asking to be rewritten.

Rewriting begins with recognition. When a person names the story they've been living, they create the possibility of revision. They can experiment with new roles, new metaphors. The fixer can become the witness. The martyr can become the boundary-setter. The rebel can become the creator. These new roles do not erase the old ones—they expand them. They allow the person to live with greater range, agency, and psychological depth.

Culture also shapes personal myth. Some roles are gendered, racialized, or class-coded. Society tells people who they are supposed to be based on appearance, status, and social positioning. These external myths often become internalized. A young man may believe he must be stoic and self-reliant. A woman may believe her worth is tied to care-taking. A person from a marginalized group may internalize myths of inferiority, danger, or perpetual resilience. These narratives are not chosen, but they are absorbed. And without awareness, they limit who a person can become.

Myth is not just a constraint—it is also a portal. The archetypes people live through can point toward deep emotional truths. The shadow, for example, represents the disowned parts of the self—anger, vulnerability, desire, need. Engaging with the shadow mythically allows a person to integrate what they have split off, without shame. The hero's journey, a common mythic structure, offers a map for transformation: departure, ordeal, return. When someone sees their depression, divorce, illness, or loss through this lens, it becomes not just suffering, but initiation.

This symbolic reframe does not trivialize pain. It dignifies it. It says: There is meaning here. There is a pattern to be understood, a story to be told differently. When a person embraces their myth not as fate but as material, they reclaim creative power. They move from character to author.

In the end, we all live by stories. Some we inherit. Some we invent. Some are whispered by the culture, others carved by experience. The task of psychological development is not to discard story, but to live consciously within it. To ask: What role am I playing? Who gave me this script? What might happen if I chose another?

Because the story is still unfolding. And at any moment, the plot can turn.

Rewriting the Self: Agency, Editing, and Renewal

To say that identity is a story is not to say that the story is fixed. In fact, the most liberating insight of narrative psychology is that stories can be revised. The self, for all its complexity, is not a static object but a dynamic process. It evolves through reflection, experience, loss, rupture, and insight. While some people remain bound to the same narrative for decades—repeating roles, recycling pain—others discover the capacity to edit the story. This act of rewriting is not cosmetic. It is foundational. It is how psychological growth becomes real.

Rewriting the self begins with one of two impulses: either something no longer fits, or something awakens. In the first case, a person begins to feel tension between their current self-narrative and their lived experience. The confident achiever feels hollow despite success. The loyal partner begins to resent how often they silence themselves. The "strong one" quietly breaks under pressure. These disruptions are not failures; they are signals. They mark the beginning of narrative dissonance—a rupture between the old story and the emerging self.

In the second case, the shift is sparked not by collapse, but by insight. A new relationship, a creative breakthrough, a spiritual experience—something opens. The person sees themselves differently, sometimes just for a moment, and that glimpse cannot be unseen. They realize, perhaps for the first time, that they have been living inside a limited version of who they are. This moment of clarity invites reexamination: If I am not who I thought I was, then who might I become?

But rewriting is not just about imagining new possibilities. It requires confronting the original story—where it came from, what it protected, and what it cost. Many people resist this process, not because they lack courage, but because the story has become intertwined with survival. If I am no longer the one who keeps the peace, will anyone stay? If I stop being the victim, do I have to take responsibility? If I let go of the story of being broken, what will be left of me? These questions are not rhetorical. They are existential.

The work of rewriting involves two simultaneous processes: deconstruction and reconstruction. Deconstruction is the process of examining the original narrative with honesty and curiosity. What parts of this story were inherited rather than chosen? What parts served a purpose but are no longer true? What stories about love, success, strength, or worth have shaped my life without my consent? This inquiry does not blame. It reveals.

Reconstruction, in turn, asks: What might a more truthful story look like? One that includes complexity, contradiction, and change. One that honors the past but is not beholden to it. One that allows the person to grow without shame. This is not about creating a fantasy or writing a triumphant memoir. It is about coherence with flexibility. A story that can stretch to include pain, joy, error, and emergence without collapsing into a single theme.

Therapeutic settings are often where this work unfolds. In narrative therapy, clients are invited to externalize the problem—separating the person from the story—and then to examine alternative narratives that have been overshadowed. Instead of "I'm a failure," the client might explore "I was surviving in a system that did not support me." Instead of "I'm too sensitive," they might say "I feel things deeply, and that has shaped how I respond." These small shifts in language reflect massive shifts in identity.

Even outside therapy, people engage in narrative revision through journaling, dialogue, creative expression, or simply by telling their story differently over time. A person who once told the story of a breakup as abandonment may come to tell it as an act of self-respect. A job loss may shift from shame to redirection. These reinterpretations are not dishonest. They are psychologically generative. They allow the person to move forward without erasing the past.

But rewriting does not mean starting from scratch. It means integrating what was fragmented, updating what was outdated, and recognizing what was once invisible. It means seeing the younger self not as an embarrassment, but as a version of the self doing the best it could with what it had. It means holding complexity: "I was both naive and brave." "I hurt people, and I was also hurting." "I didn't know then what I know now." These acknowledgments are markers of maturity. They signal the transition from story as defense to story as truth.

There is also a communal aspect to rewriting. Identity is not shaped in isolation. It is reinforced—or resisted—through relationships. When a person begins to change their story, others may struggle. Friends and family may prefer the older version: the agreeable one, the funny one, the caretaker. Changing the story may require boundary-setting, loss, or even departure from environments that cannot accommodate the growth. This is painful. But it is also part of the process. A story that is not lived is just a script. It becomes real through action.

Renewal does not mean arriving at a final version of the self. It means committing to a relationship with the self that is ongoing, honest, and compassionate. It means accepting that identity is always under construction—that the person one is becoming deserves as much attention as the person one has been. It also means understanding that rewriting is not linear. People return to old stories under stress. They forget their progress. They revert. But even this is part of the narrative. Regression does not erase growth. It reveals where the story still holds pain.

In some cases, rewriting involves claiming a story that was never allowed. Queer people, trauma survivors, adult children of dysfunctional families—many must write stories that were actively erased or denied. This act of reclamation is powerful. It says: My experience matters. My truth deserves to be named. I exist beyond what others saw, beyond what they allowed me to be. This kind of storytelling is not just healing. It is radical.

Ultimately, rewriting the self is not about perfection. It is about integration. It is the recognition that we are composed of many selves, many chapters, many voices. The task is not to silence the ones we regret, but to place them in context. To say: That was a part of me. And now, this is too.

In a culture obsessed with performance, rewriting the self is an act of resistance. It says: I am not a brand. I am a becoming. And while the story of who I am will continue to shift, what matters most is that I am the one telling it.

* * *

24

Consciousness, Awareness, and Self-Reflection

What does it mean to be aware of being aware? Unlike basic perception or automatic thought, self-awareness is recursive. It allows us not only to think but to notice that we are thinking. This recursive quality is what gives consciousness its strange texture—its reflective depth, its narrative coherence, and its burden of responsibility. We are not just reacting to life; we are observing ourselves doing it. And from that observation, something profoundly human emerges: reflection, choice, and meaning.

In psychological terms, consciousness is not one thing but a layered system. At the most basic level, it refers to the state of being awake and responsive to stimuli. At a higher level, it includes focused attention, intentional action, emotional insight, and metacognition—the ability to think about thinking. This layered architecture of the mind is what allows humans to plan, evaluate, fantasize, regret, and imagine. But it also opens the door to ambivalence, shame, confusion, and existential doubt. Self-awareness is both a gift and a wound.

Philosophers have long wrestled with the nature of consciousness—what it is, where it resides, and why it matters. Is it a byproduct of complex neural computation? A window into something more fundamental about reality? A survival adaptation that gave rise to meaning-making? Science has made progress in mapping the correlates of consciousness in the brain, but it cannot yet explain how subjective experience arises from matter. What we do know is that consciousness plays a central role in psychological health. Without the capacity to reflect on our emotions, to examine our motives, to witness our thoughts, we are little more than instinct wrapped in memory.

This chapter explores the psychological dimensions of consciousness and self-reflection: how awareness develops, what shapes it, and what it makes possible. We'll examine how the "observing mind" evolves from early childhood to adulthood, how people develop (or fail to develop) metacognitive insight, and why certain forms of inner knowing are so difficult to access. We will also explore the relationship between awareness and identity, showing how consciousness can both stabilize and disrupt the stories we tell about ourselves.

At the heart of this chapter is a paradox: the more we become aware of ourselves, the more we confront the limits of what can be known. Insight does not guarantee accuracy. Reflection does not always lead to change. Awareness can invite humility, but it can also bring self-conscious paralysis. Knowing oneself is not a straightforward achievement. It is an ongoing process marked by ambivalence, revision, and ethical tension. As the psychoanalyst Adam Phillips once noted, people want to know themselves—but not too much.

Still, the capacity for self-reflection is one of the most powerful tools in human psychology. It is what allows us to grow from experience rather than be flattened by it. It is what helps us choose who we become, rather than merely react to who we've been. And it is what gives us access to something deeper than cognition—conscience, integrity, and the ability to witness our lives with clarity rather than delusion.

This chapter will not offer an answer to the mystery of consciousness. But it will explore how that mystery operates in ordinary life, how it can be cultivated, and how it becomes the foundation for psychological maturity. Because if we are ever to become more than our conditioning, we must learn not just to live—but to observe ourselves living.

The Architecture of Consciousness

At first glance, consciousness seems obvious. You are awake. You are reading these words. You are aware of what you're thinking—or at least you believe you are. But under the surface of this familiarity lies one of the most intricate and least understood functions of the human mind. Consciousness is not a simple light switch that flicks on in the morning and off when you sleep. It is a layered, dynamic process involving attention, memory, sensory integration, language, and reflective awareness. To understand the self, we must begin by understanding the structure of awareness itself.

At its most basic level, consciousness can be divided into two broad categories: phenomenal consciousness and access consciousness. Phenomenal consciousness refers to subjective experience—the vividness of what it feels like to hear music, to see red, to feel sorrow. It is the texture of being alive. Access consciousness, by contrast, refers to the mental content that is available for reasoning, speech, and intentional action. You may hear a song and feel nostalgic—that is phenomenal—but the moment you begin to think about *why* the song evokes those feelings, reflect on the associated memory, and articulate it to someone else, you are engaging access consciousness. Both forms are always present, but they operate on different levels.

Within the brain, consciousness is not housed in a single region but emerges from the integrated activity of multiple networks. The thalamus regulates sensory input; the prefrontal cortex manages executive control and reflective thinking; the default mode network becomes active during self-referential thought and daydreaming. Neuroscience continues to explore how these regions interact to generate the seamless experience of "being me"—but no single structure explains it. What we call consciousness is an emergent phenomenon: a whole that is more than the sum of its parts.

Cognitive psychologists often speak of consciousness as layered. The lowest layers are automatic and implicit—reflexes, conditioned responses, ingrained habits. Above that are the processes of selective attention: what we notice, what we tune out, what grabs our focus. Further up are deliberate thought, decision-making, and problem-solving. And hovering at the top—sometimes engaged, sometimes dormant—is meta-awareness: the capacity to monitor one's own mind. These layers are not fixed like geological strata. They are fluid and interactive. What starts as unconscious can become conscious through insight; what is conscious can slip into automation through repetition.

Attention plays a key role in shaping consciousness. It is the gatekeeper of awareness, determining what enters the spotlight of the mind. You are bombarded with sensory information every second, but only a fraction reaches your conscious awareness. The rest is filtered out, either as noise or background context. This filtering is both necessary and dangerous. It keeps you from being overwhelmed, but it also means your conscious experience is always a partial view. You are aware of only what your brain allows you to be aware of—and that allowance is shaped by habit, emotion, and expectation.

Emotion also influences the content and direction of consciousness. It colors perception, draws attention, and provides meaning. A fearful person will notice danger more readily. A hopeful person will see opportunity. These emotional filters do not distort consciousness so much as define it. What we feel often determines what we see. And because we are usually unaware of these emotional filters, they operate like invisible lenses. This makes consciousness deeply subjective, even when it feels objective.

Language enhances the complexity of consciousness by allowing humans to name, symbolize, and share experience. The capacity to narrate one's thoughts—to turn a sensation into a word, a reaction into a story—is central to psychological development. Children acquire this ability gradually, as language scaffolds their internal world. Adults refine it through reflection and dialogue. But language can also trap consciousness in conceptual loops. We start to think about thinking, worry about worrying, and create narratives that take on a life of their own. The very capacity that gives us insight can also become a source of confusion and suffering.

Sleep, dreaming, and altered states of consciousness reveal just how fluid awareness can be. In deep sleep, consciousness fades. In dreams, it becomes strange—symbolic, associative, nonlinear. In states induced by meditation, hypnosis, or psychedelics, the boundaries of self and time may dissolve altogether. These altered states demonstrate that ordinary waking consciousness is not the only—or even the most profound—form of awareness available to the human mind. It is simply the one we are most accustomed to.

What makes human consciousness unique is not just the ability to experience the world, but the ability to represent that experience to ourselves. We are able to think about our own thinking, to imagine different versions of ourselves, to plan for futures that do not yet exist, and to revisit past events through memory and emotion. This recursive loop—consciousness reflecting on itself—is what makes identity, ethics, creativity, and introspection possible.

But consciousness is not inherently benevolent. It can be used to deceive, to rationalize, to self-sabotage. It can amplify suffering by making pain inescapable through rumination. It can become compulsively self-referential, leading to anxiety, paralysis, or narcissism. Awareness alone is not a virtue. It is a tool. Its value depends on how it is used, what it is connected to, and whether it is balanced by empathy, humility, and emotional integration.

In many ways, consciousness is like a mirror. It shows us what is there—but only if the mirror is clean, well-lit, and free from distortion. Most of the time, the mirror is smudged. We see parts of ourselves, but not the whole. We react to reflections without understanding their source. Cultivating consciousness means learning to clean that mirror—to recognize its biases, to sharpen its focus, and to use it not only to see ourselves but to understand others.

This architecture of consciousness—its layers, filters, and limitations—forms the foundation for all psychological inquiry. Without it, there is no insight, no transformation, no self. But with it comes a burden: to be aware is to be responsible. Once we see, we cannot unsee. Once we know, we are accountable.

And that is the quiet cost—and promise—of being conscious.

The Emergence of the Observing Mind

The capacity to observe one's own mind is one of the most remarkable developments in human psychological evolution. It is what allows us not only to think, but to know that we are thinking. This meta-awareness—what psychologists call metacognition—opens the door to reflection, regulation, and self-inquiry. It is the beginning of inner life as something we can witness, shape, and engage with intentionally. Without it, we remain fused with our thoughts and emotions, reacting to the world as if our perceptions were facts. With it, we gain the ability to pause, to reflect, and to ask: Is this true? Is this mine? Is there another way?

Metacognition doesn't emerge fully formed. Like most psychological capacities, it develops in stages. Early in life, children operate in what developmental psychologists refer to as egocentric cognition. They feel emotions, act on impulses, and form thoughts—but they are not yet aware that these inner events can be observed or questioned. Around age four or five, something begins to shift. Children develop what is known as theory of mind—the ability to recognize that other people have thoughts, beliefs, and emotions separate from their own. This marks the early seeds of the observing mind: the awareness that minds exist as entities, including one's own.

By adolescence, this capacity expands. Teenagers begin to reflect on their own thinking, analyze their motivations, and even critique their internal narratives. They become acutely self-conscious, often painfully so, because the ability to observe the self also comes with the ability to judge it. They start to ask who they are, what others see, and whether the self they perform aligns with the self they feel. This capacity can be unstable in adolescence—sometimes profound, sometimes performative—but it signals a fundamental shift from mere consciousness to reflective self-awareness.

In adulthood, the observing mind can become a powerful ally—or a source of torment. Some people strengthen it through education, dialogue, and introspection. They develop a consistent habit of observing their reactions, questioning their assumptions, and adjusting their behavior based on insight. Others avoid this process, either because it was never modeled or because it feels threatening. To observe the mind is to become aware of contradiction. It is to see one's envy, defensiveness, or cruelty alongside one's compassion and intention. It is to know, in real time, that you are not always who you wish to be.

One of the most psychologically liberating insights a person can have is the realization that a thought is not a command. The observing mind allows us to hold space between impulse and action, between feeling and interpretation. When anger rises, we can feel it without becoming it. When fear whispers disaster, we can question its logic. This inner witness does not erase emotion, but it provides perspective. It allows us to respond rather than react.

But cultivating this perspective is not easy. The observing mind is often drowned out by the volume of automatic thought. In daily life, most people operate on mental autopilot, driven by habit, emotion, and situational cues. The mind comments, critiques, predicts, and remembers—but rarely stops to reflect. The observing mind must be deliberately strengthened, like a muscle. Practices such as mindfulness, journaling, cognitive restructuring, and reflective dialogue all serve to engage it. They invite us to look *at* our thoughts rather than *from within* them.

Psychological models have tried to capture the mechanisms that enable this kind of self-observation. Aaron Beck's cognitive theory identified the importance of automatic thoughts and core beliefs, while more recent acceptance-based approaches emphasize defusion—the process of separating from one's thoughts in order to observe them more clearly. In Dialectical Behavior Therapy, the skill of "wise mind" represents a synthesis of emotional and rational awareness, made possible through reflection. These models all point to a similar truth: that mental health depends not just on what we think, but on our ability to *see ourselves thinking*.

There are also barriers to the observing mind. Trauma, in particular, can fragment awareness and make self-observation feel unsafe. When the mind associates certain thoughts or feelings with danger, it often shuts down reflective awareness in favor of dissociation or hypervigilance. In such cases, developing the observing mind requires not just cognitive skill, but emotional safety. The goal is not to force self-reflection, but to create a compassionate space where the mind can be observed without judgment.

There is a cultural dimension as well. Some societies and environments encourage introspection and dialogue; others prize conformity and emotional control. Children raised in households where feelings are named, validated, and explored are more likely to develop reflective awareness. Those raised in environments where emotional expression is punished or minimized may learn to shut down observation altogether. In this way, the observing mind is not only a personal skill but a relational inheritance.

Importantly, the observing mind is not neutral. It can take on different tones depending on internalized messages. For some, it is a harsh critic—always watching, always judging. For others, it is a calm narrator, offering insight without condemnation. The tone of this inner voice is shaped by early attachment, modeled behavior, and later cognitive habits. Part of psychological growth involves reshaping the observing mind into something more compassionate, accurate, and attuned.

The emergence of the observing mind also intersects with identity. When we observe ourselves, we begin to question the roles we play, the stories we believe, and the images we project. This can be destabilizing. It can threaten the illusion of coherence. But it is also the path to freedom. Because when we recognize that we are not our thoughts, not our emotions, not even our roles—we begin to sense that there is a self beneath performance. A self that observes, that chooses, that grows.

The observing mind is not mystical. It is a natural psychological faculty that can be strengthened, sharpened, and deepened over time. It allows us to look inward with clarity, to engage life with intention, and to revise the story of who we are as we grow. It does not offer certainty, but it offers awareness. And from awareness, everything else becomes possible.

Insight, Illusion, and the Limits of Self-Knowledge

We live in a culture that celebrates insight. We praise those who seem self-aware, who can speak with clarity about their past, name their patterns, or admit their flaws with poise. We encourage reflection, promote therapy, and valorize emotional intelligence. And yet, insight—real, sustained, transforming insight—is one of the rarest and most elusive achievements in human psychology. It requires more than information. It demands more than analysis. It calls for the courage to dismantle illusions that have, for many people, become essential to survival.

Insight is often confused with intellectual understanding. A person may be able to describe their behavior in detail, recount their childhood trauma, and even name their defense mechanisms, all without any meaningful change in how they live. This is what psychoanalyst Karen Horney once called "intellectual insight" as opposed to "emotional insight." Intellectual insight explains; emotional insight transforms. It pierces the armor of rationalization and touches the nervous system. You feel it in your chest, not just in your head. It rewires not only how you think, but how you react, how you remember, and what you believe about yourself.

But this kind of transformation is difficult because self-knowledge is not neutral. The mind resists it. It is not simply that we *can't* see ourselves clearly—it's that, on some level, we often *don't want to*. Insight threatens the familiar. It reveals contradiction. It forces confrontation. And for many people, especially those with a history of emotional invalidation, trauma, or rejection, insight can feel dangerous. It might suggest that the persona they've worked so hard to construct is less stable than they believed. Or that the identity they've defended for decades is built on protective distortion.

This resistance to insight is not a flaw. It is a psychological defense. Freud called it resistance; contemporary therapists might call it emotional self-protection. We avoid what is too painful to know. We deny what might unravel us. We rationalize, distract, displace, and split off awareness in the name of functionality. These are not signs of pathology—they are adaptive responses to inner conflict. But they come at a cost: the more rigid the illusion, the less space for growth.

Illusions serve a purpose. A child may grow up believing that their parents were perfect because the alternative—recognizing neglect or cruelty—would be too destabilizing. An adult may believe they are unlovable because that belief explains why people have left, and gives coherence to a painful pattern. These narratives, however false, provide order. They make suffering predictable. To question them is to invite chaos. And so many people cling to their illusions not because they are foolish, but because they are afraid.

The challenge of self-knowledge, then, is not simply to dig deeper. It is to approach the self with both precision and compassion. Too much scrutiny without safety leads to shame. Too much comfort without honesty leads to stagnation. The middle path is reflection with gentleness: to ask not just "What is true?" but "What am I ready to know, and what would I need in order to face it?"

Even the most insightful people carry blind spots. These are the parts of self that remain hidden despite therapy, introspection, or feedback. They are maintained by unconscious processes—defense mechanisms, trauma memory, social conditioning. They are also shaped by culture. A person raised in a collectivist environment may overlook how deeply they sacrifice personal needs. A person raised in an individualistic society may fail to recognize how much their autonomy rests on invisible privilege.

Insight requires not only inward gaze but contextual understanding. Who you are is shaped by where and with whom you have lived.

Moreover, insight is nonlinear. It does not arrive in a single moment and stay forever. People often discover the same truth multiple times, each time at a deeper level. You may realize you are conflict-avoidant in your twenties, and then again in your thirties, and again in your forties—each time discovering a new layer of why. This spiral of recognition is not a failure. It is how growth actually unfolds. The mind integrates truth slowly, in steps, often through repetition and lived experience rather than instant revelation.

There is also a paradox at the heart of self-knowledge: the more we know ourselves, the more we realize how much remains unconscious. This is not a failure of insight but a feature of the human condition. The self is not a fixed entity to be fully known; it is a moving process, layered and shaped by time. New relationships, crises, roles, and contexts reveal new facets. To know the self is to remain open to discovery—and to accept that some parts of the self may always remain out of reach.

This acceptance is itself a kind of insight. It allows for humility. It tempers the ego's desire for mastery with the recognition that self-understanding is always partial. We are not static beings to be solved. We are living organisms, in motion, unfolding.

And so, insight is not an endpoint but a practice. It is something we return to again and again, each time seeing with slightly more clarity, slightly more depth. It is less about acquiring truths than about loosening illusions. Less about control than about connection. And in its most profound form, it is not about fixing the self—but about witnessing it with compassion.

Cultivating Reflective Awareness

If the observing mind gives us access to awareness, then reflective awareness is what we do with that access. It is the process of intentionally pausing, looking inward, and making meaning out of experience. Reflective awareness is not passive. It is not the same as daydreaming or mental drifting. It is an active stance toward the self—one that seeks coherence, understanding, and alignment. While it often arises in moments of solitude, it is ultimately a relational act: how we reflect shapes how we relate, and how we relate shapes what we reflect upon.

At its most basic level, reflective awareness is the habit of asking internal questions. Why did I react that way? What am I feeling right now? What part of me is speaking? These are not questions we are typically taught to ask. Many people grow up in environments that prioritize performance over reflection, control over curiosity. Emotional responses are often judged, minimized, or dismissed. Over time, people learn to focus outward: on what others want, how they appear, what should be done. Reflection atrophies. Awareness narrows.

To cultivate reflective awareness is to reverse this narrowing. It means turning attention inward not to ruminate, but to witness. It is different from overthinking, which loops through the same patterns without resolution. Reflection has direction. It seeks to understand. It integrates past and present, thought and feeling, reaction and intention. And it does so with a particular kind of tone: honest but not harsh, curious but not invasive.

There are many pathways to reflective awareness. One of the most accessible is journaling. When we write about our experiences, especially by hand, we slow down cognition. We give shape to scattered thoughts. We move from reaction to representation. Over time, consistent journaling builds a kind of inner map. We begin to notice patterns: triggers, coping mechanisms, beliefs we didn't know we held. And in naming them, we loosen their grip. We create space between stimulus and story.

Dialogue is another powerful tool. Talking with someone who can reflect back not just our words but our emotional subtext helps us see ourselves more clearly. This is the essence of therapeutic work: a mirror with memory, someone who can hold both the present moment and the broader arc of your story. But even outside of therapy, reflective dialogue is possible—with friends, mentors, partners—if the container is safe. The key is not advice or analysis, but resonance. Reflection requires space, not solutions.

Mindfulness practices also strengthen reflective awareness, particularly when framed in psychological rather than mystical terms. By noticing sensations, thoughts, and feelings without judgment, we learn to observe the mind as a process. This observational stance allows us to become less fused with any single thought or emotion. We recognize that moods pass, that pain can be witnessed, that thoughts are not commands. This perspective is foundational to psychological flexibility.

Cognitive-behavioral approaches offer a more structured path to reflection. By identifying cognitive distortions—such as black-and-white thinking, catastrophizing, or personalization—we learn to examine the beliefs that shape perception. We shift from assuming to inquiring. This is not about positive thinking, but about accurate thinking. Reflective awareness involves seeing reality more clearly, not more optimistically.

Importantly, reflection requires emotional regulation. We cannot reflect deeply if we are flooded with fear, anger, or shame. This is why practices that ground the nervous system—breathwork, physical movement, sensory regulation—are essential companions to reflection. They create the internal stability needed to look inward without collapsing.

Cultural and developmental factors shape who has access to reflective awareness. Children raised in environments where emotions are named, modeled, and explored are more likely to develop it. Those raised in environments of chaos, neglect, or emotional suppression may have to learn it later, often with effort. But it can always be learned. Reflective capacity is not fixed. It is a skill, and like any skill, it strengthens with use.

There is a moral dimension to reflective awareness. To see oneself clearly is to become accountable. Once we notice our impact, our intentions, our contradictions, we can no longer pretend we didn't know. Reflection calls us to maturity. It asks: How do I want to live? Who do I want to become? What do I need to repair? This kind of reflection is not self-indulgent. It is foundational to ethical life.

But reflection is also personal. It is how we make sense of our lives. It is how we metabolize experience into meaning. A heartbreak becomes more than pain; it becomes insight about how we love. A mistake becomes more than regret; it becomes clarity about our values. Reflection gives narrative shape to the raw data of living. It turns experience into wisdom.

At its deepest level, reflective awareness is not just about knowing the self. It is about befriending it. This requires kindness. Many people, once they begin to reflect, encounter an inner critic so loud that it drowns out any possibility of growth. Compassion is not a luxury in this process. It is a necessity. Without it, reflection becomes rumination. With it, reflection becomes restoration.

To cultivate reflective awareness is to commit to a lifelong practice. Not a destination, but a rhythm: pause, look, understand, integrate. And then live. Not perfectly, not always consciously, but more intentionally. More humanely. More whole.

* * *

25

The Search for Truth

From our earliest years, we are driven by questions. Why is the sky blue? What happens when we die? Can you still love someone who lies to you? These are not idle curiosities. They are attempts to place ourselves inside a coherent map of existence. To be human is to search for truth—not only factual truth, but personal, emotional, and moral truth. We want to know what is real, what can be trusted, and how to navigate life in a way that makes sense. This search defines both our greatness and our fragility. It propels scientific discovery and philosophical inquiry. It also fuels dogma, denial, and delusion.

Psychologically, truth operates on many levels. There is sensory truth: what we see, hear, and feel. There is emotional truth: how something affects us or resonates. There is interpersonal truth: what we believe about others and what they believe about us. And there is existential truth: what we decide life means and how we assign value. These truths do not always align. A person may feel unloved while being deeply cherished. They may recall a past injustice that others insist never happened. They may be certain of a spiritual reality that cannot be proven or shared. To live honestly is not to resolve these contradictions, but to hold them with discernment.

The need for truth is also the need for coherence. Our brains are wired to seek patterns, explanations, and consistency. When something does not make sense, we feel anxiety. This is why we sometimes cling to falsehoods: because they offer clarity. They protect us from ambiguity. They reassure us that the world is knowable and that we are not helpless in it. In this way, the search for truth is not always noble. It can be driven by fear, control, and the desire to be right. People often say they want the truth, but what they really want is to feel certain.

This chapter is not about truth as an abstract ideal. It is about the psychological dimensions of truth: how we pursue it, distort it, defend it, and surrender to it. It explores why knowing is so emotionally charged, why unknowing can feel threatening, and how maturity often involves tolerating ambiguity rather than eliminating it. The goal is not to define what is true in any metaphysical sense. It is to understand what it means to *search* for truth—to engage with reality as best we can, knowing that our tools are flawed and our motives are mixed.

We will begin by examining the human desire to know, and why it is as much emotional as it is cognitive. From there, we will explore the limits of knowing, and the ways in which the mind distorts or constrains perception. We will then turn to the relationship between truth and power—how culture, identity, and authority shape what people consider real. And finally, we will explore epistemic humility: the ability to hold truth with open hands, to revise beliefs without shame, and to stay grounded even when certainty is out of reach.

The Desire to Know

The human mind is not content with sensation alone. It craves structure, explanation, and order. This drive to know is not a modern invention; it is fundamental to our survival and to our identity. From infancy, we are natural pattern-seekers. Babies will track faces, detect voice-tone differences, and seek cause-and-effect relationships. By childhood, we've begun forming internal theories about how the world works. These aren't always accurate, but they serve a powerful function: they help us orient, predict, and respond. The desire to know is rooted in this psychological need for coherence.

In psychology, this drive is often described through the lens of cognitive consistency. Leon Festinger's theory of cognitive dissonance, for instance, suggests that when our beliefs, behaviors, or emotions are in conflict, we experience internal tension. To resolve it, we seek explanations that restore harmony. This is not always a search for truth—it is often a search for equilibrium. When people say they want the truth, they often mean they want a version of reality that makes emotional sense. One that is bearable. One that confirms what they already believe or hope is true.

This helps explain why the same fact can land so differently with different people. If someone has constructed an identity around being the wronged party, a new piece of information that complicates that story can feel not just surprising, but threatening. Truth is not just data. It is identity-relevant. It is emotionally sticky. The desire to know is filtered through the need to belong, to feel safe, to make meaning. It is never purely intellectual.

This is why insight often arrives in stages. People are not blank slates waiting to receive facts. They are meaning-makers with emotional ecosystems. A man may spend years believing his father was cruel because he cannot yet face the grief of having needed him. A woman may insist she's "fine" in her marriage because she is not ready to confront the loneliness that would rush in if she admitted otherwise. The truth waits for readiness. Or more precisely, the *willingness* to hold it.

Psychologically, knowledge is never neutral. It can empower or destabilize. It can free us, but it can also fracture us. The adolescent who discovers a parent's affair does not just acquire a new fact—they experience a rupture in trust, identity, and family mythology. The adult who uncovers their own self-deception doesn't merely change a belief—they must reckon with the consequences of having lived under a false premise. To know something new is to often feel something new: grief, anger, guilt, or liberation.

This emotional terrain is part of what makes truth-seeking such a delicate psychological task. People vary in their tolerance for complexity.

Some need answers to feel safe. Others need uncertainty to feel alive. Some will rewrite memory to maintain coherence. Others will tolerate dissonance in order to stay loyal to what feels emotionally real. These differences are not moral judgments—they are developmental responses. The capacity to want to know depends on what one believes they can survive.

Education, too, plays a role in how the desire to know is shaped. In some environments, knowledge is transactional—memorize, perform, and forget. In others, it is relational—a tool for inquiry, for questioning, for self-expansion. Children who are taught to ask why, to tolerate not knowing, to reflect rather than recite, grow into adults who are more likely to pursue truth with humility rather than ego. But many are taught the opposite: that to know is to dominate, to win, to control. In such systems, the pursuit of truth becomes a contest rather than a conversation.

Culture adds another layer. In societies that prize certainty, ambiguity is often treated as weakness. People are rewarded for confidence, even when it's misplaced. Politicians, pundits, and public figures who speak in absolutes are more likely to be trusted—even if their claims are dubious—because they project control. This has real consequences. It creates an emotional economy in which doubt is seen as failure, and nuance is dismissed as indecision. In such environments, the desire to know becomes entangled with the desire to appear certain.

Relationally, the desire to know plays out in intimacy. We want to know our partners, our friends, our children. But we also want to be known in return. And that kind of mutual knowing requires vulnerability. It means letting go of performance. It means allowing others to see us as we are—not just as we wish to be seen. This is difficult. Many people hide behind roles, personas, or curated versions of themselves because the truth feels too exposed. To be known is to risk rejection. But it is also the only path to genuine connection.

Ultimately, the desire to know is a yearning for orientation. It is how we anchor ourselves in a confusing and often contradictory world. But the quality of that knowing—whether it is open or defensive, humble or rigid—shapes not only what we see, but who we become. The truth is not just something we find. It is something we must learn to *live with*.

The Limits of Knowing

For all our drive to know, the human mind is a deeply fallible instrument. It constructs reality from incomplete data, filtered through memory, emotion, bias, and culture. Our knowledge is never pure; it is shaped as much by what we believe as by what we observe. The limits of knowing are not just epistemological—they are psychological. They live in how we process, protect, and preserve our view of the world, often without realizing we are doing it.

Cognitive psychology has long demonstrated that perception is not passive. We do not see the world as it is; we see it as our brains interpret it. Visual illusions reveal this clearly: the brain fills in gaps, corrects for shadows, and makes assumptions based on context. But this principle extends far beyond vision. We fill in emotional gaps too. We assign meaning where there is ambiguity. We construct stories to explain behavior—our own and others'—and then forget that they were just stories.

Memory, for example, feels stable and trustworthy. But it is anything but. Studies by Elizabeth Loftus and others have shown that memory is highly suggestible and reconstructive. What we recall is often a blend of fact, emotion, later experiences, and narrative coherence. We don't replay memories like films—we remake them like myths. And once we tell a story often enough, it becomes hard to separate what happened from what we've come to believe.

Emotion further complicates knowing. When we are afraid, angry, or ashamed, our cognitive processing narrows. We become less likely to entertain alternatives, less able to tolerate complexity. This is known as affective realism—the phenomenon in which emotional states shape what we believe to be true. If we feel unsafe, we are more likely to see others as threatening. If we feel rejected, we are more likely to interpret neutral behavior as hostile. Emotion does not merely color our perception; it actively directs it.

Then there are cognitive biases—those predictable errors in thinking that affect all of us. Confirmation bias leads us to favor information that supports what we already believe. Anchoring bias makes us cling to the first piece of information we receive. The availability heuristic causes us to overestimate the importance of things that are most easily recalled—often because they are dramatic, recent, or emotionally charged. These biases are not signs of stupidity. They are adaptive shortcuts. But they also mean that what we think we know is often a distortion of what is actually there.

Social context compounds these limitations. We are deeply influenced by group norms, authority figures, and cultural narratives. Solomon Asch's conformity experiments showed that people will deny obvious truths if the group disagrees. Stanley Milgram's obedience studies revealed how authority can override moral judgment. More recent work on motivated reasoning shows that when identity is at stake, people will reject even overwhelming evidence if it threatens their worldview. In other words, we often believe not what is true, but what protects our belonging.

This leads to a paradox: the more intelligent or educated a person is, the better they may be at rationalizing their false beliefs. Intelligence is not a safeguard against bias; it can become a tool for more sophisticated self-deception. This is why deeply entrenched ideologues are often the most articulate. They don't lack reasoning ability—they've trained it to serve their preconceptions.

Technology further muddies the waters. The internet offers access to unprecedented amounts of information—but without filters for accuracy, credibility, or context. Algorithms feed us what we already engage with, reinforcing our existing views. In such an environment, knowledge becomes tribal. People trust not based on evidence, but on source loyalty. The phrase "do your own research" often means "find something that confirms what I already suspect."

And yet, to acknowledge these limits is not to surrender to relativism. It is to take responsibility for how we know what we know. It means recognizing that certainty is a feeling, not a fact. That our convictions must always be subject to review. That humility is not a sign of weakness, but a requirement for growth.

There is a developmental arc to this awareness. Children are often taught that truth is binary: right or wrong, good or bad, fact or fiction. Adolescents begin to confront ambiguity, and many respond with cynicism or rebellion. Mature adults, when supported by self-awareness and emotional regulation, begin to see that knowledge is layered. That multiple perspectives can contain partial truths. That not knowing is not failure—it is the beginning of wisdom.

To live within the limits of knowing is to practice what psychologists call *epistemic humility*. It means resisting the lure of quick conclusions. It means noticing when we are emotionally invested in being right. It means being willing to revise, update, and sometimes dismantle our beliefs in the face of new evidence. And it means understanding that clarity is not always possible—or necessary. Sometimes the most honest answer is "I don't know."

But this is not an invitation to passive uncertainty. It is a call to active discernment. To learn how to weigh evidence, to tolerate ambiguity, and to seek coherence without clinging to simplicity. To become the kind of person who holds beliefs responsibly—not because they are beyond questioning, but because they have been earned through reflection.

The limits of knowing are real. But they are not failures. They are the conditions in which psychological maturity is formed.

Truth, Power, and Perspective

The idea that truth is objective, singular, and discoverable appeals to our need for certainty. But in psychological and social reality, truth is often filtered through power, perspective, and emotional allegiance. People do not merely see the world—they are positioned within it. That position shapes what they consider real, whose experiences they trust, and what facts they find persuasive. The pursuit of truth, then, is never just about logic; it is about identity, affiliation, and the invisible structures that shape belief.

From a psychological standpoint, every person operates within what might be called an interpretive frame. This frame includes past experience, emotional expectations, cognitive biases, and cultural context. But it also includes power dynamics—who is allowed to speak, who is believed, who is dismissed. What counts as truth in a courtroom, for example, often has more to do with credibility, social standing, and rhetorical skill than it does with accuracy. The same is true in classrooms, boardrooms, and media debates. People with authority are granted the power to define what is real. And those without it often internalize the idea that their truth does not count.

This is why truth and power are always entangled. Michel Foucault, the French philosopher and social theorist, argued that knowledge is never neutral. It is produced within systems of power that shape what is seen, what is said, and what is possible. The stories societies tell about what is true—about gender, sanity, morality, intelligence—are often mechanisms for maintaining control. When people say "the truth came out," they usually mean it aligned with a dominant narrative. But history is filled with truths that were silenced because they disrupted power: scientific facts that challenged religious dogma, survivor accounts that contradicted institutional interests, cultural knowledge that colonial systems erased.

In group psychology, this plays out through the dynamics of in-groups and out-groups. People are more likely to believe information that confirms their group's worldview and to dismiss contradictory information as biased, false, or dangerous. This is called motivated reasoning. It's not just that people believe what they want to believe. It's that they believe what protects their identity within the group. If a piece of information threatens group cohesion, it will often be rejected—

not because it is false, but because it is inconvenient.

This explains why fact-checking rarely changes minds. In fact, it often backfires. When people are confronted with evidence that contradicts their beliefs, they may double down. This is known as the backfire effect. The correction is perceived not as clarification, but as attack. And because the belief is tied to identity, letting go of it feels like a betrayal. Belief systems are rarely undone by logic alone. They are relational, emotional, and embedded in status hierarchies.

Social media amplifies this effect. Online platforms do not reward accuracy—they reward engagement. Outrage spreads faster than nuance. Simplistic narratives outperform complex ones. And because people curate their feeds, they are increasingly exposed to information that mirrors their perspective and excludes others. This creates epistemic silos—echo chambers where each group becomes more convinced of its own righteousness and more suspicious of those outside it. In such environments, truth becomes tribal.

Even science, often seen as the gold standard of objectivity, is not immune to power and perspective. Scientific research is shaped by funding priorities, institutional norms, publication biases, and social values. What gets studied, who gets cited, whose voices are included—all reflect larger cultural forces. This doesn't mean science is unreliable. It means science is a human enterprise. And like all human endeavors, it must be examined for the ways in which it centers certain truths while excluding others.

In personal relationships, the link between truth and perspective becomes deeply intimate. Two people can recount the same argument in entirely different ways, each feeling truthful. That's because memory is selective, emotion is interpretive, and perception is shaped by history. The mistake is to assume that only one of them is "right." Often, both are expressing a partial truth shaped by their vantage point. The goal in such moments is not to win the argument, but to understand the frame.

This brings us to a critical insight: psychological maturity involves learning to hold multiple truths at once. It means recognizing that your perspective is valid, but not exhaustive. That someone else's experience may contradict yours and still be real. This is not moral relativism. It is epistemic generosity—the ability to remain grounded in your own reality while making space for others.

Power complicates this further. Not all perspectives are equally weighted in the social world. Marginalized people are often asked to prove their truths while dominant voices are assumed to be objective. A woman reporting workplace harassment may be asked for evidence. A CEO denying it may be believed without question. This asymmetry is not just unfair—it is psychologically corrosive. It teaches people that truth is not about what happened, but about who gets to decide what happened.

Repairing this requires more than just better evidence. It requires a different orientation to knowledge. It means listening without defensiveness. Valuing testimony. Understanding that truth is co-created through dialogue, not declared by fiat. It means developing what psychologist Jennifer Freyd called "institutional courage": the willingness to face uncomfortable truths, especially when doing so threatens one's status or security.

Ultimately, truth is not just a matter of content. It is a matter of relationship. It lives in how we treat each other's experiences. How we hold our convictions. How we respond when reality challenges our comfort. And how willing we are to trade certainty for connection, simplicity for complexity, and power for understanding.

Epistemic Humility as Maturity

To know something is powerful. To admit you might be wrong is more powerful still. Epistemic humility—the recognition that our knowledge is always partial, provisional, and subject to revision—is not the absence of intelligence; it is the presence of psychological maturity. It reflects a mind that values truth over ego, curiosity over control, and learning over victory.

Children, understandably, crave certainty. It provides safety, structure, and predictability. They want to know the rules, the reasons, and the right answers. Adolescents often push against this by embracing skepticism, defiance, or relativism. But adulthood, at its most integrated, involves learning to live inside complexity. To remain open without being naïve, firm without being rigid, and discerning without being arrogant.

This is not easy. Western culture tends to reward confidence more than accuracy. People who speak with force, assert their opinions, and never waver are often perceived as more competent, even when they're wrong. Politicians, pundits, and influencers thrive by projecting certainty—because it sells, not because it reflects reality. In such a landscape, humility can appear weak or indecisive. But in truth, it requires far more strength to say, "I don't know," or "I was wrong," than to defend a position you no longer believe.

Psychologically, epistemic humility rests on several core capacities. The first is metacognition: the ability to think about your own thinking. To step back and observe your assumptions, emotional investments, and mental habits. Without this self-awareness, it's easy to mistake belief for fact, or defensiveness for principle.

The second is emotional regulation. People cling to false certainty not just because they are misinformed, but because they are afraid. Uncertainty can feel like chaos. Doubt can feel like failure. Admitting you're wrong can feel like shame. To practice epistemic humility, one must tolerate these feelings without being ruled by them. That takes emotional maturity.

The third is identity flexibility. When beliefs are fused with self-worth, any challenge feels personal. But when identity is grounded in deeper values—like integrity, compassion, or growth—then beliefs can evolve without threatening the self. You are not your opinions. You are the person evaluating them.

In practice, epistemic humility means pausing before reacting. Asking questions before making judgments. Seeking out perspectives that challenge your own. It means holding space for ambiguity, resisting the urge to explain everything, and allowing reality to be more complicated than your first take. It also means being willing to update your view as you learn more—without needing to retroactively justify your previous beliefs.

This orientation has profound implications for relationships. People who practice epistemic humility tend to listen better, argue less defensively, and repair ruptures more effectively. They are more capable of saying, "I see your point," or "I missed that," or "Thank you for helping me see it differently." These are not admissions of defeat. They are expressions of respect—for the other person, and for the evolving nature of truth.

In education, epistemic humility transforms teaching from transmission to dialogue. The best educators do not just deliver facts—they model inquiry. They show students how to think, not just what to think. They reward good questions, encourage intellectual risk, and frame learning as a lifelong pursuit. When students are taught to value exploration over performance, they become more resilient, curious, and open-minded.

In leadership, epistemic humility builds trust. Leaders who admit their limits, seek counsel, and revise strategies in light of new evidence are more respected over time—not less. They create cultures where feedback is welcomed, error is not punished, and continuous learning is possible. This is especially critical in times of disruption, when rigid certainty can lead to catastrophic decisions, while adaptive humility allows for course correction.

Culturally, a mature society is not one that has resolved all its debates. It is one that can hold disagreement without collapse. That requires a collective commitment to epistemic humility. The willingness to listen to those with less power. The courage to examine one's own blind spots. The discipline to distinguish between conviction and dogma. And the capacity to remain grounded in values even when facts are in dispute.

There is a quiet dignity in saying, "I don't know enough yet to have a strong opinion." Or, "My understanding has changed." Or, "I was certain, but I'm less so now." These are not signs of wavering. They are signs of wisdom. In a world flooded with loud certainty, they are revolutionary acts.

The search for truth is not a straight line. It is a spiral. We revisit the same questions with new eyes, new data, new insight. Epistemic humility is what keeps that spiral from becoming a circle. It turns stubbornness into growth, debate into dialogue, and belief into inquiry. Not because we abandon the desire to know—but because we understand what it means to know well.

* * *

VI

PART VI: PAIN, TRAUMA, AND DISCONNECTION

Pain, trauma, and disconnection touch all of us at some point, shaping how we see ourselves and relate to the world. In this part, I want to explore with you how disruption fractures our inner life, how suffering can isolate, and how healing begins with understanding those breaks. These experiences are deeply human and complex, but by learning how they work, you can find pathways toward repair, resilience, and reconnection.

26

What Is Psychological Pain?

Pain is one of the oldest messengers in human experience. Physical pain warns us of injury. It demands attention, halts action, and forces care. Psychological pain does the same, but in ways more complex, more internal, and far more misunderstood. We have learned to treat emotional pain as a failure—either of mental health, of moral character, or of coping skill. But pain is not the enemy. It is a signal. It tells us what matters. It alerts us to threat, loss, boundary violation, or inner dissonance. And if we listen, it tells us what needs to change.

This chapter reclaims psychological pain from the margins of dysfunction and places it at the center of human intelligence. To feel distress in a world of instability, loss, and disconnection is not a sign of illness—it is a sign of awareness. The capacity to hurt is not a liability. It is a form of responsiveness. Yet we live in a culture that frames pain as pathology. Depression is medicated without context. Grief is scheduled into bereavement leave. Anxiety is treated as a chemical glitch rather than an emotional barometer. We have come to fear our own emotional signals as if feeling them were evidence of weakness.

This confusion has roots in both language and medicine. The rise of diagnostic models has provided clarity and validation for many, but it has also fostered a dangerous conflation between pain and disorder. If you're suffering, you must be broken. If you're not okay, you must be sick.

But emotional pain is not always a malfunction. Often, it is a reflection of reality. A mind in conflict. A life out of alignment. A value betrayed. A loss endured. It is not always something to be removed. Sometimes it is something to be honored.

Psychologically, pain serves many roles. It prompts introspection. It surfaces unmet needs. It forces a reckoning with what we can no longer ignore. Even unbearable suffering can hold the seeds of transformation—if it is met with understanding rather than avoidance. But this requires a shift in how we frame distress. We must stop asking, "How do I get rid of this?" and start asking, "What is this trying to tell me?"

This chapter will explore four dimensions of psychological pain. First, we'll examine pain as signal, not symptom—a perspective rooted in both evolutionary psychology and emotional theory. Then, we'll look at how discomfort gets mislabeled as pathology, especially in modern cultures that prize performance over presence. The third section investigates the function of suffering in personal growth and meaning-making. And finally, we'll explore what happens when pain becomes stuck: when it no longer signals but loops, distorts, and overtakes. There is a difference between pain that teaches and pain that traps.

To understand psychological pain is to understand what it means to be human. It is to respect the organism's call for attention, not to anesthetize it. It is to hear what the mind is trying to say through its discomfort, confusion, or despair. And above all, it is to stop seeing pain as the problem—and start seeing it as a portal.

Pain as Signal, Not Symptom

Psychological pain is often treated as an error. Something has gone wrong, and the presence of emotional suffering is assumed to be evidence of internal dysfunction. But this assumption is relatively new. Historically, and across many wisdom traditions, pain was seen not as a glitch in the system, but as an essential feature of being human. It is a message, not a malfunction. It calls our attention to something that

WHAT IS PSYCHOLOGICAL PAIN?

matters.

From an evolutionary standpoint, pain is an adaptive signal. Physical pain protects the body by interrupting behavior that could cause injury or death. Emotional pain serves a parallel role in the social and psychological domain. It alerts us to threat, disconnection, exclusion, loss, or internal dissonance. Shame cues us that we may be at risk of rejection. Anxiety prepares us for uncertainty or danger. Grief forces us to confront the finality of absence. These feelings are not irrational. They are forms of intelligence—internal communication designed to help us survive and adapt.

The mistake lies in mistaking the discomfort of the signal for pathology itself. Imagine a smoke detector that beeps in the presence of fire. The sound is unpleasant, even piercing, but disabling the alarm doesn't solve the problem. The same is true for psychological pain. Numbing it—whether through medication, distraction, or avoidance—may bring temporary relief, but if the underlying fire still burns, the system is working as it should. The pain is not the problem. The problem is what the pain points toward.

The nervous system is exquisitely sensitive to cues of safety and danger. Stephen Porges' Polyvagal Theory proposes that our autonomic responses are attuned not just to physical threats, but to relational and emotional ones. This means that psychological pain arises not only from trauma, but from misattunement, disconnection, boundary violations, or internal contradiction. These are not trivial stimuli. They threaten the coherence of the self, the stability of meaning, and the security of attachment. Pain is the bodymind's way of saying: something essential is out of sync.

In clinical settings, emotional suffering is often framed as disorder. But what if, in many cases, the pain is a sign of coherence rather than collapse? A person who feels depressed after losing a job is not broken. They are accurately registering a loss of identity, purpose, or structure. A teenager who feels overwhelmed by the climate crisis is not mentally ill. They are responding to a world that feels unstable, unjust, or doomed.

In both cases, the pain is not an overreaction—it is a truthful reaction to destabilization.

Of course, not all pain is equally informative. Chronic or disproportionate distress can suggest patterns that need intervention. But the rush to interpret pain as dysfunction often short-circuits its signal value. When someone is anxious, we ask how to make it stop rather than what it might be protecting. When someone is grieving, we ask how long it will last instead of how deeply they loved. When someone is angry, we assume they are dysregulated rather than asking what boundary may have been crossed.

Pain becomes meaningful when it is contextualized. A panic attack in isolation seems irrational; a panic attack after months of emotional suppression in an abusive relationship makes perfect sense. Meaning gives pain coherence. Coherence gives pain direction. And direction turns pain from chaos into communication.

Children instinctively treat pain as signal. A child who feels excluded on the playground doesn't diagnose themselves. They seek explanation. They seek repair. They cry, they speak, they protest. Over time, many adults lose this instinct. They learn to hide, suppress, or reframe their pain in ways that invalidate it. They learn to override their own signals in favor of appearing fine. And in doing so, they lose access to a critical source of guidance.

Psychologically, this disconnection from pain often shows up as dissociation, numbness, or misattributed anger. A person may lash out not because they are aggressive, but because they are unaware of the hurt beneath. Another may become emotionally flat, not because they are indifferent, but because they have unconsciously shut down their capacity to feel pain that once overwhelmed them. When pain is silenced, it doesn't disappear. It recirculates in disguised forms: fatigue, irritability, chronic indecision, or relational sabotage.

Restoring the signal value of pain requires reestablishing trust in one's inner system. It involves learning to sit with discomfort long enough to understand what it's saying, without rushing to silence it. This is not indulgence. It is discernment. Pain that is listened to tends to move. Pain that is dismissed tends to deepen.

The therapeutic process, at its best, does not aim to erase pain. It aims to translate it. A good therapist is not someone who fixes you. They are someone who helps you decode your own messages—who asks what the depression might be saying, what the anxiety might be guarding, what the anger might be grieving. This approach does not deny the legitimacy of diagnosis or the utility of medication. But it refuses to make pain the enemy.

The body, too, carries these signals. Somatic symptoms—tight chests, clenched jaws, shallow breathing—are often the nervous system's attempts to flag psychological strain. Listening to these signals does not mean becoming hypervigilant or obsessed with inner states. It means cultivating enough internal awareness to register when something needs attention.

Psychological pain is not always pleasant. It is not always clear. But it is often true. And in a culture that too often confuses composure with health and silence with stability, learning to hear pain as signal is a radical act of self-respect.

The Mislabeling of Discomfort

There is a growing tendency in modern culture to conflate ordinary discomfort with clinical dysfunction. Emotional states that once fell within the normal range of human experience—grief, worry, sadness, discontent—are now quickly pathologized, labeled as symptoms to be treated rather than signals to be understood. This mislabeling doesn't just distort our relationship with suffering; it dulls our emotional intelligence and erodes our tolerance for the very experiences that shape maturity.

Psychological discomfort is not a mistake. It is part of how we learn, grow, and adapt. But when people are taught to fear their own feelings, they begin to treat any internal unrest as a crisis. A student overwhelmed before an exam wonders if they have an anxiety disorder. A man grieving his father's death is prescribed medication after two weeks of tearfulness. A teenager navigating heartbreak wonders if something is wrong with her ability to regulate emotion. These examples aren't hypothetical. They're representative of a cultural trend that frames negative feeling as failure.

The reasons for this are complex. Diagnostic language has become part of public conversation, often in ways that blur the line between experience and illness. Terms like depression, anxiety, trauma, and bipolar are used colloquially to describe everything from moodiness to inconvenience. The language of psychiatry has filtered into everyday life, offering a sense of explanation—but at the cost of nuance.

Social media compounds this by turning diagnosis into identity. Posts and videos claiming "I have high-functioning anxiety" or "I finally realized I have trauma" attract engagement and validation. For some, this brings relief—a long-overdue recognition of struggle. For others, it becomes a way to collapse complexity into a label, bypassing the slow work of understanding context. While these platforms can de-stigmatize mental health, they also incentivize over-identification with discomfort and under-inquiry into its source.

This trend reflects a deeper discomfort with ambiguity. We crave clear explanations for our pain. And in a medicalized culture, those explanations often come with prescriptions. But not every emotional state requires treatment. Many require reflection, context, support, and time. When sadness is framed as disorder, we forget that it can be a valid response to loss. When anxiety is treated solely as a malfunction, we ignore its role in alerting us to misalignment or danger.

The mislabeling of discomfort also reveals how intolerant we have become of slowness, messiness, and emotional ambiguity. We live in a performance culture that prizes control. Productivity is valorized; rest is suspect. Emotional discomfort threatens this rhythm. It slows us down. It makes demands we don't want to answer. So we rush to fix it, categorize it, or medicate it. Not out of malice, but out of fear—fear of vulnerability, fear of complexity, fear of losing momentum.

There is also a gendered dimension to this. Girls and women, in

WHAT IS PSYCHOLOGICAL PAIN?

particular, are often socialized to suppress anger and doubt, while being allowed sadness or anxiety. As a result, emotional discomfort is filtered through narrow channels: instead of saying "I'm enraged," a woman might say "I'm anxious." Instead of saying "I'm furious at how I've been treated," she might say "I'm overwhelmed." These emotional translations are then pathologized rather than explored, reinforcing a cycle in which valid emotional data is invalidated.

The educational system mirrors this. Children who fidget, resist, or disengage are increasingly diagnosed with disorders before other possibilities are explored—boredom, mismatch, unaddressed trauma, or simple personality differences. The question is no longer "What is this child reacting to?" but "What disorder explains this behavior?" This diagnostic shortcut removes context and flattens individuality. It also teaches children that discomfort is unacceptable rather than part of growing.

This is not a call to reject diagnosis. For many, receiving a clinical diagnosis is a turning point—a way to understand long-unmet needs and finally access appropriate care. But the pendulum has swung too far when common distress is no longer seen as part of the human condition. When we pathologize discomfort, we rob it of its instructive power. We discourage introspection. We teach people to fear themselves.

Psychological discomfort is not always a problem to be solved. Sometimes it is a truth to be lived through. A period of transition. A signal of incongruence. A response to change, loss, betrayal, or awakening. If we meet it only with suppression or pathologization, we miss its message. But if we make space for it—listen to it, reflect on it—it becomes a form of self-contact.

Culturally, this shift requires a re-education of emotional life. It means teaching children not just how to feel better, but how to feel deeply. It means helping adults distinguish between depression and mourning, between anxiety and awakening, between emotional discomfort and true dysfunction. It means restoring the capacity to tolerate distress without collapsing into fear.

Discomfort is not the enemy of well-being. In many cases, it is the path to it. The urge to label and eradicate it reflects a misunderstanding of what it means to be whole. To live fully is to feel broadly—to encounter emotional weather in all its forms, and to respond with curiosity rather than panic.

When we mislabel discomfort, we not only confuse ourselves—we weaken our ability to discern what needs healing from what simply needs holding. And that discernment is the cornerstone of emotional maturity.

Meaning, Maturation, and the Function of Suffering

Psychological pain, while often unwanted, plays a developmental role far beyond survival or symptom. It has the capacity to reorganize identity, clarify values, and deepen one's orientation to life itself. When pain is held with awareness, not bypassed or numbed, it becomes a catalyst for transformation. This is one of the paradoxes of human development: the very states we try most to avoid—grief, despair, guilt, heartbreak—often force the growth we otherwise resist.

From the lens of existential psychology, suffering is not only unavoidable, it is instructive. Viktor Frankl's *Man's Search for Meaning* stands as one of the most enduring texts in this tradition, articulating the idea that pain without meaning is unbearable, but pain in the service of meaning is survivable. Frankl, who endured Nazi concentration camps, observed that those who could find some sense of purpose in their suffering were more likely to endure. His insight was not sentimental; it was clinical. The psyche can endure agony when it has somewhere to place it—when the suffering points toward something larger than itself.

Suffering, then, becomes part of the architecture of maturity. In early developmental stages, pain is externalized—it is something done to us. A child scrapes a knee or is scolded unfairly. But as we age, pain becomes internalized. We begin to suffer not just from injury or injustice, but from awareness. We suffer because we recognize complexity. We suffer because we are aware of our contradictions, our moral failings, the fragility of life, the passage of time. This form of suffering is not pathological. It is the cost of consciousness.

In many ways, pain is what teaches us depth. People who have moved through significant suffering often carry with them a kind of gravity—not necessarily solemn, but grounded. They are less reactive, more tolerant of nuance, and more attuned to the invisible struggles of others. This is not because pain made them better, but because they allowed it to change them. The pain didn't go away; it reshaped the vessel.

Developmentally, this process is echoed in post-traumatic growth theory. While trauma can create long-term damage, it can also generate a reordering of priorities, a new sense of self, and a renewed connection to meaning. Importantly, this growth is not linear, and it does not suggest that pain is good or necessary. It only affirms that when suffering is metabolized—when it is integrated rather than rejected—it can leave behind strength, clarity, and purpose.

Pain is also a moral tutor. Guilt, for instance, is one of the most socially functional emotions humans possess. When it functions appropriately, it signals that we've violated our own ethical code or caused harm to another. In this way, pain acts as a compass. It points us back toward alignment, urging repair, apology, or change. Without the sting of guilt, many would continue behaviors that fracture relationships and erode integrity. The discomfort of guilt teaches responsibility.

Likewise, heartbreak teaches us about attachment, vulnerability, and the cost of love. It shows us what mattered. It teaches us boundaries. It humbles us. And often, it clears the way for a more honest self to emerge—one that is less performative, less defended, and more capable of mature connection.

In many rites of passage across cultures, suffering is ritualized as a gateway. There are ceremonies of grief, solitude, physical pain, or endurance meant to mark the threshold between adolescence and adulthood. These rituals don't celebrate pain for its own sake; they recognize it as a necessary process of shedding old identity and stepping into new responsibility. Modern Western cultures, however, have largely abandoned these structured transitions. Without them, individuals are left to navigate the meaning of pain alone—often without language, community, or guidance.

Therapeutically, making meaning from suffering is one of the most powerful mechanisms of healing. Narrative therapy, for example, helps individuals reframe their pain into a coherent story—one in which they are not just victims, but agents of growth. This does not deny the reality of harm. It simply restores the individual's capacity to interpret that harm in a way that doesn't freeze them in time. The story changes, and with it, so does the self.

At a cultural level, however, we often fail to support this process. Suffering is either minimized—"just think positive"—or over-pathologized—"you'll never recover from this." Both extremes disempower. What's needed is a middle path: one that honors the depth of pain while affirming the possibility of evolution. This path does not rush healing. It respects timing. But it also refuses to treat pain as identity.

Spiritual and contemplative traditions offer additional insight into this process. Buddhist psychology, for example, distinguishes between pain and suffering: pain is inevitable, suffering arises from resistance to that pain. This distinction is powerful. When pain is met with openness, curiosity, and presence, it can pass through. When it is met with judgment, avoidance, or clinging, it calcifies. The process of maturation involves learning to stay with pain long enough to see what it reveals—without drowning in it or prematurely escaping it.

None of this is to romanticize suffering. There is pain that crushes, overwhelms, and scars. Not all pain leads to growth, and not everyone has the resources or support to transform their suffering into something meaningful. But when those resources exist—when the pain is witnessed, named, and held—then something remarkable can happen. People change. They reorder their values. They stop lying to themselves. They forgive. They say no. They make art. They become more human.

Psychological pain, then, is not only a signal—it is a sculptor. It shapes the edges of our character. It reveals what we care about. And it deepens our capacity to live with compassion, insight, and moral gravity. The function of suffering is not to destroy us. It is to wake us up.

When Pain Becomes the Identity

While suffering has signal value and transformative potential, it also carries a psychological risk: the possibility that a person will begin to organize their identity around their pain. This shift is subtle at first. What begins as a legitimate cry for understanding, validation, or support can, over time, harden into a framework for self-definition. Instead of pain being an experience the person is moving through, it becomes the lens through which they see the world, the story they tell about who they are, and the explanation they use for why they cannot change.

This process is not driven by weakness or melodrama. It is a protective strategy. When someone has endured long periods of invalidation, neglect, or chronic stress, pain may become the most consistent part of their inner life. It becomes familiar, known, and in a strange way, stabilizing. The suffering is real, but so is the relief of finally having a narrative that makes sense of it. The danger comes when that narrative becomes so central that it begins to eclipse all other aspects of identity.

In psychological terms, this can be understood as an overidentification with the wound. Rather than being someone who has suffered, the person becomes the suffering itself. "I was betrayed" becomes "I am unlovable." "I experienced trauma" becomes "I am permanently broken." These are not conscious decisions. They are internal conclusions formed through repetition, reinforced by how others respond, and solidified by how safe or unsafe it feels to imagine being something else.

Trauma literature speaks of this phenomenon in terms of frozen identity. When a person experiences trauma—especially developmental trauma that occurs in childhood—the nervous system may anchor in the emotional age at which the pain occurred. The self then orients around that imprint, making it difficult to experience life outside the parameters set by the original injury. The world is interpreted through that filter.

Relationships are managed through it. Emotional regulation is shaped by it. And attempts at healing can be unconsciously sabotaged, because letting go of the identity that formed around pain feels like abandoning the only self that ever felt honest.

There is a further complication: social and digital environments now reward the performance of suffering. In online spaces, especially, pain becomes content. The more visibly someone suffers, the more engagement they receive. Algorithms prioritize distress; followers respond to vulnerability. What begins as honest self-disclosure can morph into a cycle of performative pain, in which the person becomes tethered to their suffering because it is the source of attention, sympathy, or identity cohesion. To disidentify from the pain would risk invisibility, or worse, irrelevance.

This is especially dangerous for younger generations, who are developing identity in real time while watching others model selfhood as a series of wounds. The result is a distorted emotional culture: one that confuses vulnerability with exhibition, growth with victimhood, and honesty with chronic exposure. Pain is real, and sharing it can be deeply healing. But when it becomes the primary language through which people relate to each other—and to themselves—it loses its function as signal and becomes something else entirely: a kind of internal gravity that pulls everything into its orbit.

This identity formation around pain is not limited to trauma survivors. It shows up in chronic illness communities, in identity-based political discourse, in support groups, and even in therapy. Again, none of this implies the pain is fabricated or the suffering insincere. What matters is whether the pain is being processed as part of a developmental arc— or whether it has calcified into a self-concept. When pain becomes a reference point for every interaction, every aspiration, and every perceived limitation, the individual is no longer healing. They are circling.

One of the most compassionate interventions a therapist or mentor can offer is to gently name this pattern. Not with accusation or dismissal, but with honesty: "What if this pain is part of your story, but not the whole story?" This reframes the individual's relationship to their suffering. It places the pain in time, rather than allowing it to sprawl across all of it. It invites a different question—not "What happened to me?" but "Who am I becoming as I learn to live with what happened?"

Moving beyond pain-based identity is not a denial of suffering. It is a reclamation of selfhood from the parts that have been organized entirely around it. This doesn't mean pretending to be fine. It means allowing the self to be more than its damage. It means developing internal capacities—curiosity, humor, ambition, tenderness—that are not in reaction to pain, but in pursuit of life. It means risking joy, not just managing symptoms.

In practice, this can be terrifying. For those who have been identified with their pain for years, even decades, the idea of selfhood apart from suffering can feel destabilizing. Who will I be if I'm not this story? Who will care for me if I stop performing it? What happens if I let it go and nothing fills its place? These are not trivial questions. They deserve respect. But they do not justify staying stuck. Growth is not guaranteed, but stagnation is, if pain becomes the only identity we are willing to claim.

Ultimately, psychological health involves integration, not erasure. Pain is not the enemy. It is a formative force. But it is meant to move. It is meant to evolve. When pain becomes identity, we stop evolving with it. We let it define the edges of our possibility. And in doing so, we lose touch with the other parts of ourselves—the parts that long for connection, creation, and continuity.

Reclaiming life from pain means telling a fuller story. One in which suffering is a chapter, not the entire book. One in which the person is seen not only for what they've endured, but for what they are still capable of becoming.

* * *

27

Trauma and Its Reverberations

Trauma is not what happens to us; it is what happens inside us as a result of what happened. This is the central insight of trauma psychology—and it marks a shift from external event to internal response. A car accident, a war zone, a betrayal, or years of emotional neglect: each may qualify as trauma, not by objective severity alone, but by the degree to which the individual's system is overwhelmed, altered, and unable to return to safety. Trauma is not measured by the facts of the event, but by its lasting footprint on the nervous system, memory, and sense of self.

In public discourse, the word "trauma" has become nearly ubiquitous. People speak of traumatic meetings, traumatic social interactions, traumatic media exposure. While some of this reflects a growing cultural fluency around emotional harm, it also risks diluting the gravity of real trauma. Psychological trauma is not simply pain, and it is not synonymous with offense, discomfort, or sadness. It is a rupture in safety—a break in the system's ability to process experience, regulate emotion, and sustain coherent selfhood. That break may be loud and violent, or it may be quiet and chronic. Either can fragment the internal world in lasting ways.

This chapter examines the reverberations of trauma—how it shapes not just memory, but identity, behavior, and bodily perception. We will explore the difference between acute trauma (a single overwhelming event), chronic trauma (repetitive or ongoing exposure), and complex trauma (especially when rooted in early relationships). Each presents unique psychological patterns, and each requires a different path toward integration.

One of the most important shifts in trauma theory over the past three decades has been the move from a purely narrative model to a somatic one. We now understand that trauma is not just something we remember—it is something we *feel*. It lodges in the body, hijacks the autonomic nervous system, and distorts the perception of present reality. Trauma survivors often find themselves reacting to today as if it were yesterday, pulled into states of hypervigilance, collapse, or disconnection without knowing why. This is not a failure of logic or will. It is a learned survival response that has become ingrained.

Equally important is the recognition that early trauma, particularly developmental trauma, can have foundational effects on identity formation. Children who grow up in environments of inconsistency, emotional abandonment, or relational threat internalize adaptive patterns that later become maladaptive. These patterns shape attachment style, stress tolerance, emotional granularity, and even the ability to interpret others' facial expressions or tone of voice. Trauma, in this sense, is not an interruption of life. It *becomes* life. It frames how one experiences the world.

Yet trauma does not mean permanent damage. It is not destiny. Recovery is possible—not through erasure, but through integration. The goal of healing is not to forget what happened, but to reclaim the self that was left behind. This process involves making space for the body to feel safe again, for the mind to tolerate complexity, and for memory to become a story that can be told, rather than a loop that controls.

In this chapter, we begin by clarifying what trauma is—and what it isn't. Then we explore how early trauma leaves developmental imprints that echo across time. Next, we turn to the body, where trauma hides and resurfaces through sensation, posture, and nervous system states.

Finally, we examine what healing entails when the goal is not to return to who we were, but to become who we were never allowed to be.

What Trauma Is, and What It Isn't

Trauma is not defined by the event itself. It is defined by the way the mind and body respond when the event overwhelms a person's capacity to process, cope, or stay connected to a sense of safety. Two people may live through the same car crash, the same natural disaster, or the same childhood environment—yet walk away with entirely different psychological imprints. What distinguishes trauma from pain is not magnitude alone, but meaning, duration, context, and whether the body and mind were able to digest the experience or had to disassociate from it in order to survive.

One of the most useful definitions comes from Dr. Peter Levine, who describes trauma as anything that is "too much, too fast, too soon," or conversely, "too little for too long." The former often results from acute trauma—events like accidents, assaults, or medical emergencies. The latter points to developmental trauma—experiences of prolonged emotional neglect, absence of attunement, or chronic environmental instability. Both conditions disrupt the nervous system, but they do so in different ways and often leave different psychological footprints.

Culturally, we have become more attuned to trauma in recent decades. Awareness campaigns, clinical education, and widespread use of terms like PTSD have helped destigmatize psychological responses that were once dismissed as weakness. But with this rise in visibility has come a flattening of meaning. Trauma has become a catch-all phrase for any distressing experience, regardless of its severity or persistence. While this shift reflects a more empathetic culture, it also introduces diagnostic confusion. If everything is trauma, then trauma loses its clinical specificity.

It is essential to preserve that specificity. Psychological trauma is not just about being hurt—it is about being overwhelmed beyond one's capacity to stay integrated. In such moments, the brain's normal processing systems shut down, and the body takes over. The prefrontal cortex, responsible for reasoning and executive function, goes offline. The amygdala, which governs fear, ramps up. The hippocampus, which organizes memory, becomes erratic. As a result, the traumatic moment may not be stored as a coherent narrative but as fragmented sensations, images, and emotional flashpoints. This is why trauma survivors often speak in disjointed stories or experience triggers that seem unrelated to the original event.

Another critical distinction is between trauma and adversity. Not all hardship is traumatic. Adversity, especially when buffered by protective factors like stable relationships or internal resilience, can strengthen a person's coping mechanisms. Trauma, by contrast, overwhelms those mechanisms and leaves the system dysregulated. The presence of post-traumatic stress symptoms—intrusive thoughts, avoidance behaviors, negative shifts in mood or cognition, and heightened arousal—suggests that the event has not been metabolized.

Further complicating this picture is the role of chronic stress. When a person is subjected to long-term exposure to stressors—such as domestic instability, community violence, or emotional invalidation—their system may enter a state of ongoing hypervigilance. This condition is often misdiagnosed as generalized anxiety or depression, when in fact it is the residue of an environment that never allowed for rest. The nervous system becomes locked in survival mode, unable to downshift. Sleep is shallow. Digestion is impaired. Emotional reactivity increases. The person may not identify their experience as trauma, but their body tells the truth.

The type of trauma matters as well. Acute trauma usually involves a singular event—something clearly delineated in time. Complex trauma, on the other hand, is cumulative and relational. It arises when a person experiences repeated breaches of trust, often by caregivers or in environments where safety was expected but denied. This kind of trauma is particularly difficult to name, because there may be no obvious villain or incident. The trauma is in the pattern, the silence, the lack of repair. And it often hides behind high achievement, perfectionism, or emotional numbness.

Misconceptions about trauma also contribute to shame and self-doubt among survivors. People may question whether their experience "counts," especially if they cannot recall specific details or believe others had it worse. But trauma is not a competition. It is not validated by public consensus. The only question that matters is whether the experience disrupted the individual's sense of safety, coherence, and self-trust. If it did, it deserves recognition.

Another common myth is that trauma always results in visible dysfunction. In reality, many trauma survivors function at a high level—managing careers, relationships, and obligations with apparent ease. But under the surface, they may experience emotional disconnection, chronic fatigue, relational ambivalence, or an inability to feel joy. This is not resilience. It is survival. And it often masks a deep loneliness that comes from living in a body that has not felt safe in years.

Modern trauma research, particularly the work of Bessel van der Kolk, Gabor Maté, and Stephen Porges, has emphasized that healing trauma requires more than talk therapy. Because trauma is held in the body as much as in the mind, recovery must include somatic awareness, sensory integration, and the reestablishment of physiological safety. The goal is not just to understand what happened, but to release the body from the grip of that past.

Ultimately, trauma is a wound of disconnection—disconnection from safety, from others, from self. And the path to healing lies not only in revisiting the past, but in restoring connection in the present: to the body, to trustworthy relationships, and to a coherent sense of self that is no longer stuck in survival.

Developmental Imprints: The Long Shadow of Early Pain

When trauma occurs in adulthood, it typically disrupts a system that has already formed. But when trauma occurs in childhood, it becomes part of the system itself. The distinction is not merely temporal—it is structural. Developmental trauma shapes the architecture of the self. It doesn't just hurt the child; it builds the adult.

At the heart of developmental trauma is relational injury. This includes experiences like emotional neglect, inconsistent caregiving, chronic invalidation, and subtle but persistent forms of misattunement. Unlike acute trauma, which tends to be obvious and isolatable, developmental trauma often hides in plain sight. There may be no physical violence or overt abandonment. Instead, the child grows up in an environment where their emotional states are not mirrored, their needs are not prioritized, and their sense of safety depends on suppressing parts of themselves to maintain connection.

These early relational dynamics have profound effects on nervous system regulation. A child who learns that their feelings are too much for a caregiver to handle will begin to minimize or disown those feelings. A child whose needs are met unpredictably may learn to stay in a constant state of alert, scanning for cues, anticipating rejection. Over time, these adaptations become traits. They solidify into patterns of relating, not only to others, but to the self. Emotional regulation becomes externally oriented—dependent on how others respond. Boundaries are blurred or absent. Self-trust erodes.

Attachment theory provides one of the clearest frameworks for understanding how early trauma manifests later in life. Secure attachment requires consistent, responsive caregiving that allows a child to explore the world while knowing they have a safe base to return to. When that base is unreliable, inconsistent, or frightening, the attachment system organizes around survival instead of trust. This gives rise to anxious, avoidant, or disorganized attachment styles—all of which reflect strategies that were once adaptive in context, but become maladaptive over time.

Disorganized attachment, in particular, is often linked to complex trauma. It develops when a child experiences their caregiver as both a source of comfort and a source of threat. This creates an impossible paradox: the person I need to run to is also the person I need to run from. The nervous system, unable to resolve this contradiction, defaults to fragmentation. This can lead to dissociative tendencies, identity confusion, and difficulty with emotional continuity. In adulthood, these individuals often struggle with intimacy, not because they don't want connection, but because connection was never safe.

The imprint of developmental trauma is not only psychological but somatic. Because the child's body is still forming, stress is encoded into posture, breath, muscle tone, and visceral states. Chronic tension, shallow breathing, digestive problems, and sensory sensitivities are not just physiological quirks—they are the residue of a nervous system that learned to brace against life. These bodily states become baseline; the person does not feel "anxious" or "shut down"—they feel normal. Which is why so many survivors of early trauma do not identify as traumatized. They have no contrast. They have only ever known themselves in a state of adaptive contraction.

Memory plays a complicated role here. Developmental trauma often occurs before the brain is fully capable of encoding explicit memory. As a result, much of what was experienced cannot be recalled in words or images. It lives instead as implicit memory: bodily sensations, emotional tones, and behavioral reflexes that arise without explanation. A person may find themselves flooded with panic during intimacy, or emotionally numb during conflict, without knowing why. These are not character flaws or evidence of irrationality. They are the body's memory asserting itself.

This is one reason traditional talk therapy is often limited in treating developmental trauma. Insight alone does not reach the body. The person may be able to articulate what happened—or what didn't happen—

but still feel stuck in patterns that make no logical sense. True healing requires methods that engage the somatic system: body-based therapies like Somatic Experiencing, EMDR, sensorimotor psychotherapy, or trauma-informed yoga. These approaches do not bypass the mind—they simply recognize that the mind is not the only site of injury, nor the only site of recovery.

One of the most damaging consequences of developmental trauma is the internalization of shame. Because the child cannot comprehend that the environment is the problem, they conclude that *they* are the problem. "If I were different, my parent wouldn't act this way." "If I weren't so needy, I would have been loved." These beliefs become identity scaffolding. The adult who emerges from such a childhood may be high-functioning, charismatic, even successful—but underneath, there is often a deep sense of defectiveness that no achievement can erase.

Importantly, this kind of trauma does not always stem from malicious intent. Many caregivers are themselves traumatized and pass on patterns they never had the tools to interrupt. Cultural norms, economic stress, and systemic oppression all play roles in shaping the caregiving environment. But understanding the source of the injury does not negate its impact. Empathy for the parent must not come at the cost of empathy for the child.

Recovery from developmental trauma is possible, but it is slow. The work involves building an internal sense of safety where none existed before. It means learning to recognize and name emotional states, to set boundaries without guilt, to feel desire without shame. It means reparenting the self—not by denying the past, but by offering the kind of presence, consistency, and care that was missing. This process can take years. It is not linear. But each moment of awareness, each act of self-kindness, is a step toward reclaiming the self from the long shadow of early pain.

Trauma Lives in the Body: Somatic Memory and Reenactment

Long after the mind has forgotten—or convinced itself it has—the body continues to respond. This is one of the central paradoxes of trauma. The narrative mind may downplay, distort, or erase the experience. But the body does not forget. It holds trauma as posture, as reflex, as a felt sense of threat that persists even in safety. To truly understand trauma, we have to move beyond cognition and examine how the nervous system itself becomes organized around fear, anticipation, and protective withdrawal.

The nervous system is built to respond to danger. When we perceive a threat, the sympathetic branch activates: heart rate increases, muscles tense, pupils dilate, breath becomes shallow. This is the classic fight-or-flight response. If the threat is overwhelming and escape is impossible, the parasympathetic system may instead trigger a freeze or collapse response—slowing everything down to minimize pain or detection. These responses are not choices; they are ancient survival mechanisms. But trauma occurs when the system gets stuck in one of these states and cannot reset.

What makes trauma particularly insidious is that the nervous system doesn't require actual danger to activate these responses—it only needs to perceive it. And when a person has experienced trauma, the threshold for perceived danger becomes distorted. A voice tone, a scent, a glance, or even a moment of stillness can trigger a flood of physiological reactivity that feels disproportionate to the situation. That's because the body is not responding to the present. It's reacting to a pattern that was laid down in the past.

This is somatic memory. Unlike explicit memory, which is narrative and conscious, somatic memory is stored in the body's sensory and motor systems. It shows up as tension in the jaw or shoulders, a racing heart when there is no danger, a sudden shutdown during intimacy or conflict. These responses are not symbolic; they are real. And they often occur outside of conscious control. This is why trauma survivors may say, "I know I'm safe, but I don't *feel* safe." The nervous system has its own logic, and that logic is based on pattern recognition, not rational evaluation.

Bessel van der Kolk's work in *The Body Keeps the Score* has been pivotal in illuminating this dynamic. Drawing on neuroscience, attachment theory, and clinical practice, he argues that trauma must be approached through the body, not just the mind. Verbal processing, while valuable, often cannot reach the implicit layers where trauma is stored. This is why trauma treatment increasingly incorporates modalities that bypass language and engage directly with sensation, movement, and breath.

One such modality is Somatic Experiencing, developed by Peter Levine. It helps clients build tolerance for sensation and learn to complete the defensive responses (fight, flight, freeze) that were interrupted during the traumatic event. Another is EMDR (Eye Movement Desensitization and Reprocessing), which uses bilateral stimulation to help the brain integrate fragmented memories. Even yoga, when trauma-informed, can help reconnect survivors with their bodies—not as sites of pain, but as sources of strength and presence.

Reenactment is another crucial concept. Traumatized individuals often find themselves drawn into relationships or situations that mirror the original trauma. This is not masochism. It is an unconscious attempt to resolve what was never resolved. The psyche seeks completion. If the original experience involved powerlessness, the person may unconsciously seek scenarios where they can either relive that powerlessness or finally triumph over it. Unfortunately, these reenactments often repeat the trauma rather than repair it, leading to cycles of victimization or control that feel inescapable.

These patterns are especially common in complex trauma, where the original injuries involved attachment figures. A person who grew up with a volatile caregiver may find themselves repeatedly drawn to partners who evoke the same unpredictability. The logic is not conscious. It lives in the nervous system's template for what intimacy feels like. Healing, then, involves not only recognizing these patterns, but slowly updating the body's expectations of relationship, conflict, and safety.

Touch is another site of complication. For some trauma survivors, especially those whose trauma involved physical violation or neglect, safe and respectful touch can be deeply healing. For others, it may be a source of panic or numbness. Understanding one's own somatic boundaries—what feels supportive, what feels invasive—is a crucial step in reclaiming bodily autonomy. And it cannot be rushed. Safety must be *felt*, not just asserted.

Dissociation is also worth examining. It is one of the most common somatic responses to trauma, particularly developmental trauma. When overwhelm becomes unbearable and escape is impossible, the mind protects itself by disconnecting from the body. The person may feel numb, floaty, unreal. Time may distort. Emotions may flatten. While dissociation is adaptive in the moment, chronic dissociation becomes a prison. The person is alive but not *in* their life. They go through the motions, disconnected from joy, pain, and presence. Reintegrating the self means helping the body feel safe enough to come back online.

A common theme in trauma recovery is the fear of embodiment. To live in a body that once felt helpless, violated, or unsafe is no small task. For many survivors, the path to healing begins with noticing. Not pushing, not confronting—but simply noticing: where do I feel tight? Where do I brace? When do I go numb? These are not signs of dysfunction. They are maps. They show us where the body has tried to protect itself. And if approached with patience, they can show us how to return.

Ultimately, the body is not the enemy. It is the site of the injury, yes—but also the site of healing. Through breath, movement, regulation, and safe relationship, the body can learn to release what it once had to hold. The nervous system can learn to recognize safety, not as a theory, but as a lived state. And in doing so, the person begins to reclaim their life from the grip of the past.

Recovery and Integration: Moving Beyond Survival

Healing from trauma is not about becoming the person you were before. It is about becoming the person who can carry what happened without being defined by it. This is one of the most misunderstood aspects of recovery. People often imagine that healing means forgetting, moving on, or eliminating symptoms entirely. But recovery is not erasure. It is integration. It is the ability to tell the story—verbally, physically, emotionally—without falling apart.

For those shaped by trauma, particularly in early life, recovery involves rebuilding the internal structures that were never fully formed: trust, self-regulation, emotional literacy, safety in the body. These are not just abstract goals. They are concrete psychological capacities, and they are built through relationship—first with others, then within the self. A central principle in trauma recovery is that healing happens in connection. If trauma is a wound of disconnection, then recovery is the process of re-establishing contact: with one's own feelings, with trustworthy others, with a coherent sense of self.

The first stage of recovery is stabilization. This includes creating external and internal conditions of safety: reducing exposure to harm, building routines, establishing reliable sources of support. The goal is not to "face" the trauma right away. It is to create the scaffolding that makes such work possible. This stage may last weeks or years, depending on the severity and chronicity of the trauma. And it is not a passive state. Stabilization often involves intensive effort: learning grounding techniques, developing emotional regulation skills, and slowly expanding one's tolerance for discomfort without dissociating or panicking.

Once safety has been established, the work of processing can begin. This may involve revisiting the traumatic material—through narrative, bodywork, or expressive modalities like art or movement—but only with the nervous system's consent. If reprocessing is rushed, it can retraumatize. Timing, pacing, and attunement are critical. Skilled therapists understand that the goal is not catharsis, but integration.

The aim is to move from fragmented sensations and implicit fears to a coherent narrative that can be held with compassion rather than dread.

Processing also means grieving. Trauma often involves not just what happened, but what didn't: the love that wasn't received, the protection that wasn't offered, the childhood that wasn't safe. Grieving these absences is painful, but necessary. It allows the survivor to honor the full extent of the loss, rather than minimizing it or carrying it silently. And through this grief, a new sense of self can begin to emerge—one that is honest, tender, and whole.

The final phase of recovery is reconnection. This is where trauma no longer sits at the center of identity. The person may still be shaped by what happened, but they are no longer driven by it. Their choices are freer. Their relationships are more authentic. They are able to feel deeply without being overwhelmed, to protect themselves without shutting down, to take risks without being ruled by fear. This is not the absence of pain, but the presence of agency.

Reconnection also involves re-engaging with life: pursuing meaningful work, building supportive communities, expressing creativity, and experiencing pleasure without guilt. These are not luxuries—they are reparative. They remind the survivor that they are more than what they endured. That life is still available. That joy is still possible.

Importantly, recovery is not linear. There are regressions, plateaus, and setbacks. Old symptoms may re-emerge under stress. Grief may surface unexpectedly. But these fluctuations are not failures. They are part of the process. Healing is cyclical, not sequential. What matters is not perfection, but persistence.

Self-compassion is essential. Many trauma survivors carry deep shame, not only about what happened, but about how they responded. They may judge themselves for dissociating, for staying silent, for using substances or shutting down. But these responses were adaptive. They were the psyche's best attempt at survival. Recovery includes recognizing this: what looks like dysfunction now was once a form of protection. And that protection deserves respect, even as it is gently released.

Another crucial part of recovery is learning to tolerate goodness. For many trauma survivors, peace, affection, or even rest can feel foreign or unsafe. The nervous system, habituated to chaos, interprets calm as danger. This is why some people unconsciously sabotage healthy relationships or resist stability. The work here is not just behavioral—it is neurological. The nervous system must be trained, slowly and consistently, to recognize safety as familiar, not threatening. This requires patience and repetition, but it can be done.

It also helps to remember that trauma recovery is not about becoming someone new. It is about recovering access to parts of the self that were exiled by fear. The playful part, the curious part, the tender part. These parts still exist. They are not lost. They are waiting. And each act of self-kindness, each moment of embodied presence, is an invitation for them to return.

For those supporting someone in trauma recovery, the most powerful offering is not advice, but presence. Trauma is often rooted in experiences of being unseen, unheard, or invalidated. Repair begins when those experiences are countered with attunement, patience, and care. You do not need to fix the trauma. You only need to stay.

In the end, recovery is not a destination but a relationship—one that unfolds over time, through setbacks and breakthroughs, grief and grace. It is the long, brave process of coming home to oneself. Of learning to inhabit the body with trust, to feel emotions without fear, to love without losing self, and to remember that what was broken can be mended, even if the scars remain.

*　*　*

28

Disconnection, Numbness, and Emotional Amnesia

Disconnection is one of the least visible, least understood, and most misunderstood psychological conditions in modern life. People often imagine emotional suffering as something loud—panic attacks, rage, sobbing, visible crisis. But a great deal of suffering happens in silence. It hides behind the appearance of composure. It lives in the quiet absence of feeling, in the hollowed-out places where emotion once lived but no longer visits. This is the terrain of numbness, shutdown, and emotional amnesia: the internal decision, often unconscious, to stop feeling as a way of staying alive.

When people say things like "I don't know what I feel," or "It's like nothing touches me anymore," they're describing this phenomenon. It can look like depression, or burnout, or a vague sense of flatness that follows someone for years. It can manifest as forgetfulness, confusion, or a troubling sense of detachment from memory itself. It can feel like drifting, like watching life happen through a pane of glass. And often, people living this way don't know why. They only know that something feels absent, and that presence—real presence—is hard to come by.

Psychologically, disconnection is an adaptive response to overwhelm. When emotional experiences are too intense, too frequent, or too unsupported, the system begins to shut itself down. This can be a response to trauma, to chronic invalidation, to a lifetime of subtle emotional neglect. Over time, it becomes automatic: feelings are bypassed before they reach full awareness. Even joy and intimacy become difficult to access. The system no longer registers them as safe.

This adaptation often begins in childhood. A child who is consistently punished for expressing emotion, or who is met with indifference instead of comfort, learns not to show sadness. A child whose fear is mocked learns to hide it. A child whose needs are never mirrored learns not to need. These early emotional injuries don't just shape behavior; they shape the nervous system's default settings. They teach the body and brain to deprioritize emotional content, to discard it before it becomes disruptive. The person appears calm, even when distressed. They function well in crisis, but collapse in intimacy. They can handle emergencies, but not eye contact.

And because the world often rewards stoicism, this pattern can go undetected. People who are emotionally disconnected are rarely called out for it; they're praised for being independent, low-maintenance, rational. But inside, they may feel lost, robotic, or deeply alone. They may crave connection but be unable to tolerate it. They may sense that something is missing without knowing what it is. And they may have no memory of who they were before the numbness set in.

Emotional amnesia refers to this fading of internal history. It's not the same as forgetting facts or events. It's the loss of access to the emotional resonance of lived experience. A person may recall that something happened, but feel no connection to it. They may describe a traumatic event with flat affect, unable to locate themselves in the memory. Or they may forget entire swaths of time, especially periods marked by overwhelm, instability, or pain. This is not a character flaw. It's a form of self-protection. When the body and mind can't safely process an experience, they store it out of reach.

But what is protective in one context can become limiting in another. Over time, the strategies that kept someone safe begin to cost them connection, vitality, and meaning. They may lose the ability to attune to others, to identify what they want, or to trust their own emotional signals. Relationships suffer. Intimacy becomes threatening. The self becomes fragmented—not by choice, but by necessity.

This chapter explores the architecture of disconnection: how it forms, how it functions, and what it costs. It looks at the difference between intentional emotional boundaries and automatic emotional suppression. It examines the phenomenon of emotional amnesia as both a neurological and psychological adaptation. And it considers what it means to live in a body that once needed to shut down in order to survive.

But this chapter is also about possibility. Disconnection is not the end of emotional life. It is the shape that emotional life takes when it has had to go underground. With care, curiosity, and patience, the patterns of numbness can be understood—not as pathology, but as wisdom formed in the context of survival. And when that wisdom is no longer needed, it can be unlearned.

Emotional presence is not a trait. It is a capacity—one that can be restored. The following sections will explore how.

The Protective Logic of Numbness

When the emotional system becomes overloaded, the mind and body do not simply keep feeling. They conserve. They guard. They withdraw from sensation the way a body retreats from an open flame. In the language of trauma studies, this is a form of dissociation—but dissociation is only one piece of the broader puzzle of emotional numbing. Numbness is not a sign of brokenness. It is a sign of adaptation. Specifically, it is an intelligent, if costly, way for the human organism to protect itself from an environment it could not change, escape, or process at the time.

The misconception about emotional detachment is that it signals a lack of depth or care. In reality, it often masks extreme sensitivity. It is precisely because the person feels so much—or once did—that they have gone numb. The child who cried and was mocked for it, the teen who reached out and was ignored, the adult who was betrayed repeatedly while vulnerable—all have learned through repetition that emotion invites pain. In such a context, feeling becomes a threat, not a signal. So the psyche does what it must: it shuts the signal down.

This can take many forms. Some people become emotionally flat—unable to feel excitement or grief, unresponsive to both joy and loss. Others disconnect selectively, numbing themselves to fear or sadness while still showing bursts of humor or anger. Still others develop highly functional personas, managing careers, relationships, and daily responsibilities while internally living behind glass. They don't break down. They don't collapse. But they are not fully present, either. And often, they can't explain why.

The protective logic behind numbness is simple: when the cost of feeling exceeds the available capacity to regulate those feelings, the mind chooses to limit input. This is the same principle at work in physical shock. When the body sustains serious injury, it often delays pain to preserve energy and focus on survival. Psychological numbness operates in much the same way. It is not denial, which requires effort. It is absence, which requires none. It is the quieting of signals before they reach the surface.

But numbness is not always global. Many people function in a kind of partial presence: they are aware of their surroundings, capable of intellectual insight, even sociable. What they lack is emotional immediacy. They do not feel feelings in real time. They may cry only after the crisis is over. They may feel joy only when remembering it, not while living it. Or they may move through their days with a chronic sense of detachment, as though their life is happening to someone else. This is not failure. It is learned protection.

Children, in particular, are prone to developing such defenses when exposed to environments that are emotionally unpredictable, frightening, or barren. A child raised by emotionally dysregulated caregivers quickly learns that their own emotions are liabilities, not guides. They suppress needs, dull affect, and prioritize external cues over internal ones. By adolescence, these patterns are often so well-rehearsed that the young person no longer notices them. They have become a personality: quiet, independent, hard to read. But beneath that presentation is often a nervous system that has never learned what safety feels like.

And because these individuals may perform well—earning praise for being "mature for their age" or "cool under pressure"—their disconnection is rarely named. Worse, it is often rewarded. The workplace values composure. Romantic partners may misinterpret numbness as emotional stability. Even clinicians can mistake dissociation for resilience. But the cost of this invisibility is high. Without recognition, the person remains stuck in a protective pattern long after the danger has passed.

It's important to understand that numbness is not only about avoidance. It is about resource limitation. The brain is a finite system. When it perceives that certain experiences cannot be managed—whether due to emotional overwhelm, relational threat, or lack of support—it reroutes. It allocates attention to task performance, to survival routines, to intellectualization. It deprioritizes feeling in favor of function. This is not a moral failing. It is a survival decision.

However, what begins as survival eventually becomes habitual. And like any habit, it resists change. Numbness becomes the baseline. The person no longer remembers what it felt like to cry freely, to laugh without self-consciousness, to feel affection without bracing for its loss. Emotional life becomes abstract. Memories lose their texture. The present feels muted. And the body follows suit: appetite may change, sleep may flatten, physical sensations may dull. The whole system narrows its range.

This is the paradox of psychological protection: the very mechanisms that helped someone endure a difficult environment may become the very things that keep them disconnected from a meaningful one. The shield becomes a barrier. The strategy becomes a prison.

Yet the system can relearn. Emotional numbness is not permanent. The brain and body are plastic; they can be retrained. But doing so requires first honoring the reason the numbness existed in the first place. It was not weakness. It was wisdom. The goal is not to tear down the walls all at once. It is to teach the system, gently and patiently, that it is now safe enough to feel again.

When people begin to thaw, the feelings that emerge are often messy, layered, and delayed. They may grieve the years they spent disconnected. They may rage at the conditions that forced them to shut down. They may fear that regaining feeling will make them too vulnerable. These reactions are not setbacks. They are milestones. They mean the system is waking up.

And with that awakening comes possibility: to connect, to express, to remember, to be whole. But it begins by recognizing numbness not as absence, but as presence—a presence shaped by necessity, formed in context, and ready, one day, to be released.

Emotional Amnesia and the Loss of Inner Continuity

Emotional amnesia is not the forgetting of facts; it is the forgetting of felt experience. It is the sensation of looking at one's own past and finding it strangely hollow. The images may be there, the timeline may hold—but the resonance is gone. Joys feel abstract, griefs feel distant, even traumas seem like they happened to someone else. The continuity of self, which depends not just on memory but on emotional access to memory, begins to fray.

This phenomenon is often described by trauma survivors as a kind of estrangement from their own life. They may know they were once happy in a particular relationship, but they can no longer access the emotional register of that happiness. They may speak about a loss that should have devastated them, yet feel no sadness in the telling. Or they may block out entire years—childhood, adolescence, periods of adult stress—as if their mind placed a fog over those chapters, leaving behind only vague outlines. This is not malingering. It is not avoidance. It is a neuropsychological and psychological strategy meant to preserve functioning in the face of unbearable emotional overload.

Emotional amnesia typically emerges in response to overwhelming or prolonged stress, particularly when the system is given no time, space, or support to process what has happened. This includes both acute traumas, such as accidents or assaults, and chronic conditions like neglect, instability, or repeated emotional invalidation. When feelings cannot be felt safely, the mind places them in storage. That storage is not always accessible later. Sometimes the key is lost. Sometimes the box is locked. And sometimes, the box never existed at all.

Children are especially prone to this kind of fragmentation. Their developing minds rely on caregivers to help them name, hold, and integrate emotional experience. When those supports are absent—or worse, when the caregivers are the source of the threat—the child learns to disassociate from emotion in order to maintain psychological coherence. This often results in spotty memory, flattened affect, and a highly functional exterior that conceals deep disconnection. As adults, these individuals may appear composed, intellectual, even high-achieving—but inside, they may feel unreal.

In many cases, emotional amnesia isn't total. It exists in degrees. Someone might remember the details of an event but feel curiously unmoved by it. Or they might feel strong emotion without being able to link it to any specific source. These are the echoes of split experience: one part of the mind carries the knowledge, another part carries the pain, and the two are never allowed to meet. This internal divide can produce confusion, guilt, and a persistent sense of inauthenticity—what trauma theorist Janina Fisher calls "the loss of the self-in-relationship."

What complicates the picture further is that emotional amnesia can also mimic or coexist with more familiar symptoms of dissociation: depersonalization, derealization, and memory lapses. But while dissociation is often episodic, emotional amnesia is more ambient. It's not that the person is *currently* disconnected; it's that they have *always* been. They may have lived their whole life one step removed from emotional immediacy and not know any other way of being. For them, the question is not "Why did I shut down?" It is "Was I ever really there?"

DISCONNECTION, NUMBNESS, AND EMOTIONAL AMNESIA

This loss of inner continuity is not just about trauma; it is also about identity. Our sense of self depends on a narrative that connects past, present, and future in a way that feels coherent. When emotional amnesia breaks that chain, the person may struggle to locate who they are. They may feel like a collection of fragments: functional at work, performative in relationships, blank in solitude. They may question whether their memories are real, or whether they made things up to survive. These are not existential indulgences. They are psychological consequences of living without full access to one's own emotional archive.

Repairing emotional amnesia does not involve "getting the memories back," as pop culture often suggests. Recovery is not about perfectly remembering what happened. It is about restoring the capacity to feel one's way through life again—to experience emotion as a guide, not a threat. Sometimes this means grieving events long after they occurred. Sometimes it means reconnecting with parts of the self that were hidden for decades. And sometimes it means acknowledging that some things will remain lost, but that life can still be fully lived going forward.

Therapeutically, working with emotional amnesia involves building safety first. Without a sense of emotional security, the system will not risk reconnecting. It also involves helping the person tolerate small doses of affect, learning to trust their own emotional reactions even when those reactions seem delayed or confusing. Over time, new memories begin to encode with greater clarity. The present becomes more vivid. The past may remain blurred, but it no longer dominates the horizon.

What is most important to understand is that emotional amnesia is not a failure. It is not repression, immaturity, or unwillingness to face the past. It is the mind's attempt to protect what was still forming when the pain began. The task of adulthood is not to relive that pain, but to expand what is now possible. Emotional life can be restored—not all at once, and not perfectly, but meaningfully.

And with that restoration comes continuity—not because the old story is fully retrieved, but because the new story begins to take shape with feeling once again at its core.

The Long-Term Cost of Emotional Disconnection

Emotional disconnection does not announce itself with drama. It is not a breakdown, an explosion, or a visible crisis. It is subtle, creeping, and often mistaken for stability. Someone who is emotionally disconnected may hold a job, maintain a family, and contribute to society without disruption. They may even be admired for their calm under pressure, their level-headedness, or their independence. But beneath that calm is often a life of low-resolution experience: muted joy, dulled sorrow, and a chronic sense that something essential has gone missing.

The long-term psychological cost of this state is profound. While numbness protects the system from being overwhelmed in the short term, over time it starves the individual of the very things that make life feel rich and meaningful. Without emotional depth, relationships feel thin. Without affective resonance, purpose becomes abstract. Even identity begins to dissolve into function rather than felt experience. The person becomes more role than self—more reliable than real.

One of the clearest consequences of emotional disconnection is a compromised capacity for intimacy. Intimacy is not just the sharing of facts; it is the willingness to be emotionally seen. When someone is disconnected, they may still perform the gestures of closeness—saying the right things, being physically present—but they may not feel accessible. Their partner may describe them as "emotionally distant," "hard to read," or "not fully there." This disconnect is often interpreted as lack of love, but in many cases, it is not about love at all. It is about emotional inaccessibility that the person themselves does not know how to undo.

This inaccessibility affects not just romantic relationships, but friendships, parenting, and self-relationship. A parent who is emotionally shut down may care deeply for their child, but be unable to attune to the child's emotional needs. They may offer structure without comfort, or advice without presence. This can replicate generational patterns of disconnection, where emotional support is substituted with material provision or rule enforcement. The child may grow up "well behaved" but emotionally underdeveloped, learning to prioritize performance over authenticity—just as their parent once did.

In the realm of self-relationship, emotional disconnection interferes with the development of self-awareness and self-trust. Emotions serve as internal signals—alerts about what matters, what hurts, what needs attention. When those signals are suppressed or unreadable, the individual loses contact with their own inner compass. Decisions become intellectualized rather than felt. Boundaries become theoretical rather than embodied. Desires are hard to name. And over time, the self begins to feel opaque, even to the person living it.

This opacity can contribute to chronic anxiety, existential confusion, and the persistent sense that one is "going through the motions." It may also feed into patterns of overcompensation: excessive caregiving, perfectionism, or compulsive productivity. These behaviors are not always conscious, but they serve a function—to create a sense of worth in the absence of felt selfhood. The person may excel in roles that reward output but feel lost when asked who they are beneath those roles. They may panic in stillness, not because they fear laziness, but because stillness confronts them with a self they can't quite feel.

Physiologically, emotional disconnection is associated with dysregulation of the stress response system. Because emotion is closely tied to the autonomic nervous system, chronic suppression often leads to baseline elevations in cortisol, muscle tension, and cardiovascular strain. Over time, this can contribute to fatigue, inflammation, digestive issues, and a host of stress-related illnesses. What begins as emotional detachment becomes full-body wear. The system runs without pause, without feedback, and without restoration.

Another long-term cost is cognitive rigidity. When emotion is suppressed, the mind often compensates by relying more heavily on fixed beliefs, routines, or external frameworks. This can reduce flexibility, creativity, and openness to new experience. The world becomes manageable only when it is predictable. Uncertainty feels dangerous not because it is inherently threatening, but because it invites feelings that the person cannot tolerate. So they cling to order, to certainty, to moral binaries. Emotional suppression and cognitive extremism often go hand in hand.

In a cultural context that prizes stoicism and productivity, these patterns are not only tolerated but encouraged. The high-functioning, emotionally shut-down individual is often seen as a success story. They're promoted. They're respected. But inside, they may feel like ghosts in their own lives. And because their suffering doesn't look like suffering, they may never be offered support—or even language—to describe what's happening.

Breaking this pattern requires more than insight. It requires the gradual reintroduction of emotion into daily life—not in overwhelming doses, but in small, tolerable moments. This might look like naming a feeling without judgment. Noticing a bodily response and staying with it. Allowing tears to come without pushing them away. Seeking relational spaces where feeling is welcomed, not pathologized. And, perhaps most crucially, learning to trust that the return of feeling will not lead to collapse, but to reconnection.

Emotional disconnection is reversible. But it requires patience, consistency, and support. The goal is not to "become emotional" in some performative sense. The goal is to live in alignment with one's emotional truth, however subtle, layered, or quiet it may be. Presence is not the opposite of composure; it is composure with feeling intact. The person who reclaims their emotional life does not become less stable—they become more whole.

Reclaiming Feeling: The Practice of Emotional Reawakening

The journey back from numbness and emotional amnesia is not a single breakthrough. It is a slow and layered practice of learning to feel again—and to trust that feeling will not destroy you. For many people, the fear is not of emotion itself, but of what it might unleash: chaos, vulnerability, shame, grief, or need. These fears are not imagined. They are the residue of real experiences in which emotion was unsafe, unwelcome, or unmanageable. So recovery begins not with emotion itself, but with context. With safety. With presence.

Reclaiming feeling is not about becoming expressive, dramatic, or sentimental. It is not about acting out emotion or forcing tears. It is about restoring the internal capacity to experience, name, and regulate affect as it arises. In practical terms, this often begins with physical awareness. The body is the first place emotions show up, even when the conscious mind doesn't register them. Tightness in the chest, tension in the jaw, a heaviness behind the eyes—these are the early signals. Learning to notice and stay with these sensations, rather than override or numb them, is the first step toward emotional reintegration.

This is where somatic approaches often prove more effective than purely cognitive ones. Talking *about* emotion can be useful, but it doesn't always reconnect a person to *feeling*. Movement, breathwork, grounding practices, and even art or music can help bypass the overdeveloped intellectual defenses and invite sensation in through the side door. The goal is not catharsis. It is coherence: the integration of physical, emotional, and cognitive awareness into a unified experience of the self.

Importantly, this reawakening is rarely linear. For many, the first return of feeling is not relief—it is grief. Grief for what was lost, what was survived, what was never allowed to be felt at the time. People may cry without knowing why. They may become irritable, anxious, or emotionally flooded. These reactions can be frightening, especially for those who have been emotionally disconnected for years or decades. But they are not regressions. They are signs of the system rebooting. They are proof that life is beginning to move again where there was once only stillness.

Therapeutically, this is where containment becomes crucial. Feeling without support can retraumatize. Feeling with support can rewire. That support might come from a skilled therapist, but it can also come from trusted relationships, safe environments, or internal resources cultivated over time. What matters is not just the emotion itself, but the experience of moving *through* it—of surviving it—of discovering that emotion is tolerable, meaningful, and even necessary for human connection and wholeness.

Reclaiming feeling also requires rethinking emotion's role. In many cultures, emotion is pathologized, feminized, or dismissed as weakness. This leads many people—particularly men, high-achievers, or those raised in emotionally barren households—to see feeling as a liability. Undoing that belief is part of the work. Emotion is not a threat to reason. It is not the enemy of strength. It is a source of information. Of depth. Of relationship. To be emotionally awake is not to be ruled by feeling, but to be in relationship with it. To listen, interpret, and respond.

In this process, small practices matter more than grand gestures. Noticing when your body tenses. Asking what you feel before you act. Naming emotions with specificity: not just "bad" or "fine," but lonely, resigned, anticipatory, nostalgic. Giving yourself permission to cry at a movie, to laugh without restraint, to feel envy without shame. These are not indulgences. They are acts of rehumanization.

And as this emotional landscape comes back online, something else often returns with it: memory. Not just events, but emotional coloration. A sense of presence in one's own past. A richer texture to the present. The fog begins to lift. The person begins to feel more *in* their life, rather than adjacent to it. This can be disorienting at first. But with time, it becomes empowering. The self, once compartmentalized, begins to cohere.

That coherence is not the same as perfection. A person who reclaims

DISCONNECTION, NUMBNESS, AND EMOTIONAL AMNESIA

their emotional life still struggles, still experiences numbness at times, still defaults to old patterns under stress. But they are no longer strangers to themselves. They know when they are disconnected, and they know how to come back. That capacity—to return—is the essence of resilience. Not avoidance. Not invulnerability. But return.

Emotional reawakening does not erase the scars of emotional suppression. But it transforms those scars into context, into insight, into wisdom. The adult who can feel is not the child who never hurt. They are the person who hurt, adapted, survived—and chose to feel again anyway.

And that choice—to reenter life with feeling intact—is one of the bravest psychological acts a person can make.

* * *

29

Shame, Guilt, and Inner Exile

Shame is not just a feeling. It is an orientation of the self against itself. It whispers, not that you've done something wrong, but that *you are* something wrong. It is a posture of emotional collapse, a sinking inward, a turning away from others and from the self. It silences, isolates, and binds. And when it takes root early or deeply enough, it becomes more than an emotion—it becomes architecture. A framework through which the entire self is filtered and judged.

Guilt, though often lumped together with shame, functions differently. Guilt says, "I did something wrong," and invites repair. Shame says, "I *am* something wrong," and invites retreat. Where guilt is tied to behavior, shame is tied to being. Both can coexist. Both can evolve. And both, when internalized without integration, lead to a kind of psychic splitting: a state in which certain parts of the self are banished, hidden, or buried—not because they are monstrous, but because they were never met with understanding.

This inner exile can be subtle. It may not announce itself as shame, especially in people who have grown used to its presence. Instead, it appears in the background hum of self-doubt. The reflexive self-interruption. The urge to overperform or disappear. The compulsive need to fix, to please, to explain. Or in more muted forms: a chronic tension in the body, a loss of spontaneity, a discomfort with stillness.

These are the quiet markers of a person living at odds with themselves, negotiating an internal border between what is allowed to be seen and what must remain hidden.

Often, this division begins early. A child whose feelings are shamed learns to disown those feelings. A child who is told they are "too much" learns to shrink. A child whose needs are unmet or mocked may begin to believe that their very neediness is shameful. Over time, they split: a "presenting self" that conforms, performs, and protects, and a hidden self that carries the banned emotions, unmet needs, or unresolved grief. This fragmentation is adaptive. It allows the child to survive emotionally unsafe environments. But it comes at a cost: the loss of wholeness.

In adulthood, this split self continues to operate beneath the surface. The person may appear confident, competent, even admired. But inside, they may feel fraudulent, hollow, or haunted by a sense that they are fundamentally flawed. No praise can fully land. No accomplishment quiets the inner critic. This is the long echo of shame: it distorts not only how we see ourselves, but how we interpret the world's response to us.

Culturally, shame is often weaponized. Entire systems are built on the shaming of nonconformity—whether through religious doctrine, social expectations, or institutional punishment. Shame polices behavior by threatening exile: if you deviate, you will not belong. This is part of why shame is so powerful. It's not just about internal worth; it's about survival through belonging. And to undo shame is not just to feel better about oneself—it is to risk standing alone.

But there is also wisdom in guilt and shame. They are not inherently pathological. Guilt can guide ethical behavior. Shame, when softened and explored, can reveal our longing to be seen, loved, and whole. The goal is not to eliminate these emotions, but to disarm their power to divide. To bring the exiled parts of ourselves back into relationship. To say: you, too, belong here.

This chapter explores how shame and guilt shape the psyche, how they create inner division, and how we begin to restore integration. It moves beyond abstract theory to examine lived experience—the moments when we collapse into self-rejection, the patterns that keep us stuck, and the slow, steady practices that lead us home to ourselves.

The Architecture of Shame

Shame is not always loud. It does not need to humiliate us in public or drag us into dramatic self-loathing to be effective. Its most enduring form is quiet and internal: the rules we learn about ourselves that seem to come from nowhere, the limitations we place on our voices, our desires, our spontaneity. These rules live inside the body, not just the mind. They constrict the chest, freeze the breath, pull the shoulders in, and avert the eyes. Shame is postural as much as psychological. It arranges the self into compliance long before anyone says a word.

But shame is not innate. It is built. Its architecture takes shape in the earliest relational environments where we learn who we are—first through what is reflected to us, and then through what is withheld. For a child, identity is not yet a solo construction; it is mirrored into being. If the reflection is warm, reliable, and attuned, the child begins to form a self that feels acceptable. If the reflection is harsh, inconsistent, or absent, the child begins to form a self that must be altered, hidden, or corrected. And it is from this alteration that shame arises—not because of what the child does, but because of what the child comes to believe they are.

Unlike guilt, which emerges more clearly in middle childhood with the development of moral reasoning and empathy, shame appears far earlier. Even toddlers can exhibit shame responses—turning away, covering their face, or withdrawing from interaction. These early shame reactions are not necessarily harmful. In fact, they can be useful regulatory cues, helping children navigate social boundaries. But when those reactions are reinforced by ridicule, rejection, or emotional abandonment, they begin to harden. The momentary flush of shame becomes a chronic affective state, and eventually, a trait.

The content of shame is culturally shaped. In some environments, vulnerability is shamed. In others, it's sexuality, anger, dependency, or intellectual expression. What gets coded as "too much" or "not enough" depends on the emotional norms of the family and the larger society. Children are exquisitely sensitive to these unspoken codes. A child doesn't need to be told outright that crying is weak or asking for help is bad; they pick it up in the parent's tone, the withholding of affection, the subtle withdrawal of approval. These patterns encode not just behavior, but identity: not *you shouldn't cry*, but *you are weak*.

Over time, shame becomes layered. It begins with the experience of being rejected for something authentic. But then the person begins to reject themselves *for having shame*. The shame becomes recursive: I'm ashamed of my shame. This layering is what makes it so difficult to access. The shame is defended against—not just because it's painful, but because it's seen as proof of brokenness. And so it is buried. But what's buried isn't gone. It continues to operate beneath the surface, shaping behavior, self-concept, and emotional expression.

Shame also distorts memory. When someone carries chronic shame, their autobiographical narrative is often punctuated by moments of perceived failure, humiliation, or inadequacy. These memories are not just recalled—they are relived. The person may blush, cringe, or contract physically while describing events from decades ago. Their shame is not a relic; it is a live wire. And because shame thrives in secrecy, it is rarely metabolized through relational repair. Instead, the person turns it inward, creating a private story of unworthiness.

In psychological terms, shame-based identity formation often leads to rigid defenses: perfectionism, people-pleasing, emotional avoidance, or control. These defenses are not random. They are attempts to earn belonging by becoming what is needed and eliminating what is not allowed. But they come at a steep cost. The person becomes less spontaneous, less authentic, less emotionally flexible. They may succeed outwardly but feel hollow inwardly. They may be loved for what they *do*, but never feel lovable for who they *are*.

It is important to understand that shame doesn't just damage self-esteem—it disrupts the *structure* of the self. When shame is deeply internalized, the person does not simply believe they are flawed; they lose access to entire emotional and relational capacities. Shame suppresses voice, dampens desire, and short-circuits emotional expression. In its chronic form, it leads not to sadness, but to silence.

Therapists working with shame often encounter resistance not because the client is defiant, but because the client is terrified. To touch the shame is to risk collapse, to expose the very part of the self that has been hidden for a lifetime. And yet, paradoxically, it is only through that exposure—gentle, titrated, supported—that healing begins. Not by flooding the person with emotion, but by offering a new relational context: one in which the shame is met not with judgment, but with presence.

At its core, shame is about disconnection: the rupture between the self and the social world, and eventually, between the self and its own inner truth. Healing shame is not about becoming shameless. It is about becoming whole. It is about remembering that the parts of the self that were cast out were never unworthy—they were unwelcomed.

Guilt as Conscience, Guilt as Burden

Guilt is often regarded as the more "mature" or "useful" counterpart to shame. It carries with it the suggestion of ethical awareness: the understanding that one's actions have consequences, that others are affected by what we do or fail to do. Guilt, in its healthiest form, invites responsibility. It can catalyze repair, promote growth, and reinforce our place in a moral community. But guilt is not always healthy. Like any emotional system, it can become distorted, excessive, or stuck. And when it does, it no longer serves the conscience—it begins to erode it.

Psychologists have long differentiated between adaptive and maladaptive guilt. Adaptive guilt is proportionate to the situation. It arises when a person genuinely violates their own moral code or harms another. It comes with an urge to make amends, not just to relieve discomfort, but to restore connection and personal integrity. In contrast, maladaptive guilt is diffuse, chronic, and often disconnected from specific actions. It may be learned in childhood from emotionally manipulative caregivers, from religious or cultural systems that equate guilt with virtue, or from early experiences in which the child was blamed for things they had no control over.

In families where guilt is used as a tool of control, children often grow up hyper-attuned to others' emotions. They learn that their job is to keep people happy, prevent conflict, or manage their parents' moods. These children become adults who apologize reflexively, who feel guilty for saying no, for setting boundaries, for putting their own needs first. Their guilt is not about wrongdoing—it is about existing in a way that feels inconvenient to others. Over time, this pattern becomes so ingrained that they begin to anticipate guilt before any conflict arises. The guilt is preemptive. It shapes behavior not to correct harm, but to prevent imagined disapproval.

Religious and cultural conditioning can intensify this experience. In many traditions, guilt is tied to purity, duty, and sacrifice. A person may be taught that wanting too much, asserting oneself, or experiencing pleasure is selfish—or sinful. In these systems, guilt becomes a marker of goodness. The more one suffers under the weight of guilt, the more morally upright they are perceived to be. This creates a perverse incentive: to feel guilty is to be virtuous. To let go of guilt is to risk moral failure. In such contexts, guilt ceases to be a signal of conscience and becomes a badge of identity.

This dynamic is especially pronounced in people with high levels of conscientiousness or empathy. These individuals are deeply invested in doing the right thing, being fair, avoiding harm. But without discernment, their guilt can spiral. They may feel responsible for other people's feelings, outcomes, or disappointments. They may ruminate on past decisions, replay conversations, or seek endless reassurance. This is not integrity—it is anxiety dressed in moral clothing. And while it may appear admirable on the surface, it often reflects an internal narrative of unworthiness: a belief that they are always one step away from being bad, selfish, or inadequate.

Chronic guilt also has physiological effects. It can contribute to tension headaches, digestive issues, insomnia, and depressive symptoms. The nervous system responds to guilt much like it does to threat: with hypervigilance, tight muscles, and shallow breathing. Over time, this wears down resilience. The person may become emotionally exhausted, cynical, or disengaged—not because they no longer care, but because caring has become too painful. This is one of guilt's hidden dangers: when overused, it erodes the very empathy it is meant to support.

In therapy, addressing guilt requires careful unpacking. Not all guilt is unjustified. But not all guilt is useful, either. The first step is differentiation: What did I do? What do I believe I did? What is mine, and what has been projected onto me? Often, this process reveals that the guilt is less about the present moment and more about old relational patterns—trying to appease a critical parent, avoid punishment, or maintain attachment by staying small. Once these roots are identified, the person can begin to examine their guilt with curiosity rather than collapse.

Forgiveness also plays a role, though not always in the ways people assume. It is not about forgetting or excusing harm. It is about releasing oneself from the constant reliving of past failures. Sometimes that means seeking forgiveness from others; other times, it means granting it to oneself. But genuine forgiveness is impossible without accountability. This is why guilt, at its best, is connected to repair. It is not performative remorse. It is not self-flagellation. It is a return to alignment between values and actions.

For people who carry persistent guilt, healing involves building a new relationship with conscience. One in which morality is not measured by suffering, and goodness is not proved by self-denial. It means learning to distinguish between responsibility and codependence, between remorse and shame, between ethical growth and emotional punishment.

In this light, guilt is not something to be eliminated—it is something to be refined. When it functions well, it keeps us connected to our humanity. It reminds us that we are part of something larger than ourselves. But it must be grounded in clarity, not confusion. In presence, not perfection. And in love—not fear.

Inner Exile and the Fragmented Self

When shame and guilt go unexamined, they don't just weigh us down—they divide us. One of the least recognized yet most impactful consequences of chronic internal conflict is the creation of a split self: a fragmented identity in which parts of us are exiled from consciousness, denied expression, or hidden behind carefully managed performances. This isn't a pathological fracture like in dissociative identity disorder. It's the quieter, more common kind of fragmentation—the kind that occurs when we tuck certain traits, memories, or emotions out of sight, not because they're dangerous, but because at some point, they made us feel unlovable.

This exile can take many forms. For some, it's the suppression of anger. For others, it's vulnerability, sexuality, creativity, grief, or joy. What gets banished depends on the relational and cultural messages we received about what was acceptable and what was not. Over time, we don't just hide these parts—we forget they were ever there. The self becomes streamlined for survival. And what is left is the version of us we believe others will tolerate.

But those exiled parts don't vanish. They go underground. They live in the body, in the unconscious, in dreams, in slips of the tongue, in inexplicable triggers and disproportionate emotional reactions. They make themselves known through longing, through discomfort, through inexplicable fatigue or sudden irritability. We may think we're moving through the world as coherent selves, but often we are navigating life with a divided internal landscape: the self that performs and the self that waits in silence.

This fragmentation often begins in childhood, especially in environments where authenticity is unsafe. A child who is scolded for crying may learn to shut down sadness. A child who is praised only when achieving may suppress rest or play. A child who is shamed for being "too much" may learn to dim their light. These early adaptations are intelligent. They serve a protective purpose. But they do so by carving off parts of the self and storing them away. By the time we reach adulthood, the authentic self is not gone—it's just buried.

Trauma compounds this fragmentation. When a person undergoes an overwhelming experience—particularly one that involves betrayal, violation, or helplessness—the mind often copes by compartmentalizing. Some memories are walled off. Certain emotions become intolerable. The self becomes splintered not only to survive others' judgments, but to survive its own pain. This is especially true in complex trauma, where repeated exposure to relational harm leaves a person feeling fundamentally unsafe in connection. The result is often a chronic state of self-monitoring and emotional constriction.

Culturally, the pressure to perform a coherent identity intensifies this split. Social media, professional environments, even family dynamics often reward a streamlined, palatable self. We are taught—sometimes subtly, sometimes brutally—that certain parts of us must be hidden to be accepted. This creates what Winnicott called the "false self": a constructed identity that protects the true self by shielding it from exposure. The false self may be functional, even socially successful, but it lacks vitality. Behind it, the person may feel hollow, disconnected, or like an imposter.

This inner exile also plays out in language. We speak of ourselves in fragments: "There's a part of me that wants to leave," or "I know it's irrational, but I still feel this way." These phrases are not just figures of speech. They reflect a deep, intuitive awareness of the self as multiple—of conflicting needs, desires, and beliefs coexisting within a single psyche. Psychological health, then, is not about eradicating these internal parts. It is about fostering dialogue between them.

The consequences of unaddressed inner exile are far-reaching. People may struggle with intimacy, not because they don't want closeness, but because they fear being seen in their entirety. They may feel chronically restless, not because they are undisciplined, but because some part of them is always trying to escape. They may sabotage opportunities or relationships, not out of malice, but because success threatens to expose the parts of them that feel undeserving. These behaviors are not flaws. They are the echoes of internal division.

Therapeutic approaches that address fragmentation often emphasize integration over eradication. Rather than "fixing" the person, the goal is to welcome home the parts that were cast out. This may involve inner child work, parts work (like Internal Family Systems), somatic therapy, or narrative approaches that allow the person to re-author their story with compassion and coherence. The healing comes not from changing who the person is, but from acknowledging *all* of who they are—especially the parts they were taught to hide.

Reintegration is slow. It involves building trust with the self. It requires unlearning the reflexive shame that has kept certain parts in exile. It asks us to expand our window of tolerance—not just for discomfort, but for authenticity. And it means grieving what was lost: not just time or opportunity, but the emotional freedom that was never allowed to develop.

Ultimately, the journey from inner exile to inner wholeness is not about becoming someone new. It is about returning to what was already there, beneath the shame, the guilt, and the performance. It is a quiet homecoming—a recognition that no part of the self is too much, too broken, or too late to be reclaimed.

Integration as the Return to Wholeness

If shame divides and guilt burdens, then integration is the process by which the self is reclaimed. It is not a reversal of injury, nor is it a tidy reconciliation of every contradictory impulse. Integration is the act of making room—of allowing all parts of the self to exist in dialogue rather than in exile. It is a shift from inner antagonism to inner companionship, from performance to presence, from fragmentation to coherence. And it is one of the hardest psychological tasks we undertake.

Contrary to popular belief, integration is not about arriving at a unified, unchanging self. The self is not singular, and it never was. We are made of multiple subselves—emotional, behavioral, relational modes that form in response to experience. There's the protector, the pleaser, the critic, the wounded child, the observer, the dreamer, and many more. Psychological maturity does not mean collapsing these into one dominant identity; it means creating an internal environment where each can be acknowledged, understood, and regulated in context.

This process often begins with awareness—recognizing the voices inside without immediately believing or obeying them. A person might notice a harsh inner critic and begin to ask, whose voice is that? Where did it come from? What does it think it's protecting me from? Integration does not mean silencing that critic, but understanding its origins, its fears, and its outdated strategies. Over time, the relationship with that part becomes less adversarial. The inner war quiets.

The same is true for emotional states. Integration means no longer splitting emotions into good or bad, strong or weak, allowed or forbidden. It means holding space for joy and grief, desire and fear, tenderness and rage—sometimes all at once. This capacity is what Bion called "containment": the ability to metabolize experience without dissociation or collapse. A contained person is not emotionless. They are emotionally literate. They can feel fully without being overtaken.

Cognitive integration also plays a role. Many people live in cognitive dissonance, holding beliefs that contradict their behavior, values they cannot enact, or identities they struggle to embody. Integration means confronting these contradictions not with shame, but with curiosity. Why do I say I value honesty, but avoid hard conversations? Why do I believe in self-worth, but tolerate mistreatment? These questions, when asked gently, reveal the places where healing is needed—not to condemn, but to align.

Relational integration is equally crucial. The parts of us that were formed in relationship—especially those wounded by disconnection—

can only fully heal in relationship. This does not require romantic partnership or even close friendship. It requires *relational safety*: a space where one can be witnessed without judgment, responded to without withdrawal, and challenged without rejection. In such spaces, we begin to risk authenticity. We let others see the parts we were taught to hide. And when those parts are met with presence rather than punishment, something profound happens. The self begins to reunite.

Integration is also a somatic process. The body holds memory—of shame, of fear, of disapproval. These memories are not always accessible through language, but they can be felt in posture, tension, breath. Practices like somatic experiencing, yoga, EMDR, or mindful movement can help release these imprints, allowing the body to participate in the return to wholeness. A person who has carried chronic shame may, for the first time, stand upright. Breathe deeply. Take up space. These are not small shifts. They are reparations of the physical self.

But integration is not a permanent state. It is a dynamic process. Life continues to fracture us—through trauma, loss, conflict, transition. Integration is the ongoing commitment to repair, to stay in relationship with the self, especially when things break. It is not about achieving perfection, but about cultivating an internal orientation of acceptance, flexibility, and truth.

And perhaps most importantly, integration is not a solo project. While the work happens inside us, it is shaped by the people around us. We are wired for co-regulation, for reflection, for mutual meaning-making. The more we are surrounded by people who honor our full humanity, the more capacity we develop to honor it ourselves. Integration, then, is both personal and cultural. It is a psychological achievement, but also a relational one. It asks not only, "Can I accept myself?" but also, "Can I live in a world that makes room for that self to breathe?"

To speak of wholeness is not to speak of purity. It is to speak of hospitality. The integrated person is not someone who has figured everything out, but someone who has made a home inside themselves—a home where no part is unwelcome, where the exile has ended, and where complexity is no longer a threat, but a truth to be lived.

* * *

30

Moving Toward Wholeness

Suffering doesn't end. It changes shape. It quiets, it returns, it teaches. Sometimes it loosens its grip and lets us breathe. Other times it appears without warning, as if it had never left. To live a whole life is not to escape suffering, but to live in relationship with it—consciously, honestly, without letting it define the entirety of who we are.

The cultural idea of healing tends to imply finality. A wound heals, and we are restored. A broken bone mends, and life goes on. But psychological pain resists such closure. Trauma, grief, abandonment, regret—these are not broken bones. They don't stitch neatly. They don't disappear. What they do, when held with care, is integrate. They become part of the landscape of the self, like scar tissue that marks where life has been difficult but survived.

Too often, healing is framed as a project of removal. Get rid of your anger. Overcome your anxiety. Let go of your grief. But real psychological growth asks something deeper: not to discard suffering, but to carry it with dignity. To stop seeing pain as a flaw in need of correction, and instead, to approach it as a feature of being human. The point is not to be untouched by suffering, but to become trustworthy with it.

Wholeness, then, is not a state of purity or perfection. It is not the absence of fear, shame, or sorrow. It is the presence of capacity—the ability to stay with what is difficult without collapsing or fleeing. The ability to be honest about one's own contradictions. The ability to feel deeply without becoming undone. Wholeness is coherence in the face of complexity. It is emotional maturity made visible.

This chapter is about the final turn: from the pursuit of healing as repair, to the deeper path of living well in the presence of what will never be undone. It builds on every chapter that came before, drawing together the threads of emotion, identity, memory, trauma, belief, and meaning to explore what it means to live a life that is honest, flexible, and complete—not because nothing is broken, but because nothing is excluded.

In a world obsessed with optimization and performance, choosing to live with suffering rather than hide or fix it is a radical act. It's an act of self-respect. It's also an act of resistance against a culture that pathologizes vulnerability and demands emotional efficiency. This final chapter is not a summary or a sendoff. It's a reckoning. A reframing. An invitation to walk forward not in pursuit of perfection, but with integrity—one step at a time, pain included.

Acceptance Is Not Surrender

Acceptance is one of the most misunderstood ideas in psychology. It is often mistaken for resignation, for apathy, or for the passive act of letting life happen without protest. In reality, psychological acceptance is none of those things. It is not giving up. It is showing up—fully, consciously, and without illusion. It is the willingness to turn toward reality, even when reality includes pain.

This distinction matters, especially for people who have been harmed. Telling someone to "accept what happened" without understanding what that truly means can sound like a betrayal. It can feel like asking them to condone injustice, to minimize trauma, or to forfeit their right to be angry. But real acceptance does not invalidate pain. It validates it. It says: this is true, and I will not pretend otherwise. Acceptance is not about saying things *should* have happened the way they did. It's about acknowledging that they *did*—and that no amount of resistance will rewrite the past.

This approach is central to several psychological frameworks, including Acceptance and Commitment Therapy (ACT). ACT emphasizes a shift away from control and toward conscious engagement. Rather than trying to eliminate difficult thoughts or feelings, ACT encourages people to hold them lightly, notice them, and take action aligned with their values anyway. In this model, acceptance is a precondition for meaningful life, not an obstacle to it.

What makes acceptance so challenging is that it often requires us to give up the hope of a better past. That hope can be seductive, even if it's subconscious. We replay conversations, imagine different decisions, wish someone had protected us, or long for the version of ourselves we might have been if life had gone differently. There is grief in letting go of those imagined realities. But that grief is clarifying. It makes space for the present.

Crucially, acceptance does not mean approval. A person can accept that they were harmed and still pursue justice. They can accept that they are grieving and still move toward connection. Acceptance is not a decision to stop caring. It's the decision to stop fighting what *is*. And when suffering stems from something ongoing—chronic illness, systemic injustice, or unresolved loss—acceptance allows the person to engage with that reality without being consumed by it.

In trauma work, this is especially important. Survivors often experience two layers of pain: the original wound, and the secondary suffering that comes from trying to deny, suppress, or undo it. Acceptance invites a different path. It does not ask the person to forget or forgive prematurely. It asks them to witness themselves honestly. To say, this happened. This hurt. This changed me. And I am still here.

The paradox of acceptance is that it often leads to the very change we seek. When a person stops trying to erase their anxiety and instead welcomes it as information, they often feel less anxious. When someone stops fighting their grief and makes space for it to move through them, they begin to breathe more freely. This is not magic; it's regulation. The nervous system responds to honesty. When we stop pretending, we stop escalating our own distress.

Of course, acceptance is not a one-time decision. It is a practice. Some days it feels accessible. Other days it doesn't. A person may accept their chronic pain on Monday and rage against it on Tuesday. This fluctuation is part of the process. Acceptance is not a permanent state of peace. It is a willingness to return—to meet the moment again and again without resistance, even when resistance is tempting.

It also helps to remember that acceptance is contextual. We don't have to accept *everything* all at once. Sometimes we begin by accepting a single feeling. Or a single memory. Or the fact that we're struggling to accept anything at all. These are all valid entry points. Integration begins wherever we are willing to stop pretending.

Finally, acceptance has a relational dimension. It's not just about making peace with our inner experience. It's about reducing the harm we do to ourselves and others when we're fighting reality. A parent who accepts their own limitations is less likely to project those unmet needs onto their child. A person who accepts their grief is less likely to numb themselves in ways that isolate them from others. Acceptance makes room for kindness.

We tend to think of maturity as mastery—of emotion, of behavior, of life. But more often, maturity is the ability to sit with what cannot be fixed and still act with integrity. It is knowing when to move, when to rest, when to speak, and when to sit quietly with what hurts. In this way, acceptance becomes not just a psychological tool, but a moral stance: a commitment to live truthfully, even when truth is painful.

Making Meaning Without Erasure

When people speak about "healing," they often mean closure—a turning of the page, a sense that the painful chapters are behind them and the story has moved on. But lived experience rarely unfolds that way. The most defining moments of our lives, especially those marked by suffering, do not disappear with time. They become part of us. And to make meaning of them is not to erase their pain—it is to allow them a place in the larger narrative of who we are.

Meaning-making is central to psychological resilience. Viktor Frankl, in *Man's Search for Meaning*, wrote that suffering ceases to be suffering when it finds meaning. He did not mean that suffering becomes enjoyable or morally good. He meant that when we can locate a larger frame—when we can say, *this pain shaped me*, or *this loss taught me something I carry forward*—then suffering does not reduce us. It becomes metabolized, absorbed into the story of a full and conscious life.

But the act of making meaning must be done carefully. Not all meaning is honest. Sometimes we rush to find silver linings in order to avoid grief. We say things like "everything happens for a reason," not because we believe it, but because we're afraid to sit with the possibility that some things just hurt. We create redemptive narratives because we think pain must be justified in order to be bearable. In doing so, we risk bypassing the truth.

This is the trap of what psychologists and trauma scholars call "toxic meaning-making." It's the tendency to impose tidy explanations on complex suffering. This can show up as spiritual bypassing, forced forgiveness, or premature positivity. It often arises in communities or relationships where discomfort is not well tolerated. When someone is grieving and hears, "At least you had the time you did," that may be meant kindly—but it asks the person to edit their experience, to replace raw grief with acceptable gratitude.

Authentic meaning-making, by contrast, is slow. It honors the wound before trying to interpret it. It lets the story remain unresolved for a long time. It does not demand that pain be transformed into wisdom immediately. It trusts that the lessons, if there are any, will emerge on their own timeline.

This kind of meaning-making also acknowledges that some pain is senseless. Not everything that happens is part of a divine plan or personal growth arc. Some experiences are simply violations of what should never have been. And yet, even in the aftermath of senselessness, we can still choose how to live. We can decide what values to carry, what boundaries to draw, what kind of person we want to be in response to the reality of loss. This is not the same as justification. It is reclamation.

Narrative psychology offers a useful lens here. According to this framework, identity is formed not just by what happens to us, but by how we make sense of it over time. The stories we tell ourselves—about who we are, what we've survived, and what matters—shape our ongoing behavior and sense of self. When people feel trapped in their suffering, it is often because the story has stopped moving. They are stuck in a single frame: victim, failure, outsider. The work of meaning-making is to gently unstick the narrative—not to deny what happened, but to enlarge the frame.

Sometimes that means shifting from "I was betrayed" to "I learned what betrayal feels like, and I know now what I will no longer allow." Sometimes it means moving from "I lost everything" to "I still grieve what I lost, and I am also discovering who I am without it." These are subtle shifts. They do not remove pain. But they allow the person to be more than their pain.

It's also important to recognize that meaning-making is relational. We rarely develop new narratives in isolation. We need reflection, witnessing, and resonance. A person might carry shame for years, only to have someone else say, "That makes so much sense," and suddenly the shame loses its grip. In this way, meaning is co-constructed. It is shaped by the people who help us see ourselves with more compassion and clarity.

One of the risks in this process is overidentification with the wound. When the story of suffering becomes the core of identity, it can calcify.

People may cling to pain not because they want to, but because it is the only version of self that feels known. This is especially common when suffering has not been witnessed or validated. The pain remains in focus because it has never been properly held.

The goal, then, is not to forget the suffering, nor to make it the centerpiece of life. It is to allow it a place of dignity within a broader, evolving story. A story in which the self is multiple: hurt and healing, limited and growing, broken and whole. That paradox is the essence of adult psychological life.

To live meaningfully is not to make every experience have a purpose. It is to live *as if* one's values matter, *as if* one's pain can be honored, *as if* even the most unanswerable questions deserve our attention. Meaning is not something we find lying on the ground. It is something we build, slowly and imperfectly, out of the materials we have.

The Discipline of Staying Human

In modern life, there is a quiet pressure to become emotionally efficient. To regulate quickly, bounce back fast, and reframe suffering into a growth opportunity before the wound has even closed. This pressure doesn't always come from outside. Often, it is internal: a learned expectation that we must be composed, productive, and emotionally self-sufficient at all times. But human beings are not machines. We are relational, meaning-making creatures. And to stay fully human—especially in the aftermath of suffering—is a discipline.

That discipline begins with presence. Psychological presence is not simply being aware of one's thoughts or emotions; it is the capacity to *remain* with them, especially when they are painful or unfamiliar. Presence means resisting the impulse to numb, deny, or rush past discomfort. It means staying grounded in the body during moments of fear or grief, not because it feels good, but because it is the only honest starting point for anything meaningful.

Staying human also means allowing complexity. Our minds are often drawn to binary thinking, especially under stress. We want our pain to be either justified or excessive, our behavior either good or bad, our relationships either nourishing or toxic. But human experience is rarely that clean. To stay human is to tolerate contradiction: to hold love and disappointment in the same hand, to feel gratitude and regret about the same person, to recognize that healing and harm can exist side by side.

One of the most powerful practices that supports this capacity is grief literacy. In many cultures, grief is poorly understood. It is treated as something to get over, rather than something to live with. But grief is not a deviation from life; it is part of life. And learning to grieve—fully, without apology—is one of the most important disciplines of emotional adulthood.

Grief literacy involves knowing what grief *is*: not just sadness, but an entire ecosystem of emotions, including anger, confusion, numbness, and even relief. It also involves recognizing that grief does not follow a linear path. It comes in waves, often unexpectedly. A person might laugh at a memory one moment and cry the next. This emotional fluidity is not a sign of instability; it is a sign that the person is still in relationship with what was lost.

Staying human also involves the practice of ritual. Not in the religious sense necessarily, but in the psychological sense: repeated, intentional acts that mark experience and create coherence. Lighting a candle for a loved one who's gone. Writing a letter that will never be sent. Walking the same path at sunset every night to mark the close of day. These small rituals are not cures; they are containers. They give form to feeling.

Another essential part of the discipline is self-respect. In the aftermath of trauma or humiliation, it can be tempting to collapse inward. To make oneself small, invisible, or accommodating in order to avoid further harm. But to stay human is to reclaim one's full emotional height. Not to dominate or retaliate, but to refuse self-erasure. This is especially important for people whose boundaries were violated in formative relationships. Relearning the right to take up space is an act of restoration.

This process is neither quick nor linear. There are days when a person feels sturdy and whole, and days when they feel fractured and raw. But wholeness is not about consistency. It is about coherence: the ability to name what is true, to stand in it without shame, and to choose one's next action based on values, not fear.

That is where emotional regulation comes in—not as a tool to suppress feeling, but as a way to channel it. Regulation is the nervous system's capacity to stay within a range that allows for connection and choice. When we are dysregulated, we are more likely to lash out, shut down, or fall into compulsive patterns. Regulation restores access to the parts of ourselves that can pause, reflect, and engage. It allows us to stay relational, even when we are hurting.

This doesn't mean we become serene at all times. Anger has its place. So does grief, so does fear. But regulation allows us to feel them without being overtaken. It gives us the internal scaffolding to stay with others in their pain too—to witness without fixing, to support without absorbing. In that way, staying human becomes a relational ethic, not just a personal skill.

Finally, the discipline of staying human includes learning when to rest. Rest is not a luxury. It is a necessity for nervous system repair, emotional integration, and long-term functioning. In cultures that prize productivity, rest is often framed as laziness or avoidance. But there is nothing avoidant about resting so you can remain present. There is nothing lazy about stepping back to preserve your humanity.

To stay human in a world that often demands numbness is a daily choice. It is a form of resistance against emotional disconnection, self-abandonment, and collective denial. And it is also an act of care—not just for oneself, but for everyone we touch. Because the more honest, flexible, and emotionally available we become, the more space we create for others to do the same.

Wholeness as a Lived Practice

The idea of wholeness often evokes an image of completion, a final state of being in which all the parts of oneself are harmonized, integrated, and at peace. It is a beautiful vision—but also a misleading one if we imagine it as a permanent destination. In reality, wholeness is not a fixed achievement. It is a lived practice. It is something we return to again and again, especially when life fractures us.

To practice wholeness is to live in relationship with all parts of the self: the strong and the scared, the healed and the hurting, the honest and the ambivalent. It means refusing to exile any part of one's experience simply because it is uncomfortable, undesirable, or unresolved. This approach stands in contrast to many cultural narratives that treat emotional pain as a deviation from normalcy. In those models, being whole means being fixed. But psychologically, being whole means being intact, even when wounded.

One of the central insights of Internal Family Systems (IFS) theory is that the self is not a monolith. It is made up of subparts: inner protectors, exiles, managers, and more. Each part has its own history, motivation, and emotional logic. When people are disconnected from wholeness, it is often because some parts of themselves have been silenced, demonized, or ignored. The work is not to eliminate those parts, but to bring them into conscious dialogue—to understand what they're protecting, what they fear, and what they need.

This is not easy work. The parts that sabotage, avoid, or numb are often doing so in service of survival. A person might procrastinate not because they are lazy, but because an inner part is afraid of being judged. They might lash out because a younger part is terrified of abandonment. When those parts are met with curiosity rather than shame, something remarkable happens: they soften. They begin to trust. And the system—the self—starts to move toward internal coherence.

That coherence is the heartbeat of wholeness. It does not require perfection, enlightenment, or mastery. It requires only truthfulness. To be able to say, "This is who I am right now," and mean it without apology. Coherence allows a person to live in alignment with their values, even when they are struggling. It makes room for sorrow without collapse, and for joy without guilt.

Wholeness also includes the body. Too often, psychological frameworks privilege cognition—what we think, what we believe—while sidelining the somatic reality of experience. But trauma, grief, and resilience all live in the body. To feel whole, we must feel at home in our skin. This does not mean loving every part of one's body. It means being in relationship with it: listening to its signals, honoring its limits, and tending to its needs.

This is especially important for people whose bodies have been sites of pain, whether through illness, violence, or disconnection. Reclaiming bodily presence is an act of courage. Practices like breathwork, movement, and grounding are not indulgences; they are forms of reentry. They say, "I am allowed to be here. I am allowed to feel."

Relationally, wholeness shows up as integrity. Not moral perfection, but psychological consistency—the ability to bring one's full self into connection without shape-shifting or hiding. This is what allows for real intimacy. When people are fragmented, they may present only the parts they think are lovable. But when they are practicing wholeness, they bring their contradictions too. They say, "I'm scared and I still want to try," or "I'm angry and I still care." This transparency is what makes trust possible.

Wholeness is also a communal practice. We cannot fully claim ourselves in isolation. We need relationships that reflect back who we are, that hold space for our growth, and that challenge us when we abandon ourselves. These mirrors are not always comfortable, but they are essential. A person becomes more whole when they are seen clearly and still loved. That experience rewires something. It tells the nervous system: you are safe to exist.

Spiritual frameworks have long intuited this. Across traditions, there are metaphors of brokenness and return: the shattered vessel, the lost sheep, the prodigal son. These stories are not about perfection. They are about reunion. They remind us that what is fragmented can be gathered. That what is lost can be remembered. And that wholeness is not the absence of pain, but the presence of integration.

In practice, this means developing habits that sustain coherence. Journaling honestly. Resting intentionally. Speaking truth, even when the voice shakes. Saying no when something costs too much. Saying yes when something is worth the risk. None of these things will eliminate suffering. But they will allow us to suffer consciously, and to live richly.

Wholeness, then, is not a trophy for the healed. It is a discipline for the living. A daily return to presence, complexity, truth, and love. It does not mean we are always okay. It means we are always welcome to come back to ourselves.

* * *

VII

PART VII: THE SOCIAL CONTEXT OF THE MIND

Our minds do not develop in isolation—they are shaped by the cultural, social, and environmental worlds we inhabit. In this part, I want to explore with you how systems, communities, and collective beliefs influence our thoughts, feelings, and behaviors. Understanding these larger forces helps us see how personal experience is connected to broader social patterns, and opens the door to greater awareness and change.

31

The Psychological Impact of Culture

Culture is not just the backdrop to our lives. It is the architecture of our psychological world—shaping how we think, what we value, and how we feel. From the moment we are born, we are embedded in a web of expectations, rituals, and emotional cues that tell us what is appropriate to express, what must be suppressed, and what it means to be a good person. These are not simply social rules; they are emotional operating systems. And like all systems, they are largely invisible until disrupted.

We often think of culture as a set of external customs or traditions—language, dress, food, holidays. But the more powerful dimensions of culture are psychological. They live in the way affection is shown, how anger is managed, which emotions are prioritized, and which are punished. Culture determines whether silence is read as respect or avoidance, whether directness signals honesty or rudeness, whether suffering is a private burden or a communal event. These interpretations run so deep that we rarely question them, until we encounter another way of being.

At the heart of culture is the idea of normativity: the sense of what is normal, desirable, and expected. These norms are not morally neutral. They shape self-esteem, identity development, and emotional fluency. A child raised in a culture that values obedience and restraint will have a different emotional landscape than one raised in a culture that prizes assertiveness and autonomy. Neither is wrong—but each creates different affordances and constraints. And those constraints do not disappear in adulthood.

This chapter explores how cultural context influences the formation of emotional life. It examines the unspoken values that define who we are allowed to be, the consequences of deviation, and the complex psychology of belonging. Culture teaches us how to be people—how to feel, how to relate, how to make meaning. But it also teaches us who is considered fully human and who is not. That distinction has consequences.

Understanding the psychological impact of culture is especially urgent in a globalized world where people regularly move between cultural contexts. The experience of cultural dissonance—when one's internal values clash with external norms—can create deep confusion, alienation, and emotional fatigue. But it can also be a site of insight. To stand at the intersection of multiple cultural narratives is to gain perspective on the constructed nature of the self.

This chapter does not treat culture as static. Cultures evolve. Values shift. Emotional dialects can be learned, adapted, or resisted. But the imprint of early cultural conditioning is strong. It defines what feels natural, what feels foreign, and what feels threatening. To understand ourselves fully, we must understand the cultures that shaped us—not just in terms of heritage, but in terms of emotional instruction.

This chapter also resists the idea that culture is something that "other people have." Everyone is cultural. Every family, every institution, every social group transmits implicit values about emotion, identity, and behavior. To see the psychological impact of culture is to begin recognizing the water we swim in—and to decide, consciously, whether to keep swimming that way.

THE PSYCHOLOGICAL IMPACT OF CULTURE

Culture as an Emotional Blueprint

When psychologists study emotional development, the conversation often begins with biology. There are, after all, universal elements to human emotion: infants cry, toddlers tantrum, and joy has recognizable facial expressions across cultures. But this is only the beginning. What matters even more than whether we can feel an emotion is whether we are taught it is acceptable to do so—and that lesson is almost entirely cultural.

Culture is the invisible curriculum that teaches us how to feel, what to feel, and when to show it. In early childhood, it shapes not only the words we learn for emotional states but also the consequences for expressing them. In some cultures, sadness is seen as a natural and even noble emotion; in others, it is viewed as a sign of weakness or indulgence. Anger, too, may be seen as either a rightful protest or a disruptive force to be tightly controlled. Children learn quickly what earns approval and what leads to rejection, not just in terms of behavior, but in emotional tone.

These lessons are absorbed long before they are ever articulated. A child does not need to be told that expressing frustration is unacceptable if every display of frustration is met with withdrawal, punishment, or shaming. Likewise, a child raised in a family where vulnerability is met with soothing will come to associate openness with safety. These early patterns form what developmental psychologists call "emotional schemas"—the internalized frameworks we use to interpret our own and others' emotional states. And these schemas are not universal. They are culturally crafted.

One of the most powerful ways culture shapes emotion is through what anthropologists call "emotional dialects." Just as spoken language has regional variations, so too do emotional expressions. A furrowed brow or a quiet sigh may mean different things in different cultural contexts. A flat affect might be interpreted as respectful in one group, and disinterested in another. The meaning of emotional expression is never simply in the gesture itself; it is in the culturally shared assumptions that surround it.

This helps explain why cross-cultural misunderstanding is often emotional misunderstanding. People are not only interpreting different signals; they are using different rules to determine what those signals mean. A Japanese student might avoid eye contact with a professor out of respect, while an American professor might read that as a lack of engagement. A Middle Eastern family might grieve loudly and publicly, while a Northern European observer might interpret that as melodrama. These are not errors in emotional communication. They are reflections of different emotional grammars.

Culture also shapes the emotional norms of entire institutions. Educational systems, workplaces, and even healthcare settings transmit implicit messages about which emotions are valid. In some school systems, stoicism is rewarded; in others, enthusiasm is prized. In corporate settings, expressions of confidence may be valued over expressions of humility—or vice versa. These norms disproportionately impact people who come from marginalized cultural groups, whose emotional expressions may be misread or pathologized by dominant frameworks.

These misreadings are not benign. They influence who is seen as competent, who is taken seriously, who is promoted, and who is penalized. For instance, research shows that Black women in professional settings are more likely to be labeled as angry or aggressive when displaying the same emotional tone as their white counterparts. This is not a matter of personality. It is a matter of cultural perception clashing with institutional norms. The cost of that clash is emotional labor—often invisible and unrecognized—that falls on the person expected to conform.

For individuals navigating multiple cultural contexts, this emotional labor can become chronic. Immigrants, third-culture kids, and people in diasporic communities often find themselves constantly shifting between emotional codes. This kind of code-switching is not merely linguistic; it is emotional. It involves recalibrating tone, affect, volume, and expression to match the unspoken rules of a given setting. Over time, this can lead to emotional exhaustion and a fragmented sense of self—not because the person lacks emotional intelligence, but because they are being forced to play by multiple, often contradictory, rulebooks.

Even within a single cultural context, subcultures and family systems create microclimates of emotional expression. One family may teach that love is shown through action, not words; another may prize verbal affirmation. One community may honor elders through deference and silence, another through storytelling and open debate. These variations are often so deep that individuals only recognize them when they leave home. The first time someone dates outside their culture, marries into a different family system, or moves to a new region, they may find that their emotional instincts are not shared—and that realization can be both disorienting and illuminating.

Cultural psychology helps us understand that emotional intelligence is not a universal skill set. It is contextual. What counts as emotionally intelligent in one culture may not translate in another. The goal, then, is not to enforce a single standard of emotional fluency but to increase cultural humility: the capacity to recognize one's own emotional blueprint as *a* framework, not *the* framework. This shift opens the door to more compassionate, flexible, and accurate interpersonal understanding.

The blueprint culture provides is neither destiny nor prison. But it is powerful. It tells us which emotions are safe, which are dangerous, and which are rewarded. It teaches us how to grieve, how to celebrate, and how to interpret silence. And perhaps most importantly, it tells us what kind of emotional life is considered acceptable in the first place.

Belonging, Shame, and the Cost of Deviance

To understand the emotional power of culture, we must begin with the basic human need to belong. Belonging is not a luxury—it is foundational to psychological development, identity formation, and survival. As social animals, humans are wired to seek inclusion in groups that provide security, validation, and meaning. Culture operates as the emotional scaffolding that signals whether we belong or are at risk of exclusion. And the chief emotional enforcer of that system is shame.

Shame is not just a personal feeling; it is a relational signal that arises when one has violated the norms or expectations of their community. It says: you are not who we expect you to be. Unlike guilt, which arises from a violation of one's internal moral compass, shame is interpersonal. It depends on imagined or real audiences and is deeply tied to our sense of visibility within social hierarchies. In every culture, shame is used—implicitly or explicitly—to maintain order and conformity.

The norms that produce shame are culturally defined. In some communities, speaking too loudly is considered disrespectful; in others, failing to assert yourself is seen as weak. In one family, a child who questions authority may be shamed for being disobedient; in another, that same behavior may be praised as independent thinking. The emotional logic behind these reactions is not random. It is structured by a shared cultural belief system that defines what kinds of people are acceptable, admirable, and lovable—and what kinds are not.

When we talk about "cultural fit" or "being raised right," we are invoking these implicit standards. People who align with dominant norms are afforded a sense of ease, credibility, and safety. Those who deviate—because of temperament, neurodivergence, sexuality, race, belief, or behavior—often pay a psychological price. That price is shame-induced self-surveillance: the chronic effort to police one's tone, affect, desires, or needs to avoid triggering disapproval or exile.

This self-surveillance is not a matter of vanity. It is a survival strategy. In group settings, whether families, schools, or societies, conformity often becomes a condition for affection, inclusion, or opportunity. Children quickly learn which parts of themselves must be hidden to remain in good standing. Adults often continue these patterns unconsciously, shaping their careers, relationships, and public identities around the pursuit of acceptance. The cost is not merely stress—it is internal division. People learn to dissociate from aspects of themselves that provoke cultural discomfort.

The cost of this division compounds over time. Repeated suppression of core aspects of self—gender identity, creative inclinations, emotional intensity, political dissent—can lead to numbness, confusion, or a haunting sense of inauthenticity. In clinical psychology, these patterns are often misread as pathology. But the root is often cultural: a person forced to contort themselves to survive in a system that does not affirm them. What looks like anxiety or depression may be the emotional residue of prolonged self-erasure.

This is especially relevant for those living within multiple, often conflicting, cultural systems. A child of immigrants may experience profound dissonance when the norms of their home life diverge from those of their school or broader society. An LGBTQ+ teenager raised in a religious community may feel irreconcilable shame for simply existing. A woman in a patriarchal society may internalize self-blame for asserting needs. These are not isolated personal struggles—they are collisions between personhood and inherited cultural codes.

Yet culture is not monolithic. Within every cultural context, there are subcultures of resistance, reinterpretation, and resilience. Artists, thinkers, caregivers, and community builders often create alternative emotional frameworks that allow people to belong without betraying themselves. These spaces—chosen families, queer communities, diaspora networks, religious reform movements—offer not only support but the possibility of emotional reintegration.

What allows people to break free from the grip of culturally induced shame is not simply defiance. It is the experience of being seen without judgment. Therapeutic spaces, open friendships, and liberatory education can offer what family or culture could not: an invitation to bring forward the exiled parts of the self. This kind of relational repair does more than heal the wound of shame. It rewrites the emotional contract. It says: you can belong as you are.

Understanding the relationship between belonging and shame also has implications for how we structure our institutions. Schools, workplaces, religious communities, and governments all serve as cultural transmitters. When they rely on shaming as a tool for control—explicitly or implicitly—they produce environments of fear and suppression. When they make space for complexity, contradiction, and growth, they become sites of psychological safety and integration.

To belong is to feel emotionally recognized within a shared framework. To deviate is to risk that recognition. The more rigid the framework, the higher the psychological cost of authenticity. But when cultural norms become more expansive—when they allow for multiple ways of being, feeling, and knowing—the need for shame diminishes. And in that space, people begin to belong not because they conform, but because they are human.

Cultural Scripts and the Construction of Meaning

Culture is not simply a container for norms; it is a machine for making meaning. Through its rituals, narratives, and language, every culture tells its members what life is about—what counts as success, what counts as failure, and what the arc of a good life should look like. These scripts are not decorative; they are foundational. They shape our identities, our expectations, and our emotional trajectories. They tell us who we are supposed to become.

These cultural scripts begin early, embedded in fairy tales, school assignments, religious teachings, and casual conversation. A child in an individualistic society may be taught to "follow their dreams" and "believe in themselves," while a child in a collectivist culture may be taught to "honor their elders" and "bring pride to the family." These messages are not mutually exclusive, but they prioritize different meanings. One script centers the self as the primary author of life. The other centers relationship, duty, and interdependence.

Psychologically, these scripts offer both structure and constraint. They help people orient themselves in time—toward milestones like marriage, education, parenthood, or retirement. They provide justification for sacrifice, meaning for suffering, and a sense of coherence in the face of chaos. But they also impose expectations that may not fit everyone. When an individual's internal rhythm does not match the cultural timeline, they may feel adrift, broken, or behind—even if nothing is actually wrong.

This discrepancy between personal experience and cultural narrative is a frequent source of emotional distress. A woman who does not want children may feel guilty or incomplete in a culture that equates motherhood with fulfillment. A man who finds success but not satisfaction may struggle to understand why he feels empty—especially if his culture equates achievement with happiness. These are not just personal crises; they are ruptures in the meaning-making process.

Cultural scripts also define the moral and emotional contours of identity. They teach people what kind of person they should be—kind, strong, humble, ambitious—and what kinds of stories they should tell about themselves. These internalized narratives form what psychologists call the "narrative self": the story we construct to explain who we are, where we've been, and where we're going. But because these stories are shaped by cultural templates, they can become cages.

For example, a culture that prizes resilience may teach people to hide their pain, creating an internal narrative of stoicism that obscures vulnerability. A culture that idolizes self-sufficiency may frame dependence as weakness, even when interdependence is a human necessity. Over time, people come to edit their autobiographies to fit the script—leaving out parts that don't align, reframing moments of confusion or failure, or overemphasizing culturally approved traits.

This editing process is not conscious. It happens through repetition, feedback, and social reinforcement. A young person who tells a story about wanting to travel the world may be praised for adventurousness—or criticized for irresponsibility—depending on their cultural context. The reaction shapes not only how the person feels but how they remember. In this way, culture does not just shape behavior; it shapes memory.

This dynamic has profound implications for identity development.

When cultural scripts are too narrow, they leave little room for complexity. A person who does not conform may feel fragmented or inauthentic, not because they lack coherence, but because the available narratives cannot hold their truth. This is especially true for people at the intersections of multiple cultural systems—immigrants, mixed-race individuals, queer people, or anyone who straddles dominant and marginalized identities. These individuals often become master translators, trying to reconcile incompatible scripts into a single life story.

But culture can also be a source of liberation. Counter-narratives—alternative scripts that challenge dominant meanings—offer people new ways to make sense of their experiences. Feminist, queer, anti-racist, and postcolonial frameworks have expanded the cultural imagination, allowing people to see themselves not as broken deviations from the norm, but as fully human in ways that were previously unrecognized. These frameworks do more than resist oppression; they offer new maps for being.

Psychologically, the most resilient individuals are often those who learn to revise the cultural script without discarding the need for meaning. They do not rebel simply to defy, nor do they conform simply to survive. Instead, they engage in a process of reauthoring: selectively borrowing, reshaping, and expanding the cultural narratives available to them. This is not an easy task. It requires both emotional courage and cognitive flexibility. But it is what allows people to live lives that feel authentic, rather than performative.

This is why cultural literacy is a form of psychological insight. To understand the emotional landscape of a person's life, one must understand the scripts they were given, the ones they resisted, and the ones they are still trying to write. Culture is not an external force to be analyzed; it is an internal force that lives in the very way people make sense of themselves.

Meaning is not simply discovered. It is constructed—within the frameworks culture provides. The challenge, and the possibility, is to recognize when those frameworks no longer serve, and to begin the quiet work of rewriting the story.

Cultural Evolution and Psychological Adaptation

Culture is not static. It evolves—through conflict, creativity, necessity, and exposure. As societies change, so do the emotional expectations they place on individuals. What was once shameful may become honorable. What was once invisible may become celebrated. From a psychological perspective, this fluidity is both a challenge and an opportunity: it destabilizes the emotional scripts people rely on, but it also creates space for new ways of being.

The acceleration of cultural change in the modern world has intensified this dynamic. Globalization, digital communication, migration, and social movements have made it increasingly difficult to inhabit a single, stable cultural identity. People are exposed to more ways of living, more value systems, and more emotional grammars than ever before. While this can foster empathy and flexibility, it can also lead to identity diffusion—especially when individuals lack the support to integrate conflicting cultural inputs.

Younger generations, in particular, often find themselves caught between inherited norms and emergent values. A teenager raised in a conservative household may encounter progressive ideals through social media; an immigrant child may be praised for cultural assimilation in school while being criticized for it at home. These tensions are not theoretical—they are felt in the body as anxiety, guilt, confusion, or alienation. Cultural evolution is experienced as personal dissonance.

Psychological adaptation to these shifts requires more than information. It requires tools for emotional regulation, narrative integration, and social connection. Without these tools, individuals may respond to cultural instability with either rigid retrenchment or disoriented disengagement. In clinical terms, this often presents as high levels of stress, internal conflict, or identity confusion. In social terms, it can manifest as polarization: the hardening of belief systems as a defense against ambiguity.

But culture does not evolve evenly. It fractures, mutates, and reforms along lines of power, privilege, and resistance. The norms that govern emotional expression in one region or community may be undergoing radical change, while others remain bound to older paradigms. This unevenness creates emotional gaps between generations, between institutions and individuals, between private experience and public discourse. These gaps are where psychological strain often emerges.

At the same time, these fractures are also the site of growth. Cultural ruptures—moments when dominant narratives break down—create openings for new emotional vocabularies. The rise of mental health awareness, for instance, reflects not only a shift in values but a shift in cultural permission: people are now allowed, even encouraged, to name and explore feelings that once had no legitimate place in public life. This is not simply therapeutic—it is revolutionary. It changes who gets to be seen, heard, and validated.

Cultural adaptation is not about abandoning the past. It is about learning to hold multiple truths. A person can honor their ancestors while questioning inherited norms. They can cherish tradition while experimenting with change. They can feel gratitude for the cultural frameworks that shaped them and still feel the need to outgrow them. Psychological maturity, in this context, means developing the capacity to differentiate— to separate one's emotional life from rigid scripts without losing the grounding that culture can provide.

This maturity also requires a form of cultural humility: recognizing that one's emotional norms are not universal, and that unfamiliar ways of being are not necessarily inferior. This attitude shifts the goal of emotional intelligence from mastery to openness. It makes curiosity more valuable than certainty. In an interconnected world, where cultural boundaries are increasingly porous, this shift is not optional—it is essential.

For therapists, educators, leaders, and caregivers, understanding the psychological impact of cultural evolution is non-negotiable. It requires us to ask: What stories are people inheriting? What emotional codes are they trying to live up to? What meanings are they being asked to carry—and which ones are they trying to rewrite? Without these questions, we risk offering solutions that ignore the problem's root. We misread pain as pathology when it is often the residue of cultural misalignment.

Ultimately, culture will continue to change—sometimes faster than the psyche can comfortably manage. But embedded in every cultural transformation is the possibility of greater integration. When we name the emotional labor of adaptation, when we legitimize the disorientation of cultural transition, and when we build frameworks that support complexity rather than suppress it, we offer people something rare: the freedom to feel fully human in the midst of change.

That is the gift of evolving culture—not the replacement of one script with another, but the expansion of emotional possibility. It is not easy. But it is how we move, individually and collectively, toward something more whole.

* * *

32

Digital Life and the Fragmented Self

Technology, identity, attention, and performative psychology
The internet was never just a tool. From the very beginning, it was a new kind of space—a psychological habitat that changed not only how we connect, but how we construct ourselves. What began as a medium for sharing information quickly became a mirror, a stage, and a marketplace. And in the decades since, we've built lives within it. Not around it, but inside it. This chapter is about what that does to the self.

In psychological terms, the self is not a static entity. It is a process—an ongoing integration of memory, awareness, behavior, and social feedback. The digital world disrupts this process at every turn. It fragments time, multiplies identities, distorts feedback, and accelerates emotional response. And while it offers unprecedented opportunities for connection and self-expression, it also introduces structural challenges to psychological coherence. The very conditions of digital life—interruption, surveillance, quantification—make it harder to feel whole.

We are now living in what some have called an "interface culture," where much of our attention is spent not on the world itself, but on representations of it. We scroll through images of people we used to know. We track our thoughts in character limits. We perform affection, outrage, joy, and grief in front of invisible audiences. And whether or not we intend to, we absorb the logic of these platforms. We begin to see our lives not just as experiences, but as content.

This shift has profound consequences. It affects how we remember, how we feel, how we relate to others, and how we see ourselves. The feedback loops created by likes, shares, and views train us to optimize for performance rather than presence. The constant availability of stimulation erodes boredom, imagination, and introspection. The hunger for visibility creates new forms of emotional labor, where identity is curated, marketed, and defended in public. In this environment, the self becomes not just expressed—but manufactured.

The fragmentation of the self in digital life is not a failure of character. It is a predictable outcome of the systems we've built. In a world of constant surveillance, it becomes adaptive to monitor oneself. In a world of information overload, it becomes necessary to divide attention. In a world of public metrics, it becomes tempting to chase approval rather than meaning. These behaviors are not weaknesses—they are survival strategies in a landscape designed for extraction, not reflection.

But this fragmentation comes at a cost. Many people report feeling scattered, empty, or emotionally overexposed. They struggle to distinguish between genuine connection and digital proximity. They experience themselves as known, but not seen. And they feel a growing distance between their inner life and the version of themselves that appears online. This is not mere nostalgia for a pre-digital world. It is a psychological reckoning with what it means to be a self in an environment that pulls us in pieces.

This chapter explores the core psychological dynamics of digital life: identity construction, attention economy, emotional performance, and the struggle for integration. It does not argue for digital abstinence or romanticize the analog past. Rather, it aims to name the invisible forces shaping our minds and offer a deeper understanding of how digital systems affect emotional development, relational depth, and narrative continuity.

Because while the internet may be a relatively new phenomenon, the questions it raises are ancient: Who am I, when no one is watching? What does it mean to be real? And how do I stay whole in a world that wants me split?

Identity in the Age of the Interface

Before the digital era, the self evolved primarily through face-to-face relationships, localized social roles, and relatively slow-moving feedback loops. Identity, while never fixed, had the advantage of continuity: people knew you across time, across contexts, and across the full range of your emotional life. There was room for contradiction. There was privacy. And there was the quiet dignity of growing without an audience.

The digital world changed that. It introduced a mirror that never turns away, a spotlight that never dims. In this environment, identity becomes visible, searchable, and performative. People don't just have selves—they manage them, brand them, and curate them. Social media platforms encourage a form of identity construction that is fundamentally different from previous models. It is not relational in the traditional sense. It is transactional, image-based, and governed by algorithms designed to reward consistency, novelty, and emotional intensity.

Psychologically, this creates a double consciousness: the internal sense of who I am, and the external sense of how I am perceived. This duality has always existed, but the digital environment intensifies it. The self becomes something to be shaped in anticipation of an audience. And because the audience is both invisible and omnipresent, the pressure to conform, entertain, or please becomes ambient—always there, even when the phone is off.

This affects not only what people share but how they feel. Studies have shown that even passive social media use—scrolling without posting—can alter self-esteem, increase social comparison, and distort perception of reality. People compare their messy emotional insides to the polished surfaces of others' digital lives. They absorb highlight reels as norms and interpret their own struggles as failures. This isn't a matter of vanity. It's a matter of narrative: the story people tell themselves about who they are and whether they're doing life "right."

For younger generations, who have grown up entirely in the presence of digital mirrors, identity formation takes place in public from the start. Adolescence—a developmental period already marked by experimentation and self-doubt—becomes even more fraught when every exploratory step can be captured, judged, or permanently archived. Mistakes lose their ephemerality. Play loses its safety. And self-expression becomes high-stakes performance.

This dynamic extends to adults as well. Many people feel compelled to maintain a consistent digital persona—whether as the thoughtful professional, the doting parent, the activist, the traveler, or the wellness enthusiast. Over time, this persona can become burdensome. It limits emotional expression, discourages change, and turns identity into obligation. The curated self must be fed, updated, and defended. And the more attention it receives, the harder it becomes to let it go.

There is also a psychological cost to managing multiple selves across platforms. The version of you on LinkedIn may not match the one on Instagram. The persona on TikTok may contradict the one your extended family sees on Facebook. This compartmentalization, while sometimes necessary, fragments the self and complicates integration. It becomes harder to answer the question: who am I, really?

This is not to say that digital identity is inherently false. Many people find authenticity and connection online that they cannot access offline. Queer youth, neurodivergent individuals, or people living in stigmatizing environments often use digital spaces to explore identities they cannot safely express elsewhere. In this sense, the internet can be liberating—a space to become. But even in these cases, the same forces of surveillance and commodification apply. Visibility can be empowering, but it can also become a trap.

The key psychological question is not whether digital identity is good or bad. It is whether it allows for wholeness. Does the platform reward emotional complexity or punish it? Does it permit change, or does it demand consistency? Does it reflect the fullness of the person, or does it flatten them into a brand? These are not theoretical questions—they are existential ones. They determine whether a person feels like a self or a simulation.

In clinical terms, we are beginning to see the emotional fallout of this split. Clients describe feeling hollow, overexposed, disconnected from themselves. They speak of "imposter syndrome" not just at work but in their friendships, their relationships, their daily lives. They fear that the version of them the world sees is not real—but they don't know how to return to something that feels more grounded. The performance has become the person.

And yet, even in this environment, people long for authenticity—not in the social media sense of being "raw," but in the psychological sense of being integrated. They want to feel whole. They want to live lives that are not staged. They want relationships that exist outside the logic of visibility. And they want to be known—not followed.

The path to that kind of integrity is not about abandoning digital life. It is about becoming conscious of the forces shaping identity and reclaiming authorship. It is about building an internal self strong enough to withstand the algorithms and an external life rich enough to make the digital one optional.

The Economics of Attention and the Collapse of Presence

If identity is shaped by how we are seen, then attention is the currency that determines what is seen at all. In the digital age, attention is not just a resource—it is a commodity. It is bought, sold, manipulated, and measured. Every platform we interact with is engineered to capture and hold attention, because attention translates directly into data, influence, and profit. But what gets harvested in this process is not only time. It is presence. And over time, the psychological cost of this extraction becomes impossible to ignore.

The human brain was not designed to process endless streams of novelty. It evolved to focus narrowly and deeply—on a face, a voice, a task, a danger. In that environment, attention was a survival mechanism: a way to prioritize what mattered. In contrast, digital platforms are designed to disrupt focus as often as possible. They use alerts, notifications, autoplay, infinite scroll, and algorithmic sorting to keep users in a state of partial attention. The result is a cognitive environment where depth is penalized and fragmentation is the norm.

This has a profound impact on the psyche. Sustained attention is not just about productivity—it is a prerequisite for reflection, empathy, and meaning-making. When attention is constantly redirected, the mind struggles to form coherent narratives. Memory suffers. Emotional processing is delayed. And the sense of inner continuity—the feeling that I am the same person across time—begins to erode. This is not a metaphor. It is a measurable neurological shift.

Psychologically, the collapse of presence shows up in several ways. People report feeling scattered, restless, and chronically distracted. They struggle to stay with a book, a thought, or even a conversation. The mind feels full but undernourished—fed by a constant diet of information but starved for insight. Many describe a sense of numbness or detachment, as if life is happening just beyond their reach. This is not because they lack willpower. It is because they are living inside systems that monetize their inattention.

One of the most damaging consequences of this economy is that it trains people to expect stimulation at all times. Boredom, once a fertile ground for creativity and introspection, becomes intolerable. Silence feels threatening. Stillness feels unnatural. The very conditions that foster psychological integration—solitude, slowness, absorption—are now experienced as friction. And so people reach for their phones—not out of desire, but out of a kind of ambient desperation. To avoid falling into themselves.

The collapse of presence also affects relationships. Attention is the foundation of intimacy. To be present with another person—to really listen, to absorb their emotional state, to respond with attunement—is one of the deepest forms of love. But in a distracted mind, this kind of presence becomes harder to offer. Conversations are punctuated by glances at screens. Moments of connection are interrupted by notifications. Emotional resonance is flattened into emojis or delayed responses. And even when people are physically together, they may not feel emotionally seen.

In clinical work, this often presents as relational dissatisfaction, loneliness, or a vague sense of disconnection that is hard to name. Couples report feeling less emotionally close, even when spending more time together. Parents worry about competing with screens for their children's attention. Friends drift apart not because of conflict, but because sustained engagement feels harder and harder to maintain. These are not small issues. They strike at the heart of what it means to be human with one another.

The attention economy also distorts emotional salience. Platforms prioritize content that is provocative, controversial, or emotionally extreme—not because it is meaningful, but because it drives engagement. This creates a psychological landscape where outrage is amplified, nuance is punished, and subtlety is lost. People become desensitized to ordinary emotion and hypersensitized to emotional spectacle. As a result, the range of emotional experience that feels "valid" becomes narrower, louder, and more performative.

In response to all this, some advocate for digital detoxes or minimalist tech practices. These can be helpful, but they don't address the underlying structure. The real issue is not that people use technology too much—it's that the design of technology undermines the psychological conditions for presence, coherence, and care. To reclaim attention is not just an act of self-care. It is an act of resistance against systems that profit from fragmentation.

Rebuilding presence requires more than unplugging. It requires reorienting. It asks us to remember what it feels like to be absorbed in a task, to listen without distraction, to move through the world with our whole minds. It calls for new forms of digital literacy—ones that include not just technical skill, but emotional discernment. And it challenges us to build lives where attention is given, not stolen.

Because in the end, attention is not just about focus. It is about what we love. What we attend to becomes our world. And if we want to feel whole, if we want to be present for our lives and for each other, then we must reclaim the right to direct our attention where it matters—not where it's monetized.

Performative Psychology and the Illusion of Intimacy

We live in an age where emotional expression is no longer just personal—it is public. Anger is posted. Grief is live-streamed. Vulnerability is shared with hashtags and filters. The rise of digital platforms has ushered in a new era of emotional visibility, where feelings are not only felt but performed. And in the process, something subtle but profound has happened: emotional authenticity has been conflated with emotional performance. The result is a kind of intimacy that looks real but often leaves us lonelier than before.

At the center of this shift is the promise of connection. Platforms invite users to "share what's on your mind," to be "authentic," to let others in. And many people do so with genuine intent. They share their struggles, their joys, their losses. They hope to be met with empathy, to find resonance, to feel less alone. But the infrastructure through which these emotions are shared is not neutral. It transforms expression into content and reception into metrics.

This changes how people express emotion. Instead of being spontaneous or relational, emotions are increasingly filtered through the question: how will this be perceived? What version of this pain is acceptable? What kind of response will it generate? Over time, even sincere emotions begin to bend toward the logic of performance—edited, framed, and often exaggerated to meet the expectations of a digital audience. It's not always cynical. But it is shaped by the medium.

The psychological consequence of this is what might be called the illusion of intimacy. A person shares something raw, and others respond—often with compassion, encouragement, or praise. The exchange feels emotionally charged. But it is also transient, detached from sustained presence, and subject to the rhythm of the feed. The person may feel momentarily seen, but not necessarily known. Their vulnerability may be acknowledged, but not held. And the connection, though warm, is often ephemeral.

This dynamic can create a feedback loop that's hard to break. People receive positive reinforcement for emotional openness—so they share more. But they also feel pressure to maintain a certain emotional tone, to keep producing content that resonates. And when real emotions deviate from that tone—when they are messy, ambiguous, or unresolved—they may be withheld. Vulnerability, once commodified, becomes curated. The inner life is shaped not by depth, but by digestibility.

Social media also flattens the emotional landscape. It encourages a narrow range of high-intensity expressions—rage, joy, heartbreak, triumph—while discouraging subtler, more ambiguous states. As a result, emotional nuance is lost. People begin to question whether their feelings are "valid" if they don't match the dominant narratives. They worry that their pain is too boring, their healing too slow, their truth too inconvenient. And so they shape their emotional stories to fit the mold, leaving out the parts that don't resonate.

This has consequences not just for individual psychology, but for collective emotional culture. Performative vulnerability can create a false sense of intimacy across a community. People feel emotionally connected to influencers, thought leaders, or even acquaintances based on what they share. But without reciprocal knowledge, without real relational context, these connections are shallow. They simulate intimacy without delivering its substance. And they can leave people feeling more isolated than before—surrounded by emotional noise, but starved for emotional depth.

The illusion of intimacy is particularly dangerous because it is self-reinforcing. It satisfies the longing for connection just enough to prevent people from seeking the real thing. It offers a dopamine hit without the emotional nourishment. And it conditions people to express emotion in ways that are increasingly stylized, reactive, and public. The more one's inner life becomes fodder for public response, the harder it becomes to feel ownership over it.

This is not to suggest that sharing emotions online is inherently bad. For many, it is a lifeline—a way to break silence, to find community, to name what was once unspeakable. But the question is not just whether sharing is helpful. It is whether it supports integration. Does it help the person feel more whole, more grounded, more connected in their real lives? Or does it leave them more dependent on the affirmation of strangers, more anxious about their own truth?

True intimacy—psychologically speaking—is not exposure. It is mutual knowing. It requires time, trust, and the slow unfolding of shared experience. It cannot be rushed, quantified, or manufactured. And it is rarely found in spaces designed to amplify performance over presence.

To reclaim emotional authenticity in a digital age means becoming conscious of the forces that shape how we express and relate. It means distinguishing between connection and contact, between resonance and reaction. And it means protecting parts of the self from the logic of display—not out of shame, but out of reverence. Some emotions are not for show. Some truths do not need an audience. And some parts of us are only safe in the quiet.

Integration in a World That Splits

The greatest psychological challenge of digital life may not be distraction, comparison, or overexposure—though all are real. It is fragmentation. The repeated splitting of attention, identity, memory, and emotion leaves many people feeling internally scattered, unsure of what parts of themselves are real, durable, or even theirs. In this final section, we examine what it means to reclaim psychological wholeness in a world that encourages constant division.

To be human is to carry contradiction. But the digital world punishes contradiction. Algorithms reward consistency, platforms demand clarity, and audiences expect you to pick a lane. A person is either this or that—never both. And so people edit. They hide the parts of themselves that don't fit the persona. They suppress complexity. They live in pieces. Over time, this becomes not just a strategic choice, but a psychological state: a self divided.

Integration is the process of undoing that division. It is the ongoing practice of acknowledging, honoring, and reconciling all parts of the self—the bright and the shameful, the public and the private, the polished and the painful. It is not about creating a consistent performance, but a coherent internal world. And in a culture that trains us to fragment, integration becomes an act of resistance.

One of the first steps toward integration is reclaiming internal authority. In digital life, people are constantly exposed to external evaluations: likes, comments, views, shares. These become proxies for worth. But over time, they corrode internal self-assessment. People begin to doubt their own judgment. They look outward to know how they feel. Integration requires reversing that current. It demands that we rebuild the capacity to know ourselves from the inside out—not the outside in.

Another key component is time. The digital world moves fast, but the psyche does not. Real integration requires slowness. It asks for unstructured time, for periods of silence, for the discomfort of unedited thought. These conditions are increasingly rare. They are not built into our tools or rewarded by our culture. They must be created deliberately—protected not as luxuries, but as necessities. Because without time to reflect, we cannot metabolize experience. And without reflection, the self remains unintegrated: a collection of inputs without cohesion.

Integration also depends on memory. Digital life encourages a kind of perpetual now, where everything scrolls, refreshes, and disappears. But memory—personal memory—is the connective tissue of identity. It provides continuity. It links who we were with who we are and who we might become. In a fragmented world, people must actively preserve memory. This might mean journaling, storytelling, or simply creating space to revisit and re-interpret the past. Because the past does not disappear. It waits to be made sense of.

Relationally, integration requires spaces where people can be fully themselves. Not just performatively "authentic," but genuinely whole. This kind of relationship is not built on constant exposure, but on mutual safety. It does not demand that people share everything, only that they can share anything. These spaces—often offline, often private—are where the divided self begins to relax. They are where complexity becomes bearable. And they are essential for healing.

Psychologically, the work of integration is often slow, subtle, and deeply personal. It is not about building a better persona or quitting social media. It is about becoming more honest internally. Noticing when a reaction isn't yours. Catching the impulse to perform and choosing not to. Naming a contradiction and holding it, without needing to resolve it. These are quiet acts. But over time, they restore a sense of being real.

The goal is not perfection. It is coherence. A life where your digital presence doesn't betray your inner experience. A life where you remember who you are, even when you're not being watched. A life where your attention, identity, and emotion belong to you again—not to the systems that try to fragment them.

In the end, wholeness is not found by logging off. It is found by logging in—to the deeper rhythms of your own mind, to the relationships that hold you, and to the stories that remind you what it means to be fully, humanly, you.

* * *

33

Emotional Culture and Collective Behavior

Emotions do not stay put. They move. They pass from person to person, often faster than words. They shape crowds, identities, and decisions. At the individual level, emotions can feel deeply personal. But when we zoom out, we see that many of our feelings are shaped by what others are feeling—what they expect us to feel, what they allow, and what they punish. This chapter explores the psychology of emotional life as a collective phenomenon, not just a private one.

We live inside emotional cultures. Every family, workplace, religious group, political movement, and nation-state has an emotional code. Some prioritize calm and restraint; others value intensity and moral urgency. Some reward emotional suppression; others encourage constant outward expression. Over time, we absorb these norms until they begin to feel like natural extensions of who we are. But they are not always ours. They are learned. And they are enforced—sometimes gently, sometimes coercively.

The dynamics of collective emotion are subtle, but powerful. Emotional contagion helps us survive as social creatures, creating alignment, empathy, and shared momentum. But that same mechanism also makes us vulnerable to manipulation, coercion, and polarization. In groups, emotions can escalate quickly, often without conscious awareness. Anger spreads. Fear multiplies. Moral outrage becomes addictive. And in environments where public expression is tightly policed—by culture, algorithm, or authority—entire emotional realities can be erased or distorted.

This chapter looks at how collective emotional dynamics shape our behavior and beliefs, often beneath our awareness. It examines the invisible rules that govern what we're allowed to feel and how we must show it. It explores how political and ideological identities are fused with emotional allegiance. And it asks what psychological integrity might look like in a world where emotional pressure is constant.

To understand human behavior in any era—including our own—we must understand not only what people think, but what they're feeling together. Emotional culture is not just a background condition. It is the operating system of collective life.

Emotional Contagion and the Amplification of Feeling

Humans are biologically wired to feel with others. This capacity for shared emotional experience is not simply a function of empathy; it's a deeply rooted survival mechanism. In early evolutionary terms, attuning to the emotional states of those around us increased our chances of avoiding danger, coordinating behavior, and maintaining social cohesion. What we now call "emotional contagion" is a core feature of group life—and a powerful, if often invisible, force shaping collective behavior.

At its most basic level, emotional contagion refers to the process by which people unconsciously absorb and mirror the emotions of others. We smile when others smile. We feel tension rise when a room goes quiet. We catch the energy of a crowd even before we've interpreted the reasons for its mood. This is more than mimicry. It involves a synchronization of neural circuits, body language, vocal tone, and even heart rate. The brain's mirror neuron system plays a role in this process, as do limbic structures involved in fear and reward.

But this contagion doesn't just passively transmit emotion; it often amplifies it. In groups, emotional states can escalate far more rapidly than in individuals. A spark of anxiety becomes panic. A flicker of anger turns to rage. Joy becomes euphoria. The more people mirror and reinforce an emotional signal, the more intense it becomes. This amplification is self-reinforcing—and in large groups, it can override individual reasoning, restraint, or moral hesitation.

We see this dynamic in countless settings: the slow-building tension at a protest that suddenly erupts into violence; the waves of euphoria at a concert that sweep through a crowd; the moral outrage that spreads across a digital feed within minutes. Often, the strength of these reactions is not proportional to the facts at hand—it is a function of how many people are feeling, and how visibly they are expressing those feelings.

The same mechanism operates in subtler contexts as well. In a workplace, a single person's mood can influence the emotional tone of an entire meeting. In a family system, unspoken anxiety can dominate the atmosphere. Emotional contagion is especially potent in hierarchies, where people are more attuned to the emotional cues of those with power. Leaders, whether consciously or not, shape group affect through their tone, posture, and expression. When they are reactive, guarded, or punitive, others become dysregulated too.

In the digital age, emotional contagion is no longer limited to physical proximity. Social media platforms act as emotional amplifiers, broadcasting feelings to wide audiences and rewarding high-intensity emotional content with visibility. Studies have shown that content expressing outrage, disgust, or moral certainty is more likely to be shared and engaged with. These dynamics incentivize emotional escalation, turning public discourse into a cycle of provocation and reaction. Even when we're not aware of it, our emotional states are being influenced by what we scroll past—and what gets repeated most.

What's more, digital contagion is often stripped of contextual cues. In face-to-face settings, we interpret emotion through a rich array of signals: facial nuance, body posture, pauses, physical environment. Online, these cues are flattened. A tweet of anger appears next to a meme, which appears next to a tragedy, which appears next to a product ad. The nervous system absorbs the intensity but loses the grounding context, creating emotional confusion or numbness.

The result is a culture in which emotions move faster than thought. And while this has always been true to some extent—emotion precedes cognition neurologically—it is now built into the architecture of public life. People are pushed to react quickly, passionately, and publicly. There is little space for silence, doubt, or complexity. Emotional contagion becomes not just an occasional phenomenon, but a way of life.

This has significant psychological consequences. People report feeling emotionally exhausted, yet unable to disconnect. They find themselves swept up in feelings they didn't choose. They become reactive in ways that surprise them. And over time, they may lose track of which emotions are theirs and which have been absorbed from the environment. This erosion of emotional autonomy is not a personal failing. It is a predictable outcome of life in a high-contagion culture.

The challenge, then, is not to shut down emotionally, but to become more emotionally discerning. To ask: Where did this feeling come from? Is it grounded in my values, my experience, or my context? Or is it the residue of someone else's signal? Emotional maturity in a collective context means being able to feel with others without losing oneself. It means recognizing when the emotional climate is shaping your state—and deciding, consciously, whether to go along with it.

That kind of discernment is essential for psychological sovereignty in a world that trades in affect. Because until we understand how emotion moves through groups, we are at its mercy—carried by waves we cannot see, and reacting to currents we do not recognize.

Polarization as an Emotional Process

When people think about polarization, they usually frame it in terms of ideology: conflicting worldviews, incompatible values, or competing facts. But beneath those intellectual differences lies something more primal—emotion. Political and cultural polarization is as much about how people feel as what they believe. And if we want to understand why societies fracture, why dialogue breaks down, and why contempt becomes a social currency, we must explore polarization as an emotional phenomenon.

At its core, polarization is about the creation and maintenance of in-groups and out-groups. This isn't a modern development. Human beings have always formed tribes, and those tribes have always had emotional functions. They create safety, coherence, and belonging. They help people regulate uncertainty and manage fear. They provide a sense of moral clarity—who we are, what we stand for, and who we're against.

But in a polarized culture, the emotional stakes are heightened. The identity of the group becomes fused with emotion: pride, anger, moral outrage, fear of annihilation. Disagreement is no longer just about policy or principle. It feels like threat. And this is not metaphorical. Neurologically, the brain responds to social threat—such as exclusion, ridicule, or status loss—with the same regions that process physical pain. When identity is fused with belief, disagreement becomes destabilizing, even unbearable.

This dynamic is worsened by the way public discourse is structured. Media, both traditional and social, thrive on emotional arousal. Anger and fear generate clicks, comments, and shares. Algorithms are tuned not for accuracy or nuance, but for engagement. And engagement is driven by emotional intensity. The result is a steady stream of emotionally charged content that reinforces existing divisions and inflames antagonism.

The psychological toll is cumulative. People begin to interpret others not as individuals, but as avatars of an opposing tribe. Empathy contracts. Curiosity diminishes. The out-group is not just wrong;

they are dangerous, immoral, stupid, or evil. In this climate, people feel constantly under attack—emotionally, morally, existentially. They respond by retreating into ideological silos, where emotions are validated and mirrored. These silos offer comfort, but also deepen division.

This is how polarization sustains itself: emotionally and socially. It becomes risky to show ambivalence, uncertainty, or complexity, even to one's own group. Nuance is punished. Dissent is treated as betrayal. The emotional climate of polarization requires not just agreement, but performance—performative loyalty, performative outrage, performative certainty. And because these emotions are contagious, group norms harden quickly. Deviating from them can mean emotional exile.

These patterns show up not only in politics, but in social movements, religious communities, and even families. They are reinforced through repetition, memory, and collective ritual. And while the content of polarization changes over time, the emotional architecture remains stable. It always involves a division of the world into "us" and "them," with moral and emotional stakes attached.

So how do people escape it—or at least resist its pull?

The answer is not to abandon conviction or strive for false equivalence. It is to develop emotional awareness and regulation in the face of difference. This begins with recognizing when emotional fusion has occurred—when your identity has become inseparable from a belief. It involves noticing the physical and emotional signs of threat response: tension, defensiveness, reactivity. And it requires the capacity to tolerate ambiguity—to stay in emotional discomfort without rushing to certainty.

Psychologically, this kind of tolerance is not a matter of intelligence or neutrality. It is a function of maturity. It depends on one's ability to distinguish between disagreement and danger, between critique and erasure. In polarized environments, people often lose this ability. Everything feels personal. Every encounter becomes a test of belonging.

The more emotionally secure someone is, the more able they are to engage across difference. This does not mean abandoning their principles. It means they don't need to be constantly emotionally reinforced to feel real. They can hear complexity without collapsing. They can allow space without feeling erased.

Ultimately, the solution to polarization is not only structural or informational. It is emotional. People need tools for managing fear, regulating anger, and recovering from shame. They need spaces where emotional honesty does not require ideological purity. And they need to relearn how to see others not just as positions, but as people—flawed, feeling, and often just as afraid as they are.

Without this emotional work, polarization will not break. Because it was never just about facts. It was about feelings—unspoken, unregulated, and constantly reinforced by systems that benefit from keeping us divided.

The Performance of Public Feeling

In every society, there are rules—spoken or not—about which emotions are appropriate, when, and for whom. These rules shape our emotional expression long before we're aware of them. They begin in childhood, are reinforced through media, school, religion, and peer groups, and eventually get codified into public behavior. Over time, they become so internalized that we mistake them for authenticity. But much of what we call genuine emotional expression is, in fact, performance: a performance shaped by culture, expectation, and power.

Public emotion has always had a theatrical element. In grief rituals, courtroom apologies, political rallies, and even weddings, there are expected emotional cues. A tear at the right moment. A calm demeanor in crisis. A well-timed laugh. These aren't insincere; they are socially legible ways of signaling feeling. But in today's emotionally saturated media environment, this performance has reached new heights—because it is now constant, broadcast, and subject to feedback.

Online platforms turn emotion into content. They reward expression that is extreme, visually legible, and quickly understood. Sadness must be dramatic. Joy must be radiant. Anger must be righteous. The most visible feelings become the most socially affirmed. And as people learn which emotions "work" in a public setting—garnering likes, support, or attention—they often begin to prioritize performability over honesty.

This is not always cynical. It can be unconscious. People learn to display the emotions that are safest in their culture or subculture. In some communities, vulnerability is rewarded. In others, stoicism is prized. In some, anger is a sign of strength. In others, it signals disrespect. These emotional norms are deeply embedded. They influence how people move through the world, what they feel permitted to show, and how others interpret their behavior.

For example, women are often culturally sanctioned for displaying anger, especially in public. They may be labeled "hysterical," "unhinged," or "too emotional"—labels that undermine credibility. Conversely, men are often culturally prohibited from expressing sadness or vulnerability, leading to emotional suppression and, in some cases, explosive compensatory behavior. These patterns aren't rooted in biology; they are products of emotional culture, enforced by subtle and overt forms of social control.

In racialized and marginalized communities, emotional performance can carry survival implications. A Black person might consciously modulate their emotional tone in public spaces to avoid being perceived as threatening. An immigrant might downplay distress to appear grateful or agreeable. A queer person might exaggerate certain affective expressions to signal safety or belonging. These are not simply choices—they are adaptations to an emotional economy that is shaped by structural inequities.

In institutional contexts, emotional performance is often expected without acknowledgment. Workers in service industries are required to perform friendliness, patience, and composure—often in the face of mistreatment. Teachers, nurses, and therapists are expected to remain calm and steady, regardless of internal distress. These performances, while often necessary, can be emotionally exhausting. When sustained over time without reprieve, they contribute to burnout, depersonalization, and emotional disconnection.

Psychologically, there is a cost to all of this. When emotion becomes a performance, people can lose access to their inner truth. They begin to doubt their real feelings. They second-guess their reactions. They ask: Am I feeling this, or am I supposed to be? They develop what some psychologists call "emotional dissonance"—a conflict between internal experience and outward expression. Over time, this can lead to numbness, confusion, and a deep sense of inauthenticity.

But the answer is not to simply "be real" at all times. Emotional authenticity is important, but so is emotional regulation, timing, and social awareness. The challenge is to reclaim a sense of emotional integrity within the boundaries of social life. This means knowing what you feel even when you can't express it fully. It means recognizing the difference between a genuine impulse and a trained reaction. It means finding spaces—interpersonal or private—where full emotional range is allowed, even if not always performed.

Ultimately, the public performance of feeling is not inherently false. It becomes damaging only when it replaces emotional reflection or silences emotional truth. In a culture that increasingly confuses expression with authenticity, the deeper psychological task is to stay connected to what we feel, even when we cannot show it. Emotional maturity means being able to perform when necessary without losing oneself in the performance.

Because what matters most isn't whether others see our emotions. It's whether we know what we're feeling, why we're feeling it, and whether our emotional life is still our own.

Fragmented Empathy and the Struggle for Emotional Integrity

In a world dominated by emotional spectacle and collective reaction, one of the greatest psychological challenges is preserving emotional integrity. This doesn't mean simply refusing to participate in collective feeling; we are social creatures, and some degree of alignment with others is inevitable. Emotional integrity means knowing when a feeling is truly yours, when it's been absorbed from the surrounding emotional climate, and when it's being subtly demanded of you by the system you're in. It means resisting the erosion of self-awareness in the face of collective pressure.

This is not an abstract ideal. It's a skill—one that's increasingly difficult to cultivate in today's emotional landscape. Many people live with a constant low-level unease, unable to articulate why they feel off. They may find themselves emotionally reactive without knowing the source. Or they may feel emotionally flat, detached, and numb, unable to access authentic emotion because their expressive system has been so conditioned by external demands. Both responses reflect a common outcome of living in emotionally coercive environments: fragmentation.

Fragmentation happens when your internal emotional signals get scrambled by external noise. When you're praised for emotions you don't feel, and punished for ones you do. When the loudest emotions in the public square become the template for your inner world. Over time, you learn to override your own instincts. You second-guess yourself. You outsource your emotional authority to the collective. And because you're still feeling things—only not coherently—the emotional life becomes disorganized, contradictory, or inaccessible.

Digital life exacerbates this fragmentation. Social media platforms demand continuous affective output, often under conditions of surveillance and judgment. Emotional boundaries dissolve when content is always visible, when reactions are always tracked, and when the algorithm rewards intensity. This creates a looping system: the more others perform certain emotions, the more they are validated; the more they are validated, the more others mimic them. Before long, a person's sense of what they *should* feel replaces any honest inquiry into what they *do* feel.

Reclaiming emotional integrity requires a deliberate slowing down. It requires space—internal and external—for noticing, questioning, and recalibrating. This might look like pausing before reacting. Asking where an emotion came from. Remembering that not every feeling that moves through you belongs to you. It means building a practice of inner observation without judgment: What am I feeling? Is this mine? What does it want me to know?

That last question—what does this emotion want me to know—is foundational. Because emotions are information. They are not always right, but they are always meaningful. And in an environment that constantly tries to shape or suppress emotional information, the ability to listen inward becomes an act of psychological resistance.

This doesn't mean disengaging from collective life. Quite the opposite. True empathy, ethical engagement, and emotional courage require people who are emotionally grounded. People who can feel with others without becoming hijacked. Who can hold moral clarity without moral superiority. Who can show up in the world not with performative outrage or hollow reassurance, but with the full weight of emotional maturity: presence, discernment, and a capacity to tolerate emotional complexity.

Collective emotional health depends on individuals doing this work. Because cultures do not change through sentiment alone. They change when enough people begin to reclaim authorship of their inner lives—and refuse to let their emotional reality be dictated by spectacle, algorithms, or inherited scripts.

To be emotionally sovereign in a fragmented culture is not to feel less. It is to feel more clearly. To feel with intention. And to create conditions, in oneself and others, where emotional truth can emerge, even when it does not conform.

That is the work of integration. And it is not only personal. It is political, cultural, and moral. Because the integrity of a society depends, in part, on the emotional integrity of the people who make it.

* * *

34

Power, Privilege, and Psychological Safety

It is tempting to treat psychology as an internal affair, as though minds are formed in isolation and feelings belong entirely to the individual. But the truth is more relational, more structural, and more uncomfortable. We are shaped not only by our families and temperaments but by the systems we inhabit. These systems—educational, legal, economic, medical, cultural—do not simply offer a backdrop to psychological life. They shape the rules of the game: who gets listened to, who is believed, who gets the benefit of the doubt, and who walks through the world braced for impact.

Power is not just something held by politicians or executives. It is embedded in assumptions, patterns, and everyday decisions. It shows up in the way meetings are run, how people interrupt or defer, who gets mentored, and whose pain is normalized. Privilege is often invisible to those who possess it precisely because the absence of psychological threat feels like normalcy. But to those without that buffer, reality registers differently. The same room, policy, or tone of voice can produce vastly different emotional consequences depending on one's history of inclusion or exclusion. Safety, it turns out, is not merely physical; it is emotional, relational, and deeply contextual.

POWER, PRIVILEGE, AND PSYCHOLOGICAL SAFETY

This chapter is about the intersection of systemic forces and psychological experience. It is about how power circulates through the psyche—not always with cruelty, but often with quiet consistency. From the formation of self-esteem to the regulation of emotion and the expression of confidence, our most personal traits are often forged in response to external cues about legitimacy, value, and belonging. For some, the world affirms worth automatically. For others, worth must be proven or protected at all times. These conditions are not abstractions. They are the lived terrain of classrooms, workplaces, clinics, and neighborhoods. They are the reason some people feel comfortable speaking their mind while others calculate every word.

The psychological literature has long emphasized individual development, sometimes at the expense of social context. But more recent work—especially in trauma studies, intersectionality, and systems theory—has begun to address how the conditions of one's environment shape what is perceived, expected, or feared. These dynamics operate beneath awareness. A person may believe they are simply being shy or anxious, when in fact they are responding to accumulated signals of marginalization. Another may feel confident and well-liked, unaware that their behavior is interpreted positively because of implicit biases in their favor. This is not a moral accusation. It is a psychological truth: social hierarchies are internalized long before they are recognized.

We will begin by examining the architecture of power and how it becomes internalized as psychological reality. Then we'll explore the mechanisms through which oppression and privilege are absorbed into personal identity and relational behavior. We'll investigate the elusive nature of psychological safety—what it means, who gets to feel it, and how its presence or absence shapes development. Finally, we will turn toward the possibility of repair: what it looks like to create environments that offer genuine safety, particularly in contexts marked by unequal histories and unequal risks.

This is not just a chapter about inequality. It is a chapter about the human mind—how it registers, resists, and reproduces the systems around it. Psychological safety is not a soft concept. It is the precondition for learning, connection, growth, and trust. And understanding how it is gained or denied may be one of the most important forms of emotional intelligence a person can develop.

The Architecture of Power: How Systems Shape Inner Worlds

Power is usually imagined as something hierarchical and external—a government, a boss, a police officer. But the most enduring and effective forms of power are often structural, distributed, and normalized. They shape expectations, allocate legitimacy, and quietly inform our understanding of what is appropriate, deserved, or possible. These forces do not operate only at the level of institutions. They penetrate the inner world, affecting not just what people do but what they think they are allowed to feel.

Psychologically, human beings rely heavily on context to interpret meaning and to assess safety. From infancy onward, cues from the environment inform not only behavior but perception itself. What counts as threatening, trustworthy, or shameful is absorbed through repeated exposure to family systems, media messaging, school interactions, and cultural assumptions. These exposures are not distributed evenly. A child born into a highly resourced and socially validated environment will experience a different psychological climate than a child born into poverty, exclusion, or chronic surveillance. Even before the development of explicit awareness, the nervous system is registering tone, access, rejection, and possibility.

This unequal climate of development is what ecological psychology calls *nested systems*: the idea that individuals are always embedded within a multilayered context—family, community, institution, and culture—each of which imposes its own pressures and rewards. Those pressures shape development in tangible ways. They determine whether children learn that the world is responsive or indifferent, fair or arbitrary, predictable or volatile. These early patterns form the foundation for what psychologists call "core beliefs": internal schemas about self-worth, agency, and the nature of the social world.

But core beliefs are not simply private psychological constructions. They are often the product of sustained systemic reinforcement. Consider a Black student in a predominantly white school who is repeatedly interrupted, misheard, or singled out for behavior correction. Over time, these experiences can crystallize into an implicit belief: "My voice is disruptive," or "I'm always on thin ice." The student may become withdrawn, self-silencing, or hypervigilant—traits easily misread as shyness, disinterest, or emotional immaturity. Meanwhile, the broader institution remains unaware that it is reproducing harm, because it reads its policies and practices as neutral.

Neutrality, however, is a mirage. Every policy reflects a value system. Every norm reflects a preference. Even the expectation of "professionalism" carries cultural assumptions about tone, posture, and expression that may align more closely with some identities than others. When those norms are enforced without reflection, they serve to advantage the already advantaged and penalize those who operate outside the dominant cultural framework. This is how power becomes invisible: not by being absent, but by being routinized.

Privilege, in this context, is not about material wealth alone. It is about *presumed belonging*—the assumption that one's presence will be welcomed, one's intentions will be understood, and one's errors will be forgiven. It functions as a form of psychological insulation. Privileged individuals are less likely to interpret feedback as personal threat, less likely to anticipate rejection, and less likely to experience chronic vigilance in public settings. This freedom—what some scholars call the "unmarked state"—allows for a more relaxed, exploratory, and assertive orientation toward the world. It facilitates confidence not because the person is inherently more capable, but because their psychological reality has been structurally supported.

For marginalized individuals, the inverse is true. The absence of privilege often creates an internal atmosphere of tightrope walking: knowing that a misstep may not be interpreted as a one-off error, but as confirmation of a stereotype. This psychological pressure contributes to emotional fatigue, identity fragmentation, and performance anxiety. The term *minority stress* captures this effect well—it refers to the chronic emotional burden that results not from one's identity per se, but from navigating a world in which that identity is persistently devalued or targeted.

These forces are not imagined. They are confirmed by decades of research. Stereotype threat studies, for instance, show that simply being reminded of a negative group stereotype (e.g., women and math, Black students and academic performance) can significantly undermine performance. This is not due to lack of ability but to the added cognitive load of managing identity under conditions of scrutiny. The brain reallocates resources toward impression management and threat monitoring, leaving less capacity for complex task engagement. In other words, power does not just shape opportunities; it shapes *how the mind functions under pressure*.

The concept of *cultural capital*, first articulated by sociologist Pierre Bourdieu, also helps illuminate how power operates beneath the surface. Cultural capital refers to the implicit knowledge, tastes, habits, and dispositions that are valued by the dominant culture—and which confer unspoken advantages to those who possess them. A student who knows how to speak in ways that mirror teacher expectations, or who dresses in ways that align with professional norms, is more likely to be interpreted as competent or mature. These interpretations matter, because they influence outcomes: recommendations, mentorships, second chances.

From a psychological standpoint, these dynamics reinforce themselves. Privileged individuals, accustomed to affirmation and interpretive generosity, may come to see their success as a reflection of merit alone. Meanwhile, those who experience persistent friction or invisibility may internalize the belief that they are inherently inadequate, rather than structurally unsupported. This is how systems reproduce themselves—

not just through laws or policies, but through the psychological experiences of those within them.

What makes this dynamic difficult to challenge is that power is often most effective when it feels like the natural order of things. People do not usually question what feels normal. But normalcy is itself a product of conditioning. When systems of advantage are mistaken for personal qualities, and systems of disadvantage are mistaken for personal failures, psychological safety becomes a privilege rather than a right.

And so we must ask: what does it mean to become aware of these embedded structures? How do people begin to see the ways their inner lives have been shaped by outer hierarchies? What changes when psychological discomfort is understood not as personal pathology but as a natural response to prolonged misrecognition?

These are not abstract questions. They affect how we interpret ourselves and others. They determine whether someone is seen as assertive or aggressive, articulate or intimidating, confident or arrogant. These interpretations have emotional consequences, and over time, those emotional consequences become identities.

To understand the architecture of power is to understand the architecture of perception. And perception is where psychology begins.

Internalized Oppression, Internalized Superiority

One of the most insidious features of inequality is how deeply it becomes embedded in the psyche—often without conscious awareness. Over time, external hierarchies are absorbed into personal identity, forming invisible templates that guide how people view themselves and others. This internalization process is not limited to those on the receiving end of discrimination. It affects everyone, reinforcing both marginalized and privileged positions through patterned thoughts, emotions, and behaviors. Internalized oppression and internalized superiority are two sides of the same psychological mechanism: the absorption of structural messages as self-definition.

For marginalized individuals, internalized oppression often begins with repetition. When a person consistently encounters messages—overt or subtle—that suggest they are less capable, less valuable, or less welcome, those messages begin to seep in. This can happen through language, exclusion, lowered expectations, surveillance, lack of representation, or even excessive praise that feels patronizing. Over time, the individual may start to self-censor, hold back, or diminish their own aspirations—not because of a lack of ability, but because they have been taught, repeatedly, to question their worth or anticipate rejection.

This process is not unique to one group or context. It can be observed in students of color in predominantly white academic institutions, women in male-dominated workplaces, LGBTQ+ individuals navigating heteronormative norms, or working-class individuals in elite spaces. Internalized oppression often shows up as chronic self-doubt, imposter syndrome, emotional withdrawal, and a persistent sense of being "less than." These are not just feelings. They are adaptive responses to environments that have communicated—implicitly or explicitly—that one's presence is conditional or suspect.

Learned helplessness, a concept introduced by psychologist Martin Seligman, provides a relevant lens here. Originally developed to explain behavioral passivity in animals exposed to uncontrollable stress, the theory also applies to human beings exposed to persistent invalidation or marginalization. When individuals come to believe that their efforts do not matter, that their voice will not be heard, or that the rules are rigged against them, they may disengage—not out of laziness or indifference, but as a protective adaptation to a hostile or indifferent environment.

At the same time, privilege creates its own psychological imprint—one that is often harder to detect because it feels like confidence, clarity, or ease. But internalized superiority is not the same as self-esteem. It is a psychological stance born from unchallenged access to resources, validation, and interpretive generosity. It shows up in subtle behaviors: speaking over others, assuming authority, interpreting one's preferences as standards, or viewing one's experiences as universal. These behaviors are rarely malicious. More often, they are unexamined. But their effects are real. They reinforce the notion that some people are naturally more competent or deserving than others.

From a developmental perspective, children raised in environments that center their identity—racially, culturally, economically—often internalize that centrality as normalcy. They may not be explicitly taught that others are inferior, but the absence of diverse representation, the framing of history through a single lens, and the privileging of certain behaviors as "professional" or "respectable" send powerful messages about who gets to define the rules. This is how internalized superiority is formed—not through overt prejudice, but through ambient reinforcement of dominance as default.

The dual phenomena of internalized oppression and internalized superiority are mutually reinforcing. When one group is consistently overvalued and another is consistently undervalued, both begin to see those roles as natural. This dynamic is especially evident in contexts like education, healthcare, or the workplace, where power differences are built into the structure but rarely named. Teachers may unconsciously expect less from certain students. Healthcare providers may listen differently depending on the patient's identity. Managers may promote confidence over competence, particularly when it aligns with cultural scripts of leadership that privilege whiteness, maleness, or class-based expression.

Stereotype threat further compounds this reality. Research by Claude Steele and others has shown that when individuals are reminded of a negative stereotype about their group—even subtly—they perform worse on tasks that require focus, memory, or problem-solving. This is not a question of intelligence. It is a question of cognitive load. Managing self-presentation, warding off anticipated judgment, and suppressing anxiety all take energy. That energy is diverted from the task at hand, leading to diminished performance that can then be misread as confirmation of the stereotype. It is a cruel loop, one that turns social bias into self-fulfilling prophecy.

Internalized dynamics can also distort interpersonal relationships. A person who has internalized oppression may defer excessively, over-apologize, or avoid confrontation even in unjust situations. They may doubt their own perceptions, fear being labeled as difficult, or second-guess their right to occupy space. Conversely, a person with internalized superiority may misinterpret assertiveness as hostility, read boundary-setting as disrespect, or experience feedback as a personal attack. These mismatches fuel conflict and misunderstanding, often along racial, gender, or class lines, and contribute to the emotional friction that undermines genuine trust and collaboration.

Importantly, internalization does not mean agreement. Many people who experience internalized oppression consciously reject the messages they have absorbed. They know they are just as capable, just as deserving. But knowing and feeling are not always aligned. The residue of marginalization often lingers in the nervous system, the body, and the unconscious. Likewise, individuals with privilege may intellectually understand inequality while still unconsciously enacting behaviors that perpetuate it. Change, in both cases, requires more than awareness. It requires deliberate, sustained effort to unlearn inherited patterns and to engage differently with one's social environment. That means noticing not just what we think, but how we move through space, who we expect to be heard, what reactions we anticipate from others, and what emotional weight we assign to different interactions. It means becoming attuned to the habits of mind that were never freely chosen but quietly installed by proximity to power, or distance from it.

The more we understand about internalization, the more we can challenge the quiet tyranny of those absorbed narratives. Because the story we tell ourselves about who we are—whether we are worthy, capable, visible, or safe—is never just a personal story. It is a social one, shaped by history, policy, and repetition. To rewrite it, we must first recognize the ink. Only then can we begin to author a more accurate and humane understanding of ourselves, one that does not mirror a broken system but reflects the truth of our shared human worth.

The Fragility of Safety: Threat, Vulnerability, and Belonging

Psychological safety is often mistaken for comfort. But they are not the same. Comfort can be superficial, even deceptive; it may reflect familiarity, agreement, or the absence of challenge. Psychological safety, by contrast, is deeper and more complex. It refers to a sense of being able to exist without fear of humiliation, retaliation, or exclusion. It means knowing you can speak, err, express doubt, set a boundary, or show vulnerability—and still be met with regard rather than punishment. It is a foundational element of learning, trust, and identity development. And yet it is not equally available to everyone.

The same environment can feel radically different depending on one's social location. A classroom may feel invigorating to one student and perilous to another. A workplace may seem collaborative to one employee and tightly surveilled to someone else. These differences are not just about personality. They are about history: the history of how people with certain identities have been treated in similar spaces, how often they've been heard or dismissed, protected or targeted, valued or tokenized. Psychological safety is never just a matter of environment. It is the result of a dynamic interaction between environment and identity.

This is where the distinction between *objective safety* and *felt safety* becomes essential. Objective safety refers to measurable conditions: absence of physical danger, clear rules, available protections. Felt safety refers to the internal experience of security. It is shaped by a host of subtle factors—tone of voice, eye contact, cultural cues, language patterns, power imbalances, even the spatial arrangement of a room. You can be technically safe and still feel threatened. Conversely, you can be technically vulnerable and still feel deeply secure, if the relational field offers consistency, care, and attunement.

For individuals with histories of exclusion, trauma, or marginalization, the bar for felt safety is understandably higher. Their nervous systems have learned to expect interruption, suspicion, or dismissal. As a result, they may scan environments more rigorously, interpret ambiguity more cautiously, and respond to microaggressions with amplified emotional cost. This is not a deficit. It is a form of adaptive vigilance. But it comes with a price: the constant background effort required to stay socially and emotionally intact.

Polyvagal theory, developed by Stephen Porges, helps us understand this from a biological standpoint. The theory proposes that our nervous system is always assessing levels of threat and safety through a process called neuroception—below the level of conscious awareness. When cues of safety are present, we remain in a state conducive to social engagement, learning, and connection. When cues of danger are detected—even subtle ones—we shift into defensive states: fight, flight, freeze, or fawn. This means that a person may appear disengaged, oppositional, or emotionally flat not because of disinterest, but because their nervous system has assessed the environment as unsafe. The response is physiological before it is psychological.

This is particularly relevant in institutional contexts—classrooms, hospitals, workplaces—where norms are often standardized without regard for diverse cultural or emotional baselines. For example, a teacher who values direct debate may interpret a student's silence as apathy or lack of preparation, not realizing that for that student, speaking up in a predominantly white classroom feels socially dangerous. Or a manager may interpret a Black employee's reserved demeanor in meetings as disconnection, without recognizing it as a protective strategy developed over years of racialized scrutiny. In both cases, the failure to distinguish between objective and felt safety leads to misjudgments that reinforce inequality.

Felt safety is also shaped by *belonging*. Not performative belonging, where one is invited to the table but remains under scrutiny—but genuine belonging, where one's presence is assumed, not conditional. Belonging is not about being liked. It is about being known and accepted as a full participant in a shared space. It includes the freedom to dissent, to be complex, to make mistakes without having one's entire identity put on trial. When belonging is absent, people become cautious versions of themselves, managing impressions, suppressing impulses, and masking discomfort. Over time, this takes a toll—not just emotionally, but cognitively and behaviorally.

The absence of psychological safety is especially corrosive in environments that claim to be inclusive but fail to embody that inclusion in structure and practice. A workplace that hosts diversity trainings but tolerates silencing behavior in meetings. A university that posts equity statements but refuses to diversify its leadership. A healthcare setting that advertises culturally competent care but ignores complaints of discrimination. In such contexts, the dissonance itself becomes a source of threat. The message received is: "You are safe here—as long as you don't actually test that claim." That kind of conditional safety is worse than none at all. It breeds cynicism, anxiety, and emotional withdrawal.

Psychological safety is fragile for another reason: it is easily shattered by small moments. A single instance of public embarrassment, racialized feedback, or unacknowledged harm can undermine months or years of relational trust. This fragility is not due to hypersensitivity; it is due to the high emotional stakes of exposure. For those whose social identities carry historical or structural vulnerability, speaking up, showing emotion, or asserting a boundary can feel like a risk to one's livelihood, reputation, or physical safety. And too often, those risks are real.

This fragility also helps explain why many people disengage emotionally in environments that appear benign on the surface. The calculation is not about today's conditions alone. It is about accumulated experience. It is about knowing how quickly inclusion can curdle into rejection, how often vulnerability has been punished in the past, how rarely those in power have stepped in to protect rather than deflect. These emotional memories live in the body. They are not simply "gotten over" through logic or policy change. They require consistent, embodied demonstrations of safety over time.

Psychological safety is also gendered, classed, and racialized in the ways it is perceived. A man who raises his voice may be seen as passionate; a woman as emotional. A white colleague who challenges authority may be admired as bold; a person of color may be labeled confrontational. These interpretive lenses are not neutral. They reflect systemic expectations about who is allowed to display what emotions, and in what quantity, without social penalty. These double standards not only constrain behavior; they distort feedback loops, making it harder for individuals to know when their discomfort is legitimate and when they are being gaslit by the system itself.

All of this makes psychological safety an essential—yet unequally distributed—resource. It cannot be willed into existence through personal resilience or overcome by sheer grit. Nor can it be reduced to warm feelings or soft-spoken leadership. True psychological safety requires structural alignment, relational consistency, and a commitment to justice—not as an add-on, but as a foundation. When these elements are absent, no amount of mindfulness, communication training, or leadership coaching will suffice. Because safety is not just what happens inside of people. It is what happens between them. And between them lies everything that systems have taught us to believe about who matters, and who does not.

Toward Repair and Equity: Reconstructing Psychological Safety in Unequal Worlds

Creating psychological safety in a fractured world is not an idealistic aspiration. It is a practical, necessary task—one that begins by recognizing the true origins of danger and mistrust. Too often, efforts to cultivate safety focus on individual attitude or interpersonal skill, overlooking the systemic conditions that made safety elusive in the first place. Repair requires more than good intentions. It requires dismantling the psychological consequences of inequality while building environments that are emotionally credible, structurally fair, and consistent in their regard for human dignity.

This begins with clarity. Safety does not mean the absence of discomfort. In fact, meaningful environments—schools, workplaces, families—must often invite discomfort in the form of challenge, accountability, or unfamiliar perspectives. But safety does mean the absence of retaliation, humiliation, and identity-based harm. It means that discomfort, when it arises, is not distributed inequitably. It means that people are not punished for speaking from the margins, for expressing their lived experience, or for naming dynamics that make others uneasy. Without this baseline, discomfort becomes a tool of domination rather than growth.

Building psychological safety in inequitable systems requires structural humility. No environment is neutral, and no leader is outside the system that shaped them. The first step toward equity is acknowledging that power distorts perception—and that the people most affected by harm are often the least likely to be believed when they name it. Repair begins by creating formal mechanisms for feedback that are protected, responsive, and not dependent on the benevolence of those in authority. It means listening not just for content, but for patterns. One complaint is a red flag. Five are a system.

In practical terms, repair also means embedding practices that normalize reflection, feedback, and emotional processing as part of the culture, not as optional extras. In education, this might mean trauma-informed pedagogy, where behavioral issues are interpreted through the lens of safety and regulation rather than defiance. In healthcare, it might involve patient-led accountability boards and systemic reviews of bias-based disparities in care. In workplaces, it means examining hiring, promotion, and retention policies for implicit bias—not just hosting an annual training on equity. Real safety is not a workshop. It is a pattern of accountability that outlasts individual discomfort.

Restorative justice offers a powerful framework for psychological repair. Rather than centering punishment, restorative models prioritize recognition, responsibility, and reintegration. When harm occurs—whether through bias, exclusion, or betrayal—the goal is not to identify a perpetrator and expel them from the group. The goal is to understand the impact, name the unmet need, and rebuild the relational fabric. This is not softness. It is rigor of a different kind—the courage to stay in relationship without minimizing harm or collapsing under guilt. It creates the conditions for belonging to be earned, not presumed.

Equally important is the psychological task of expanding one's tolerance for discomfort. For those with social privilege, this often means resisting the urge to deflect, center oneself, or rush to solutions when confronted with inequality. It means listening past defensiveness and accepting that one's good character does not negate the reality of impact. For those with marginalized identities, it may mean honoring emotional boundaries, naming harm with clarity, and practicing the difficult art of staying open in the face of repeated misrecognition. Neither position is easy. Both are essential. The work of repair is relational, and no one gets to remain untouched.

At the individual level, equity work often involves internal rewiring. For privileged individuals, this may mean learning to decenter one's assumptions, speak less, and develop interpretive flexibility. It means becoming aware of when "confidence" is actually entitlement, or when "objectivity" is a mask for bias. For marginalized individuals, it may mean rejecting internalized narratives of inadequacy, reclaiming the right to take up space, and building relationships rooted in mutuality rather than survival. Healing, in this sense, is not only personal. It is collective. It happens in community, in policy, and in the subtle rewrites of everyday interaction.

One of the most difficult aspects of this work is that psychological safety cannot be created by any one person. It is emergent. It arises when enough people commit to making a space emotionally sustainable—for themselves and others. It is fragile, because it depends on shared integrity. But it is also renewable. When broken, it can be repaired. When denied, it can be named. And when taken seriously, it can change the entire trajectory of a person's development, identity, and relational possibility.

Equity is not a destination. It is an ongoing psychological recalibration. It asks people to resist the gravitational pull of familiarity and to stay in contact with the truth of other people's experience. That truth is not always easy to hear. It may implicate systems we trust, values we were raised with, or roles we've grown comfortable in. But psychological safety is never created by avoiding discomfort. It is created by staying with it long enough to reach understanding.

The reconstruction of safety is not about restoring a lost ideal. It is about building something stronger—an emotional infrastructure that can hold the complexity, tension, and variation of real human life. That is the task of our time: to create environments, institutions, and relationships where more people feel free to think, speak, and exist without fear. Where safety is not something one must earn by assimilating or pleasing, but something one can rely on simply by being human.

* * *

35

The Self in Society: Agency and Resistance

The individual is never truly separate from the system. This is not a metaphor, it is a psychological reality. Every person is shaped, constrained, and enabled by the social forces around them: culture, class, law, family, ideology, and history. Yet within those constraints, people act. They survive, adapt, resist, and—at times—transform their conditions. The tension between the self and society is not merely political or philosophical; it is a deep psychological tension that sits at the heart of human identity. How do we retain a sense of self in a world that constantly tells us who we are supposed to be?

This chapter explores that question from the inside out. It begins with the recognition that adaptation is not weakness. Many of the behaviors dismissed as submission or passivity are, in truth, brilliant strategies for navigating impossible contexts. Code-switching, emotional suppression, people-pleasing, silence—these are not signs of brokenness. They are survival techniques, honed in response to systems that punish difference or disobedience. To understand human behavior in context is to see adaptation not just as coping, but as creativity under pressure.

But survival is not the same as freedom. And humans are not merely shaped by their environment—they push back. Resistance, in its many forms, is a central part of psychological agency. It might be loud and public, or quiet and internal. It might look like protest, refusal, storytelling, boundary-setting, or the decision to remain whole in a world that fragments people by design. Not every act of resistance changes the system. But every act of resistance protects the self from total erasure. In that protection lies the seed of transformation.

Still, resistance comes at a cost. To push against the grain of a dominant narrative, to speak when silence is expected, to leave when staying is rewarded—these choices often require courage, clarity, and sacrifice. They also require conditions that make resistance possible: access to resources, emotional support, community, or even the belief that change is possible. Not everyone can afford to resist openly. And those who do often carry the emotional consequences long after the moment has passed.

This chapter does not romanticize resistance. Nor does it pathologize adaptation. Instead, it takes seriously the inner negotiations people make every day as they navigate systems that are indifferent—or hostile—to their full humanity. Some conform, some resist, and many do both in different moments. The self is not static. It is responsive, layered, and shaped by context. Understanding how agency operates in constrained environments requires us to move beyond binary judgments of strong or weak, brave or afraid. It requires a deeper inquiry into what people are up against, and what tools they have available.

Finally, this chapter turns toward transformation—not as an abstract hope, but as a psychological process. When people reclaim authorship over their lives, when they refuse the roles they've been assigned, when they create something new from what they were told to suppress, they do more than heal. They disrupt. They signal what is possible, not only for themselves, but for others watching closely, wondering if freedom is possible for them too.

This is the psychology of resistance. It is not found only in moments of protest or rupture, but in the slow, daily decisions to remain real in a world that rewards performance. To be human is to contend with the forces that would shape you—and, whenever possible, to shape them in return.

Adaptive Selves: How People Learn to Survive

Human beings are fundamentally adaptive. We learn to read our environments, sense the rules of engagement, and adjust ourselves in ways that increase our chances of inclusion, protection, or success. This adaptability is a feature, not a flaw. It is what allows people to survive in environments that are emotionally unpredictable, structurally hostile, or culturally mismatched. But over time, adaptations can become mistaken for personality. They begin to feel like fixed traits rather than the intelligent responses they originally were.

Children do not enter the world with a blank slate. They arrive with temperamental tendencies and biological sensitivities—but it is their environment that teaches them how to behave. A child raised in a loud, expressive family will learn different emotional cues than one raised in a reserved or authoritarian home. A child who grows up navigating multiple cultural codes will develop fluidity and vigilance that others may never need. These skills are not innate; they are acquired through observation, correction, reward, and repetition. They reflect the brain's basic principle: efficiency. Adapt to survive.

Psychologically, adaptation often begins as a form of protection. When the environment signals that certain emotions are unwelcome, children learn to suppress them. When curiosity is punished, children learn to self-censor. When difference is met with ridicule or danger, children learn to blend in, to mirror, to mute themselves. These behaviors are often misread in adulthood—as insecurity, passivity, coldness, or inauthenticity. But they are rarely chosen freely. They are conditioned responses to relational threat. And in many cases, they were necessary.

In marginalized communities, adaptive behavior can be the difference between safety and harm. Code-switching—the practice of alternating language, tone, or behavior depending on the social context—is a powerful example. While often exhausting, it functions as a form of self-preservation, allowing individuals to maintain credibility, reduce conflict, or avoid surveillance in dominant-culture settings. This is not deception. It is strategy. It reflects a nuanced understanding of social power and an effort to protect one's position, dignity, or livelihood.

The same applies to emotional management. A child who grows up in a chaotic or dismissive household may become hyper-attuned to others' moods, learning to regulate their own behavior to minimize conflict. This can manifest later in life as people-pleasing, over-responsibility, or emotional numbness. Again, these are not personality flaws. They are adaptations. In the language of trauma psychology, they are sometimes referred to as *fawn responses*—a lesser-known survival mode that prioritizes appeasement over fight or flight. When safety depends on being agreeable or invisible, many people learn to disappear from themselves.

But adaptation does not always look quiet. Sometimes it looks like overperformance. Perfectionism, hyperachievement, relentless self-monitoring—these too are forms of adaptation. When people internalize the belief that their worth must be earned or constantly proven, they may develop behaviors that seem ambitious on the outside but are driven by fear beneath. These adaptations are often praised by society, especially when they produce visible success. But inside, the psychological toll can be immense: chronic anxiety, self-alienation, and a fragile sense of value that depends entirely on doing rather than being.

Importantly, adaptations are not always conscious. People often do not realize they are adapting in real time. The shifts are subtle: a change in tone, a swallowed opinion, a posture adjusted to appear less threatening. Over time, these small calibrations accumulate, forming a version of self that is optimized for survival in a particular context—but may not reflect the fullness of who the person really is. And when these environments persist across years or decades, the adapted self can begin to feel permanent.

Culturally, many adaptations are shared. Whole communities learn to survive within dominant systems by developing collective codes: how to speak in white spaces, how to navigate public institutions, how to avoid drawing the wrong kind of attention. These adaptations are often passed down intergenerationally—not only through instruction, but through modeling. Children see their parents become smaller in certain rooms. They hear the change in their voices at work or with authority. These adaptations become part of what is silently taught: how to stay safe, how to be palatable, how to succeed without triggering someone else's discomfort.

But adaptation is not submission. It is agency in constrained form. Even in the most controlling environments, people find ways to retain some measure of self. A child who draws to escape a chaotic home. A queer teen who creates an online identity for exploration. A worker who jokes under their breath about management. These are not minor details. They are fragments of agency—psychological footholds that allow people to maintain some sense of coherence when external conditions threaten to dissolve it.

In psychology, we often use the language of coping mechanisms to describe these behaviors. But this can pathologize them, reducing meaningful adaptations to symptoms. A more accurate lens would be *contextual intelligence*: the ability to read power, interpret risk, and modulate behavior for survival. People who live with structural marginalization often possess this intelligence in abundance. They learn early how to move between worlds, how to translate themselves, how to anticipate rejection without collapsing under it. These skills are rarely celebrated—but they are feats of emotional engineering.

Still, there is a cost. The longer one must adapt, the harder it becomes to remember what was there before the adaptation. The self can become so entangled with the performance that it becomes difficult to disentangle need from strategy, truth from survival. This is the psychological paradox of adaptation: it protects, but it can also obscure. It allows people to remain in harmful systems longer than they should. It makes certain forms of mistreatment feel normal. And over time, it can make resistance feel dangerous—even when it is exactly what is needed.

To see adaptation clearly, then, is to hold two truths at once: the behavior may be constrained, but the person is not without intelligence or agency. What looks like passivity may be self-protection. What looks like compliance may be the price of feeding a family or avoiding violence. Judging people without context is not just inaccurate—it is psychologically unjust.

Before we ask why someone is not resisting, we must ask what they have had to survive.

The Quiet Power of Everyday Resistance

Resistance is often imagined as a grand gesture: a march, a speech, a rupture. But most acts of resistance are small, quiet, and personal. They happen not in headlines but in classrooms, workplaces, homes, and even within one's own mind. These are the daily moments when people assert their humanity in systems that try to make them forget it. When they choose not to assimilate entirely. When they hold onto something—an accent, a value, a truth—that dominant culture has told them to shed. This is everyday resistance, and it is one of the most psychologically significant ways human beings retain agency under pressure.

Sociologist James C. Scott coined the term *infrapolitics* to describe these hidden forms of dissent: the subtle refusals, private acts, and symbolic gestures that allow people to subvert power without directly confronting it. Infrapolitical acts may not be legible to outsiders, but they are deeply meaningful to those who enact them. A student who refuses to laugh at a racist joke. A nurse who takes five extra minutes with a patient no one else wants to care for. A worker who wears culturally significant clothing in defiance of dress code expectations. These choices may appear minor, but they carry psychological weight. They allow individuals to preserve a sense of moral alignment and personal authorship, even within constraining systems.

One reason these acts matter is because they interrupt internalized narratives. When a person chooses to resist—even in small ways—they reject the script that tells them they must conform completely in order to survive. That rejection, even if symbolic, restores a sense of boundary between the self and the system. It says: I am still here. I have not disappeared into this role. I have not agreed to all of this. That assertion is powerful not because it changes the system overnight, but because it prevents the self from being erased.

Everyday resistance also functions as a form of psychological regulation. In environments where direct opposition would invite punishment or exclusion, subtle forms of resistance offer a way to express anger, grief, or dignity without escalation. For example, Black professionals often describe the mental negotiation involved in deciding whether to correct a mispronunciation of their name. Speaking up risks being labeled as overly sensitive. Staying silent risks reinforcing erasure. In such moments, the choice to pause, repeat one's name with precision, or simply hold eye contact may serve as a quiet refusal to accept being misnamed. It is a small reclaiming of space.

Humor is another potent form of everyday resistance. It allows people to expose hypocrisy, challenge authority, or communicate critique in socially acceptable ways. Satire, sarcasm, and coded language have long served as tools of survival in oppressed communities. These forms of expression often fly under the radar of dominant power, allowing truth to be spoken without direct confrontation. But psychologically, the effects are clear: laughter becomes a release valve for tension, a connector between people who share a subtext, and a signal that one's inner life has not been colonized by external control.

Language itself is a site of resistance. People who switch between dialects, reclaim slurs, or create new linguistic expressions are doing more than communicating—they are asserting identity. They are refusing to allow dominant language norms to dictate meaning. In doing so, they maintain psychological coherence in spaces that would otherwise fragment or flatten them. This is particularly significant for bilingual or bicultural individuals, whose fluency in multiple codes often reflects not just education, but resilience. Choosing when and how to use language is a way of deciding how to be seen—and by whom.

Not all everyday resistance is expressive. Some is strategic silence. Choosing not to engage in a conversation, not to reveal personal details, or not to participate in rituals that feel performative can be acts of self-preservation. In psychology, silence is sometimes pathologized as avoidance or repression. But in many contexts, silence is intentional. It is a refusal to play a role that feels false. It is a shield. And like all resistance, it is relational—it gains meaning in contrast to what is expected or demanded.

These quiet acts may not be visible to those in power. But they are often recognized by those who share the experience. A knowing glance across a boardroom. A nod between students after a teacher's microaggression. A meme that signals solidarity. These signals create emotional pockets of belonging in systems that otherwise isolate or homogenize. They say: I see you. I know what this is. You are not alone. That kind of recognition is its own form of resistance against the psychological violence of invisibility.

It is important not to romanticize everyday resistance. These acts do not eliminate risk. They do not guarantee systemic change. And sometimes, they are the only options available precisely because larger forms of resistance would be too costly. But their psychological function should not be underestimated. They help people stay intact. They create emotional distance from oppressive systems. They allow individuals to retain a sense of internal freedom, even in contexts where external freedom is limited.

In developmental terms, these acts of resistance help prevent learned helplessness. They provide opportunities for choice, however constrained. And they reinforce a sense of moral agency—the belief that one can still act in alignment with one's values, even in systems that devalue those values. This belief is critical. When people lose it, they often disengage not just from systems, but from themselves. They go through the motions. They numb out. Resistance, however small, can be the thread that keeps them tethered to a sense of purpose.

Moreover, everyday resistance is often the seedbed for larger movements. Many social transformations began with private refusals, personal awakenings, or informal conversations. What feels like a quiet no today may become tomorrow's public stance. And even if it does not, it still matters. Because in that moment, a person chose to remain whole in a system designed to divide them.

The psychology of resistance is not always dramatic. Sometimes, it is the simple decision to stay real when the world demands a performance. That, too, is power.

When Agency Costs Too Much: The Psychology of Risk and Resistance

There is a popular belief that those who do not resist injustice are complicit, weak, or morally indifferent. But this view lacks psychological nuance. It fails to account for what it actually costs a person to challenge systems from within—emotionally, socially, financially, even physically. Resistance is never a pure moral act; it is a risk calculation. And for many people, the costs are simply too high. This is not because they lack courage. It is because they have already endured enough.

Agency, like safety, is unequally distributed. It is shaped by power, proximity to resources, and access to protection. A person who feels secure in their job, supported by their community, and buffered from retaliation will experience their agency differently than someone who is isolated, precarious, or targeted. This is not a matter of willpower. It is a matter of context. The same act—raising a concern, saying no, setting a boundary—can carry wildly different consequences depending on who performs it and where.

From a psychological standpoint, the decision to resist is often mediated by one's perceived margin for error. Individuals with marginalized identities frequently live with the knowledge that they are operating under increased scrutiny. Their mistakes are more likely to be remembered, their emotions more likely to be misread, and their competence more likely to be questioned. This creates what sociologist Elijah Anderson calls "the white space": a domain in which non-dominant individuals must constantly navigate the rules of dominant culture just to be tolerated, let alone respected. In such spaces, resistance can feel not only dangerous, but futile.

Risk, however, is not only external. It is also internal. People who have experienced trauma, rejection, or punishment for speaking up may develop deep emotional associations between visibility and harm. Even when conditions change, those associations persist. What looks like passivity may in fact be a protective freeze response—what trauma theorists call a form of learned inhibition. The nervous system remembers, even when the mind tries to override it. This is why telling someone to "just speak up" often misses the point. For many, that speech carries the residue of pain.

The theory of *pluralistic ignorance* helps explain how this unfolds in group settings. It describes situations in which individuals privately disagree with a dominant norm but assume that others agree—leading everyone to remain silent despite shared discomfort. This silence reinforces the appearance of consensus and discourages dissent. In workplaces, schools, or communities, pluralistic ignorance can maintain harmful practices long after people have stopped believing in them. Breaking that silence requires someone to tolerate the possibility of standing alone. And for many, that risk is unbearable.

Even when resistance is possible, it is rarely clean. People must consider trade-offs: Will I lose my job? Will I damage this relationship? Will I be labeled as difficult, ungrateful, or angry? These questions are not hypothetical. They reflect real histories of retaliation, misrepresentation, and exclusion. And so, people weigh their values against their vulnerability. They assess whether the cost of staying silent is greater than the cost of being seen. And often, they conclude that the most psychologically sustainable choice is to endure.

That endurance, too, can be misunderstood. People who stay in unjust systems are often accused of betrayal—by others or by themselves. But many remain not because they agree with the system, but because they are trying to protect something else: a dependent child, an aging parent, their immigration status, their mental health. In such cases, survival is resistance. It is an act of care for the self and others. It is a bet on the long game. Not every war is winnable. Sometimes, living to fight another day is the strategy.

It is also important to name emotional exhaustion as a barrier to resistance. Activism, dissent, and advocacy are emotionally expensive. They require sustained energy, repeated confrontation, and a willingness to be misunderstood. For individuals who are already carrying the weight of systemic inequality, this additional burden can become too much. Burnout is not failure. It is the body and mind signaling that the cost of continued exposure outweighs the potential gain. In these cases, retreat is not surrender—it is self-preservation.

Social support plays a pivotal role in determining whether resistance feels possible. People who have mentors, community, or aligned peers are more likely to take risks. They know someone will believe them, defend them, or help repair the damage. Those who are isolated—whether emotionally, geographically, or culturally—often have no such safety net. Their silence is not complicity; it is what happens when no one is there to catch them if they fall. Psychologically, the presence of even one ally can radically shift the equation.

Belief in change is another factor. For some, resistance feels worth it because they believe it might work. For others, years of disappointment have created a kind of learned futility—a sense that systems are too entrenched, too indifferent, or too corrupt to be moved. This is not cynicism for its own sake. It is a rational response to evidence. When efforts to speak up are repeatedly met with denial or punishment, the brain learns to conserve energy. Hope, like agency, must be cultivated—and for many, it has been systematically starved.

There is also the emotional cost of being the one who names the problem. In systems that rely on denial or decorum, the truth-teller is often scapegoated. Whistleblowers are punished. Boundary-setters are pathologized. Those who expose dysfunction become its target. This reversal is not accidental; it is part of how systems protect themselves. Psychologically, it is devastating. It isolates the very people who are most awake to injustice, reinforcing the illusion that silence is safer than truth.

None of this is to suggest that resistance is impossible or unwise. But it is to say that resistance is a layered psychological event. It involves identity, emotion, memory, risk, and support. It is not simply about what a person believes, but about what they can afford—financially, socially, and emotionally. And when that cost is too high, people do what they have always done: they adapt, they endure, and they find other ways to protect what matters.

The challenge, then, is not to judge who resists and who does not. It is to understand the terrain on which people are walking. To ask not "Why don't they speak up?" but "What happens when they do?" Only by mapping the emotional cost of agency can we begin to make space for more of it. Not through moral pressure, but through structural and relational support.

Because resistance is not a single moment. It is an ecosystem. And ecosystems do not grow in isolation.

Disruption and Transformation: Reclaiming the Self in a Controlling World

There comes a moment in many lives when adaptation no longer feels tenable. The performance wears thin, the silence grows heavy, and the roles that once ensured survival begin to suffocate. For some, this moment arrives suddenly—a rupture, a betrayal, a loss. For others, it builds gradually, through the slow accumulation of misrecognition and constraint. Either way, something shifts. The question is no longer, "How can I fit myself into this system?" but "What kind of self can exist beyond it?" This is the threshold of psychological transformation: the reclaiming of identity not just from personal history, but from social scripting.

Transformation is not the opposite of adaptation; it is its evolution. Where adaptation asks, "How do I survive here?" transformation asks, "What do I want to become?" It is the movement from externally shaped identity toward self-authorship. But this movement does not begin in freedom. It begins in friction—in the recognition that one's internal truth and external behavior are no longer aligned. This internal dissonance, often experienced as anxiety, restlessness, or depression, is not always pathology. It may be the early sign of awakening.

Narrative identity theory suggests that human beings make meaning through the construction of life stories. These stories are not fixed. They are revised continually in response to new experiences, new relationships, and new frameworks for understanding. Psychological transformation often involves rewriting the story one has been living—not by denying the past, but by reinterpreting it. What was once seen as weakness may be reframed as resilience. What was once seen as failure may be understood as refusal. Through this lens, even suffering becomes a site of authorship.

Liberation psychology, a tradition rooted in Latin American thought and popularized by thinkers like Ignacio Martín-Baró, insists that healing must involve both personal insight and systemic awareness. According to this view, transformation is not complete unless it includes a recognition of how systems have deformed the self—and a commitment to resisting that deformation. It is not enough to feel better. One must also become more free. This freedom is not absolute. But it is meaningful. It allows individuals to define themselves on their own terms, to reclaim parts of the self that were once hidden, and to act in ways that align with their values even under constraint.

For many, this reclaiming begins in the body. Trauma research shows that long-term adaptation to unsafe environments can produce physical symptoms: tension, numbness, gastrointestinal issues, sleep disruption. When people begin to feel safe enough to reconnect with their own bodies—through movement, breath, rest, or care—something begins to loosen. The body becomes less of a battleground and more of a home. From there, people often find it easier to access intuition, anger, joy, and desire—all of which are necessary for transformation.

Creativity is another powerful pathway. Art, music, writing, and performance provide ways to express truths that cannot yet be spoken plainly. In communities where voice has been historically suppressed, creative acts often serve dual purposes: they are personal and political, emotional and epistemological. They allow individuals to name themselves and their world in ways that dominant systems cannot contain. This naming is not symbolic alone. It is structural. It builds emotional infrastructure for others. It shows what is possible.

Transformation is also relational. Rarely does a person become themselves alone. They need others—witnesses, mentors, companions—who affirm their emerging identity and hold space for the messiness of transition. Transformative relationships do not demand consistency; they tolerate flux. They ask not, "Who were you before?" but "Who are you becoming now?" These relationships are often found in community spaces that center healing, justice, or liberation. But they can also emerge quietly: a friend who listens differently, a partner who affirms change, a teacher who names your potential.

Disruption, in this context, is not destruction. It is the refusal to perform roles that deny one's complexity. It is the choice to stop apologizing for being inconvenient, emotional, ambitious, tired, or different. It is saying no to a version of the self that was only ever built to make others comfortable. And that no, when spoken clearly, can be a form of psychological release. Not all systems collapse in the face of disruption. But sometimes, they bend. And in that bending, new pathways appear—not just for the individual, but for those watching, waiting to see if change is survivable.

There are risks, of course. People who transform often lose relationships. They may face backlash, misunderstanding, or loneliness. They may grieve the version of themselves that once made everything easier. But the trade is rarely regretted. Because on the other side of disruption is something more vital than comfort: integrity. The sense that one's inner life and outer life are in conversation, if not in full harmony. That one's existence is not borrowed, but claimed.

The work of reclaiming the self is ongoing. Systems will always try to reassert themselves. There will be pressure to return to the familiar role, the manageable version of identity. But transformation, once it begins, is hard to reverse. The mind remembers what it felt like to speak in one's own voice. The body remembers what it felt like to exhale fully. These memories become anchors—points of reference that help a person navigate future challenges with greater clarity and resistance.

In the end, disruption is not only for the self. It ripples outward. A child sees their parent stop apologizing. A student watches their teacher name harm. A colleague refuses to laugh at a degrading joke. These moments accumulate. They challenge what is normal. They shift what is expected. And slowly, the system—whether a family, a school, a culture—begins to loosen its grip.

To reclaim the self in a controlling world is not a solitary act. It is a contribution. It reminds everyone else that control is not destiny, that survival can become freedom, and that we are all more than the roles we were assigned.

* * *

VIII

PART VIII: TOWARD A PSYCHOLOGICALLY INTEGRATED LIFE

Living a psychologically integrated life means bringing together insight, complexity, and compassion—not just as ideas, but as guiding forces in your daily experience. In this final part, I want to walk with you through how to weave everything you've learned into a coherent whole. This is about embracing the fullness of who you are, navigating life's challenges with grace, and moving forward with clarity and kindness toward yourself and others.

36

Integration: The Goal of Psychological Maturity

At the center of every meaningful psychological journey is a longing for integration. Not to become someone else, not to perfect or purify the self, but to gather the scattered parts and live from a place of internal coherence. Integration is the opposite of fragmentation. It is what happens when the contradictions, complexities, and conflicts within a person are no longer treated as evidence of failure, but as material for understanding. It is the developmental achievement of recognizing: I am all of this.

Psychological maturity is often mistaken for composure, emotional control, or having all the answers. But maturity is not about always being right or always being calm. It is about capacity—the capacity to stay present with emotion, to recognize competing needs without collapsing into confusion, to act with integrity even when discomfort is high. Maturity is what allows a person to remain in dialogue with themselves. It allows for contradiction without rupture, grief without despair, desire without recklessness. It is not the eradication of struggle; it is the integration of it.

This chapter marks a transition point in the book. We have explored cognition, emotion, development, culture, trauma, systems, power, identity, and resistance. Now we ask: what does it look like to live as a psychologically integrated person in the world? What does it mean to build a life that honors the full spectrum of the human experience—our limitations, our intelligence, our longings, and our pain? Integration is not the reward for being good. It is the process of becoming real.

The human psyche is not one thing. It is a constellation of parts, voices, memories, needs, fears, and hopes. Some of those parts are visible and welcomed. Others are hidden, suppressed, or pathologized. Integration requires contact with all of them. Not indulgence, not domination—but honest relationship. This means being able to sit with anger without being consumed by it. To hear shame without letting it dictate your worth. To recognize joy without turning it into a performance. Integration allows for emotional range because it trusts in the stability of the whole.

There is no single path to this place. Some people find integration through therapy, others through creative expression, spiritual practice, or rigorous self-reflection. But what they share is a shift in orientation—from managing parts of the self as problems to be solved, to understanding them as messengers, protectors, and fragments of something deeper. This is not easy work. It requires patience, emotional honesty, and a willingness to stay in the room with oneself, even when discomfort rises.

This chapter begins by revisiting the concept of wholeness—not as an abstract ideal, but as a lived experience of internal alignment. From there, we'll explore how emotional intelligence emerges from integration, and how coherence—not consistency—becomes the hallmark of a maturing self. Finally, we'll turn to what it means to live this way in practice: to carry integration not only within, but into relationships, work, and the ethical decisions that shape our lives.

Integration is not the end of the psychological journey. It is the beginning of a different kind of living—one rooted in honesty, presence, and the refusal to abandon oneself.

Beyond Fragmentation: What It Means to Become Whole

To be human is to be divided. We hold opposing desires, conflicting memories, contradictory beliefs. We want closeness and freedom, truth and protection, mastery and rest. We grieve and laugh in the same breath. We fear what we long for. These tensions are not signs of dysfunction; they are signs of life. But when those tensions become overwhelming or incompatible with our roles, we often split. We compartmentalize, suppress, deny, or disown aspects of ourselves that feel dangerous or unmanageable. Fragmentation begins not as failure, but as strategy. It is a way of maintaining order in a complex and often unaccommodating world.

Psychological fragmentation can take many forms. A person may appear cheerful and competent at work while struggling with rage or despair in private. Another may be emotionally articulate in friendship but shut down in romantic partnership. Still another may have a spiritual life rich in reflection but remain disconnected from their body. These disconnections are not always visible. Often, the person living them has adapted so well that they no longer notice the gaps. But over time, the cost reveals itself—through burnout, relational strain, emotional numbness, or a pervasive sense of inauthenticity.

To move toward psychological integration is to begin reversing the logic of fragmentation. It is to say: All of these parts—my ambition, my shame, my fear, my anger, my tenderness—belong here. Not because they are all right, but because they are all mine. Integration does not mean indulging every impulse or affirming every belief. It means recognizing what is there, making contact with it, and allowing it to be metabolized into a coherent sense of self.

Carl Jung was one of the earliest psychologists to frame integration as the core task of maturity. His concept of individuation described the process by which a person comes to know, accept, and unify the disparate parts of the psyche. This includes not only the parts we present to the world but also the *shadow*—those aspects of ourselves we reject or repress. For Jung, wholeness required shadow work, not moral purity. It meant turning toward what is hidden, not as a threat, but as a portal to deeper self-understanding.

Contemporary psychology echoes this view, though in different language. Internal Family Systems (IFS), for instance, posits that the mind is made up of parts—some protective, some exiled, some wounded—and that healing comes not from eliminating these parts but from bringing them into relationship with a centered, compassionate core. From this perspective, symptoms like anxiety, procrastination, or emotional reactivity are not pathologies. They are signals from parts that have taken on burdens beyond their design. Integration involves listening to these parts without judgment, understanding their function, and helping them rejoin the internal system in harmony.

Another relevant model is self-complexity theory, which suggests that individuals with a more differentiated and interconnected sense of self are more resilient to stress. When a person sees themselves only in narrow terms—say, as a high achiever—they are more psychologically vulnerable when that identity is threatened. But when the self is richly textured, when multiple identities, roles, and emotional truths are available, there is greater flexibility. A failure at work does not collapse the self when the self also includes artist, parent, friend, or seeker. Integration provides psychological scaffolding for difficult times.

What these theories share is a movement away from binary thinking. The goal is not to become all light or all calm, but to hold contradiction without collapse. To be whole is not to be without tension. It is to have a relationship with that tension that is conscious, compassionate, and curious. Wholeness is not a fixed state. It is a dynamic process of dialogue between parts. It is the ability to say, when confronted with difficulty, "There is more than one voice in me, and I can listen to them all without losing myself."

This is especially important when considering the role of culture and systems in fragmentation. Many people disown parts of themselves

INTEGRATION: THE GOAL OF PSYCHOLOGICAL MATURITY

not because those parts are inherently dangerous, but because their environment could not hold them. A queer child learns to hide their desire. A Black professional learns to suppress frustration. A sensitive boy learns to mask his tears. These disowned parts are not defects. They are exiled for social survival. Integration, then, becomes an act of reclaiming what the world told us to abandon—not blindly, but deliberately, with discernment and care.

To begin integrating is to ask: What parts of me have been sent into exile? What stories have I told to make myself acceptable? What truths have I minimized to stay safe? These questions are not accusatory. They are invitations. They open the door to a deeper kind of self-honesty—one that does not measure maturity by how well a person fits a mold, but by how fully they know themselves.

Importantly, integration is not about becoming fully self-contained. It is not the fantasy of needing no one, of being emotionally invincible. True integration increases our capacity for intimacy, because it reduces the need for performance. When we are not at war with ourselves, we are better able to be present with others. We do not require them to affirm the parts we refuse to see. We can listen more clearly, offer more authenticity, and accept feedback without shattering.

The process of integration is slow. It often begins in moments of disruption—when the old strategies stop working, when a symptom refuses to be ignored, when a relationship exposes a truth we can no longer suppress. But those disruptions are not endings. They are openings. They reveal what has been fragmented, and they call us toward a more honest self.

To become whole is not to fix everything. It is to stop disowning ourselves. It is to say: I can be ambitious and uncertain. I can grieve and still feel joy. I can carry old wounds and still live forward. I can hold all of it—not perfectly, but with presence.

Emotional Intelligence as Integrative Capacity

Emotional intelligence is often described as a social skill: the ability to read a room, regulate emotion, empathize with others, and communicate clearly. And it is that. But beneath the interpersonal outcomes lies something more foundational—an internal process of integration. Emotional intelligence is not just how we handle relationships. It is how we relate to ourselves. It reflects the degree to which we are in contact with our own emotional life, able to tolerate its intensity, discern its meaning, and respond to it without distortion or collapse.

At its core, emotional intelligence requires the integration of cognition and affect. Thought and feeling are not separate domains; they are interactive systems. But for many people, the relationship between them is fractured. Some lean heavily on logic to avoid feeling. Others are consumed by emotion without clarity or containment. Emotional intelligence develops when these faculties begin to collaborate—when thought can name and organize emotion, and emotion can inform and deepen thought. This collaboration is a hallmark of psychological maturity.

The first step in that process is self-awareness. It seems simple, but it is rare. Many people experience emotion without recognizing it. Irritability masquerades as fatigue. Envy hides behind judgment. Fear shows up as control. The ability to name one's internal state—without minimizing, exaggerating, or externalizing it—is a profound act of integration. It requires contact with the body, with memory, and with social context. It asks: What am I feeling? Where is it coming from? And what is it asking of me?

Self-awareness alone, however, is not enough. The next layer is self-regulation: the ability to stay with emotion without being overwhelmed or reactive. This does not mean suppression. Regulation is not the shutting down of emotion; it is the modulation of it. It is the difference between having anger and being consumed by it. Between feeling anxious and collapsing into panic. Between sadness and paralysis.

INTEGRATION: THE GOAL OF PSYCHOLOGICAL MATURITY

Emotional intelligence allows for emotion to move through the system—acknowledged, expressed, and metabolized—without hijacking the self.

Developmentally, this capacity is forged through co-regulation in early life. When a caregiver helps a child make sense of their feelings—naming them, soothing them, staying present with them—the child begins to internalize that process. Over time, they learn to do for themselves what was once done for them: to sit with distress, to interpret its message, to choose a response rather than be driven by impulse. When those early experiences are absent or inconsistent, emotional development may be delayed or distorted. But the capacity for regulation can still be cultivated in adulthood—through therapy, safe relationships, and practices that increase emotional literacy.

Another crucial component of emotional intelligence is empathy. But empathy, too, is rooted in integration. To genuinely empathize with another person, we must be able to access the corresponding feeling within ourselves. A person who is cut off from their own sadness will struggle to recognize it in others. Someone who disowns their anger may mistake assertiveness for aggression. Empathy requires internal range. It requires that we not exile parts of ourselves simply because they are inconvenient or uncomfortable. The more whole we are internally, the more clearly we can see others.

Importantly, emotional intelligence also involves boundaries. A highly empathic person who lacks boundaries may become enmeshed, overextended, or resentful. True emotional intelligence is not about merging with others. It is about staying connected without being consumed. It involves knowing what feelings are ours and what belongs to someone else, recognizing when to lean in and when to step back. This is integration in practice—holding contact without collapse, connection without confusion.

From a neuroscientific perspective, emotional intelligence reflects healthy integration across brain systems. The prefrontal cortex, responsible for executive function and reasoning, must be in communication with the limbic system, which processes emotion. When these systems are out of sync, people may either intellectualize emotion (understanding it without feeling it) or be flooded by it (feeling without clarity). Integration fosters flexibility, allowing the brain to toggle between emotional depth and rational perspective as needed. This flexibility is the neurological basis of psychological resilience.

In clinical psychology, emotion-focused therapy emphasizes the value of turning toward emotion rather than away from it. Emotions are seen as adaptive information—not problems to fix, but signals to interpret. Anger may point to violation. Sadness may reflect loss. Anxiety may indicate misalignment between self and context. When emotions are dismissed or bypassed, they do not disappear. They go underground, becoming symptoms, resentments, or defensive behaviors. Emotional intelligence invites those emotions back into the room, not to take over, but to contribute.

In the workplace, emotional intelligence is often celebrated for its role in leadership, collaboration, and conflict resolution. But the deeper value lies in its ability to humanize power. A leader with high emotional intelligence does not avoid hard conversations. They approach them with presence and nuance. They understand that people are not interchangeable parts but emotional beings with histories, fears, and hopes. This understanding allows for cultures of trust and repair—key features of psychologically safe environments.

In intimate relationships, emotional intelligence allows for rupture and repair. Every close relationship includes misattunement, misunderstanding, and disappointment. What matters is not the absence of conflict, but the capacity to navigate it without shame, withdrawal, or escalation. Emotionally intelligent individuals can express needs without accusation, hear feedback without defensiveness, and return to connection after disconnection. This is not magic. It is integration at work.

Finally, emotional intelligence supports meaning-making. When we can sit with emotion long enough to understand its function, we become more capable of drawing insight from experience. We stop organizing our lives around avoidance. We stop chasing only the feelings that are pleasant or affirming. We begin to see pain, anger, and even confusion as part of a larger emotional ecology—one that makes room for growth, honesty, and transformation.

Emotional intelligence is not a trait to possess. It is a relational capacity—a way of being with ourselves and others that reflects integration, maturity, and moral seriousness. It does not guarantee ease. But it does make life more livable. Because when we are not running from ourselves, we can finally begin to live with intention.

Coherence Over Consistency: Making Meaning Across Time

In modern culture, consistency is often treated as a moral ideal. We are told to be the same person in every room, to "know who we are," to be unwavering in our values and predictable in our behavior. But psychologically, this demand is both unrealistic and misguided. Human development is not linear. Our values shift, our roles evolve, our beliefs mature. We respond differently in different contexts—not because we are inconsistent, but because we are complex. Psychological maturity is not marked by sameness. It is marked by coherence: the ability to make meaning across change.

Coherence means being able to look at one's life and say, "This all belongs." Even the contradictions. Even the mistakes. It does not mean explaining everything away or forcing a false harmony. It means recognizing that our lives contain multiple selves, formed under different conditions, and that each of those selves carried something true. The person we were at seventeen may seem unrecognizable now, but that person was trying to survive with the tools they had. Integration involves honoring that, rather than disowning it.

Narrative psychology helps us understand this process. The stories we tell about ourselves shape our identity, not only in hindsight but in real time. When we edit our history to make it neater, we lose access to the parts that hold emotional truth. When we deny certain chapters or minimize our past pain, we narrow our capacity for compassion—toward ourselves and others. Coherence is the ability to tell the truth about our lives, even when that truth includes contradiction or regret.

Importantly, coherence is not achieved by locking into a fixed identity. It is maintained through flexibility. Research on life-span development, particularly the work of Dan McAdams and others, shows that psychologically healthy individuals revise their narratives as they age. They incorporate new insights, reinterpret old wounds, and integrate previously disjointed experiences into a broader sense of meaning. These revisions are not self-deceptions; they are updates that reflect a deeper understanding of self and context.

Trauma often disrupts coherence. When experiences are too overwhelming to process, they are stored in memory as fragments—sensory impressions, emotional residues, or isolated images disconnected from narrative. These fragments can intrude on present life without context or explanation. Part of trauma recovery involves re-establishing coherence: linking those fragments to a story that holds them, gives them language, and places them in time. This does not make the trauma disappear, but it reduces its power to disorient the self.

Similarly, identity transitions—coming out, deconstructing faith, ending a long-term relationship, leaving a high-status role—can produce temporary incoherence. The person no longer fits the story they've been telling about themselves. In these moments, the pressure to restore consistency can be intense. But rushing to redefine oneself too quickly can create a brittle identity, one that feels safe but lacks depth. Coherence is built not by rebranding the self, but by expanding the story to include what no longer fits.

This is why maturity often looks like contradiction to the outside world. A person who used to be fiercely independent now seeks interdependence. A once-skeptical mind opens to wonder. A rigid moralist softens into humility. These shifts are not betrayals of principle; they are signs of growth. Integration means allowing for contradiction without losing the thread. It says, "Yes, I believed that then. And this is what I see now. And

INTEGRATION: THE GOAL OF PSYCHOLOGICAL MATURITY

both are part of me." That is coherence.

Psychologically, coherence provides stability without rigidity. It allows for the kind of self-trust that can tolerate change. People who are overly attached to consistency often struggle with self-compassion. They view mistakes as moral failings, growth as betrayal, and uncertainty as weakness. In contrast, coherent individuals understand that transformation is not a sign of confusion—it is a sign of contact. They have met life honestly and let it shape them.

This has important implications for relationships. People with a coherent sense of self are better able to communicate across change. They can explain how they've evolved without invalidating who they used to be. They can apologize without collapsing into shame. They can set new boundaries without pretending the old ones were foolish. This flexibility builds trust—not just with others, but within the self. It creates a continuity of identity even as the content of identity shifts.

In parenting, coherence allows caregivers to raise children with integrity. Rather than modeling perfection, they model growth. They show that adults are not finished products. That mistakes are inevitable. That values evolve. This honesty is far more grounding than false consistency. It teaches children that they, too, can become someone new without losing who they've been.

Socially, we are often penalized for perceived inconsistency. Public figures are ridiculed for changing positions. People are called hypocrites for evolving. This punitive stance discourages reflection and traps individuals in outdated identities. But from a psychological standpoint, growth requires revision. The question is not whether someone has changed. The question is whether that change reflects deeper alignment, greater clarity, and more honest relationship with the self.

Ultimately, coherence allows us to live with complexity. It lets us say: I am not who I once was, but that person matters. I have changed, but I am still me. I contain contradictions, and they are not errors. They are evidence of a life fully engaged.

In a culture that demands consistency, coherence is a quiet rebellion. It says, "I choose to be whole, not simple. I choose to grow, even if it makes my story harder to tell."

Living Integrated Lives: Practices and Commitments

Psychological integration is not a singular event. It is a sustained practice—an orientation toward the self and the world that prioritizes coherence, authenticity, and emotional depth. To live an integrated life is to move through the world with a certain kind of honesty: not the brutal kind that weaponizes truth, but the grounded kind that refuses to perform false versions of the self in exchange for acceptance or approval. It is a daily commitment to staying in relationship with your own internal life, especially when that life feels messy, contradictory, or unresolved.

Living this way requires intention. It does not happen automatically, especially in a world that rewards performance and penalizes vulnerability. The dominant culture often pulls people toward fragmentation—rewarding emotional suppression in the name of professionalism, encouraging identity curation in the name of branding, and reducing moral life to soundbites and slogans. Integration asks something different. It invites people to live from the inside out: to let their values, emotions, and relational truths shape behavior, rather than conforming to scripts imposed from the outside.

One of the most powerful practices that supports integration is reflection. This includes journaling, voice recording, contemplative walks, or any form of honest self-inquiry that creates space for the inner world to speak. Reflection is not about solving problems. It is about noticing what is alive in you, without rushing to fix or categorize it. It allows for contact with emotions that may have been bypassed, and with parts of the self that may have gone quiet. Over time, reflection becomes less about introspection and more about integration—a way to stay in touch with the evolving whole.

Another key practice is values alignment. Many people live according to inherited values they've never questioned. Others swing between roles and expectations without a clear internal compass. Integration requires that we identify what truly matters to us—and then begin to shape our lives around that. This does not mean becoming rigid or dogmatic. It means clarifying the principles that help us stay in relationship with ourselves, especially under stress. When decisions are difficult, values become the anchor. They help us choose not just what is easy, but what is congruent.

Boundaries are also essential. Integration is not only about being open—it is about being structured. An integrated person knows what they can offer and what they cannot. They recognize when a situation asks them to split off a part of themselves to be accepted. They notice when a relationship requires them to shrink, deny, or perform. And they are willing, when necessary, to say no. Not out of cruelty, but out of fidelity to the self. These boundaries protect the integrity of the inner world, and they signal to others that connection will be real or not at all.

Embodiment supports this work in ways that cognition alone cannot. Many people live in their heads—analyzing, interpreting, narrating—but remain disconnected from their bodies, where much of their emotional truth resides. Somatic practices like breathwork, movement, body scanning, and even stillness can bring the self back into relationship with sensation. This allows for the full range of emotional experience to emerge—not just in words, but in felt sense. Integration requires this kind of embodiment. Without it, insight remains theoretical.

In relationships, living an integrated life means showing up with presence rather than persona. It means being willing to be seen—not just in your strengths, but in your complexity. It means taking responsibility for your impact without collapsing into shame. It means inviting repair when harm is done, and choosing accountability over defensiveness. Integrated relationships do not eliminate conflict. They make space for it, knowing that rupture is part of intimacy—and that repair deepens trust.

Socially and professionally, integration often requires courage. Institutions and organizations are not designed for wholeness. They are built for efficiency, hierarchy, and image management. To live with integrity in these spaces means being willing to speak difficult truths, to challenge norms that fragment others, and to accept the discomfort that comes with real leadership. Integrated people do not always rise quickly through systems. But they leave an imprint that lasts: a reminder that wholeness is possible, even here.

Integration is also about continuity. In times of transition—illness, aging, grief, transformation—it is easy to lose sight of the self. These are the moments when people often say, "I don't recognize myself anymore." But the goal is not to return to who you were. It is to remember that you are still here. That your life, though different, is still yours to shape. Integration offers a thread of coherence across change. It says, "This, too, belongs."

And finally, integration is not a solitary endeavor. While much of the work happens internally, it is sustained through connection. We need spaces where we can be fully ourselves. Where we are not required to explain away our pain or sanitize our joy. Where others reflect back to us not who we were told to be, but who we are becoming. In these spaces—be they friendships, communities, partnerships, or therapeutic relationships—integration is not just maintained. It is multiplied.

To live an integrated life is to be unwilling to lose yourself to convenience, performance, or fear. It is to orient each day, however imperfectly, toward coherence. And when fragmentation returns—as it will—it is to notice, to pause, and to begin again. Not to become whole once and for all, but to keep choosing wholeness whenever the world offers you the chance to forget it.

* * *

37

Becoming Ourselves

Who are we, really? Not who we were taught to be, or who we've learned to perform, but underneath all of it—what remains? This question sits quietly beneath much of psychological life. It hides inside ambition, perfectionism, insecurity, and even resilience. Identity is one of the most personal experiences we have, yet much of it is shaped socially, historically, and unconsciously. We inherit it before we understand it. We adapt it before we question it. And for many, the self becomes a kind of performance—fluent, effective, even admired—but not entirely true.

This chapter is about what it means to become ourselves. Not in the aspirational, future-focused sense of self-improvement, but in the deeper psychological sense of reclaiming authorship over who we are—beneath roles, beyond trauma, and outside of performance. It is about the difference between living as a reflection of context and living as a coherent, internally aligned presence. Becoming ourselves is not something that happens once. It is a process of remembering, unlearning, emerging, and choosing.

Identity often begins as a negotiation. In childhood, we learn quickly which behaviors bring us connection and which ones provoke distance. We absorb cues from caregivers, peer groups, media, and institutions. We discover what earns approval, what keeps us safe, what gets us hurt.

And from those cues, we build a working model of self. This is not disingenuous. It is adaptive. But over time, the adaptations solidify. We become the role. We confuse survival strategy with essence.

For some, trauma accelerates and intensifies this process. When the environment is emotionally unsafe, identity is often formed around what will reduce threat. A child might become hyper-responsible to avoid chaos, emotionally numb to avoid pain, or invisible to avoid punishment. These strategies work. But they leave residue. Decades later, the person may no longer need the strategy, yet still feel tethered to the identity it created. Healing, then, becomes a process not just of recovering from what happened—but of rediscovering who they were before the performance began.

But identity is not only shaped by pain. It is also shaped by opportunity. By the stories we're told about who people like us are allowed to be. By what the culture rewards, what it ignores, what it pathologizes. People from marginalized communities often grow up with limited identity scripts—roles that are flattening, reductive, or punishing. Escaping those scripts can feel like betrayal. Staying inside them can feel like suffocation. Becoming oneself in such contexts is not a luxury. It is a radical act of psychological self-definition.

The most profound moments in a person's life are often those in which the performance breaks down. The job no longer makes sense. The relationship is based on someone they no longer are. The identity they've lived for years begins to feel like a costume. These are not moments of crisis—they are moments of emergence. Something inside begins to ask, not "Who am I supposed to be?" but "Who am I, actually?" That question is both terrifying and liberating.

This chapter will begin by examining how identity is shaped through performance—how roles, scripts, and social context inform our sense of self, often without our awareness. Then we will turn to trauma and its lasting influence on identity formation, exploring how survival strategies become mistaken for personality. Next, we will explore the unsettling but generative space of identity unmaking: what it means to release old roles without yet knowing what will take their place. Finally, we'll reframe becoming not as a destination, but as a practice—a lifelong willingness to live from the inside out.

To become ourselves is not to reject all that we've been. It is to reclaim the self from the conditions that once defined it. It is to live as something more than a reaction to context—and to allow our identities to grow as widely, wildly, and precisely as our truth requires.

The Performance of Self: How We Learn Who to Be

Identity does not emerge in a vacuum. It is cultivated in context—through observation, feedback, reward, and repetition. From infancy onward, we are watched, mirrored, named, corrected, and applauded. We absorb messages not only about what behavior is acceptable, but about who we are allowed to be. Identity, then, begins as a kind of performance. We learn the roles that secure approval and the postures that minimize risk. We adjust ourselves in response to others. And over time, those adjustments begin to feel like the self.

This is not inauthenticity. It is adaptation. Children instinctively seek attachment, security, and belonging. When a child cries and is met with tenderness, they learn that vulnerability is safe. When they are met with indifference or shame, they learn to suppress emotion. When creativity is encouraged, it blooms. When it is ignored, it retreats. These early lessons about what parts of the self are welcomed and what parts are punished form the foundation of self-concept. And because children are egocentric in their early development, they do not interpret rejection as the environment's failure. They interpret it as their own.

This conditioning continues in more complex ways throughout life. Schools reward obedience and conformity far more than curiosity or emotional depth. Peer groups often reinforce narrow standards of masculinity, femininity, or cultural normalcy. Religious communities, families, and media impose layered narratives about what is virtuous, lovable, or dangerous. These signals may be subtle, but their repetition gives them power. Identity, under these conditions, becomes an unconscious performance: a way of moving through the world that minimizes rupture and maximizes social approval.

Sociologist Erving Goffman famously framed social life as a stage in which we present different "faces" depending on the audience and the expected script. While some degree of role-shifting is normal and even necessary, problems arise when the performance becomes compulsory—when we no longer know how to access parts of the self that do not fit the script. A person may become so practiced at being "the strong one," "the funny one," or "the high achiever" that they lose access to sadness, fear, vulnerability, or uncertainty. Over time, the role consumes the person. The mask fuses with the face.

In psychology, this kind of internal disconnection is often linked to *false self syndrome*, a concept introduced by Donald Winnicott. The false self emerges when a person feels chronically unable to express their real emotions or needs. Instead, they develop a personality that conforms to external demands. While this false self may appear socially successful, it is often accompanied by emptiness, depression, or a pervasive sense of inauthenticity. The person is performing life rather than inhabiting it.

Even culturally celebrated identities can be performative. A student praised for being exceptional may begin to overidentify with competence, suppressing any signs of struggle. A leader admired for composure may feel unable to express confusion or doubt. A caregiver applauded for selflessness may neglect their own needs until resentment or burnout sets in. These identities are not false in the moral sense. They are partial truths mistaken for wholeness. And when people begin to outgrow them, they often feel disoriented or guilty, unsure whether the change is growth or betrayal.

For individuals from marginalized communities, the performance of identity is further complicated by social pressure to assimilate. Code-switching, emotional suppression, and role containment become necessary strategies for safety and survival. A Black woman in a corporate environment may feel pressure to appear nonthreatening. A queer teenager may conceal their attraction to avoid rejection. A disabled person may downplay their needs to avoid pity or exclusion. These performances are intelligent. They reflect high emotional awareness and contextual sensitivity. But they also carry emotional cost: self-monitoring, exhaustion, and disconnection from the fullness of identity.

The most insidious part of identity performance is that it often goes unrecognized. Because roles are reinforced by praise, security, and inclusion, people may not even realize they are performing. The mask becomes the only face they remember. And when dissonance arises—when the inner world begins to diverge from the social script—it is often dismissed as confusion or crisis. In reality, that dissonance is the beginning of emergence. The self is beginning to outgrow the performance.

Psychologically, this moment is both threatening and essential. It challenges long-held beliefs about who we are and what we must do to be loved or accepted. It surfaces emotions that have been exiled in the name of functionality. And it forces a reckoning: Is this identity still serving me? Is it still mine? For many, this question emerges not in therapy or reflection, but in the quiet fatigue of repetition. The role becomes unsustainable. The script begins to feel hollow. And in that space of discomfort, the possibility of self-reclamation begins.

The goal is not to abandon all roles. Human life requires some degree of performance. We play different parts in different relationships and settings. The problem is not the roles themselves, but the fusion of role and identity. When we forget that we are more than what we perform, we become psychologically rigid. We reduce the self to a job description, a personality trait, or a coping strategy. And in doing so, we lose access to what is spontaneous, evolving, and deeply personal.

To become ourselves, we must first recognize what we've been performing. We must ask which roles were chosen, and which were assigned. Which behaviors are congruent with our values, and which are holdovers from old scripts that no longer serve us. This is not an act of judgment. It is an act of contact. A way of returning to the question:

What part of me has not been living?

When we stop performing long enough to listen, the answer often comes—not as a sudden truth, but as a faint voice beneath the noise. A voice that says: I'm still here.

Identity Under Siege: The Residue of Trauma

Trauma is not just something that happens to us—it is something that organizes us. It alters how we interpret the world, how we feel in our own bodies, how we relate to others, and crucially, how we come to understand who we are. When the environment is persistently unsafe, inconsistent, or emotionally violating, people do not just develop coping strategies. They develop identities around those strategies. The self becomes structured around survival. And over time, the strategies that once protected a person become confused with their nature.

This is how trauma hides in plain sight. A person who is always accommodating may not seem distressed—they may be praised for their kindness, their flexibility, their emotional availability. But beneath that compliance may be a history of punishment for having needs. Another person might be hyper-independent, emotionally detached, fiercely self-reliant. This, too, may be admired. But it may have been forged in a context where trusting others was unsafe, or vulnerability was met with betrayal. These identities are not simply preferences. They are emotional blueprints drawn under pressure.

In psychological terms, trauma interrupts the development of an integrated self. Under threat, the nervous system prioritizes immediacy—what must be done to stay safe, to stay connected, to avoid harm. This often leads to dissociation, fragmentation, and role-based self-definition. A child in a chaotic household might become "the fixer" to maintain a sense of control. Another may become invisible, learning that silence equals safety. Others might adopt precocious maturity, becoming emotionally attuned to the needs of volatile caregivers. These roles are intelligent. They reduce threat. But they also narrow the range of identity.

Internal Family Systems (IFS) provides a helpful framework here. In IFS, the self is understood as composed of parts—some of which carry burdens from traumatic experiences. These parts often take on protective roles: managers that control behavior to avoid vulnerability, firefighters that numb emotion or distract from pain, exiles that carry shame, fear, or grief. Over time, these parts become so dominant that they obscure access to the core self. Identity is no longer a flexible constellation—it becomes a series of reactive stances, each organized around avoidance or protection.

What complicates this further is that these trauma-formed identities often "work" in the external world. A hyper-vigilant employee may be praised for attention to detail. A people-pleaser may rise quickly through institutions that reward deference and emotional labor. A self-silencer may be seen as agreeable or low-maintenance. The reinforcement of these patterns makes them hard to recognize as trauma responses. They are validated socially while costing the individual emotionally.

Over time, these identities can become rigid. Not because the person lacks insight, but because the alternative feels too dangerous. Letting go of hyper-responsibility might invite chaos. Expressing anger might trigger abandonment. Naming a need might evoke shame. These internal associations are often pre-verbal, held in the body and nervous system rather than in conscious thought. The person may not remember the origin of the threat, but the body remembers the stakes. And so they remain in the role—even as it begins to erode their well-being.

This erosion often presents as anxiety, depression, disconnection, or chronic fatigue. Not because the person is flawed or broken, but because the role they are living was never designed to nourish a full self. It was designed to manage risk. Eventually, the strategy collapses under its own weight. What once felt protective begins to feel suffocating. What once ensured connection begins to undermine intimacy. This is not failure. It is a signal that the self is ready to emerge from behind the defense.

But that emergence is rarely straightforward. Trauma survivors often struggle with guilt or disorientation when they try to relinquish old roles. A caretaker who sets boundaries may feel selfish. A performer who rests may feel lazy. A dissociated person who reconnects with their body may initially feel overwhelmed by the emotional material it carries. These are not regressions. They are signs that the self is coming back into contact with experiences it was once too dangerous to feel.

This is where trauma work becomes identity work. The goal is not just symptom relief. It is self-reclamation. It is the slow process of distinguishing between what is true and what was learned in order to survive. This involves grieving—not just what happened, but what was never allowed to develop because of it. The spontaneous parts. The playful parts. The vulnerable parts. The parts that didn't fit into the trauma-formed role.

Healing does not erase the past. It doesn't restore a pure, original self untouched by pain. But it does expand the present. It allows for a wider range of responses, a more flexible self-concept, and a deeper connection to desire, agency, and choice. It enables a person to say: I am not what happened to me. And I am not only who I had to become in response.

One of the most liberating moments in trauma recovery is when a person begins to feel not just safe—but free. Free to change, to rest, to explore, to disappoint others, to speak differently, to live from something other than protection. That moment is often subtle. It might come as a new choice made without panic. A feeling of spaciousness where there used to be tension. A quiet thought: I don't have to do it that way anymore.

Identity formed under siege is intelligent. But identity reclaimed in safety is expansive. It is not about rejecting the parts that protected us. It is about thanking them—and letting them rest.

The Unwritten Self: What Emerges When We Stop Performing

There is a strange silence that follows the loss of a long-held identity. A parent after the children have grown. A worker after retirement. A student after graduation. A survivor after the danger has passed. The roles that once gave shape to daily life dissolve, and in their absence, many people are met not with freedom, but with disorientation. Who am I without this role? Without this purpose? Without the performance that once made me legible to others—and to myself?

This is the territory of the unwritten self. It is the moment when identity is no longer defined by reaction or expectation, but by something more fragile and emergent. It is a space between scripts—after the performance, before the new story has taken shape. And while it is often frightening, it is also where genuine becoming begins.

Existential psychology has long recognized this moment as essential to the human journey. Viktor Frankl wrote of meaning as something we must choose, not inherit. Rollo May described authenticity as a confrontation with the anxiety of freedom. In these frameworks, the self is not discovered like a buried treasure. It is created through relationship, reflection, and risk. To stop performing is to step into a space of unknowing. It requires a tolerance for identity disorientation, and a willingness to be real even when that reality does not yet have a name.

What makes this process difficult is that the cultural scaffolding for becoming is thin. We are encouraged to brand ourselves, to pick a lane, to package our experiences into digestible narratives. But true identity emergence is often slow, nonlinear, and not easily shared. It may include weeks, months, or years of emotional ambiguity. Joy without clarity. Grief without explanation. A quiet sense of "not this anymore," without a clear sense of what comes next.

Many people rush to fill this gap. After ending a role or relationship, they take on a new one immediately. After shedding a belief system, they adopt another with equal conviction. This is understandable. The unwritten self can feel unbearably exposed. But something is lost when we replace performance with another performance too quickly. We lose the opportunity to ask deeper questions: What do I value now, without the reward system of the old role? What emotions arise when I am no longer being watched, needed, or defined?

To live through this space without rushing to resolution requires emotional stamina. It means facing the parts of ourselves that have long been silenced or distorted. The self that feels awkward. The one that is unsure. The one that carries grief for the years lived behind a mask. These parts are not signs of regression. They are signs of emergence. They have been waiting, sometimes for decades, to be invited into the room.

In this stage, many people find themselves reaching for practices that are less outcome-driven and more attuned to presence: walking without a destination, journaling without structure, sitting in silence, creating without an audience. These are not productivity habits. They are relational acts—ways of being with the self without the overlay of performance. In this space, we begin to hear quieter voices within us: desire that had gone dormant, values that had been borrowed, curiosities that had no place in the old role.

This is also when grief comes to the surface. The unwritten self carries grief for all the selves that were written by necessity. The one who had to smile through pain. The one who became the comic relief to keep peace. The one who stayed quiet to avoid rejection. Grief, in this sense, is not only about loss. It is about recognition. It is what allows us to say: That was not the whole of me. And I want something more.

One of the paradoxes of this stage is that others may struggle to understand it. Friends, family, colleagues may say, "You seem different," or "You've changed," with discomfort. They may want the old version of you—the one they could rely on to behave a certain way. This external pressure can make the unwritten self retreat. But it can also clarify what kind of support is truly supportive. The people who can witness your becoming without needing to name it are rare. And essential.

Psychologically, the process of identity emergence can feel like a shedding. Not a collapse, but a gentle dropping away of what no longer fits. The voice that used to say yes automatically falls silent. The smile that used to hide sadness fades. The impulse to explain yourself diminishes. In its place, a different kind of self-awareness emerges—not the one built for performance, but the one grounded in presence. A self that feels less polished but more true.

This is not the kind of transformation that comes with fanfare. It is not easily posted or explained. It often feels like nothing is happening at all—until you notice that your choices are different. That you're no longer pleasing people to stay safe. That you're speaking with a new kind of clarity. That your life, though less defined, feels more alive.

The unwritten self is not empty. It is spacious. And in that spaciousness, the possibility of a more integrated identity begins to take shape—not in reaction to the world, but in relationship with the truth of who you are becoming.

Becoming as a Lifelong Practice

There is no final self waiting at the end of the psychological journey. No ultimate version of who we're meant to be, fully realized, fully certain, unchanging and complete. That fantasy—common in self-help culture and developmental myths—can create more pressure than peace. In reality, becoming is not a destination. It is an orientation. A way of staying in relationship with the self as it changes, softens, sharpens, and expands across time.

To become ourselves, then, is not something we do once. It is something we commit to again and again. Through transitions, through losses, through revelations. Through moments of rupture and moments of clarity. It is not about consistency in identity, but continuity in integrity—the sense that, no matter where we are in the unfolding, we are being honest with ourselves.

This requires letting go of arrival fantasies. Many people postpone self-acceptance until they've earned a particular title, healed a particular wound, or reached a particular milestone. But the most profound shifts in identity often happen not at the peak, but in the quiet aftermath—when a goal has been reached and the old self feels distant, or when an identity no longer organizes life in a meaningful way. These are the moments when the question resurfaces: What is true for me now?

Humanistic psychology has long emphasized the importance of self-actualization—not as a linear process of improvement, but as an ongoing unfolding of one's deepest values, capacities, and presence. Carl Rogers described the good life not as a state of contentment, but as "a process, not a state of being—a direction, not a destination." In this view, psychological maturity is marked by openness to experience, flexibility in identity, and trust in the self's capacity to grow.

But becoming is not always graceful. It often involves shedding layers that once felt like skin. Letting go of roles that secured praise. Facing emotions that were once buried beneath functionality. This shedding can feel like loss. It is loss. Loss of certainty. Loss of belonging in old systems. Loss of coherence in the story we used to tell. But what emerges in its place is spaciousness. And in that space, we begin to rebuild—not in reaction to pressure, but in alignment with presence.

For survivors of trauma, this process can be especially complex. Because identity was so often shaped by what needed to be done to stay safe, becoming requires a new template—one not built around protection, but possibility. This does not mean abandoning caution or pretending the past didn't happen. It means expanding the self beyond the architecture of survival. It means asking: Who am I when I'm not managing threat? What do I want, now that I don't have to fight for every moment?

Post-traumatic growth theory offers a helpful lens here. Research shows that many people who endure trauma report increased clarity of values, deepened relationships, and a renewed sense of meaning—*not because of the trauma itself*, but because of the inner work it necessitated. This growth is not guaranteed, nor is it linear. But when conditions allow for integration—safety, reflection, support—the person who emerges is often more aligned, more attuned, and more internally free.

Becoming also involves revisiting earlier versions of the self with new compassion. Many people look back on past choices with shame or regret, wishing they had known then what they know now. But the work of becoming includes remembering that the self at each stage was doing the best it could with what it had. To become ourselves now does not require condemning who we were. It requires integrating who we were into the wider arc of who we are becoming.

Practically, becoming involves ongoing practices: listening inward before speaking outward. Slowing down in moments of emotional overwhelm. Naming what feels true, even when it's inconvenient. Releasing identities that feel brittle. And allowing new language to emerge for parts of the self that have long gone unnamed. These practices are not dramatic. But they are transformative. Because they anchor us in the present without requiring that we remain static within it.

Relationally, becoming means surrounding ourselves with people who make room for our evolution—who do not freeze us in past roles, who do not require performance in exchange for love, and who do not interpret growth as abandonment. These people may not always be easy to find. But even one relationship rooted in authenticity can nourish the courage required to stay in contact with a living, changing self.

To become ourselves is not to declare who we are and hold that line forever. It is to stay in conversation with who we are now. To be willing to say, "I see that differently today." To revise a belief when it no longer fits. To soften an identity when it starts to constrict. This is not instability. It is psychological maturity.

The goal is not to be impressive. It is to be real. Realness may be quieter than performance, less rewarded in certain circles, harder to explain. But it is more sustainable. Because it is not built on impression—it is built on contact.

When we live this way, our identities become less about containment and more about expression. Less about surviving and more about unfolding. And in that unfolding, we find not a perfect self, but a present one. Not certainty, but clarity. Not a single answer, but an ongoing relationship.

That is what it means to become.

* * *

38

Living With Uncertainty

Uncertainty is one of the most consistent features of human life—and one of the most difficult to tolerate. We want to know what's next. We want clarity, resolution, closure. We want our questions answered, our relationships labeled, our feelings sorted. And when these things are unavailable—when life remains unresolved, when emotions contradict themselves, when outcomes cannot be predicted—many people experience distress that is deeper than frustration. It feels like groundlessness. Like something essential is missing. Like we're not safe.

But uncertainty is not inherently unsafe. It is uncomfortable, disorienting, and often unwelcome—but it is not a threat in itself. Much of the suffering we associate with uncertainty comes not from ambiguity itself, but from our efforts to eliminate it prematurely. We rush to define emotions that are still unfolding. We demand decisions before the conditions for choice are clear. We insist on black-and-white answers to questions that require nuance, patience, and moral humility. In doing so, we often bypass the very process through which understanding might emerge.

This chapter is about the psychology of uncertainty—not just as an external condition, but as an internal experience. It is about how human beings relate to ambiguity, how we construct meaning in the face of the unknown, and what it takes to live with paradox rather than resolve it. It is about building emotional range—not by achieving mastery over life's complexity, but by learning how to hold that complexity without collapsing under it.

From a developmental perspective, the capacity to tolerate ambiguity is a marker of maturity. Children and adolescents often demand clarity and fairness because their emotional systems are still developing the tools to navigate contradiction. As adults, we are expected to carry more nuance. To love people who have hurt us. To grieve what was good and bad at the same time. To make decisions in the absence of guarantees. But while the need for certainty may soften over time, it never disappears entirely. Under stress, people often regress to absolutism—not because they are simple-minded, but because their nervous system is seeking ground.

Emotionally, uncertainty is often misread as failure. Not knowing what you feel is interpreted as emotional incompetence. Feeling two things at once is seen as being unclear. Struggling to make a decision is taken as evidence of confusion or weakness. These judgments are not only unfair—they are psychologically counterproductive. They turn complexity into shame, and shame narrows awareness. To live with uncertainty requires not only skill, but permission: the internal permission to be where you are, even when where you are is murky.

This chapter begins by exploring why we are so drawn to certainty—how our brains, relationships, and cultures have been shaped to prefer clarity, even when it's illusory. We then turn to paradox, not as a problem to solve, but as an integral part of psychological truth. From there, we explore emotional ambiguity—the internal experience of feeling contradictory or unclear emotions—and how staying present with those states deepens self-understanding. Finally, we offer a vision of not-knowing not as deficiency, but as capacity: a way of being in the world that honors process over resolution and complexity over premature conclusions.

To live with uncertainty is not to embrace chaos. It is to live with reverence for the parts of life that do not resolve cleanly, for the emotions that refuse to be named in isolation, for the truths that sit beside each other in tension. It is to make peace with the paradox that some of the clearest moments of wisdom come not from knowing, but from remaining open when knowing has not yet arrived.

The Need for Certainty: Why Ambiguity Feels Threatening

Human beings are wired to seek clarity. Our brains are pattern-making machines, constantly interpreting, categorizing, and simplifying the complexity of life into something manageable. This drive is not a flaw. It is an evolutionary advantage. In early human history, the ability to detect danger quickly—based on limited information—meant the difference between survival and death. A rustle in the grass could be the wind, or it could be a predator. The ambiguity itself was a threat, and the mind learned to resolve uncertainty as fast as possible.

That impulse hasn't gone away. In modern life, the uncertainty we face is rarely about physical danger, but the psychological machinery remains the same. We feel discomfort in situations that are ambiguous: when relationships are undefined, when medical tests are pending, when someone we love sends mixed signals, when we don't know how we're being perceived. Uncertainty activates the brain's threat response. It creates a kind of internal static that demands resolution. We want to *know*, not because knowing always helps, but because not knowing feels intolerable.

Psychologically, this intolerance is compounded by what's known as *cognitive closure*—a term introduced by Arie Kruglanski to describe the desire for a firm answer to a question and an aversion to ambiguity. People vary in their need for closure, but under stress, most of us lean harder into that desire. We rush to judgment. We prefer familiar explanations over nuanced ones. We interpret neutrality as threat. And we become more susceptible to oversimplified narratives, moral binaries, and emotionally charged decision-making.

This is especially evident in emotionally vulnerable moments. A person waiting for a diagnosis may prefer a terrible certainty over continued ambiguity. A partner unsure about where a relationship stands might provoke a rupture just to get an answer. A person grieving a loss may cling to anger because it offers a clear emotional anchor, even if it's painful. These responses aren't irrational—they're attempts to restore psychological control. Certainty, even when unwelcome, gives us something to stand on.

But certainty, when pursued too quickly or too rigidly, becomes a psychological trap. It can prevent growth, distort reality, and shut down emotional intelligence. The desire for quick resolution can make us intolerant of complexity in others: we want people to be either good or bad, right or wrong, in or out. We lose the capacity to hold ambiguity in relationships—to accept that someone can love us and hurt us, that we can disappoint others and still be worthy of love, that we ourselves can feel conflicted without being broken.

This rigidity shows up socially and culturally as well. In polarized environments, ambiguity is often equated with weakness or betrayal. People who express uncertainty are labeled indecisive. Those who acknowledge both sides of an issue are seen as disloyal or unclear. But these judgments reflect more about collective anxiety than individual clarity. In cultures that prize certainty, nuance is threatening. It suggests that the world is more complicated than we'd like it to be.

From a developmental perspective, the need for certainty is part of how we learn to make sense of ourselves and others. Children think in binaries—good/bad, safe/dangerous, true/false—because their cognitive structures are still forming. As they mature, they (ideally) develop the capacity for integrative thinking: the ability to see multiple perspectives, hold competing truths, and tolerate emotional dissonance. But this process can stall. Trauma, rigid cultural norms, and environments that punish emotional complexity can halt the development of this capacity, leaving adults with childlike responses to ambiguity.

In therapy and personal growth work, one of the most challenging and important steps is helping individuals tolerate "not knowing." Not knowing why they feel what they feel. Not knowing how someone else feels about them. Not knowing how the future will unfold. This kind of openness can feel like failure in a culture that conflates knowledge with competence. But in reality, the ability to stay with uncertainty is a sign of maturity. It reflects a nervous system that is no longer hijacked by the unfamiliar, and a mind that can remain curious without collapsing into confusion.

Emotionally, the need for certainty often hides deeper fears—of rejection, abandonment, humiliation, or loss of control. When those fears are activated, people seek emotional anchors. They want answers not because the answers are meaningful, but because the waiting is unbearable. But if we can learn to name the underlying fear—rather than rush to resolution—we can begin to shift our relationship with uncertainty. We can start to ask not, "How do I get out of this discomfort?" but "What is this discomfort trying to show me?"

It's important to distinguish between clarity and control. Seeking clarity is healthy. It means we want to understand ourselves and others. But when clarity becomes confused with control, it turns coercive. We demand answers from others to regulate our own anxiety. We rush decisions so we don't have to feel uncertain. We interrupt emotional processes because we can't tolerate ambiguity in ourselves. And in doing so, we sacrifice depth for relief.

The work, then, is not to eliminate the desire for certainty—it is to build a nervous system and a mindset that can hold uncertainty without shutting down. That can notice the urge to resolve, and pause. That can say, "I don't know yet," and mean it—not as a failure, but as a place of possibility.

Because the truth is, some of the most meaningful parts of life—love, change, healing, becoming—are uncertain by nature. They do not arrive all at once. They unfold. And if we are too busy chasing answers, we miss what is actually happening.

Holding the Tension: Paradox as a Feature, Not a Flaw

Psychological maturity is not defined by how well we eliminate contradiction. It is defined by how well we carry it. Life does not always line up in clean, logical sequences. People are not wholly good or bad. Emotions are rarely pure. Our beliefs evolve. Our needs compete. Our relationships fracture and heal in ways that defy linear narrative. And yet, so much of our inner conflict comes from trying to make experience simpler than it is.

We are taught—explicitly and implicitly—that coherence means clarity. That if we feel conflicted, we must be confused. That if we haven't made up our mind, we must be stuck. But many emotional truths coexist in tension. You can love your family and still feel smothered by them. You can feel gratitude for your job and still resent what it costs you. You can miss someone and know you're better off without them. These are not contradictions to resolve. They are truths to hold.

Philosopher Søren Kierkegaard described anxiety as the "dizziness of freedom"—the experience of being suspended between possibilities, aware that more than one thing could be true, but unsure which to follow. This space of paradox can be terrifying because it requires us to live without resolution. But it is also the space in which freedom emerges. Because it invites us to move beyond preselected scripts and into direct engagement with what is actually real.

Dialectical behavior therapy (DBT), developed by Marsha Linehan, centers this idea by teaching clients how to hold opposites: to accept themselves as they are and work toward change. To feel overwhelmed and still move forward. To validate their suffering while still holding themselves accountable. This approach is not about forcing reconciliation between two sides—it is about creating space for both to be honored. In DBT, dialectics are not a problem. They are a foundation.

Similarly, Carl Jung believed that psychological growth requires holding the tension of opposites until a new synthesis can emerge. He described this process as "enantiodromia"—the tendency for extreme states to give rise to their opposite. A person who represses anger may eventually explode. A person who idealizes others may crash into disillusionment. Jung saw this not as failure, but as the psyche's way of restoring balance. Integration, in his view, comes not from collapsing the paradox, but from bearing its weight long enough for something deeper to emerge.

This principle applies just as strongly to social and cultural experience. Many people struggle to hold complexity in public discourse because the emotional stakes are high. We want to know who the good guys are. We want our values to be unassailable. We want the people we admire to be free from contradiction. But they are not. No one is. And when we demand purity—of others or ourselves—we flatten the very humanity we claim to care about.

This can be especially painful for those raised in high-demand environments—religious systems, political ideologies, or family cultures that demand allegiance to a single truth. In such systems, ambiguity is framed as weakness. Questioning is betrayal. And emotional tension is something to be resolved quickly, not explored deeply. For people coming out of those systems, learning to tolerate paradox is not just a psychological task—it is a form of liberation.

But it is not easy. Holding paradox requires emotional range. It means being able to sit with dissonance without demanding that it resolve. It means resisting the urge to collapse experience into a single narrative just to feel better. And it means trusting that reality does not need to be simple to be meaningful.

One of the most profound paradoxes in human life is that we are always changing and always ourselves. Identity is both stable and fluid. Grief is both a form of love and a sign of loss. Joy can be accompanied by guilt. Success can feel empty. Even in intimate relationships, we hold paradox: we want closeness and space, freedom and safety, newness and familiarity. These are not problems to be solved. They are tensions to be respected.

Therapists often help clients name this experience by saying, "Both things can be true." This deceptively simple phrase opens up a wider emotional field. It makes room for contradiction without collapse. It lets people stop defending one side of the truth and start exploring the whole landscape. It also reduces shame—because it validates that ambivalence is not a character flaw, but a sign that something matters deeply.

In leadership, parenting, teaching, and partnership, the ability to hold paradox is what allows us to respond instead of react. A parent might feel both love and anger toward a child. A teacher might support a student while feeling frustrated by their resistance. A leader might make a difficult decision with both confidence and doubt. These moments don't make us hypocrites. They make us whole.

Even in spiritual traditions, the wisest teachings are often paradoxical. In Zen Buddhism, one must surrender to effort and effort to surrender. In Christian mysticism, loss becomes gain. In secular philosophy, the examined life is full of unresolvable questions. These teachings are not meant to confuse. They are meant to remind us that truth often lives in the tension, not in the resolution.

In the end, paradox is not something to be feared. It is something to be practiced. Like a muscle, our capacity to hold emotional complexity grows with use. The more we allow contradictory truths to coexist, the less brittle our minds become. The more we allow ambivalence to speak, the more honest our emotional lives become. And the more we live from this place of tension, the more space we create—for others, for reality, and for ourselves.

The Ambiguity Within: Emotional Complexity and Internal Conflict

Emotions are rarely singular. Even in moments that appear simple from the outside, the inner landscape is often crowded with contradiction. A person might smile through grief. They might cry from relief. They might feel guilt in the middle of joy or resentment underneath love. Emotional life is layered, nonlinear, and often difficult to name. And yet, our culture tends to demand clarity. People are expected to know what they feel, express it coherently, and act accordingly. But real emotional life resists such neat packaging.

Psychologically, this demand for clarity can create unnecessary pressure. When someone cannot identify exactly what they're feeling, they may assume they are emotionally unintelligent or avoidant. When they feel two things at once, they may believe they are confused or inconsistent. When their emotions shift rapidly, they may interpret that as instability. But in truth, emotional ambiguity is normal. It reflects a mind that is alive to nuance, a body that is responding to multiple cues at once, and a history that does not always line up cleanly with the present.

The work of emotion theorists such as Lisa Feldman Barrett has shown that emotions are not fixed biological responses. They are constructed experiences, shaped by context, memory, interpretation, and cultural training. What we feel is not just what happens to us—it's also how we make sense of it. And that sense-making process is often messy. The same event might evoke pride, shame, fear, and affection simultaneously. That doesn't make the emotion less real. It makes it more human.

Still, many people internalize the belief that emotional clarity is a sign of psychological health. They seek one definitive feeling to explain their state, and when that doesn't emerge, they grow frustrated. This is especially common in therapeutic spaces, where clients are asked, "What are you feeling right now?" with the implicit expectation that an answer should follow. But sometimes the truest answer is: "I don't know yet." That response is not evasive. It's honest.

Emotional complexity becomes particularly difficult when people believe they *should* feel a certain way. After achieving a goal, they may expect joy—but feel emptiness. After a breakup, they may expect grief—but feel relief. After confronting a toxic parent, they may expect empowerment—but feel guilt. These discrepancies create dissonance, not just between emotion and expectation, but between identity and reality. "What kind of person feels this way?" they might ask. And beneath that, often: "What's wrong with me?"

Nothing is wrong. The emotional system is working. It's just working in a complex situation. Feelings are data, not declarations. They speak to values, needs, and past experiences. They are not always rational, but they are always relevant. Emotional ambiguity signals that something important is happening—something layered, unresolved, or sensitive to time and context. Instead of demanding immediate coherence, we can learn to listen longer.

This is not always comfortable. Ambiguity brings vulnerability. It can feel like floating without direction, especially in a world that rewards quick decisions and emotional certainty. People may worry that if they don't know how they feel, they can't trust themselves. But this is a misunderstanding. Self-trust is not about knowing everything. It's about being willing to stay with what's true, even when it's not yet clear.

Internal conflict is one of the most common forms of emotional ambiguity. We want opposing things. We feel drawn in more than one direction. We carry competing values. This is not immaturity—it's life. A parent might want both to protect and to let go. A leader might feel both responsible and resentful. A person recovering from trauma might feel both compassion and rage toward those who hurt them. The question is not how to eliminate one side of the conflict, but how to carry both with integrity.

Psychodynamic psychology has long recognized the presence of multiple internal voices—parts of the self that hold different needs, fears, and perspectives. Rather than aiming to silence those voices in favor of a single, unified identity, many therapeutic approaches now focus on integration: creating enough internal safety that these parts can speak without being exiled or hijacked. Emotional ambiguity, in this view, is not a problem to fix—it's a conversation to attend to.

Practically speaking, this means creating internal conditions for reflection. Naming the ambiguity without rushing to resolve it. Sitting with mixed emotions without trying to declare a winner. Giving feelings time to unfold, deepen, or even change. This also means resisting cultural narratives that equate decisiveness with strength. In many cases, pausing is not avoidance. It's discernment.

Language can be a powerful ally here. People often find themselves stuck because they lack the words to describe what they're feeling. Terms like bittersweet, ambivalent, tender rage, or joyful sorrow can help name the in-between states that are otherwise hard to express. Poetry, music, and metaphor also serve this purpose: not to explain emotions, but to evoke them, to honor their complexity, and to invite resonance.

In relationships, naming emotional ambiguity can be deeply connecting. Instead of pretending certainty, a person might say, "I'm still sorting out what I feel," or "Part of me wants to reach out, and part of me feels hurt." These statements don't create confusion; they create clarity about the process. They also make space for others to be complex. When we model emotional range, we give others permission to do the same.

Ultimately, the goal is not to always know what we feel, but to remain present with ourselves while we figure it out. Emotional ambiguity is not the absence of intelligence. It's the presence of depth. It means that our inner world is alive and responsive to the nuance of life. And when we stop treating it as a flaw, we can start to experience it as what it really is: the language of a mind that refuses to lie to itself for the sake of simplicity.

Not Knowing as Wisdom: The Psychological Strength of Open Awareness

In a culture that prizes answers, certainty is often mistaken for competence. We admire confidence, even when it's misplaced. We reward people who speak in absolutes. We elevate the quick and decisive over the slow and reflective. But psychological maturity is not defined by how much a person knows; it is defined by how they relate to what they don't know. It is not the absence of uncertainty that signals wisdom—it is the capacity to live with it, to listen to it, and even to learn from it.

To be clear, this is not the same as apathy or passivity. It is not disengagement or helplessness. Open awareness is active. It is an attuned, receptive stance that allows for complexity, contradiction, and nuance to remain in view without rushing to collapse them into a singular answer. It requires ego strength: the ability to withstand the discomfort of ambiguity without grasping for control. And it requires emotional regulation: the capacity to notice rising anxiety or urgency and stay grounded instead of reactive.

In this way, not knowing becomes a discipline. It is the practice of withholding premature closure. Of resisting the psychological temptation to lock down a narrative. Of honoring process over product, unfolding over conclusion. This stance allows space for new data, deeper reflection, and more honest insight to arise. It is what allows a person to say, "I'm still figuring this out," and mean it not as a sign of weakness but as a mark of care.

This openness is particularly important in relationships. So many interpersonal ruptures occur not because people don't care, but because they assume too quickly what the other person meant, felt, or intended. The mind fills in gaps. Assumptions harden into certainty. And certainty shuts down curiosity. By contrast, when people hold space for not knowing—when they say, "Help me understand," or "I'm not sure what you're feeling"—they open the door to deeper connection. They allow others to remain full, complex people rather than characters in a fixed internal script.

There is also a developmental quality to open awareness. Young children ask questions incessantly because they live in a state of wonder. But by adolescence, many have already learned that certainty is safer. That not knowing gets you laughed at, left out, or shut down. Reclaiming the capacity to not know is, in many ways, a return to a more curious self—a self that values understanding over performance, inquiry over ego.

This is not easy in a culture built on definitive opinions. Social media, in particular, incentivizes instant certainty. People are rewarded for taking strong stances, declaring judgments, and projecting confidence even when nuance is warranted. In that environment, admitting "I don't know" feels radical. But it is also deeply human. It interrupts the performance of omniscience and makes room for mutual learning.

Psychologically, living with uncertainty allows people to grow beyond rigid identity structures. When people define themselves narrowly—by roles, ideologies, or fixed beliefs—uncertainty feels threatening. It destabilizes the constructed self. But when identity is understood as flexible and ongoing, uncertainty becomes less of a rupture and more of a resource. It becomes a space in which new parts of self can emerge.

In cognitive science, this is sometimes referred to as *epistemic humility*: the recognition that knowledge is always partial, that perception is limited, and that the mind interprets more than it observes. This humility is not self-deprecation. It is accuracy. It is an honest reckoning with what it means to be a human animal navigating an infinite world with finite tools.

Practicing open awareness also supports emotional regulation. When people can stay with the unknown without shutting down, they create more space between stimulus and response. They become less reactive, less compulsive, and more capable of responding from values rather than fear. This is especially important in moments of emotional overwhelm, when the urge to do something—anything—is strongest. The ability to say, "I don't need to act yet. I can wait, watch, and feel," is a powerful psychological tool.

This does not mean that clarity is bad or that certainty should be avoided. Clarity is essential in many domains: boundaries, ethics, decisions. But clarity that emerges from open awareness is different from clarity imposed by fear. One is earned; the other is grasped. One leads to coherence; the other leads to defensiveness. Open awareness allows clarity to arrive on its own timeline—when enough information, experience, or emotional readiness has accumulated to make it real.

Some of the most profound experiences in life—grief, love, transformation—begin in a state of not knowing. They ask us to surrender to the unknown, to feel our way forward, to hold contradictory truths without choosing one over the other. And in doing so, they reveal that not knowing is not the absence of wisdom. It is its birthplace.

To live in open awareness is not to float in vagueness. It is to ground ourselves in reality as it is—not as we wish it were, not as we fear it might be, but as it continues to unfold. It is to stay soft when the world demands hard answers. To stay curious when certainty feels like safety. And to trust that the mind, when given time and permission, can arrive at clarity that is real, not rushed.

Because the most profound truths are not those we declare, but those we live into. And the path to them is rarely a straight line. It is a spiral of unfolding, unlearning, returning, and remaining open—again and again—to what we do not yet fully know.

* * *

39

Psychological Wisdom

There is a kind of understanding that does not arrive quickly. It does not come from reading a book, hearing a lecture, or receiving advice—no matter how true the content may be. It settles in slowly, over years, through trial and error, through lived contradiction, through patterns that repeat until they are finally seen clearly. This kind of understanding is not about acquiring information. It is about becoming someone who can hold that information in a meaningful way. It is psychological wisdom.

Psychological wisdom is distinct from intelligence. A person can be brilliant—articulate, perceptive, analytically sharp—and still remain emotionally immature. They may know exactly how the mind works but behave in ways that betray self-deception, fragility, or relational recklessness. Wisdom is not about cognitive capacity. It is about how that capacity is directed and tempered over time. It involves humility, depth, and a kind of internal pacing that values resonance over reaction.

This chapter is not about becoming wise in a lofty or moralistic sense. It is about the slow, interior process by which people develop psychological discernment: the ability to see clearly, act thoughtfully, and live with increasing alignment between values and behavior. It is about what the mind learns over time—not just about the world, but about itself. What is worth holding onto. What needs to be released. What keeps breaking us open, and what helps us stay intact.

Psychological wisdom tends to arrive quietly. It does not announce itself. Often, we only recognize it in hindsight: in the way we no longer fall for the same story, react with the same urgency, or chase the same approval. We notice we pause more. We speak more carefully. We see more clearly when something isn't ours to fix. These are the fruits of long inner work—often invisible to others, but unmistakable in the shape of a life.

Developmentally, this process cannot be rushed. People gain psychological insight at the pace they are ready to metabolize it. It is one thing to know that boundaries are healthy; it is another to set one in a moment of emotional risk. It is one thing to understand trauma responses; it is another to notice them mid-pattern and choose differently. Wisdom lives not in our theories, but in our nervous systems. It becomes visible in the gap between impulse and response. In the decision to stay silent, to speak truthfully, to walk away, or to remain present.

Across cultures, traditions, and therapeutic modalities, there is broad agreement that wisdom includes qualities like emotional regulation, perspective-taking, self-knowledge, tolerance for ambiguity, and compassion—for self and others. These are not traits we are born with. They are built over time, often through the very experiences we would not have chosen. Grief, failure, heartbreak, betrayal—these moments can become teachers, not because suffering is noble, but because they expose what we could not see before.

This chapter will trace how psychological wisdom forms. It begins by looking at the slow accumulation of insight—how repeated emotional experiences eventually cohere into understanding. Then we examine how people learn to extract principle from pattern, developing internal rules not dictated by others but by hard-won truth. From there, we explore the shedding of false certainty as a sign of wisdom—not confusion. And finally, we ask what it means to live what we know—to embody our insights in real-time, in the hard moments, when it counts.

Psychological wisdom is not the absence of struggle. It is the quiet presence of clarity within it. It is the deepening of perspective, the softening of judgment, and the growing ability to stay steady when life does not go to plan. It is not perfection. It is coherence. And while it may not come quickly, it comes—if we are willing to stay present, to learn honestly, and to carry what life has taught us with care.

The Slow Learning of Life

There is a deep difference between knowing something intellectually and understanding it psychologically. Most of us can articulate basic truths about boundaries, emotional regulation, and relational patterns long before we can consistently live them. We know we shouldn't take things personally, but still feel wounded by offhand remarks. We know we should rest, but still push ourselves to exhaustion. We know what healthy love looks like, but still find ourselves pulled toward old wounds dressed in familiar clothing. Psychological wisdom is not what we can recite. It is what we slowly, stubbornly, and imperfectly begin to live.

Much of what the mind learns over time cannot be taught in advance. Experience must be metabolized. Insight must be earned through repetition, reflection, and discomfort. This is one reason why growth often feels circular rather than linear. People find themselves in the same emotional situation again and again—not because they are broken, but because something deeper is still trying to be understood. Each loop offers a new angle, a new capacity, a new possibility for learning. But only if we're paying attention.

This kind of learning is slow because the nervous system learns slowly. The brain is not designed to update immediately when given new information. It is designed to protect stability, to preserve prior learning, to reduce uncertainty. This means that emotional change often lags behind cognitive insight. We might know, for instance, that a certain relationship is unhealthy, but still feel drawn to it. That lag is not a sign of weakness. It is a sign that the body has not yet caught up with the mind—and that healing needs to happen in both.

Many therapeutic traditions emphasize the importance of this slowness. Depth psychology, for example, has long recognized that inner change often begins unconsciously, long before it shows up in behavior. In Internal Family Systems, insight into one's parts may come quickly, but unblending from those parts takes time. In somatic approaches, the body's readiness to release trauma is gradual, nonlinear, and unpredictable. These modalities remind us that wisdom does not arrive all at once. It gathers. It unfolds. It settles in like sediment in a river, slowly clarifying what the waters once kept cloudy.

Culturally, we are not conditioned to respect this kind of timeline. We are encouraged to seek rapid transformation, to consume self-help in digestible snippets, to equate speed with success. But real wisdom has no shortcuts. The kind of insight that lasts—the kind that reshapes how we treat ourselves and others—comes only when we're willing to stay in the long middle: the stretch of time when we know better but still struggle to do better. It is in that middle that character is formed.

Often, the turning point in this process is not a grand epiphany, but a quiet shift in interpretation. The moment we no longer see an old behavior as "just how I am," but as something learned and therefore changeable. The moment we recognize a familiar feeling not as truth, but as a signal from a younger part of self. The moment we catch ourselves mid-pattern, pause, and choose differently—even slightly. These micromovements accumulate. They are the slow weave of wisdom into the fabric of personality.

The role of memory is also central here. Psychological wisdom involves the capacity to look backward, not with shame or regret, but with honest reflection. It means noticing what we've done before and how it ended. It means being able to say, "I've been here before, and I remember how it felt." This kind of remembering is not about judgment. It's about pattern recognition. It's about protecting our future selves by honoring what our past selves have lived.

This slow accumulation of experience is what allows people to begin trusting themselves. Not in a superficial, affirmational way, but in the grounded sense that they have seen enough, felt enough, and learned enough to navigate life with clarity. Trust built on repetition is different from trust built on fantasy. It is earned. And because it is earned, it holds up under pressure.

None of this happens automatically. Time alone does not create wisdom. Plenty of people grow older without growing deeper. What makes the difference is the degree of attention we bring to our own lives. The willingness to reflect, to revise, to take responsibility. Wisdom is not a natural consequence of aging. It is the fruit of intentional living. Of asking hard questions. Of noticing when we're tempted to bypass discomfort. Of telling the truth to ourselves, even when no one else would know the difference.

Importantly, psychological wisdom does not eliminate struggle. It changes the quality of the struggle. The wise person is not someone who no longer suffers; they are someone who suffers with more clarity, more dignity, and more grace. They see what's happening while it's happening. They recognize their own patterns in real time. They don't pretend to be unaffected—but they don't get lost in the storm the way they once did.

This is the slow learning of life. It does not come from always doing the right thing. It comes from noticing, over and over, what the wrong thing costs—and deciding, eventually, to stop paying that price. It comes from observing one's own behavior with enough curiosity to interrupt it. And it comes from holding ourselves in compassion while we fail, because wisdom that is built through self-punishment rarely sustains.

Psychological wisdom begins not with mastery, but with the willingness to remain present through discomfort. It builds not through intellectual shortcuts, but through emotional honesty. And it becomes visible, over time, in the gentleness with which we treat others—not because we have never been hurt, but because we understand what it means to hurt and still choose not to harm.

From Pattern to Principle

Wisdom does not emerge from isolated events. It emerges from patterns—emotional, relational, behavioral—that repeat until they are seen clearly enough to become principles. These principles are not externally imposed rules. They are internal recognitions: quiet, settled truths we carry with us because we've lived the consequences of ignoring them. They arise not from doctrine, but from lived reality. Not from theory, but from pain, resilience, and reflection.

In psychological terms, a principle is a distilled form of pattern recognition. A person notices that whenever they ignore their early feelings of discomfort in a relationship, they end up compromising themselves. Or they observe that each time they avoid difficult conversations, resentment builds until it spills out sideways. These are not singular insights. They are realizations earned through emotional mileage. And once internalized, they begin to function like compass points—orienting future decisions without needing to consult external approval.

Most people do not arrive at these principles on the first or second encounter with a situation. In fact, some of the most deeply ingrained insights come only after years of repetition. The woman who keeps saying yes when she means no. The man who confuses intensity with love. The adult who still feels responsible for their parent's emotions. These patterns repeat until something in the system—the mind, the body, the soul—says: enough. That threshold is the birthplace of principle.

These principles take many forms. Some are about boundaries: "I do not explain myself to people committed to misunderstanding me." Others are about trust: "When someone shows me who they are, I believe them." Some are about energy: "Peace is more important than being right." Others are about self-worth: "I don't chase what has to be convinced to value me." They are not mantras. They are mile markers. They indicate that the road behind us taught us something too costly to forget.

Importantly, these principles are not one-size-fits-all. What feels like wisdom to one person may not apply to another's path. Psychological insight is always context-sensitive. A person who spent years in silence may need to learn to speak. A person who spoke without reflection may need to learn to pause. A principle, to be wise, must emerge from within. It must match the contours of one's own life. Otherwise, it becomes a borrowed truth—easy to say, hard to embody.

Principles also evolve. What once felt like a necessary defense—"Never let your guard down"—may eventually soften into a more nuanced truth: "Trust is earned, but vulnerability is not weakness." This evolution is a sign of integration, not contradiction. It reflects the mind's growing capacity to hold tension, to incorporate new data, to revise its own maps. Wisdom is not static. It adapts. It refines. It welcomes complexity without losing coherence.

This transition from pattern to principle often occurs quietly. There is rarely a clear before-and-after moment. More often, it looks like choosing differently one day—not because you should, but because you finally can. It looks like noticing a familiar emotional hook and walking away from it. Like hearing the voice of old conditioning and choosing not to follow it. These are not dramatic acts. They are subtle shifts that carry enormous psychological weight.

Neuroscience supports this process. The brain learns through repetition. Each time we respond differently to an old trigger, we weaken one neural pathway and strengthen another. Over time, those new responses become more accessible. But the bridge between pattern and principle must be built intentionally. It requires reflection: Why do I keep doing this? What do I believe it's protecting me from? What does it cost me? When insight answers those questions, principle begins to form.

Therapy often accelerates this process by offering a reflective mirror. A skilled therapist helps a person see their patterns not as failures, but as protective adaptations—and then guides them toward principles that better serve their current life. But this process also happens outside the clinical space. It happens in solitude, in journal entries, in long walks, in the ache that returns until we finally listen.

What distinguishes psychological principle from rigid belief is its flexibility. A principle can hold tension. It does not demand uniform application. It guides rather than dictates. It is self-authored, but not self-righteous. This makes it sustainable. It does not collapse under contradiction, because it was born of contradiction.

As we accumulate principles, our inner landscape changes. We no longer need to deliberate endlessly about every situation. Some decisions become clearer, not because life is simpler, but because we have oriented ourselves more clearly within it. That orientation creates an internal coherence—a sense that our choices reflect our lived understanding. This is one of the most reliable markers of psychological wisdom: a felt alignment between what we know, what we believe, and how we behave.

Of course, we still fall short. We still act against our own principles at times. But the recovery is quicker. The repair is cleaner. The return to self is more available. Wisdom does not mean never deviating. It means knowing how to return—and why the return matters.

From pattern to principle is the path of insight. It is the bridge from experience to meaning, from repetition to discernment, from reaction to intention. It does not happen quickly. But when it happens, it changes everything—not by altering the world around us, but by changing the way we meet it.

Letting Go of Certainty

There is a period in psychological development when certainty feels like safety. We cling to what we know, or think we know, because it provides structure. It offers relief from the chaos of ambiguity. Clear answers give us a sense of control; defined identities give us a sense of stability. In early stages of life—cognitively, emotionally, even morally—certainty serves a purpose. But as the psyche matures, those same rigid forms begin to suffocate. The very certainty that once helped us survive starts to keep us from evolving.

Letting go of certainty is not about becoming aimless or indecisive. It is about expanding our capacity to hold complexity. It means recognizing that most truths are layered, that many situations resist binary conclusions, and that emotional growth often requires sitting inside ambiguity rather than resolving it too quickly. Psychological wisdom arises not when we know everything, but when we stop needing to.

This transition is deeply uncomfortable. Certainty, even when painful, is familiar. People often stay in rigid beliefs or roles not because they work, but because they are predictable. A man might cling to the idea that vulnerability is weakness because it protects him from the shame of exposure. A woman might hold tight to the belief that conflict means failure because it preserves an image of relational harmony. These forms of certainty are not intellectually chosen. They are emotionally inherited. And relinquishing them can feel like betrayal.

What replaces certainty is not confusion. It is nuance. It is the psychological ability to say, "Both of these things are true," or "I don't know yet, but I can wait." This is not moral relativism or passivity. It is maturity. It is the understanding that inner conflict is not a flaw—it is a signal that more than one part of the self is speaking. That contradiction is often a precondition for integration.

Jean Piaget, the developmental psychologist, described a process called equilibration: the mind's continual effort to balance assimilation (fitting new information into existing frameworks) and accommodation (changing frameworks to fit new information). Psychological wisdom requires a greater capacity for accommodation. It means being willing to update the self—to revise not just opinions, but identities. To recognize that who we were is not who we must continue to be.

This kind of flexibility is not encouraged in most social environments. Institutions, ideologies, and even families often reward consistency over truth. Once a person declares a belief, any change can be viewed as weakness, hypocrisy, or disloyalty. In such environments, psychological growth becomes an act of quiet resistance: a refusal to stay frozen in ideas that no longer serve, a willingness to disappoint others in service of a more integrated self.

Letting go of certainty also changes the way we listen. Rather than preparing our next argument, we begin to truly hear. We ask better questions. We become more interested in understanding than in proving. This shift is not just interpersonal—it's intrapsychic. We stop fighting with ourselves. We allow conflicting emotions to coexist. We make space for parts of us that were silenced by the demand for clarity.

Many people reach this point through disillusionment. A system they believed in fails. A person they trusted betrays them. A role they clung to collapses. These moments, while painful, are psychologically fertile. They break the illusion of certainty and force a deeper kind of seeing. Not always immediately, but eventually, they can lead to a wiser relationship with reality—one that is less about control and more about responsiveness.

Importantly, letting go of certainty does not mean letting go of values. In fact, it allows values to emerge more clearly. When we no longer need to defend a rigid belief system, we can ask deeper questions: What do I really care about? What kind of presence do I want to be in the world? How do I want to show up when life doesn't go as planned? These are not questions that yield simple answers. But they are the questions that orient us inwardly, when outer structures are in flux.

Therapeutically, this process often shows up as a softening. Clients begin to speak with more curiosity, more compassion, more awareness of the parts of themselves they once judged. They begin to notice their need for certainty without collapsing into it. They say things like, "I'm not sure yet," or "That used to feel true, but now I'm questioning it." These are not signs of regression. They are signs of growth.

In spiritual traditions, this state is often called humility. Not the kind that diminishes the self, but the kind that recognizes the limits of human understanding. It is the wisdom that knows when to act and when to wait, when to speak and when to listen. It is the spaciousness that allows insight to arise without force.

Letting go of certainty is also what makes empathy possible. When we no longer need the world to match our inner map, we can allow others to have their own. We can tolerate disagreement without defensiveness. We can recognize the dignity of difference. This doesn't mean abandoning discernment. It means anchoring discernment in presence rather than in fear.

At its core, this is a shift from control to contact. From clenching to allowing. From defending a fixed truth to living inside an evolving one. Psychological wisdom does not ask us to be right. It asks us to be real. To remain open. To stay grounded in the not-knowing long enough for deeper knowing to find us.

Living What You Know

At some point in psychological growth, the distance between insight and action becomes the real frontier. We know what's happening. We recognize our patterns. We understand the stories we tell ourselves, the roles we play, the reflexes we've inherited. But understanding is not the same as integration. Knowing what is happening and choosing differently in the moment it matters—that is the work of wisdom. It is where psychology moves from concept to character.

To live what you know is to behave in alignment with your internal reality, even when it is inconvenient, uncomfortable, or invisible to others. It means asserting a boundary without overexplaining. Naming your need without shame. Admitting a mistake without collapsing into self-loathing. Choosing silence when silence serves growth more than vindication. These are not instinctive behaviors for most people. They are practiced. Rehearsed. Built through time, awareness, and many failed attempts.

Cognitive insight alone is a weak predictor of behavioral change. Research across psychotherapy outcomes has repeatedly shown that clients often understand their issues long before they can change them. This gap—between knowing and doing—is not a flaw in intelligence. It is a matter of readiness, regulation, and emotional safety. The body must feel safe enough to enact new behavior. The nervous system must trust that the world will not collapse if it abandons the old script. That trust is not built in theory. It is built in action.

Living what you know begins with small, ordinary choices. The moment you pause before answering out of obligation. The moment you say no, not with anger, but with steadiness. The moment you recognize your urge to prove, perform, or appease—and choose instead to stay grounded. These moments don't always feel triumphant. Sometimes they feel anticlimactic or even disorienting. But they are where wisdom takes root. Not in the dramatic, but in the consistent.

Emotionally, these choices are difficult because they often violate old contracts. The unspoken agreements we made in childhood or early adulthood—be easy, be agreeable, be perfect, be invulnerable—don't dissolve just because we've outgrown them. Living differently threatens those contracts. It means risking relational tension, professional misunderstanding, or internal guilt. Which is why so many people continue to live out patterns they know are harmful: not because they lack awareness, but because they fear the fallout of change.

To move through this, we need more than willpower. We need emotional scaffolding. This might come in the form of therapy, community, spiritual practice, or deep inner dialogue. Something that reminds us, especially in the shaky moments, that it is safe to be different now. That we can survive without the armor. That our truth does not have to be justified to earn its place.

Psychological wisdom is not just about self-expression. It is also about restraint. Sometimes living what you know means holding your tongue, not from fear, but from discernment. It means understanding the difference between reacting and responding. Between venting and communicating. Between winning an argument and preserving a relationship. The wise person does not stop feeling the impulse to defend, retaliate, or dominate. They simply notice it—and make a different choice.

This kind of maturity is hard to quantify. It won't earn applause. It rarely looks impressive. But it builds a life of coherence. A life in which values, emotions, and behavior begin to align. That alignment is not perfection. It is not the absence of struggle. It is the presence of inner clarity: a sense that even in difficulty, we are acting from something grounded and real.

Importantly, this alignment is not static. Living what you know requires continuous recalibration. The wisdom that served us at one stage may need to be revised at another. A boundary that once protected us might now limit us. A truth that once felt urgent may no longer apply. Wisdom honors the present. It does not cling to old versions of the self in the name of consistency.

Over time, living in alignment builds self-trust. Not the kind of trust that says "I'll always get it right," but the kind that says "Even when I mess up, I'll come back to myself." This is one of the deepest psychological shifts a person can experience: moving from performance-based worth to presence-based worth. From living to prove to living in truth.

This transformation shows up in subtle ways. In how we speak to ourselves after failure. In how we interpret someone else's silence. In how we show up when no one is watching. It is visible not in what we declare, but in how we live. In the congruence between what we say matters and how we behave when it is tested.

Ultimately, wisdom is not a trait to possess. It is a practice to embody. It is a way of moving through the world with increasing honesty, humility, and compassion—for ourselves and for others. And the more we live what we know, the more our presence becomes steadying for those around us. We become, in quiet ways, a source of clarity in a noisy world.

This is not something that happens all at once. It is something we grow into. One moment, one choice, one conversation at a time. That is how psychological wisdom lives—not in theory, but in practice. Not in perfection, but in the slow, steady work of becoming the person we already understand ourselves to be.

* * *

40

The Invitation of Psychology

Psychology is not a passing field. It is not a trend, a subset of medicine, or a clinical sidebar to the "real" work of science or philosophy. It is the disciplined, evolving attempt to understand what it means to be human—from the inside out. And for as long as people experience emotion, conflict, confusion, longing, joy, memory, or suffering, psychology will remain essential. This chapter closes the book not by summarizing its contents, but by naming the enduring relevance of psychology itself: why it matters, why it continues to grow, and what it invites each of us to carry forward.

Every generation faces different cultural challenges, political tensions, and existential questions. But beneath those surface variations lies something constant: the human mind trying to make sense of experience. That mind wants safety. It wants meaning. It wants to belong and to stand apart, to connect and to protect, to find coherence in a world that rarely hands it over easily. The questions we ask may take new forms, but the underlying currents remain stable. What do I do with my pain? Who am I in the eyes of others? Why do I feel like this? What does it mean to grow up? To fall apart? To become myself? Psychology does not provide fixed answers to these questions. But it provides a structure for inquiry, a vocabulary for exploration, and a framework for staying honest as we navigate them.

THE INVITATION OF PSYCHOLOGY

This book has approached psychology not as a body of knowledge to memorize, but as a lens—one that sharpens focus and softens judgment at the same time. To see a person psychologically is not to reduce them to a diagnosis or a set of traits. It is to regard them with context, with complexity, and with the understanding that every behavior has a reason, even if it is unconscious or maladaptive. It is to see not just what someone is doing, but why it might make sense given their history, their beliefs, and the emotional logic of their inner world. That stance—of curiosity over condemnation, of explanation over assumption—is at the heart of psychological thinking. And it remains one of the most humane postures we can bring to our personal and public lives.

In today's world, psychology often gets flattened into self-help slogans, motivational clichés, or aestheticized versions of healing. But in its truest form, it is neither a shortcut to happiness nor a prescription for constant wellness. It is a discipline of witnessing: observing the forces that shape us, interrupting the patterns that confine us, and developing the capacity to hold emotional truth without collapsing into it. That kind of strength—emotional, cognitive, relational—is not built through inspiration alone. It is built through understanding. Through the daily work of noticing what's happening inside us and around us, and meeting it with both insight and compassion.

The invitation of psychology is not simply to know more. It is to live more fully awake. To question reflexes that no longer serve. To examine assumptions that have never been challenged. To relate to others as layered, complex beings rather than symbols of our projections. And perhaps most important, to relate to ourselves in the same way: not as problems to be fixed, but as stories to be understood. That act of understanding changes people. It softens them. It makes space for contradiction. And in a world as divided and fast-moving as ours, that softening is a form of strength.

As we reach the end of this book, the goal is not to close a chapter on psychology, but to open a door. This discipline is not just for students or clinicians. It is for anyone who has ever struggled with themselves, wondered about others, or hoped to live with more clarity and care. It is for those who want to do the deep work of becoming—who want to grow not only in knowledge, but in wisdom. Psychology can't offer certainty, but it can offer clarity. It can't prevent pain, but it can give that pain language. And in doing so, it allows us to live with more integrity, more understanding, and more connection—to ourselves, and to one another.

Understanding the Human Condition

Psychology has always been, at its core, an attempt to understand the human condition—not from the outside, as history or biology might, but from within. It studies what it means to feel, to choose, to relate, to suffer, to heal. It offers us a structured way to examine our motivations, our contradictions, our habits of thought and emotion. In doing so, psychology reveals not just how people behave, but why—and what internal logic their behavior might follow, even when it appears irrational or self-defeating.

This is not a small contribution. For centuries, explanations of human behavior were left to philosophy, religion, or moral judgment. If someone suffered from melancholy, they were thought to have weak character or sinful thoughts. If a child couldn't concentrate, they were labeled lazy or disobedient. If a person struggled with fear or compulsions, they were seen as spiritually deficient or socially deviant. Psychology challenged that interpretive frame. It said: What if there is a reason? What if pain is not a failure, but a signal? What if our behavior makes sense in ways we haven't yet understood?

That shift—from blame to curiosity, from moralizing to mapping—was transformative. It gave people tools to examine themselves without shame, and to make sense of others without contempt. The question became not "What's wrong with you?" but "What happened to you?" or "What pattern are you enacting?" or "What need is being protected here?" That reframe opened doors for compassion, for accountability, and for change.

THE INVITATION OF PSYCHOLOGY

Understanding the human condition through psychology doesn't mean abandoning responsibility. It means locating behavior in its appropriate psychological context. A person who lashes out may still be accountable for their behavior, but we can also ask what emotions they were managing, what attachment history they're carrying, what distortions shaped their interpretation of a given moment. The aim is not to excuse harm, but to understand the forces that contribute to it—so we can interrupt them.

This complexity matters. It matters in how we raise children, how we resolve conflict, how we design systems, how we relate to ourselves when we fall short. Without a psychological lens, people tend to rely on binary thinking: good versus bad, strong versus weak, normal versus broken. But psychological thinking resists that flattening. It teaches us to think in spectrums, in contexts, in dynamic systems. It shows us that traits can be adaptive in one setting and maladaptive in another. That a coping mechanism might be both helpful and harmful. That what looks like dysfunction might actually be the mind's best attempt at self-preservation, given the tools it had.

Over time, this lens helps us become more honest and more generous—not just with others, but with ourselves. We begin to see that our reactions are shaped by something. That our defense mechanisms, while perhaps outdated, once served a purpose. That our shame, our fear, our envy, our numbness—none of it is random. All of it is interpretable. All of it speaks. And if we learn how to listen, we can respond more wisely.

This interpretive power is what makes psychology indispensable across domains. In medicine, it helps physicians understand patient compliance, stress reactivity, and communication patterns. In education, it informs how children learn, regulate, and develop motivation. In the workplace, it clarifies leadership styles, team dynamics, and interpersonal friction. In justice systems, it offers insight into trauma, aggression, rehabilitation, and the long arc of behavioral change. Even in the arts, psychology helps us understand why stories move us, why music stirs us, why beauty feels redemptive.

But perhaps its most profound application is still the personal one.

Psychology gives us language for our inner lives. It offers structure to what once felt chaotic. Terms like projection, rumination, emotional regulation, trauma response, and internalized shame are not just technical jargon. They are ways to name experience—ways to say, "Yes, that's what this is," and in doing so, to reduce isolation. When people have words for what they feel, they suffer less. Not because the feelings vanish, but because they become navigable. Because they begin to make sense.

This is why psychology, as a discipline, is not bound by time. The language may evolve, the models may shift, but the core project remains: to understand the human mind in context. To explore how thought, feeling, memory, behavior, and environment interact. And to translate that understanding into greater clarity, deeper compassion, and more intentional living.

In this way, psychology is not a luxury. It is a foundation. It is one of the few fields that helps people make coherent meaning out of their own experience—and invites them to extend that same understanding toward others. That invitation does not expire. As long as there are people asking why they feel the way they do, why they repeat certain patterns, why they long for what they do not have, why they fear what hasn't yet happened—psychology will have a role to play. And it will be one worth playing well.

The Mirror and the Map

Psychology offers two gifts at once: reflection and orientation. It holds up a mirror so we can see ourselves clearly, and it provides a map so we can begin to choose where we go next. These roles—mirror and map—are not separate. They are sequential. We cannot move with wisdom until we see with honesty. And we cannot see with honesty until we have language for what we've been living through.

The mirror reveals what is already present: our thought patterns, our defenses, our impulses, our contradictions. It helps us recognize what we've inherited and what we've constructed. Some of this reflection is affirming. We see our resilience, our growth, the parts of us that have worked hard to protect our dignity. But some of it is confronting. We see the ways we avoid, the pain we carry, the habits we've built around fear. This is the moment when many people turn away—when they treat the mirror as a threat rather than an opportunity. But it is here, in the discomfort of honest recognition, that transformation begins.

Unlike pure introspection, psychological reflection is structured. It doesn't simply encourage people to feel more; it helps them interpret what those feelings mean. Someone might say they feel anxious in relationships. Psychology helps them see that what they're calling anxiety may be an attachment response formed in childhood. That their avoidance may be protective, not pathological. That their patterns aren't failures, but strategies. Suddenly, the mirror isn't just showing symptoms. It's revealing systems.

This kind of seeing can't be done alone. While self-awareness begins in solitude, it matures in relationship. Therapy, dialogue, even meaningful reading can serve as forms of external mirroring. They allow us to see ourselves through the eyes of another—not distorted by judgment, but clarified by context. When the mirror is grounded in psychological insight, it doesn't humiliate. It illuminates.

From there, the map becomes possible. Not a rigid formula, but a flexible framework: a way to trace the territory of selfhood with more precision. The map says, "Here's what avoidance looks like," "Here's how trauma shapes cognition," "Here's how developmental history influences adult intimacy." It doesn't tell you what to do, but it helps you understand the lay of the land. And once you know where you are, you can begin to decide where to go.

Importantly, psychological maps are not about escape. They are about engagement. The goal is not to leave the self behind but to inhabit it more fully. Not to eradicate flaws but to understand their origin. To approach our inner landscape with the same curiosity we would bring to an unfamiliar city. To ask not only, "What's wrong here?" but "What's happened here?" and "What needs tending?"

This map also helps us track progress—not in linear milestones, but in shifts of perception. The ability to pause instead of react. The decision to speak a truth that once felt dangerous. The moment we recognize that our fear doesn't match the present moment, and we choose to stay anyway. These are not dramatic changes. They are quiet reroutings. But over time, they change the entire path.

The dual role of psychology—as mirror and map—also extends to how we relate to others. When we understand our own patterns, we become more capable of seeing the patterns in others without condescension. We begin to notice that someone's criticism is a defense, that someone's silence is a scar, that someone's control is a form of fear. This doesn't mean we tolerate harm. It means we engage with more discernment and less reactivity. With more clarity and less projection.

In a broader sense, the mirror and map metaphor challenges how we think about change. Western culture often promises transformation through willpower or behavior modification alone. But without understanding, change is unsustainable. It becomes performance. The real engine of transformation is self-knowledge paired with intentionality. And psychology, at its best, provides both.

It's worth noting that neither mirror nor map offers shortcuts. Both require patience. We do not understand ourselves all at once. We learn in layers. We uncover. We resist. We forget. We remember again. And as life changes, we are asked to update the map and revisit the mirror. What used to be true may no longer be. What once felt unbearable may now be survivable. The psychological journey is never static because the self is never finished.

In this way, psychology doesn't just support individual growth. It shapes how we imagine growth itself. Not as achievement, but as integration. Not as a march toward certainty, but as a slow, humbling commitment to truth. The mirror grounds us in what is. The map helps us move toward what might be. Together, they orient us—not to perfection, but to presence.

THE INVITATION OF PSYCHOLOGY

A Discipline for the Disrupted Age

In an era defined by instability—politically, ecologically, technologically—psychology becomes more than personal. It becomes a form of civic literacy. We are living in a time when people are overwhelmed not only by their inner lives, but by the emotional chaos of the world around them. Outrage cycles dominate media. Misinformation spreads through emotional contagion. Loneliness is widespread despite constant digital connection. Polarization is no longer just ideological; it is psychological. And in the face of all this, we need something sturdy. Psychology offers that sturdiness—not in the form of easy solutions, but in the form of interpretive tools that help people stay anchored, discerning, and humane.

The modern world is emotionally disorienting. We are exposed to more information, more suffering, and more social comparison than at any other point in history. Our nervous systems are overclocked. Our attention is fragmented. Our sense of self is often tied to online performance. We are simultaneously hyperconnected and emotionally under-resourced. And for many, this leads to a subtle but chronic sense of unreality—a feeling that life is happening to them, not with them.

This is the terrain psychology is uniquely suited to address. While sociology can explain structural trends, and politics can shift laws, only psychology speaks directly to the inner cost of dislocation. Only psychology examines how people absorb cultural anxiety, how they make sense of loss, how they defend against shame, how they seek control when the world feels ungovernable. These are not just mental health questions. They are existential ones.

One of the most pressing needs of the moment is emotional regulation. Not just in children, but in adults, leaders, institutions. The inability to pause, reflect, and respond rather than react is one of the central drivers of social dysfunction. Psychology helps people build that capacity. It teaches the difference between a thought and a fact, a feeling and an action, a trigger and a truth. It shows us how to delay gratification, how to tolerate discomfort, how to listen without collapse or counterattack. These are not just therapeutic goals. They are prerequisites for any functioning society.

Consider the rise of conspiracy thinking. It is tempting to treat it as a political phenomenon, but it is also a psychological one. Conspiracies often take root in people who feel disempowered, unseen, or emotionally disregulated. The narrative offers coherence, identity, and control—all things the human psyche craves when overwhelmed. A psychologically informed response doesn't just debunk falsehoods. It asks what emotional needs are being met by the belief. What fears are being soothed. What sense of belonging is being offered that reality has failed to provide.

Similarly, the epidemic of burnout—once thought to be a workplace issue—is increasingly recognized as a psychological crisis. It stems from chronic emotional overload, unmet relational needs, and the internalization of productivity as self-worth. Solving burnout isn't about better time management. It's about restoring a sense of internal safety and identity apart from performance. Psychology makes that visible.

Even interpersonal conflict, in homes or workplaces or public spaces, often hinges on basic psychological blind spots: projection, transference, misattuned communication. Without a shared psychological vocabulary, people argue about content when the real tension is about emotion. They escalate because they don't recognize their own fear. They punish because they misread another person's silence. A psychologically literate culture doesn't eliminate conflict, but it transforms how conflict is understood and managed.

This is why the discipline matters now more than ever. Because the world is not getting simpler. Because people are not getting less stressed, less fragmented, less reactive. If anything, the need for inner steadiness is growing in proportion to outer volatility. And yet many people are still trying to navigate modern life without the tools to understand what's happening inside them.

Psychology helps people reclaim their agency. It teaches them to name their experience, to recognize their patterns, to own their projections. It invites them out of reactivity and into reflection. That shift alone—being able to pause and ask, "What is really happening here?"—can prevent relational damage, personal regret, or the deepening of unconscious loops. In a world where speed and spectacle dominate, that pause is revolutionary.

To be clear, psychology alone cannot fix everything. It cannot override structural injustice, cure societal inequality, or replace collective action. But it equips people to show up to those challenges with more resilience, clarity, and integrity. It strengthens the emotional infrastructure upon which all other change depends.

In this sense, psychology is not a luxury of the privileged. It is a necessity for the disoriented. It is the practice of staying human in a world that increasingly incentivizes performance over presence, rage over reflection, certainty over curiosity. And while the field itself must continue evolving—becoming more inclusive, more culturally attuned, more willing to confront its own biases—the foundational aim remains sound: to understand the mind, so that we might suffer less, relate better, and live more fully.

The Ongoing Invitation

There is no end to this work. No final state of enlightenment, no psychological finish line, no moment when a person becomes fully formed and free from contradiction. But there is a path, and that path is both intimate and shared. It is the path of self-understanding, of emotional maturity, of psychological integrity. And psychology, as a discipline and as a lens, offers a steady invitation to walk it.

This invitation is not about becoming perfect. It is about becoming honest. It asks us to meet our experience with clarity rather than denial, to face our contradictions without shame, and to engage our emotional lives with both curiosity and responsibility. It says: What you feel matters. What you believe shapes how you live. What you carry from the past affects how you respond in the present. Let's pay attention to that. Let's understand it—not to control it, but to relate to it more wisely.

Psychology does not promise happiness. It offers something sturdier: coherence. The ability to see yourself clearly, to understand your patterns, and to navigate life with a sense of grounded presence even when things are hard. That coherence is not rigid. It adapts. It grows. But it keeps you connected to something real—something that doesn't vanish the moment a relationship ends, a job changes, or a belief is questioned. In a fragmented world, coherence is a form of emotional anchor.

The ongoing invitation of psychology is also an invitation to compassion. Not the kind that bypasses accountability, but the kind that says, "I see the why." When you understand how someone became who they are, even their most frustrating behaviors start to make psychological sense. That doesn't mean you excuse harm. It means you stop assuming that malice is the only explanation. It means you gain the ability to stay present with people's complexity instead of splitting them into heroes and villains. It means you hold yourself to the same standard.

That inner posture—of discernment without condemnation, of boundaries without dehumanization—is not just personally transformative. It is socially protective. In times of division and dehumanization, psychologically mature people are the ones who resist emotional contagion. They do not scapegoat. They do not collapse into helplessness. They do not confuse intensity for truth. They stay grounded, reflective, and capable of empathy without gullibility. And those people are needed.

This is not about being above it all. It is about being inside life more skillfully. Feeling more deeply without drowning. Thinking more clearly without dissociating. Acting more consciously without performing. That is what a psychologically integrated life offers: the capacity to be both vulnerable and steady, aware and active, open and wise.

To live this way is to resist the reduction of humanity into roles, algorithms, or ideologies. It is to insist that each person contains more than what is visible. That behavior has roots. That emotions have logic. That the psyche is not something to be hacked or bypassed or branded, but something to be understood and cared for.

THE INVITATION OF PSYCHOLOGY

That is the final invitation of psychology: to remain human in the fullest sense. To keep exploring the mind not because it makes us special, but because it makes us real. To pursue understanding not as an escape from pain, but as a way to meet it with integrity. To engage the world not just through intellect, but through insight, humility, and care.

You have now walked through the many dimensions of psychological life: from attachment to identity, from trauma to meaning, from systems to selfhood. What you carry forward is not a set of conclusions, but a deeper way of seeing. That way of seeing—clear, complex, compassionate—is the heart of psychological maturity.

And it is never finished.

* * *

Afterword

No Finish Line, Just Forward

There is a longing in many of us for completion. For the chapter to be closed, the wound to be healed, the identity to be settled. We want to arrive somewhere—clear, certain, intact. But psychology, if it teaches anything enduring, teaches this: we are always becoming.

This book began with a question about what it means to be human. Not in the abstract, but in the lived, often messy, contradictory experience of being a person in the world. What you've read is not a manual. It is a map of possibilities. It names what often goes unnamed. It gives structure to what can feel unstructured. But it does not offer a formula for wholeness. Because there isn't one.

Psychological growth is not linear. It loops, it doubles back, it pauses, it surprises. It's not about getting somewhere and staying there. It's about returning to yourself again and again with more honesty, more steadiness, and more skill. It's about recognizing the mind as a system—dynamic, adaptive, protective—and learning to work with it instead of against it. It's about listening closely to what your patterns are trying to say. And when needed, rewriting them.

If you have reached the end of this book with a sense of open questions, that's a good sign. It means something in you is still alive to the work. Still curious. Still listening. And that is what matters most. Not whether you feel finished. But whether you feel engaged.

Let yourself keep evolving. Let yourself revise what you once believed. Let yourself hold what hurts without collapsing into it. Let yourself

AFTERWORD

celebrate what is working, even in the midst of what's not. Let yourself grow in directions no one taught you were possible.

There is no final state of clarity, no perfect version of yourself waiting to be uncovered. There is only the next moment. And in that moment, you choose how to see, how to respond, how to participate in your own becoming.

This book is finished. But you are not.

Keep going.

* * *

References

- American Psychiatric Association. (2013). *Diagnostic and statistical manual of mental disorders* (5th ed.). https://doi.org/10.1176/appi.books.9780890425596
- Ariely, D. (2008). *Predictably irrational: The hidden forces that shape our decisions*. HarperCollins.
- Asch, S. E. (1951). Effects of group pressure upon the modification and distortion of judgments. In H. Guetzkow (Ed.), *Groups, leadership, and men* (pp. 222–236). Carnegie Press.
- Bowlby, J. (1969). *Attachment and loss: Vol. 1. Attachment*. Basic Books.
- Bowlby, J. (1982). *Attachment and loss: Vol. 1. Attachment* (2nd ed.). Basic Books.
- Brach, T. (2003). *Radical acceptance: Embracing your life with the heart of a Buddha*. Bantam Books.
- Brown, B. (2012). *Daring greatly: How the courage to be vulnerable transforms the way we live, love, parent, and lead*. Gotham Books.
- Brown, B. (2015). *Rising strong: The reckoning, the rumble, the revolution*. Spiegel & Grau.
- Cacioppo, J. T., & Patrick, W. (2008). *Loneliness: Human nature and the need for social connection*. W. W. Norton & Company.
- Clear, J. (2018). *Atomic habits: An easy & proven way to build good habits & break bad ones*. Avery.
- Cron, I. M., & Stabile, S. (2016). *The road back to you: An Enneagram journey to self-discovery*. InterVarsity Press.
- Deci, E. L., & Ryan, R. M. (2000). The "what" and "why" of goal

pursuits: Human needs and the self-determination of behavior. *Psychological Inquiry, 11*(4), 227–268. https://doi.org/10.1207/S15327965PLI1104_01
- Dweck, C. S. (2006). *Mindset: The new psychology of success*. Random House.
- Erikson, E. H. (1980). *Identity and the life cycle*. W. W. Norton & Company.
- Fogg, B. J. (2019). *Tiny habits: The small changes that change everything*. Houghton Mifflin Harcourt.
- Frankl, V. E. (1959). *Man's search for meaning*. Beacon Press.
- Frankl, V. E. (2006). *Man's search for meaning*. Beacon Press.
- Fromm, E. (1941). *Escape from freedom*. Farrar & Rinehart.
- Gilbert, P. (2009). *The compassionate mind: A new approach to life's challenges*. Constable.
- Goffman, E. (1959). *The presentation of self in everyday life*. Anchor Books.
- Goleman, D. (1995). *Emotional intelligence: Why it can matter more than IQ*. Bantam Books.
- Haidt, J. (2006). *The happiness hypothesis: Finding modern truth in ancient wisdom*. Basic Books.
- James, W. (1890). *The principles of psychology* (Vol. 1). Henry Holt and Company.
- Jung, C. G. (1968). *Archetypes and the collective unconscious* (R. F. C. Hull, Trans., 2nd ed.). Princeton University Press.
- Jung, C. G. (1980). *The archetypes and the collective unconscious* (R. F. C. Hull, Trans., 2nd ed.). Princeton University Press. (Original work published 1959)
- Kabat-Zinn, J. (1990). *Full catastrophe living: Using the wisdom of your body and mind to face stress, pain, and illness*. Delacorte Press.
- Karen, R. (1998). *Becoming attached: First relationships and how they shape our capacity to love*. Oxford University Press.
- Kegan, R. (1982). *The evolving self: Problem and process in human development*. Harvard University Press.

- Maslow, A. H. (1943). A theory of human motivation. *Psychological Review, 50*(4), 370–396. https://doi.org/10.1037/h0054346
- May, R. (1950). *The meaning of anxiety*. Ronald Press.
- McAdams, D. P. (1993). *The stories we live by: Personal myths and the making of the self*. Guilford Press.
- Milgram, S. (1963). Behavioral study of obedience. *Journal of Abnormal and Social Psychology, 67*(4), 371–378. https://doi.org/10.1037/h0040525
- Miller, A. (2008). *The drama of the gifted child: The search for the true self*. Basic Books.
- Neff, K. (2011). *Self-compassion: The proven power of being kind to yourself*. William Morrow.
- Porges, S. W. (2011). *The polyvagal theory: Neurophysiological foundations of emotions, attachment, communication, and self-regulation*. W. W. Norton & Company.
- Rogers, C. R. (1961). *On becoming a person: A therapist's view of psychotherapy*. Houghton Mifflin.
- Sartre, J.-P. (1943). *Being and nothingness* (H. E. Barnes, Trans.). Washington Square Press.
- Selye, H. (1956). *The stress of life*. McGraw-Hill.
- Skinner, B. F. (1953). *Science and human behavior*. Macmillan.
- Tajfel, H., & Turner, J. C. (1979). An integrative theory of intergroup conflict. In W. G. Austin & S. Worchel (Eds.), *The social psychology of intergroup relations* (pp. 33–47). Brooks/Cole.
- Tolle, E. (1999). *The power of now: A guide to spiritual enlightenment*. New World Library.
- van der Kolk, B. A. (2014). *The body keeps the score: Brain, mind, and body in the healing of trauma*. Viking.
- Vygotsky, L. S. (1978). *Mind in society: The development of higher psychological processes*. Harvard University Press.
- Watts, A. (1951). *The wisdom of insecurity: A message for an age of anxiety*. Vintage Books.
- Winnicott, D. W. (1965). *The maturational processes and the facilitating*

environment: Studies in the theory of emotional development. International Universities Press.
- Yalom, I. D. (2003). *The gift of therapy: An open letter to a new generation of therapists and their patients.* Harper Perennial.

Recommended Reading List

On Attachment and Early Bonds

- Bowlby, J. (1982). *Attachment and loss: Vol. 1. Attachment* (2nd ed.). Basic Books.
- Karen, R. (1998). *Becoming attached: First relationships and how they shape our capacity to love.* Oxford University Press.
- Winnicott, D. W. (1965). *The maturational processes and the facilitating environment: Studies in the theory of emotional development.* International Universities Press.

On Identity and Meaning

- Frankl, V. E. (2006). *Man's search for meaning.* Beacon Press.
- Cron, I. M., & Stabile, S. (2016). *The road back to you: An Enneagram journey to self-discovery.* InterVarsity Press.
- Miller, A. (2008). *The drama of the gifted child: The search for the true self.* Basic Books.
- Erikson, E. H. (1980). *Identity and the life cycle.* W. W. Norton & Company.
- McAdams, D. P. (1993). *The stories we live by: Personal myths and the making of the self.* Guilford Press.

On Emotional Growth and Complexity

- Goleman, D. (1995). *Emotional intelligence: Why it can matter more than IQ*. Bantam Books.
- van der Kolk, B. A. (2014). *The body keeps the score: Brain, mind, and body in the healing of trauma*. Viking.
- Brown, B. (2015). *Rising strong: The reckoning, the rumble, the revolution*. Spiegel & Grau.
- Neff, K. (2011). *Self-compassion: The proven power of being kind to yourself*. William Morrow.

On Psychology and the Human Condition

- Jung, C. G. (1980). *The archetypes and the collective unconscious* (R. F. C. Hull, Trans., 2nd ed.). Princeton University Press. (Original work published 1959)
- Yalom, I. D. (2003). *The gift of therapy: An open letter to a new generation of therapists and their patients*. Harper Perennial.
- May, R. (1950). *The meaning of anxiety*. Ronald Press.

On Living with Uncertainty

- Watts, A. (1951). *The wisdom of insecurity: A message for an age of anxiety*. Vintage Books.
- Brach, T. (2003). *Radical acceptance: Embracing your life with the heart of a Buddha*. Bantam Books.
- Sartre, J.-P. (1943). *Being and nothingness* (H. E. Barnes, Trans.). Washington Square Press.

On Self-Discovery and Lifelong Growth

- Rogers, C. R. (1961). *On becoming a person: A therapist's view of psychotherapy*. Houghton Mifflin Harcourt.
- Brown, B. (2012). *Daring greatly: How the courage to be vulnerable transforms the way we live, love, parent, and lead*. Gotham Books.
- Clear, J. (2018). *Atomic habits: An easy & proven way to build good habits & break bad ones*. Avery.
- Deci, E. L., & Ryan, R. M. (2000). The "what" and "why" of goal pursuits: Human needs and the self-determination of behavior. *Psychological Inquiry, 11*(4), 227–268.
- Fogg, B. J. (2019). *Tiny habits: The small changes that change everything*. Houghton Mifflin Harcourt.

On the Social Nature of the Self

- Asch, S. E. (1951). Effects of group pressure upon the modification and distortion of judgments. *Groups, Leadership, and Men*, 222–236.
- Milgram, S. (1963). Behavioral study of obedience. *Journal of Abnormal and Social Psychology, 67*(4), 371–378. https://doi.org/10.1037/h0040525
- Goffman, E. (1959). *The presentation of self in everyday life*. Anchor Books.
- Cacioppo, J. T., & Patrick, W. (2008). *Loneliness: Human nature and the need for social connection*. W. W. Norton & Company.

About the Author

RJ Starr is an academic psychologist, professor, educator, and author whose work delves deeply into the emotional and existential challenges at the heart of human experience. His scholarship and writing explore how we create meaning, shoulder responsibility, and maintain groundedness amid uncertainty and complexity. Known for a voice that is both intellectually rigorous and deeply accessible, Starr invites readers into greater self-awareness, emotional clarity, and purposeful living. Drawing from a broad interdisciplinary background, he integrates psychological theory with cultural insight to illuminate the inner workings of identity, emotion, and resilience.

Beyond his academic and writing pursuits, Starr dedicates himself to exploring the rich inner lives that shape how we think, feel, and relate. He brings this exploration into his teaching and public lectures, fostering curiosity, critical thinking, and emotional intelligence. Through his work and his website, https://profrjstarr.com/, which offers hundreds of pages of free tools, courses, essays, frameworks, papers, letters from readers, podcasts, and products, he encourages individuals to engage honestly and courageously with the complexities of the human condition—supporting a journey toward integration, growth, and lasting psychological well-being.

You can connect with me on:

- https://profrjstarr.com
- https://linktr.ee/profrjstarr

www.ingramcontent.com/pod-product-compliance
Lightning Source LLC
Chambersburg PA
CBHW020529030426
42337CB00013B/785